Czech Republic
Toward EU Accession

Main Report

The World Bank
Washington, D.C.

CONTENTS

Tables

Figures

Boxes

Abstract

This country study is based on the findings of several missions that visited the Czech Republic during the second half of 1998. The report analyzes economic developments in the Czech Republic since 1997. It focuses on assessing the status of the Czech Republic's economy from the perspective of its pursuit for European Union membership.

The report is composed of two volumes. Volume I is the Summary Report that condenses main findings and conclusions. The report focal point is mainly on the need to recover a sustainable output growth path, and the elimination of the remaining structural weaknesses as means to maintain macroeconomic stability while increasing the competitiveness of the Czech economy.

Volume II is the Main Report. It provides the assessment and technical analysis of selected key sectors of the Czech economy. While each chapter is sector-specific in nature, the EU accession process dominates them. Volume II has fourteen chapters and is structured as follows: Chapter I reviews the economic performance since the 1997 currency crisis, focusing on the stabilization and recovery efforts, macroeconomic vulnerabilities and the fiscal stand. Chapter II analyzes growth and income convergence in relation with the EU accession process. Chapter III studies contingent liabilities and their impact on the fiscal front. Chapter IV focuses on inter-government fiscal relationships. Chapter V studies labor market trends, policies and performance. Chapter VI provides an assessment of the foreign trade sector, focusing on trade policy, foreign direct investment, export penetration in the EU and contestability of domestic markets. Chapter VII covers the challenges of the financial sector, evaluating mostly banking, but also capital market issues. Chapter VIII reviews the challenges in the enterprise sector: it concentrates on the changing structure of industry, the unfinished privatization agenda, efforts to attract more foreign direct investment (FDI) and challenges to meet EU quality and environmental standards. Chapter IX analyzes the agriculture and rural sectors in light of the competitive pressures from EU accession. Chapter X reviews the challenges from meeting EU environmental directives. Chapter XI studies public administration performance and reform options. Chapter XII reviews social sector development, focusing on the social safety net, ethnicity and exclusion, and the evolution of the education system. Chapter XIII reviews the challenges in health sector reform. Finally, Chapter XIV analyzes policy reform options in key economic infrastructure sectors, namely telecommunications, energy, gas and transportation.

The report was prepared by a World Bank team composed of Carlos Silva-Jauregui (ECSPE, team leader), Emily Andrews (ECSHD, social sectors), Joel Bergsman (CFAFI, FDI), Julia Bucknall (ECSSD, environment), Sara Calvo (PRMEP, macro vulnerabilities), Rita Cestti (ECSSD, environment), Amadou Cissé (WBIEP, inter-government relations), Csaba Csaki (ECSSD, agriculture), Michel Debatisse (ECSSD, agriculture), Simeon Djankov (FSPEU, enterprise sector), Bernard Drum (EASPS, enterprise sector), Robert Ebel (WBIEP, inter-government relations), Orskar Honisch (consultant, agriculture), Gordon Hughes (ENV, environment), Burchak Inel (ECSPF, sub-national credit market), Bart Kaminski (DECRG, foreign trade and FDI), Ioannis Kessides (ECSPE, infrastructure), Maureen Lewis (ECSHD, health sector), Zhicheng Li (ECSPE, fiscal and contingent liabilities), Andrew Lovegrove (consultant, banking), Tina Mlakar (ECSPE, enterprise sector and capital markets), John Nellis (PSDEN, enterprise sector), David Newberry (consultant, energy), Barbara Nunberg (EASPR, public administration), Jana Orac (ECSPE, public administration), Janusz Ordover (consultant, telecommunications), Hana Polackova (ECSPE, contingent liabilities), Rossana Polastri (ECSPE, growth and macro vulnerabilities), Gary Reid (ECSPE, public administration), Katherine Terrell (consultant, labor market and social security), Anthony Wheeler (ECSHD, education and Roma issues), Clifford Winston (consultant, transportation) and Ilham Zurayk (ECSPF, banking).

The report benefited from valuable comments and suggestions received at different stages from Hafez Ghanem, Michelle Riboud, Jan Svejnar, Jana Matesova, Sweder van Wijnbergen, Mandeep Bains, Roberto Rocha, Roger Grawe, Sanjay Pradhan, Gerard Viatte, Vaclav Vojtech, Thomas Laursen, Pradeep Mitra, Kyle Peters, Czech government officials, and participants at the ECSPE-Czech Republic CEM seminars on enterprise sector, foreign trade, contingent liabilities, public administration reform, regulatory aspects of infrastructure, agriculture sector, and environment sector. The report also benefited from helpful comments, suggestions and discussions from Czech government officials and participants from non-government organizations during the plenary discussions on the Czech CEM held in Prague.

The authors profited from the effective collaboration with government officials, in particular with Deputy Prime Minister and Minister of Finance Pavel Mertlik, ex Minister of Finance Ivo Svoboda, and Deputy minister of Finance Jan Mladek. Mission members had the opportunity to discuss the main findings of the different missions at the Office of the Deputy Prime Minister, Czech National Bank, Ministry of Agriculture, Ministry of Industry and Trade, Ministry of Labor and Social Affairs, Ministry of Environment, Ministry of Finance, Ministry of Foreign Affairs, National Property Fund, Czech Statistical Office, Research Institute for Agriculture Economics, CzechInvest, Trade Promotion Agency, Antimonopoly Office, and the Securities Exchange Commission.

The missions' members had the opportunity to discuss key issues with academicians at Charles University and CERGE-EI. The report also benefited from discussions with representatives from the Czech and Moravian Chamber of Trade Unions, Banking Association, Komercni Banka, Ceska Sporitelna, Ceskoslovenska Obchodni Banka (CSOB), Investicni a Postovni Banka (IPB), Expandia, Patria Finance, CA/IB Securities, European Commission, International Monetary Fund, Organization for Economic Cooperation and Development, and European Bank for Reconstruction and Development.

The different mission members would like to express their gratitude to all our Czech counterparts in the government, academia and business community, for the time they spent with us in open and friendly discussions. Their cooperation made this report possible. In particular, special thanks are due to Jiri Vetrovsky, Dimitrij Loula and Veronika Znamenackova from the Department of International Financial Relations, Ministry of Finance, for his effective support and organization of the multiple mission agendas. Special thanks also to Milos Vecera, IFC representative in Prague, for his hospitality and support to mission members during the preparation of this report and to our colleagues at the IMF for close collaboration. Tina Mlakar and Zhicheng Li provided research support. John Karaagac, Usha Rani Khanna and Wendy Guyette provided editorial assistance. Dolly Teju processed the report.

CURRENCY AND EQUIVALENT UNITS

Currency Unit = Czech Koruna (CZK)

	1993	1994	1995	1996	1997	1998
CZK/USD	29.16	28.78	26.55	27.14	31.71	32.27
CZK/DEM	17.64	17.75	18.52	18.06	18.28	18.33
CZK/EUR	34.11	34.06	34.31	34.00	35.80	36.16

WEIGHTS AND MEASURES

Metric System

ACRONYMS AND ABBREVIATIONS

AB	Agrobanka
ALMP	Active Labor Market Programs
ALMPs	Active Labor Market Policies
APPs	Auto Power Producers
AT&T	American Telephone and Telegraph
BAT	Best Available Techniques
BATNEEC	Best Available Techniques Not Entailing Excessive Costs
BCM	Billion Cubic Meters
BIS	Bank for International Settlements
CAP	Common Agricultural Policy
CED	Central Electric Dispatching
CEE	Central and Eastern Europe
CEECs	Central and Eastern European Countries
CEFTA	Central European Free Trade Agreement
CEM	Country Economic Memorandum
CEZ	Ceske Energeticke zavody
CF	Ceska Financni
CHP	Combined Heat and Power
CI	Ceska Inkasni
CMEA	Council of Mutual Economic Assistance
CNB	Czech National Bank
CO	Carbon Monoxide
CPI	Consumer Price Index
CPP	Czech Gas Works Group
CR	Czech Republic
CS	Ceska Sporitelna (Czech Savings Bank)
CSA	Czech Airlines
CSB	Czechoslovak State Bank
CSFR	Czech and Slovak Federal Republic
CSO	Czech Statistical Office
CSOB	Ceskoslovenska Obchodni Banka
CU	Customs Union
CZK	Czech Crown
DCG	Domestic Credit Growth
DEM	German Mark
DLOs	District Labor Offices
DPM	Deputy Prime Minister
EAA	Europe Association Agreement
EBRD	European Bank for Reconstruction and Development
EC	European Commission
EEC	European Economic Community
ECU	European Currency Unit
EMAS	Environmental Management Assessment Standard
EMU	Economic and Monetary Union
EOP	Elektrarny Opatovic
ESI	Electricity Supply Industry
EU	European Union
EUR	European Union Currency
EUROSTAT	European Union Statistical Office
FDI	Foreign Direct Investment
FOBAPROA	Mexican Banking Fund for the Protection of Savings
FSU	Former Soviet Union
GACR	Grant Agency of the Czech Republic
GARCH	Generalized Autoregressive Conditional Heteroskedastic
GATT	General Agreement of Tariffs and Trade
GDCs	Gas Distribution Companies
GDI	Gross Domestic Investment
GDP	Gross Domestic Product
GDR	Global Depository Receipt
GE	General Electric
GOCR	Government of the Czech Republic
GS	Goods and Services

GSM	Groupe Speciale Mobile	NIS	Newly Independent States
GSP	General System of Preferences	NO_x	Nitrogen Bioxide
Ha	Hectare	NPF	National Property Fund
HEO	Hungarian Energy Office	NTB	Non-Tariff Barriers
HIF	Hungarian Communications Authority	O&M	Operation and Maintenance
		OECD	Organisation for Economic Co-operation & Development
HR	Human Resource		
HRM	Human Resource Management	OLPA	Office of Legislation and Public Administration
ILO	International Labor Organization		
		OTND	Objective, Transparent and Non-Discriminatory
ICORs	Incremental Capital-Output Ratios		
		P	Private Sector
IEA	International Energy Agency	p.e.	Population Equivalent
IFC	International Finance Corporation	PAR	Public Administration Reform
		PAYG	Pay-As-You-Go
IFS	International Financial Statistics	PCBs	Polychlorinated biphenyls
		PCTs	Polychlorinated terphenyls
IMF	International Monetary Fund	Pee	First Quarter
IMV	Index of Macroeconomic Vulnerability	P/E	Price Equity Ratio
		PECAA	Pan-European Conformity Assessment Agreements
IPB	Investicni A Postovni Banka		
IPFs	Investment Privatization Funds	PGRLF	Agricultural and Forestry Guarantee and Support Fund
IPPC	Integrated Pollution Prevention and Control		
		PHARE	Poland Hungary Assistance for Economic Reconstruction
IPPs	Independent Power Producers		
ISO	International Standard Office	PPI	Producers Price Index
ISP	Index of Speculative Pressure	PPP	Purchasing Power Parity
KB	Komercni Banka	PRIBOR	Prague Inter-banking Offer Rate
Kg.	Kilogram		
KoB	Konsolidacni Banka	PSE	Prague Stock Exchange
KW	Kilo-watt	pse	Producer Subsidy Equivalent
LAC	Latin America and Caribbean	R&D	Research and Development
LDC	Less Developed Country	RCA	Revealed Comparative Advantage
LFPRs	Labor Force Participation Rates	RECs	Regional Electricity Companies
		REER	Real Effective Exchange Rate
LFS	Labor Force Survey	RIAE	Research Institute of Agricultural Economics
M	Municipal or Local Government Budget		
		RIF	Restitution Investment Fund
MATAV	Hungarian Telephone National Operator	RILSA	Research Institute for Labor and Social Affairs
MFN	Most Favorable Nation	RMS	RM-System
MIT	Ministry of Industry and Trade	ROW	Rest of the World
MLS	Minimum Living Standard	S	State Budget
MoF	Ministry of Finance	S&P	Standard and Poor's
MoL&SA	Ministry of Labor and Social Affairs	SB	Single Buyer
		SBM	Single Buyer Model
MPP	Mass Privatization Program	SEF	State Environment Fund
MTPL	Motor Third Party Liability	SFA	State Financial Assets
MVM	Hungarian Grid Company	SFMR	State Fund for Market Regulations
MW	Mega Watts	SGFFF	Support and Guarantee Fund for Farmers and Forestry
N/C	Non Convergence		
NATO	North Atlantic Treaty Organization	SITC	Standard International Trade Classification
NAV	Net Asset Value	SO_2	Sulfur Oxide
NGOs	Non-governmental Organizations	SPJs	Socially Purposeful Jobs
		STE	Stedoceska energeticka, a.s.

xv

STET	Italian Telecom Company	UN	United Nations
TO	Transmission Operator	US	Unites States
TOZ	Perpetual Inventory Revolving Credits	USAID	United States Agency for International Development
TPA	Third Party Access	USD	United States Dollar
TSO	Transmission System Operator	UWWT	Urban Wastewater Treatment Directive
Twh	Tetra-watt		
UCS	Unemployment Compensation System	VAT	Value Added Tax
		VOCs	Volatile Organic Compounds
UK	United Kingdom	WTO	World Trade Organization
ULC	Unit Labor Cost	ZB	Zivnostenska Banka

FISCAL YEAR

January 1 to December 31

Vice President:	Johannes Linn
Country Director:	Roger Grawe
Sector Director:	Pradeep Mitra
Sector Leader:	Hafez Ghanem
Team Leader:	Carlos Silva-Jauregui

Chapter I. Economic Performance on the Road to EU Accession

Introduction

Until 1996, the Czech Republic was perceived as the most successful transition economy in Central and Eastern Europe (CEE).[1] Given the Czech Republic's favorable initial conditions on a number of key economic policy variables -- Czechoslovakia maintained, even during communism, a prudent monetary, fiscal and debt strategy; macroeconomic stability seemed to have been firmly established just a few years after the *Velvet Revolution* of 1989. The structural transformation of the economy, from command to market, was perceived as going ahead at remarkable speed. The innovative voucher privatization program was a tool to redefine the role and size of the State, transferring a large amount of assets to the private sector. The so-called Czech miracle -- economic transformation with minimum unemployment and no hyperinflation -- was seen by many as a role model, but one unable to be reached by other transforming economies.

While the mass privatization program was able to reallocate a large amount of property into private hands in a very short period of time, it did not induce the needed fundamental changes in enterprise behavior. The seemingly strict fiscal discipline of the Czech government was not present in the enterprise sector, particularly in large enterprises, some of which were persistent loss makers. The banking sector continued to be dominated largely by state banks, which did not play the role of efficient financial intermediators. The symbiotic relationship between state banks and large quasi-private enterprises remained in place, in part because state banks were unwilling to impose hard budget constraints on the enterprise sector, but also due to the inability of legislative reforms to set the proper conditions for the use of market based solutions to enterprise restructuring. Weak corporate governance compounded the problem by allowing wages to grow above productivity increases, eroding competitiveness abroad.

The so-called Czech miracle came to a halt in May 1997. At that time, a speculative attack on the crown -- driven in part by the international communities' perception of an unsustainable current account balance -- forced the authorities to abandon the exchange rate policy maintained since 1991 and to introduce a strict austerity program, including tight fiscal and monetary policies. The macroeconomic imbalances behind the crisis served to highlight the deficiency in microeconomic restructuring. By November 1997, Prime Minister Vaclav Klaus had resigned, a caretaker government had been appointed and, in mid-1998, general elections had brought down the government. The lack of comprehensive restructuring, and the events that followed the May crisis, brought the economy to a halt. As a result, the Czech Republic is now experiencing its first post-transition recession, with a decline in output by 2.3 percent in 1998 and with low prospects of economic growth in 1999. Moreover, unemployment has doubled, reaching over 8 percent in the first half of 1999.

---

[1] During this period, most articles written on the Czech Republic transition from command to market economy were overly optimistic, including some written by World Bank staff. Few voices of dissent highlighted the fragility of the Czech transition model. The international community's attraction for the Czech Republic's model was based, to a large degree, on the voucher privatization method, a radical approach to rapid or mass privatization. An economic research report from a very well known investment bank said in February 1995 that "...mass privatization, balanced finances, an export orientation, a reliable currency, and low unemployment have laid a superb foundation for a stable, prosperous, and democratically-supported market economy." This image of success was shared by many and was fueled by the Czech authorities, who officially refuted any potential weaknesses of their process of transition. Only a few hinted of the intrinsic weaknesses of the Czech model. In hindsight, time would prove them right.

In the midst of the economic crisis, the Czech Republic is seeking accession to an enlarged European Union (EU), a task that in itself is demanding. To seize the benefits from accession, the Czech Republic needs to stabilize its economy and to recover its growth potential by setting the foundations for sustainable development. This, in turn, will foster the likelihood of an early accession to the EU. However, the process of accession also implies costs, which need to be balanced with the demands of stabilization and restructuring. These are the great challenges that are ahead of the Czech policy makers.

Stabilization and Recovery: Beyond the Velvet Divorce

Macroeconomic Performance during 1993-95

The Czech Republic had an impressive macroeconomic performance after the *Velvet Divorce* that dissolved the Czech and Slovak Federal Republic (CSFR) at the end of 1992. Recovery from the transitional recession started in 1993 and gathered momentum in the following two years. Growth in the 1993-95 period was accompanied by a decline in the already low rate of unemployment, as well as by a decline in the inflation rate to single digit levels. The current account shifted from a surplus in 1993 to a deficit thereafter, but the level of the deficit remained moderate relative to GDP, giving the impression that the Czech Republic had entered a sustainable high growth path (see Table 1.1).

Table 1.1. Inflation, Growth and Current Account Balance in Selected CEE Countries, 1993-99

	1993	1994	1995	1996	1997	1998	1999[1/]
	Annual Inflation Rate (average CPI, percent)						
Czech Republic	20.8	10.0	9.1	8.8	8.5	10.7	2.2
Estonia	89.0	47.7	28.9	23.1	11.2	10.6	6.0
Hungary	22.5	18.8	28.2	23.6	18.3	14.3	9.0
Poland	35.3	32.2	27.8	19.9	14.8	11.8	6.8
Slovak Republic	23.2	13.4	9.9	5.8	6.2	6.7	10.0
Slovenia	32.9	21.0	13.5	9.9	8.4	7.9	8.0
	Real GDP Growth (percent)						
Czech Republic	0.6	2.7	6.4	3.8	0.3	-2.3	-1.0
Estonia	-8.5	-1.8	4.3	4.0	11.4	4.3	2.0
Hungary	-0.6	2.9	1.5	1.3	4.4	5.0	4.0
Poland	3.8	5.2	7.0	6.1	6.9	4.8	4.0
Slovak Republic	-3.7	4.9	6.9	6.6	6.5	4.4	2.0
Slovenia	2.8	5.3	4.1	3.5	4.6	3.9	3.5
	Current Account Balance (percent of GDP)						
Czech Republic	1.3	-1.9	-2.6	-7.4	-6.1	-1.9	-0.7
Estonia	1.3	-7.1	-4.7	-9.1	-12.0	-8.6	-8.0
Hungary	-9.0	-9.5	-5.6	-3.7	-2.2	-4.8	-5.0
Poland	-2.7	-1.0	4.6	-1.0	-3.5	-4.2	-5.6
Slovak Republic	-5.0	4.8	2.3	-11.1	-6.9	-9.7	-4.5
Slovenia	1.5	4.2	-0.1	0.2	0.2	0.0	-0.2

1/ Ministry of Finance projections.
Source: Central Statistical Office of Respective Countries.

The success in rapid output recovery and in reducing inflation to single digit levels was due to a comprehensive stabilization program implemented during the early years of the transition. The stabilization program included a basket-pegged exchange rate at competitive initial level, after a

113.5 percent devaluation of the crown in 1990, tight fiscal policy and initial wage discipline leading to a compression of real wages in 1991-92.[2]

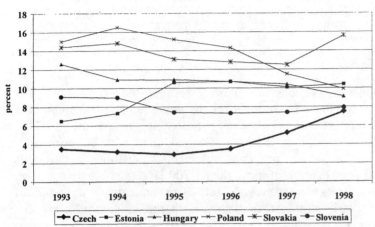

Figure 1.1. Unemployment Rate in Selected CEE Countries

Czech — Estonia — Hungary — Poland — Slovakia — Slovenia

The stabilization program did not prevent the economy from achieving rapid recovery. On the contrary, the very competitive exchange rate (see Table 1.2) and the favorable external conditions contributed to a strong growth of exports and investment, leading GDP to grow at 2.7 and 6.4 percent in 1994 and 1995, respectively.[3] The growth recovery led the unemployment rate to drop below 3 percent by end-1995. This was seen as a remarkable achievement, given that most transitional economies had experienced an increase in unemployment to levels of around 7 to 15 percent during the same period (see Figure 1.1).

At the end of 1995, the Czech Republic was regarded as the clearest success story in the region. It had one of the lowest rates of inflation and the lowest rate of unemployment. The high GDP growth rate looked sustainable, as it was accompanied by a moderate current account deficit, balanced fiscal accounts, and seemed to be underpinned by important structural reforms. Major achievements in the structural area included the liberalization of wages, prices and foreign trade, as well as an innovative mass privatization program centered on the distribution of vouchers to Czech citizens that enabled a massive transfer of enterprises to the private sector in a very short period of time.

Table 1.2. Relation between Purchasing Power Parity and Current Exchange Rates in 1993 and 1997

	Czech Republic	Estonia	Hungary	Poland	Slovenia
1993	2.8	2.3	1.9	2.2	0.9
1997	2.3	2.2	2.1	2.1	1.4

Source: World Bank Atlas (1996) and EUROSTAT.

These achievements, in conjunction with a low debt level, led the Czech Republic to enjoy the highest credit rating among all transitional economies, even though a number of important questions and puzzles still surrounded its performance. By 1997, the Czech Republic's debt was rated at Baa3 by Moody's and BBB+ by Standards and Poor's; both ratings were investment grade. The credit rating grades continued to improve until late 1998 (see Table 1.3).

---

[2] Since September 28, 1992, the crown was allowed to float on a narrow band of (+/-) 0.5 percent around a central parity rate. The central rate was pegged to a currency basket comprised by the German mark, US dollar, Austrian Schilling, Swiss Franc and French Franc between 1993 and May 1997.

[3] The competitiveness levels are assessed by a simple comparison between Purchasing Power Parity (PPP) and current exchange rates among the most advanced transitional economies in Central Europe. Within this sample, the Czech Republic was second only to the Slovak Republic, which shared the same initial stabilization program, and which devalued its currency relative to the Czech crown at the time of its independence.

Table 1.3. Sovereign Long-term Foreign Currency Credit Ratings, September 1998

	Moody's	S&P	Fitch IBCA
Czech Republic	Baa1	A	BBB+
Estonia	Baa1	BBB+	BBB
Hungary	Baa2	BBB-	BBB
Poland	Baa3	BBB-	BBB
Slovak Republic	Ba1	BB+	BBB-
Slovenia	A3	A	A-

Source: Moody's, Standard and Poor's and Fitch IBCA.

The Czech transition success, however, raised some questions among those few skeptics of the Czech miracle. First, the unemployment rate looked extremely low by any international comparison, and particularly low in comparison with other transitional countries undergoing restructuring, suggesting perhaps the existence of redundant labor in large enterprises. Second, the major commercial banks remained in State hands and were experiencing severe problems in their loan portfolios. Third, although the voucher scheme had allowed a rapid privatization of more than 1,700 large and medium enterprises, there were doubts as to whether the new owners were exercising active corporate governance and driving restructuring. These doubts were particularly strong in the case of enterprises controlled by the new investment funds, created during the voucher scheme to prevent excessive fragmentation of ownership and to exercise governance on behalf of millions of voucher holders.

The Emergence of Macroeconomic Imbalances

The Czech Republic experienced increasing macroeconomic imbalances in the middle of the 1990s. This was partly as a result of the perceived early success in stabilizing the economy, but also partly a result of arbitrage opportunities resulting from inconsistent monetary and exchange rate policies. Large amounts of capital flowed into the Czech Republic, hindering the capacity of the Central Bank for monetary policy management. The flows were significant in 1994 but intensified in 1995 to US$8.2 billion, or 15.8 percent of GDP (see Figure 1.2). While these flows were mostly driven by medium- and long-term credits, short-term credits also

Figure 1.2. Financial Account of the Balance of Payments

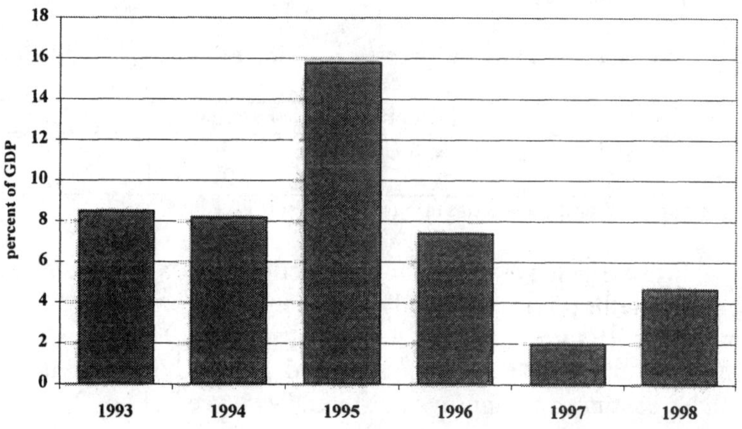

increased. The capital flows stimulated excessive growth in domestic demand which, combined with disproportionate wage increases, overheated the economy; as a result, the current account deteriorated.

The Central Bank reacted to the capital inflows with a number of policy options that included costly sterilization and restriction on short-term flows. But these policies did not prevent overheating of the economy. At the end of February 1996, the Czech National Bank (CNB) decided to widen the exchange rate band to (+/-) 7.5 percent around the central parity, in an effort to allow more flexibility to the crown.

Table 1.4. Selected Economic Indicators, 1993-98

	1993	1994	1995	1996	1997	1998
Real Economy						
Real GDP (growth rate)	0.6	2.7	6.4	3.8	0.3	-2.3
Share of Private Sector in GDP	45.1	56.3	63.8	74.0	74.3	75.0
Unemployment rate (end of period)	3.5	3.2	2.9	3.5	5.2	7.5
Inflation (CPI, period average)	20.8	10.0	9.1	8.8	8.5	10.7
Inflation (PPI, period average)	9.2	5.4	7.6	4.8	4.9	4.9
Private Consumption/GDP	48.9	50.6	50.1	50.9	52.4	51.5
Gross National Savings/GDP	28.4	28.2	29.9	28.1	27.1	28.1
Gross Domestic Investment/GDP	28.5	29.6	32.8	33.0	30.7	28.1
Balance of Payments						
Trade Balance/GDP	-1.5	-3.4	-7.1	-10.1	-8.6	-4.6
Merchandise Exports (volume growth rate)	-	6.5	15.5	0.0	14.0	11.5
Merchandise Imports (volume growth rate)	-	20.2	26.8	11.1	7.5	9.0
Current Account Balance/GDP	1.3	-1.9	-2.6	-7.4	-6.1	-1.9
Financial Account/GDP	8.5	8.2	15.8	7.4	2.0	4.7
Gross Official Reserves (billion US$, end-year)	3.9	6.2	14.0	12.4	9.8	12.6
Reserve Cover (months of imports of GS)	-	3.4	5.5	4.4	3.6	4.4
Gross External Debt/GDP	27.8	28.9	33.1	36.9	44.5	39.6
External Debt Service (percent of exports of GS)	-	13.1	9.2	10.7	15.6	15.1
Public Finances						
General Government Balance/GDP	2.6	0.8	0.3	-0.3	-1.2	-1.5
Gross Public Debt/GDP	19.1	17.6	15.3	13.1	12.9	13.2
Interest Rates						
Interbank offer rate (3 month PRIBOR, in percent)	13.1	9.1	10.9	12.0	16.0	14.3
Average nominal lending rate (in percent)	14.1	13.1	12.8	12.5	13.2	12.9
Average real lending rate (deflated by PPI, in percent)	5.5	7.1	5.2	7.9	7.1	10.4
Average nominal deposit rate (in percent)	7.0	7.1	7.0	6.8	7.7	8.1
Average real deposit rate (net, deflated by CPI, in percent)	-7.5	-1.1	0.8	-0.5	-1.1	2.0
Money and Credit						
Broad Money (M2, annual growth)	19.8	19.9	19.8	9.2	10.1	5.2
Quasi-Money (M3, annual growth)	23.3	24.4	24.6	12.8	22.5	9.7
Credit to Enterprises and Households	-	16.6	12.7	9.7	8.7	-1.0
Net Foreign Assets	-	4.0	-1.7	1.9	-0.5	2.0
Labor and Wages						
Labor Productivity (percentage change)	-	1.6	5.5	3.5	1.7	-1.2
Nominal gross wage growth (period average)	-	17.8	19.1	16.8	8.0	8.1
Real gross wage growth (period average)	-	7.1	9.1	7.3	-0.4	-2.3
Exchange Rates						
Nominal Exchange Rate (CZK per US$, average)	29.2	28.8	26.5	27.1	31.7	32.3
Nominal Exchange Rate (CZK per DEM, average)	17.6	17.8	18.5	18.1	18.3	18.3
Nominal Effective Exchange Rate (previous year=100)[1/]	99.3	99.9	100.0	99.1	106.5	100.8
Real Effective Exchange Rate (ULC, previous year=100)[1/]	87.3	91.8	93.0	91.6	101.1	92.0
Memo						
Gross Domestic Product (current US$ billion)	31.2	41.1	52.1	58.0	53.0	56.4
Per Capita Income (US$)	3,300	4,017	5,016	5,636	5,198	5,527

1/ Growth of the exchange rate indices indicates depreciation of the Czech crown.
Source: Ministry of Finance, Czech National Bank, Czech Statistical Office and IMF.

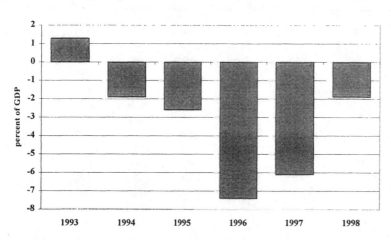

Figure 1.3. Current Account Balance

Macroeconomic performance started to falter in 1996, when the current account deficit recorded an unsustainable large deficit of 7.4 percent of GDP (see Figure 1.3). The external imbalance apparently did not have fiscal roots -- the fiscal deterioration was minor (0.6 percent of GDP) relative to the current account deterioration (4.8 percent of GDP).[4] Instead, the current account imbalance was due to a sharp drop in export growth and to a strong expansion of private consumption and investment, which pressured import demand up.

The export slowdown was partly due to a contraction of the Czech Republic's main export markets in the West, primarily Germany, but also due to the erosion of competitiveness, over the years, caused by the fixed exchange rate. The real effective exchange rate appreciated by 36 percent between 1992-96 (see Table 1.5). There were doubts as to whether enterprise restructuring had proceeded at a pace sufficient to offset the real appreciation that occurred during this period with productivity gains. Real wages increased by 31 percent during 1992-96, without significantly affecting unemployment. The growth of real wages above productivity growth was more severe in State enterprises, but also affected privatized enterprises, raising doubts about the quality of corporate governance in the private sector. Fast wage growth not only affected competitiveness, but also explained, to a large degree, the consumption boom observed during this period. Gross national savings declined from 29.2 percent in 1992 to 27.1 percent in 1997. Finally, there were doubts as to whether the high investment ratio observed in the Czech Republic -- around 33 percent of GDP in 1996 -- provided room for optimism, or whether there were many poor and inefficient projects still being financed.

Table 1.5. Real Effective Exchange Rate (REER) and Real Wages, 1993-98

	1993	1994	1995	1996	1997	1998
REER	100	92	85	78	79	73
Real Gross Wages	100	107	117	125	125	122

Note: A decline in the REER index indicates appreciation of the crown.
Source: Ministry of Finance.

The external imbalances led to a fast build up of external debt, raising doubts about the sustainability of the current account deficit. Gross external debt increased from US$9.6 billion in 1993 to US$21.2 billion in 1996 (see Figure 1.4). Short-term debt increased threefold, from US$2 billion to US$6 billion in the same period. While the current account deficit declined slightly in 1997, the external

---

[4] While this statement is in principle true, it is, however, difficult to tell to what degree the current account deterioration was the result of fiscal pressures. The official general government fiscal balance did not show a strong correlation with the deterioration in the current account deficit. Nonetheless, a number of extrabudgetary activities and the buildup of contingent liabilities may have increased the contribution of the fiscal deficit by an extra one percent of GDP. See the chapter on contingent liabilities in this report.

imbalances persisted, leading to a high perception of risk. The increasing uncertainty eventually culminated in a speculative attack on the Czech crown in May 1997.

The 1997 Currency Crisis and the Policy Response

With the widening of the exchange rate band and strong inflows of capital, the crown appreciated by as much of 6 percent over its central parity during the second half of 1996 and the early months of 1997. The strong crown induced a further deterioration of the capital account deficit, which reached its peak during the first quarter of 1997, at almost US$5 billion.

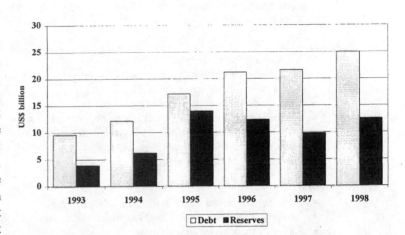

Figure 1.4. Gross External Debt and Official Reserves

Foreign reserves, however, started to decline during 1996, as expectations of the unsustainability of the external imbalance accumulated. By this time, the CNB had stopped intervening in the foreign exchange market to avoid both liquidity increases and the high cost of sterilization.[5] Instead the CNB issued statements about the inconsistency of the exchange rate levels with the fundamentals in an attempt to influence exchange rate behavior.

By February 1997, weakening economic activity due to the deterioration of competitiveness abroad and the continuing deterioration of the current and trade accounts -- exports of goods actually stopped growing by mid-1996 while imports continued to grow -- prompted a negative reaction from market participants. The crown started to weaken as capital flew out of the Czech Republic and as investors made portfolio shifts to short term maturities. With the decline of economic activity, the fiscal stance also deteriorated, prompting the authorities to introduce a package of fiscal austerity measures in April 1997 (see Box 1.1). This package, however, failed to reverse the market perception of an imminent crisis.

The fragility of the economic situation became evident a few weeks later. The turmoil in the financial markets in Asia, as a result of the currency attacks on the Thai baht, intensified the pressure on the crown to depreciate in late May. While the volatile international conditions also affected other transition economies, the Czech crown was more exposed due to the external imbalances and the greater openness and globalization of the Czech economy.[6] An attack on the Czech currency followed when both foreign and domestic investors ran from the crown into other hard currencies. Despite massive foreign exchange interventions by the CNB -- amounting to sales of US$2.5 billion -- and despite steep increases in interest rates -- 75 percent for the two-week repo and 35 percent on the three-month PRIBOR -- to defend the crown and contain the attack, the CNB was forced to abandon its foreign exchange regime in favor of a managed float. The crown depreciated by 12 percent with respect to the central basket parity.

---

[5] At its peak in the last months of 1995, cumulative sterilization of capital inflows reached 24 percent of M2, just under CZK240 billion.

[6] In April 1997, the foreign exchange turnover of the Czech Republic was US$5.5 billion against US$0.4 billion for Hungary and Poland.

Box 1.1. Austerity Measures Introduced in April-May 1997

The government introduced a series of fiscal measures, regulatory reforms and structural reform intentions to cope with the impending currency crisis. The measures included:

April 1997
- A freeze in government sector real wage bill;
- a 25 percent reduction in public-sector capital expenditures;
- savings in non-investment subsidies;
- introduction of an import deposit scheme;
- a pledge to accelerate the privatization of banks and strategic enterprises;
- a pledge to increase transparency and regulation of capital markets;
- a recommendation to give preferential treatment to domestic suppliers in public procurement; and
- an increase in funding for export promotion activities.

May 1997
- a freeze in nominal wages in the state sector in 1998;
- an appeal for wage moderation in firms with state participation;
- a reduction in social expenditures;
- a reduction in capital expenditures;
- a reduction in budget-financed imports; and
- a pledge to accelerate the structural measures announced in the April package.

Source: Organisation for Economic Co-operation and Development (OECD).

While the currency crisis may have been triggered by an external event such as the turmoil in Asia, the market fundamentals in the Czech Republic were prompt to a crisis. As in Asia, the Czech Republic suffered from an unsustainable (and expanding) current account deficit, a fixed exchange rate regime, a banking sector burdened by bad loans, non-standard accounting practices, lack of regulation in financial markets, an investment boom (albeit with weak growth), a high asset to GDP ratio in the banking sector and an unhealthy relationship between State banks and loss making enterprises. The fiscal balance was also deteriorating; contingent liabilities, especially in the financial sector, were increasing. The prompt reaction of the CNB served to contain the crisis and to stabilize the crown a few months later.

The May currency crisis triggered additional policy reforms. The Government introduced a second package of austerity measures including further spending cuts, to avoid an increase in the fiscal deficit. The Government started implementing a stricter wage policy in the public sector, and announced additional reforms in the financial sector (see Box 1.1). These included plans to privatize the State-owned banks, and to undertake further reforms in the capital market. Expenditure cuts were also planned for 1998. The fiscal measures, equivalent to 2.5 percent of GDP, were implemented in a difficult environment, due to problems generated by the July floods in Moravia and East Bohemia. The floods affected more than 10,000 people and produced damages estimated at about 3-4 percent of GDP. The government covered CZK18 billion in flood relief expenditure, and insurance companies covered CZK10 billion. The remainder was borne by private citizens.

The Aftermath of the Currency Crisis

The 1998-99 Recession

The slowdown in economic activity intensified after the currency crisis, in part as a result of the austerity measures introduced and the impact of the floods. The heavy flooding lowered output growth by an estimated 0.5 percentage point. As a result, the overall economic performance during 1997 was disappointing and GDP growth slowed down to just 0.3 percent (see Figure 1.5). This slowdown was driven by the slow down in domestic demand growth to 0.3 percent as consumers' confidence plummeted in the second half of 1997 and as investment projects stopped. The

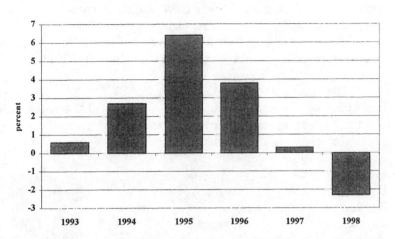

Figure 1.5. GDP Growth Rate, 1993-98

growth in private consumption fell from 7 percent in 1996 to 2.1 percent in 1997. Government consumption increased by 3.4 percent in 1997. Investment (fixed capital formation) declined by 4.3 percent as a result of high interest rates and the cancellation of public infrastructure projects.

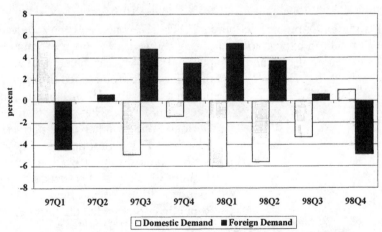

Figure 1.6. GDP Components Annualized Growth Rates

The slowdown in economic activity turned into a full-fledged recession during 1998 as the downturn deepened during the second half of the year. As a result, GDP declined by 2.3 percent in 1998. Domestic demand declined by 3.4 percent, with household consumption falling by 3 percent and gross capital formation by 5.7 percent (fixed capital formation by 3.8 percent). Foreign demand helped to mitigate the recession, especially during the first half of 1998. The strong appreciation of the crown in 1998 eroded competitiveness abroad and eliminated the cushion provided by the foreign balance. As a result, during the last quarter of 1998, output declined at an annualized rate of 3.9 percent, and the growth of imports of goods and services surpassed exports by 4.9 percent (see Figure 1.6).

One of the most damaging impacts of the current recession has been the effect on employment and, consequently, on the unemployment rate of the economy. For the first time since the *Velvet Divorce*, the Czech Republic experienced a decline in employment with a rapid rise in unemployment. The rate of unemployment remained at around 3 percent until mid-1996 (see Figure 1.1). By 1998, unemployment increased to 7.5 percent. This trend continued during the first half of 1999, with unemployment reaching over 8 percent.

While tight monetary and fiscal policies may have helped deepen the recession, the fundamental cause of the slowdown resided in unresolved structural problems in the real and financial sectors. The change in ownership structure induced by the voucher privatization program was insufficient to produce the changes in governance needed to promote deep restructuring. A good deal of the enterprise sector continued to operate with losses during the transition years; and the banking sector, mostly dominated by large state banks, did not enforce hard budget constraints to promote the needed restructuring. This was complicated by the lack of a regulatory system that helped the development of the emerging market economy. Moreover, privatization investment funds did not play the expected positive role in improving corporate governance.[7] As a result of the macroeconomic crisis, microeconomic deficiencies surfaced.

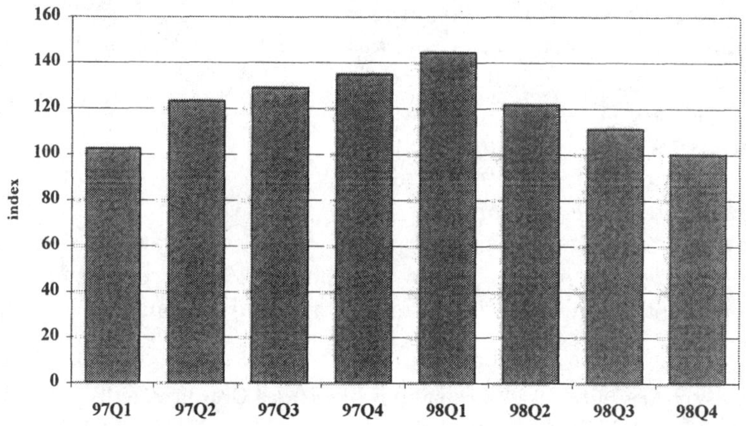

The external situation has improved significantly since the speculative attacks on the crown. The current account deficit declined from 6.1 percent in 1997 to 1.9 percent in 1998 (see Figure 1.3). This adjustment on the current account was, in part, the result of the weak import demand and strong export growth that followed the currency crisis. The adjustment of the current account, however, is amplified by a strong cyclical component. Other factors also contributed to the adjustment. The decline of world commodity prices in 1998,

Figure 1.7. Annualized Growth in Exports of Goods, 1997-98

in particular oil, improved the terms of trade by as much as 5 percent. These events, and the renewed demand from Europe, led to a significant growth in export volume during the year. Export performance slowed down in the second half of 1998, as capital inflows and the appreciation of the exchange rate after

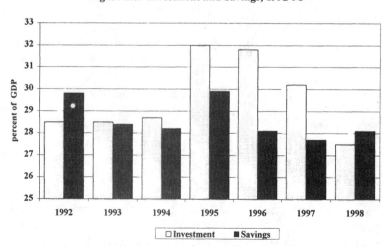

Figure 1.8. Investment and Savings, 1992-98

the crisis in Russia eroded the wedge produced by the 1997 devaluation (see Figure 1.7). The slowdown in Germany and in other trade partners in the EU diminished export performance during 1999. A large decline in exports to transforming countries like Poland and Slovak Republic compounded the problem.

The recent slowdown in growth reduced the average growth rate of the Czech economy during the whole post-independence period (1993-98) to a disappointing 1.9 percent on average. This growth performance looks particularly low,

---

[7] See the enterprise sector chapter of this report.

considering the high average investment ratio (above 30 percent of GDP) maintained throughout this period (see Figure 1.8). This implies incremental capital-output ratios (ICORs) much higher than other countries with similar per capita incomes, and higher than the other CEE countries as well (see Table 1.6). The comparison with other transitional CEE countries is admittedly based on a short period, during which there were macroeconomic cycles affecting the growth performance of CEE countries in different ways. However, it does suggest that the Czech economy is growing well below its potential, and that there is scope for both further efficiency gains and for the achievement of higher growth rates for the same investment levels.

Table 1.6. Average Implicit Incremental Capital-Output Ratios

	Czech Republic	Hungary	Poland	Slovak Republic	Slovenia
1993-98	13.5	8.7	3.2	7.7	5.7
1994-98	12.0	7.1	3.0	5.7	5.5

Source: The World Bank.

One of the possible causes of the high ICOR in the Czech Republic is likely to be the composition of investments. A large share of investments in the past went to environmental cleanup, highways, railway corridors, telecommunications and the atomic power stations Temelin. In 1996, for instance, energy, transport and telecommunications took about half of the investments in non-financial enterprises. The investments have a long-term return and do not have the fast output response as traditional investments do, thus increasing the ICOR.

Inflation Targeting

Against the background of an impending recession and growing inflation, the Central Bank introduced a new monetary policy in early 1998, targeting a narrow definition of inflation. Net inflation, a correction of the CPI inflation that excludes the impact of changes in regulated prices and indirect taxes, has been the instrument of choice. While the CNB set a target for 1998 in the range of 5.5-6.5 percent, unusual circumstances helped push inflation down sharply during the year (see Figure 1.9). The decline in inflation rates was a result of both the CNB's tight monetary policy, and the impact of a declining domestic demand and commodity prices, including food and oil, during the year. Net inflation declined to 1.7 percent by December, well below the CNB target. At the same time, CPI inflation declined to 6.8 percent at the end of the year. This trend continued in early 1999, with CPI inflation declining to 2.9 percent and net inflation to minus 0.4 percent in March.

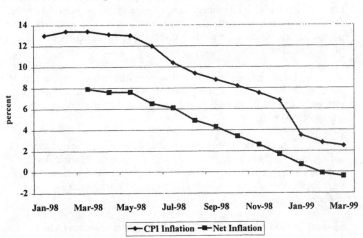

Figure 1.9. Annualized Inflation Rates

With the sharp decline in inflation, the CNB engaged during the second half of 1998 in an aggressive policy to reduce interest rates. The cut in interest rates started after the elections in June, but accelerated in the last part of 1998 and the beginning of 1999. Between July of 1998 and March of 1999,

CNB two-week repo rate was cut ten times, by a total of 750 basis points, from 15 percent to 7.5 percent. Further reductions took place in April and May. The easing of monetary policy was done amidst a deteriorating external environment, due to the crisis in Russia. Commercial bank lending and borrowing rates also declined, but to a lesser degree. At a result, real interest rates have actually increased for both deposits and credits (see Table 1.7).

Table 1.7. Interest Rates on Deposits and Credits, 1998-99

	January 1998		January 1999	
	Nominal	Real	Nominal	Real
Deposits Total	8.47	-4.63	6.44	2.94
Short-term	11.88	-1.22	8.44	4.94
Medium-term	12.20	-0.90	10.46	6.96
Long-term	5.09	-8.01	4.16	0.66
Credits Total	13.68	7.58	10.06	9.26
Short-term	13.76	7.66	10.04	9.24
Medium-term	14.47	8.37	10.31	9.51
Long-term	12.97	6.87	9.91	9.11

Note: Deposit rates are deflated by CPI. Lending rates are deflated by PPI.
Source: CNB.

Given the weakness of economic activity and the level of net inflation the CNB could set official short-term interest rates to the lowest level consistent with the net inflation target of 3.5–5.5 percent set for 2000. A close eye on foreign exchange market developments should, however, be maintained. In fact, some further small depreciation would not be a source of concern and could actually help strengthen external competitiveness, but a pronounced downward move could endanger the inflation target.

Box 1.2. Inflation Targeting

Inflation targeting is a framework for monetary policy characterized by the public announcement of official inflation rate targets over a specific time horizon. The ultimate goal of inflation targeting is to reduce inflation uncertainty. Inflation uncertainty is costly: it exacerbates the volatility of relative prices and increases the risk of financial instruments and contracts set in nominal terms. By making explicit the central bank's medium-term policy intentions, inflation targets reduce volatility in financial markets, improve planning in the private sector, enhance the public debate about the direction of monetary policy, and increase the accountability of the central bank.

Inflation targeting has had important benefits for the countries that have used it. Inflation targeting countries have achieved lower inflation rates and lower inflation expectations; typically enjoy lower nominal interest rates as a result of the lower inflation expectations; and have been able to sustain price stability despite unexpected shocks.

It should be noted however that as long as inflation targets coexist with other objectives of monetary policy, e.g., exchange rate stability, and the central bank lacks the means to convey to the public its policy priorities and its operating procedures in a credible and transparent way, tension between the inflation target and the other policy objectives is unavoidable. In such circumstances, the benefits of inflation targeting may be lower.

Source: The World Bank Knowledge Management System (KMS).

Fiscal Performance during the Transition

Since the beginning of the transition, the Czech government has maintained a fiscal policy aimed at achieving a nearly balanced budget. This policy of seemingly strong fiscal prudence is tainted, in part, by the fact that a number of budgetary operations have been carried outside the budget.[8] These operations have been conducted by extrabudgetary funds, financed directly from privatization proceeds coming from the National Property Fund (NPF) or from the State Financial Assets (SFA).[9] Once the budgetary and extrabudgetary operations of the central government are consolidated with the finances of the local authorities and the public health insurance funds, then the accounts of the general government reflect a different story, with the general government fiscal budget reflecting small deficits during 1994-98.

The fiscal performance of the Czech Republic during the transition seems to be favorable when compared with most CEE transition countries. All of these countries undertook price liberalization and privatization reform, albeit at different paces and using a variety of methods. As a result, all of the countries went through cycles of sharp recession followed, in most cases, by private sector-induced recovery. A central feature of the liberalization packages was a set of policies intended to affect fiscal accounts that, in many cases led to fiscal crises -- a rare phenomenon in these previously socialist economies.

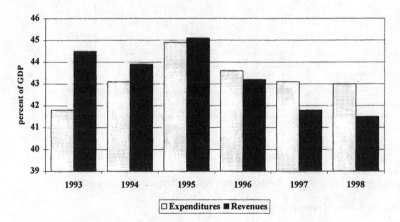

Figure 1.10. General Government Expenditures and Revenues

A close look at the behavior of public finances in the Czech Republic shows that the widening of the official fiscal gap between 1993-98 was caused by a reduction on the revenue side -- equivalent to 3 percent of GDP -- while the expenditure side experienced a structural recomposition with no attrition, remaining at around 43 percent of GDP (see Table 1.8). Since the 1993 tax reform, discretionary cuts in direct tax rates and changes in tax regulations resulted in a progressive fall of revenue, from 44.5 percent of GDP in 1993 to 41.5 percent in 1998 (see Figure 1.10).

The share of capital expenditures decreased from 7 percent of GDP in 1995 to 5.1 percent in 1998. With the recession, public investment projects have been postponed, reducing capital expenditures even further. The share of transfers to households increased from 11.8 percent of GDP in 1995 to 13 percent in 1998. In the same period, the share of subsidies to enterprises and financial institutions increased from 3.1 percent of GDP in 1995 to 3.6 percent in 1998 (see Table 1.8). The increase in subsidies reflected in the general government fiscal accounts, however, does not reflect the increased net transfer to the real and financial sector coming from transformation institutions which built a large degree of contingent

---

[8] Extrabudgetary funds include the Czech Land Fund, the National Property Fund, the State Fund for Culture, the State Fund for Environmental Protection, the State Fund for Soil Fertilization and the State Fund for Support and Development of Czech Cinematography.
[9] State Financial Assets (SFA) comprise the central government's account at the Czech National Bank, in which the state budget surpluses from previous years are deposited.

liabilities during the 1996-98 period. Moreover, when these operations are taken into consideration in the consolidated accounts, the fiscal deficit exploits during 1997-98.[10]

Table 1.8. General Government Operations, 1995-99

	1995	1996	1997	1998	1999[8]
	percent of GDP				
Total revenue	45.1	43.2	41.8	41.5	40.7
Tax revenue	38.8	37.8	37.3	36.8	36.9
Direct taxes	9.8	9.1	8.5	8.9	8.7
Corporate profits	4.9	4.0	3.3	3.7	3.3
Personal income tax	5.0	5.1	5.2	5.2	5.5
Indirect taxes	12.2	12.1	11.7	11.0	11.0
VAT	6.9	7.0	7.0	6.6	6.7
Excise	4.1	3.9	3.8	3.7	3.6
Customs duties	1.3	1.3	0.9	0.7	0.6
Social insurance contributions	15.4	15.4	15.8	15.6	16.0
Social security	11.2	11.1	11.4	11.2	11.6
Health funds	4.3	4.3	4.5	4.4	4.4
Other budgetary tax revenue[1]	1.3	1.2	1.2	1.2	1.2
Non-tax revenue	6.3	5.4	4.5	4.7	3.8
Total expenditure	44.9	43.6	43.1	43.0	43.2
Current expenditure	37.5	36.9	37.6	36.9	37.8
On goods and services[2]	21.3	21.0	20.1	19.8	20.0
Interest Payments	1.2	1.0	1.2	1.2	1.4
Transfers	15.1	14.9	16.4	15.9	16.4
Enterprises and banks	3.1	3.0	3.3	2.8	3.0
Households[3]	11.8	11.8	12.9	13.0	13.0
Others[4]	0.2	0.1	0.2	0.2	0.4
Capital expenditure[5]	7.0	6.5	5.5	5.1	5.0
Net lending	0.4	0.1	0.0	0.1	0.1
Bank restructuring[6]	0.0	0.0	0.1	0.8	0.5
Balance including privatization revenues	0.2	-0.4	-1.4	-1.5	-2.5
Balance excluding privatization revenues and bank restructuring costs	-2.5	-2.3	-2.3	-1.6	-2.8
Hidden Fiscal Balance[7]	-1.1	-1.5	-4.1	-3.5	
Overall Implicit Fiscal Balance	-0.9	-1.9	-5.5	-5.0	
Overall Implicit Fiscal Balance excluding privatization revenues and bank restructuring costs	-3.6	-3.8	-6.4	-5.1	

Note: Comprises Central Government, Local Authorities, Extra-budgetary Funds (excluding Fund for Market Regulations, including Czech Land Fund), State Financial Assets, the National Property Fund, and Health Fund.
1/ Includes property, gift and inheritance taxes, motor vehicle tax, and other tax revenues.
2/ Includes government consumption, current spending by extra-budgetary funds, transfers to subsidized organizations and health fund expenditures.
3/ Includes social security, unemployment, and general income support benefits.
4/ Includes transfers abroad and other transfers.
5/ Includes capital transfers to enterprises and subsidized organizations as well as other transfers from local governments.
6/ Financed by Central Government and the NPF.
7/ Hidden fiscal deficit comes from transformation institutions and state guarantees.
8/ Budgeted.
Source: IMF, Ministry of Finance and World Bank staff estimates.

The 1997 crisis, and the severe floods that followed in July, put considerable pressure on public finances. The two rounds of expenditure cuts implemented in April and May (see Box 1.1) were not

---

[10] Fiscal performance in the Czech Republic encompasses a significant amount of government activities financed outside the budgetary system by transformation institutions. For instance, in 1998, in addition to the reported budgetary cost of CZK10.4 billion to cover losses at Konsolidacni banka (KoB) and the cost of state guarantees to Ceska Sporitelna, the estimated losses covered by sources outside the budgetary system would be CZK62.9 billion, or 3.5 percent of GDP, which will bring the total 1998 fiscal deficit as percent of GDP from a reported 1.5 to an estimated implicit deficit of 5 percent of GDP. In addition, the accumulated hidden public liabilities not included in the government debt report are estimated at CZK359 billion in 1998.

sufficient to contain the deterioration of public accounts. As a result, the deficit widened to 1.4 percent of GDP.[11] At the same time, transformation institutions engaged in operations that built an estimated "hidden" deficit of 4.1 percent of GDP.[12] This deficit resulted from operations in the financial and enterprise sectors as tighter regulations from the CNB limited the capacity of the state banks to roll-over bad debts. The overall picture, after these estimates of the "hidden" deficit are considered, shows a deep deterioration of the fiscal stand in 1997-98, on the order of 3.6 percent of GDP in 1997. As a result, the implicit fiscal deficit of the Czech Republic reached 5.5 percent of GDP in 1997 and 5 percent in 1998, damaging the image of fiscal prudence that the Czech Republic maintained during the transition.

There is no doubt that, when looking at the budget, the fiscal policy was tight in 1997, and remained tight in 1998 despite the severe downturn in the economy. The government deficit was limited to 1.5 percent of GDP in 1998. Transformation institutions, however, continued to build implicit liabilities in 1998, softening the budget constraint. While the government is now fully aware of the dangers in building up implicit liabilities, it needs to take measures to contain this non-transparent behavior of extrabudgetary institutions.

Against the background of the current recession, the fiscal stance has become less restrictive. Parliament approved a state budget for 1999 with a deficit of 2 percent of GDP, implying a deficit for the general government of about 3 percent of GDP. To avoid the buildup of hidden liabilities, the authorities should develop policy options for addressing the structural weaknesses and for consolidating public finances over the medium- term. Fiscal policy must consider the recovery of economic growth as a priority, but it must also avoid the temptation of unsustainable fiscal stimulus to the economy. The development of a comprehensive medium-term fiscal strategy should be a priority. This is needed, not only as part of the EU accession process, but also to address the mounting pressures from mandatory expenditure programs, from risks associated with the "hidden debt" and bank and enterprise restructuring costs, and from the need to make room for additional expenditures on the environment, infrastructure, and defense. The government must also be concerned about the deterioration of demographic conditions that could destabilize the pension system soon after EU accession.

The Czech Republic started from the advantageous position of a low debt and a fairly small deficit. Nonetheless, the medium-term fiscal prospects could be unfavorable in the absence of new reforms. Once additional expenditures related to adopting the *Acquis Communautaire*, North Atlantic Treaty Organization (NATO), bank and enterprise restructuring, and the realization of contingent liabilities are taken into account, the medium-term fiscal position becomes worrisome, even after accounting for increased EU transfers and privatization revenues. To put public finances on a sustainable path, the government needs to undertake reform of the tax system and to contain, as well as reform, expenditure programs. The government should also continue to reduce wasteful subsidies such as those to enterprises and certainly not introduce new expenditure programs that work against the reform process such as providing new guarantees. The increased attention to enhancing fiscal transparency and the inclusion of contingent liabilities and off-budget activities in the budgetary process is a significant step forward.

Appropriate measures need to be taken to start fixing the pension system. While better conditions for a comprehensive reform of the pension system are not present, measures to make the current system more sustainable could be implemented. This implies further increasing the retirement age, to take account of changes in life expectancy, improving the actuarial fairness of early retirement provisions; it implies eliminating the accrual of benefits during periods when people are not in the labor force, and

---

[11] Excluding privatization revenues and including bank-restructuring costs would have driven the fiscal deficit to 2.3 percent of GDP in 1997.

[12] See the chapter on contingent liabilities in this report.

limiting the indexation of past earnings used to calculate pension benefits as well as pension payments solely to inflation. The link between contributions and benefits should be strengthened, and consideration could be given to partially pre-funding the pension system to spread the burden of retirement financing more equally across generations and enhance fiscal discipline. Once measures to strengthen banking and capital markets are in place, consideration should be given to broad reforms that include a multi-pillar pension system with higher participation form the private sector.

Coping with Vulnerabilities

Currency Crisis and Early Warning Systems

Vulnerability to sudden reversals in international capital flows has been a distinctive worldwide emerging market feature of the 1990s. The Czech Republic has been no exception -- suffering from sharp capital inflows and sudden capital outflows. The result was an economic boom in the mid-1990s, followed by a currency crisis in 1997 and a painful adjustment process that produced a fall in GDP, increased unemployment rates, and general discontent with the reform process.

The currency crisis revealed the extent to which a country like the Czech Republic is vulnerable to a change in investor confidence. As the fundamentals deteriorated, the market perception of the sustainability of the government's policy mix eroded. Confidence in the exchange rate was lost, forcing the government to abandon the exchange rate regime.

The Czech Republic is a very open economy and, therefore, vulnerable to external economic fluctuations. The business cycle of its major trading EU partners, especially Germany, affects its output performance. In an integrated world, the Czech Republic faces an exceptionally volatile international environment. What was, at most, an Asian regional crisis in 1997 turned into a global crisis in 1998 (see Box 1.3). The world faced unsustainable economic conditions in key emerging market countries in Asia, Latin America and the Former Soviet Union (FSU).

The impact of the Russian crisis on transition economies in CEE has so far been relatively contained, albeit to different degrees.[13] The Czech Republic coped remarkable well with the recent developments in Asia and Russia. As a result, the crisis has not had an appreciable long-term effect on its financial markets. There were, however, sizable short-term effects.

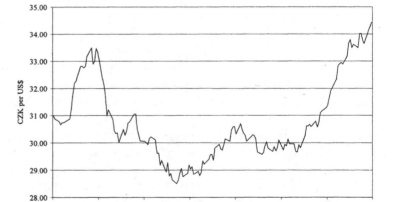

Figure 1.11. Daily Exchange Rate Movement

Spreads in the Eurobond market rose sharply and become volatile; however, they declined as the international financial markets stabilized. The Czech Republic's exchange rate appreciated after the crisis

---

[13] On August 17, faced with unsustainable market pressure, decreasing international reserves and a sizable amount of short-term debt payments, the Russian government abandoned its pegged exchange rate regime, the anchor of its stabilization policy over the preceding 3 years. Simultaneously, it announced a 90-day moratorium on private external obligations, a restructuring of domestic government debt, and the imposition of foreign exchange controls.

as a result of portfolio shifts from risky regional markets to countries with perceived lower vulnerability (see Figure 1.11).

The 1998 world financial crisis has served to highlight the relative strengths and weaknesses of the region's economies. Although the leading acceding countries have seen their equity markets decline sharply, pressure on their exchange rates, interest rates and external spreads has been quite moderate. The crisis, however, has raised concern among policy makers regarding macroeconomic and financial sector vulnerabilities that could lead to disruption of growth, to pressure on its currency regime, or that could hinder the operating capacity of the real and financial sectors.

Box 1.3. International Financial Crises in the 1990s

"The financial crises that have gripped developing countries and the global economy in the recent years have exposed several weaknesses that individually and in concert have contributed to these crises.

In East Asia surging capital inflows and weak financial regulations contributed to booms in domestic lending, often to high-risk sectors such as real estate, resulting in fragile domestic financial sectors. Excessive corporate leveraging and some deterioration in returns made firms highly vulnerable to shocks affecting cash flow and net worth. In Thailand [as well as in Mexico in 1994], an ailing financial sector, export slowdown, and large increases in central bank credit to failing banks helped trigger the run on the domestic currency. The crisis spread to other countries in the region because of common vulnerabilities -- high short-term foreign currency debt on the balance sheet of private agents, financial sector weaknesses, spillovers through international trade linkages, and contagion effects of changes in capital market sentiment. Real activity in the region began a sharp decline as private investment suffered a massive shock -- due to increased uncertainty, the withdrawal of external financing, and the impact of higher interest rates and currency devaluations on the cash flow and balance sheets of banks and firms.

The financial crises that have hit emerging markets do not mean that developing countries should retreat from globalization. The benefits of greater openness in trade and to external savings are among the more important ways in which countries can achieve faster long-run growth. The main lessons of the crisis are that countries need to build and strengthen regulatory and institutional capacities to ensure the safety and stability of financial systems, especially at the interfaces with international financial markets, while the international architecture to prevent crises and deal with them more effectively needs to be strengthened."

Source: The World Bank (1999), Global Economic Prospects, 1998/99.

The integration of the Czech Republic with international markets makes it more sensitive to changes in investors' confidence than other CEE economies. The Czech Republic acceded to the IMF article VIII requirements for current account convertibility in 1995; the OECD membership that year required significant openness of the capital account. While these facts may have made the country more vulnerable during the 1997 currency crisis, the management of the financial instability generated by the events in Russia showed that market fundamentals matter more than capital account convertibility. The policy mix this time was not committed to maintain an exchange rate policy that was inconsistent with the fiscal and monetary policy stand.

The Czech Republic's relative degree of vulnerability can be analyzed by a formal measure. An index that quantifies periods of unusual market volatility and macroeconomic vulnerability was computed. When the index exceeds a defined threshold value and when there is persistence for a certain period, this is interpreted as a "warning signal." The indicator is called *Index of Speculative Pressure (ISP)*, and is constructed as follows:[14]

$$\text{ISP}_t = \Delta\%\text{exchange rate}_t + \Delta\%\text{ interest rate}_t - \Delta\%\text{ international reserves}_t$$

Each variable is calculated in monthly percentage changes and is standardized to have mean zero and unit variance. The threshold is defined as the mean plus 1.5 times the variance of ISP. If the index is larger than this threshold, then it is taken as a signal that there is excessive market volatility. Figure 1.12 shows the index and the threshold, which were calculated for January 1993 to December 1998. There are few episodes of *"excessive market volatility"* according to the index. The most important ones occurred in early 1993 and during the May 1997 crisis. The index also captures some of the after-effects of the Russia crisis. Overall, the ISP index reveals no systemic problem with speculative pressures on the crown outside the mentioned episodes.

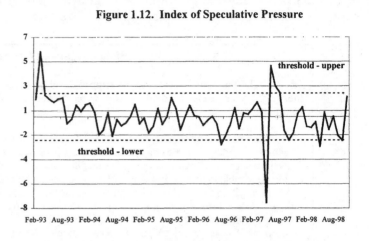

Figure 1.12. Index of Speculative Pressure

Another measure of macroeconomic vulnerability was estimated for the Czech Republic. The *Index of Macroeconomic Vulnerability* (IMV) is constructed by using a set of variables that have proven to be leading indicators of a crisis. The variables used to calculate the IMV are the ratio of M2 to international reserves (M2/R), which measures the degree of exposure to sudden shifts in capital flows, real domestic credit growth (DCG), inflation (π) and the real effective exchange rate index (REER).

The index of macroeconomic vulnerability is constructed using monthly data and the following equation:

$$\text{IMV}_t = \text{REER}_t + \text{DCG}_t + \text{M2/R}_t + \pi_t$$

The index is based on the deviations of the long run trend of each one of the variables. The method used here is the Hodrick-Prescott filter. After de-trending the variables, the index is constructed as the sum of the standardized new series. To account for volatility changes on the IMV, the threshold is computed as a time varying variance of the IMV. This is done by estimating the conditional variance of the IMV series based on a Generalized Autoregressive Conditional Heteroskedastic (GARCH) model.[15] The index is plotted against time, with the estimated time varying threshold level. Periods when the index is above the threshold indicate increased macroeconomic vulnerability.

The IMV index was calculated for the Czech Republic during the 1993-98 period. The results are shown in Figure 1.13. The index clearly captures an increase in macroeconomic vulnerability in the Czech Republic starting around May 1996, but more persistently since September 1996, that is 6-12

[14]   See Herrera, Santiago and Conrado Garcia (1998), "A User's Guide to an Early Warning System of Macroeconomic Vulnerability for LAC Countries," mimeo.
[15]   See Herrera and Garcia (1998) op. cit.

months before the crisis. The IMV index also captures some increasing vulnerability at the end of 1998.[16] No other periods of sustained vulnerability are reflected by the IMV index.

Figure 1.13. Index of Macroeconomic Vulnerability

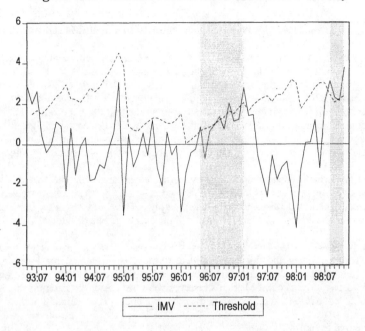

Sources of Vulnerability

During 1996-97, the Czech Republic received substantial capital flows; at the same time, however, the CNB lost international reserves. Reserve losses were the outcome of speculative attacks that led to exchanges of foreign currency assets for domestic currency asset. Foreign exchange was provided by the CNB in an attempt to sustain the exchange rate level, without success. Reserve losses during 1996 were accompanied by an increasing current account deficit, suggesting that the prevailing consumption boom was the result of lack of credibility in exchange rate sustainability. In the end, the exchange rate regime collapsed. This is the type of scenario that prevailed during the early 1980s in Latin America and that eventually led to schemes such as Argentina's currency board, to eliminate uncertainty about the evolution of the exchange rate and inflation.[17]

Both currency crisis literature and the recent country experiences suggest that inconsistent macroeconomic policies, and sudden changes in expectations about the sustainability of the exchange rate regimes, have been at the heart of speculative attacks in developing countries (see Box 1.4). In the Czech Republic, inconsistent macroeconomic policies appear to have been the mid-1990s source of macroeconomic vulnerability identified by the IMV index (see Figure 1.13). During this period, attempts to solve banking problems by means of official emergency financing resulted in reserve losses, given the prevailing fixed exchange rate. In May 1997, contagion of Thailand's incipient crises -- due to perceived vulnerability from a large and unsustainable current account deficit -- triggered a speculative attack in the

---

[16] With the series ending in 1998, this higher vulnerability could be the result of the use of a GARCH model for the threshold level. Further data is needed to identify if this vulnerability is persistent.

[17] Under a currency board system, the monetary authority cannot increase domestic credit to finance public sector deficits or bail out firms.

Czech Republic's crown. In contrast to other regions like Latin America and Asia, in the Czech Republic there was no evidence that the currency crisis of 1997 had been driven by investor refusal to rollover debt or fear of debt default. The average maturity of the external debt was 6 years, long when compared to other emerging markets (e.g., 8 months in Brazil before the 1998 crisis) and the CNB had enough foreign exchange reserves to back the debt up (see Table 1.9).

Box 1.4. Sources of Vulnerability to Capital Outflows

Sudden capital outflows can occur when market agents believe the domestic currency will depreciate. What leads to this belief? Empirical studies have identified two broad sources: inconsistent macroeconomic policies, for example monetization of the budget deficit in a financially integrated economy with fixed exchange rates, and sudden changes in expectations about the sustainability of macroeconomic policies. Other sources of the sudden shift of perceptions include the expectation of realized contingent liabilities, a drop in tax revenues associated with business cycles driven by capital inflows, and investor refusal to rollover the debt in countries other than the crisis country, an effect known as contagion. Contagion was evident in many emerging markets after Russia devalued the ruble in August 1998.

In mid-1992, in Sweden, international events led to an attack on the Swedish krona. Sweden's Riksbank defended the currency by borrowing abroad, but this defense was extremely unpopular as it increased unemployment and raised interest rates sharply. Three months later, however, another attack occurred. This time the defense was unsuccessful and the exchange rate devalued.

Similarly, Mexico's 1994 crisis provides a good case of a sudden change in expectations. An increase in US interest rates and domestic political turmoil led to capital outflows and sudden deposit withdrawals. To prevent a credit crunch and a banking crisis, the Central Bank injected liquidity, leading to further reserve losses. At this point Mexico's reserves were insufficient to back up short-term public debt. This vulnerability led investors to refuse to roll over the debt and to a depreciation of the currency

Source: The World Bank KMS.

Sources of vulnerability still remain in the Czech Republic. An indication of this is depositors' preference for a larger share of savings denominated in foreign exchange, as indicated by an increased share of foreign currency deposit to total deposit since 1997 (see Table 1.9). This share, however, is still small compared to that of other emerging markets.

Table 1.9. Macroeconomic Vulnerability Indicators, 1995-98

	1995	1996	1997	1998
External Sector Indicators				
Short Term External Debt/Reserves (percent)	35.7	48.4	72.5	68.3
Average maturity of External Debt (years)	13.9	14.7	4.7	5.6
External Debt/GDP (percent)	34.1	37.7	41.6	44.2
Current Account Deficit/GDP (percent)	-2.6	-7.4	-6.1	-1.9
Bilateral Real Exchange Rate Index[1]	100.0	102.3	119.6	121.9
International Reserves (US$ billion)	14.0	12.4	9.8	12.6
Financial and Banking Sector Indicators				
Domestic Debt (public)/Reserves (percent)	27.5	32.9	38.2	45.2
Non-performing loans/Reserve (percent)	..	..	100.8	62.2
M2/Reserves (percent)	272.9	329.1	391.9	314.7
Foreign Currency Deposits/Total Deposits (percent)	6.6	7.2	12.6	12.4
Foreign Currency Deposits/M2 (percent)	5.3	6.0	11.4	11.1
Real Sector Indicators				
GDP growth rate (percent)	6.4	3.8	0.3	-2.3
Industrial production growth rate (percent)	8.8	2.0	4.4	1.6
Manufacturing Production growth rate (percent)	9.0	1.7	16.0	2.5
Industrial Wage rate or Earnings	18.5	18.4	10.5	9.3
Unemployment rate (percent)	2.9	3.5	5.2	7.5

1/ Index with respect to the US. Increase in the index means depreciation.
Source: IMF-IFS, Ministry of Finance, Czech National Bank, OECD, CSO and the World Bank.

The current recession has served to highlight deficiencies in the structural front, particularly those related to the banking and enterprise sectors.[18] The financial conditions of the banks remain weak. Sources of weakness include poor corporate governance; significant non-performing loans, poor ability to assess risk, and the belief that the Czech authorities would not let banks fail. In an environment of increasing guarantees, bank managers have little incentive to do proper risk assessment, thus helping increase financial sector vulnerability. Moreover, firms do not face hard budget constraints, thus reducing their need for restructuring and increasing efficiency. The need to impose harder regulations in the banking system concerning collateral provisioning for non-performing loans revealed the weak status of the portfolios of state banks. As a result, the past behavior of the state banks vis-à-vis rolling over bad loans stopped. This change in behavior, in conjunction with the need to build sizable cash collateral, produced a severe credit crunch that reduced the availability of new credit to the real sector. This means that firms that had planned their future operations based on credit availability cannot continue operating. The result of this has been an increase in bank non-performing loans, particularly from small and medium firms in the non-tradable sector that have virtually no access to foreign loans. In 1997, around 70 percent of loans from firms operating in this sector were non-performing.

The fragile financial situation of a large segment of the enterprise sector is another source of concern. The poor state of many of the large, domestically-owned industrial conglomerates has been a drag on the economy and the banking sector throughout the transition. The lack of corporate governance, disregard of investor protection, poor lending decisions by banks, and a failure to close non-viable production units have resulted in the survival of large, inefficient, politically powerful, socially important and excessively indebted corporations. This lies at the heart of the current economic malaise. Addressing the problems of the corporate sector in a manner that does not generate a wrong incentive structure will be one of the key policy dilemmas of the current administration. This legacy of the past must be cleared and an efficient industrial system reconstructed.

While the adjustment on the external sector closed the current account deficit -- from 7.4 percent in 1996 to 1.9 percent in 1998 -- the external adjustment may not have been complete. The cyclically adjusted current account deficit is estimated by the IMF to be in the order of 4-5 percent of GDP, due to a large real output gap, indicating that some strengthening of external competitiveness is still needed. Wage moderation would facilitate further monetary easing and would also improve the external competitiveness of the economy. Public sector wage increases of 13 to 15 percent have been decided, and wage agreements in the private sector appear to be in the range of 7 to 8 percent. Under these circumstances, a firm stance in any remaining wage negotiations in the government sector and state-controlled enterprises is needed for the remainder of the year. Productivity increases need to be promoted and wage growth needs to be maintained below such increases in productivity.

At the heart of the recovery of the Czech economy lies the privatization of remaining control in state-own banks, and the severance of the symbiotic relationship with large industrial conglomerates. Strategic foreign investors need to be brought in to establish a sound banking culture. This, in turn, will encourage enterprise restructuring, by imposing true hard budget constraints to the real sector. The government's program to revitalize the real sector needs to be tailored to avoid moral hazard and the perpetuation of non-viable enterprises.[19]

---

[18] See the enterprise and financial sector chapters in this report.
[19] See the enterprise sector chapter in this report for further description of the enterprise revitalization program recently announced by the government.

Economic Recovery and EU Accession

The Czech Republic faces significant challenges as it seeks to lay the basis for economic recovery, sustainable growth, and EU accession. An imperative is to recover growth and redirect the economy towards its potential. The required macroeconomic and structural policies needed to achieve these objectives will entail difficult political choices and considerable economic and social stress in the short run, but they are likely to set the foundation for sustainable development and to enhance the prospects for EU accession.

Provided that prudent monetary policy and a sustainable fiscal stand are in place, and provided that the structural reform process is vigorously pursued, there should be scope for economic recovery starting in the latter part of 1999 and continuing into 2000. The Czech Republic has potential for relatively high rates of growth over the medium term, in the order of 4-5 percent of GDP, driven by productive investment, deep structural reform and improved export performance. For this to be sustainable, risks need to be reduced and real output cycles minimized or avoided.

Stronger fiscal discipline, especially concerning off-budget activities, and better monetary and fiscal policy coordination, will be needed to maintain a sustainable current account deficit, which could be covered by foreign direct investment, and to converge towards EU inflation levels. Relatively rapid productivity growth in the tradables sector and wage growth restraint in the non-tradables sector will be essential to maintain macroeconomic stability and generate long-term sustainable growth.

The post-crisis experience of emerging markets suggests that limited credit availability, as well as inflexible labor markets, have contributed to sluggish economic recovery (see Box 1.5).

Box 1.5. Post-Crises Growth Recovery - Emerging Market Experiences

Limited credit availability to the non-tradables sector, non-performing bank loan overhang and inflexible labor markets have slowed economic recovery in emerging markets, despite a booming trade sector. In Mexico, for example, the share of non-performing loans to total loans increased to 30 percent in 1997 from 10 percent before the 1994 crisis. These figures do not include bank loans that have been transferred to the Central Bank in exchange for government bonds under Mexico's post-crisis bank restructuring program FOBAPROA.

Small and medium firms operating in the non-tradables sector were the source of the bad loans; these firms did not have access to capital markets after the crisis, hence growth in the non-tradable sector was sluggish. By contrast, the tradable sector became Mexico's engine of growth after the 1994 financial crises. GDP growth, however, did not help lower the share of non-performing loans to total loans.

Non-transparent ineffective bankruptcy procedures, poor corporate governance and limited bank credit funds: the combination of these factors has created disincentives for some debtors, with the capacity to service their debts -- since nonpayment would be severely punished.

In the case of Argentina, which enjoys a strong banking system, high production costs including labor costs, prevented a fast recovery of the economy.

Source: The World Bank KMS.

Today, the Czech Republic is experiencing the real effects of its first post-transition economic crisis. It enjoys relative price stability, low inflation and interest rates, and stable terms of trade. Furthermore, contingent liabilities and off-budget activities are gradually being included in the medium-term fiscal projections. The exchange rate is flexible, hence greater freedom exists to accommodate capital flow volatility. The current weaknesses of the Czech enterprise and financial systems -- due to non-performing loans -- need to be resolved both to reduce vulnerabilities and to set the Czech Republic on a positive path towards EU Accession.

In the past decade, there has been an enormous effort put forward by the Czech government and the Czech society at large to transform the economy from command to market. The Czech Republic is one of the most open economies in the region with low import tariffs, limited non-tariff barriers, an open capital account, sizable trade flows accounting for a large part of the economic activity -- most of them with the EU -- good levels of FDI -- most coming form the EU -- and educational levels comparable to those in the EU. The current recession is likely to be costly in terms of output and employment; however, it should not deprive us from recognizing the sizable progress in economic development made so far. While the Czech Republic is a prime candidate for EU accession, the authorities should not lose sight that other CEE transition economies are competing with the Czech Republic in this endeavor.

The extensive reform agenda for the pre-accession period will require a concentrated effort by all levels of government. The implementation period is being determined by the government's EU accession strategy. The accession process, however, will not wait for the Czech Republic as it moves forward. Other leading transition economies are likely to position themselves at the front of the pack unless the Czech Republic moves forcefully to recover its leading position and advance the implied structural reforms that are needed for a successful EU membership. Implementing the reforms needed in the key sector analyzed in this report will help the Czech Republic to maximize the benefits from accession while minimizing the costs of transposing and applying the *acquis*.

Chapter II. Sustainable Growth and Income Convergence

Introduction

Prior to accession, former applicants to the European Union (EU), such as Spain, Portugal, Greece and Ireland, all had market economies and all had been extensively exposed to competition in the Europe-wide economic arena. By contrast, the transition economies face a twofold challenge: to complete the transition from a command to a market economy, and to concurrently prepare for integration into the EU. Since the *Velvet Revolution* in 1989, the Czech Republic has made substantial progress in advancing in this systemic transformation and, until recently, in stabilizing its economy, yet the process is far from complete and does not approach the situation of earlier entrants which had their regulatory systems and market institutions more developed than current accession candidates.[1] The overarching aim of this transformation process is to improve both the living standards and the quality of life of its ten million citizens but also of future generations. A crucial element for the Czech Republic's development agenda is thus returning to a sustainable growth path (see Figure 2.1) and joining the EU at the earliest possible date. Accession to the EU is thus not merely an objective in itself, but rather the means to create the momentum necessary to accelerate the reform agenda and to implement needed structural changes to strengthen economic growth prospects.

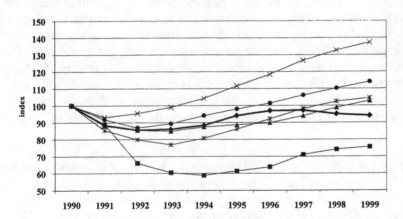

Figure 2.1. GDP Recovery in Selected CEE Countries

There are two important reasons to believe that the income gap with the EU can be reduced over the next decade. First, economic history has shown that countries with lower income per capita that are closely integrated with richer countries tend to grow more rapidly than the richer countries, thereby reducing the gap in per capita income. The divergence in per capita income between member states of the EU has been significantly reduced during the last decade. Second, the former Czechoslovakia used to be one of the most prosperous industrial economies before the Second World War. In 1955, measured at purchasing power parity, Czechoslovakia's estimated per capita income was 3.5 times that of Greece and 2.3 times that of Spain.[2] The command economy exercise of the post war era, however, proved to be disastrous to the Czech economy. By 1993, the Czech Republic's PPP per capita income was only 64 percent of Spain's. To a certain extent, the Czech Republic had already enjoyed the benefits of high-income country

---

[1] Joining the EU has become a much more complicated process since the *acquis* has been substantially expanded by the Single Market Program and the plans for Economic and Monetary Union (EMU) contained in the Maastricht Treaty (the Treaty on European Union signed at the Maastricht summit). Under the EU Single Market, the EU becomes a space where laws, regulations, standards, and institutions are approximated, harmonized and/or mutually recognized in order to ensure a leveled play field and free competition on an EU scale.

[2] B. Balassa (1970), "Growth performance of Eastern European Economies and Comparable Western European Countries," Economics Department Working Paper, No.5., The World Bank.

in the past; this is an enormous potential that should not be wasted. The number of years that will take the Czech Republic to recover its past position, i.e., to close the economic gap with Western Europe, depends to a great extent on the policy framework and its impact on output growth rates.

This chapter discusses strategy options for the Czech Republic to accelerate its income convergence with the EU. While during the period 1993-95 the Czech Republic recovered the output growth momentum after the breakup of the Czechoslovak federation, in 1996 macroeconomic performance started to slow down; by 1998, the economy was in recession. Assuming an average growth rate of 3.9 percent, i.e., similar to the rate achieved in 1996, the growth accounting model presented in this chapter estimates that the Czech Republic will reach the average income level of the EU in 25 years, essentially at the same time as Poland (with an income per capita 32 percent below that of the Czech Republic) if the latter maintains its growth momentum. The time to close the income gap, however, could be dramatically reduced. For example, if the Czech Republic increases its GDP growth rate by just one percent, it will reduce the time to achieve EU average income by ten years. Moreover, assuming a model with diminishing returns of scale of production factors, the Czech Republic could cut the time to reach EU average income by six years if growth is accelerated through the implementation of liberal structural reforms.

Past European Integration: The Experience of Ireland, Greece, Spain and Portugal

The benefits from economic integration are many, but the most important one is raising the welfare of the population by increasing the growth capacity of the country. The two main channels through which economic integration can affect growth are accumulation of physical and human capital and technology or knowledge creation.[3] Economic integration has the advantage of improving the investment climate by reducing the risk premium. For both domestic and foreign investors, confidence can be boosted by several factors. In particular, joining the EU makes the country potentially less risky. EU membership assures well-defined property rights, levels of competition and a coherent state-aids policy. Through the four freedoms, the EU promotes the efficient allocation of resources, thereby securing market contestability and trade and capital account liberalization. On the technology side, integration brings the benefits of international spillover of knowledge through foreign direct investment. This reduces the duplication of innovation efforts and increases competition, thereby bringing efficiency gains and welfare.

The growth effects of economic integration with the EU can be illustrated by the experience of Ireland, Greece, Portugal and Spain. It is relevant to look at the experience of these four countries for at least two reasons. First, because they are among the countries that joined the EU during the 1970-80s -- enlargements with an income per capita relative to the EU similar of that of the Czech Republic. Their performance can provide some information about income convergence.[4] Second, sufficient time has passed since these countries joined the EU to derive conclusions about the medium-run growth effects of economic integration. Table 2.1 and Figure 2.2 show that the income gap between the EU and these four countries has narrowed, although at different degrees. The exception being Greece, whose income per capita relative to the EU-15 remains in 1998 at about the same level as in 1981, and below its peak before accession.

---

[3] Baldwin, R. and E. Seghezza (1996), "Growth and European Integration: Towards an Empirical Assessment", Centre for Economic Policy Research, No.1393.
[4] Ireland joined the EU in 1973, Greece in 1981, and Spain and Portugal in 1986. By the time they joined the EU their GDP per capita was, relative to the EU average, at 69 percent for Greece, 59 percent for Ireland, 70 percent for Spain and 54 percent for Portugal.

Table 2.1. Income Convergence of Ireland, Greece, Spain and Portugal

	1960	1970	1980	1985	1990	1995	1998	Relative Index[1/]
	GDP per capita (EU-15 average=100)							
Ireland *(1973)*	61	60	64	65	74	96	108	183
Greece *(1981)*	44	63	70	64	58	66	68	99
Spain *(1986)*	57	71	70	70	77	79	81	116
Portugal *(1986)*	40	50	55	53	61	71	72	133

1/ The relative index measures the improvement (or decline) of the respective country's income per capita vis-à-vis the EU average, between the year of accession and 1998. Since 1991, the EU average includes East Germany.
Source: European Commission (DGII) and World Bank.

The pattern of income convergence has been highly sensitive to the policy framework implemented by the individual countries. Ireland's income per capita convergence accelerated only in the late-1980s, about 14 years after entry. Spain and Portugal have been more or less converging at the same pace -- Portugal a bit faster due to its lower initial position. Greece's income gap widened after entry and it was not until the late 1990s that it started catching up (see Figure 2.2).

Except for Greece, these four countries experienced investment booms upon accession to the EU. Capital formation was boosted in three of the entrants -- Ireland, Portugal and Spain -- while Greece instead experienced a consumption boom. There is also

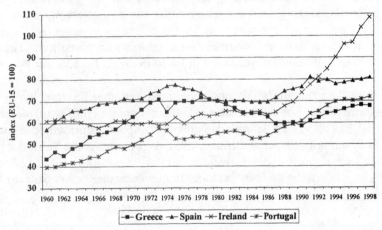

Figure 2.2. Per Capita Income Convergence with the EU-15

evidence that these countries (with the exception of Greece) experienced a stock market boom.[5] The investment boom was driven primarily by the reduced political risk, the restructuring of the capital stock in view of new production patterns, and the introduction of new technologies accompanied by increased FDI. The opening of the capital account played an important role, as entry was generally accompanied by an increase in capital inflows.

In summary, the income gap of the countries that joined the EU in the 1970-80s enlargement has been reduced -- except for Greece. The benefits on growth from accession, however, were not automatic. Gains from economic integration have been contingent on the choices made by policy makers. The commitment and implementation of reforms played a key role in the relative performance of the acceding countries, a reason why Greece lagged behind the others.[6] Income convergence has not been the artifice

---

[5] Baldwin, J. Francois and R. Portes (1997), "The Costs and Benefits of eastern enlargement: the impact on the EU and Central Europe," *Economic Policy: A European Forum*, No.24, 127-76, April.
[6] Baldwin and Seghezza (1996) found that for three period averages (1971-90, 1971-74, and 1975-90) European countries experienced higher total factor productivity growth than the sample average that included non-European countries. Another important finding is that European countries that resisted deep integration had systematically worse productivity growth than the EU members. They argue that because European integration has substantially liberalized trade, it has promoted growth.

of exchange rate valuation, but of real output growth rates that have exceeded those of the richest members of the EU.

Bridging the Income Gap with the EU

The capacity to bridge the income gap with the EU depends, not only on achieving higher growth rates than the EU, but on the ability to sustain these rates of output growth for long periods of time without generating macroeconomic imbalances through domestic (fiscal) or external (current account) sources.

At current nominal exchange rates, the Czech Republic had, in 1997, a per capita income of US$5,169 -- higher than that of Estonia, Poland and Hungary, but only 56 percent of Slovenia's per capita income. Compared to the EU-15, the situation is quite different: the Czech Republic has only 23 percent of the EU average income per capita. For international comparisons, however, these relationships are more informative if income is measured in terms of a common unit that eliminates the country specific price (and exchange rate) distortions, such as purchasing power parities (PPP). However, PPP calculations are based on major price surveys covering a basket of goods and services that are both comparable and representative for the countries in analysis. These two requirements make it difficult to establish reliable PPP numbers for economics in transition. Therefore, for comparison here we use per-capita GDP numbers measured in EUROSTAT's Purchasing Power Standards (PPS).[7]

Per capita GDP numbers measured in PPS tend to be somewhat lower than their US$-PPP alternatives. For the Czech Republic, per capita GDP was in 1997 measured at 12,000 in PPS terms and US$13,100 in PPP terms. This level of income represented 63 percent of Germany's GDP per capita in PPS, but only 59 percent if measured in PPP terms (see Table 2.2).

Table 2.2. Per Capita GDP in Purchasing Power Standard (PPS) and Parity (PPP), 1997

	Per Capita GDP PPS	Per Capita GDP US$PPP	Ratio of PPS to PPP Values
Czech Republic	12,000	13,100	0.92
Hungary	8,900	10,000	0.89
Poland	7,500	7,500	1.00
Slovak Republic	8,900	9,500	0.94
Slovenia	13,000	14,200	0.92

Source: EUROSTAT and Ministry of Finance.

When measured in PPS terms, the Czech Republic's 1997 income per capita sharply rises vis-à-vis the EU average. At the same time, the difference in income per capita among the other transition economies declines markedly. Table 2.3 shows the 1997 GDP per capita, both at current exchange rates and at PPS levels for EU countries and for the leading five Central and Eastern European Countries (CEECs) seeking EU accession. According to the PPS estimates, in 1997 the Czech Republic is the second most affluent country among the group seeking EU membership -- just below Slovenia -- and its gap with the average EU income per capita is significantly reduced. Moreover, the Czech Republic's per capita income is only 8 percent below that of Greece. An important feature is that the difference between

---

[7] See EUROSTAT (1998), Statistics in Focus. PPS numbers are used in the European Union and by the European Commission to make comparisons of GDP per-capita due to the unreliability of PPP numbers. Primary results of the 1996 European Comparison Program from EUROSTAT on PPP calculations show significant differences in PPP numbers extrapolated for 1996 from the basis of 1993 than the ones calculated in 1996. PPPs represent spatial comparisons and are not intended for time series analysis.

the Czech Republic's income at current exchange rates and that at PPS is the largest of all first wave candidate countries. Given that for most of the candidate countries a significant progress has been made in trade liberalization, this could imply that the difference in non-tradable prices between the Czech Republic and the EU is more severe than in the other countries.

Table 2.3. GDP Per Capita in Europe, 1997

	Per capita GDP		Per capita GDP – PPS	
	1997 US$	% of EU avg.	1997 PPS	% of EU avg.
Austria	25,555	112	21,300	112
Belgium	23,799	105	21,500	113
Denmark	32,143	141	21,800	115
Finland	23,314	102	18,700	98
France	23,787	104	19,800	104
Germany	25,605	112	20,900	110
Greece	11,402	50	13,100	69
Ireland	19,981	88	18,300	96
Italy	20,294	89	19,200	101
Netherlands	23,108	101	19,800	104
Luxembourg	40,791	179	31,500	166
Portugal	10,422	46	13,400	71
Spain	13,512	59	14,800	78
Sweden	25,735	113	18,700	98
United Kingdom	22,118	97	18,900	99
EU Average	22,771	100	19,000	100
Czech Republic	**5,169**	**23**	**12,000**	**63**
Estonia	3,168	14	7,000	37
Hungary	4,305	19	8,900	47
Poland	3,509	15	7,500	39
Slovak Republic	3,625	16	8,900	47
Slovenia	9,161	40	13,000	68

Source: EUROSTAT, Statistical Office of the European Commission and World Bank.

Simulating Alternative Growth Accounting Scenarios

Closing the income gap and facilitating convergence will ultimately depend on the differential output growth rate between the Czech Republic and the EU. If the Czech Republic grows only slightly faster than the EU, income convergence could take several decades, while high sustainable growth rates will close the income gap in much shorter time. To appreciate the consequences of apparently small differences in growth rates when compounded over long periods of time, we have calculated the per capita income path of the first five applicant countries, assuming slightly different growth rates. Table 2.4 shows some of the results of these simulations.[8] We assume that per capita income in the EU grows on average at 2 percent per year -- a reasonable assumption given the average output growth of the EU in the previous decades. For the applicant countries we assume two scenarios. In one, the country grows at the

---

[8] All the calculations are done with income per capita measured in PPS terms. These calculations are intended for illustration purposes and do not reflect forecasts on the growth paths of the acceding countries.

average rate over 1994-97, the four years previous to our base year.[9] In the other scenario, we assume that the country grows at a sustained rate of 5 percent. The latter implies a 3 percent differential in income per capita growth rate with the EU.

Table 2.4. Years Required to Close Per Capita Income Gap with the EU

	Average Growth Rate μ	EU Average Scenario 1 Avg. μ	EU Average Scenario 2 μ = 5%	75% of EU Average Scenario 1 Avg. μ	75% of EU Average Scenario 2 μ = 5%	Low End EU Average Scenario 1 Avg. μ	Low End EU Average Scenario 2 μ = 5%
Czech Republic	**3.5**	**32**	**16**	**12**	**6**	**10**	**5**
Estonia	4.5	42	35	30	25	28	24
Hungary	4.0	39	26	24	16	23	15
Poland	6.3	23	32	16	22	15	21
Slovenia	4.1	19	13	5	3	3	2

Note: Assumes EU per capita growth rate at 2 percent. Low End EU is the average of Greece, Portugal and Spain. Base year for the calculation is 1997.
Source: EUROSTAT and own calculations.

If the Czech Republic's per capita income grows at a sustained rate of 3.5 percent, it would take 32 years to bridge the income gap with the EU average. By growing at its average rate, it would take the Czech Republic thirteen years more than Slovenia and nine more than Poland, which has about 60 percent the per capita income of the Czech Republic but in the last four years has been growing at an average rate of 6.3 percent. On the other hand, if it manages to grow at 3 percent above the EU, that is at 5 percent per annum, then the time to close the income gap would be sharply reduced to 16 years. Note that the Czech Republic will reach 75 percent of the EU average in 12 years at current growth rates, and the lower end of the EU (Spain, Portugal and Greece) in 10 years.[10]

Another way of looking at income convergence times is to set a target date and find out the required growth rate for closing the income gap. Table 2.5 below presents the summary of these simulations. By growing at a constant rate of 6.7 percent per year over a period of 10 years, the Czech Republic will achieve parity with the EU average. It will take only 4 years to reach 75 percent of EU average at this growth rate. Notice that this growth rate is close to Poland's average for the last four years.

Table 2.5. Growth Rate Required to Achieve EU Parity

	EU Average Scenario 1 10 years	EU Average Scenario 2 20 years	75% of EU Average Scenario 1 10 years	75% of EU Average Scenario 2 20 years	Low End EU Average Scenario 1 10 years	Low End EU Average Scenario 2 20 years
Czech Republic	**6.7**	**4.3**	**3.7**	**2.9**	**3.4**	**2.7**
Estonia	12.7	7.2	9.5	5.7	9.1	5.5
Hungary	10.0	5.9	6.9	4.4	6.5	4.2
Poland	11.9	6.8	8.7	5.3	8.4	5.1
Slovenia	5.9	3.9	2.9	2.5	2.6	2.3

Note: EU per capita growth rate at 2 percent. Low End EU is the average of Greece, Spain and Portugal.
Source: World Bank staff estimates.

For the Czech Republic, the growth rates required to catch up with 75 percent of the EU average income per capita in ten years is 3.7 percent, easily within its reach. This is not the case for the other

---

[9] For Hungary, we assume instead a 4 percent growth rate due to the impact of structural reforms on the growth performance of the economy in the last two years.
[10] The threshold of 75 percent of the EU average income per capita is important because a number of development fund transfers from the EU budget to its member countries are directed to regions with per capita incomes below that threshold.

leading candidate countries -- with the exception of Slovenia -- that require very high sustained growth rates. This is, in good part, the result of the high starting point of the Czech Republic vis-à-vis other transition economies. Although the 1997 estimates of per capita income in PPS (or PPP) value show that the Czech Republic is starting with a privileged position relative to other acceding countries -- second just below Slovenia -- the 1998 recession and its aftermath has reduced its comparative advantage position with respect to the others members of the first group candidates. The Czech Republic is the only member of this group of countries with negative output growth rate in 1998-99. To bridge its income gap with the EU, the Czech Republic needs to implement a strategy that enhances efficiency through microeconomic reforms, thus allowing the country to recover its growth impetus, to reach a sustainable output growth rate close to its potential and to fully benefit from a successful integration into the EU.

The Impact of the Lost Growth Momentum and the 1998-99 Recession

Contrary to other leading transition economies, the Czech Republic is involved in its first post transition recession. In 1998, GDP declined by 2.3 percent, after a modest growth of just 0.3 percent in 1997. Output growth is not expected to recover significantly until 2000. As a result, the income gap with the EU has been expanding since 1997, instead of closing. The cost of this disappointing growth performance is twofold. On the one hand, other leading transition economies like Estonia, Hungary and Poland have been growing at relatively high rates in recent years, closing their income gap with the Czech Republic and the EU. The Czech model of transition has left too many structural issues unfinished; after an impressive performance in the early years of the transition, the country has lost momentum. On average, output growth in the Czech Republic has been around 2.3 percent during 1994-98. Other leading accession countries have performed much better in this respect. By growing at rates of 6 and 5 percent on average over the last four years, in 1997 Poland and Estonia have reached a per capita income that is equivalent to 63 and 58 percent of the Czech Republic's, respectively. The per capita income of both countries was 58 and 53 percent of the Czech Republic's in 1994. Slovenia, on the other hand, has increased its gap with the Czech Republic.

Figure 2.3. GDP Per Capita Relative to Germany (PPP)
(Base 1992=100)

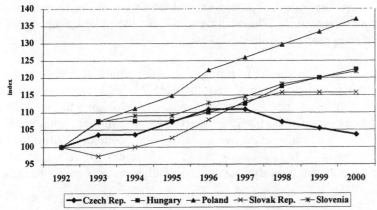

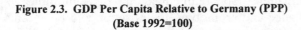

Using 1997 as base year and assuming no major changes in price structures, a simple calculation shows that the Czech Republic's PPP per capita income in 1998 is about 59 percent of Germany's per capita income, down from 61 percent in 1996. This expansion of the income gap with the EU is expected to continue in 1999-2000. Since the 1997 crisis and its aftermath, the Czech Republic has lost momentum in terms of catching up with the income per capita in EU countries. While its income per capita remains the second largest of the CEE leading transition group, relative to the EU, the gap with Estonia, Hungary and Poland is closing and that with Slovenia is expanding (see Figure 2.3).

The current recession has implications for the timing of income convergence with the EU. As the simple growth accounting exercise showed (see Table 2.4), the Czech Republic would have taken 32 years to converge to the median EU income if its output growth rate had been maintained at

Figure 2.4. Convergence in Per Capita Income

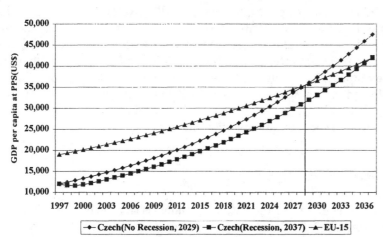

3.5 percent per annum (sixteen by growing at 5 percent per annum). The output growth rate, however, was 0.3 percent in 1997 and -2.3 percent in 1998. Current estimates of the output growth rate in the Czech Republic indicate a small decline in 1999 -- on the order of 1 percent of GDP -- and a gradual recovery thereafter. Assuming this output growth pattern and a long-term growth rate of 3.5 percent, the same long-term growth assumed in the original exercise, we computed the new time frame for convergence to the EU average income per capita.

As Figure 2.4 shows, growing at a constant rate of 3.5 percent, the Czech Republic's income per capita would have converged to the EU average in 32 years, that is in the year 2029. When we introduce the 1998 recession and the gradual recovery path,[11] the convergence takes place in 2037, that is, 8 years later. This simple exercise illustrates the impact of the current recession on the convergence time and the need for the Czech Republic to recover positive and sustainable output growth rates.

Simulating Alternative Policy Reform Scenarios

Meeting the challenges of accession and benefiting from membership in the EU are among the most important tasks that the Czech Republic authorities are facing today and will continue to face in the future. Sustainable high growth will enhance the Czech Republic's perspective to meet these two challenges. The policies needed to achieve high sustainable growth rates and to meet the requirements of the EU accession process are closely interrelated. Both aim at setting the conditions to improve efficiency, at maintaining macroeconomic balance and promoting liberalization and integration with the goal of improving the welfare of the population. The previous section has highlighted the importance of achieving faster growth rates for the Czech Republic. We paid special attention to the impact of the current recession on the speed of income convergence. This section describes the policy alternatives to speed income convergence with the EU through long-term balanced growth.

In recent years, there have been a large number of empirical studies aimed at identifying the correlation between growth, endowments, initial conditions, and the role of the government policy regime.[12] These studies have identified key features that distinguish countries with high and low rates of economic growth. Most of the studies have been based on the neoclassical growth model which predicts that within a group of economies with roughly similar tastes, technologies and political institutions and policies, those with lower per capita income will tend to grow faster. This is known as the *absolute convergence* hypothesis, which is based upon the assumption of diminishing returns to reproducible capital.[13]

---

[11] The exercise assumes growth rates of -2.3 percent in 1998, -1.0 percent in 1999.
[12] See Barro, R. (1997), "*Determinants of Economic Growth, A Cross-Country Empirical Study,*" The MIT Press, Cambridge Massachusetts.
[13] Known in the neoclassical growth literature as β convergence.

A less strict version of convergence, which assumes that all countries are not equal and in fact differ in many aspects is the so-called *conditional convergence*, also known as σ convergence.[14] This type of convergence implies declining cross-sectional dispersion of per capita income across units, as measured by the coefficient of variation or other measures of dispersion. The basic difference is that while absolute convergence relates to the relationship with initial levels of income and subsequent growth rates, conditional convergence implies that each country has its own steady state level of income and will grow faster the farther away it is from this level. Growth is thus affected by a number of things, including the policy framework a country chooses to implement.

Box 2.1. Equation and Parameters used for Convergence Simulation

The model produces an estimate of the long-run (steady state) annual growth rate by using a growth equation. The equation is estimated using a large cross-section of countries over the period 1965-89. The reduced form growth equation is the following:

$$Y = b0 + b1\, X1 + b2\, X2 + b3\, X3 + b4\, X4 + b5\, X5$$

where X1 is the logarithm of the initial income per capita of the country, X2 is the logarithm of the average level of fixed investment over GDP, X3 is a proxy of the level of human capital measured as the logarithm of the level of educational attainment, X4 is the logarithm of a quality adjusted labor force growth rate and X5 is the logarithm of a policy index that summarizes the existing policy framework. In the equation above, b0 to b5 are the parameters of the model. The estimated reduced form equation is given by:

$$Y = 0.0879 - 0.0190\, X1 + 0.0170\, X2 + 0.0098\, X3 - 0.0267\, X4 + 0.0250\, X5$$

The index of liberalization (X5) is composed of ten different indicators reflecting the current state of policies in the economy. It includes, among other variables, indicators of monetary policy, fiscal policy, trade liberalization, and other factors that strengthen the enabling business environment of an economy. The Index of Economic Freedom is used as a proxy for this policy index, modified to incorporate a broader definition of trade liberalization.[15] This index is based on ten different indicators, namely: (i) the degree to which tariffs and quotas hinder the free flow of commerce; (ii) the extent to which taxes burden economic activities; (iii) the share of government consumption in output; (iv) the rate of inflation as a proxy for monetary policy; (v) the degree to which a country is receptive to FDI; (vi) the extent of government involvement and level of distortions in the financial sector; (vii) the importance of market forces in determining prices and wages; (viii) the degree to which property rights and rule of law are perceived to be supportive of an enabling business environment; (ix) the role that government regulations might play in hindering private sector development; and (x) an estimate of the size and importance of the underground economy. Its scale goes from one, reflecting a low degree of liberalization, to five, reflecting full liberalization. Some of these indicators are measurable and some are not. In the latter case, Johnson and Sheehy assign values according to scales based on non-quantifiable criteria.

Source: Barbone and Zalduendo (1997).

We base the analysis on the simulation of different policy scenarios and their impact on the growth prospects of the Czech Republic. To measure the impact on the long-term growth of the economy, we used the estimation results of a cross-section growth model (see Box 2.1).[16] Investigating the growth performance of a large number of countries over a long period of time allows the assessment of any country's long-term growth potential under key assumptions about the levels of capital, both physical and human, endowments and policy variables. The model enables us to make comparisons between the Czech Republic's future growth rates relative to those of the EU under different policy

---

[14] Barro, R and X. Sala-i-Martin (1995), *Economic Growth*, New York: McGraw-Hill Inc.
[15] Johnson, B. and T. Sheehy (1996), *Index of Economic Freedom*, The Heritage Foundation, Washington, DC.
[16] Barbone L. and J. Zalduendo (1997), "EU Accession of Central and Eastern Europe: Bridging the Income Gap," Policy Research Working Paper No.1721, The World Bank. This growth model is an extension of Sachs, J. and A. Wagner (1996), "Achieving Rapid Growth in the Transition Economies of Central Europe," Harvard Institute for International Development, Cambridge.

scenarios. As a result, we can estimate the time of convergence to EU income levels and the impact of changing policy variables on the growth rate of the economy.

The growth determinants for the Czech Republic and the other candidate countries are presented in Table 2.6. According to these determinants of growth, the Czech Republic ranks second in all variables except in the level of investment (fixed capital formation) and the policy index of market reforms, in which it ranks first along with Poland. Paradoxically, the Czech Republic's average income growth rate over the period 1994-97 has been only 3.3 percent (2.2 percent if we include 1998). Though good by EU growth standards, it is much slower than in countries such as Estonia or Poland. According to the model, the higher starting per capita income, which the Czech Republic enjoys, explains a good part of this development. On the other hand, although market reforms moved initially faster than in other countries, in the last years the pace of reforms slowed down; the turmoil in emerging markets has put the quality of these reforms to a test.

Table 2.6. Growth Determinants for EU Candidate Countries

	Average Growth Rates 1994-97	GDP per capita 1997 PPS level	Average Investment as % of GDP	Human Capital Stock 1985	Structural Policy Index, 1996	Adjusted Labor Index 1984-89
Czech Republic	3.3	12,000	30	N/A	4.00	5.4
Estonia	4.5	7,000	27	N/A	4.00	5.3
Hungary	2.5	8,900	22	10.75	3.10	4.9
Poland	6.3	7,500	17	8.41	2.95	5.6
Slovenia	4.1	13,000	24	N/A	2.65	5.3

Note: For the simulations the human capital index was set to 9.6 in the Czech Republic, Estonia and Slovenia, corresponding to the average of Hungary and Poland.
Source: Barbone and Zalduendo (1997), EUROSTAT and World Bank staff estimates.

In this section, we analyzed two policy scenarios. The first scenario assumes no further policy reform, hereafter referred as current status. The second policy scenario assumes that the Czech Republic accelerates its structural reform agenda and adopts policies that replicate those of fast growing economies. Under this second scenario we evaluate the impact of independent changes of the key policy variables on both the growth prospect of the economy and the joint effects. In addition, we assume that the Czech Republic's convergence (steady-state) income per capita level is the EU average. We also assume an investment rate of 26 percent, closer to the expected rate for the next years and in line with other candidate countries. Furthermore, we assume that the EU income per capita level will grow at a constant 2 percent per annum. The results of these simulations are presented in Table 2.7 below.

The model predicts that, under the current policy framework, it would take 23 years for the Czech Republic to converge to the EU average income per capita, 10 years to 80 percent of the EU average (Spain's current level) and 7 years to 75 percent of the EU average. If we hold all the other variables constant and assume that the policy liberalization index takes the value of the fastest growing economies (4.22 instead of the current 4.00), then the time period to converge to EU average income per capita is reduced by 22 percent to 18 years. To reach the 80 percent of the income per capita of the EU average it takes 8 years.[17]

Given the already high level of capital accumulation in the Czech Republic, the model predicts the strongest impact on growth performance coming from changes in the policy framework. Of course, higher accumulation of productive capital can accelerate growth. The model predicts a high return to physical investment, although not as high as the impact of changing the policy framework altogether (see Box 2.1). When we assess the individual impact of the other growth determinants, either the ratio of

---

[17] The relative lower speed of convergence is due to the implicit assumption of diminishing returns.

investment to GDP or to the human capital stock, the results are also important. By increasing the human capital stock to Hungary's level, that is by 12 percent, the number of years needed to reach the average EU income per capita is reduced by 2 years. This is, in part, the result of an already high level of human capital in the Czech Republic, thus making the return to human capital lower than it would otherwise be. The combination of policy improvements generates interactions and accelerates growth performance to a slightly faster rate. As a result, income convergence can be reached in 17 years instead of 23, a gain of five years.

Table 2.7. Years Required to Close Per Capita Income Gap with the EU under Alternative Policy Scenarios

	Current Status	Policy Index Of Fastest Growing	High Investment Rate	Human Capital Candidate Highest	Combination GDI & Policy Index	Combination of all Reforms
Czech Republic						
EU Average	23	18	23	21	18	17
80 percent EU average	10	8	10	9	8	8
75 percent EU average	7	6	7	7	6	6
Germany's level	26	21	26	24	21	20
Memorandum						
Estonia	29	20	26	31	18	17
Hungary	66	28	37	66	22	24
Poland	N/C	50	103	N/C	34	28
Slovenia	37	18	24	32	15	14

Note: For the simulations, the policy index is set at 4.22; the investment rate is set at 30 percent; and the human capital index is set at 9.6. N/C means no convergence. The memorandum rates refer to convergence to the average income in the EU.
Source: World Bank staff estimates.

By comparison, we also estimate the number of years that it would take the Czech Republic to converge to the income per capita of its major trade partner, namely Germany. If the Czech Republic is to converge to Germany's level of per capita income then, under the current policy stand, it would take almost three decades to bridge the income gap. By accelerating the structural reform agenda through increased liberalization, the model predicts that the period of time is reduced from 26 to 20 years.

Finally, the growth equation can be used to simulate the growth potential by replacing the key growth determinants as of 1997. Based on 1997 as initial per capita income, the projected long run per capita growth rate for the Czech Republic is 6.8 percent. This seemingly high projected per capita income growth rate is due to the fact that the Barbone and Zalduendo model used in the simulations gives a relatively high weight to the human capital variable. Other models that estimate growth equations predict a lower long-run per capita income growth rate, in the order of 5.4 percent per annum. Regardless of which model fits the data better and produces a more accurate long-term growth estimate, the growth performance of the Czech Republic, particularly during recent years, has been disappointing and well below its potential.

The growth effects of economic integration can be substantial, as shown through the experiences of Spain, Portugal and Ireland. The positive impact of EU accession on growth, however, is not automatic, as demonstrated by Greece's performance since accession. Benefiting from accession and achieving higher output growth rates depends, to a large degree, on the policy framework that a country like the Czech Republic chooses to implement. The fact that the policy environment can influence growth performance is critical.

The Czech Republic made a remarkable effort in stabilizing and transforming its economy during the early years of the transition. The Czech model of transition, however, was not fault free. As a result of the 1997 crisis, the implicit fragility of the transition model has surfaced in a number of areas. The current recession will be costly in terms of production and employment, and the lack of solid economic performance will delay the time of convergence to EU income levels. Additional efforts are required to bring the Czech economy back on track to the high and sustainable growth scenario that accelerates and facilitates convergence to the EU.

First and foremost is the need to recover macroeconomic stability and output growth to ensure an economic environment that facilitates output as well as employment growth, without generating macroeconomic imbalances in key areas such as the current account of the balance of payments or a broadly defined fiscal balance that includes hidden deficits and contingent liabilities. On the structural area, the Czech Republic must deepen reforms and must address key deficiencies in areas such as the financial sector, both in banking and capital markets, enterprise sector reform, public administration, the regulatory framework of infrastructure, agriculture and environment. However, addressing problems in these crucial areas should be done in a way that minimizes distortions and reduces the likelihood of moral hazard. Market mechanisms should be used to the degree possible to set the right incentive structures and to avoid the recurrence of crises.

Chapter III. Dealing with Contingent Liabilities

Introduction

The Czech Republic has been known for balanced government budgets. In contrast to most European Union countries, however, the fiscal performance in the Czech Republic encompasses a significant amount of government activities financed outside the budgetary system. These activities generate fiscal risks. Recently, these off-budget fiscal risks have become more visible, as state guarantees and agencies that are either explicitly or implicitly guaranteed by the government have generated significant claims on the budget. Still invisible in fiscal records, but already officially recognized by the government, is the stock of hidden public liabilities, which has emerged outside the budgetary system as a result of borrowing by these various agencies to finance off-budget activities of the government.

Given the amount of off-budget activities, fiscal analysis in the Czech Republic needs to identify all main activities of fiscal nature and to determine the country's implicit fiscal deficit. Having done that, fiscal analysis must then focus on two questions: (a) is the dynamic in the budget and in off-budget fiscal risks sustainable; and (b) are public finance institutions, the rules and decision making processes, developed in a way to prevent government obligations from causing fiscal strain in the future?

It turns out that the implicit fiscal deficit in the Czech Republic, though significantly higher than the deficit calculated through conventional methods, is comparable with deficits of other EU applicant countries. However, the trend outside the budgetary system is troublesome. While the reported government debt has declined, government off-budget obligations, resulting from financing hidden deficits, have been growing rapidly. In the future, these obligations will impose significant pressures on the budget. Their further growth may truly endanger future fiscal stability, perhaps more so than other important pressures emerging from pensions and other mandatory programs under the budget. Moreover, if left without analysis, the off-budget risk to future fiscal stability will not be foreseen. Presently, there is no institutional mechanism to monitor government off-budget obligations and the ensuing fiscal risk, and demands on new guarantees and further programs to be financed through various off-budget agencies are growing. That is why the following analysis of fiscal performance in the Czech Republic mainly focuses on contingent liabilities.

Contingent liabilities are a much greater problem in the Czech Republic than in other advanced EU acceding countries such as Hungary and Estonia. This is not necessarily because the Czech Republic would have faced greater problems for which the government has paid, but because state assistance in the Czech Republic has often been accounted for outside the government books. For example, like the Czech Government, the government of Hungary has also arranged assistance to the banking sector in the amount of approximately 10 percent of GDP since 1991. But unlike the Czech budget and debt, the Hungarian budget and debt actually have reflected this amount almost fully. In the Czech Republic, such amounts have been kept in the books of "transformation agencies" and have not been reflected in fiscal analyses. So while Hungary had reported large fiscal deficits, the Czech Republic reported budgetary balance.

Estimating the Magnitude of the Hidden Fiscal Problem

The Implicit Fiscal Deficit

Table 3.1 below shows that the *implicit fiscal deficit in the Czech Republic has been significantly higher than reported deficit levels*. Excluding quasi-fiscal activities of the Czech National Bank, the "hidden" part of the fiscal deficit comprises of two main components: (a) net spending on fiscal programs by transformation institutions Konsolidacni Banka (KoB), Ceska Inkasni (CI), Ceska Financni (CF) and National Property Fund (NPF); and (b) a hidden subsidy extended through state guarantees. For a given year, net public spending by transformation institutions includes cash outlays on new programs in the form of directed credits and asset purchases,[2] and interest expenditures; it is adjusted for debt collection and other revenue from programs and for interest revenue. The hidden subsidy of state guarantees reflects the amount and default risk of the guaranteed loans. To avoid double accounting, the net hidden subsidy is adjusted for guarantee claims paid from the budget and reported in the budget deficit in a given year. Table 3.2, show the components of "hidden" deficit.

Table 3.1. Government Implicit Fiscal Deficit, 1993-98
(percent of GDP)

	1993	1994	1995	1996	1997	1998
Reported state budget fiscal deficit	-0.5	-1.3	0.3	0.5	1.1	1.4
"Hidden" fiscal deficit in transformation institutions (KoB, CI, CF and NPF)	3.2	1.9	1.0	0.5	1.0	2.0
"Hidden" fiscal deficit in guarantees net hidden subsidy (risk-adjusted)	0.0	0.0	0.1	1.0	3.1	1.5
Implicit fiscal deficit (including transformation institutions and guarantee net hidden subsidy)	**2.7**	**0.6**	**1.4**	**2.0**	**5.2**	**4.9**

Source: Ministry of Finance and World Bank staff estimates.

Recent as well as Past Banking Problems have been Financed Outside the Budgetary System. Until 1993, off-budget programs had mainly dealt with pre-transition problems inherited by the banking sector. These programs had been financed through Konsolidacni Banka, which was capitalized by the National Property Fund, and borrowed CZK39 billion from Czech National Bank.[3] In 1993, the Ministry of Finance established Ceska Inkasni, a non-banking financial institution, to clean up the portfolio of a state-owned bank (CSOB). Covered by a guarantee issued by the National Property Fund, Ceska Inkasni took a credit from CSOB and used this credit to purchase CSOB's bad assets at face value.

During 1996-98, a new bank consolidation program and a stabilization program have been launched to deal with the newly emerging problems of the banking sector. To implement these programs, the Czech National Bank established Ceska Financni, a non-banking financial institution. In 1998, Ceska Financni had, in its portfolio, very low quality assets, purchased at face value from small and medium-

---

[1] Ceska Financni has financed two blocks of programs geared toward bank revitalization. One block, in the total amount of approximately CZK35 billion, is financed and guaranteed by the Czech National Bank. The other, called the Stabilization Program, in the amount of about CZK12 billion is financed through Konsolidacni Banka, and thus guaranteed by the government. Only the latter block is considered in the implicit deficit calculation. It is included as an activity of Konsolidacni Banka.

[2] The assets purchased through off-budget programs are of extremely low quality. Therefore, the analysis considers asset purchases as a spending program rather than a financial transaction.

[3] Debt to Czech National Bank by Konsolidacni Banka amounted to CZK32 billion by the end of 1998, which is about 1/5 of total liabilities of Konsolidacni Banka.

sized banks, in the amount of about CZK50 billion, a liability of about CZK15 billion to Konsolidacni Banka, and about CZK35 billion to Czech National Bank.

Table 3.2. Sources of "Hidden" Fiscal Deficit, 1993-98
(CZK billion)

	1993	1994	1995	1996	1997	1998
Konsolidacni Banka (KoB)[1/]	7.7	7.3	4.5	0.9	10.6	28.8
net public expenditures						
Ceska Inkasni (CI)	20.1	6.6	4.9	4.8	3.1	2.7
net public expenditures						
Ceska Financni (CF)					0.6[2/]	1.8[2/]
net public expenditures						
National Property Fund (NPF)	4.2	8.2	4.3	1.9	2.0	2.6
net public expenditures (excluding KoB, CI)						
State guarantees	0.1	-0.4	1.3	14.9	51.5	26.7
net hidden subsidy (risk-adjusted)						

1/   Activities of KoB include a credit to finance Stabilization Program of CF. Therefore, the table includes only interest payments by CF (which are then reported as interest income of KoB).

2/   These figures are interest payments to KoB on credit taken by CF from KoB to finance Stabilization Program. In addition, CF paid interest CZK0.8 billion and CZK2.8 billion in 1997 and 1998, respectively, to Czech National Bank on its credit from Czech National Bank to finance Consolidation Program.

Source: Ministry of Finance, Konsolidacni Banka, Ceska Financni and National Property Fund.

The Czech National Bank also financed other bank rescue operations, which have become the source of CZK161 billion of low quality, non-standard assets remaining in its portfolio at the end of 1998.[4] Out of these, the government covers the risk for CZK22 billion assets. Furthermore, CZK32.4 billion of these assets are in the form of the remaining credit from Czech National Bank to Konsolidacni Banka and thus are indirectly also covered by the government.

Aside from the bank rescue operations, Konsolidacni Banka and, less directly, National Property Fund have also financed government programs to support troubled insurance companies, public hospitals and Czech Railways, to build infrastructure, and to clean up industrial enterprises for privatization (see Table 3.3). The National Property Fund has partly financed these programs from privatization revenues but also partly from its issuance of obligations. Calculations of the implicit fiscal deficit exclude principle repayments and thus do not reflect on-going financing of pre-1993 programs by the National Property Fund. In addition, both the Konsolidacni Banka and National Property Fund have accumulated their own contingent liabilities in the form of various guarantees. Since risk assessment of these guarantees is not available, calculation of the implicit fiscal deficit excludes the implicit subsidy extended through these guarantees.

Significant fiscal risk also emerges from the Agricultural and Forestry Guarantee and Support Fund (PGRLF). Similar to the National Property Fund, obligations of PGRLF are not explicitly guaranteed by the state. PGRLF was created as a "private" self-sustaining fund to guarantee loans to farmers in combination with interest subsidies provided by the state. As with Konsolidacni Banka, PGRLF was initially capitalized with state funding and shares transferred from the National Property Fund. The Minister of Agriculture is the sole shareholder, and the staff of the Ministry of Agriculture operate the Fund. The market, however, assumes that PGRLF is a beneficiary of an implicit government subsidy and

---

[4] Of the CZK161 billion, CZK32 billion are redistribution loans, CZK51 billion are guarantees, CZK26.1 billion are receivables from the National Bank of Slovakia and CZK51 billion are bad assets -- which include CZK0.65 billion in receivables purchased from banks, CZK13 billion in receivables from banks, CZK0.41 in receivables from CNB clients and CZK37.1 billion from Ceska Financni.

values its guarantees in similar terms as guarantees issued by the government. The perception of an implicit state guarantee may generate pressure on the budget in the future. Table 3.4 shows that claims on PGRLF guarantees have more than doubled each year since 1995. Although defaults are likely to increase further as the portfolio grows and as loans become effective, the Fund is not building adequate reserves to cover future guarantee claims.

Table 3.3. Programs Covered by National Property Fund, 1993-98
(CZK billion)

	1993	1994	1995	1996	1997	1998
Financing environment rehabilitation	0.0	0.1	0.8	1.0	1.4	2.1
Financing the development of railway routes				0.1	0.0	0.2
Support to state-owned enterprises (including liability clean up)	2.1	0.5	0.9	0.3	0.2	0.3
Support to agricultural businesses		6.1	1.0			
Bond Interest	2.1	1.5	1.6	0.5	0.4	0.5
NPF Source of "hidden" fiscal deficit (excluding transfers to KoB, CI and CF and transfers according to state budget law)	4.2	8.2	4.3	1.9	2.0	3.1
Others, already included in hidden deficit calculation:						
Health insurance companies (through KoB) [1]				0.8	0.4	0.4
Support to aviation companies (via KoB) [1]					0.1	0.02
Provisions to Ceska Inkasni (CI) [1]			3.4	10.3	5.5	6.0
Stabilization program of CF (through KoB) [1]					0.6	1.8
Others, included in the reported budget deficit:						
Transfers according to state budget law	9.5	19.4	10.7			

[1]   These items are excluded from the implicit deficit calculation. NPF expenditures related to KoB, CI and CF are accounted for as financing items of these institutions.
Source: NPF Annual Reports.

Table 3.4. Summary of the Agricultural and Forestry Guarantee and Support Fund Subsidies and Loan Portfolio

	1994	1995	1996	1997	1998	Total
1. State appropriations (CZK billion)	2.7	2.1	2.9	3.5	3.6	14.8
2. Interest subsidy commitments (CZK billion)	1.1	2.4	4.7	3.6	2.5	14.3
Overdraft (1 - 2) (CZK billion)	1.6	-0.3	-1.8	-0.1	1.1	0.5
Loans guaranteed[1] (CZK billion)	6.1	9.7	14.8	15.0	9.6	55.2
Loans guaranteed (number)	2,358	2,711	3,249	2,382	1,754	12,454
Average loan size (CZK million)	2.6	3.6	4.5	6.3	5.4	4.4
Total amount guaranteed (CZK billion)	1.5	4.0	8.2	5.1	2.8	21.6
PGRLF average guarantee coverage (percent)	24.4	41.8	55.4	34.1	29.2	39.1
Guarantee claim payments (CZK billion)	0	0.03	0.07	0.17	0.66	0.93
Guarantee claim payments (number)	0	9	19	61	119	208
Average claim amount (CZK million)	0.0	3.1	3.6	2.7	5.5	4.5

[1]   This amount includes the total amount of loans, which are fully or partly guaranteed by the Fund. The amount actually subject to a guarantee is shown in a line below as Total amount guaranteed.
Source: Agricultural and Forestry Guarantee and Support Fund (PGRLF).

Off-budget Obligations and Claims on Future Budgets

The first troubling fact implied by the above discussion is the sharp increase in the amount and risk of guarantees issued by the state. The bulk of the increase has emerged from the government's support to banks and to the Czech Railways. In 1997 and 1998, the government issued a CZK22 billion guarantee to the Czech National Bank on some of its very risky lending for bank restructuring and CZK31 billion guarantee to a bank (CSOB) on its claim against a Slovak financial institution (Slovenska Inkasni). To support the Czech Railways, the government issued two guarantees, each over CZK20 billion with a very high default risk in 1996 and 1997 on railway modernization. The hidden cost of guarantees has already started to show as a growing claim on the budget emerging from guarantee defaults. Claims on the budget increased from about CZK1 billion annually during 1993-96 to CZK2 billion in 1997, and almost CZK7 billion in 1998.[5]

Another, Related, Troubling Fact is the Rapidly Increasing Level of Hidden Public Liabilities. These liabilities have been accumulated outside the budgetary system mainly by transformation institutions as these had to borrow to finance government programs.[6] Table 3.5 shows approximate levels of hidden public liabilities, excluding non-guaranteed quasi-fiscal operations of the Czech National Bank.

Table 3.5. Hidden Public Liabilities
(CZK billion)

	1993	1994	1995	1996	1997	1998
Konsolidacni Banka (KoB)[1/] (net of provisions and reserves)	79	81	79	70	86	98
Ceska Inkasni (CI) (net of provisions and reserves)	20	27	25	17	8	7
National Property Fund (NPF)	29	33	40	22	17	15
State guarantees (risk adjusted guarantees outstanding)	3	3	6	28	74	107
Hidden public liabilities (net of provisions and reserves)	131	144	150	137	185	226
Hidden public liabilities (percent of GDP) (net of provisions and reserves)	13.1	12.1	10.8	8.7	10.9	12.4
Provisions and reserves of KoB and CI	19	24	42	59	71	84
Gross hidden public liabilities (not adjusted for provisions and reserves)	150	168	192	196	256	310
Reported gross government debt	159	162	154	155	173	194
Reported gross government debt (percent of GDP)	15.8	13.7	11.2	9.8	10.3	10.6

1/ Activities of Konsolidacni Banka include financing of the Stabilization Program of Ceska Financni. Therefore, the table does not include Ceska Financni as a separate entity.
Source: Konsolidacni Banka, Ceska Inkasni and National Property Fund.

Off-budget programs, such as guarantees and support extended through Konsolidacni Banka, National Property Fund, PGRLF and other, possibly new, agencies and guarantee funds, *impose cost on taxpayers with a delay but with no discount.* It is already evident that, past hidden deficits and servicing of the hidden public debt outside the budgetary system gradually generates claims on government budget.

---

[5] Since the guarantee claims paid from the budget have contributed to the reported deficit, the "hidden" deficit that emerges from guarantees only includes the difference between the hidden subsidy extended by the government through new guarantees and the claims mostly on guarantees issued in previous years. Unadjusted for guarantee claims, the hidden subsidy through guarantees has actually reached CZK55 billion and CZK32 billion in 1997 and 1998, respectively.

[6] Hidden public liabilities are calculated on gross basis. The analysis focuses on gross liabilities because the quality of directed loans extended and assets purchased through off-budget programs is extremely low and their potential value is on average estimated around 10 percent (3 percent for CI, less than 10 percent in CF and under 20 percent in KoB).

One Source of Budget Claims are State Guarantees. Assuming no new state guarantees issued, the budget may need to cover about CZK4 billion annually in the coming years, and CZK33 billion in year 2002, if the debt of Slovenska Inkasni to CSOB is not resolved. Figures in Table 3.6 are obtained by multiplying the default risk by annual scheduled payments. More conservative assumptions for default risk would increase the estimated claims on budget resources.

Table 3.6. Estimated Guarantee Claims on the Budget
(CZK billion)

1998 Guarantees out-standing	Default risk	Total Claim	1999	2000	2001	2002	2003	1999-2003	1999-2030
284.8[1]	Avg. 38%	107.4	3.3	4.9	5.4	33.3	3.7	50.5	97.8

1/ This amount excludes most recent loan guarantee commitments in the amount of CZK17.6 billion that are
   expected to be implemented in 1999.
Source: Ministry of Finance and World Bank staff estimates.

Another source of future claims on the budget is Konsolidacni Banka. Konsolidacni Banka experienced about a CZK14 billion loss in 1998, which will be covered by state bond issue. Assuming no new programs, the analysis of Konsolidacni Banka's asset portfolio indicates that its future losses and its potential claims on the state budget are likely to stabilize in the neighborhood of about CZK6 billion in 1999-2001. However, new government programs that require further borrowing by Konsolidacni Banka without generating adequate revenues will further increase Konsolidacni Banka's debt service and, thus, losses.

Without further privatization revenues, the National Property Fund will need to further borrow to meet its commitment vis-à-vis Ceska Financni, Ceska Inkasni, environmental recovery and railway development, and to cover principle repayments for its obligations.[7] To meet its obligations, analysis of the National Property Fund's commitments, excluding those vis-à-vis Konsolidacni Banka, suggests that the Fund will annually need about CZK15 billion during 1999-2003 and about CZK33 billion in 2004.

The Agricultural and Forestry Guarantee and Support Fund (PGRLF), even if it issues no new guarantees in future years, will under a conservative 25 percent default assumption, suffer from reserve shortage to cover future guarantee claim payments. Analysis of its guarantee portfolio implies that PGRLF will need between CZK1 and 2 billion in the next four years, after depleting its available capital of CZK1.5 billion.

In the medium to long run, off-budget financing of government activities, guarantees and other contingent liabilities, surface as increases in government debt. In the Czech Republic, the expected increase in public debt by the amount of hidden public liabilities estimated around 12.4 percent of GDP in 1998 (see Table 3.5) is significant but not disastrous. What does appear as disastrous is the dynamic in the rise of hidden public liabilities. Clearly, the levels of new guarantees issued and new government programs entrusted for financing to Konsolidacni Banka are not sustainable. Their continued growth at the current pace may, in a few years, endanger fiscal stability, and thus play against the country's objective of EU accession. The situation will appear more serious if implicit government liabilities were included in the deficit and debt calculations.

The Banking Sector Remains a Major Source of Claims on Government Financial Support. The above calculations of true fiscal deficit and hidden public liability exclude banks other than Konsolidacni Banka. Whether or not activities of the other banks have been politically motivated, the three large banks

---

[7] The initial issuance of NPF's obligations had been used mainly to capitalize Konsolidacni Banka. The following ones were to cover its other commitments.

residually owned by the state suffer from weak portfolio and continue to rely on state support. These troubled banks include Czech Savings Bank, Komercni Banka and CSOB. The activities to support Czech Savings Bank illustrate the problem: In December 1998, Konsolidacni Banka purchased bad assets in the amount of CZK6.5 billion from the Czech Savings Bank (their nominal value was CZK10.5 billion). The provisions made for the low quality of assets purchased, increased the losses of KoB by CZK4 billion to a total of CZK14.4 billion.[8] In addition, Konsolidacni Banka issued subordinated debt for Czech Savings Bank in the amount of CZK5.5 billion so that Czech Savings Bank meets its capital adequacy requirement.[9] Table 3.7 shows the development in government exposure to the risks emerging in the three large state-owned banks. In the context of past developments, the table indicates that the process toward privatization of these banks is likely to absorb further public resources, possibly exceeding any revenues realized from their privatization.

Table 3.7. Government Implicit Risk Exposure in Large Banks: Amounts of Loss and Classified Loans

		1997		1998	
	State ownership share	Total loss loans	Total classified loans	Total loss loans	Total classified loans
		CZK billion			
Czech Savings Bank	45.0	33.4	44.7	8.4	31.1
Komercni Banka	48.7	56.1	102.1	27.2	59.4
CSOB	65.7	19.2	52.8	10.6	40.2
Total		**108.7**	**199.6**	**46.2**	**130.7**
Government exposure (% of GDP)		6.6	12.1	2.6	7.3

Source: Banks' Annual Reports.

Though not explicitly included in the calculation of the implicit fiscal deficit above, the Czech Railways is a large loss-making state-owned enterprise, which seems to enjoy an implicit state guarantee on its continued operation.[10] Losses and investment requirements have been growing; the Railways has been unable to cover both operating cost and to service old debt, and has been rapidly accumulating new debt (see Table 3.8). The increasing debt has raised the cost of debt service and has deteriorated the Railways' financial outlook. The Railways does not expect to be able to fully service its debt: it is already a major beneficiary of government guarantees and Konsolidacni Banka's support. Analysis of the Railways' performance and outlook indicates that government guarantees on Railways' debt simply substitutes government subsidy at face value. Non-guaranteed Railways' debt is yet another source of "hidden" deficit and fiscal risk -- mainly financed by the Czech Savings Bank, CSOB, Komercni Banka and Konsolidacni Banka, all of which have been discussed above.

Off-budget programs contribute only marginally to achieving the main policy objectives of the government and, in some instances, may even undermine these objectives. What are the results of off-budget programs in the Czech Republic? To support reforms and to prevent problems from recurrence or simply to pay for failures that are likely to occur again? A brief overview suggests that many off-budget programs, such as bailouts of banks and health insurance companies, have done the latter. Sometimes, programs which did not qualify for budgetary support (for example an additional subsidy to Railways), did in fact qualify for assistance outside the budget (such as a very risky guarantee extended to Railways).

---

[8] The estimated market value of these purchased assets has been only CZK2.5 billion. Konsolidacni Banka by purchasing them covered around one half of the expected loss for the Czech Savings Bank (i.e., CZK8 billion).
[9] See the financial sector chapter in this report.
[10] Czech Railways employs over 90,000 people. Profits generated in freight transport are used to subsidize the transport of passengers -- transport on which a large part of the population depends. The enterprise suffers from major undercapitalization and, in a related way, is known for its notoriously low productivity.

Moreover, these programs have often implied that the government will help again in case of future failures, and will thus have generated moral hazard among market agents, reducing their incentives to improve productivity and competitiveness. Accordingly, the objective of EU accession and integration with European markets -- which poses high requirements on competitiveness of banks and enterprises in the Czech economy -- may have been undermined.

Table 3.8. Czech Railways: Debt Outstanding, 1996-98
(CZK billion)

	1995	1996	1997	1998
Loss	3.1	4.7	4.7	3.5
Debt outstanding	1.6	5.8	15.3	20.6
o/w covered by state guarantees	0.0	2.5	8.0	12.4

Source: Czech Railways.

The Need to Resolve Institutional Problems

This section discusses the institutional problems behind the hidden deficit and hidden public liabilities in the Czech Republic and outlines suggestions on how to deal with these problems. In particular, the suggestions aim at developing a mechanism to enhance the processes of decision-making and control with respect to government off-budget activities and contingent liabilities. The government in the Czech Republic has already taken several important steps toward better fiscal management, particularly in trying to identify, classify, and understand the full range of fiscal risks facing the country, and to analyze the consequences of these risks for future public finances. The next steps should aim at introducing a medium-term strategic fiscal framework. This would open up key macroeconomic questions and policy choices, which relate to contingent liabilities as well as to mandatory and other budgetary expenditures in the budget process.

Government Pays Little Attention to Dealing with Off-budget Fiscal Risks

The present system in the Czech Republic, in which the government undertakes a large amount of off-budget activities, generates two main weaknesses: (a) the hidden public liabilities generate sudden, and not entirely expected, claims on the budget thus endangering future fiscal stability; and (b) off-budget government programs do not explicitly relate to the strategic choices made in the budget process. These weaknesses can be broadly explained by the low transparency of government operations, by fragmentation of the budget process, and by the weak position of Parliament in public finance decision making and fiscal control. The budget process does not require, and fiscal reports do not provide, information about government off-budget operations of a fiscal nature or about their financing. This creates scope for fiscal opportunism; policy makers may too easily launch low-priority activities outside the budget and thus commit future budgetary resources to their financing. The paragraphs below give more detail, focusing on state guarantees. Other forms of pursuing government programs outside the budgetary system, such as requesting Konsolidacni Banka to support health insurance companies, appear to have no limits.

Transformation institutions are available to government to pursue programs without much scrutiny and in a costly manner. Compared to budgetary decisions, there is very little scrutiny on government decision-making about activities to be pursued by transformation institutions. Without Parliamentary and public scrutiny, the government has the authority to pursue programs of all sorts and in unlimited amounts. Since the government guarantees its obligations, for example, Konsolidacni Banka is able to borrow in the markets and to finance as many programs as requested, even though it is unable to repay its debts without future support from the state budget.

Almost no Statutory and Regulatory Procedures Guide the Government's Exposure to Risks. Compared to other European countries, such as the Netherlands or the United Kingdom, the government in the Czech Republic has very broad authority to issue state guarantees and to accept other off-budget obligations. With respect to state guarantees, section 36 of the Law of December 20,1990, No. 576 authorizes the government to extend state guarantees "designed to finance government-approved developmental programs" without requiring estimates of future potential budget claims and, more broadly, without any public policy framework for issuing guarantees or a process for comparing programs of direct state assistance to state guarantees. This shortcoming has created an incentive for those entities and spending ministries unable to secure the desired level of state assistance through the budgetary process to seek such assistance outside the budget process through loan guarantees. The additional state assistance provided via guarantees is perceived as cost free and is not included in the overall financial support provided to a given sector (e.g., agriculture and transport). In some cases, the Ministry of Finance has extended guarantees that are not authorized under the broad authority of No. 576/90. These guarantees include a CZK22.5 billion guarantee to the Czech National Bank in 1997 and a CZK31.0 billion guarantee to the CSOB in 1998.

Guarantees Issued are Subject to no Meaningful Limits. Law No. 576/90 sets that the sum of installment payments due within a calendar year not exceed 8 percent of expected state budget revenues. This limit is extremely high and not very meaningful. For 1999, the limit allows for about CZK46 billion of installment payments, compared to the scheduled CZK12 billion. Other EU applicant countries place much tighter limits on guarantees, such as 1 percent of budget revenues as a limit for new guarantees issued in a given year in Hungary.

Guarantee Approval Process is Weak. Proposed guarantees are presented to the Ministry of Finance by the spending ministries. The Ministry of Finance then analyzes the viability of the proposed project and the borrower's potential ability to repay the proposed guaranteed loan to reject or accept further consideration of the proposed project. However, no mechanism encourages the Ministry of Finance to pronounce a high-risk project non-viable. Once a project is determined to be viable, the state guarantee typically receives parliamentary approval before it is granted. In this process, guarantees are often extended as a result of emergency and eminent political pressure rather than as a result of a strategic decision to support certain outcomes at a given price and against other competing claims on public resources.

The government requires almost no risk sharing by the lending institution, which creates moral hazard under guarantee contracts. The government typically guarantees 100 percent of the loan principal and interest. In addition, many guarantee contracts require the government to pay penalties to compensate the lender for the loss of profits due to early repayment due to default. As a result of the government's acceptance of virtually all credit risk, the role of the private lending institution is reduced to that of a loan servicer. The lender disregards the credit quality of the borrower. Borrowers tend to neglect risks of projects, which are covered by government guarantee. In the event of default, the borrower negotiates with the government rather than with the lender, because the lender does not have a stake in the loan performance.

Banks are well compensated for their loan servicing role. Even though the government almost always accepts 100 percent of the credit risk, domestic banks typically charge the borrower interest rates that are only marginally (e.g., 150 basis points) lower than the rates charged to borrowers for unguaranteed loans. Since the government is accepting the total credit risk, the interest rate charged to the borrower should equal the interest rate that would be charged on comparable government loans with some small premium to compensate for prepayment risk. In addition to profits earned from the interest rate charged to the borrower, lenders also charge the government a servicing fee. As mentioned above, the lender also often charges the borrower penalties in the form of higher interest rates after a missed payment. These penalties are then passed on to the government when the government honors the guarantee claim.

Risks are not Monitored. The Ministry of Finance provides only limited oversight of outstanding guaranteed loans. Borrowers are required to notify the Ministry of Finance 30 days in advance if they intend to default on their state-guaranteed repayment obligation. Prior to this notification, it is unclear how closely the Ministry of Finance monitoring outstanding guarantees.

No Reserves are Set Aside in Advance for Expected Guarantee Claim Payment. Each year the Ministry of Finance estimates the expected claim payments in the upcoming year. Given the pressure to present a balanced budget, incentives are created to make an optimistic estimate of expected claims in the upcoming year. Actual claims in 1997 were CZK2.0 billion compared to the CZK0.5 billion budgeted; and CZK6.7 billion in 1998 contrasted to the CZK0.8 billion budgeted.

The lack of reserves to cover future guarantee claims results in guarantee defaults producing "shocks" to the state budget, resulting in a disruptive budget process that thwarts medium-term fiscal strategy. As guaranteed loans default, resources must immediately be found within the state budget, potentially requiring substantial and unexpected reductions in other state programs.

The lack of a requirement to establish loan loss reserves allows loan guarantees to avoid the discipline of the budget process; it creates tremendous incentives to issue guarantees, because they do not require budgetary resources in the current year. As a result, substantially higher budgetary resources may be required in future years to pay for defaulted guarantees. Therefore, the current guarantee structure distorts the decision making process and encourages policy makers to make decisions today that may severely limit the options of future policy makers.

The focus on cash payments for guarantee claims creates strong incentives to meet annual guarantee claims payments through options that increase the cost of guarantees over the long term. For example, loan defaults would generally be less expensive over the long-term if the government immediately purchased a defaulted loan and refinanced it by government debt. Cash-based accounting and reporting, however, create opposite incentives -- as documented by the case of defaulted guarantees to Czech Railway. In 1997, the Czech Railway failed to make scheduled payments on its three state guaranteed loans. The state made these payments, but did not declare the loans to be in "gross default." By only making the scheduled payments of CZK0.2 billion, rather than paying off the entire guaranteed loan balance of CZK8 billion, the state significantly reduced cash demands for guarantee claims in 1997. However, if the Railway cannot realistically repay this debt, by continuing to make payments on annual installments the state is making unnecessarily high payments: the interest rate paid to the lender is higher than the government's cost of borrowing. For example, if the average interest rate on the guaranteed Railway loans were 6.25 percent and the state could issue comparable debt with a 6.00 percent interest rate, continuing to make the payments for the Railway at the 6.25 percent interest rate would result in an increased cost to the state of approximately CZK0.2 billion over the remaining life of the Railway loans through 2017 on a cash basis (e.g., the sum of the annual difference in interest costs).

Introducing Comprehensive Medium-term Strategic Fiscal Framework

To introduce a medium-term strategic fiscal framework in a comprehensive manner, the government will need to integrate all activities of a fiscal nature into its standard processes for policy making, budget allocation, control and reporting. Whether it is an activity to be pursued through a state guarantee or an "independent" agency, such as Konsolidacni Banka, it must be subjected to the same level of scrutiny as that for spending programs. The scrutiny process would mainly aim at ensuring a truly stable fiscal outlook and at using the current and future public resources for policy priorities.

To strengthen future fiscal stability, it may be useful for the government to formalize its medium-term strategy by establishing a fiscal framework for each of the next three years, and to include contingent government liabilities in the underlying fiscal analysis. The three-year fiscal framework would show more clearly what are the medium-term fiscal implications of government decisions. Not only decisions directly involving public expenditures, but also those decisions creating a contingent government liability, should be considered. Fiscal analysis must factor in the cost of implicit subsidies provided by contingent support programs, including the potential future claims on public resources that may emerge from arrears and other obligations of state-guaranteed and state-owned institutions. Medium-term fiscal forecasts need to incorporate all expected contingents as well as direct outlays.

To enhance the Government's strategic choices, programs of contingent support, as well as budget allocations, should clearly relate to policy priorities and to specific results rather than to bottom-up, often partial, pressures. The trend in public finance institutional development in EU member and applicant countries, including Sweden, United Kingdom, and Hungary has been toward linking decisions about expenditure and contingent support programs with the cost of delivering specific services and with specific policy objectives to be accomplished. Recent experiences emerging from this trend to improve strategic allocation within public expenditure management suggest the following features of the budgetary process in the Czech Republic.

The three-year fiscal framework can become a tool enabling policy makers to relate decisions about guarantees, budget allocations and other forms of government support to policy choices. At a stage early within the budget cycle, the Cabinet should make a collective, binding decision on the core elements of public finance strategy, both at the macroeconomic level and at the level of inter-sectoral allocation. A multi-year framework for budget preparation would encourage building a stable consensus around medium-term policy strategies -- a consensus which should, as far as possible, embrace the Cabinet, legislature and civil society. A transparent decision-making process for public finance strategy is a key factor to enhance stability in budget allocations and to reduce the tendency to transfer commitmentsoff-budget. Linked to policy objectives and desired outputs (results and services to be delivered), the Ministry of Finance would set sectoral ceilings. Sectoral ceilings would apply to the same extent to budget allocations and contingent support programs. Line ministries would have the responsibility to determine which spending and contingent support programs would best contribute to accomplishing the policy priorities. Each guarantee proposed by the line ministries in this process would be subject to risk analysis by the Ministry of Finance and to further scrutiny as any other budget item. The Ministry of Finance would set the reserve requirement for each particular guarantee, which ideally would be the amount of hidden subsidy (the present value of the future potential fiscal cost) of the guarantee. The sector ministry would then have to transfer the required reserve amount to central reserve fund. The central reserve fund would be earmarked to exclusively cover future guarantee claims on the budget.

To minimize future claims emerging from contingent liabilities, the government will need to implement new limits and rules for issuing and dealing with off-budget programs. Specifically, the government will need to introduce effective regulations with respect to the amounts of, and the government risk exposure to, contingent liabilities, with respect to the design of programs of contingent support. Special requirements should apply to the status and responsibilities of agencies, such as credit and guarantee funds, which are entrusted with implementing government programs. Special reporting requirements should apply to all programs and institutions, including non-banking financial institutions and funds that may either explicitly or implicitly generate fiscal risk in the future.

New Budget Rules and practices may specify government responsibilities vis-à-vis off-budget government commitments and fiscal risks around the following imperatives:

- Identify, analyze and regularly report off-budget government commitments, including hidden and contingent government liabilities that may affect future public expenditures (guarantee claims and residual obligations of state-guaranteed agencies) and revenues (tax exemptions). Require that analysis of fiscal risks be added to fiscal reports. In this respect, the inclusion of the Fiscal Risks Table in the 1999 state Budget proposal is a step in the right direction.

- Place tighter limits on state guarantees and off-budget programs, on government implicit obligations, and both direct and contingent liabilities resulting from extra-budgetary funds and other agencies associated with government policies. Also, regulate more tightly financial management by subnational governments to limit their exposure to unsustainable debts and excessive commitments. Potential fiscal risks may emerge from guarantees issued by local governments, from enterprises and banks owned by local governments, and from inadequate maintenance of delivery systems of core public services at the local level.

- Before approving off-budget assistance, recognize its risks and its full potential cost. Consider, for instance, the determinants and size of default risk of state guarantees; risk exposure of extra-budgetary funds and other agencies supported by the government. It is important that policy makers and the public understand that state guarantees and off-budget programs implemented through extra-budgetary funds and various other agencies, such as Konsolidacni Banka, National Property Fund and PGRLF, represent a real claim on future public resources. Programs that do not require cash from the current state budget may require significant budgetary resources in the future. The new Budget Rules should mandate that probability and size of these future claims be recognized before decisions are made about new programs. From the macroeconomic viewpoint, tight control over all potential government liabilities is more important than a budget balance accompanied by increasing hidden public debts.

- Link decisions about guarantees and off-budget programs to the medium-term strategic fiscal framework and to budget allocations; based on potential cost estimates, set aside reserves. To prevent potential bias toward excessive use of off-budget programs, the new Budget Rules should require that off-budget programs are subject to the same scrutiny as budgetary programs throughout the entire budget process. Overall spending ceilings for sectors and budget chapters, for instance, could cover both budget expenditures and guarantees. Sector ministers would propose the forms of pursuing their sectoral policies -- for instance, whether to extend a subsidy, loan or guarantee. On the basis of risk analysis, the Ministry of Finance would require that guarantees and off-budget programs be limited and that the amount of their expected fiscal cost be deducted from the proposed medium-term ceilings and budget allocations and be transferred to guarantee reserve fund. The Ministry of Finance would be responsible for publishing estimates of the potential cost of state guarantees and off-budget programs, for building adequate reserves over time, and for using the reserves exclusively to cover future claims associated with such programs.

- Create proper incentives for the borrower, lender, and program manager by requiring significant risk sharing under state guarantees and other programs. New Budget Rules may advise that state guarantees do not cover risks that are controlled by the borrower and lender, such as various specific commercial risks, and do not cover the full amount of the underlying asset. Appropriate design and risk treatment of government programs can become the responsibility of the Ministry of Finance.

- Improve reporting of actual performance of programs under state guarantees and outside the budgetary system, set specific performance criteria and review the process for such programs and demand accountability similar to that for the state budget. The new Budget Rules should strengthen the role of Parliament and public audit with respect to the decisions about, and performance oversight of, government programs implemented both outside, as well as within, the budgetary system.

- Set completion dates for guarantee programs and off-budget activities. The new Budget Rules should require that all agencies and programs established by the government with specific objectives outside the budgetary system, be subject to termination dates of, and re-authorization requirement for, their existence, and to tight limits on their activities.

To address the pressure for more extra-budgetary funds and further fragmentation of the budgetary system will require two measures. First, part of the motivation for establishing such funds should be removed by the broad agenda of actions designed to enhance the stability of budgetary allocations. Second, the Budget Rules should include:

- a short positive list of legitimate extra-budgetary funds, primarily in the area of social insurance, where a clear rationale for separate funding can be identified;

- in the context of the principle of a comprehensive budget, a clear statement of presumption against recourse to extra-budgetary funds; and

- tight restrictions on the establishment of new extra-budgetary funds, including requirement of Parliamentary approval.

Budget Rules should ensure that any borrowing and creating liabilities by extra-budgetary funds (as well as state-guaranteed agencies) be tightly restricted, and revenues of extra-budgetary funds be collected mainly from the beneficiaries of their activities (for example, establishing a fund to maintain roads may be justified if the fund is financed directly from user fees rather than from general taxes).

Chapter IV. Inter-government and Local Finance

Introduction

The Czech Republic chose the decentralization program to be an important part of its transformation process, thereby complementing other reforms. Under the overlapping trends of privatization and fiscal decentralization, the Czech Republic has been transformed since 1990 from one of the most centralized and command oriented former communist countries into one resembling a market economy. At present, the assigned local public finance system represents approximately one-third, in terms of GDP shares, of the central government: revenue and expenditure.

As local governments have become significant players, analyzing their fiscal functions is key to understanding the extent of fiscal adjustment in the country, while the roles and responsibilities of both central and sub-national governments need to be assessed in order to address the overall risks to stability of the decentralized system. There are several areas for discussion and analysis:

- the central government's dominant role in inter-governmental relations;

- the fragmentation problem of local government;

- better definition of revenue assignment, as no proper revenues exist for local governments;

- more transparent rules for inter-governmental transfers to replace the current practices based on political pressures; and

- the lack of a comprehensive regulatory framework for sub-national credit and the lack of proper monitoring and control by the Ministry of Finance.

This chapter is organized as follows. The first part provides a brief historical review of the development of decentralization and local administration, followed by an analysis of fiscal arrangements. Revenue assignment and expenditure responsibilities will then be discussed, as well as the inter-governmental transfers, local government credit markets, and fiscal equalization. The section concludes with an analysis of the potential of local tax systems in terms. The last part provides a discussion on relevant future issues to be considered for local government development.

Public Sector History and Organization

Under the communist regime, the government was organized as a multi-tier system, yet fiscal decentralization was not promoted, and local authorities acted as agents of the central government. After the *Velvet Revolution* in 1989, successful joint transformation institutions characterized the period 1990-93. The federalist experience of Czechoslovakia failed in 1993 under the force of nationalistic pressures. Since then, the separate course of the Czech Republic has been characterized by the progress of local self-government (*samospráva*).

The basis of local self-government is enunciated in the Constitution of December 16,1992.[1] The rules governing the status and scope of municipal activities are found in Act no. 367/1990 on municipalities, amended by Act no. 403/1992. The law on municipalities was enacted on May 6, 1992, and other basic documents on their budgets were adopted over the 1990-93 period. The process of restructuring the public sector in the Czech Republic was animated by the idea of decreasing the total tax burden in the country and maintaining a balanced budget. The favorable macroeconomic context opened the way for a major tax reform in 1993.

Organization of the Inter-governmental System

The Czech governmental and fiscal system is organized as a two-tier system composed of the national center and the local governments (see Table 4.1). The upper level is controlled by an elected Parliament, while local governments are led by mayors elected by local councils, which are themselves elected by the people. There are 6,234 independent municipalities, the majority of which are small, with fewer than 500 residents. Between the two levels of government, 77 district offices[2] act as intermediaries, performing state administration, without self-government functions. The district budget and that of its constituent local municipalities together form the local budgets.

Past centralization, and the fragmentation of the fiscal landscape have made it a challenge to assure a competent administration of local units, due in part to resource and personnel limitations. Accordingly, in 1997 it was decided to establish 14 regions with regional self-administration. Once this proposal is approved, the new regions and regional governments will form an intermediate tier to assist in the interaction of municipalities with the center.

Table 4.1. Inter-governmental System in the Czech Republic

	Executive Branch	Legislative Branch
Central Government	Ministry of Finance Ministry of Interior	Parliament
(Regions)	*Establishment of a decentralized tier underway*	
Local Governments **District** **Municipalities**	District Government Mayor City/ Municipal Council	District Assembly Municipal Board of Representatives

Source: Ministry of Finance.

According to the new framework, the district government will conduct state functions at the local level. Its representatives are to be appointed by the central government; the Ministry of Interior will prescribe the quota of staff for the district authority. Members of a district assembly are to be elected by municipal councils, with the number of members proportional to the size of the respective municipalities. A district assembly will approve the district budget and annual accounts, will decide on the allocation of state subsidies, especially the equalization grant, and will allocate the district budget surplus. However, as district authorities provide similar local services as municipalities, their financing is to be included in local budgets.

---

[1] Chapter 7 (Articles 99-105).
[2] Including the four largest cities, called magistrates: Prague, Brno, Ostrava, Pilsen. Unlike the districts, these cities also have self-governing functions.

District budgets coalesced into municipal budgets by insignificance. The district share of expenditures declined from 35 percent in 1992 to 15 percent by 1994, and the share of capital expenditures fell from 50 percent to 7 percent. A large number of municipalities are very small in size, with more than 80 percent having less than 1000 people and almost 90 percent having less than 2000 people (see Box 4.1) -- thus typically too small to efficiently provide all the required public goods and services.

Box 4.1. Local Governments at a Glance

Summary Statistics on Local Governments

1950: 13 regions, 179 districts, 11,051 municipalities
1998: 14 regions, 77 districts, 6,234 municipalities

Average area of municipality:	1,337 ha
Largest municipality (Prague):	49,614 ha
Smallest municipality (Zavist):	42 ha

Average population of municipality:	1,636
Number of municipalities with more	
than 10,000 inhabitants:	133 (1997)
Largest municipality (Prague):	1,204,953 (1997)
Smallest (Brezina):	9 (1991)

Source: Czech Statistical Office.

This fragmentation problem is typical of transition countries. Trying to establish closer links to population, the central government may prove unable to maintain direct bilateral contact with atomistic local units, and the latter may lose political clout in the process. As a country without a prevailing rural settlement, the Czech Republic faces the potential contradiction between the structure of demand for public goods induced by urban tastes, requiring large scale infrastructure, and a fragmented supply base. A solution to the problem could come by regrouping municipalities for providing services.[3] Although a union of cities does exist in the Czech Republic, there is almost no cooperation between cities in delivering services or administrative functions.

To complicate matters, the small size of municipalities further slows the decentralization of real responsibility for services. The absence of an upper coordinating tier of government

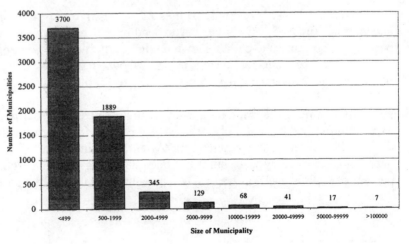

Figure 4.1. Municipalities by Population Size, 1993

---

[3] The law on municipalities allows regrouping of municipalities after authorization of the central government.

gives scope for significant administrative power in the center. The new sense of identity and independence actually slows the development of cooperative associations among local areas.

The Inter-governmental Budget System

The general public budget includes the state and local budgets complemented by five extra-budgetary funds.[4] The budgetary system is further complemented by the National Property Fund, the Land Fund, and the National Health Fund. In connection with the tax reform of 1993, health care was excluded from the general budget, and 27 health insurance services were set up, financed by mandatory contributions of 4.5 percent for employees and 9 percent for employers. The present tax system has several features similar to western countries (see Table 4.2). The main revenue sources are the VAT, excises, and direct taxes that include personal and corporate income taxes. Aside from the tax system, there are social security contributions (pension, illness and unemployment insurance) in addition to the above mentioned health care contributions.

While the new system did not include any significant local taxes, it introduced the *shared tax principle*. All taxes are collected by the central government through over 200 regional tax offices, while audits are done mostly by districts. Independent auditors are authorized, but there is a lack of auditors who specialize in municipalities.

Fiscal Analysis of Local Governments

Before 1992, municipal budgets were primarily dependent on transfers from the state, and almost all capital investments at the municipal level were financed through central government grants or subsidies. In 1993, a new tax and municipal financing system introduced "own revenues" from shared taxes and local taxes, paving the way for greater local financial and fiscal autonomy. The present inter-governmental structure reflects important changes in the tax revenue allocation made in 1996.[5] As a result of reductions in operational and capital subsidies, municipalities have come to rely increasingly on own budget surpluses in financing their capital expenses. In addition, they have financed their expenditures through credits, both from commercial and state sources.

During 1994-1997, municipalities ran a positive current balance before subsidies (defined as tax and non-tax revenues minus current expenditures) in every year, except for 1996. On average for the period, the current balance has shown a slight deficit of 0.1 percent of GDP. After operational subsidies are taken into account, the current balance shows a strong -- albeit declining -- surplus over the whole period, and is on average 2.0 percent of GDP (see Table 4.3.).

In contrast, the capital balance without subsidies (defined as capital revenues minus capital expenditures) has been sharply negative every year in this period, averaging a deficit of 3.0 percent of GDP, although the deficit is narrowing. After taking into account capital subsidies, the capital balance has been negative in every year, but it has been declining steadily, from -2.5 percent of GDP in 1994 to -1.8 percent of GDP in 1997, averaging -2.2 percent of GDP over the period.

---

[4] The two most important of which are the Fund for Market Regulation in Agriculture, a marketing board for stabilizing the markets of selected agricultural products, and the Fund for Environmental Protection, focusing on co-financing capital projects and environmental protection activities.

[5] The personal income tax allocation for municipalities was reduced from 55 percent to 30 percent while a new corporate income tax allocation of 20 percent was established.

Table 4.2. Main Taxes of Inter-governmental System in the Czech Republic, 1996

Personal Income Tax Incomes of residents and income from Czech sources of nonresidents, taxed progressively from 15 percent in the lowest bracket to 40 percent in the highest bracket.	Shared by central (40 percent) and local governments (60 percent) Exemptions are annual pensions payments up to CZK120,000, and all insurance compensations. Various deductions as per taxpayers social conditions and dependents.
Corporate Income Tax Profits of legal entities headquartered in the Czech Republic. Rate of 35 percent for all companies. Taxable income of pension funds, individual funds, unit trusts – 25 percent.	Shared between central (80 percent) and local governments (20 percent). Exemptions are incomes of charity and non-profit organizations. Tax-deductible expenditures consist of asset depreciation up to 45 years, social security contributions.
Value Added Tax (VAT) Levied on taxable supplies, while the tax on inputs are refunded. The basic rate is 22 percent on most goods and services, and the reduced rate of 5 percent applies to foodstuffs, pharmaceuticals, books and newspapers.	Assigned to central government.
Excises Levied on petroleum products, alcohol, tobacco and spirits. Specific rates apply.	Assigned to central government. Exemptions include education, health, cultural activities, etc.
Real Estate Tax Levied on owners of land, buildings and structures. Tax based on area, type and quality of the land, and usage. Basic rate for housing is CZK 1-3/m.sq., and for commercial varies from CZK 5 to 10/m.sq. Specific coefficients are applied to correct for value (e.g., number of floors, location).	Assigned to local governments, which can only determine some coefficients applicable to the tax rates, to reflect appropriate property values or revenue targets. Exemptions include churches and non-profit community properties, property used for health, education, social and cultural uses, etc.
Property Transfers, Gifts, and Inheritance Taxes Transfer tax is 5 percent on real estate, and inheritance and gift taxes are progressive according to family relationships (1-5 percent for direct relatives, 3-12 percent for indirect relatives, 7-12 percent for unrelated and legal entities.	Assigned to central government. Exemptions include deeds transferred within state organizations, transfers from the National Property Fund, deed transfers related to privatization.
Road Tax Annual rates CZK1,200-50,400. Levied on companies and individuals in the transportation business, for each vehicle	Assigned to central government Exemptions cover public transportation, public safety cars, etc.; vehicles operating within specified emission limits.
Tax Administration Annual returns are filed by individual or recognized accountants. Ministry of Finance is highest authority for both tax legislation and administration. Second tier are regional financial authorities, followed by local financial offices. Taxpayer can appeal decisions by local authority to regional authority, but is not suspensive of payments. Appeals at regional level are made to the MoF. But, MoF is judge to appeals against itself.	All taxes are state taxes, and are administered by the central government bodies, especially MoF. Local governments administer transfers and fees. Municipalities administer local fees and fines, while district offices administer administrative fees and fines.
Real Estate Taxation consists of: Land Tax: On land in the Real Estate Cadastre, paid by its owner/user (0.25-0.75 percent of the official price); Land tax for which building permission was granted (CZK1 per square meter). Building Tax: Calculated according to the registered ground area of the building (CZK5-10/m2 for businesses, CZK1-3/m2 for residential, increased by CZK0.75/m2 for each additional floor; rates are also multiplied by a coefficient according to locality (0.3-3.5, 4.5 in Prague).	Assigned to local governments.

Source: Ministry of Finance.

The gross balance, the sum of current and capital balances, was positive in 1994, but turned negative in 1995 and remained negative, averaging a slight deficit of 0.2 percent of GDP. With expenditure on lending minus repayments, the overall borrowing requirement for local governments amounted to a slightly higher deficit, still averaging 0.2 percent of GDP, or 2.3 percent of total revenues.

Table 4.3. Municipal Budget Balance
(CZK million)

	1994	1995	1996	1997	Avg 94-97
Current balance without subsidies (current balance)[1/]	5,365	8,454	-23,377	1,112	--
Percent of GDP	0.5	0.6	-1.5	0.1	-0.1
Current balance with operational subsidies	29,368	30,201	25,505	25,097	--
Percent of GDP	2.6	2.2	1.7	1.5	2.0
Capital balance without subsidies	-35,144	-45,012	-44,043	-42,147	--
Percent of GDP	-3.1	-3.3	-2.9	-2.6	-3.0
Capital balance with capital subsidies (capital balance)	-28,167	-31,956	-31,421	-30,260	--
Percent of GDP	-2.5	-2.4	-2.1	-1.8	-2.2
Gross balance (current+capital)	1,201	-1,755	-5,916	-5,163	--
Percent of GDP	0.1	-0.1	-0.4	-0.3	-0.2
Expenditure: Lending minus repayments	1,072	518	1,365	-396	--
Overall balance	**129**	**-2,273**	**-7,281**	**-4,767**	**--**
Percent of GDP	**0.0**	**-0.2**	**-0.5**	**-0.3**	**-0.2**
Percent of Revenues	**0.1**	**-1.8**	**-4.4**	**-3.3**	**-2.3**
Current balance with Grants/Capital Balance with Grants (percent)	-104.3	-94.5	-81.2	-82.9	-90.7

1/ Current Balance w/o Grants = Tax Revenue + Non-Tax Revenue - Current Expenditure.
Source: Budgets of local governments, Ministry of Finance.

Over the period 1994-1997, tax revenues of local governments have grown on average 12.2 percent, non-tax revenues have grown 6.2 percent, subsidies have grown 15.8 percent, while capital revenues have grown 15.0 percent. Overall, revenues have grown 10.2 percent. Over the same period, current expenditures have grown 15.3 percent on average, while capital expenditures have increased 7.6 percent. Overall, expenditures have grown 12.1 percent on average.

As a result of these trends, the overall budget deficits of municipalities were driven mostly by capital expenditures. The share of municipal investment financed by "own sources" surpluses generated from operating budgets has been high, but declining. Operating surpluses financed on average 90.7 percent of the capital deficits in this period. In other words, all long-term borrowing was used for investment outlays, indicating prudent financial management at the local level. However, it is important to note that these figures are aggregate, and results show variance across municipalities. Also, since municipal revenues are composed mostly of revenues over which the municipalities do not have any control, the existence of operational surpluses is heavily dependent on factors outside the control of municipal management. This is especially true in the case of transferred operational subsidies from the central government, which, in the face of declining capital subsidies, have come to play an important role in financing municipal capital outlays.

Local nominal revenues and expenditures have also grown faster than central revenues and expenditures (at 10.2 percent vs. 9.6 percent for revenues, and 12.1 percent vs. 10.5 percent for expenditures). Moreover, local revenues and expenditures are equally dispersed at 4.8 percent -- slightly higher than those of the central budget, respectively at 4.4 percent and 4.9 percent.[6] Hence, on nominal

---

[6] The dispersion rates are measured by the standard deviations of each item, and reflect their general degree of instability.

terms, the central budget appears more stable and convergent than its local counterparts. These trends suggest that, on nominal terms, local governments face a harder task at stabilization, despite the important transfers from central to local levels. The transfers amounted on average to 2.9 percent of GDP, especially in 1996 when they peaked at 4 percent of GDP as a result of changes in methodology of payments of some state social benefits -- effective since October 1995.

The above dynamic trends translated in real terms for local budgets in a slightly better budgetary outcome compared to the central budget. At 1994 prices, local budget revenues actually fell by an average of -5.2 percent over the 4-year period; local expenditures also fell in real terms by -4.8 percent, suggesting a 0.4 percent rate of deficit growth. For the central budget, revenues actually increased by 0.7 percent in real terms, despite positive real transfers to local governments at the average annual rate of 6.8 percent. Central expenditures also increased in real terms by 1.5 percent, i.e., with a resulting growth rate of the deficit of 0.8 percent. Thus, the built-in structural real deficit of central finance grew two times faster than the one of the local counterpart, suggesting that local governments appear to have made better fiscal decisions than the national average.[7]

Local public finance in the Czech Republic faces constant challenges. Municipalities have little discretion over taxes and expenditures. On the expenditure side, since 1997 only about 5 percent of budgetary transfers can be freely spent. On the revenue side, all taxes are centrally set (income and corporate tax). For the latter, localities can influence the location of firms on their territories. The real estate tax will offer some limited tax power. The municipalities set, within the limits of the law, the amounts for local fees and charges.

The lack of genuinely local taxes prevents tax competition, and bargaining the local tax burden. The shared tax principle limits the ability of local governments to respond optimally to expenditure developments. The dynamics of the local public finance system generates a structural budget deficit which, short of local control of important taxes, burdens the narrow tax bases (real estate, non-tax revenues) and increases debt financing.

The sources of deficit financing for Czech municipalities are: 1) commercial bank credits and municipal bonds; 2) interest-free loans from the State and other state agencies including the State Environment Fund (SEF); and 3) loans from multilateral and bilateral institutions. Table 4.4 shows the breakdown of the financing of deficit by categories of local government budgets. In all years except for 1994, the major source of financing was the domestic market. In 1994, when the Prague Eurobond was issued, the proceeds of this bond were used to offset the outstanding domestic bank credit, thus resulting in a net outflow from the sector.

Table 4.4. Sources of Deficit Financing
(CZK million)

	1994	1995	1996	1997
Overall Balance	129	-2,273	-7,281	-4,767
Borrowing from abroad	7,294	0	0	256
Borrowing from the domestic market, o/w:	-7,423	2,273	7,281	4,511
Non-bank credit	0	2,284	1,614	2,799
Bank credit	-7,423	-11	5,667	1,712
Total deficit financing	-129	2,273	7,281	4,767

Source: Budgets of local governments, Ministry of Finance.

---

[7] On spending: recall that revenues are essentially a central government affair.

Table 4.5. shows a more detailed breakdown of municipal borrowings on a flow basis which are defined as net increases (decreases) in the outstanding values of debt owed by municipalities under each type of instrument. Overall, the nominal inflow to the sector has fallen from 1994 to 1997 (from CZK11.2 billion to CZK6.9 billion).

Table 4.5. Credit to Municipalities (Flow)
(CZK million)

	1994	1995	1996	1997
Commercial Bank Credits	2,429	3,742	2,943	1,901
Municipal Bonds	7,617	897	3,367	1,293
Debt of Small Municipalities	170	424	463	618
Reimbursable Financial Assistance from district offices and the State budget	0	1,804	1,092	2,304
Loans from SEF	1,000	1,665	1,625	800
Total Debt Inflows	11,217	8,532	9,490	6,916

Source: Ministry of Finance and World Bank staff calculations.

The composition of debt has also undergone changes. A clear trend is that the share of commercial credits in overall credit flows to municipalities has been declining, in both absolute terms and relative to non-commercial state credit. Bank loans have accounted for 22 percent of borrowings in 1994, 44 percent in 1995, 31 percent in 1996, and 27.5 percent in 1997. Municipal bonds have accounted for 68 percent of total borrowings in 1994 (year of Eurobond), 11 percent in 1995, 35.5 percent in 1996 and 19 percent in 1997. The aggregate share of bank credits and municipal bonds in total new borrowings has fallen from 90 percent in 1994 to 46 percent.

Reimbursable state loans, on the other hand, have shown a steady increase over the period, from a level of 0 in 1994 to CZK2.3 billion in 1997, accounting for one-third of new borrowings. Debt of small municipalities, reported separately, has shown a steady growth: The debt of these municipalities accounted for only 1.5 percent of net borrowings in 1994, but 9 percent in 1997, rising from CZK0.2 billion to CZK0.6 billion. Finally, loans from the SEF increased sharply from 1994 to 1995 (9 percent to 19.5 percent of borrowings, respectively), and ended at 12 percent of borrowings in 1997.

Similar trends can be observed in outstanding stock of debt (see Table 4.6.). Outstanding bank credit has remained at a stable level (about 34.5 percent of outstanding debt in both 1994 and 1997), while from 1995 to 1997 (excluding Prague's Eurobond), share of municipal bonds in total debt has decreased from 38 percent of debt to 34 percent. In contrast, reimbursable state loans and loans from the SEF have increased, accounting for 27 percent of total outstanding debt in 1997 together. Debt of small municipalities has grown modestly, from 3.5 percent of debt in 1994 to 5 percent in 1997.

Table 4.6. Credit to Municipalities (Stock)
(CZK million, end-year)

	1993	1994	1995	1996	1997
Commercial Credits	2,485	4,914	8,656	11,599	13,500
Municipal Bonds	26	7,643	8,540	11,907	13,200
Debt of Small Municipalities	324	495	919	1,382	2,000
Reimbursable Financial Assistance	0	0	1,804	2,897	5,200
Loans from SEF	109	1,110	2,774	4,400	5,200
Total Debts	2,945	14,162	22,694	32,184	39,100
As percent GDP	-	1.2	1.7	2.1	2.4

Source: Ministry of Finance.

Local Government Revenues

The municipalities' own revenues, i.e., non-transfer revenue, make up the bulk of local revenues. They amounted to 7.1 percent of GDP in 1994 and then decreased to 6.6 percent in 1997. This decline in "own" revenues between 1994 and 1997 indicates the aggregate role of fiscal transfers (2.2 percent of GDP in 1997). Between the two main sources of revenue, the personal income tax has declined by 7 percent over the period, thus reducing the overall local tax yield, whereas budgetary transfers grew at 1.8 percent, albeit insufficiently to stem the overall fall.

In terms of GDP share, revenue dynamics do not favor the fiscal equilibrium of local entities. GDP shares of local tax revenues have declined, on average, by 0.7 percent over the 4-year period, by contrast to more than 11 percent for the central government. Moreover, the lower standard deviation of 0.2 percent for local taxes, as compared to 4.8 percent for central government taxes, suggests that local taxes are more stable on their declining trend, thus yielding an increased divergence between the two revenue systems.

Most of tax revenues are tax shares are both determined and collected centrally. With the tax reform introduced in 1993, the property tax (mostly the real estate tax) was assigned to localities, albeit with missing degrees of freedom for municipalities (see Table 4.1).[8] National authorities expect it to triple when it will be assessed on an ad-valorem basis in 1999. Property taxes amounted, on average, to 0.3 percent of GDP. In 1996, the corporate income tax also became a shared tax (0.5 percent of GDP). Additionally, non-tax revenues are an important local revenue source (1.6 percent of GDP), and include local fees, administrative fees, proceeds from sales and rent of municipal property, user charges, etc.

The lion's share of local revenue is the personal income tax, which represented 37 percent in 1997 (3.8 percent of GDP). Its most important part, a tax on wages, is shared with constituent municipalities. The sharing rule for the tax on wages collected in a district is determined by a ratio set by Parliament. A partial re-centralization of the wage tax was introduced in 1996, with local governments sharing 60 percent of their wage tax. The district authority gets 30 percent of the yield collected within the district, and municipalities share 20 percent according to the size of their population. The remaining 10 percent goes to the municipality where wages were originally paid.[9] In 1996, 20 percent of the corporate income tax (collected in the whole country) was assigned to the municipalities, according to the number of their population. However, if the discrepancies in per capita tax revenue among districts are thought to have been narrowed, it is still expected that the discrepancies among municipalities within a district will probably rise.

Local Expenditures

Budgetary expenditures by local governments amounted to 9.1 percent of GDP in 1997, and represented 21.6 percent of the consolidated general government budget. The growth of spending, however, does not have a high income generating potential, as the growth of recurrent spending at 15.3 percent is twice as important as that of capital spending, which is 7.6 percent. The main drivers of the growth of recurrent spending are welfare (46 percent), order, safety, and general public services (20 percent), recreation and culture (17 percent), and education and health (11 percent).

The main tasks of local government include pre-school and primary school education (joint tasks of both levels, as wages are paid centrally), social services including care for the elderly and for the disabled,

---

[8] The proposal of the new law on property tax is expected to come into effect by 2001.
[9] The four magistrates (Prague, Brno, Ostrava, and Pilsen) initially received 100 percent of their wage tax. With tax reform in 1996, the magistrates retain 70 percent.

housing, planning, refuse collection, water supply and waste water treatment, parks and recreational facilities, local road maintenance and local transportation. The major single expenditure items are capital expenditures (34 percent), such as drinking and wastewater treatment facilities, schools, dumps, hospitals, and social care facilities. They are financed by operating revenue, specific subsidies from the central government, and loans. The maintenance of communal housing represents about 11 percent of expenditures since the ownership of previously state-owned housing was transferred to localities. Education is the third local expenditure item (primary and pre- school facilities), with the state assisting by a subsidy. The system of expenditure assignment reflects a shift of once national activities to local governments.

Some types of expenditure responsibilities are sprinkled throughout the budgets of all levels of government. The scale of provision is determined by the benefit area principle and the relative wealth and political independence of the individual communities. These include consumer price subsidies, subsidies for vulnerable groups, welfare programs for pensioners and the disabled, family and child allowances, and support for the homeless. These subsidies are financed by the central government and are transferred to the districts, which in turn disburse these funds to the localities.

Budget-financed investments are also notably decentralized. The central government has progressively cut its subsidies to the "productive" sector (capital grants to state enterprises and subsidized organizations), and this role has been taken up by sub-national governments. The capital grants and subsidies are in the form of economic services rendered, the mainstay of which is road construction and maintenance.

The absence of detailed codification of the assignment of expenditure and policy decision responsibilities among levels of government leaves a number of murky areas. First, the distinction between funded and non-funded mandates under the same expenditure category is unclear. Central authorities influence the delegated functions to local governments in ways that cannot be legislated. For example, the central government sets and pays the wages of civil servants, including those working in local governments, but the other operating expenditures are paid by local budgets. Second, the devolution of expenditure responsibilities to locals was unmatched by the corresponding tax authority to assume their efficient provision.

Government Transfers

The principle of budgetary independence at all levels of government, enshrined in the basic budget law, ended the reliance of lower levels of government on higher levels to automatically finance deficits incurred in implementing programs. It also ended the practice of transferring surpluses to the next higher level of government. However, as the central government is responsible for macroeconomic results, it uses tax sharing as an instrument of control over local governments, and as an automatic mechanism to correct fiscal disparities. Since the economic and tax revenue base in some regions was too weak to finance their expenditures, the central government re-centralized the personal income tax, the largest source of local revenue.

The amount of explicit central transfers the local governments would obtain were negotiated with the central government on an ad hoc basis. The transfers from the state budget represent, on average, 2.9 percent of GDP (2.2 percent in 1997). About half of these budgetary transfers are *general grants*; they include a contribution for state administrative activities delegated to local government, the education grant per student per year at primary and pre-school facilities, the health grant per bed per year, social welfare subsidies, and an equalization subsidy aiming to compensate municipalities with very low per capita tax base. The special subsidies are earmarked for specific capital expenditures, such as housing development, schools, hospitals, and environmental projects.

The overall system of transfers to localities is multi-channeled, and the criteria of distribution are often non-transparent, with some horizontal equalization purpose in mind. The determination of cost differentials and distress-related grants is often driven by political influence and interests. The system of inter-governmental transfers established after the 1993 reform did not sufficiently account for regional differences in revenue capacity, spending needs, or the need for equalization.

So far, there is an amendment of the budget rules concerning the allocation of the equalization fund between districts and municipalities. The equalization formula is calculated as the difference between the per capita tax revenue of a particular district, and the national average excluding the four largest cities. The grant is received by districts, which, in turn, determine inter-municipality allocation in the district assembly. The main drawback of this arrangement is that it is determined by political means. Therefore, the more fiscally-distressed the district, the less it would be willing to allocate to municipalities.

Although desirable, the shift from a system of tax shares and transfers to decentralized taxation powers is problematic in that the central government fears irresponsible tax increases by local governments, and that it is hard to find important taxes that can be used locally.

Local Government Credit Market

In addition to the local tax revenue, tax sharing and government transfers, Czech municipalities have also enjoyed access to long-term credit since 1993. The growth in commercial credit can be seen as a positive development for the municipal sector borrowers as well as for the domestic financial market. Access to borrowing is becoming increasingly important for Czech municipalities, as their need for outside financing has increased with cuts in revenue sharing and subsidies.

Nonetheless, further development of this market requires overcoming a set of obstacles. The issue of fragmentation, already addressed above, affects the financial efficiency of the projects that municipalities undertake and thus their overall creditworthiness. However, even very small municipalities are known to try to access credit markets, and have obtained loans for investments. In a limited number of cases, several municipalities cooperate to carry out and finance joint investments, but these arrangements are not systematic because of the lack of a legal framework.

A way of overcoming the problem of fragmentation is increased private sector participation in infrastructure. In fact, as there are many gains from private sector participation in local and regional utility services, some of these sectors have been opened up to privatization, especially in the water and wastewater and heating sectors.[10] However, privatization in other sectors, such as gas and electricity distribution, has been slow, and a framework for full cost recovery tariffication in these sectors is missing. Consequently, while municipalities have been able to raise water and wastewater tariffs (over which they have control) in order to capture the cost of their investments in the infrastructure leased by private entities, other municipalities who have invested in extension of gas distribution lines or coal-to-gas conversion projects have found it difficult to recover their investments through tariffs once the projects were turned over to state or regional utilities.[11]

---

[10] In both Brno and Ostrava, a French water company has purchased the majority shares of the municipal water company, which leases the infrastructure from the municipality and pays a rental that covers the full cost of the city's investments. The water tariffs, which are set by the municipality, are adjusted to cover the full cost of the investments. Several municipal solid waste companies were also sold to foreign companies.

[11] MUFIS, June 1998 Report.

Another obstacle relates to the lack of revenue autonomy for Czech municipalities. Since the system of tax allocation has been by and large unchanged over the period (except for one major adjustment in 1996), the large share of non-local revenues in local budgets has not led to the kind of instability that one observes in other transition countries. In fact, some banks cite the size of transferred revenues as a source of comfort, especially when dealing with very small municipalities who might otherwise, in their view, not maintain a stable own revenue structure over a period of time. Nonetheless, over the longer term, it will be necessary to consider giving municipalities more control on the revenue side in order to improve their stand-alone creditworthiness and to strengthen the market lenders' incentives to assess them on this basis.

In fact, in relative terms, the share of commercial credit in total municipal borrowings has fallen since 1994, while that of noncommercial credit has increased. Coupled with a high percentage of non-performing loans in the portfolio of major state lenders such as the SEF (73 percent according to a recent external audit), a growing reliance on state-allocated loans to municipalities could prove to crowd out private credit. If allocated to uncreditworthy municipalities or projects that are not commercially viable, such loans may: (a) add to contingent liabilities by introducing soft budget constraints and raising the expectation of state bail-outs for even commercial loans, especially if the SEF loans are systematically forgiven at the expense of the central government budget; and (b) inhibit the development of the commercial credit market by eliminating the need for the municipalities to produce projects that will pass the market test.

Similarly, a lack of transparency in the existing capital grant system may have distortionary effects on the evolution of private credit for municipal investments. The capital grant system should be reviewed to ensure that it is based on rationale and transparent economic criteria so as not to crowd out private credit and that scarce public resources are used for real externalities. Institutional capacity for allocating, monitoring, and evaluating the use of capital grants will need to be strengthened at different levels of the government to ensure an effective and transparent implementation of the EU pre-structural and structural funds.

Moreover, the introduction of a comprehensive regulatory and supervisory framework for municipal debt, including prudential regulations to be passed under the tutelage of the Ministry of Finance, as well as financial sector disclosure and investor protection regulations that would cover municipal bank loans and bonds, is urgently needed. The benefit of this framework would be not only to provide a control mechanism for the central government, but also to prevent unpredictable and administrative interventions in the market.

The Czech municipalities have a constitutional right to manage their budgets without state intervention, and until 1997, there were no legal or executive restrictions on municipal borrowing. The lack of restrictions has given municipalities considerable flexibility in their borrowing decisions. However, it has also led to intermittent case-by-case interventions by the central government, particularly in the area of bond issuance. In the case of bonds offered in the international markets, the central government has imposed restrictions on the use of proceeds (Prague 1994) and rejected an issue altogether (Prague 1997), while in the case of domestic bonds, there has been a moratorium on all issuance since 1997, mainly as a reaction to the macroeconomic crisis. These interventions have proven to be a rather ineffective tool for controlling municipal indebtedness or foreign currency risk exposure, since external and internal bank loans have remained outside the scope of these interventions.

In addition, the budgetary classification applied to municipalities should be revised to aid municipalities -- and commercial intermediaries -- in better assessing municipal debt carrying capacity, particularly through a clear distinction between the current and capital accounts. Information disclosure and auditing rules will need to be standardized and strengthened. Finally, the legal framework for investor protection mechanisms for municipal borrowing must be revised by allowing municipalities to use revenue pledges or intercepts and extending the commercial bankruptcy law to municipalities.

Despite successful previous programs of support by external institutions such as the USAID, which provided technical assistance to municipalities and lenders, there is a need for further assistance in debt management capacity of municipalities. Apart from basic asset-liability management and multi-year investment planning, which must be attuned to the different needs of smaller and larger municipalities, they would also benefit from training programs in private sector participation in infrastructure at the local level.

Addressing the set of problems identified above is key to the continuing growth of the Czech municipal credit market on a fiscally and financially sustainable trajectory. This, in turn, is an objective that is closely linked with EU accession. Continuing access to financial markets is critical for Czech municipalities as they prepare to undertake significant infrastructure investments delegated to them. A tier of healthy municipal sector borrowers should add to the competitiveness and profitability of the domestic financial sector. On the other hand, ensuring the fiscal sustainability of municipal borrowing is important for the central government, which is concerned with not allowing general government borrowing beyond levels compatible with Maastricht criteria. Given these multi-sectoral links, any reform of municipal borrowing should be undertaken within a unified framework which balances these multiple development needs.

A key goal of this reform should be to develop the municipal commercial debt sector as a well-regulated, competitive, and transparent segment of the domestic market. At the present time, the government is planning a sweeping territorial reform, as well as the introduction of a regulatory framework for municipal borrowing for the first time. These upcoming changes, concurrent with preparation for EU accession, could provide an opportunity for the government to take stock of the progress made in this market so far and to identify the remaining gaps, in view of their various sectoral priorities. Since major international donors who have been active in this area -- most notably, USAID -- are preparing to exit the Czech Republic, this could be considered a propitious moment for the Bank to offer to the Czech government, if requested, policy advice and other assistance in the framework of a broader financial sector assistance program, which would be carefully coordinated with the country's fiscal/macroeconomic objectives and EU integration reform agenda.

Taxable Capacity and Fiscal Equalization

Some counter-equalization actually occurred in the Czech Republic, as demonstrated by the decision of national authorities to re-centralize personal income tax in an attempt to prevent districts and municipalities from growing apart. The increasing proportion of districts applying for the equalization grant is another indication: from 58 percent in 1995, it jumped to 92 percent by 1997. The dynamics of the sharing rule between districts and municipalities also favors counter-equalization between districts, because in addition to being at the political discretion of the district assembly, it is based on the district average rather than a national average. The counter-equalization is fueled by the differential in the personal income tax between individual districts, due to different unemployment rates and wage levels, and different concentration of businesses in districts.

Tying transfers to both taxable capacity and tax effort can ensure the predictability of transfers, in addition to providing desirable stabilization features. Tax financing of local public goods is more appealing than alternative financing sources such as inflationary finance, or borrowing. These alternatives have the important drawback in that they are either prohibited or rendered difficult by central authorities. Therefore, the determination of taxable capacity and tax effort should prove useful as parameters for a formula based-transfer system. Taxable capacity depends on the ability of residents to pay taxes, generally measured by per capita income, and on the ability of municipalities to collect them. Tax effort is the degree to which taxable capacity is used. In order to measure fiscal equalization, (normalized) per capita local expenditure should be compared with the counterpart per capita local revenue. However, the corresponding detailed local data is unavailable to assess the fiscal disparities among the communities of the Czech Republic, and only some indirect conclusions could be drawn from the aggregate data.

Income Responsiveness of Local Public Finance

The analysis of tax system elasticity is useful to identify the budgetary items most likely to boost revenue during the course of economic growth, and therefore most likely to act as automatic stabilizers. The concept of buoyancy is used to analyze the flexibility of taxes and expenditures to changes in income. Since the tax reform occurred in 1993, Czech rates and bases have not changed. Thus, the only discretionary changes are the changes in sharing rules and assignments that occurred during the 1996 reforms. Accordingly, the elasticity measures of the personal and corporate income taxes have been calculated only for 1997.[12]

Taxes with high income-flexibility are desirable for local budgets as they decrease their dependence on discretionary inter-governmental transfers. They make the tax system cyclical as more taxes are withdrawn from the income stream as the economy grows, and less when in a downturn, which facilitates automatic stabilization. The gross elasticity concept[13] yielded negative estimates in general, as most budgetary items have experienced negative growth during the 4-year period of analysis, while the economy registered an average real growth of 4.1 percent.

The local tax system as a whole is negatively income-elastic with a coefficient of -1.28. Only central governmental transfers are income-elastic with a coefficient of 1.67. This suggests that the local tax system is adequately flexible, but highly distorted by the sharing principle. For instance, personal income tax has an elasticity of -2.74, suggesting a highly regressive effect in its local destination, even though by design it has progressive features (see Table 4.2). Thus, the sharing rules truncate the local tax system, making it pro-cyclical (accentuating booms and aggravating slumps), which perpetuates the need for compensating inter-governmental transfers for stabilization purposes. This is partly intentional, as Czech authorities want to retain central control in the absence of controlling instruments on municipalities.

For the spending side of the budget, an alternative elasticity concept was utilized, that of revenue-elasticity,[14] which indicates the responsiveness of expenditures to changes in revenue. When macroeconomic control of local government is the main concern of central authorities, a revenue-inelastic spending system is desirable because it has the potential to automatically restore fiscal equilibrium over time.[15] For the period of analysis, total expenditures are moderately revenue-inelastic with an index of 0.92. The revenue-inelasticity of expenditure assures that, during the course of economic growth, spending will grow proportionately less than revenue. However, the expenditure path of individual local goods will depend on their consumption characteristics as well.

---

[12] The point elasticity will provide the responsiveness of the tax system to changes in economic growth for the terminal years of 1996 and 1997 only. Longer observations of the whole tax system are necessary to provide elasticity estimates for long run tax behavior.
[13] Calculated as the average percentage change in tax revenue divided by the average real GDP growth rate.
[14] As both revenue and spending fell over the period, the revenue-elasticity concept will be positive.
[15] Note that the converse is true when macroeconomic management is set on long run growth.

Fiscal Risks in Inter-government Relations

Implicit and Explicit Liabilities

The intergovernmental fiscal relations define financial liabilities between local and central governments. The central government transfers tax revenues, gives grants, provides direct loans and loan guarantees to local governments to fill the financing gap or for equalization purposes. Any local defaults on services of these loans and calls on loan guarantees could create liabilities for the central government. While the law stipulates that the central government has no financial responsibility for local governments' financial imbalance, including borrowing and debt service, the central government is likely to take on contingent, or implicit liabilities generated by local authorities. So far, however, the central government has not been involved in bailouts.

Fiscal risks can take the form of explicit or implicit contracts. On the one side, fiscal risks are explicit when the Government liability is recognized by law or contract. On the other side, fiscal risks are implicit when there is a "moral" obligation by the Government due, for instance, to public expectations or pressure form interest groups. Both types of risks are associated with direct liabilities -- those obligations that need to be fulfilled in any event -- and contingent liabilities -- those obligations that need to be fulfilled in case a particular event happens.

Direct Explicit Liabilities. The law stipulates formulas for inter-government transfers of revenues. Beyond that, the central government does not have an explicit responsibility for sub-national finances.

Contingent Explicit Liabilities. State governments provide loan guarantees for local government borrowings. In particular, the State Environment Fund provides direct loans, interest grants, loan guarantees to environment related local investment projects. Default of such activities could pose financing problems to the central government.

Direct Implicit Liabilities. Factors that affect fiscal imbalances of local governments include the assigned tax and other revenue, assigned expenditures, and intergovernmental transfers. The dynamics of the sharing tax rule does seem to favor wealthy municipalities, reducing the scope for equalization.

Contingent Implicit Liabilities. During the last few years, local government non-guaranteed borrowings have increased. In addition, local governments provide loan guarantees to local entities. The default or calls of these debts could pose dangers to local government finance.

Evidence of Potential Fiscal Liability Buildup by Local Governments

Contingent Explicit Liabilities. The State Environmental Protection Fund (SEPF) provided local governments with direct loans and loan guarantees for environmental related projects since 1992. In the next four years, SEF has assigned about 41 percent of its total expenditure and about 46 percent of total capital expenditure to provide direct loans to local government (see Table 4.7).

Table 4.7. Projected Budget of the State Environmental Protection Fund, 1998-2002

	1998	1999	2000	2001	2002
			CZK million		
Total Revenue	3720	4070	3672.3	3544.7	3545.8
Total Expenditure	3720	4070	3672.3	3544.7	3545.8
Non-capital subsidies to local gov't	276	319.2	295	282.1	289.2
Capital expenditure	3364	3660.8	3316.3	3196.7	3190.6
Investment subsidies to local gov't	1815	2010.4	1783	1735	1729.8
Investment loans to local gov't	1549	1650.4	1533.3	1461.7	1460.8
(as percent of total expenditure)	41.6	40.6	41.8	41.2	41.2
(as percent of total capital expenditure)	46.0	45.1	46.2	45.7	45.8

Source: State Environmental Protection Fund.

The risk exposure of the SEPF loans is high. From 1992 to 1997, 13 loans out of a total of 128 loans -- about 10 percent -- defaulted. The total value called was CZK276.4 million, about 30 percent of total loan value (see Table 4.8).

Table 4.8. State Environment Protection Fund Loans, 1992-97
(in million CZK & in percent of total)

Default				Non default	Total
Unpaid principal	Unpaid interest	Other Book-debt	Total (13 cases)	Repaid (115 cases)	(128 cases)
91.5	70.6	114.3	276.4	647.5	923.9
9.9%	7.7%	12.4%	29.9%	70.1%	100.0%

Source: SEPF, 1997 Annual Report.

The SEPF has also issued guarantees. By November 1998, the SEPF had issued CZK1.4 billion of loan guarantees, of which CZK710 million or 50 percent of total guarantees were for the Eco Gaia project -- now in court. Until the court investigation is over, the potential financial risks must be covered by the Fund.

Direct Implicit Liabilities. Although the overall local government fiscal deficit is under control, imbalances exist, especially among poor municipalities. The overall local government deficit was about 0.1 percent of GDP in 1999, after a surplus in 1998, and a sizable deficit in 1997, in part as a result of the floods. The disparities among local governments are, however, growing. Municipalities have little discretion over taxes, thus resulting in the widening of the gap between rich and poor district on tax income (see Table 4.9). Although the central government uses equalization transfers to minimize such gaps, the transfers imperfectly compensate for them.

The average growth rate of expenditure over the period is 12.1 percent, higher than the revenue growth of 10.2 percent. The revenue-inelastic expenditure items, and the de facto assignment of expenditures among levels of government, poses a number of problems which can drive local governments into deficits. The low-revenue districts and municipalities are the most affected.

Contingent and Implicit Liabilities. The non-guaranteed borrowings and indebtedness of local governments have increased since 1993. The total debt outstanding for local governments grew from CZK2.9 billion in 1993 to CZK41.6 billion in 1997. Total debt outstanding of local governments reached 19 percent of total general government debt, and its growth rate is the highest among the different general government borrowing. Local governments borrowed over 65 percent of their debt total from commercial banks, credits and municipal bonds. Their debt service increased accordingly. In a few cases, the municipalities' debt service reached more than 50 percent of their total expenditures. This has imposed risks of financial failure to the local governments, and potential liabilities to the central government.

Table 4.9. Per Capita Income Tax Revenue of Selected Districts, 1996–99

	1996	1997	1998[1]	1999[2]
	CZK			
A. National average	6,826.7	7,027.8	7,643.1	8,352.1
B. National average[3]	5,446.4	5,456.2	5,811.9	6,245.3
C. Highest tax revenue p.c. in district				
Mladá Boleslav	8,043.5	9,036.9	11,476.0	12,709.8
(as percent of National average-B)	147.7	165.6	197.5	203.5
D. Lowest tax revenue p.c. in district				
Jeseník	4,105.5	3,889.3	4,466.6	4,723.7
(as percent of National average-B)	75.4	71.3	76.9	75.6
(as percent of Mlada Boleslav-C)	51.0	43.0	38.9	37.2
Plzeň – sever	4,022.6	4,303.9	4,451.2	4,727.9
(as percent of National average-B)	73.9	78.9	76.6	75.7
(as percent of Mlada Boleslav-C)	50.0	47.6	38.8	37.2
E. Other District and Municipalities				
District Písek	5,783.7	6,219.5	6,317.1	6,593.0
(as percent of National average-B)	106.2	114.0	108.7	105.6
(as percent of Mlada Boleslav-C)	71.9	68.8	55.0	51.9
Municipality Písek	4,600.3	5,087.0	5,167.0	5,393.7
(as percent of National average-B)	84.5	93.2	88.9	86.4
(as percent of Mlada Boleslav-C)	57.2	56.3	45.0	42.4

1/ Preliminary.
2/ Budgeted.
3/ Excluding magistrate towns: Praha, Brno, Ostrava and Plzeň.
Source: Ministry of Finance.

Challenges and Future Issues for Fiscal Decentralization in the Czech Republic

On a path to establish a well-functioning market economy, the Czech Republic nonetheless faces some challenges regarding efficient fiscal decentralization for the future. The first challenge of *extensive fragmentation* can be overcome by the implementation of an intermediate level of government provisioned by the Constitution. Experience elsewhere shows that certain issues, such as environmental protection, unemployment, the privatization process, and development planning are better handled within a regional context. The fragmentation problem can also be addressed by regrouping municipalities through the promotion of joint projects, or the creation of special districts.

Revenue composition and revenue sharing constitute the second challenge to the fiscal decentralization in the Czech Republic. The composition of revenue leaves little room to make independent revenue decisions, and it prevents competition between municipalities. As the revenue side cannot be used significantly, local entities resort to debt financing to balance the budget. Thus, there is a need for a system of legal standards to harmonize the financial decisions made by local representatives. The decisions regarding the magnitude of local tax burden would be efficiently located in the communities who would no longer be "passive" recipients of funds.

The need for deficit reduction has induced the central government to maintain, for the most part, the principle of tax sharing and the inter-governmental transfer systems of the past. Further deficit control by the central government is done either directly, by setting annual caps for local expenditures or local debt, or indirectly, by assigning some fiscal policy goals such as restrictions on foreign loans. However, mounting sentiments of individuality and independence make control increasingly conflictual. Moreover, tax shares are allocated to the municipality of origin, not to the locality that most needs it. Thus, revenue sharing needs to be redirected via equalization schemes. The current tendency for counter-equalization, both in terms of differentiation of district to municipality and of municipality to municipality, must be replaced by better formulae to strengthen horizontal and vertical equity. The inclusion of indicators of taxable capacity and tax effort, and of the local budget situation, will likely fill this need.

On both efficiency and equity grounds, it appears that decentralization of taxation powers to local authorities appears a better pursuit for the Czech Republic. The equity objective eliminates the tendency of local politicians in rich areas not to have the same desire as the state to transfer funds to poorer areas. Tax decentralization may enhance local accountability, but it has the potential to lead to over-taxation in the lower tiers of government. Alongside decentralization of taxation power, the continual adaptation of the revenue sharing principle needs to be emphasized, in order to provide a better balance between central and local government tax revenues. This is particularly important with respect to the increased responsibilities of local governments. In the future, negotiations should replace central control. Macroeconomic control of local governments through annual negotiations has been an effective tool in some countries to cap local tax increases.[16]

A third challenge for the future is *the development of local tax administration capacity*, which is necessary before undertaking further devolution of revenue. The low level of "professionalism" at the local level consists of the lack of regular exchange of information among municipalities concerning their fiscal flows, the absence of regular evaluation of the impact of the changes or the revenue system and the shift in responsibilities. Thus, there is insufficient data to carry out a proper fiscal analysis of a growing local budget system.

A related issue, and a fourth challenge, is *the lack of a comprehensive regulatory framework for sub-national credit*. Despite no defaults so far, commercial credit accessed by Czech municipalities has caused concern, because of its relatively fast growth in the absence of regulations and the potential risks to the central government. These risks include possible bail-outs of defaults, if hard budget constraints are not in place, and contribution to excessive general government indebtedness. The reaction of the government has been to slow down the growth of the market and to prepare a legal framework for this debt, which has not yet been passed. It is urgently needed to introduce a prudential framework, complemented with central monitoring capacity, in order to limit risky or excessive municipal borrowing and to prevent unpredictable and administrative interventions in the market. It is also necessary to strengthen market discipline through introduction of information disclosure rules for sub-national debt, a legal framework for investor protection and collateral, as well as the maintenance of a clear signal to the market that municipalities operate under hard budget constraints.

At the same time, the flows of state-allocated loans and grants to the municipalities also constitute a risk. Reliance on a variety of state-allocated loans to municipalities has grown more rapidly than commercial credit. This could lead to under-cutting of the commercial market as well as weakening of budget constraints. Both the capital grant and the subsidized loan system should be reviewed to ensure that they are based on rationale and transparent economic criteria. Additionally, institutional capacity for allocating, monitoring, and evaluating the use of capital grants will need to be strengthened at different levels of the government to ensure an effective and transparent implementation of the EU pre-structural and structural funds.

---

[16] For example, Sweden and Denmark have managed through negotiations with local associations to avoid local tax increases better than England and Norway, where local governments retain no taxation of any importance.

Finally, *the role of the private sector* in the provision of public goods needs to be strengthened. Currently, the financing and allocation of public goods is done through political means, not market mechanisms. As most public goods in the Czech Republic are financed or provided by the central government, the unpredictable nature of various revenues results in vast inefficiency. A desirable feature would be the generalization of formula-based allocations of resources. However, in addition to grants, regional deconcentrated government, and cooperation between communes, an important direction towards the solution of small municipalities could be the shifting of responsibilities from governments to markets. The private sector could be used as contractor to acquire economies of scale, but subject to local regulations, to provide local public goods.

Chapter V. Labor Market in Transition

Introduction

During the transition from a command to a market economy, the Czech Republic's labor market experienced some of the same stylized trends as other Central and Eastern Europe (CEE) economies did, in terms of a reduction in participation rates (especially of women), a decline in employment, and fall in real wages. Yet the country did not experience the rise in the level of unemployment with persistent long-term unemployment, as other CEE economies did. This characteristic set the Czech Republic apart from other transition economies where real output contraction was accompanied by increasing unemployment. In most CEE economies, the unemployment rate reached double digits during the transition. In the Czech Republic, however, unemployment remained below 4 percent until 1997.

The Czech unemployment paradox was maintained during most of the transition years. However, the slowdown in economic activity in 1997 -- and, more dramatically, the 1998-99 recession -- has begun to generate a sizable increase in unemployment and a fall in job vacancies. For the first time, the Czech Republic is experiencing rising unemployment, although this is happening nine years after the collapse of the communist block. Although unemployment in the Czech Republic remains lower than most transition economies, the unemployment rate has more than doubled in the past two years, reaching 7.5 percent in 1998 and over 8 percent in the first months of 1999.

Nonetheless, the first post-transition recession is not affecting everyone to the same degree: different groups must cope with the changes in market characteristics in different ways. Women are being hurt more than men during the recession, as their unemployment rate has increased relative to that of men in recent years. This chapter aims at understanding the dynamics of the Czech labor market.

A prosperous integration into the European Union (EU) will require significant increases in productivity and a reallocation of labor supply. These increases in productivity are key for the Czech Republic to compete, in equal terms, in the EU single market. Efficient mechanisms to allow the labor market to operate, and to facilitate the adjustment, are necessary. For this purpose, the policy mix has to be such that proper incentives exist to human capital development, thus allowing for the labor market to operate efficiently and to set the proper returns to education and experience-, labor market flexibility -- minimizing regulation that impede the market operation -- and a targeted safety net to cope with dislocations. As with other transition economies, the Czech Republic has initiated the process of adjustment.

Overview of the Emerging Labor Market

Main Characteristics

Demographic Trends. The population in the Czech Republic has remained relatively stable during the transition, experiencing only a minimum decline. In 1989, there were 10,362,000 people. In the first quarter of 1998, an estimated 10,295,000 lived in the country. The birth rate, however, has declined dramatically, from 12.4 live births per 1,000 inhabitants in 1989 to 8.8 in 1996. Hence, the base of the population pyramid has narrowed substantially over this period. In the first quarter of 1998, children under the age of 15 represented 18 percent of the population. The working age population (ages 15-64) accounted for 68 percent of the population, while retirees accounted for 14 percent. The proportions in each five-year age group are fairly evenly distributed between the ages of 15 and 54 (with about 7-8 percent of the population in each age category), whereas the proportion in the age groups beyond 55 tapers off precipitously. The implication of these demographic dynamics is a concern. With the decline in the birth rate, the aging of the population is increasing the burden on the tax and pension systems.

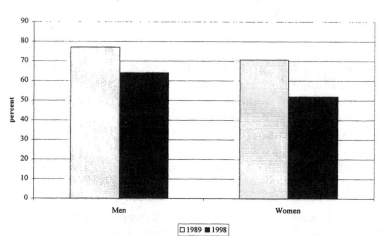

Figure 5.1 Labor Force Participation Rates

Labor Force Participation. During the early part of the transition, labor force participation rates (LFPR) fell substantially in the Czech Republic, as in all transition countries. Because women had artificially high labor force participation rates under socialism, they were clearly expected to withdraw from the labor force in large amounts. However, the withdrawal of women from the labor force was only somewhat greater than that of men. In the Czech Republic, male labor force participation rates for the population 15 years and older fell from 77.1 percent in 1989 to 70.7 percent in early 1998. For women, rates declined from 64.1 percent in 1989 to 52 percent in 1998 (see Figure 5.1).[1] Since 1994, the decline in the LFPRs has slowed down for women and virtually come to a halt for men.[2] Much of the early decline in LFPRs was among older workers. The labor force withdrawal of workers entitled to old-age pension was encouraged by government measures aimed at combating unemployment. In fact, the departure of older workers from the labor force affected women more than men, largely because the female retirement age is five years lower in most countries. In the Czech Republic, until January 1996, the retirement age was 60 years for men and between 55 and 57 for women, depending on the number of children they raised.

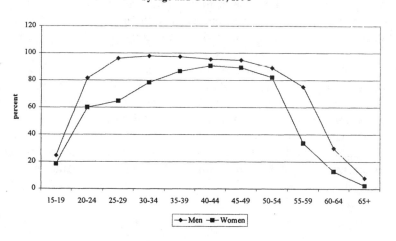

Figure 5.2. Labor Force Participation Rates by Age and Gender, 1998

---

[1] This pattern is also observed in Hungary, where the LFPR declined by about 16 percentage points for men and 20 percentage points for women, and in Slovakia, where the decline was 5.2 percentage points for men and 7.7 percentage points for women over the 1989-94 period. See Paukert, L. (1995), "Economic Transition and Women's Employment in Four Central European Countries, 1989 - 1994," Labor market paper No. 7, International Labor Office Geneva.

[2] The decline in women's participation in recent years seems to be due to changes in measurement definitions. Until 1996, women who were on maternity leave for more than six months were no longer considered employed. Starting in 1997, they were counted as being out of the labor force. Accounting for this adjustment, which decreased LFRP of women by 5 percentage points (from 57 to 52 percent) it appears that the trend in female LFPRs has been fairly constant since-mid 1993.

The decline in LFPRs depends on the age structure of the population. Since 1993, however, there has been a decline in both men's and women's LFPRs in the youngest (15-19 year) age group but not in the older generation (as was the case in the earlier period). This decline reflects the increasing numbers of young people enrolled in school over this period (see discussion below). There are also declines in the LFPRs of women in their childbearing years over the 1994-98 period -- declines that are partially driven by the change in the definition. For example, in the first quarter of 1994, about 74.8 percent of the women in the 20-24 group were participating in the labor force. In the same first quarter of 1998 only 60.0 percent of the women in this age group were participating. The LFPR of women 25-29 fell even more over this period, from 83.2 percent to 64.8 percent.

Education Attainment

The Czech labor force has traditionally been well educated. The minimum level of education required by law is currently nine years (junior high school). However, as of 1998, about ninety percent of the workforce has an educational attainment that continued beyond the basic education, including about eleven percent of the employed having university or higher education levels. The educational attainment of the labor force is higher than that of the population at large, since the participation rates of the least educated (those with no education plus junior high school graduates) is very low (33 percent for men and 23 percent for women). The proportion of women who participate in the labor market increases with education (the increases are large from basic to secondary to tertiary levels of education).

With the transition, enrollment rates in secondary and tertiary education have increased. The proportion of individuals 15 to 18 years old who are enrolled in any form of secondary school (apprenticeships, or vocational or academic high school) has increased from 84 percent to 96 percent from 1989 to 1996. The proportion of 19 to 23 year olds in university or higher levels of education has risen from 17 to 20 percent.

Table 5.1. Returns to Education in the Czech Republic

	1989		1996	
	Men	**Women**	**Men**	**Women**
Years of Education	0.027	0.038	0.058	0.070
Highest Level Attained				
-apprentices w/2years	0.063	0.074	0.094	0.104
-apprentices w/3-4 years	0.077	0.079	0.112	0.166
-vocational H.S. w/4years	0.127	0.206	0.294	0.394
-academic H.S. w/4years	0.135	0.116	0.351	0.380
-university	0.283	0.389	0.544	0.656

Note: Figures are reported coefficients from Mincerian earnings functions.
Source: Munich, Svejnar and Terrell (1998).

Seeking additional education is a rational behavior given that during the transition there have been outward shifts in demand for higher educated labor relative to less educated workers. The evidence is found in the lower incidence of unemployment among the more educated and the increasing returns to education, not only in the Czech Republic but in most CEE countries. A year of education raised earnings by about 3 percent for men and about 4 percent for women during socialism whereas it raised earnings by 6 percent for men and 7 percent for women, respectively, in 1996.[3] It is worth noting that, whereas the

---

[3] See Munich, D., J. Svejnar and K. Terrell (1998), "Returns to Human Capital During Communism and in the Transition to Capitalism: Retrospective Evidence from the Czech Republic," unpublished manuscript, University of

returns to education have been higher for women, the returns have been rising faster for men than for women so that the gender gap is closing during the transition. For example, between 1989 and 1996 the rate of return of a year of education for men rose by 116.7 percent while the rate of return for women rose by 83.5 percent.

Wages and Productivity

Real wage declined sharply during the early years of the transition but after the initial adjustment they have increased above productivity gains. The real wage fell by 5.5 percent in 1990 and 26.3 percent in 1991 because of very high inflation (56.6 percent in 1991). It began to rise in 1992 reaching the pre-transition level in 1996. In 1997, wages grew at a slower rate than in the previous five years -- by 1.9 percent to be 3.3 percent above the 1989 level. From 1992 to 1996, wages were increasing at a faster rate than productivity.

Analysis of Unemployment

Unemployment rates rose sharply into double digits in all the transition economies except the Czech Republic, where the registered unemployment rate grew rapidly from 0.1 percent in January of 1990 to 3.2 percent in January of 1992. The unemployment rate then stabilized, fluctuating between 3 and 4 percent between the middle of 1993 and the end of 1996. With deteriorating demand conditions, unemployment began to rise in 1997; the registered unemployment rate stood at 5.6 percent and the Labor Force Survey (LFS) unemployment rate was 7.5 percent in 1998. By the early months of 1999, the rate of unemployment reached 8 percent.

Characteristics of the Unemployed

Unemployment in the Czech Republic is concentrated among the young, women, the low skilled, the handicapped, Romanies and in certain regions of the country.

Figure 5.3. Unemployment Rates by Age and Gender, 1998

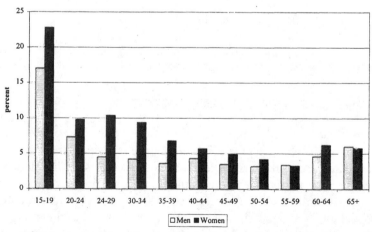

Unemployment by Age. The unemployment rate of the youngest age group, 15-19 years old, was 17 percent for men and 22.8 percent for women. The rates fall rather quickly for higher cohorts for men, but remain relatively high for women, until after their child bearing years. Women's rates are higher than men's in most age groups (except the older ones) and the gender gap is the greatest among the 25-29 years old (see Figure.5.3).

Unemployment by Gender. It appears that in most transition countries women have been affected more than men. Unemployment rates in the Czech Republic, as measured by LFS, show this characteristic. Men's unemployment rates have been lower than women's

Michigan, September. Other authors find similar and sometimes higher rates of return to education in the Czech Republic during the transition.

rates. During the period covering the second quarter of 1993 to the first quarter of 1998, the average unemployment rate for men was 3.2 percent whereas for women it was 4.5 percent.[4] What is notable is the extent to which the gap between men's and women's rates has risen in the last three quarters, that is the current slowdown.[5] The women's unemployment rates are now more than 50 percent greater than men's. In the first quarter of 1998, the women's unemployment rate was 7.3 percent whereas the men's was 4.8 percent.

Unemployment by Region. The variance in the unemployment rates by region has always been high in the Czech Republic, with Northern Bohemia and Northern Moravia typically having rates two to three times that of Prague. The remaining regions have unemployment rates between 60 and 80 percent higher than Prague. The regional gaps represent structural unemployment and a mismatch between vacancies and unemployed that cannot be easily resolved until there is more regional mobility in the country. However, the gap between the regional unemployment rates is not growing.

Unemployment by Education. The unemployment rate of people with minimum education (mandatory by law) or with no education has always been the highest of all groups. In the first quarter of 1998, the unemployment rate was 15.7 percent among this least educated group, compared with 1.9 percent for the university educated. This 9:1 ratio between the unemployment rates of the most to the least educated has been fairly persistent in the past five years.

Table 5.2. Unemployment Rates by Education, 1994-98

	1994	1995	1996	1997	1998
Junior High School and without schooling	8.1	10.2	11.1	12.2	15.7
Apprenticeship (Trade) school	3.8	3.7	3.7	4.1	5.7
Secondary vocational	3.2	4.2	3.0	3.7	5.3
Apprenticeship school with GCE	4.0	2.6	2.8	2.4	4.0
Secondary vocational with GCE	2.4	2.4	2.1	2.7	4.2
Secondary general with GCE	3.5	4.2	2.8	4.2	5.7
University	1.4	1.2	0.6	1.3	1.9
Total	3.7	4.0	3.8	4.3	5.9

Note: Data measured during the first quarter of the year.
Source: Czech Statistical Office.

Duration of Unemployment

The Czech Republic is renowned for its short unemployment spells. About half of the unemployed had spells of six months or less, with more than half up to early 1995 and slightly less than half since then. Long term unemployment (of one year or more) affected about one fifth to one-quarter of the population until the first quarter of 1995 and, since then, almost one-third of the unemployed have very long spells.

Mean unemployment spells, approximated for the whole population and for men and women indicate that the average unemployment spell in the Czech Republic was rising from approximately 8.5 months in the second quarter of 1994 to 11.6 months in the second quarter of 1995. Since then, it has remained

---

[4] The unemployment rates for single people are considerably higher than those for married, but the gender gap is not as large for singles as it is for the married (0.3 percent vs. 1.6 percent, respectively).

[5] It should be noted that married women's unemployment rates are biased downward, compared to those calculated under conventional measure, because in the Czech Republic (and in many transitional economies), women on maternity leave were (until 1997) considered as employed. As noted above, since the first quarter of 1997, women on maternity leave have been counted as out-of-the labor force.

between 11.6 to 12.1 months, with signs of a decline in duration in the last two quarters ending in early 1998.

Women's average unemployment spells have been longer than men's spells: the proportion with spells greater than one year is higher for women than for men. The average spell was 8.8 months for women and 7.9 months for men in 1994, and it rose to 11.2 and 12.4, respectively, in 1996. However in early 1997, men's and women's mean spells were nearly equal: 11.4 and 11.1 months, respectively.

How Much Adjustment has Occurred in the Labor Market?

The benefits from competing in the EU single market will be maximized, to a large degree, if the labor market operates efficiently and if it allocates resources to their best possible uses. A number of factors indicate that the labor market in the Czech Republic has adjusted to a certain degree. The adjustment continues as the current recession is forcing enterprises that did not adjust in the past to reduce their so-called hidden unemployment.

Change in Employment Structure

The adjustments in the structure of employment by economic activity have been significant, as in all CEE economies (see Table 5.3). In the first four years of transition, as total employment dropped by 12 percent, the proportion employed in agriculture dropped by almost one-half. One-fifth of all manufacturing jobs were lost, and there were significant reductions in public health, social work and other services. Not surprisingly, the growing sectors were in trade, tourism and financial services. Public administration and defense also grew significantly over this period: its share of total employment rose from 1.6 percent in 1989 to 3.0 percent in the first quarter of 1993. It continued to grow from 1993 to 1998, according to the LFS quarterly data.

Table 5.3. Employment Structure by Sectors, 1989-98

	1989	1993	1994	1995	1996	1997	1998
Agriculture, Hunting and Forestry	11.5	7.9	7.0	6.6	6.1	5.1	5.7
Industry	38.9	35.0	33.7	33.2	32.6	31.6	31.2
Manufacturing	33.9	30.2	29.7	29.2	28.8	27.9	27.5
Construction	7.8	8.3	9.0	8.8	9.2	9.7	9.7
Wholesale and Retail Trade	9.3	10.6	11.8	12.6	13.0	13.4	13.1
Hotels and Restaurants	1.8	3.0	3.1	3.1	3.1	3.3	3.5
Transport, Storage & Comm.	6.5	8.1	7.5	7.6	7.7	7.8	7.8
Financial Intermediation	0.5	1.3	1.6	1.8	1.9	1.9	2.0
Real Estate	7.3	4.5	4.8	4.9	5.1	5.1	5.0
Public Adm. and Defense	1.6	5.1	5.6	5.5	5.3	6.5	6.5
Education	5.7	6.7	6.7	6.4	6.6	6.3	6.2
Health and Social Work	5.2	6.1	5.8	6.0	5.9	5.5	5.7
Other Service Activities	3.8	3.3	3.3	3.4	3.3	3.2	3.6
Total (percent)	**100**	**100**	**100**	**100**	**100**	**100**	**100**
Total (in thousands)	**5,433**	**4,946**	**5,025**	**5,077**	**5,096**	**4,935**	**4,881**

Note: Measured at end of period for 1989, second quarter for 1993-97, first quarter for 1998.
Source: Czech Statistical Office.

Total employment rose between 1993 and 1996 (albeit by a weak average of just one percent a year). However, as the economy began to slow in 1996, the declines in employment were significant: 3.2 percent from 1996 to 1997 and another 1.1 percent decline from 1997 to 1998. Hence net employment growth since 1993 has continued to be negative (at -1.3 percent per annum). The same patterns in the shifts in employment composition continued, although at a slower pace. In the first quarter of 1998, agriculture accounted for 6 percent of total employment (down from 12 percent at the end of 1989) and industry (manufacturing and utilities) accounted for 31 percent (down from 39 percent in 1989). The tertiary sector (from construction to services) generated 63 percent of the jobs at the beginning 1998 when it only accounted for 50 percent of all jobs at the end of 1989.

Labor Turnover

Another way to capture the extent of adjustment in the labor market is to examine the amount of turnover, that is, the movement from and to employment (e), unemployment (u), and out of the labor force (o). The pools of employed and out-of-the labor force remained fairly stagnant in 1994-97. The transition probability that an individual stayed employed throughout the year, given that he/she was employed in the first quarter (Pee) is between 0.95 and 0.96 throughout these four years. These estimates are higher than the estimates in the literature for the CEE economies (see Table 5.4). The probability that one stays out-of-the labor force in the Czech Republic is also relatively high (approximately 0.94 every year) compared to those for the other transitional economies. Obviously, it follows that the exits from employment or from out-of-the labor force were relatively small. Flows into unemployment from employment were highest in 1994, but even then the probability was merely 0.02. Hence, there was less mobility out of these states over time in the Czech Republic than in the above-mentioned transitional economies.

Table 5.4. Job Turnover in Selected Transition Economies

	Pee	Peu	Peo	Pue	Puu	Puo	Poe	Pou	Poo
Czech Republic (1994)	0.947	0.021	0.032	0.506	0.319	0.174	0.046	0.018	0.936
Czech Republic (1995)	0.952	0.015	0.032	0.467	0.361	0.172	0.048	0.011	0.941
Czech Republic (1996)	0.955	0.013	0.032	0.426	0.418	0.147	0.046	0.010	0.944
Czech Republic (1997)	0.953	0.019	0.024	0.429	0.435	0.124	0.041	0.016	0.938
East Germany (1990-91)	0.836	0.093	0.071	0.350	0.373	0.277	0.160	0.041	0.799
Russia (1992)	0.908	0.033	0.059	0.512	0.328	0.160	0.090	0.017	0.893
Poland (1993-94)	0.897	0.040	0.063	0.354	0.487	0.159	0.074	0.043	0.883

Note: (e) = employment, (u) = unemployment, (o) = out of labor force. The table measures transition probabilities. For instance, Peu is the transition probability from employment into unemployment.
Source: Terrell, K. (1998), "Czech Republic: Key Developments in the Labor Market", The World Bank, mimeo.

Counter to the stagnant nature of the pools of employed and out-of-the labor force, the pool of unemployed experienced tremendous turnover in these three years.[6] In 1994, a person who was unemployed in the first quarter had a 0.68 probability of leaving unemployment sometime during the year. However, this probability fell in the three successive years to 0.64, 0.58 and 0.54. The declining trend is due primarily to a decline in the probability that an unemployed person finds a job -- a probability which fell from 0.51 in 1994 to 0.43 in 1996 and 1997. Nevertheless, these transition probabilities from unemployment to employment are high in light of the probabilities for the other CEE countries in the early 1990's (0.350 for East Germany in 1990-91 and 0.361 and 0.354 for Poland in 1992-93 and 1993-94, respectively). They are, however, similar to those found for Russia.

It is, of course, also possible to move from one job to another without either passing through unemployment or leaving the labor market. Estimates of job-to-job flows grew during 1994-96, as the economy pulled out of the transition recession and as labor markets began to operate as markets. The

[6] This seems to have been true in the Czech Republic in the earlier stage of the transition as well.

probability of changing one's job during the year (without becoming unemployed) grew from 0.025 in 1994, to 0.059 in 1995 and 1996.

This finding of increased flexibility in the labor market as the transition proceeds is corroborated by demand elasticities. In the Czech Republic, the short run elasticity of demand with respect to output (measured in terms of sales) was 0.0 before transition, 0.12 in the first year (1990-91) and only began to grow, becoming more elastic, in 1991-92 and 1992-93 (when it was estimated to be between 0.50 and 0.59).[7]

Adjustment in Wages

It is a well-known fact that the wage structures of centrally-planned economies were compressed and distorted in comparison to market economies. Ideology dictated that wage differentials between the skilled and unskilled be kept small. Moreover, the socialist systems failed to allocate workers to sectors in which their potential productivity was highest and to elicit high levels of worker performance within organizations.

There is a great deal of evidence suggesting that wage setting became increasingly more responsive to market forces as the transition proceeded in the Czech Republic and other CEE countries. Although unions play a role in wage setting, they have not been contentious. Government intervention in wage setting has also been minimal. Regarding practical evidence, firms in the Czech Republic are relying more and more on the data collected by private firms (e.g., Trexima) on compensation of managers and employees by occupation, education, experience, etc. to set wages. Studies have shown that there have been significant changes in labor demand elasticities and wage dispersion over time.

Estimates of the labor demand elasticities with respect to own wage in the manufacturing sector suggest that these elasticities had been negative in all the CEE countries before the transition started and that they became more pronounced as the transition took place. The pre-transition estimates are on the order of -0.4 in the Czech Republic, -0.3 in Slovakia, -0.3 in Poland, and -0.2 in Hungary. Within one to two years after the transition was launched, these estimates rose to around -0.6 to -1.0 in the Czech Republic, -0.8 in Poland, and -1.0 to -2.3 in Hungary. In Slovakia, the estimates stay at about -0.3. Hence, in the Czech Republic, labor demand has become more elastic over time, indicating that employers are laying workers off at a higher rate in response to a given percentage increase in wages.

Evidence on increased wage dispersion in the Czech Republic can also be found in other measures. Using *Household Budget Survey* data the Gini coefficient on wage income rose from 0.3 in 1989 to 0.4 in 1993.[8] Private firm level data collected by Trexima shows that ratio of wages in the ninth decile to the first decile was 2.6 in the first quarter of 1996 and that the ratio of earnings of senior manager to unskilled labor was 5.7 in 1996. The increased wage dispersion is being brought about, in part, by increasing rates of return to education, which were held artificially low during communism.

The other notable finding is that the inter-industry wage differentials are shifting. The sector where wages are rising most rapidly is, of course, the financial sector, where the average wage had been below the agricultural average wage in 1990, but from 1993 onward, it was more than double the average wage in agriculture. The other sector which is driving wages up are public administration and defense. Since 1993, average salaries in public administration and defense have been between 36 and 47 percent higher than the

---

[7] See Basu, S., S. Estrin and J. Svejnar (1998), "Employment and Wage Behavior of Enterprises in Transitional Economies," University of Michigan, Unpublished paper.

[8] See Garner, T. and K. Terrell (1998), "A Gini Decomposition Analysis of Inequality in the Czech and Slovak Republics During the Transition," *The Economics of Transition*, 6 (1) May.

average in agriculture and always above the average for the nation, but below industrial and financial sector wages. Wages in real estate and construction have also risen above the national average.

On the other hand, it appears that, except for Prague and Central Bohemia where the capital is located, there has been relatively little change in the dispersion of average salaries across the main regions of the Czech Republic. The ratio of the average wage in Prague to the average wage in East Bohemia grew from 108 percent to 133 percent during 1990-97, but the wage ratios of all other regions to East Bohemia were smaller -- ranging between 102 percent to 110 percent -- and remained stable over time. The fact that wage dispersion did not rise across the seven main regions is curious, and may reflect lack of adjustment in the labor markets. One would have expected larger differentials given the relatively small amount of migration across these regions and the large differentials in the regional unemployment rates.

Male-female wage differentials have also grown with the transition (see Table 5.5). Since 1994, men's wages have been rising faster than women's (at an average annual rate of 16.0 percent vs. 12.7 percent for women). Hence the gender gap has grown: men's average wage was 40 percent higher than women's average wage in 1996, whereas they were 30.7 higher in 1994. This is in part the result of education returns rising faster for men than women.

Labor market outcomes are a result of many different factors on the demand and supply side, including household decisions about market vs. home production. The extent to which labor market outcomes in the CEE countries are a result of gender discrimination was the subject of an International Labor Organization (ILO) study that surveyed manufacturing establishments in Hungary and the Czech and Slovak Republics in 1993. The results of the survey show an absence of gender bias in layoffs at the establishment level in Hungary and Slovakia but significant gender bias in layoffs in the Czech Republic. The survey also found the highest amount of gender bias in recruitment to be in the Czech Republic and the lowest in Hungary.[9]

Table 5.5. Average Hourly Wage by Gender, 1994-96

	Men	Women	Ratio Men to Women
	CZK		
1994	41.15	31.49	1.307
1995	51.29	37.47	1.369
1996	60.85	43.46	1.400

Source: Ministry of Labor and Social Affairs.

These findings for the Czech Republic are supported by evidence that married women have a lower probability than married men of leaving unemployment for a job in a given quarter, over the 1993 to 1996 period.[10] Moreover, married women have a higher probability of leaving employment for unemployment in a given quarter. Finally, single women's transition probabilities to, and from, unemployment are not significantly different from men's probabilities. Hence, the higher female unemployment rate in the Czech Republic is due to the fact that married women are more likely to become unemployed and less likely to leave unemployment than married men.

Further analysis of the reasons for these flows is warranted if appropriate policy decisions are to be made. If employers are discriminating against women, one might begin by examining the labor market legislation that may make women more costly relative to men. However, this is only one of many reasons

---

[9] See Paurkert (1995), op. cit.

[10] See Stefanova, J. and K. Terrell (1998), "Gender Differences in Flows across Labor Market States in the Czech Republic," unpublished manuscript, University of Michigan, November.

for discrimination. Moreover, as noted above, these flows may be the result of many other factors which have not been analyzed, such as declines in sectors and occupations which hire relatively more women, or choices based on household welfare maximization, among others.

Constraints to Labor Market Performance

In any economy, but particularly in transition economies, labor policies and incentives set by those policies are key to facilitating the labor market in the adjustment process. Maintaining an environment that is conducive to work, to investing in human capital and to matching skills and qualifications with those demanded by the new economic environment is critical. Labor legislation can hinder or facilitate labor adjustment, as can wage settling mechanisms, by allowing or deterring the market's signals to allocate resources efficiently. Non-wage costs and by-law fringe benefits can also limit the capacity of the labor market to operate efficiently, by imposing an extra burden on production.

Labor Legislation

The current Labor Code No. 65/1965, as subsequently amended, is not highly restrictive, except perhaps in the mandate on hours of work. The maximum number of hours of work per week are 43.5, with a 30 minute break for lunch every day. Working time of employees younger than 16 years shall not exceed 33 hours. An employee must not work more than eight hours of overtime in any one week (with some exceptions). In a particular calendar year, an employee may be ordered to work overtime up to a maximum of 150 hours. Minimum annual leave is a period of three weeks [Section 102].

Few requirements are placed on wage levels, other than minimum wages, premium for hazardous work conditions and overtime work, which are low by international norms: 25 percent if the work is done during the day and 50 percent if done at night.

What may be a more important constraint on the labor market is Chapter (7), Sections 149-162, that is focused on 'working conditions for women.' The protections offered to women include:

- the prohibition of certain types of work (e.g., underground in extracting minerals or "in jobs which are inappropriate for them physically or which are harmful to their bodies, especially in the kinds of work which endanger their maternal calling");

- The requirement that employers "reassign her temporarily to other work which is suitable for her" if her work poses hazard to her pregnancy [Section 153];

- "If a woman taking care of a child younger than 15 or a pregnant woman requests shorter working time or some other suitable adjustment to the prescribed weekly working time, the employer is obliged to grant her request" [Section 156]; and

- Entitling women to 28 weeks of maternity leave in connection with child birth; "the employer is obliged to grant a woman additional maternity leave until her child reaches three years of age if she asks for it" [Section 157]; "the employer is obliged to grant a mother who is breast-feeding her child a special [paid] break for this purpose." [Section 161]

Czech society places a high value on maternal care of children. However, as economic theory predicts and as studies in other countries show, labor protection laws in market economies can actually hurt women as they make them more expensive than men to hire. The extent to which recruitment practices in the Czech private sector are influenced by laws that protect women and stress maternity leave is something that requires further analysis at the firm level.

Wage Policy Framework: Minimum Wage Law and Wage Controls

Government intervention in wage setting is not heavy handed nor is it unlikely to create any serious constraints on the labor market performance.

Minimum Wage. A minimum wage was established in 1991.[11] Levels are set for both workers paid on an hourly basis and for workers paid on a monthly basis.[12] The rate has been changed three times since it was first set, with the most recent change in January 1998. As in most countries, there is no formula for increasing the minimum wage. Until recently, the minimum was set by a tripartite social agreement but it is currently adjusted by the Ministry of Labor and Social Affairs (MoL&SA) when deemed necessary. The law requires that no worker receive less than the minimum wage.

Table 5.6. Minimum Wage (CZK), 1991-98

Date Set	Feb. 1991	Jan. 1992	Jan. 1996	Jan. 1998
Hourly	10.80	12.00	13.60	14.80
Monthly	2,000	2,200	2,500	2,650

Source: Ministry of Labor and Social Affairs.

The real minimum wage has eroded significantly over time, so that in 1997 it was only two-thirds of its real value in 1991. On the other hand, the real average wage has been rising, and in 1997 was fifty percent higher than its 1991 value. Hence, the ratio of the minimum wage to the average wage fell from 52.7 in 1991 to 23.4 percent in 1997. With the increase in 1998, it is now 24.8 percent of the average wage. By international standards, this is quite low. In the U.S., where the minimum wage is set relatively low, it has been between 33 and 40 percent of the average hourly wage in manufacturing since 1990.

With the minimum being set so low, the MoL&SA estimated that less than 10 percent of the labor force is earning the minimum wage. Hence, increases in the minimum wage are unlikely to have significant negative employment effects. However, since the minimum wage is the base for calculating many social benefits (unemployment benefits, pensions, etc.) changes in its level will affect the social safety net for a portion of the population. Hence, these changes directly affect government expenditures and for some, they affect labor supply decisions.

It appears that in the Czech Republic, the low minimum wage is having some unusual effects in the labor market, i.e. increasing the size of the informal economy. Employers -- especially in the construction sector -- use the minimum wage as a means to get around the law for hiring foreign workers. Since foreign workers can only be hired if no Czech worker will take the job, employers advertise jobs at the minimum wage knowing that an insufficient number of Czech workers will accept them: this enables the employers to get authorization to hire foreign workers.

---

[11] In addition to the minimum wage, the employment legislation defines the so-called *minimum tariffs*. These were originally dependent on the tenure of a worker, his/her education and a type of job. Tariffs are applied in the firms with no collective agreement between the trade union and employer on wages. From 1992 to 1995, there were 12 such wages and, since 1995, there are two in addition to the basic minimum wage for unskilled workers: 1) for jobs which require a secondary education with the CGE exam; and 2) for jobs requiring a university education (CZK5,350 in 1997). Although the law states that no employee can earn a wage lower than the minimum tariff, it is not binding as no penalties are stated.

[12] Workers on partial disability benefits get 75 percent of the minimum wage and those on full disability receive only 50 percent of the minimum wage.

Wage Controls. Wage controls were first put into effect in 1991 and then intermittently in the ensuing years, with several changes in design. They have not been in effect since 1996. When they were in effect, wage controls limited the wage bill growth in an enterprise so that it was equivalent to the product of the total number of employees in the enterprise at the beginning of the year and the economy-wide average wage. Hence, some adjustment of relative wage levels within the enterprise was possible. Moreover, it is not clear just how effective wage controls were because fines were not imposed until the enterprise exceeded the norm by five per cent. Moreover, in 1992, more profitable firms were allowed to raise their wage bill at a higher rate than the norm. For most of the period, the policy only applied to the large-scale state sector, although in 1993 the government extended coverage to all enterprises with more than 25 employees. Given that a) the targeted population and goals changed often in a short time period; and b) monitoring and enforcement were considered to be weak, it is unlikely that wage controls had a significant effect on wage growth or wage dispersion.

Non Wage Costs

Non-Wage costs are in line with those of the European Union. Wages represent about 64 percent of total gross wage costs. The bulk of non-wage cost are statutory social security contributions -- about 26 percent. Approximately 7 percent of the cost of labor is for paid leave (national holidays and vacation, which by law amounts to a minimum of three weeks per year). Conversely, taxes, contributions, fringe benefits and personnel costs increase the cost of labor to about 156.5 percent of gross wages. It should be noted that subsidies are still given by the government, and that they rose in 1997. Subsidies can be for 'job creation,' but they have also been given to assist firms in downsizing redundant labor.

Social Security contributions are paid by employers and employees to cover expenses for compulsory social security: old age and disability pensions, sickness benefits, and unemployment insurance (see Table 5.7). The majority of this contribution (19.5 percent by the employer and 6.5 by the employee) is towards the pension fund. The parliament rejected a proposal to increase these rates to 21.3 percent and 7.1 percent, respectively, but it is generally agreed that they will be raised this year. Health insurance comprises an additional contribution of 13.5 percent.

Table 5.7. Social Security and Health Insurance Contribution Rates in 1998

	Employee	Employer	Total
Total Social Security	8.0	26.0	34.0
Pension	6.5	19.5	26.0
Sickness Insurance	1.1	3.3	4.4
Unemployment	0.4	3.2	3.6
Health Insurance	4.5	9.0	13.5
Total Social Security & Health Insurance	**12.5**	**35.0**	**47.5**

Note: Percentage of gross wages.
Source: Ministry of Labor and Social Affairs.

Personal income tax rate is quite progressive, beginning at 15 percent for those earning less than CZK84,000 (approximately US$2,800) a year. The top category, those who earn more than CZK756,000 must pay CZK211,680 plus a marginal rate of 40 percent for any income above CZK756,000. However, the tax base is reduced by the following major annual allowances: i) CZK28,800 for every taxpayer; ii) CZK14,400 for each dependent child (up to four); and iii) CZK16,800 for a spouse (unless the spouse's income exceeds CZK28,800).

Regional Mobility

As shown above, unemployment is unevenly distributed across regions, and the pattern has been persistent at least since 1994. Moreover, wage differentials have also been persistent over time. Regional disparities in the labor market could have been expected in the early years of the transition, given the inherited geographical distribution of economic activities and the inevitable inequalities accompanying periods of fast structural change. However, the fact that they have persisted up until 1998 is a sign that the labor market is not responding sufficiently to equilibrate these imbalances. Moreover the gap between vacancies and the number of unemployed has widened tremendously in the past years (see Figure 5.4).

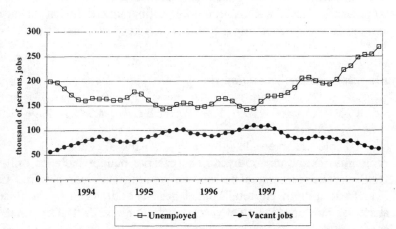

Figure 5.4. Unemployment and Vacant Jobs, 1994-97

In some regions, the number of unemployed greatly exceeds the number of job offers. Prague comprises the extreme case, where the number of vacancies exceeds the number of unemployed. When the unemployed and vacancies are broken down by skill level, the degree of mismatch within and across, regions appears more sharply. In the Czech Republic, regional mismatch also varies with education.[13] The unemployment of junior and vocational high school graduates is driven primarily by deficient demand as there were very few districts where vacancies for these educational levels exceeded the number of unemployed, although facilitating regional mobility could alleviate the problem to some extent. However, measures to increase regional mobility could have improved matching significantly for those with apprenticeship training. The (already very low) unemployment of university-educated individuals could have been reduced even further by both better matching of the unemployed with the vacancies within districts as well as by higher geographic mobility.

A study of regional mobility, both in terms of migration (change of residence) and commuting, is quite illuminating.[14] The study shows that the amount of migration across regions is relatively small (only about 3 percent of the population migrate a year) and it declined over the 1989-93 period. On the other hand, the magnitude of commuting is much higher: approximately 17 percent of the population is commuting each year. As expected, the majority of commuting takes place around large cities, and there are major commuting flows across the border to Germany. Econometric analysis of the data on commuting flows among 76 micro regions suggests that workers are responsive to real wage differentials and that flows are highest among the districts with the highest unemployment. Hence, workers are willing to commute, often long distances, in response to changes in the allocation of employment opportunities.

---

[13] See Munich, D., J. Svejnar and K. Terrell (1995), "Regional and Skill Mismatch in the Czech and Slovak Republics," in S. Scarpetta and A. Worgotter (eds.), *Regional Dimension of Unemployment in Transition Countries--A Challenge for Labor Market and Social Policies*, Paris: OECD.

[14] See Erbenova, M. (1994), "Regional Unemployment Differentials and Labor Mobility: A Case Study of the Czech Republic," paper presented at the OECD-IHS Vienna joint Technical Workshop on "Regional Unemployment in Central and Eastern Europe," Vienna 3-5, November.

So why is there relatively little migration compared to commuting? The study concludes that the most serious obstacle to migration is the housing shortage in the Czech Republic. In the first four years of the transition there was a steep decline in the number of finished residential dwellings and the number of new constructions. In 1993, about 264,000 households which wanted to have their own dwelling were unable to have it. The housing problem is a result of the withdrawal of the state in construction and, at the same time, the continued involvement in the ownership of housing and the regulation of rent. The state has been allowing rents to gradually increase every year, e.g., in June 1998 rents were allowed to rise 50 percent. Until the housing market is liberalized, the shortage of housing will continue to be a problem, and the lack of inter-regional mobility will keep regional disparities from withering away.

Programs for the Unemployed

Expenditures on Active and Passive Labor Market Programs

Table 5.8. presents information on the allocation of funds to the active and passive employment programs for the unemployed. The passive budget includes only unemployment benefits. As a share of GDP, these expenditures are relatively small when compared to OECD countries. For most of the period, over two-thirds of the total budget has been allocated to the unemployment compensation system. This share has increased in recent years, reaching 82 percent of the total allocation.

Table 5.8. Budget Allocation to Active and Passive Labor Market Programs, 1991-98

	Total		Active Policy		Passive Policy		Share of Total	
	Mil. Of Crowns	Index 1991=100	Mil. of Crowns	Index 1991=100	Mil. of Crowns	Index 1991=100	Active	Passive
1991	2450.3	100	773.0	100	1677.3	100	31.5 %	68.5 %
1992	3145.0	128	1721.7	223	1423.4	85	54.7 %	45.3 %
1993	2166.1	88	749.4	97	1416.7	84	34.6 %	65.4 %
1994	2562.6	105	718.3	93	1844.3	110	28.0 %	72.0 %
1995	2416.6	99	634.8	82	1781.8	106	26.3 %	73.7 %
1996	2664.5	109	558.1	72	2106.4	126	20.9 %	79.1 %
1997	3972.0	162	552.0	71	3420.0	204	13.9 %	86.1 %
1998	5096.7	208	903.0	117	4193.7	250	17.7 %	82.3 %

Note: Excluding public employment and administration expenditure.
Source: Ministry of Labor and Social Affairs.

Unemployment Compensation System

In January 1990, Czechoslovakia introduced an unemployment compensation system (UCS) which was generous when compared to the U.S. but not liberal when compared to West European systems. The UCS was adjusted to be less generous, first in 1991, and then again in 1992. Since then, there has been only one major adjustment in 1998.

The eligibility requirements have moved from being quite broad to narrow, to broad again. All along, anyone who worked for at least twelve months in the preceding three years is immediately eligible for unemployment benefits, unless the person was fired for cause. However, people who were dismissed for redundancy are eligible for benefits. The twelve months of work can be substituted with a number of different situations (such as care for one's own child until the age of three, imprisonment, registered unemployment, full time study, and military service).

To remain eligible, people must report to the district labor office at least once every two weeks and be willing to take a suitable job. If the unemployed do not cooperate with the district labor office, they are removed from the register and they no longer receive monetary benefits or assistance in looking for jobs. In general, the Czech district labor offices have a reputation for enforcing the unemployment compensation system.

In 1990-91, all eligible unemployed were entitled to twelve months of benefits. On January 1, 1992, entitlement was reduced to six months. This condition holds today. Periods of sickness, maternity leave or participation in government-subsidized job placement programs (during which benefits are replaced by other sources of income) are not deducted from the entitlement period.

Benefits are established on the basis of a fixed "replacement rate" with respect to previous wages and do not vary with length of employment. In 1990, the replacement rate for those who were laid off because of redundancy was 90 percent for the first six months and 60 percent for the remaining six months of entitlement. For all others -- those who had quit or were fired for other reasons -- it was 60 percent throughout. For those who had not worked before, it was a function of the social welfare benefit. During that period, the unemployed were allowed to have paid jobs as long as they did not earn more than 20 percent of the minimum wage. In 1991, for the first six months of unemployment, the replacement rate was reduced to 65 percent for the redundant, and maintained at 60 percent for all others. For both groups, the replacement rate fell to 50 percent in the second six months of the entitlement period. On January 1, 1992, the replacement rates became 60 percent for all workers during the first three months and 50 percent during the second three months of their unemployment spell. While undertaking a training course, workers are allowed to receive 70 percent of their previous wage. Since January 1998, the replacement rates have fallen to 50 percent and 40 percent for the first and second half of the entitlement period, and to 60 percent for those in retraining.

From 1992 to 1995, the maximum level of benefits was set at 1.5 times the minimum wage (1.8 times for those in retraining). In January 1, 1996 the base for the maximum changed to the minimum living standard for an adult in a one-person household. There is no minimum benefit since 1992. Benefits are not indexed to inflation, nor are they taxed.

Until the end of 1995, the wage base for the unemployment benefit received by labor force entrants was the minimum wage. As of January 1, 1996 the base has been changed to the minimum living standard for an adult in a one person household (CZK2,660 at that time, CZK2,890 currently).

A family can also receive social assistance (welfare), in addition to unemployment compensation, if the sum of the unemployment benefits and the income of other household member is less than the household minimum living standard (MLS).[15] Once benefits expire, the unemployed are eligible for social assistance if their household income is below the MLS.

A significant number of the registered unemployed individuals do not receive unemployment benefits. Some of these individuals are ineligible (e.g., because the work requirement was not met, or because they are not available to take a job in the next two weeks) or simply because they have been removed from the register. Some of these individuals have exhausted their benefits, and they may re-register in order to obtain the assistance of the district labor office in finding a job. Others are receiving severance pay and cannot collect unemployment benefits simultaneously. Finally, others may be on a public works job, an active labor market program (described below). For those whose families are below the poverty line (i.e., MLS), registration is a prerequisite for receiving welfare.

The proportion of the total registered that receives benefits has fluctuated tremendously over time. In 1991, the percentage rose from 54 in January to 72 in December. With the tightening of eligibility

---

[15] See social sector chapter in this report.

requirements, and with the reduction in entitlement (the number of months of benefits the unemployed person could receive), the percentage fell dramatically, to 58 in January of 1992. It continued to fall throughout that year and, during 1993-1995, the percentage fluctuated between 45 and 50. In the middle of 1996, the percentage began to climb again and remained around 50 until March 1998, when it began to fall again.

The UCS is parsimonious by European standards and only slightly more generous than the U.S. and Canadian schemes. Hence, most would not expect it to have serious disincentive effects. Studies have demonstrated that the unemployment compensation system has only a moderately negative effect on the rate that men and women exit from unemployment.[16] Using a random sample individual data from district labor offices (DLO) registers, these studies find an elasticity of unemployment duration with respect to benefits of 0.3 for men and a rate that is insignificant for women. The elasticity with respect to entitlement was estimated to be between 0.3 and 0.4 for men and about 0.4 for women (depending on the year of study). A comparison of these elasticities with those for the U.S. and Canada shows they are in the middle to low range. Hence, these elasticities represent a moderate disincentive effect. When carrying out the drastic experiment of "reducing benefits and entitlement to zero," i.e., making a recipient a non-recipient, the studies found that moving an individual from the recipient to the non-recipient category reduces his unemployment duration by 23.5 percent, or 4.2 weeks. Alternatively, when moving a man from the non-recipient to the recipient category, they found it increases his unemployment duration by 9.8 percent. As a result, policy makers may have latitude in providing an adequate social safety net without jeopardizing efficiency.

Active Labor Market Programs

In December 1990, the Czech Republic enacted legislation governing Active Labor Market Policies (ALMPs). The Law on Employment stipulated that the Ministry of Labor and Social Affairs had the responsibility of "...implementing the state employment policy to propose measures designed to influence the supply and demand of labor and to create harmony between resources and needs for the labor force on the nationwide scale." In further amendments and laws, five types of programs were designed to help unemployed jobseekers find employment.

Socially Purposeful Jobs (SPJs): This program subsidizes the creation of new jobs with funds going either to an existing employer (who creates new jobs for the unemployed) or to the unemployed who strive to become self-employed entrepreneurs. These funds were meant to be for long-term jobs. The length of the contract was originally for one year; in 1992 it was increased to two years. Employers or entrepreneurs receive a lump sum in advance at the time the contract is signed. The subsidy can be either in the form of a loan, a grant or interest payments on the firm's bank loan, or it can be in some combination of these three. If a person is not retained for the length of the contract, the employer (entrepreneur) is supposed to be penalized by returning the entire grant or interest payments.

Welfare Work. These are short term jobs, lasting for a period up to six months, and renewable for a second six-month period after a brief waiting period. These jobs are provided primarily by local authorities and are usually for public works, requiring little skill. However, they can be filled with highly skilled

[16] See Ham, J., J. Svejnar and K. Terrell (1998), "Unemployment and the Social Safety Net During the Transition to a Market Economy: Evidence from Czech and Slovak Men," *American Economic Review*, forthcoming in December; Ham, J., J. Svejnar and K. Terrell (1999), "Factors Affecting Women's Unemployment Duration During the transition the Czech and Slovak Republics" *Economics of Transition,* forthcoming in January; and Sorm, V. and K. Terrell (1999), "Labor Market Policies and Unemployment in the Czech Republic," *Journal of Comparative Economics,* forthcoming in April.

individuals. They have also been used as a screening device to test how cooperative and willing to work the unemployed person is.

Program for Secondary School Graduates. This program came into being in 1993 in response to high unemployment rates among young secondary school graduates. The structure of the program is similar to that of the SPJs except that it is tailored to the educational background of the new graduates, and the duration of their employment contracts has always been for one year.

Retraining. The program offers vocational training (from several weeks to several months) to interested unemployed persons. The majority of the training (about three-quarters) is "specific" to the needs of an employer, requiring the prospective trainee to have a letter of intent to hire from an employer. "Non specific" training (i.e., training not requested by employers) in highly demanded skills such as accounting and computers is also offered to recent school graduates. Various private and public institutions provide the training; the bulk of the training provides white-collar skills.

Programs for Disabled and Disadvantaged. The disabled (as identified by the Social Welfare Office) are assisted in obtaining jobs with either a quota system or a subsidy. All enterprises with more than twenty employees must have at least 5 percent of their employees disabled (of which .5 percent must have a "serious" disability).

Relative Importance of Each Program in Terms of Enrollment and Expenditures

The relative importance of the various ALMPs, in terms of the numbers of participants and expenditures, has changed over the years (See Table 5.9.). The largest item on the expenditure side has constantly been the administration and services costs, which accounted for more than half of total expenditure for the ALMPs, with the figure amounting to almost 72 percent by 1997. At end 1998, the administration cost was still high at 62 percent of total. In 1991-92, the SPJ program category, and within it the subsidies for regular employment in private sector, was the largest of the ALMPs. By end 1993, priority emphasis was placed on welfare work in terms of placements but not in terms of expenditures, where youth measures accounted for the largest amount of total expenditure (excluding administration costs). In the ensuing years welfare work predominated in terms of expenditures, and training in terms of placements.

The labor market policies are implemented and enforced through a network of 78 District Labor Offices (DLOs) and about 160 auxiliary branch offices, which are subordinate to the MoL&SA. Although the MoL&SA has ultimate control over all operations, the DLOs tend to be fairly autonomous with regard to several decisions.

The average district office was staffed with approximately 50 people in 1991 and the number has grown to approximately 60 people in 1997. Moreover, each district has about two auxiliary districts with about four staff members each. The bulk of the staff in the average DLO is occupied in administering the unemployment benefits or job brokering.[17]

The burden of work, measured in terms of number of job seekers per staff member, seems to be similar to those calculated in Belgium, Germany, the Netherlands and Scandinavian countries, but the burden is lower than it is in almost all other OECD member countries. In 1991, there was an average of 50.5 unemployed per DLO staff member. This ratio fell in 1992 to 38.5 and, in 1993, to 26.0. In 1994, there were on average 37.9 unemployed per staff member in a DLO. The job-brokering function is the most staff-intensive and if one uses only this staff, the ratio rises to over 100 in 1993.

---

[17] See OECD (1995), *Review of the Labor Market in the Czech Republic*, Paris, France.

Table 5.9. Expenditures and Number of Unemployed Placed in Active Labor Market Programs

	1991	1992	1993	1994	1995	1996	1997	1998
Placements (in thousands)	67,900	160,200	42,955	45,350	36,820	31,220	30,730	46,550
	Shares							
Training	7.8	11.0	24.4	32.6	36.4	38.8	37.1	35.2
Youth Measures	21.2	13.7	17.2	15.4	14.4	16.3	11.4	19.8
Socially Purposeful Jobs:								
Subsidies for regular employment	32.0	40.1	19.4	17.2	14.4	9.9	8.5	14.8
Enterprises startup	17.7	16.2	9.3	4.6	3.5	1.6	2.6	2.8
Welfare works	21.4	18.2	27.4	28.4	29.3	31.4	38.7	25.6
Handicapped	0.0	0.9	2.3	1.7	2.0	2.0	1.7	1.8
Expenditures (CZK million)	1,286.2	2,359.3	1,682.8	1,822.2	1,923.2	1,932.9	1,930.1	2,327.8
	Shares							
Public Empl. Services and Admin.	47.9	29.3	55.7	60.6	67.2	71.5	71.9	62.4
Training	3.1	4.0	4.4	5.7	5.2	4.7	4.7	6.3
Youth Measures	3.7	13.7	14.6	7.0	6.1	5.2	5.3	5.1
Socially Purposeful Jobs:								
Subsidies for regular employment	25.7	31.3	10.1	10.8	6.4	3.8	2.3	6.3
Enterprises startup	13.0	9.8	2.8	2.4	2.1	1.5	1.1	2.3
Welfare works	6.1	9.5	9.5	10.1	9.9	10.3	11.7	12.1
Handicapped	0.6	2.4	2.9	3.4	3.1	3.0	3.1	5.5

Note: Including public employment and administration expenditure.
Source: Ministry of Labor and Social Affairs.

In terms of the ratio of unemployed per vacancy, the work of job brokering in the Czech Republic is relatively easy as compared to OECD member countries (except for Japan) and its neighbor Slovakia. The ratio for Prague is consistently far below the eight regions, with 0.1 unemployed per vacancy for most of the 1992-1996 period. The ratios for the five Bohemian regions are fairly similar -- in the range of 1 to 4 unemployed per vacancy. The average ratios for the two Moravian regions are far higher -- between 2 to 9 unemployed per vacancy -- for the majority of the period. However, compared to the Slovak Republic, where the unemployment/vacancy ratios fall in the zone of 20-50, the Czech ratios are quite low.

Impact Evaluation of Active Labor Market Policies

In broad terms, the goal of ALMPs is to shorten the spell of unemployment and to place people in long-term employment. Evidence on the effectiveness of ALMPs in the Czech Republic in terms of number of "jobs created" per dollar expended comes from matching function studies, which estimate the elasticity of an increase in per capita expenditures on ALMPs with respect to outflows to jobs. The findings from several studies[18] are that, depending on specification and data coverage, the elasticities are very low, ranging from zero to 0.18.[19] Although these extremely low elasticities do not bode well for ALMPs, they would be defensible if the programs are assisting the hard-to-employ, long-term unemployed.

---

[18] See Boeri, Tito (1997), "Learning from Transition Economies: Assessing Labor Market Policies Across Central and Eastern Europe," *Journal of Comparative Economics*, 25, (3): 366-384; Burda, Michael, and Martina Lubyova (1995), "The Impact of Labor Market Policies: A Closer Look at the Czech and Slovak Republics." Centre for Economic Policy Research, London, Discussion Paper No. 1102; Munich, D., J. Svejnar and K. Terrell (1997), "The Efficiency of Worker-Firm Matching in the Transition: (Why) Are the Czechs More Successful than Others?," The William Davidson Institute Working Paper No. 107, October; and Svejnar, J, K. Terrell and D. Munich, (1995), "Unemployment in the Czech and Slovak Republics," in Jan Svejnar (ed.), *The Czech Republic and Economic Transition in Eastern Europe*. New York: Academic Press.

[19] For review of these studies see Terrell K. and D. Munich (1995), "A Review of the Evidence on the Effectiveness of the Passive and Active Labor Market Policies in the Czech Republic", *In:* OECD Symposium Series, *Labor Market Policies in the Central and East European Countries*. Briefly, the matching function studies indicate that the estimates

Another study focusing on programs that help the unemployed find jobs through job search assistance (job brokering) as well as through job subsidies[20], concludes that DLO assistance in job brokering appears to have lowered unemployment duration of the groups that have longer unemployment spells, namely, women, Romanies, handicapped, less educated, and those who have been unemployed before. Moreover, the ALMPs assisted individuals who were receiving unemployment benefits more than it assisted those who were not receiving unemployment benefits. This finding is intriguing in that it is consistent with the hypothesis that the DLOs were motivated to reduce costs of the programs. Overall, from the political economy standpoint, the results suggest that the ALMPs increased the social acceptability of the transition by improving the chances of certain groups to reintegrate to the labor market.

Compliance with the EU Acquis Communautaire

Social policy development was not a high priority at the union level until the early 1970s when the European Commission launched legislative initiatives in the field of employment laws, equality of opportunities, health and safety at work. Following the adoption of the single market program in 1985, and the signing of a Social Charter[21] in October 1989, successive action programs were adopted. They pointed to a more ambitious plan for action covering, in addition to previous items, working conditions and worker rights to information and consultation. The principles of the Social Charter were incorporated into a social chapter attached to the Maastricht Treaty. This established "social policies," mainly employment policies, at the heart of the process of EU integration.

More recently, the 1994 White Paper on social policy and the latest Action Program (1998-2000) define future directions for social policies, with employment as the main theme. They aim at the development and full implementation of minimum social standards to underpin the single market. They stress the need for applicant countries to bring their legislation and policies in line with that of the EU.

Box 5.1 below summarizes the main requirements for harmonization for the Czech Republic. These EU requirements focus on four main issues: (a) equal opportunity for men and women; (b) coordination of social security schemes; (c) health and safety at work; and (d) labor laws and working conditions.

---

are sensitive to model specifications in terms of the inclusion of regressors, treatment of dynamics, estimation methods, and changes of parameters during the different stages of the transition (the Lucas critique). There is an intense debate in the literature as to whether ALMPs can generally increase flows to jobs or create jobs (see e.g., Calmfors, Lars, and Skedinger, Per, (1995), "Does Active Labor-Market Policy Increase Employment? Theoretical Considerations and some Empirical Evidence from Sweden." *Oxford Review of Economic Policy,* 11 (1)). Some argue that their impact is more likely to be positive in countries which are undergoing tremendous structural adjustment, such as in the CEE (see e.g., Lehmann, Hartmut (1998), "Active Labor Market Policies in Central Europe: First Lessons." In Regina T. Riphahn, Dennis J. Snower and Klaus F. Zimmermann, eds., *Employment Policy in Transition: Lessons from German Integration.* Berlin and London: Springer), or in periods when economic conditions are relatively strong.

[20] See Terrell and Sorm (1999), op. cit.

[21] The Charter was signed by 11 governments. The UK declined to do so.

Box 5.1. Czech Republic's Labor Market and the *Acquis Communautaire*

I. Equal Opportunities for Men and Women. Stage I key measures require that the country complies with the contents of Directives 75/117/EEC and 76/202/EEC, which contain provisions on (i) equal pay and (ii) equal treatment for men and women in access to jobs, promotion, training and working conditions. Stage II key measures require the country to comply with Directives 79/7/EEC and 86/378/EEC, which apply the principle of equal treatment for men and women to statutory and occupational social security schemes.

The Czech constitution ensures fundamental rights and freedoms to every person regardless of sex (Section 3, para 1 of the 'Charter of Fundamental Rights and Freedom'). Under Section 28 of the Labor Code employees are entitled to fair compensation for their work and for satisfactory labor conditions. Apart from these general constitutional principles, there is no other definition of equal opportunities in the Czech law. It is generally recognized that women are favored in the Labor Code. However, the Czech Government also recognizes that developments in the labor market have not been favorable for women. In order to comply with the EU guidelines on equal opportunities, the Ministry of Labor and Social Affairs has recently proposed revisions to the Labor Code that include: (a) unification of parents' leave and the differentiation of this time-off from regular maternity leave; (b) introduction of the principle of equal compensation for jobs of the same value and ensuring the enforcement of this principle; and (c) prohibition of discrimination in advertisements of jobs.

II. Co-ordination of Social Security Schemes. Although no harmonization in the social security schemes needs to be carried out, certain rules that prevent workers who are moving from one Member State to another from losing their social security rights have to be in place. There are no Stage I measures, but is advised to begin adaptation at an early stage. The Community provisions on the legislation are based on four principles: (i) only one legislation can be applicable (to avoid double social security contribution); (ii) equality of treatment (same obligations and same benefits as nationals); (iii) retention of rights acquired; and (iv) aggregation of periods of insurance or residence.

According to the Research Institute for Labor and Social Affairs, the status of the Czech legislation in the area of social security is at an acceptable level when compared to that of the EU. The Czech Republic has acceded to a number of international conventions on human rights, including the right to social security, and these conventions have already become part of their legislation. For example, regarding the principle of equality of treatment, foreigners can participate in the health and pension systems if they so choose.

III. Health and Safety at Work. Measures at Stage I require compliance with Directive 89/391/EEC, which stipulates that the employer has to assess the risks to safety and health at work, to make sure that workers receive appropriate safety and health information and to provide workers with adequate safety and health training. Legislation should also include provisions regarding protective and preventive services, health surveillance and the participation of workers on health and safety issues at work. At Stage II, countries are required to examine and comply with a set of 13 Directives which contain regulations on the achievement of a satisfactory level of health and safety of workers in the most critical areas (workplace equipment, safety signs, chemical exposure).

The Ministry of Labor and Social Affairs has been drafting amendments to the Labor Code that will provide for the application of the EU framework. Some amendments that are being considered are: prevention and settlement of serious accidents, nomination of employee representatives concerning the issues of labor safety, disability insurance, adoption of certain recommendations for technical standards. In addition to these legal measures, the adoption of the EU standards for health and safety at work will require some administrative changes in the state administration, oversight of safety and protection, and some organizational changes within the firms, as employees must elect "labor safety" representatives who must be trained in health and safety. Since about 70 percent of the norms are in compliance with EU law already, Stage 1 is nearly complete.

IV. Labor Law and Working Conditions. At Stage I, countries are required to comply with the contents of four Directives which provide protection of worker rights on the issues of: (i) collective redundancies; (ii) undertakings, businesses, or part of businesses; (iii) insolvency of employers; and (iv) young people at work. At Stage II, they are required to comply with the contents of three additional Directives, which regulate terms and working conditions, working time, and information and consultation.

The Czech regulations meet the requirements of EU guidelines in many standards (e.g., working hours, rest hours, overtime work, etc.). In some areas, Czech regulations are a bit more flexible than EU guidelines. For example, in Czech law, no youth employment, under the age of 15, is allowed except for special conditions. Working contracts will become less flexible as the complete conditions of work will be required to harmonize with the EU. Two areas that are not currently included in the Czech labor law and are being drafted for the new Labor Law for harmonization with the EU are: employees representation and guarantee institutions. For example, the new Czech law will meet the EU requirement that employees be represented at negotiations with employers in procedures preceding collective dismissals and in ensuring the employee's rights in case of enterprise transfers. An "insolvency fund" is being created that employers must pay into in order to ensure workers' salaries if the firms go bankrupt.

Source: The European Commission and the World Bank.

Conclusion

The Czech Republic was unique in coping with the reallocation effects on employment during the initial years of the transition. While other transition economies suffered from high and persistent levels of unemployment, the Czech economy did not experience this painful aspect of transition. Significant reallocation of labor took place in the early years of the transition.

The 1997 currency crisis and the follow-up recession is slowly changing the face of the Czech economy in general and its labor market in particular. The uniqueness of the Czech labor market is slowly vanishing. Unemployment has been growing rapidly since the 1997 crisis and the gap between vacancies and jobs has widened. At the current speed, unemployment is likely to reach 10 percent during 1999. While this level of unemployment is low in comparison with many transition economies, particularly Slovakia, it is, however, worrisome since the short-term perspectives for economic recovery are slim.

Available evidence suggests that the Czech labor market has been subject to rapid transformation Notwithstanding the gains achieved so far, what lies ahead to ensure a successful integration into the EU remains a challenge.

Migration flows are not likely to ease the pressure on the labor market. A number of factors induce analysts to think that labor flows within the Czech Republic and toward EU countries will probably remain small.[22] First, regional mobility in the Czech Republic is weak due, in part, to housing shortages. Second, the income differences between the EU and acceding countries tend to be smaller than those that have been observed to generate sizable migration.[23] Third, the unemployment problems faced by many EU countries discourage migration even at the country level. Finally, during the last wave of accession, the potential migration flows expected from Greece, Portugal or Spain toward previous EU members never materialized despite the elimination of national borders.

Pursuing a strategy conducive to the recovery of a sustainable growth path and, therefore, towards job creation and continuous adjustment and innovation is essential for the Czech Republic. Wage moderation would improve external competitiveness. The public sector needs to take the lead in signaling this intention to the market.

While the recession has made labor market conditions more difficult, it has by no means affected everyone equal. Women have been affected more than men. Already, during the transition the income differential between men and women has increased and women have been more likely to move to unemployment and less likely leave unemployment for a job. While the Czech society places a high value to family, labor policies are making women "more expensive" than men, thus sending the wrong incentives to the labor market. Consideration should be given to redesign labor policies affecting women to sustain the social value without introducing the incentive distortion.

With increasing unemployment and the potential to develop long term unemployment, there is still room for improvement of programs in support of unemployment. The unemployment compensation system should be reviewed to avoid threshold effects and poverty traps. Work-tests should be enforced to avoid a waste of scarce public resources. Efforts to evaluate and improve the effectiveness of active policies should be continued. To reduce the gaps between regional unemployment rates, consideration should be given to

---

[22] See Borjas G. (1998), "Economic Research on the Determinants of Immigration: Lessons for the European Union", World Bank, mimeo.

[23] Measured in PPP terms, the income per capita of the Czech Republic was 63 percent of the EU average and 92 percent of Greece's income in 1997.

other types of policies, complementary to labor market programs, in particular those fostering the development of public transportation, housing and mortgage financing.

As the process of accession to the EU advances, the authorities are making a considerable effort to adjust the regulatory framework of the labor market to EU requirements. The Copenhagen criteria require the Czech Republic (and any other signatories to Europe Agreements) to: have a functioning market economy, have the capacity to cope with competitive pressures and market forces within the EU, and adhere to the aims of political, economic and monetary union in the EU. This requires an efficient labor market capable of both absorbing shocks and reallocating resources during the pre-accession period and beyond. The Copenhagen criteria also require that members have established stable institutions guaranteeing democracy, the rule of law, human rights and the respect for, and protection of, minorities. As all EU members, the Czech Republic will be required to eventually adopt the entire *acquis*.

In the area of the labor market, the Czech Republic's compliance with the *acquis communautaire* implies recognizing both a set of minimum rights for workers and standardized labor conditions resembling those prevailing in the EU. The White Paper prepared by the EU identified four areas of social legislation (linked with labor markets) where legal harmonization and convergence is needed, namely: (a) equal opportunity for men and women; (b) health and safety at work; (c) labor law and working conditions; and (d) coordination of social security schemes.

Compliance with some EU regulations could increase labor costs and adversely affect labor demand and enterprise competitiveness. Implementing such regulations also means setting up ways to monitor compliance by firms (labor inspection, for instance) and allowing workers to exercise their rights (through administrative and judiciary bodies). Budgetary resources will need to be devoted to these activities Once the broader impact of reforms is factored in, however, the net impact on economic efficiency and welfare is likely to be positive. The pre-accession strategy should thus focus on: a) the early adoption of those EU norms that would make labor market institutions more flexible; b) the gradual adoption of those reforms/or enforcing the compliance with existing laws in cases where benefits exist but also entail transitional costs (health and safety at work); and c) delaying adoption of EU norms which will restrict flexibility (the case of firing costs).

In the run-up to accession, there is an opportunity to make the Czech Republic's labor markets more efficient. In a time of rapid economic change, labor market flexibility would ease the reallocation of factors of production from non-competitive to competitive firms, thus feeding economic growth while reducing unemployment. Moving quickly towards mutual recognition of educational and training systems and professional qualifications with the EU will help the Czech Republic strengthen its human capital. Investments in education are likely to have the highest returns. The rapid professionalization of its civil service needs to be part of this process. Preparing for, negotiating, legislating, and implementing EU norms requires intensifying the training of civil servants, including intermediate and technical staff.

Another impediment to a successful labor market lies in the resistance of employers to high social insurance contributions and to other types of payroll taxation. At a time when the government is concerned about employment, the Czech Republic has a tax system that is pro-capital when it comes to the selection of production technique. This may be an outcome of the need to promote modernization of the industrial sector. The tax system labor bias is due to the high social security contributions and high personal income tax rates (relative to corporate income tax rates). All add up to a substantial bias against labor, thus limiting the creation of new job opportunities.

Table 5.10. Statutory Social Contribution Rates in the Czech Republic, Europe, and the OECD
(Percent of Gross Wage Bill)

	Employers	Employees	Total	o/w Pensions	Share of Pensions
Czech Republic	**35.0**	**12.5**	**47.5**	**26.0**	**55**
European Union[1]	23.6	12.9	36.5	20.6	56
Western Europe[2]	22.1	11.7	33.8	19.3	57
OECD[3]	16.2	8.6	24.8	13.2	53

1/ Un-weighted average of the EU-15 excluding Denmark.
2/ The above plus un-weighted average of Iceland, Norway, and Switzerland.
3/ The above plus un-weighted average of Australia, Japan, Mexico, New Zealand, and the US.
Source: Ministry of Finance and OECD, *The Tax and Benefit Position of Production Workers,* Paris.

Surveys of small employers[24] suggest that excessive labor taxation, including social security contributions, represent an important impediment to the development of small enterprises (in addition to a lack of credit and to severe procedural obstacles to the start-up of new businesses). Total social security contributions in the Czech Republic amount to 48 percent of gross wages, whereas the average contribution rate for the EU countries is 36 percent.

As the fiscal situation permits, there should be efforts to reduce taxes on labor, in particular the social security contributions for health, pensions, sickness and employment insurance. High taxes on labor are not only harmful to job creation but may also encourage tax evasion. While it is likely that this is currently less a problem in the Czech Republic than in other transition economies, small firms typically cannot afford the same compensation costs as larger enterprises; they are more difficult to target for audit and enforcement. Thus, if taxes are too high, fewer small firms will be established, wages will tend to be under-reported, and the size of the informal sector will tend to increase. The experience of other transitional economies suggests that, in an economy undergoing rapid structural change, a vicious circle of increasingly high tax rates and a shrinking tax base could be set in motion.

The Czech Republic's bid to join the EU provides an opportunity for a new "push" of profound structural reforms that will accelerate adjustment and modernization of policies and institutions. Membership will require the Czech Republic to adjust its policies and laws to the norms set out in the EU's treaties, directives and regulations, known collectively as the *Acquis Communautaire.* This will also require the development of human and institutional capacity to implement and enforce the *acquis* in a sustained and systematic way. For some EU directives, compliance will mean sizable investments. The *acquis* will act both as a benchmark and a powerful lever for advancing structural reform. The Czech Republic's membership in the EU will not only require massive restructuring and modernization of most sectors, but will encourage a crucial reallocation of resources in the economy. Labor markets will thus play a crucial role, not only in the process of adjustment, but for the Czech Republic to compete in the EU internal market.

---

[24] OECD (1996), *Small Business in Transition Economies,* Working Papers, Vol. IV, Paris.

Chapter VI. Foreign Trade Sector

Introduction

Following the 1989 *Velvet Revolution*, Czechoslovakia began its journey back to capitalism with a mixture of liabilities and assets. Czechoslovakia had one of the least reformed systems of central planning among Council of Mutual Economic Assistance (CMEA) members in 1989; the scope of central controls over the economy was vast. In contrast to Hungary or Poland, where a significant shift of economic decision making responsibility to enterprises had produced cadres of managers better equipped to cope with challenges of moving to a demand-constrained economy, Czechoslovak enterprise managers were ill-prepared for the new tasks. On the other hand, domestic balances and very low international indebtedness were clearly assets, as was the political determination to break decisively with central planning. This assured strong support for moving swiftly to a new economic regime.

Initially, assets seemed to have prevailed over liabilities. The Czech economy rebounded in the third year of the transition, following a similar pattern of other quick reforming countries. Expansion of exports to the EU -- facilitated by geographical proximity and by liberalized access to EU markets -- had driven economic recovery. By 1997, however, it became apparent that reform measures had not been enough to establish a foundation for sustainable economic growth. Having peaked at 6.4 percent in 1995, the growth rate of real GDP fell to 3.8 percent in 1996 and 0.3 percent in 1997. The faltering macroeconomic performance was accompanied by large current deficits in 1996-97. These expanding external imbalances were seen by the international financial community as unsustainable and eventually helped to trigger the currency crisis of April-May 1997. While exports rebounded in 1997 and the first half of 1998, export performance declined in the second half of the year. As a result, GDP contracted by 2.3 percent in 1998. The question is how can the export sector regain its momentum and become the growth engine of the economy.

Quick Adjustment of Foreign Trade Flows during the Early Transition Period

The stabilization *cum* transformation program, launched on January 1, 1991, after yearlong preparations, set the policy framework for establishing a market economy and for engineering the former Czechoslovakia's reintegration into the world economy. These measures replaced the central planning regime and led to a reversal of the earlier trends of declining Czech competitiveness in world markets.

Reorientation of Foreign Trade Patterns

Czech foreign trade developments have gone through two distinct phases: the first phase occurred over 1989-95 and was characterized by exceptionally rapid growth, much higher than in other transition economies; the second phase which occurred from 1996 was characterized by a considerable slow-down in exports to the EU. Although the growth rates still remained respectable, the increase in 1996 barely kept pace with the growth of EU import demand. The triple-shock of the collapse of the Soviet Union and the CMEA, the dissolution of Czechoslovakia and a shift towards market-based regime in foreign trade contributed to the initial expansion. The disappearance of political factors that had shaped foreign trade patterns in the CMEA led to the collapse of "Eastern" trade, and sizable portion of this trade was redirected to EU markets: the value of Czech exports there grew at an average of 30 percent annually over 1990-95.

Although the value of total exports fell in 1990 and 1991 by approximately 16 and 13 percent respectively, this was exclusively due to the fall in the value of exports to the CMEA. These fell by 52 percent between 1989 and 1991. Over 1992-95, total exports in terms of US dollar value grew at double-digit rates. So did imports, after an initial contraction in terms of value by one-third over 1989-91.

Between 1989 and 1991, the value of EU trade increased from one third to one half of the Czechoslovak total trade. The share of the former CMEA fell from 51 to 34 percent during the same period.[1] Exports to CMEA economies fell by about 53 percent over 1989-91. A considerable portion of these exports was shifted from the CMEA to markets in highly developed economies -- the EU in general and Germany in particular (see Table 6.1). By 1991, the EU replaced the CMEA, and Germany replaced the former Soviet Union as Czechoslovakia's major trading partners.

Table 6.1. Geographic Reorientation of Czech Foreign Trade, 1989-98

	1989	1990	1991	1992	1993	1994	1995	1996	1997	1998
	percent									
EU	32	39	50	60	54	59	61	61	61	64
CEFTA[1/]	..	..	..	..	23	19	19	18	18	17
of which Slovak Republic	..	..	..	..	18	14	13	12	10	9
CIS and other European Transition Economies[2/]	51	41	34	23	9	8	8	8	8	6
Other	18	20	16	17	14	13	12	13	13	12
Total	100	100	100	100	100	100	100	100	100	100

1/ CEFTA data includes trade with Hungary, Poland, Slovak Republic and Slovenia. For 1997-1998 it also includes Romania.
2/ Includes Former Soviet Union Republics, countries of the Former Yugoslavia (Slovenia until 1992), Romania (until 1996), Bulgaria, and Albania.
Source: Czech Statistical Office (CSO).

The split with the Slovak Republic -- with its potentially negative impact weakened by the establishment of the Customs Union -- increased registered foreign trade. For statistical purposes, what was domestic trade became foreign. Because of the erection of state borders, trade with the Slovak Republic became subject to the same considerations as that with other preferential partners. The diversion of this trade towards richer neighboring economies -- Austria and Germany -- became inevitable once exclusively economic considerations (i.e., the relatively small size of a Slovak market) came to the fore.

Thus, in contrast to other Central and Eastern Europe countries (CEECs), two shocks, i.e., that of the dissolution of both the CMEA and Czechoslovakia, have shaped Czech export performance. Both seem to have contributed to the Czech surge in exports to third markets, mainly the EU. In fact, it appears that some fraction of an 18 percent-increase in Czech exports to the EU in 1993 may be attributable to diversion of sales from the Slovak Republic.

Huge Increase in Exports to the EU: One of the Best Performers in the Group

Over 1989-97, Czech exports to the EU increased in terms of value more than those from Hungary or Poland did. Because of its more rigid central planning, the undertrading of Czech firms with the West prior to 1989 was much larger than in the case of more "liberal" Hungary and Poland. The scope for redirection of exports from CMEA and developing countries markets was therefore initially much larger. Until 1992, Poland -- which was the first country to fully liberalize its foreign trade and exchange rate

[1] Since the trade statistics from the CSO aggregate data from the Democratic Republic of Germany and West Berlin into figures for Germany, the actual shares of Czechoslovakia's trade with CMEA in 1989 would have been higher.

regimes -- recorded the largest increase in the value of exports to the EU since 1989. While the value of exports from both Hungary and Poland fell in 1993, Czech exports -- in part driven by the demise of Czechoslovakia -- increased by 18 percent. By 1997, the value of Czech exports stood at 464 percent of its 1989 level, Hungarian exports stood at 362 percent, and Poland's, at 311 percent.

How does the overall export growth performance of the Czech Republic compare with that of other first wave applicants to the EU? The most notable difference is that other applicants experienced a one-time contraction in their exports to the EU in terms of value, if not in market share, whereas the Czech Republic did not. The decline was particularly steep in the case of Estonia and Hungary; it was relatively mild for Slovenia. Interestingly, the contraction for Estonia, Hungary and Poland occurred simultaneously in 1993. It is not clear whether the Czech Republic avoided the contraction thanks to the split effect or thanks to an estimate of Czech exports to the EU in 1992, i.e., before the velvet divorce, being too low.

Table 6.2. Exports to the EU of First Wave EU Accession Candidates, 1992-97

	1992	1993	1994	1995	1996	1997
	percent					
Czech Republic	22	25	26	27	26	26
Estonia	1	1	2	3	3	4
Hungary	26	22	22	23	24	27
Poland	41	38	36	35	34	32
Slovenia	10	14	14	13	12	11
Total (US$ billion)	**25.1**	**26.1**	**33.0**	**43.8**	**46.2**	**49.8**

Source: Derived from EU trade statistics in UN COMTRADE database.

Rapid growth in exports to the EU, which began in 1990, continued until 1995. In 1996 and 1997, however, the rates of growth fell to single digit levels. Both Hungary and Estonia registered much larger increases: their respective shares in EU-directed exports of the group increased in 1997, while that of the Czech Republic remained flat (see Table 6.2). Quarterly data indicate a considerable increase in these exports in the last quarter of 1997, and in the first quarter of 1998. Thus, it would seem that Czech exporters were able to respond forcefully to a strong recovery in EU import demand in that period; this may be the sign that exports have regained some of their lost vigor.

Customs Union with the Slovak Republic: Contracting Trade

The Czech and Slovak Customs Union (CU), which came into effect in January of 1993, is unusual in two important respects. First, the decline in economic integration has characterized its subsequent evolution. The share of the Slovak Republic in Czech total trade turnover has fallen rather precipitously since 1993 (see Table 6.1). While this comes as no surprise, it clearly sets this CU apart from other cases of regional integration.

Second, despite a common external border, the existing arrangements have allowed for considerable discretion in decisions affecting imports. While the CU agreement does not allow for a free flow of trade originating in third countries, the value of imports from developing countries on GSP basis, as well as the volume of imports eligible for in-quotas rates, have varied between two countries. So have import limits on products subject to non-automatic import licensing.

Nonetheless, a significant degree of the coordination of foreign and customs policies has been maintained. A common customs tariff, in effect since 1993, had duties that were applicable in the former Czechoslovakia on December 31, 1992. It also held unchanged all concessions initially granted by the former Czechoslovakia to General Agreement of Tariffs and Trade (GATT) contracting parties. The Council of the Customs Union pursues common commercial policy towards third countries and ensures that the same legal norms are adopted regarding customs procedures, statistics, intellectual property, countervailing and antidumping.

Should the Customs Union be Dissolved?

Considering that the European Commission has not approved the Slovak Republic to be among the first-wave entrants to the EU, an interesting question is how might the earlier accession of the Czech Republic impact the customs union arrangements. In economic terms, this should not raise major problems. First, the Slovak Republic is a party to the Pan-European Cumulation Agreement, which will -- through adopting schedules of tariff reductions of the European Association Agreement (EAA) -- remove all tariff barriers on manufactures by the year 2001. Hence, as far as manufactures are concerned, the Czech accession will have little impact on their CU.

Second, similar provisions as in the EAA, which the Slovak Republic also signed, cover a number of areas relevant from the point of view of deeper integration. Both countries are expected to converge towards the *Acquis Communautaire* of the EU. As in the EAA, anti-competitive practices and the abuse of monopoly power are incompatible with the CU agreement. Similarly, the national treatment as well as Most Favorable Nation (MFN) treatment are applied to intellectual property protection. However, the EU's trade and internal market rules will have to apply to all new member states and this could create problems because the Czech Republic wishes to retain the customs union with the Slovak Republic.[2]

Changes in EU Oriented Export Basket

As in other first-wave EU-candidates, manufactures drove the growth of the Czech Republic's EU-oriented exports. Their value more than doubled, increasing by 107 percent. (The value of other exports increased only by 43 percent over the same period.) As a result, the share of manufactures in total EU-oriented exports increased from 81 to 86 percent, and is slightly higher than in the Czech Republic's exports to the Rest of the World (ROW).

Second, exports of agricultural products peaked in 1995 and contracted both in 1996 and 1997. While the contraction in 1996 was due to bad weather, this was not the case in 1997. Restrictions in access to EU agricultural markets did not seem to be responsible for it. Both foods with a highly restricted access and agricultural materials which face few restrictions in EU markets contracted.

Reshuffling within Manufactures: Automotive Exports a Success Story

During the first phase of the increase in Czech total EU-oriented exports came from redirecting exports from the former CMEA, mainly the Former Soviet Union (FSU); by contrast, growth must now come from either new or restructured industrial capacities. Firms which have not modernized are likely to face difficulties, not only in expanding, but maintaining their share in foreign markets. The evidence from the Czech performance in EU markets suggests that the machinery and transport equipment sectors had undergone significant industrial restructuring.

Indeed, since 1995, the Czech export performance has become critically dependent on machinery and transport equipment. Between 1994 and 1997, their share in EU-oriented exports increased from 24

---

[2] See Financial Times, June 23, 1999.

to 38 percent. The value of exports of manufactures, excluding machinery and transport equipment, was flat in 1996-97; that of agricultural products declined.[3]

Transport equipment was thus the major driving force of export growth. The dollar value of exports increased by 98 percent between 1995 and 1997; its share in Czech EU-oriented exports rose by 6 percentage points, from 8 to 14 percent. Exports of passenger motor vehicles alone increased from US$416 million in 1995 to US$946 million in 1997, or by 127 percent.

In fact, the increasing volume of machinery exports to the EU over 1995-1997 indicates that this expansion came from new (or revamped) industrial capacities. First, in 1993 among the top 50 exports in terms of four-digit Standard International Trade Classification (SITC.) Rev 1 items, there were only twelve SITC.7 (machinery and transport equipment) products accounting for 24 percent of exports of this group (the share of top 50 in total export was 58 percent). In 1997, the number of SITC.7 products increased to 19, and their share in exports of top 50 products increased to 49 percent (the share of top 50 in total export was 63 percent). Even more significantly, among the top ten exporters, there were only two SITC.7 products in 1993, while in 1997 this number rose to six.

Second, the automotive industry has been mainly responsible for this change. For instance, exports of motor vehicle parts, ranked seventeenth in 1993, moved to a third position in 1997. The value of these exports increased from US$74 million to US$515 million, and their share in total exports rose from 1 to 4 percent. While passenger cars (SITC. 7321) were among top exporters already in 1993 (ranked second after textile clothing -- SITC. 8411), they moved to the top, with the share of 7.2 percent of total exports. The value of these exports increased over the 1995-97 period of sluggish growth by 127 percent. Even if only those exports falling in the top 50 are included, the automotive industry -- generating earnings of approximately US$1.7 billion -- accounted for 20 percent of the top 50 exports and 13 percent of total EU-oriented exports in 1997.

The estimates of Revealed Comparative Advantage (RCA) indices confirm a continuing shift in Czech status in EU markets to the role of exporter specializing in machinery and transport equipment. Although the Czech Republic's revealed specialization remains in "old" industrial products such as iron and steel or metal manufactures, machinery and transport equipment have registered the largest gains in RCA. The RCA index exceeded unity for electric machinery in 1997, indicating a shift in comparative advantage. But most spectacular was the increase in specialization of the automotive sector, which is clearly re-emerging, after an interim of more than 50 years, as a flagship of the Czech economy.

Shift Toward Human Capital and Technology Intensive Products

Considering the relatively high level of GDP per capita, the well-developed physical infrastructure and the large pool of highly skilled labor, one would expect that dismantling of vestiges of central planning would produce a shift in Czech export baskets towards human capital-intensive products and technology-intensive products. The developments over 1993-97 fully corroborate this expectation. From 1993 to 1997, the fastest growing exports were those of human capital -- and technology-intensive products. Their combined share increased from 50 percent to 61 percent of total exports with technology-intensive products recording the largest increase in the 1993-97 period. This change was mainly at the expense of natural resource-intensive products, although the share of unskilled labor intensive products also declined.

Although calculations of Czech RCA indices in EU markets indicate that emerging specialization entails human capital-intensive and technology-intensive activities, those calculations come with a caveat.

---

[3] See agriculture sector chapter in this report.

The Czech firms still remain at a comparative disadvantage in trade of technology-intensive products in EU markets (see Table 6.3, panel A).[4] This holds true despite a large increase in the value of RCA index and despite the 80 percent increase in the share in EU imports of these products. Although starting from a low base, this was the largest increase among relative factor intensity groups (see Table 6.3, panel B).

The Czech economy has a large revealed comparative advantage in human capital-intensive products. Given its long industrial tradition, its highly educated labor force and its low wages relative to the EU, this is not surprising. The revealed comparative advantage index of skilled labor-intensive products recorded the largest increase among relative factor intensity groups and has the largest value. In contrast to Hungary and Poland, the RCA index for unskilled labor-intensive products has only slightly declined, indicating slow progress in restructuring of these industries.

Table 6.3. Revealed Comparative Advantage Indices and Shares in EU Imports of Major Product Groups, 1993-97

Relative Factor Intensity Group	1993	1994	1995	1996	1997	Index 1997, (1993=100)
A. Revealed Comparative Advantage Indices						
Natural Resource Intensive	0.76	0.74	0.66	0.59	0.54	71
Unskilled Labor Intensive	1.57	1.57	1.54	1.55	1.54	98
Technology Intensive	0.63	0.68	0.75	0.80	0.99	157
Human Capital Intensive	1.76	1.80	1.90	1.99	2.20	125
B. Shares in EU Imports, in percent						
Natural Resource Intensive	0.90	1.05	1.08	0.98	0.96	107
Unskilled Labor Intensive	1.86	2.24	2.52	2.58	2.59	139
Technology Intensive	0.75	0.97	1.22	1.33	1.35	180
Human Capital Intensive	2.09	2.56	3.10	3.30	3.75	180
All goods	1.19	1.43	1.63	1.63	1.68	141

Source: Derived from trade data reported by the EU to the UN COMTRADE database.

The Level of Commodity Processing: Stagnation?

Although their share has been on the decline, commodities still account for around one-fifth of EU-destined exports. The most important commodity processing chain is based on wood, accounting for about 40 percent of commodity exports to the EU.

The commodity processing chains do not seem to have undergone significant restructuring. First, the composition of these exports has remained remarkably stable with primary commodities accounting for 13 percent, intermediate for 26 percent, and final stage commodities for 61 percent. Second, only exporters of primary stage products have increased their share in their EU-imports. On a positive note, exporters of intermediate and final stage commodities are at comparative advantage in EU markets. Furthermore, insofar as the costs are internationally competitive, there is nothing worrisome about it.

Exports have not Become 'Environmentally' Cleaner

A high level of industrialization at the outset of communism, combined with the legacy of misdevelopment under central planning as well as less stringent environmental measures in the Czech

[4] The methodology for classification of commodity groups is based on Krause, L. B. (1988), *U.S. Economic Policy toward the Association of Southeast Asian Nations. Meeting the Japanese Challenge*, The Brookings Institution, Washington DC.

Republic than in the EU, would suggest a very high share of environmentally dirty products in Czech EU-directed exports. Although falling since 1995 (see Table 6.4), the share of "dirty" products in Czech exports to the EU has nevertheless remain high at 22 percent in 1997.

Table 6.4. Revealed Comparative Advantage Indices and the Share of Environmentally Dirty Products in Czech Exports to the EU, 1993-97

	1993	1994	1995	1996	1997
Exports (in millions of US dollars)	1,691	2,266	3,103	2,879	2,903
Share in Czech exports (in percent)	26	26	27	24	22
Share in EU "dirty" imports (in percent)	2.43	2.83	2.91	2.94	2.86
RCA	2.09	2.02	1.82	1.79	1.70

Source: Derived from the UN COMTRADE database.

The mere existence of dirty industries does not automatically amount to a dirty environment; intervening factors include environmental policy and technologies. While an assessment of whether clean or dirty technologies prevail is not possible, it seems that since 1995 there have been some shift away from "dirty" industries. But the fact that the weight of dirty industries remains high suggests that the Czech Republic may have to face higher costs of adjustment to EU environmental standards than countries where this share has declined (e.g., Hungary).

Assessment: An Overall Impressive Performance

Although some developments in Czech commercial interaction with the EU may raise concerns, the overall picture remains bright. The share of "made in the Czech Republic" imports in EU external imports has increased every year since 1993, with machinery and transport equipment registering the highest growth. Its export basket has undergone significant change, in line with Czech endowments in factors of production. Moreover, it appears that the process of industrial restructuring has produced internationally competitive industrial capacities in several sectors of the economy.

Factors Accountable for Impressive Export Performance

Several factors have contributed to an impressive export response following the collapse of central planning throughout the region. Leaving aside well-developed infrastructure and superb geographical location, a radical approach to economic reforms, at least during the initial phases of the transition, liberal policies that have increased contestability of domestic markets and foreign investment stand out.

Dismantling Orthodox Central Planning: 'Big Bang' Approach

Czechoslovakia began its path towards competitive markets by launching a stabilization-cum-transformation program in 1991. The program simultaneously pursued stabilization and liberalization tracks, decontrolled prices and dismantled the state monopoly over foreign trade. The removal of central controls provided a powerful incentive to decentralized solutions. Strong devaluation -- although followed by real appreciation as inflation took off -- helped to expand exports. As in other bold reformers, the first benefits came from foreign trade performance: because of a less-reformed central planning and more suppressed trade with non-communist countries, the Czech reorientation was larger in scope than that of Hungary, Poland or Slovenia. (For similar reasons, Estonia's foreign trade reorientation was larger than of all the above.)

Ultimately, Czech export expansion extended well beyond the period following the implementation of the program. This suggests that reforms have led to the emergence of some firms that are responsive to market signals and are competitive in international markets. It seems that economic-opening to external markets, as well as foreign investment, have played an important role in microeconomic restructuring.

Liberal Foreign Trade Policy and Contestable Domestic Markets

The desired outcome of the transition from central planning is the emergence of competitive and contestable markets. A market is contestable when relationships among firms are not unduly distorted by anti-competitive governmental or private action and when there is an open market access for foreign goods, services and investment. Liberalization of regulatory regimes, strict adherence to the principle of national treatment of foreign investors, the reduction in tariffs and the removal of non-tariff barriers increase the contestability of domestic markets.

Czechoslovakia, and then the Czech Republic, have pursued an active policy to open its domestic markets to foreign competition. This policy has consisted of both unilateral liberalization and bilateral free trade agreements with the most important trading partners, including the EU and Central European Free Trade Agreement (CEFTA). As a result, the degree of protection afforded to domestic production (or factors of production) has significantly declined.

Tariffs. Not only have tariffs declined but they have been at levels comparable to those in the EU, and are in fact much lower than in other first-wave candidates (excluding Estonia). In marked contrast to Hungary or Poland, the Czech Republic did not seek to bind its MFN tariff rates at the highest allowable levels when it joined the World Trade Organization (WTO) in 1995. Instead the Czech Republic bound its rates at currently applied MFN rates. Nor did it seek to limit the scope of bindings -- all tariff items are bound. Post-Uruguay tariff bound rates averaged across major product categories do not diverge significantly from those of the EU, in fact they are very similar.

MFN rates apply to a small portion of Czech imports. Imports subjected to tariff preferences account for around 80 percent of Czech total imports. A large share of these imports, especially of non-agricultural products, into the Czech market is already duty-free. By the year 2001, all industrial products from these partners will have duty-free access. Furthermore, unlike Hungary, the Czech Republic grants MFN treatment either autonomously, or on the basis of bilateral agreements, to practically all trading partners, who are not WTO members including most of the former Soviet republics.

Non Tariff Barriers (NTB). The Czech Republic has not resorted to anti-dumping or countervailing duty actions, nor has it taken any safeguard actions. Except for a short period between April 21, 1997 and August 21, 1997, when the 20 percent deposit on the invoice price of imports was in effect, there were no measures taken to address balance of payment problems.

Nonetheless, the Czech foreign trade regime is not entirely NTB-free. There are some technical barriers to trade as well as regulations limiting access to domestic markets. Although the desire to become a full-fledged member of the EU Single Market has driven developments in standards and technical regulations, the Government has not been able to resist the temptation to use technical certification as a barrier to trade. According to the European Commission, the list of products subject to special local tests conducted by the State Testing Laboratory has recently increased, thereby erecting a new barrier to trade.

Competition Policy. Leaving aside the initial stages of the transition (1990-92), the Czech Republic has pursued a moderately liberal and passive foreign trade policy: that is, no special protection was afforded to firms or factors of production. It has not resorted to trade measures to attract FDI. The passive trade policy reduces the importance of competition rules and policies that help offset welfare losses due to the reduction in contestability of domestic markets by foreign firms. It does not, however, make it irrelevant as many spheres of the economy are not exposed to external competition (non-tradables).

The Czech Republic's competition policy framework, rules and enforcement capacities, have yet to be fully harmonized with that of the EU. The competition rules, as laid down in the 1991 Competition Law, largely comply with EU competition legislation, that is, its substantive rules (restrictive practices, block exemption and merger control) as well as procedural rules. There are some gaps, but proposed amendments to the Competition Law go a long way to close them. Overall, combined with liberal foreign trade policy, producers have remained under relatively strong competitive pressures.

State Aids. Subsidies, or state aids, distort competition. They give "national champions" an unfair advantage in competing with other firms, domestic or foreign. While it would be impossible to quantitatively assess the distortions in competition due to state aids, state aids -- in the form of direct transfers of funds, foregone revenues (tax concessions or credits), etc., -- have been a feature of Czech state interventionism. But the share of subsidies fell from around 16 percent over 1990-92, to around 2.5 percent of the GDP in 1996-97. These estimates, however, do not include 'soft' loans to large firms by state-controlled, if not state-owned, banks. State aids are still administered by various ministries and government agencies according to different procedures.

Government Procurement. General government's total expenditure accounted for 43 percent of GDP in 1998. A sizable portion of general government spending goes to public procurement of goods and services. As the total "market" for procurement is quite substantial practices governing government procurement policies may alter conditions in the contestability of domestic markets.

As is the case in many countries, government procurement regulations discriminate -- both implicitly and explicitly -- against foreign firms. The provisions of the procurement regulation stipulate that contracts to domestic firms (i.e., domestically or foreign-owned firms registered in the Czech Republic) may receive up to 10 percent preference. If a bid is submitted jointly by a domestic and foreign firm, it is considered to be submitted by a non-resident foreign firm. Even though tendering procedures seem to be transparent, such conditions introduce a bias in favor of resident firms, and may effectively prevent non-resident foreign firms from obtaining government contracts. This bias, however, seems to be less severe than in other transition economies.

Opening the system to foreign contractors along the lines of the WTO Agreement on Government Procurement would yield at least two important benefits: it would reduce the cost of services provided by the state, and it would improve the competitiveness of domestic contractors. The latter should also allow them to compete for government contracts abroad, especially in EU member countries. According to the Ministry of Industry and Trade, access of the Czech Republic to the agreement on government procurement will be resolved in the context of the EU accession process. It is expected, however, that the Czech Republic will become a signatory of the agreement and will fully follow its provisions.

Significant Inflows of Foreign Direct Investment

An excellent geographical location with its easy access to EU and Eastern markets, low relative unit labor costs, a large pool of a highly skilled labor force, and investment "guarantees" provided by the EAA and OECD membership have offered unique advantages to foreign investors. Nonetheless, the magnitude of FDI suggests that the Czech Republic has not been the star performer among CEECs. By no means, however, has the Czech Republic been a poor performer. In terms of FDI flows, aggregated over 1990-97, the Czech Republic ranks second among first-wave candidates in terms of FDI per capita and third in terms of share in GDP. From 1993 to 1997, FDI increased to CEECs, yet the Czech Republic retained its high position, albeit in terms of FDI share in GDP its ranking slightly fell. Estonia was the second FDI recipient in terms of the GDP, but third on a per capita basis. The 1997 crisis did not have a significant impact on FDI: they fell by US$100 million to US$1.3 billion in 1997. Foreign direct investors remained confident. In 1998, FDI increased to US$2.5 billion, the highest in per GDP terms among the leading five CEE candidates for EU accession (see Figure 6.1). This increase on FDI took place in spite of the deep recession, indicating the investors confidence on the future prospects of the Czech Republic. The strong trend continued in the fist half of 1999.

FDI inflows have already made an important contribution to the development of the Czech economy, and its reintegration into world markets. FDI accounted for about 10 percent of average annual investment expenditures from 1990 to 1997. Since FDI inflows were rather evenly spread over the whole period, many foreign firms have already been reinvesting their profits locally. As a result, the share of firms with foreign participation in total investment outlays is likely to be high.

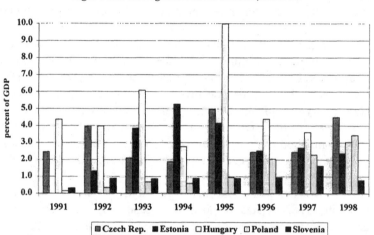

Figure 6.1. Foreign Direct Investment, 1991-98

FDI has contributed to the expansion of stable commercial and production links with firms located in the EU. FDI has contributed to the export success of the Czech automotive industry. It has thus far attracted around 13 percent of total FDI. For instance, Skoda Auto, part of the Volkswagen Group, already the largest firm in the Czech Republic, is now also the largest exporter accounting for 7 percent of exports to the EU. It has contributed to the development of forward (cost) and backward (demand) linkages among domestic firms. Skoda suppliers have become exporters. Although indirect effects related to restructuring and productivity spillovers are difficult to capture, competition from foreign firms and their more stringent quality requirements has resulted in improved performance.

Measures to Increase Contestability

There are several measures, which might increase the contestability of domestic markets and thereby increase the competitiveness of Czech firms. These measures can be summarized as follows:

- To improve competition policy framework, as well as rules and enforcement capacities of competition authorities, one may consider granting anti-trust authority to a single independent institution. This institution would be empowered to assess the competition and welfare impact of important policy decisions, as well as actions taken by firms affecting the contestability of domestic markets and monitor their impact *ex post*;

- To improve the current framework of state aids. This would involve establishing transparent monitoring mechanisms, streamlining and reducing the scope of subsidies. State aids should be also subjected to scrutiny by a competition authority once it is reformed;

- To open government procurement to foreign contractors over the next years along the lines of the GATT Agreement on Government Procurement. Among other things, this would entail the elimination of preferences offered to resident firms; and

- To align MFN tariff rates on industrial products with those levied by the EU. This would not necessarily involve a formal lowering of statutory tariffs but might simply entail the change in applied rates.

Sustainability of External Performance

Among first-wave candidates to accede the EU, the Czech Republic ranks only second to Estonia in terms of liberal foreign trade institutions and policies. Tariff rates are close to those in the EU. The broadly conceived business climate -- including the financial sector, conditions in entry for domestic and foreign firms, legal framework enforcing property rights and contracts -- has been favorable to foreign investment and private activity. Relationships among firms are not distorted by governmental or private actions; there is free market access -- as stipulated in the EA -- for foreign goods, services and investment. Investments account for around one-third of the GDP. Thus, with relatively low foreign debt and macroeconomic stability firmly in place, one would expect a flourishing economy. But since 1997 this has not been the case and the current recession has negatively affected economic performance at all levels.

Some developments in Czech commercial interaction with the EU may indeed raise concern. There are indications that its sustainability may be in jeopardy. In fact, they may presage serious difficulties in sustaining expansion in foreign trade without sacrificing the standard of living. Total exports of manufactures other than capital and transportation equipment were flat in 1996-97: the question remains how fast other sectors of the economy will restructure. With the rapidly progressing reductions in tariff rates on industrial products from the EU and with harmonization of technical regulations and standards, these other sectors will incur growing competition from imports. Without progress in restructuring, many of them may be unable to survive in the long-term.

The problem is that a large number of private or semi-private, domestically-owned firms, have accumulated substantial debt without undergoing significant restructuring. Their sales declined and losses increased. Without restructuring, their survival is doubtful at best. Their sales during restructuring may further decline before rebounding. While the government's intentions to revitalize the failing industry are commendable, it is too early to know if they will be successful.[5]

Thus, the most important tasks for improving the competitiveness of Czech firms are establishing a viable banking sector as well as transparent capital markets. The banking sector has not exerted pressures on firms to restructure. To the contrary, banks have been a source of soft financing. Capital markets have discouraged investors, thus preventing firms from raising capital there; they have also failed to influence the behavior of firms.

---

[5] For a description of the government's restructuring program see the enterprise sector chapter in this report.

Chapter VII. Financial Sector

Evolution of the Banking System

Changing Structure of the Banking Sector

The Czech banking sector has changed significantly since 1989 -- displaying characteristics common to many Central European transition countries. Prior to 1990, the sector included the Czechoslovak State Bank (CSB), which provided central banking, as well as enterprise commercial banking services; Ceska Sporitelna (CS), a savings bank; Ceskoslovenska Obchodni Banka (CSOB), the foreign trade bank; and Zivnobanka (ZB), a foreign currency transaction bank. In 1990, the commercial banking activities of CSB were split into two new banks, Komercni Banka (KB), a commercial bank, and Investicni Banka which later merged with the postal savings system to form Investicni A Postovni Banka (IPB). The successor to CSB, the Czech National Bank (CNB), became the country's central bank.

Table 7.1. Structure of the Banking Sector, 1995-99

	1995	1996	1997	1998	1999[1]
Total Assets (percent)					
Large Banks	76.42	72.94	68.57	66.04	66.15
Small Banks	3.47	3.64	3.47	3.48	2.28
Foreign Banks/Branches	17.86	20.15	23.46	25.03	25.97
Specialized Banks	2.25	3.27	4.50	5.45	5.60
Credit (Gross) (percent)					
Large Banks	82.25	80.15	76.89	74.03	73.55
Small Banks	4.07	3.62	2.92	2.80	2.38
Foreign Banks/Branches	13.26	15.46	18.66	20.46	21.25
Specialized Banks	0.42	0.76	1.53	2.70	2.82
Deposits (percent)					
Large Banks	83.69	81.84	77.42	72.91	74.22
Small Banks	4.08	4.66	4.24	4.51	2.99
Foreign Banks/Branches	9.65	9.55	12.69	15.56	15.95
Specialized Banks	2.58	3.96	5.64	7.02	6.84

1/ Data until end-March 1999, for the banks with valid license as of March 31, 1999. Large banks: Ceska Sporitelna, Ceskoslovenska Obchodni banka, Investicni a Postovni banka, Komercni banka, Konsolidacni banka; Small banks: Banka Hana, Moravia banka, Plzenska banka, Prvni mestska banka, Union banka, Expandia banka; Specialized banks: Ceska exportni banka, Cm. zarucni a rozvojova banka, Cm. hypotecni banka, and building societies.
Source: Czech National Bank.

CNB began issuing licenses in 1990, however, the licenses for branches of foreign banks have been issued since 1992, when the Act on Banks came into force. Liberal licensing practices led to a rapid expansion in the number of banks and allowed the entry of foreign capital in the form of wholly or majority foreign owned banks and foreign bank branches. The number of banks and foreign branches peaked at 55 in 1994 and then fell to 45 by end 1998. Despite the rapid proliferation of licenses after 1990, the banking system remains highly concentrated. As of the end of 1998, the five largest banks (KB, CS, IPB, CSOB and Konsolidační banka - KoB) had a combined market share of 66 percent of assets (see Box 7.1.).

Increasing their share of total assets from 13 percent to 25 percent between 1994-1998, foreign-owned banks steadily eroded the market share of the big five. With the acquisition of IPB by Nomura and with the planned privatization to foreign strategic investors of CS and KB during 1999-2000, the foreign-owned banks' market share is expected to increase to about 90 percent of total assets in the system. As in other countries, foreign banks initially started operations in order to support the activities of their home country corporate clients; subsequently, they expanded into servicing Czech corporate and retail customers. In penetrating the market, the foreign-owned banks enjoyed significant advantages over their Czech competitors. They began operations with a "blue chip" customer base, rapidly building up their portfolios of high quality customers and gaining the critical mass required to achieve profitability. They did not have the inherited burdens of the large state-owned banks; they had access to experienced staff and management and a tradition of control and credit analysis. The foreign banks also had indirect access to the deposit base through the Czech inter-bank market, which helped reduce the funding problem that could have constrained their growth.

Box 7.1. Structure of the Banking Sector in the Czech Republic

⇒ 63 commercial banks, of which 43 banks are active (March 1999).
• 1 state financial institution (Konsolidacni Banka).
• 23 foreign-owned banks and branches, accounting for 25 percent of total banking assets (expected to increase to 90 percent with the future privatization of large state-owned banks).
• 19 domestic banks.
• 15 banks in liquidation or bankruptcy proceedings.
• 5 banks wound-up without liquidation.
⇒ five largest banks account for 66 percent of total assets, 74 percent of gross loans, 73 percent of deposits, 80 percent of employees, and 95 percent of branch offices.
⇒ 2 large state-owned banks (CS, and KB) launched privatization programs, expected to be concluded by end-1999/ 2000.
Profitability Ratios (December 1998):

• Return on assets	-0.41 percent
• Return on core capital	-13.44 percent
• Net interest rate margin	2.59 percent
• Deposit rates	6.66-9.13 percent
• Lending rates	10.51-11.65 percent
• Non-performing assets	27.2 percent of total assets (Konsolidacni Banka excluded)

Source: Czech National Bank.

The small bank segment of the system also developed rapidly from 1991 to 1995. The small banks drew their customers from the emerging small and medium-sized private enterprise sector, providing working capital and acquisition financing to entrepreneurs. Thus, they came to be closely associated with a volatile economic sector. The small banks suffered from weaknesses, consisting of a lack of skilled professional and managerial staff and a lack of operational experience; weaknesses in controls (particularly for credit) and systems; and inadequacies in governance arrangements which encouraged imprudent connected lending. These weaknesses were compounded by the high cost structures inherent in start-up banking operations, a corresponding need to expand quickly to generate revenues, and dependency on high cost wholesale funding. The entry of criminal elements, who were quick to exploit the banks for their own ends, only exacerbated the situation. Since 1996, the combination of these negative factors has led to widespread failures within the small bank segment and has impeded the growth of this segment of the system.

At the end of 1998, the stock of credits granted amounted to about CZK1,135 billion, or about 60 percent of GDP. Changes in the allocation of credit from 1992 to 1998 reflected two factors: transfer of credit to the private enterprise category increased from 33 to 70 percent of total credit due to privatization; and growth of credit to the enterprise sector increased from 79 to 86 percent due to the focus of Czech banks on enterprise lending (see Table 7.2.). The retail banking business remains relatively small, although the rapid development of specialized banks, primarily building savings banks, in recent years indicates that this sector may be poised for strong growth.[1]

Table 7.2. Allocation of Credit by Sector

	1992	1995	1997	1998
	percent of total credits			
Government (Net)	9	3	1	3
Private Enterprises	33	64	72	70
State Enterprises	46	20	14	11
Households & Small Business	12	12	10	10
Other	0	1	3	6

Source: Czech National Bank.

Performance of the Banking System

Banking sector profits from banking activities in 1998 were about CZK96 billion.[2] However, the sector ended with an overall net loss of about CZK9 billion, after taking account of operating costs of about CZK90 billion (net of extraordinary revenues), net provisions of about CZK12 billion, and taxes of about CZK3 billion. The level of the sector losses is clearly affected by the level of provisions taken to cover potential losses on the banks credit portfolios, and, especially in 1998, by huge write-offs of bad credits against provisions.

Table 7.3. Performance Measures for the Banking System

	1996	1997	1998
	Percent		
Return on Assets	0.60	-0.18	-0.41
Net Interest Margin	3.05	3.21	2.59
Return on Core Capital	19.61	-6.34	-13.44

Source: Czech National Bank.

Nevertheless, the poor performance of the banking system as a whole masks some encouraging improvements (particularly in 1997 and 1998) in other measures of performance, which indicate that the sector was becoming more efficient. Per employee operating margins increased by 39 percent between 1996 and 1998 (from CZK692 thousand to CZK963 thousand) as the number of employees remained stable (at about 53,000), while total assets and revenues grew. The ratio of operating costs to operating income also began to improve, declining from 49.42 percent in 1996 to 45.33 percent by end-September 1998.

Improvements in some measures of operating performance were overwhelmed, however, in 1997 and 1998 by the impact of new provisions against credit losses. The new provisions are being driven by a

---

[1] The core business of six building saving banks consist in collecting long-term deposits from the public and granting long-term housing loans, in majority bearing fixed rates. The state subsidizes the natural persons' deposits with these banks up to a limit set by the law (the Act on Building Saving Banks). The core business of building saving banks is thus different from that of mortgage banks, which consist of issuing mortgage bonds and granting mortgage loans bearing floating rates. One specialized mortgage banks exists in the Czech Republic, and four other banks are allowed to issue mortgage bonds, resulting with an increase of the stock of mortgage credit bearing floating rates. All these banks are also entitled to provide state-supported housing mortgage loans to natural persons.
[2] Includes branches abroad and excludes KoB.

combination of factors: (a) a new regulation requiring banks to gradually -- until the end of 2001 -- stop netting off the value of real estate collateral against the balance of loans classified as loss loans; (b) improvements in external auditing and internal loan classification procedures (driven in part by the prospect of privatization); and (c) the gradually increasing scope of CNB on-site examination activities.

The first of these factors primarily affects the provisions taken by the large state-owned banks, which hold the major part (84 percent at the end of 1998) of the system's classified assets, while the first and second factors may be expected to continue to depress results throughout 1999, as CS and KB clean up their balance sheets in advance of privatization. By the end of 1997, fully 90 percent of classified credits were held by the five large banks. The comparative quality of credit portfolios is reflected in the ratio of provisions and reserves to gross credits, with large banks holding 12.98 percent of credits in reserves, small banks holding 15.65 percent, and foreign banks holding only 4.42 percent.

From 1995 through the end of 1998 the return on average assets of large banks declined from 0.91 percent to minus 0.80 percent, and that of small banks from a minus 2.03 percent to minus 6.89. During the same period, the return on assets of foreign owned banks improved from 0.18 percent to 0.55 percent.[3] The trend is consistent with a picture of growing recognition and incidence of asset quality problems in the small and large Czech banks. The performance of foreign banks is consistent with an expected pattern of low profitability during their start up period (due to high initial costs), moving to significant profitability as these banks reach critical mass without encountering major asset quality problems.

The existence of a relatively undeveloped retail market indicates that Czech banks should be able to improve their financial performance by taking advantage of the much wider spreads and lower loss experience in this type of lending. Typical transition market retail intermediation spreads of 12 to 15 percent compared to the Czech banking system average intermediation spread of only 5.4 percent in 1997, thus giving the Czech banks a substantial scope for improvement. The return on assets and total capital in the specialized banks reached 2.80 and 40.75 percent respectively by the end of 1998 (a period during which the enterprise-focussed large and small banks incurred losses). It is, therefore, reasonable to expect that the structure of lending will move over the next few years towards better balance between retail and commercial activities. The privatization of CS may help drive this process, as the bank has the strongest retail franchise in the Czech Republic but has to-date focused mainly on interbank and commercial lending rather than on the development of its untapped retail market potential.

Bank Restructuring

Since adequate functioning of the banking sector is the necessary condition for successful transformation of the Czech Republic into a market economy, the CNB found it necessary to solve the problems of banking sector so that a potential systemic crisis would be prevented.[4] Accordingly, there have been successive attempts by the authorities to resolve the problems of the banks. These included programs for the large banks initiated during 1991-1993 and for the small and medium banks in 1996 and 1997. The focus of these programs has been on the provision of balance sheet assistance to the banks in

---

[3] During the same period, returns on total capital declined from 15.57 percent to minus 17.68 percent for large banks, and from minus 8.7 percent to minus 44.63 percent for small banks. Return on total capital for foreign bank improved from 3.87 percent to 12.60 percent.

[4] According to the law, it is a primary objective of the CNB to ensure stability of the Czech national currency and for this purpose perform supervision over the execution of banking operations and take care of the prudential and purposeful development of the banking system in the Czech Republic (Article 2, Act of the CNB No.6, 1993).

the form of asset carve outs and additional capital provided by the State, rather than on institutional restructuring.[5]

The Large Banks[6]

In 1991, the authorities established Konsolidacni Banka (KoB)[7] for the purpose of taking over those loans made on non-commercial terms that the large banks inherited from the former economic system (Consolidation Program I). In the first instance, this involved carving out the "TOZ" revolving perpetual inventory loans which had been provided as working capital to a large number of Czechoslovak enterprises. Since then, KoB has directly undertaken other restructuring operations including the purchase of "social loans" from IPB prior to its privatization. As indicated below, it has also financed a major component of CNB's program for small and medium banks.

KoB's approach to asset work out is influenced more by its "developmental" role as a State institution rather than by private sector approaches to the workout process. The bank itself notes that its work-out operations are governed by "the aim of allowing clients an opportunity to develop their businesses so that conditions are created in which they can pay off their debt to the bank".[8] While 319 bankruptcy actions, representing about 21 percent of the loan portfolio, had been taken by the end of 1997, KoB management emphasize that this method is only utilized where enterprise managers are completely uncooperative. KoB has more typically used debt restructuring and debt to equity conversions, unaccompanied by full restructuring of the enterprises.

By mid-1998, KoB still had relationships with more than 4,000 Czech enterprises (the majority of which were TOZ clients); it had accumulated significant equity stakes in a number of large "strategic" enterprises. The bank had ceased to function only as an "asset hospital", while expanding its operations to include development finance activities (acting as an intermediary for European Investment Bank loans) and as a commercial bank accepting deposits and making loans to commercial customers. Funding for these activities was provided by means of bond issues and deposits. Since KoB's activities in bank restructuring have been carried out at Government direction, they have normally relied for funding on "future privatization proceeds" from the National Property Fund (NPF). KoB's annual operating losses are funded by an ex-post contribution from the State budget.

In addition to the KoB, the Consolidation Program I included another agency, which focused on debt obligations of the foreign trade companies (almost exclusively to CSOB) in the former Czechoslovak Republic. Ceska Inkasni (CI) was formed by the Ministry of Finance in 1993 to take over the debts and corresponding claims of these companies which corresponded to trade obligations of low rated (i.e., high sovereign risk) countries, including the countries subject to United Nations embargoes. In 1997, the obligations of the Slovak trade companies were added to these obligations in order to facilitate the privatization of CSOB.

---

[5] Since banking sector in the first stage of transition lacked capital, the financial injection by the state was unavoidable.

[6] Some of the large banks operated already in the period of centrally planned economy, while some of them emerged with the break-up of the state mono-bank system into two-tier system after 1989.

[7] Konsolidacni banka s.p.u. was founded by the Czechoslovak Ministry of Finance in 1991. Konsolidacni banka Praha s.p.u. was founded by the CR Ministry of Finance in 1992 and took over Czech-related assets and liabilities of the federal Konsolidacni banka s.p.u. (Slovak-related assets and liabilities were transferred at the same time to Konsolidacni banka Bratislava s.p.u.).

[8] KoB 1997 Annual Report, page 12.

By the end of 1997, CI had total assets of CZK27.3 billion, of which CZK19.5 billion had been provisioned. The high loss experience on the portfolio is consistent with high sovereign risk of debtors. The assets are administered by a unit of CSOB, which pursues collection by means of litigation, settlements, and netting off of counter-claims. The portfolio is funded by CSOB with a corresponding guarantee from the NPF. The principal net of collections is amortized over a 10 year period.

Consolidation Program I had positive impacts for the banks and for the economy as a whole. Recapitalization and partial consolidation of the financial situation enabled the large banks to fulfil their intermediation functions during the first years of the transition period.

The Small Banks

The small banks began to experience severe problems in late 1995. The scale of their asset quality problems became more apparent in 1996, when the generous privatization loans which allowed full accrual until 1994 and 1995 became due, and following stepped up on-site examination by the CNB, and more stringent external audits. Indications of problems in the small banks caused depositor concern and resulted in increasing and unsustainable liquidity pressures on this segment of the banking sector.

In response to these problems, the CNB first initiated a program of supervisory actions designed to encourage the banks to help themselves (Consolidation Program II). The program consisted of an evaluation of the quality of loan portfolio, including the impact of the bad loans on a bank's profitability. In addition, the capacity and willingness of shareholders and management of a bank to stabilize the financial situation was assessed. This program established targets for forcing either the liquidation of a bank which could not meet the 8 percent capital adequacy standard at the end of 1996, its recapitalization by existing or new shareholders, its merger with or sale to a better-capitalized bank, or an imposition of conservatorship. In 1993, there were 22 operating small banks. Until the first quarter of 1999, the number of small banks had substantially decreased, since 14 of them entered into bankruptcy proceeding or were liquidated, and one small bank was merged.

In addition to Consolidation Program II, the liquidity crisis of one medium sized private bank (Agrobanka) was solved by the loan granted by the CNB in 1996, and put under conservatorship. In 1998, the bank was split into "good part" and "bad part". Good assets together with portfolio of deposits were sold to GE Capital, while the bad assets remained in former Agrobanka, which went into liquidation. Most of losses of this operation bear the CNB as lender of last resort. However, since Agrobanka's equity was lost, private shareholders incurred losses as well.

This process of consolidation of banking sector was accompanied by a decrease of general public confidence in the banks. Small banks in particular experienced unsustainable outflow of deposits. It became clear during 1996, that CNB's supervisory actions alone would not be sufficient to solve the segment's problems. In order to prevent the risk of liquidity crisis in the subsector of small banks, which could potentially de-stabilize the whole banking sector, the government approved another program in October of 1996 (Stabilization Program). At the same time, to increase depositor confidence in the small banks, deposit insurance coverage has been temporarily extended from CZK100,000 to CZK4 million.[9]

---

[9] Clients' deposits of five small banks were compensated in amounts in excess of that covered by the deposit protection scheme (above CZK100,000). In the case of four banks, the facility granted by the CNB covered the difference between compensation covered by Deposit Insurance Fund and the sum of CZK4 million for natural persons, as well as the extension of the deposit insurance to the legal persons. However, both natural and legal persons with special relations with the banks were exempt from this additional compensation, and were compensated only to the limits set by deposit insurance scheme. The fifth case (Ceska banka, a.s.) was different since the depositors, both natural and legal persons, were reimbursed up to CZK4 million. This additional

In October 1996, the CNB established Ceska Financni (CF) as a subsidiary of the CNB, for the purpose of financing the Stabilization Program. As part of the Stabilization Program, CF purchased poor quality assets from the banks, at book value for cash up to 110 percent of a bank's capital. The banks are required to repurchase the residual amount of these assets in the period of next 5 to 7 years. The return of funds that CF used to purchase poor quality assets is assured by a guarantee issued by each bank participating in the program. In order to further assure the return of funds to CF, the banks were required to each year create provisions in the amount representing at least 1/7 of the amount of assets purchased by CF. These provisions were fully funded by the interest subsidization provided on the cash received.[10] Refinancing of CF is assured by the loan granted by KoB. The possible losses of KoB due to this operation shall be covered by NPF.

Assets acquired by CF are managed by the originating bank under the supervision of CF personnel. Asset liquidation in the first half of 1998 produced revenues amounting to only about 2 percent of CF's total assets, indicating that progress in this area may be somewhat slow. However, CF managementnote that many of the assets being managed are the result of criminal activity, and so recovery is likely to be very limited.

In order to qualify for the Stabilization Program, banks had to commit to programs of institutional strengthening, limits on credit activities and improved risk control, and possible replacement of management. By 1999, only two of six banks that originally participated in the Stabilization Program remain in business and participate in the program. Four banks did not comply with the requirements of the program and went out of business. By late 1998, a total of approximately CZK12.3 billion had been spent by CF for the "Stabilization Program," and approximately CZK35.5 billion for the "Consolidation Program II and for receivership of Agrobanka".

Cost of Restructuring to Date

In April 1998, the Government produced a paper which summarized the extent of the off budget financing provided by the transformation institutions.[11] The principal objectives of this proposal were to increase the transparency of State finances and to end the system of off-budget financing of banking system losses incurred as a result of bad lending decisions which created an environment of moral hazard. The Government's paper notes that "any kind of explicit and implicit promise of State financial aid violates the stimuli of market entities. Primarily, the State promise to absolutely take over commercial risks gives rise to irresponsible risk-taking on the part of market entities. Consequently, the repurchase of bad claims at full accounting value and the provision of State guarantees can expressly deform the conditions in financial and real markets and lead to moral hazards on both sides".[12]

---

compensation was covered by Deposit Insurance Fund, and was based on a temporary provision of the Article II of Act on Banks, which was part of the amendment of this Act approved in 1998.

[10] The lack of an interest charge creates a subsidy in the range of 11.5 to 17.6 percent per annum (CF's own cost of funds to finance the cash provided to the bank). As the interest free funding is provided over 7 years, the effective rate of subsidization is approximately equal to the book value of assets transferred.

[11] MoF document reference 08/22 372/1998: *Hidden Debt Financing and Conceptual Proposal Regarding the Functional Standing and Substantive Focus of the So-called Transformation Institutions and the System for Financing Them.* See contingent liabilities chapter in this report for further discussion of this issue.

[12] Two particular aspects of this are worth noting. The CNB recognizes that CF's activities give rise to questions of moral hazard regarding the CNB's supervisory and monetary activities. The CNB is now in a position of supervising banks in which it has a direct economic interest and has resumed the role of direct lender to the real sector performed by the former CSB. Neither of these developments is desirable, and the consolidation of CF with KoB would be a useful method of removing the moral hazards faced by the CNB. By contrast, CI presents no particular moral hazard as it is focussed on dealing with historically-acquired sovereign risks. There is minimal duplication of

Table 7.4. Estimated Bank Assistance Funding Provided by Transformation Institutions, 1991–98
(Excluding Future Pre-privatization Assistance)

	Amount	
	CZK Billion	percent of 1998 GDP
Konsolidacni banka[1]	113.20	6.37
Ceska financni[2]	47.84	2.69
Ceska inkasni	27.28	1.54
Total	**188.32**	**10.60**

Note: Excludes operating losses funded by state budget.
1/ Adjusted to exclude CZK36.30 billion provided to CF.
2/ Includes CZK36.30 billion provided by KoB.
Source: Czech National Bank and World Bank staff calculations.

The Government's paper also proposes consolidating the three main institutions (KoB, CF and CI) into KoB in order to eliminate the duplication of operating costs resulting from multiple work; the paper proposes creating an environment in which the institution responsible for enterprise assets is motivated to act forcefully to resolve them. The proposals in the paper, which was prepared by the previous Government, are now under consideration by the current Government.

Despite its negative aspects, the financial assistance provided has helped maintain the stability of the financial system, and has allowed the exit of a number of banks. Despite significant legal constraints, some progress has also been made by transformation institutions, and by the large banks in working out problem assets. The human resources required to move work-out activities forward at an accelerated pace have now been developed. These could provide a foundation for meaningful progress in creditor-led enterprise restructuring once the problems of the legal environment and incentive structures have been addressed.

Nonetheless, the fact that the State has had to repeatedly provide financial assistance tends to bear out the argument that the moral hazard of this type of restructuring program carried very real costs. The Czech authorities now recognize that to minimize this cost, any further assistance should be coupled with the major strengthening of bank corporate governance and comprehensive institutional restructuring that can only be expected from sales of controlling stakes in the banks to strategic investors.

Privatization of State Banks

Evolution and Remaining Agenda

The initial privatization of Czech banks was carried out as part of the mass privatization program. The voucher privatization of the 5 state-owned banks (KB, Zivnostenska Banka (ZB), CS, IPB, and CSOB) did not result in a full transfer of State control to the private sector; it was not until 1992 that the first state-owned bank was fully privatized, with the sale of 52 percent of ZB to the IFC and Berliner Handels-und-Frankfurter Bank. Until the privatization process for IPB began in 1996, State control over

operating costs as the specialized work-out functions involved in these types of debt (international litigation and settlement procedures) have little in common with the domestic enterprise debt work-out functions of the other transition institutions. As many government-to-government issues are involved in this type of debt workout, retention of these claims within the legal ownership of the Ministry of Finance would seem reasonable. But there is reason for concern that the off budget financing mechanism used for CI (the NPF) makes its operations less than transparent.

the 4 largest banks was seen by key Government officials as a means for maintaining financing of the enterprise sector and for ensuring that the transition to a market economy would be irreversible.[13]

Table 7.5. Ownership of Major Czech Banks, 1992-98

	1992		1997		1998	
	State	Private	State	Private	State	Private
	Percentage		Percentage		Percentage	
CS	60	40	60	40	60	40
KB	49	51	49	51	49	51
IPB	51	49	36	64	0	100
CSOB	66	34	65	35	65	35

Note: State ownership is defined as including shares owned by ministries, the CNB, NPF, restitution funds, and Czech towns and municipalities. Slovak ownership of CSOB (24 percent) is excluded.
Source: Czech National Bank.

The Czech Government has successfully sold two banks under state ownership to foreign investors in the past years. In 1998, the privatization of IPB was completed by means of a simultaneous sale of state-owned shares (36 percent of pre-transaction capital) and a new capital subscription which transferred control to Nomura.[14] The transaction passed the bulk of IPB's asset risk to the State by means of substantial pre-privatization provisions and by a heavy discount on the price of shares sold by the State to Nomura. Nomura was required to maintain its control over the bank for a period of not less than 5 years. During the same year, Agrobanka (no state ownership) was "sold" to GE Capital, after CZK22 billion of classified assets was transferred to the CF under the consolidation program.[15]

In mid-1998, the Government decided to initiate the privatization process for the remaining three state-owned banks (CS, CSOB, and KB) and retained financial advisers for all three banks. The timetable under discussion envisions privatizing, CS by the end of 1999, and KB at some point in 2000. The privatization of the state's 65 percent stake in CSOB, the fourth largest bank in the Czech Republic, took place in July 1999. The government decided to sell this stake to Belgium based KBC Bank for CZK40.05 billion, or CZK11,942.20 per share, nominal value of which is CZK1,000 (or in dollar term, US$1.1 billion for the stake, or US$341 per share), IFC bought 4.3 percent of CSOB.

The privatization process for CS and KB, with tenders opened in April and June 1999, respectively, presents significantly greater challenges than that for CSOB. Both banks have fundamentally different franchises from CSOB; both have significant asset quality problems, which are likely to require complex transactional solutions. CS has an attractive retail deposit franchise and a countrywide network of branches. Its management has made significant steps towards restructuring and rationalizing the bank's retail operations, and expanding the retail franchise by offering card and new deposit products. KB's franchise value for foreign investors derives from its pre-eminent role in the Czech corporate sector, a

---

[13] With the exception of KB, during the last 6 years some dilution of the State's shareholdings in the banks has occurred as a result of raising additional capital from the private sector, but in any case the State's shareholding has remained large enough to ensure management control of all four banks. Also, CSOB was privatized in July 1999 by a sale to foreign investor.

[14] This discount could not be taken in the price of newly created shares sold to Nomura because the sale price of newly issued shares may not be less than the nominal value of existing shares.

[15] This transaction was not a 'real' privatization since Agrobanka never was a state-owned bank but a private bank under state conservatorship. The technique used in this transaction was to (a) first place Agrobanka in receiverships, and then, (b) conduct a purchase and assumption transaction to transfer deposits, good assets, and cash to the "new" Agrobanka. The cash was provided by the purchase of bad assets from the new bank by CF (see section on Bank Restructuring in this chapter).

fairly large network of branches, new investments in technology to support the introduction of card products designed to improve fee income and reduce operating costs, and recent efforts by management to centralize risk decision-making as well as improve the bank's cost/income ratio by reducing staff. A final, and perhaps critical, advantage is that it is expected to be the last large banking franchise available for purchase by foreign strategic investors thereby giving it scarcity value.

Despite attractive features, the privatization of CS and KB will involve substantial costs. CS has a very large commercial portfolio -- a large part of which is classified -- and which incorporates substantial high risk country exposures. The minimum cost of sterilizing the risk of classified assets is hard to estimate due to a history of lax accounting for classified loans.[16] At the end of September 1998, CS's uncovered classified loans amounted to CZK24.3 billion. CS's classified loans to customers rose by 50 percent from January 1997, to reach 34 percent of total loans the end of September 1998. Further significant portfolio deterioration is indicated by a CZK3 billion increase in the bank's projected loss for 1998 to CZK10.5 billion. The bank required a capital injection of CZK5.7 billion[17] to remain above minimum regulatory capital levels through year end 1998. It experienced a significant loss of US$250 million in the third quarter of 1998 as a result of speculation in Russian debt securities and derivatives. The State has recently committed CZK20.5 billion in further support to CS to cover the purchase by KoB of approximately CZK15 billion of social loans[18] and subscription to approximately CZK5.5 billion of CS subordinated debt.

In September 1998, CZK66 billion (27.5 percent) of KB's CZK241 billion customer loan portfolio was classified, and only CKZ150 billion of its customer loans were graded "standard." Tier 1 capital had fallen to 6.6 percent of risk weighted assets and total capital to only 9.4 percent of risk weighted assets. With additional losses expected in the last quarter of 1998, plus further large provisions against real estate collateral required in 1999, the bank will require substantial infusions of capital from the State if it is to remain in compliance with regulatory capital requirements. While management appears to be attempting to address the problems of the bank, further strong measures are clearly required, including efforts to reduce non-interest expenses (which have been rising in nominal terms in 1998) and to reduce staff.

Structure of the Privatization Transaction

Privatization transactions can be structured in a variety of ways, which have a profound impact on the net cost of the transaction to the State.[19] In the IPB privatization, "an as is and where is" no-recourse sale was used. In this type of transaction, the purchaser performs very extensive due diligence and seeks to identify all assets that have a risk of loss. If more than one bidder is competing, it is usually possible to structure a set of rules for asset valuation. If only one bidder is present, then every valuation may become a subject for negotiation. The bank then writes off its capital through provisions against these potential losses and the purchaser takes control by means of a new capital subscription. In case of the IPB, however, there was no write-off of equity. The sale of the state's stake to Nomura International was accompanied by subscription of new emission of shares by Nomura International as well as by capital injection provided by Nomura International. Afterwards, when the state's stake was privatized, an increasing of equity by subscription of second emission of IPB shares has followed. The first round of

---

[16] For example, CS classifies only according to the CNB's minimum standards, whereas KB places all new loans on watch status for 6 months.

[17] Expected to be provided in the form of a subordinated loan from KoB.

[18] Low interest loans given under the Communist regime for purposes such as housing.

[19] Careful analysis by appropriate experts of the impact of tax benefits embedded in the various options needs to be undertaken before the selection of a transaction structure. Failure to take account of tax benefits passed to the purchaser of a bank may have serious negative consequences for the net cost of each type of transaction.

this subscription was opened to existing shareholders,[20] while the second round was opened to general public. After privatization, the new owner of the bank is free to maximize value from the provisioned assets, with the gains being a windfall profit from the transaction.

The transaction structure has positive features from the perspective of the State. If undertaken under conditions of competitive bidding, the purchaser is likely to incorporate some portion of his estimate of the liquidation value of the classified assets in the price paid for the bank. The State can influence the valuation of classified assets by improving the legal environment for work out operations. The State faces no post-privatization administrative demands to administer or oversee the liquidation of the classified assets; the purchaser is likely to move ahead as rapidly as possible with working out assets, thereby providing impetus to the process of enterprise restructuring. In the Czech case, post-privatization events, such as a change in the legal environment for work out operations may occur, providing potential windfall profits to the purchaser by improving the prospects for collecting classified assets. Finally, in this type of transaction purchasers require very extensive due diligence (as all risks are to be retained on balance sheet), slowing down the privatization process and increasing the chances of a single bidder negotiation.

A second option is a *Ring Fenced* privatization transaction which is structured so that either: (a) the classified assets of the bank remain on the balance sheet of the bank but under a State guarantee-the "ring fence"; or, (b) the classified assets are carved out of the bank in exchange for either cash, a State guaranteed security, or a combination of both. The purchaser of the bank may also receive the right to "put" additional assets which become classified during a defined time period to the seller. The transaction may also be structured with a "call" provision which allows the purchaser to buy back assets from the classified asset pool according to previously agreed pricing rules. In both cases, the bank purchaser receives a contract to manage the classified asset pool and is paid a management fee plus incentive fees to administer and work out the assets. If the transaction is structured using a State guarantee, rather than cash or interest bearing security, then the purchaser is also paid for the cost of funding the asset pool.

This transaction structure is attractive to investors in that it allows them to purchase the bank on a "clean" balance sheet basis. Although the classified assets may be held on balance sheet, the existence of a State guarantee results in a nil capital weight; the fees arising from management of the classified assets may provide a substantial source of income to enhance the profitability of the post-privatization bank. From the perspective of the State, the structure may prove attractive in several ways. The potential use of a government security or guarantee allows a reduced initial cash outlay. The State retains beneficial ownership of the classified assets and thus captures the benefit (net of costs and incentive payments) of any value realized from them. The bank purchaser cannot capture windfall profits from these assets. If the incentives in the asset management contract are structured correctly, the State will receive the benefit of private sector asset management skills and significantly higher net proceeds from liquidation than if it attempted to carry out this activity by itself.

However, the ring fence structure also carries risks. The incentives incorporated in an asset management contract are extremely complex. If incentives are incorrectly structured, the State may find itself paying substantial fees to an asset manager pursuing a "do nothing" strategy. The incorporation of asset put and call features requires the State to maintain the technical ability to challenge puts and correctly value calls. In the event that errors are made in the structuring of either of these features, the bank purchaser may be able to either engage in risk-free speculation, or capture the economic benefit of improvements in external circumstances at the State's expense. The asset management contracts normally require the State to maintain an institutional structure designed to (and capable of) defending its

---

[20] Before the subscription started in August 1998, Nomura International publicly announced in May, that it would not participate in it.

interests during the life of the asset management contract, which may be several years. Where the classified assets are retained under guarantee on the bank's balance sheet, substantial tax benefits may accrue to the purchaser which need to be addressed via a synthetic tax estimation agreement. Finally, this type of transaction structure is complex and requires a seller with a strong base of experienced professional staff (or with access to such staff) to administer successfully.

A third option is a *Carve Out Privatization.* This transaction structure is similar to the "ring fence" concept with key exceptions that the bank's classified assets are purchased by the State in exchange for cash or securities. The carved out assets are then placed under the management of an independent contractor. The contractor works under a well structured incentive contract which is designed to align his interests with the interests of the asset owner (the State) and to encourage the highest net present value for the pool. The bank purchaser receives no special call rights on these assets (but is free to purchase them on an arms length basis from the independent -- and unrelated -- asset management contractor). Asset puts may be incorporated into the bank privatization structure.

This type of transaction is attractive in that it eliminates many of the conflicts of interest which may arise under the ring fence structure. Provided the incentive structures for the asset management contractors are well designed, administrative oversight can be limited (the asset manager's interests are the same as the owner's) in scope. In Czech circumstances, the carve out arrangement may also be susceptible to extension to the assets of the transformation institutions.

In May 1999, the government approved an enterprise revitalization program, supported by a creation of the Revitalization Agency. The program will include the carve-out of debts (recapitalization and/ or debt restructuring) held by the KB, CS and KoB, with a renowned international investment bank as the administrator of the Agency. While the final details are still under development, Banks are expected to play an active role in the program.[21]

Reform of the Collateral and Bankruptcy Framework

Creditors in the Czech Republic face a legal environment which is hostile to their interests and which impedes effective debt workout and collection (bankruptcy and foreclosure). Problems exist, both in the current legislative framework, and in the ability of the courts to function as effective administrators of the law. This negative legal environment for creditors imposes significant direct and indirect costs on the economy, it reduces the corporate governance (discussed below), and it is likely to increase the cost of privatizing the remaining three large state-owned banks.

In the economy as a whole, a negative creditor environment increases credit risk for lenders; it distorts the supply of credit by negating the value of otherwise appropriate collateral for loans. Banks respond to the lack of acceptable (i.e., realizable) collateral in a number of ways: (a) by maintaining high lending spreads because every loan is de facto unsecured, and therefore high risk; (b) by requiring alternative forms of collateral (e.g., cash) which raise the effective cost of borrowing without directly impacting the loan spread; and (c) by refraining from lending to certain sectors where collateral based lending cannot be avoided (e.g., commercial real estate transactions).

The impact of these collateral and bankruptcy law derived distortions in lending behavior is significant. More "difficult" forms of finance (e.g., loans to facilitate enterprise restructuring) become simply unavailable because the risk of default cannot be offset by a reasonable probability of recovery from collateral or bankruptcy. Asset prices tend to fall due to a lack of liquidity in the markets, increasing

---

[21] See the enterprise sector chapter for further details of the revitalization program.

banking losses.[22] Even for good borrowers, financing costs are higher either as a result of higher rates (because all loans are unsecured) or because of the limited types of collateral acceptable in this environment. Moreover, capital investment is reduced as enterprises must now self-finance investments such as machinery.

Laws on Collateral and Foreclosure

In the Czech Republic, it is recognized that liens on real property of all types are basically unenforceable without the consent of the debtor. Problems in the existing law on collateral thus fall into four main areas: (a) the lack of an effective lien enforcement system to prevent debtors from selling or transferring non-real estate collateral for their own benefit; (b) lack of an effective foreclosure procedure for all types of collateral; (c) lack of a registration system for liens to maintain debtors' claims; and (d) the delays and court costs attendant upon court procedures.

A law on extra-judicial auctions has been drafted. It is now in the discussion stage (but not yet submitted to Parliament), with the objective of passage towards the end of 1999. The proposed law would provide for the timely seizure and sale of collateral without the consent of the debtor. Creditor claims would be prioritized according to the date of each lien and subordinated to tax arrears on the date of the first lien (thus enabling creditors to fix the tax liability against the collateral for credit analysis purposes). The process of foreclosure would be initiated by a creditor after a debtor defaults on an obligation by means of a filing with an auctioneer licensed for this purpose. The proposed law represents a significant step forward and should greatly improve both the speed and the effectiveness of the foreclosure process.

Bankruptcy Law

The Czech bankruptcy law (revised in 1991 and in April 1998) suffers from problems in three main areas: (a) the court-driven process is extremely slow and expensive; (b) creditors have little voice in the bankruptcy proceedings, making creditor-driven or "Chapter 11" style debt restructuring very difficult;[23] and (c) it results in extremely low recoveries as a result of the two preceding factors.[24]

Although a comprehensive new bankruptcy law is envisaged, it is still in the conceptualization stage. The structure of the present law, which focuses on liquidation, is not optimal for restructuring enterprise debtors (where the value of a firm normally deteriorates sharply if it ceases to be operated as a going concern). Given the large number of enterprises which are potential bankruptcy candidates, inclusion in the new legislation of provisions to permit Chapter 11-style bankruptcy[25] and a provision to facilitate debtor in possession lending[26] may both be appropriate. Moreover, the capacity of the courts to handle bankruptcy work must be strengthened. Consideration should be given to the creation of specialist courts to handle this type of business, and to the implementation of effective training programs for bankruptcy judges and court officials.[27]

---

[22] The value of assets such as commercial real estate is the present value of net cash flow. Thus, as the proportion of price which can be financed falls as a result of lenders refusing to lend, so a higher proportion of the discount rate is made up of the required return on equity (normally higher than the interest rate on borrowings), and asset value falls.
[23] The bankruptcy process is essentially a liquidation by means of periodic auctions of assets.
[24] CNB op cit. says that a recovery rate of 5 percent after 5 years is representative.
[25] This type of bankruptcy (common in the United States) normally involves a restructuring agreed upon by a qualified majority of creditors who then receive bankruptcy court certification to make the agreement binding on all unsecured creditors and the debtor itself.
[26] This type of credit is designed to keep a company in bankruptcy proceeding in going concern status. The creditor receives first preference protection as an inducement to make a high risk loan of this type.
[27] World Bank (1999), Czech Republic Capital Market Review.

Credit Information

In the Czech Republic, there is no separate Bank Secrecy Act. Bank secrecy is regulated by Article 38 of Act on Banks and by some other Acts, especially by the Act to Prevent Money Laundering. The second Amendment of Act on Banks, which came into force in 1998, removed the legal barriers preventing the exchange of information among banks. According to the Article 38a, "banks may provide each other with information on the bank connection, identification of account holders and matters testifying to the financial standing and credibility of their client, even through a legal entity which is not a bank." The ad hoc exchange of information exists, and in some individual cases of large debtors banks now co-ordinate their policies. However, banks have not yet reached the agreement on establishing a general and systematically actualized credit information database, largely due to strong competition. For example, banks with well developed retail banking franchise are not prepared to share information with banks whose franchise is in this respect less developed.

While corporations are required to enter significant facts and events in the commercial court register, the process is slow; given the lack of enforcement and penalties, it is essentially voluntary. Publicly-traded companies are subject to Securities and Exchange Commission disclosure requirements, but for many companies these requirements are not applicable. A final adverse factor is that the tax authorities are not required to make publicly available information regarding specific tax liens.[28]

One impact of making credit information freely available is that it allows lenders to operate in a more transparent environment which greatly reduces the risks, and hence the risk premium that must be paid by borrowers. A number of measures to improve credit information include: (a) extensively revising bank secrecy provisions to allow the operation of credit bureaus; (b) establishing a publicly-accessible electronic database of tax liens; and (c) enforcing criminal penalties on the management of borrowers for failing to disclose material information in credit applications.

Development of Banking Regulation and Supervision

Banking Act

The basic thrust of the Banking Act and its subsequent amendments has been to harmonize Czech banking law and regulation with that of the European Union. It is expected that a comprehensive and fully harmonized banking law will be introduced in 2000 to replace the existing law. The Banking Act (and its subsequent amendments) places the powers of banks firmly in the universal bank model adopted in much of Western Europe. Banks and branches of foreign banks operate within a system of universal banking and may carry on both commercial banking and investment banking activities. However, the banking license granted to an individual bank or branch of a foreign bank may restrict the scope of its banking activities, especially the scope of its foreign exchange operations.[29] Banks are allowed to

---

[28] The tax authorities are required to disclose the existence of a tax debt (Act 337/1992) but: (a) only at the request of the debtor; and (b) are not required to disclose the existence of liens.

[29] The law (Act on Banks, Act on Building Savings Banks, etc.) together with the banking licenses and statutes of individual banks may also determine the particular profile of the banking activities of each individual bank. This can be done through restrictions on the scope of its banking activities, the setting of a special objective for the bank derived from the public interest, or through a license to offer special products supported by a state contribution or guarantee. Such banks are specialized banks operating within the system of universal banking. Therefore, the Czech banking sector consists of several types of banks. First, banks and branches of foreign banks which, by the scope of their activities, can be characterized as universal banks. Second, banks with special products and services profile, namely: KoB (established to administer long-term poorly performing state claims); Czech-Moravian Credit and

internalize the insurance business, the business of investment funds as well as the business of pension funds through their subsidiaries. A bank must not perform control (defined in accordance with 89/646/EEC Directive) over a legal entity other then banks, financial institutions or enterprises of auxiliary services. Banks are allowed to invest in non-financial companies, however a bank's qualifying holding (defined in accordance with 89/646/EEC Directive) in such a legal entity should not exceed 15 percent of the bank's capital in a single legal entity, or a total of 60 percent of the bank's capital in the sum of all legal entities.

The Banking Act was amended twice in 1998. The first ("small") amendment became effective in January 1998 and was directed at resolving problems arising from the close inter-relationship between banks and enterprises. The banks have one year to divest direct or indirect controlling stakes in non-financial enterprises and three years to divest direct or indirect[30] controlling stakes in non-financial enterprises representing more than 15 percent of a bank's capital. Moreover, members of bank managerial boards and bank employees are prohibited from being members of the boards of non-financial enterprises. The amendment also requires banks to separate their commercial and investment banking activities.[31] The small amendment also enhanced the powers of the CNB to handle banks in receivership by authorizing it to order a reduction in the nominal value of shares (allowing new shares to be issued at realistic prices for recapitalization purposes) and increased the deposit insurance ceiling to CZK300,000 per depositor.

The second ("large") amendment became effective in August 1998 and was directed at a more general harmonization of Czech banking law with the European Union by strengthening the supervisory powers of the CNB by imposing new obligations on the bank shareholders. It focused on eradicating the criminal ownership element, which had played a significant role in the development of the small bank crisis. Bank shares are now required to be held in registered, rather than bearer form. The CNB's approval is required for any stake in a bank exceeding the limit of 10, 20, 33 and 50 percent share in voting rights. The Act also set forth the duty to report to the CNB if a investors' stake is going to decline below these levels. The CNB is empowered to remove the voting rights of shares controlled by persons it considers unfit. Further provisions to strengthen bank governance were included in the amendment, including changes in the membership criteria for members of statutory bodies. These provisions now require the board of directors, i.e., managerial board, to be composed exclusively of bank executives, and the supervisory boards to be elected by shareholders rather than employees. Changes in the membership of these boards are now required to be reported to the CNB. The large amendment also expanded the CNB's oversight by enhancing its early intervention powers to allow the appointment of a receiver once a bank's capital falls below 2/3 of the regulatory minimum. It also required the court to decide on appointment of a receiver (i.e., on the removal of management) within 24 hours of a receipt of a request from the CNB. Finally, this amendment expanded the deposit insurance scheme to include corporations, as well as individuals, to increase deposit insurance ceiling to CZK400,000 per depositor, and to exclude bank insiders and money launderers from coverage.

Regulation

CNB regulations are modeled on both the Basle Committee's recommendations and European Union banking directives. The regulatory framework has undergone a process of gradual but continuous

---

Development Bank Ltd (established to support small and medium-sized private businesses); Czech Export Bank Ltd (export support bank); Building savings banks, and mortgage banks.
[30] Indirect control exercised through bank-owned investment funds cumulated with bank owned (directly-owned) shares.
[31] The amendment also included a more general provision to require securities traders to meet standards of professional care directed at halting the practice of tunneling (asset stripping).

evolution since the adoption of the Banking Act in 1992, as regulations are brought into line with international best practice. In 1997, a total of eight prudential regulations were in effect. Most of these aimed at covering credit risk, which currently represents the principal risk in the Czech banking sector. Regulations covering credit risk include those on capital adequacy, credit exposures, and credit classification and provisioning. Other regulations cover liquidity and market risks, including those governing the foreign exchange positions of banks, and investment in securities. A September 1997 regulation has improved reporting requirements (both public and prudential returns). The amendment of regulation on credit classification and creation of provisions, effective in August 1998, has forced banks to recognize high risk related with securing of loans by real estate in current legal environment by requiring banks to progressively provide against the portion of classified loans secured by real estate over three years. During the same year, a special regulation on year 2000 issue came into force. Finally, new regulations are being prepared to incorporate market risk in the calculation of a bank's capital adequacy and to mandate banking supervision on a consolidated basis.

Bank Supervision

The supervisory responsibilities of the CNB and the basic regulatory framework were established by the Act on the Czech National Bank and the Banking Act, both effective from January 1993. Under this legislation, the CNB was mandated to supervise commercial banks along with its monetary policy responsibilities, and was made independent of the Government (reporting directly to Parliament).

The CNB's bank supervision activities are carried out through the bank supervision department reporting to a responsible member of the CNB board. The supervisory approach focuses on the use of a balanced on- and off-site activity. The bank supervision function has been reorganized a number of times, most recently in June of 1998, in line with the general reorganization of the CNB. The bank supervision division has 87 positions, 47 of which are assigned to off-site and on-site inspectors.[32] Supervisory staff are organized into five sections, four to handle day-to-day supervision and one to handle conservatorships and receiverships. Regulatory affairs (preparation and analysis of regulations) are handled by a separate division within the bank supervision department.

Despite the seemingly adequate number of positions within the bank supervision division, the CNB's lack of external training assistance[33] has contributed to the slow development of effective bank supervision. At the present time, only two examination teams are fully functional, with the remaining two expected to be operational by mid-1999. To offset this weakness, the CNB has adopted a strategy of regular meetings (at least three times per year) with the external auditors of the banks, who are now required to audit prudential returns as well as statutory financial statements. The CNB intends to focus as much of its resources on carrying out on-site inspections as possible in the future. As the ability of the CNB to identify and regulate risk improves, consideration could also be given to developing minimum capital requirements for banks, which reflect their overall risk profile. Consideration should also be given to assigning a composite supervisory rating to each bank for purposes such as the prioritization of supervision and determining deposit insurance premium levels.

The supervisory strategy adopted by the CNB calls for developing consolidated supervision of financial institutions (in line with BIS and European Union practice). A major step towards

---

[32] A team which really performs examination in a bank is based on on-site team, however, includes also at least an inspector whose responsibility is off- site surveillance of the examined bank. When necessary, this team is strengthened by other inspectors as well as by IT specialists. The other employees are managers, specialists and clerical staff.

[33] Caused at least in part by the rigidity of legislation on Bank Secrecy Act which makes the types of technical assistance provided to bank supervisors in other countries difficult to implement.

implementing this strategy was taken in November of 1998 by signing a cooperation agreement between the Securities and Exchange Commission, the Ministry of Finance, and the CNB. The agreement allows for information sharing between the institutions, for operational cooperation, and for joint development of regulations. However, implementation of consolidated supervision is likely to continue to be hampered at the operational level due to the restrictions of the Bank Secrecy Act, which limits the ability to share information. Considerable duplication of effort is likely to be one result of this constraint; this is an area where amending legislation to allow the free flow of information between regulators would prove useful.

The CNB is committed to addressing remaining gaps in the regulatory framework in areas where there is, as yet, no full compliance with Core Principles for Effective Banking Supervision developed under the leadership of the Basle Committee for Banking Supervision. These include: systems which measure, monitor, and control market risks; supervision on a consolidated basis; verification of the existence of complex risk management in banks; enhancement of the chart of accounts and accounting principles; and establishment of regular contacts and exchange of information with supervisory bodies in other countries. Progress in these areas is important for the preparation of the negotiations for accession to the EU. Recently, on June 17, 1999, Bank Board of the CNB approved the "provision on capital Adequacy incorporating credit and market risk", coming into force on April 1, 2000. Through implementation of this provision, which requires the banks to cover with capital not only credit risk but also market risk, the Czech regulation will make essential step to reach full compatibility with international standards.

Recommendations for the Banking Sector

Now that the Czech banking reform program has gained momentum and is addressing the key shortcomings in the sector, it is important to minimize any risk that it would be derailed by the possibly high short-term cost of certain elements of the reform. Many bank privatizations in transition economies involve costs arising from cleaning up the banks' balance sheets that are far in excess of any income from the sale of the bank. Therefore, the objective of the bank privatization process should be to minimize the net cost to the State of the privatization viewed as a whole.

Acceleration of Legal Reforms

In the Czech context, the legal environment is a powerful external variable which impacts the net cost of privatization transactions. If the Government acts quickly to alter the legal conditions surrounding the seizure and sale of collateral and the bankruptcy process, the value of the classified assets of both CS and KB could be increased significantly, with equally significant potential benefits to the post-privatization owner of those assets.

To demonstrate the costs to the Government -- and the potential benefits if the legislative timetables for corrective measures were to be sharply accelerated -- a simple example using the classified assets of CS and KB can be used to illustrate the absolute sums involved. Using very modest assumptions regarding possible recoveries as a result of early adoption of the new law on extra-judicial auctions, produces fiscally significant results. Improving collections on substandard, doubtful and loss assets to 40 percent, 30 percent, and 20 percent, respectively, produces potential savings (or increased revenues) of about CZK28.7 billion for the two banks. The actual benefits resulting from improved asset prices, as a result of the restoration of liquidity to commercial and other real estate markets, may prove to be significantly greater.

In view of the importance of this law to the economy, and the Government's direct financial interest in its implementation (both for tax collection and bank privatization purposes), consideration should be given to placing the legislation on a much-accelerated timetable. Similarly, consideration should be given to accelerating the timetable for adoption of a new bankruptcy law.[34]

Administration of the Privatization Process

The bank privatization process is administered by a steering committee composed of representatives of the NPF, the Ministry of Finance, and CNB. The committee supervises the activities of those investment banks retained to act as financial advisers to the NPF, it receives recommendations from the investment banks, and, in turn, it makes recommendations to the Minister of Finance. The final decisions regarding the privatization process are made by the Government. The placing of the steering committee within the Ministry of Finance is logical given the expenditures that are likely to be associated with the privatization process. The breadth of institutions involved in the committee is also useful in giving the various constituencies involved in privatization a voice in the proceedings and in producing consensus.

Given the likely technical complexity of the CS and KB privatizations, to contain costs it may help to retain the services of an outside adviser in order to enhance the committee's strengths. The adviser would provide support for analyzing the broader implications of the bank-specific recommendations made by the banks' financial advisers. This may be particularly useful given the other obligations of committee members.

Pre-privatization Governance of the State Banks

While the management of both KB and CS is moving ahead with plans to improve the banks' performance in the pre-privatization period, the length of the periods involved (perhaps up to 12 months for CS, possibly up to 24 months for KB) indicates that a more structured governance framework would be useful to ensure that the time available to improve the banks is used to the greatest advantage, and to ensure that new asset quality problems do not have an impact on either the cost or pace of privatization.

The Czech Commercial Code follows the German model and establishes a two-tier board structure including a management board and a supervisory board for joint stock companies including the banks. The management board is responsible for day-to-day management, and the supervisory board for monitoring compliance with the law. Although the Commercial Code makes it possible for the company by-laws to empower the supervisory boards to appoint and remove members of the management board, few companies apply this option. For this reason, the role of the supervisory board in monitoring the board of directors is limited. In other countries, using similar German inspired legislation, the powers of the supervisory boards of state-owned or controlled banks have been strengthened by using the owner's power to amend bank statutes and by being willing to confront management resistance to necessary supervision and control.

A number of additional steps could be taken to improve bank governance in the pre-privatization period. The NPF or the supervisory boards could retain advisers to assist them in defining targets for placing the banks on a time-bound program of operational and asset quality improvement and by monitoring the achievement of each bank's operational restructuring program. The governance structure of the banks could be amended to ensure that credit decisions and the effectiveness of controls are

---

[34] There have been concerns that calculations of possible recoveries of CS and KB classified assets might be too optimistic, especially since the existing government's bill on the law on extra-judicial auctions does not completely meet the expectations: it contains some articles, which in many cases effectively protect the debtor against the extra-judicial auction. For example, according to the bill it would not be possible to put an enterprise as a whole in the auction, since an enforceable court decision would be necessary to start auction, which is a very lengthy procedure.

monitored Given the scope for improvement in the banks' performance, relatively small investments in good governance could bring large benefits by the time the banks are privatized.

Recovery of Assets of Transformation Institutions

In the Czech Republic, large amounts of classified assets are in State hands in the transformation institutions. Consideration should be given to how to structure the work out arrangements of these assets in a way which maximizes recovery, for example, by selling the assets or by contracting the work out to appropriately incentivate independent contractors. There should be a clear separation of functions between the economic development role which is currently delegated to KoB and the handling of the non-performing assets of this bank. Development banking activities should be clearly brought under the supervision of CNB. The workout function should be wound down as rapidly as possible.

Capital Market Development[35]

Introduction

The overreliance on the banking sector to provide credit to enterprises in the Czech Republic raises questions on the role of capital markets in the enterprise restructuring and, consequently, in industrial production growth. In the bank-based systems, such as Germany or Japan, the enterprises are usually highly leveraged and establish significant links to the respective banks, which can become active shareholders and influence the decision-making in the enterprises. By contrast, in the market-based systems, such as the United States, the enterprises are more likely to access funds on the capital markets, which can perform an important role in improving corporate governance and the overall performance of the enterprises. In the Czech Republic, where the banking sector has currently been restructuring and consolidating, the latter model of capital market development presents a crucial counterpart to the banking sector reform, with both of them aiming to improve enterprise performance.

At the beginning of the transition period in the early 1990s, the Czech Republic performed better than other transitional countries. An innovative voucher privatization program enabled the fast privatization of a large number of enterprises. However, the regulatory framework for enterprises and capital market institutions contained flaws that ultimately hindered the efficiency gains expected from privatization. Moreover, as already shown, there was much less progress in privatizing the state banks, and in setting up a functional mechanism for the resolution of bad debts. These deficiencies help explain the mixed restructuring record and low growth performance.

The designers of the voucher program were aware that a pure distribution of vouchers would lead to both fragmented ownership and weak corporate governance. In order to combine fast privatization with a rapid improvement in corporate governance, investment funds were introduced, and the regulatory framework in the capital market was designed so as to facilitate secondary trading and the consolidation of ownership (see Box 7.2). Secondary trading in shares led effectively to a consolidation of ownership by funds and strategic investors. The greater concentration of ownership was a positive development, as the presence of large shareholders is one of the essential components of a sound governance system. However, ownership concentration was not complemented by other elements essential for sound corporate governance.

---

[35] This section draws heavily from the World Bank (1999) Czech Republic Capital Market Review.

Box 7.2. Capital Market Development in the Czech Republic

⇒   Market capitalization of 30.1 percent of GDP (bond market capitalization of 10.5 percent of GDP); Turnover of 34.7 percent of GDP; Turnover/Capitalization ratio of 115.6 percent (all end-1997), Price/Earnings Ratio of 12.2 percent, but figures not realistic:
•   Multiple counting and non-transparent transactions;
•   Public ownership of important enterprises not traded (12 percent of GDP);
•   Adjustments to market capitalization ratio: 13.7 percent of GDP;
•   P/E ratios of small- and medium-sized firms between 1-3 percent due to the low profitability, and low demand for purchase of minority shares due to lack of adequate disclosure, weak minority shareholder protection, and take-over obstacles.
⇒   Multiplicity of channels: the Prague Stock Exchange trading (PSE), RM-System trading, and off-exchange broker trading (settlement through the PSE's Univyc subsidiary), while private off-market trading prohibited since mid-1997:
•   PSE and Univyc account for 89.8 percent of trading;
•   Total off-market trading of 43.5 percent (mid-1998);
•   Different pricing across marketplaces (in March 1998, 50-100 percent premium on stock shares on the off-market, comparing to the official PSE).
⇒   Number of traded securities: 2179 end-1997 (about 1,700 companies privatized through the voucher scheme, and 400 investment funds and unit trusts).

Investment Funds
Established to create ownership concentration as part of the voucher privatization.
⇒   After April 1992, proliferation of management companies (200) managing about 600 funds:
•   Weak corporate governance: Management companies (banks in some cases) have incentives to realize gains related to insider deals and fraud instead of fee of 2 percent of new asset value of each fund (by law);
•   Investment funds collected vouchers with the value of shares of 12 percent of GDP;
•   Investment privatization funds (IPF) (closed) collected 80 percent of vouchers, closed mutual funds 12 percent, and opened mutual funds 8 percent.
⇒   Investment Fund Act (July 1996) improved disclosure provisions, and applied stricter rules regarding conversion of funds into holding companies to escape regulatory control:
•   77 funds converted into holding companies before the Act took effect (or 131 funds by 1998), representing 25 percent of total investment fund assets (3 percent of GDP); fraud continued, their shares trading stopped, and their prices collapsed.
⇒   Current situation: 112 management companies, 105 IPFs, 86 closed unit trusts, 145 open unit trusts:
•   High discount rates for the fund shares: 67 percent over net asset value for IPFs, and 78 percent for closed-end trusts.
⇒   New amendments to the Investment Fund Act (July 1998): mandatory openings of all existing funds (by end 2002):
•   Allowed to hold 11 percent of company's equity (reduced from 20 percent);
•   Real estate investment allowed;
•   Creation of independent Securities Commission tasked with supervision of funds.

Pension Funds
44 supplementary pension funds (with a state contribution) were authorized, but during 1998 the number declined to 30, expected to fall to 20 or 15:
•   1.72 contributors in the third quarter of 1998, or 35 percent of labor force;
•   around 3 percent of own wage contribution, of which 28 percent is contributed by the state;
•   assets of funds of 1.3 percent of GDP (end 1997);
•   5 largest funds account for 60 percent of participants and client funds.

Insurance Companies
⇒   40 insurance companies (end 1997) plus the State Health Insurance Company:
•   State-owned Ceska Pojistovna converted into a joint-stock company, with a dominant market share of nearly 60 percent;
•   18 companies operate as universal insurance companies, 18 specialize in non-life insurance, and 4 in life business; one universal company changed into a non-life company in 1998;
•   19 companies have no foreign ownership participation, 14 have foreign participation, and 7 are foreign-owned or controlled;
•   There is no local reinsurance company, although the largest three domestic companies are authorized to act as active reinsurers;
•   Total premiums in GDP (1997) accounted for 2.9 percent (EU average 6 percent), of which life premiums 0.8 percent (EU average 3.1 percent), and non-life premiums 2.1 percent (EU average 2.9 percent);
•   Entry of large European companies stimulated competition, innovation and efficiency;
•   Legal monopolies in some segments exist; smaller companies financially weak and may be insolvent;
•   Restructuring needed, especially moving from traditional substantive approach to insurance regulation, and emphasizing prudential and solvency monitoring approach.

Source: Czech National Bank and The World Bank.

The traditional market indicators overestimate the size and liquidity of the Czech capital market. After correcting for problems of multiple counting and special factors related to the voucher privatization program of 1993/94, the tradable equity market is found to be only half of the total, to have been a negligible source of finance for industrial enterprises, and to remain illiquid for all but a handful of shares. The traditional price indicators suggest that securities are correctly valued and that the equity prices are to some extent integrated with international equity markets. However, these indicators do not capture the divergence of security prices across different marketplaces.

The finding that the market is moderately sized relative to GDP and that liquidity is still low should come as no surprise, as the market has been operating for only five years. A more fundamental problem is the absence of transparency in pricing and inadequate corporate disclosure. It undermines confidence in securities as a medium of investment, distorts credit assessment and the valuation of savings intermediaries, and may also pervert the allocation of risk capital.

The unreliability in pricing in the last few years reflects the exploitation, by fund and enterprise managers, of flaws in the regulatory and supervisory framework, as well as the fragmented structure and organization of the securities market. Secondary trading was frequently conducted in a non-transparent way, involving fraudulent transactions by fund and enterprise managers. The transfer of assets at the expense of fund shareholders was facilitated by the closed-end structure of most funds, weaknesses in the regulatory framework, lax supervision, and the multiplicity of trading channels. The perception of widespread fraud was ultimately reflected in the low prices of fund shares, which were almost fully discounted in the case of funds converted into holding companies. Although many individuals may have at the end obtained some return from these vouchers (acquired at a symbolic cost), this return was far below the expectations generated by the program, and tarnished the image of capital market institutions in general.

Moreover, these developments also led to the creation of a distorted environment for the emergence of corporate governance. Namely, ownership concentration through investment funds did not necessarily imply the emergence of strong governance. Investment funds do not seem to have performed well their governance role, as indicated by the evidence that enterprises primarily controlled by investment funds restructured less than enterprises controlled by strategic investors. Even in the case of the latter enterprises, there are many cases where the new controlling shareholder has exercised control for personal gain, at the expense of the financial health of the enterprise and the interests of minority shareholders. Finally, the external mechanisms of governance, such as the financial sector and legal framework, remained weak during the post-privatization years. The major banks remained subject to political influence, suffered from a weak capital base, while legal framework was not adequately developed (for example, foreclosure and bankruptcy laws).

Recent Efforts to Strengthen the Capital Market Regulatory Framework

The Government reacted to the emergence of problems in the capital market by strengthening the regulatory framework in several steps. In 1996, several amendments to the Commercial Code and the Investment Fund Act were introduced. These amendments improved disclosure and minority shareholder protection rules, and prevented a further conversion of investment funds into holding companies. However, it became apparent in 1997 that these amendments were insufficient to significantly improve governance of investment funds and to arrest fraud. For this reason, new amendments were drafted in 1997 and enacted in 1998. They included amendments to the Act on Banks, the introduction of an autonomous Securities Exchange Commission, and amendments to the Investment Fund Act:

The amendments to the Act on Banks attempt to minimize conflicts of interest which may arise when banks are creditors and owners at the same time, by introducing more restrictive board rules and investment rules (discussed above).

The creation of a Securities Commission outside the Ministry of Finance is another very important step towards a sound capital market. Although the new Commission does not yet enjoy full regulatory independence (the regulations have to be issued as Government Decrees), it has substantial enforcement power, and has proved the willingness to use it in the first months of operation.

The new Investment Fund Act has introduced radical changes in the capital market, by mandating the opening of all investment funds within a period of three years. This change is justified by the poor performance of these funds and the need to rebuild confidence in capital market institutions. The opening will allow better exit opportunities for a large number of individual investors, will eliminate the weakest institutions, and will generally improve fund management, because under-performers will, for the first time, face the threat of net redemptions.

In addition to these changes, the Government is also preparing improvements in the regulatory framework for pension funds and insurance companies that may significantly affect the way these institutions operate, and could have a positive impact in the overall efficiency of the capital market. The central question faced by Czech policy-makers is whether these changes will enable the capital market to perform all its functions efficiently and contribute to the development of the Czech economy.

Gaps in the Regulatory and Institutional Framework for the Capital Market

The Securities Market. Despite the initial impression that may be given by the traditional indicators of size and liquidity, the Czech capital market has effectively a moderate size, has been a negligible source of finance, and is largely illiquid, except for a small number of traded shares. The traditional price indicators are also misleading and do not capture the divergence of security prices across different marketplaces. While the increase in market size and liquidity can be seen as long-term goals, the lack of price integrity undermines confidence in securities as a medium of investment, it distorts credit assessment and the valuation of financial intermediaries, and it perverts the allocation of risk capital.

The achievement of price integrity will require further progress on two parallel tracks. The Commission must continue improving the regulatory framework and must strengthen its enforcement capacity, as most of the fraudulent operations with securities have been breaches of existing laws. Improvements in regulation and enforcement should be accompanied by parallel improvements in the organization of the market. Market regulators have to face the failure of the Prague Stock Exchange (PSE) and RM-System (RMS) to provide transparent trading systems (a consolidated price display, co-ordinate settlement and freedom in order-routing) and to assure unified pricing. The schism in settlement facilities also inhibits arbitrage between markets, increases overhead costs and frustrates true delivery versus payment on share transactions.

Investment Funds. The mandatory opening of funds introduced by the new Investment Fund Act is a radical but a basically sound decision. However, more detailed guidelines to orient institutions during the opening process may still be lacking. The present regulatory framework is essentially adequate to guide the operations of open funds, but some deficiencies still remain, primarily in the area of pricing, taxation, and custodian services. Although there is a role for genuine venture capital funds exerting active governance, the regulatory framework may not allow these funds to emerge. The law allows new closed-end funds to be formed, but subjects them to the same regulation of open funds. Unless the regulatory framework is adapted, the new closed-end funds will not play the role of venture capital funds, and may draw little interest from investors.

Corporate Governance. Although the internal mechanisms of governance have been considerably improved since 1996, minority shareholder rights are still inadequate, corporate controllers are not fully accountable to shareholders, and the quality of financial reporting is not consistent across enterprises. Holding companies constitute a challenge, as they are still a collective investment vehicle, but have escaped the more stringent regulatory framework that applies to these institutions.

There is also wide scope to strengthen the external mechanisms of governance. Although one state bank was privatized in early 1998, another one in July 1999, the two largest state-owned commercial banks, awaiting privatization, still hold a very large amount of bad loans in their portfolios. Moreover, the rules on collateral and foreclosure as well as on the bankruptcy framework remain cumbersome (discussed above).

Finally, enforcement capacity needs to be strengthened. Although the introduction of a Securities Commission is a very important step towards stronger enforcement capacity, the Commission still has limited financial and regulatory independence; it still needs to implementa well-articulated training and institutional development program. Moreover, enforcement of the legal framework does not depend on the Commission alone: it also involves the police and the court system, both of which are poorly equipped to deal with commercial disputes and bankruptcy cases.

Pension Funds. The private pension sector suffers from a number of weaknesses. First, the institutions may fail to promote supplementary pensions, as they effectively offer short-term savings policies. Second, because the funds have a relatively short time horizon, they may not become providers of long-term resources and will contribute less effectively to capital formation and resource allocation. Third, participants are not required to save a minimum percentage of their earnings, thereby leading to a low average contribution and constraining the growth of the system. Fourth, there are no clear rules on accounting standards and information disclosure, and no guidelines on advertising. As a result, the system is opaque, and the public cannot make informed decisions. Finally, the supervisory function is very weak, and appears to focus on ensuring that no participant receives multiple state contributions, thereby overlooking the importance of prudent and transparent policies. The Ministry of Finance prepared a perceptive analysis of the current system, and the Government has already drafted various amendments to the Pension Fund Law that address several of the problems identified above.

Insurance Companies. The main weaknesses of the current situation are the presence of financially weak companies, the feeble enforcement of the prudential provisions of existing legislation, the continuing monopoly of some basic classes of business, and the continuing approval requirement of general policy conditions. The requirement for prior supervisory approval discourages innovation as well as the introduction into the Czech market of insurance contracts that meet specialized needs and have been successfully launched in other more advanced countries. Future amendments to insurance legislation have already been proposed.

Policy Recommendations

Securities Market

The broad objectives of the Commission for the security market should be to restrict the number of publicly tradable companies (to those that really fit this profile and those that may benefit from open access to the capital market), to integrate the different trading channels, and to ensure compliance with the regulatory framework, while also proposing and implementing further improvements in legislation.

These actions would ensure the achievement of price convergence, increase market liquidity, restore confidence, and open more possibilities for new equity issues.

The reduction in the number of publicly tradable companies would be naturally achieved if the controlling shareholder is induced to buy the shares of stranded minority shareholders and transform the company into a privately-held company. This could be achieved by strengthening the enforcement of the existing rules and by introducing further improvements in the internal mechanisms of governance, particularly in the area of minority shareholder protection. These two sets of actions would make it costly to remain public and would encourage several firms to change their legal status. The reduction in the number of tradable shares would "clean the market," thereby allowing the Commission to supervise fewer companies more effectively, and would contribute to more transparency in trading.

The measures required to improve the regulatory framework and the enforcement of the trading rules would include: (i) reviewing the jurisdiction of the Securities Commission, particularly in relation to its powers over the Stock Exchange; (ii) incorporating conduct of business rules for the protection of investors, as required by the Investment Services Directive; (iii) introducing a better compliance regime by attaching an audit trail so that trading operations can be exposed to regulatory inspection; (iv) developing procedures for criminal prosecution for those who dishonestly misappropriate corporate or fund assets; (v) applying administrative sanctions available to the Commission, for reprimand, fine, or suspension of license; and (vi) exploring the self-regulatory powers of the Stock Exchange, to allow for summary treatment of complaints against member firms and provision for restitution of profits arising from misconduct.

The measures that would deal with market fragmentation and contribute to a better market structure would include: (i) establishing the universal clearing center; (ii) requiring facilities for order routing which ensure that investors obtain best execution, and prohibiting "cross-listing" on more than one organized market when this is not possible; (iii) enforcing timely and comprehensive price disclosure, both pre-trade and post-trade; (iv) enforcing comprehensive disclosure by issuers, in accordance with a strict interpretation of the disclosure requirements of the Securities Law; (v) providing guidance to publicly traded companies on notifiable events and appropriate information release to events of varying importance; and (vi) establishing quality of market monitoring for breadth, depth and liquidity of the market and quality of price discovery.

Investment Funds

Managing the Opening of Investment Funds. The Securities Commission should ensure an orderly opening process and a fair treatment of investors during the opening. This would include: (i) issuing guidelines clarifying the different stages of the opening process; (ii) allowing the temporary suspension of redemptions in situations of illiquidity and issuing guidelines for the execution of outstanding requests at the same price; (iii) retaining exit opportunities during the temporary suspension by allowing secondary trading; (iv) providing temporary regulatory forbearance during the opening, and (v) providing standardized texts for articles of association and prospectuses to facilitate the transition from closed to open funds.

Improve Pricing Rules by: (i) replacing historical pricing by forward pricing; (ii) granting some leeway for managers to price securities issued by enterprises in bankruptcy or not traded, subject to approval by the depository and the auditors; (iii) ensuring that there is single pricing of open fund shares, when the shares are also traded in secondary markets, by de-listing or mandating that the shares be negotiated at Net Asset Value (NAV) minus/plus a margin; and (iv) shortening the maximum period of redemption, or accruing interest on NAV to compensate for the delay.

Adjust the Regulatory Framework for Integration into the EU by: (i) obliging fund managers to publish detailed portfolio composition for all holdings; (ii) reducing the maximum holdings of individual equities, from 10 to 5 percent of a fund's net assets; (iii) strengthening the role of the depository; (iv) removing the tax disadvantage affecting Czech funds by exempting them from VAT, and by removing the taxation on income and capital gains (which implies double taxation); and (v) preparing regulations preventing abusive or fraudulent sales practices, and encouraging self-regulatory bodies to establish and enforce codes of conduct on their members.

Handle Holding Companies by: (i) improving the internal mechanisms of corporate governance for all joint stock companies along the lines suggested below; and (ii) imposing additional disclosure rules in the case of holding companies -- similar to those imposed on investment funds.

Open Space for Genuine Venture Capital Funds. Introduce separate investment guidelines for closed-end funds formed in the future, allowing them to hold much larger portions of equity and to exert active governance, subject to well-written prospectuses and articles of association.

Corporate Governance

Privatize Enterprises Still Controlled by the State, Mainly Banks and Utilities. Comprehensive regulatory reforms should be undertaken, thereby opening the ground for the privatization of utilities.

Strengthen Further Minority Shareholder Protection by: (i) reducing the threshold for shareholders to call a general meeting -- from 10 percent of the share capital to 5 percent, and to a still lower percentage for the largest companies; (ii) entitling any shareholder to obtain a full copy of the list of all shareholders of the company, upon request and payment of the costs; (iii) requiring any general meeting to include the participation of, not only large shareholders, but also a minimum proportion of the total number of shareholders; (iv) allowing cumulative voting to strengthen the influence of small shareholders in the board; (v) reducing the threshold at which large shareholders must offer to buy-out of minority shareholders, from 50 percent to 25-30 percent; (vi) requiring prior shareholder approval of "vulnerable" transactions such as those relating to the purchase or disposal of substantial assets; and (vii) encouraging proxy arrangements.

Clarify the Duties of Directors to the Company. The "bright-line" rules designed to ensure that directors are aware of their obligations would include: (i) a duty to act with diligence, and in what the director believes to be the best interests of the company; (ii) a duty to disclose to other directors any personal interest in a transaction to be entered into by the company and not to vote on that transaction; and (iii) a duty to ensure that the business of the company is not carried on in such a way as to create a substantial risk of loss to creditors. These duties should be enforceable by the company, or by any shareholder.

Improve Disclosure and the Quality of Information. (i) The Government should introduce the obligation to disclose consolidated financial statements and, especially, to enforce disclosure requirements; (ii) the Government should consider transferring the responsibility for setting accounting and auditing standards to independent and self-regulating bodies, although the Commission should retain the authority to impose supplemental reporting requirements; (iii) the removal of an external auditor should not be permitted, except with the prior approval of the shareholders voting at a general meeting; (iv) supervisory boards could be required to establish an audit committee, and the committee would oversee the internal audit function; it would meet periodically with the external auditors, and would propose to the general meeting the appointment or removal of the external auditors; and (iv) external auditors should owe a duty of care to both the company and the shareholders and should be able to be sued for negligence in the performance of their duties.

Improve Monitoring of Boards by Shareholders. Consider modifying the board system so that the supervisory board is elected by the shareholders, and the management board members are appointed or removed by the supervisory board.

Address the Problem of Holding Companies. All the measures proposed above to protect minority shareholders and to improve transparency would also benefit the minority shareholders of holding companies. Nonetheless, additional measures to deal with these companies are justified. Any company with more than a minimum number of shareholders (e.g., 100 shareholders), and with a substantial proportion of its assets invested in publicly tradable securities, should provide to its shareholders a level of disclosure that is comparable to that required for investment funds.

Address the Problem of Unit Trusts. Consider changes in order to allow investors to convene meetings and to remove the management company in the same manner as the shareholders of a company can remove a director and appoint a replacement. Management contracts should be terminable at any time by a suitable voting majority of investors in the fund.

Strengthen Enforcement Capacity. Further improvements to the independence of the Securities Commission would be desirable; the Commission would need to develop and implement an institutional development program, including substantial training, to develop the skills of its staff. Court judges and officials also need to receive training and resources in order to handle commercial disputes more efficiently.

Enhance the credibility and actual prospects of take-overs by entitling investors to obtain a full copy of the list of all shareholders of the company, upon request and payment of the costs. If this action is considered to violate shareholder privacy, the authorities should consider legal ways that would allow outsiders to ask for the shareholders' permission to reveal their identity and address in order to formulate a buyout offer. This communication could be carried out by the board of directors or the securities registrar.

Enhance the banks' capacity to handle problem debtors through the following measures: (i) privatizing the State banks as fast as possible, through sales to strategic investors; (ii) reviewing tax rules to allow a faster build-up of provisions already in the pre-privatization stage; and (iii) allowing the Konsolidacni Banka to auction its classified loans, or to outsource collection and restructuring in exchange for collection fee.

Streamline the bankruptcy process through the following measures: (i) improving the capacity of courts to decide whether or not to grant a bankruptcy petition;[36] (ii) enhancing the function of the administrator;[37] (iii) making the fee structure based on performance than is currently the case; (iv) allowing debtors suffering from liquidity difficulties to seek reorganization under court protection; (v) removing the obligation for debtors to demonstrate that a minimum proportion of liabilities will be

---

[36] The Act on Bankruptcy stipulates that if there is evidence that a debtor is insolvent and if other conditions required by the law are met too, the court is obliged to grant a bankruptcy petition, i.e., declare the debtor to be bankrupt and order to start bankruptcy procedure. There are numerous conditions to be met, however, these conditions are reasonable according to CNB. For example the court shall not grant bankruptcy petition if there is clear evidence that assets of debtors are insufficient to cover administrative costs of bankruptcy procedure, not to speak to at least partly honor creditor's claims. Another example is that a municipality cannot be declared bankrupt.
[37] The Act on Bankruptcy stipulates that an eligible person could be every fit and proper person with adequate skills (an accountant or a lawyer or also a person with managerial experience etc.), who has no special business or personal relation, which prevent his/her appointment in given individual case. Each court has the list of these persons, who can be appointed as the administrator.

able to be repaid, allowing debtors and creditors to develop any solution they think best preserves their interests; including swaps of debt for equity in restructured firms; and (vi) improving the courts' capacity to handle bankruptcy work, and creating specialist bankruptcy courts and training programs for bankruptcy judges and court officials.

Pension Funds

Measures that would Improve the Voluntary Private System without Changing its Basic Character. The Government should enact the amendments that have already been drafted, as these would greatly contribute to improving the regulatory framework for private pension funds. The amendments would: (i) require a minimum term of 36 months for pension contracts; (ii) increase the cut-off date for old age pensions from the current 50 to 55; (iii) raise the minimum capital of pension funds from CZK20 to 50 million; (iv) force pension funds to hire an independent bank as a depository; (v) require official approval of any significant transfer of shares of pension funds; (vi) allow pension funds to invest in bonds and equities listed in approved foreign markets (most or all OECD countries are expected to be approved); (vii) impose a fiduciary duty on pension fund managers; and (viii) allow the MoF to publish reports with information on individual pension funds obtained during the supervision process.

In addition to promptly enacting the amendments, the authorities should also consider implementing the following measures as soon as possible: (i) encouraging the merger process to ensure that small funds do not undermine the integrity of the whole system; (ii) creating an independent and well-staffed supervision agency; (iii) banning investments in illiquid securities and banning or severely restricting holdings of real estate assets; (iv) introducing mandatory solvency reserves; (v) requiring a separation of own funds from participant balances, defining the treatment of unrealized capital gains, and improving asset valuation rules; (vi) segregating the assets of participants from those of the founders, the asset managers, and custodial institutions; (vii) requiring the use of one authorized custodial institution; (viii) requiring either the use of licensed individual asset managers on a full-time basis, or the hiring of licensed companies as external asset managers; (ix) requiring a minimum size for pension funds to directly offer annuities, and subject annuity products to actuarial review; (x) requiring the distribution of statements to participants three or four times a year, and the provision of detailed data to the Supervision on a quarterly basis; and (xi) introducing standards on advertising, such as requiring disclosure of returns over a pre-specified set of terms and comparison with the sector. Note that most of these measures could be simply added to the amendments already drafted, and submitted to Parliament in a short period of time.

Measures that would Change the Character of the Voluntary Private System. The measures described above do not address some basic weaknesses of the current scheme, such as its short-term orientation and its functioning on endowment insurance principles. To address these problems, the regulators may consider the following changes: (i) formally linking the current scheme to retirement; (ii) imposing a minimum contribution of around 5 percent of income; (iii) redesigning the tax treatment of pension funds with a view to adopting the EET system, and lowering the State contribution; and (iv) considering a more structural move from the endowment insurance model to the mutual fund model.

Insurance Companies

The authorities are considering a number of amendments designed to strengthen the regulatory framework for the sector and to ensure much greater compliance with EU directives. These would include: (i) ending the issuance of new licenses to state-owned insurance companies; (ii) ending the licensing of universal insurers and limiting licensing to separate life, non-life and reinsurance subsidiaries; (iii) replacing the security deposit by minimum capital requirements; (iv) applying a "fit and proper" test on the founders, directors and senior officers of insurance companies; (v) eliminating the prior approval of policy conditions; (vi) spelling out in detail the content of business plans; (vii) applying the standard EU solvency margins, separated by life and non-life; (viii) introducing the "prudent man rule" for asset management; (ix) strengthening disclosure requirements; and notification of management changes; (x) eliminating the discriminatory treatment of brokers acting for a foreign insurance company; (xi) requiring the employment of an actuary and independent audits; and (xii) strengthening supervision.

The proposed amendments should be implemented without delay, as they would address most of the problems affecting the sector, and would bring the regulatory framework much closer to the EU directives.   The authorities should also consider the following additional measures: (i) abolishing monopolies in motor third party liability (MTPL) and workers' compensation (the problem caused by the inadequacy of reserves for MTPL could be handled by a one time transfer from the state budget, or by imposing a special tax on motor insurance); (ii) offering tax incentives for long-term life insurance (to be determined in conjunction with the redesign of the tax treatment of pension funds); (iii) strengthening consumer protection by the creation of an ombudsman office or similar body, and by promoting the use of insurance company ratings; and (iv) adapting regulation and supervision to the growing presence of financial conglomerates (this would require implementing the co-operation agreement between the central bank, the securities commission, and the insurance supervision department, and might also require amendments to the insurance, banking and securities legislation to allow the supervisory authorities from the three sectors to exchange information and co-operate between themselves and with supervisors in other countries).

Chapter VIII. Enterprise Sector Reform

Introduction

The Czech Republic's enterprise sector is going in 1998-99 through a difficult period which roots are entrenched in the policies chosen during the early years of the transition. While at the beginning of the transition, the Czech Republic seemed to got off to a very good start, such perception of a good beginning has soon been discarded when the first signs of reform deficiencies emerged in the mid-1990s. The macroeconomic imbalances behind the 1997 crisis served to highlight the deficiency in privatization design and microeconomic restructuring in the Czech Republic.

The mass privatization program implemented by the authorities in the early years of the transition was able to reallocate a large amount of property into private hands, it did not, however, help in introducing the needed fundamental changes in management behavior and corporate governance to a large and important segment of the enterprise sector. A sizable part of the privatization was leveraged, thus generating firms that had no capital and large debts. The voucher system, moreover, generated disperse ownership, thus given the de-facto command to managers, not to shareholders. This may have contributed to the narrow vision of some of the new owners and managers, which opted for short-term personal gains instead of long-term enterprise development.

The banking sector continued to be dominated largely by state banks, which did not play the role of efficient intermediation of financial resources. As a result, state banks did not impose the needed hard budget constraints on the enterprise sector. This behavior was compounded by the inability of legislative reforms to set the proper conditions for the use of market based solutions to enterprise restructuring. At the end, the symbiotic relationship between state banks and large conglomerates remained in place, limiting the incentives for deep restructuring. Weak corporate governance compounded the problem by allowing wages to grow above productivity increases, eroding competitiveness abroad.

In 1996 and 1997, a package of reforms attended to a number of the more costly policy errors and shortcomings, but there is still a great deal to be done in terms of enterprise and bank restructuring, improving productivity, and spreading the good practice seen in some Czech firms to a larger and wider number. The correct way forward is by pursuing and perfecting the reform path, which should mean completing the unfinished agenda in privatization, particularly of the banks, employing financial and policy mechanisms that will spur market-led restructuring, improving the regulatory and legal environment under which firm operate, and attending to those measures required to bring Czech industry in line with European Union (EU) requirements.

This chapter examines the industrial and manufacturing sectors in the Czech Republic. It describes their evolution since 1989, assesses their readiness to survive and thrive once the country becomes part of the EU, reviews how close Czech firms are to EU quality and environmental standards, and looks in some detail at two related areas of concern: the unfinished process of privatization, and the environment for attracting more FDI.

Macroeconomic Stability with Microeconomic Weaknesses

By the end of 1995, and indeed well into 1996, the general assessment was that the Czech Republic had successfully managed the transition from plan to market. Czechoslovakia had, in the past, been one of the most rigidly planned economies. Private sector output as a share of GDP was very low in 1990, at around 2 percent, which was on a par with that in the most statist portions of the communist world: Russia, Albania and Belarus[1]. But by 1995, the Czech Republic led all transition countries on this account, as private sector share in GDP approached 70 percent (it was almost 80 percent by the end of 1997). Extensive and rapid privatization accounted for much of this shift. Strong growth in new start-up companies, especially in the small and medium categories -- with a fair amount of this coming from foreign direct investment (FDI) -- accompanied privatization and contributed greatly to the explosive growth in private sector share, especially services.[2]

By 1994, unemployment exceeded 10 percent in all Central and Eastern Europe (CEE) -- except for the Czech Republic, which persistently recorded jobless rates of around 3 percent. There were several explanations about such low rate. One of them argued that labor costs expressed in dollar terms were low enough to prevent some of the painful lay-offs. However, such relative low costs were not unique to the Czech Republic, yet only the Czech unemployment rate remained at such a low level. While there was substantially more job turnover in the Czech Republic than in other CEE transition economies, observers also began to hypothesize that the unusually low rate of unemployment could not be totally explained by job creation in the private sector, nor by a flexible labor market as demonstrated by the explosive growth of the service sectors, especially the tourism sector. Instead, low unemployment figures must have resulted from a lack of exit, restructuring and labor-shedding in firms (private and public), mainly due to the factors contributing to a softening of the budget constraint, such as:

- continued heavy state involvement in banks and, in turn, their ownership of some of the largest and most important privatization investment funds created conflicts of interests, and resulted in the extension of credits to the failing enterprises owned by the bank-related funds;

- deficiencies in the collateral/bankruptcy/insolvency mechanisms that facilitated the survival of companies that should have been either forced to restructure or disappear;

- non-transparent and non-regulated capital markets, leading to weak corporate governance, and a "third wave" of questionable corporate takeovers in 1995-96; and

- fraud by the managers of the privatized companies and/or privatization investment funds, interested in maximizing short-term profit by asset stripping, while avoiding any labor layoffs or restructuring which were necessary for the long-term productivity and efficiency.

The rate of growth of GDP began to slide in the last quarter of 1995, and only reached 0.3 percent in 1997. The situation further deteriorated in 1998, when GDP contracted by 2.3 percent. In the industrial sector, some worrisome aggregate numbers started to surface: from 1993 through 1997, wages consistently outpaced productivity.[3] By 1997, average Czech productivity change lagged behind that prevailing in Poland, Hungary and Slovenia, while unit labor costs increased steeply from 1994 through 1997 (see Table 8.1).

---

[1] In every other country in Central and Eastern Europe, including the Baltic states and Slovenia and Croatia, the private sector share in 1990 was at least double, and in Poland's case, five times this amount.

[2] While success cases of FDI in the Czech Republic are well known -- like Skoda Volkswagen -- there were also failures like CAGIVA and CZ Strakonice or Air France and CSA.

[3] The Economic Strategy of EU Accession, approved by the Government of Czech Republic on May 17, 1999, argues that higher wage growth in the recent years is not a factor of concern, since the Czech competitiveness should be primarily based on qualitative factors, such as education and skills of workforce, and not on low wages.

Table 8.1. Labor Productivity and Unit Labor Cost, 1994-98

	1993	1994	1995	1996	1997	1998	Average 1993-97
Labor Productivity[1]			Annual percentage change				
Czech Republic	-1.6	5.1	11.3	8.3	9.2	-	6.4
Hungary	18.2	19.9	11.1	6.2	-1.8	-	8.6
Poland	12.9	14.3	7.2	10.1	12.5	-	11.4
Slovenia	5.6	12.1	8.2	6.0	2.0	-	6.7
Unit Labor Cost			Index (Base 1993 = 100)				Ratio[2]
Czech Republic	100	111.4	118.3	127.8	124.4	130.8	100
Hungary	100	90.4	76.1	72.1	69.9	63.7	49
Poland	100	97.3	102.5	109.6	107.8	110.6	85
Slovenia	100	97.6	107.0	100.9	101.8	103.7	79

1/ Labor productivity measures are in the manufacturing sector.
2/ The ratio measures the relative unit labor cost (ULC) of the country vis-à-vis the Czech Republic in 1998. Hungary's unit labor costs are about half of those in the Czech Republic.
Source: The Vienna Institute for International Economic Studies (WIIW).

By the mid-1990s, Czech firms were revealed to be highly leveraged -- many of them lacked capital -- with the average company carrying twice as much debt as enterprises elsewhere in Central and Eastern Europe.[4] Total domestic credit amounted to more than 70 percent of GDP -- the highest ratio in the transition economies. About three-quarters of this debt is in private firms, and a very significant portion is not being serviced. Non-performing or dubious credits in the banks rose rapidly after 1993. At present, by conservative estimate, total bank classified credit exceeds 22 percent of GDP[5] (and inter-enterprise credits amount to another 15 percent).

After 1995, what one sees in the Czech Republic is a perception that the privatization process as well as the insufficiently regulated capital market led to the enrichment of a few, not only at the expense of the average voucher investor, but also to the detriment of operational performance in many firms. External imbalances and current account problems emerged in 1996-97, as did the increasingly visible weaknesses in the banking system. This convinced many observers that the restructuring process in Czech industrial and manufacturing firms failed to sustain its promising start, and that it has slipped, particularly since 1996, relative to its principal regional comparators. Accordingly, one can identify a segmentation of industrial performance into three categories:

- a small number of large, very well-performing firms, usually linked with foreign investment/ownership and producing for export to the EU (Skoda-Volkswagen);

[4] In 1997, the total debt/equity ratio for the 700 largest Czech firms, excluding banking and financial institutions, stood at 2.12; compared to Slovenia's 1.09, Poland's 1.24, Hungary's 1.21, and Bulgaria's 1.34. Contrast this to Thailand, where the average D/E ratio over the period 1988-96 was 2.00, or to Indonesia's 1.95. Bulgaria, Romania, Hungary and to some extent Poland, all wrote-off some corporate debt in the period 1993-95, but this accounts only partly for Czech (and Slovak) firms being much more highly leveraged. Note that the numbers reported here may be higher than the averages for the whole non-financial sector in each country as smaller enterprises (not accounted for here) typically have lower leverage ratios (World Bank data and calculations). A part of the large debt in the Czech Republic has also been a result of the revolving credits (TOZs) from the previous regime.
[5] According to the Czech National Bank, classified bank debt in 1997 totaled CZK272.9 billion or 16.45 percent of 1997 GDP. But this excludes credits in state institutions such as Konsolidacni Banka and Ceska Financni and in banks under receivership, in which there is an estimated additional CZK100 billion of non-performing paper. Adding the two yields a figure of 22.6 percent of GDP in classified debt, and it could easily go higher if, as many suspect, the CZK100 billion estimate is too conservative.

- a larger number of medium and small firms that are doing well mainly by serving as suppliers to the leading companies such as Skoda-Volkswagen, or because of links as suppliers to foreign, often German manufacturers; and

- a mass of firms that are struggling with inadequate restructuring, lack of capital and excessive indebtedness, and that have been kept alive through the rolling over of credits by the state-owned or controlled banks.

Data from company surveys reveals that, through 1997, the Czech Republic appears to still possess the highest percentage of well-performing firms of any country in Central and Eastern Europe.[6] There are, however, several reasons to treat this conclusion with caution. Czech accounting data were reportedly very suspect in the first few years of transition, and are often still subject to qualification today. Moreover, Czech firms, facing frequent rollovers of non-performing loans by the bankers, devoted a relatively low share of earnings to debt servicing. Finally, it may simply be that the enterprise performance lags macroeconomic trends. During 1998-99 the performance of many Czech firms slided as a result of accumulated debt problems, the continuing decline of output growth, the steep drop in internal demand, and credit shifts in the financial sector that will end the soft credit regime of the past.

It is against this difficult backdrop of declining growth rates that the new Czech decision-makers who came to power in July 1998 must choose their course of action for both the short and medium term. A more activist approach seems justified in light of the economic downturn, and, with it, a steep rise in unemployment, to an unprecedented 7.5 percent by the end of 1998. However, the correct way forward is by pursuing deep structural reforms. For example, an increasing unemployment rate already provides indirect evidence that some restructuring has been taking place, especially in the case of large enterprises once credits have dried up. The next steps of the reform, such as completing the unfinished agenda in privatization, particularly of the banks, and urgently attending to those measures required to bring Czech industry in line with EU requirements, are treated in detail in the following sections.

The Changing Czech Industrial Structure

The legacy of central planning left the structure of the Czech economy with large-scale industrial production based in state-owned enterprises. The service sector was underdeveloped, and small industrial enterprises were scarce. Enterprises were managed by directors appointed not on leadership qualities or business acumen, but on the basis of party affiliation. These initial conditions, similar to those in other Central and Eastern European countries, made restructuring a daunting task.

The first challenge was the privatization of assets. As privatization unfolded, with the initiation of market reforms and the new opportunities for private business underway, a large shift towards services and away from traditional industrial production took place. Accordingly, the share of employment in industry shrunk from 42 percent in 1990 to 32 percent in 1997. This shift came about through:

- Small-scale privatization, which allowed Czech entrepreneurs to become owners of establishments (mostly in the service sector) without the need for much external capital;

- Few legal hindrances to open a small business; and

---

[6] As measured by percentage of firms in the samples classed in the first or best category; i.e., those showing a positive cash flow.

- The explosive expansion of the tourist industry, which provided many possibilities for lucrative employment. Employment in services increased from 39.4 percent in 1990 to 53.5 percent in 1997.

A second noteworthy development is the shift from large-scale production to small- and medium-size enterprises. Starting from an extreme concentration relative to the norm of a market-oriented economy, the Czech government pursued policies that, in effect, reduced the size of firms, through the exit and/or break-up of state-owned firms. The number of very large enterprises (with more than 2,000 employees) fell by half -- from 133 to 69 companies. At the opposite end, the number of small enterprises (between 20 and 99 employees) quadrupled -- from 1192 to 4953 companies. In 1990, there were fewer than 1,000 micro enterprises employing less than 20 workers; by 1997, that number had exceeded 100,000. The movement towards smaller industrial units is further reflected in the dwindling share of workers employed by very large enterprises. Between 1993 and 1997, the share of workers in enterprises with more than 2,000 employees fell from 37 percent to 19 percent, while the share of employment in small firms (with 20 to 99 employees) tripled to 13 percent of the workforce.

The third phenomenon of note was the change in top management. In 1990/91, prior to the first wave of privatization, the management of all Czechoslovak companies changed: general directors who were communist party members were removed from management. In the majority of cases, the new general manager appointed at that time was the old technical director, i.e., an internally promoted manager. Very few outside directors were appointed, in part due to the limited supply of superior managers and the poorly functioning market for managers. The Czech mass privatization program did not give preferential access to insiders, thus preventing managers from becoming the legal owners, or even significant stakeholders, of their respective firms.[7] Indeed, in a recent survey of 706 companies the average share of equity holdings of general managers was only 3.4 percent of total equity (at the end of 1997), with only 2.2 percent of managers holding 20 percent or more.[8] The small direct holdings of managers may have been insufficient to align their interests with those of the new owners. This might be another factor contributing to the widely reported stripping of assets by managers, in cases where the return on such activities was much higher than the return on (frequently illiquid) equity holdings. In the absence of concentrated outside ownership and hence good monitoring, managers had ample opportunities to increase their private rents and not those of the shareholders. It is, however, difficult to trace actual holdings of managers. In several cases, managers would possess indirect holdings through companies. At least in some companies managers played an important role (Skoda Plzen, CKD, Chemapol, etc.).

The fourth major development in the transformation of the industrial sector was the entry of foreign firms, either through FDI, through joint ventures, or simply through contracting agreements. The aggregate numbers indicate that, at the end of 1997, 15 percent of GDP and 18.5 percent of employment were in FDI firms. Empirical studies indicate, however, that the number of joint venture and contracting projects with EU partners is significantly higher in the Czech Republic than in either Hungary or Poland.[9] This is in part explained by the large number of medium-scale Czech manufacturers who supply

---

[7] In other transition economies, the privatization method aimed at making insiders preferential owners of the enterprises. For example, in Slovenia, the insiders had a preemptive right to become owners of their enterprises, thus, more than 90 percent of the companies ended up in the hands of managers and employees. The Czech voucher privatization system resulted in the highly dispersed ownership patters, lacking a strategic owner, which enabled the managers to in fact take control of the enterprise.

[8] See Claessens, S., and S. Djankov (1999)., "Ownership Concentration and Corporate Performance in the Czech Republic," Journal of Comparative Economics, September.

[9] See Djankov, S. and B. Hoekman (1999), "Foreign Investment and Productivity Growth in Czech Enterprises," World Bank Economic Review, October.

intermediate products to Austrian and German firms across the border, or to large foreign firms in the Czech Republic.

A recent survey[10] measured the amount of foreign entry (not only FDI) in 513 large and medium-size firms employed in the analysis. Of these firms, 24 percent of companies concluded one or more joint ventures with foreign companies, and 18 percent attracted FDI. Aggregate statistics confirm this trend, since 39.8 percent of all manufacturing firms with more than 10 employees participated in joint ventures or attracted FDI. Interviews with enterprise managers indicate an evolutionary process in their partnership with foreign companies -- an evolutionary process starting with a contracting arrangement, and if successful, continuing with a joint-venture contract, and then equity investment. These survey findings suggest that the attraction of foreign investors may not come, primarily through tax incentives and duty-free entry of capital goods, but through establishing a long-term relationship with foreign companies.

Finally, Czech manufacturing firms have been successful in reorienting their exports to Western European markets. Significant reorientation took place in the initial years of transition (1989-92) in the former Czechoslovakia. By 1997, Czech firms exported the largest share of exports towards Western Europe than any transition economy (68.9 percent). Equally important, the share of Czech exports to Russia stands at a minute 2.4 percent in 1997, suggesting that the direct economic effects of the financial crisis in Russia are unlikely to be large. Nevertheless, given the Czech first post-transition recession, and the increasingly evident problems of the Czech banking system, the timing of the Russian (and, more generally, emerging markets) crisis could prove complicated.

The Unfinished Privatization Agenda

Privatization Progress and Results

In 1991, privatization began in what was then Czechoslovakia -- using a multi-track approach to divest the 7,000 medium and large enterprises and more than 25,000 small business units. Most of the small firms and business units were sold by public auction; their sales generated revenues of over CZK31 billion (well over US$1 billion at then prevailing exchange rates). Implementation of small scale privatization was largely the responsibility of local or municipal privatization committees. In medium and larger firms, a variety of divestiture methods were employed, while the centerpiece and best-known feature of the Czech approach was the innovative mass privatization program (MPP) which used coupons or vouchers.

The Ministry of Privatization, established in 1990, determined policy. Once the decision to sell was taken, medium and large entities were turned over to the National Property Fund (NPF), established in 1991, which was responsible for both the disposition of the firms and the voucher program. The Ministry of Privatization ceased to exist on June 30, 1996; its policy responsibilities were transferred to the Ministry of Finance. To date, the NPF remains as the government sales agency and the body responsible for corporate governance through the appointment of corporate directors.

The MPP was employed for approximately two-thirds of the shares (by number) of the medium and large enterprises, which initially entered the privatization program in 1991. For a subset of more than 350 firms, in which strategic investors -- both foreign or domestic -- expressed keen interest, conventional case by case methods were used, usually tenders, and direct negotiated sales. A large amount of property was transferred to the municipalities or restituted to previous owners; a small number of management and employee buyouts was allowed.

---

[10] See Djankov and Hoekman (1999) op. cit.

The MPP was carried out in two waves, the first in 1992/93 and the second in 1994/95 after the dissolution of the Federation. The MPP granted no preferences to insiders; this was unlike voucher schemes in other countries, many of which took account of strong ownership claims and the political clout of enterprise managers and employees. To help diversify ownership risk, and to counteract the risk of ownership fragmentation as well as the consequent *de facto* control by enterprise insiders, the government allowed investment privatization funds (IPFs) to act as intermediaries in the MPP. Registered IPFs were allowed to buy vouchers from citizens and then to acquire block holdings of shares offered.

Many IPFs, including some of the largest and most important, were owned by banks in which the state held a majority or controlling stake. Each IPF was required to invest in at least ten enterprises; no more than ten percent of its portfolio could be accounted for by any single enterprise. Each IPF was also prohibited from owning more than 20 percent of the shares of any single firm. The program started with considerable popular support, as about two-thirds of voucher holders invested their vouchers in IPFs.[11] The fourteen largest funds collected 78 percent of the voucher points sold to IPFs in the first wave and 60 percent in the second. Of these fourteen, nine were owned by financial institutions. The result was that by the end of the two waves, four large state-dominated Czech banks -- Ceska Sporitelna, Komercni Banka, Investicni Banka and Ceskoslovenska Obchodni Banka (CSOB), together with the state insurance company, Ceska Pojistovna -- owned IPFs that had acquired 32 percent of all voucher points.

There was, at the outset, much debate about the design of the MPP; more recently, there has been much discussion about its outcomes.[12] The contentious issues are the approach's effect on corporate governance, its contribution to the much criticized post-privatization behavior of the IPFs, and the ease with which -- in the absence of prudential regulation in capital markets -- minority shareholders were defrauded and many privatized firms were saddled with unproductive debt. While fund involvement in the Czech Republic contributed to rapid ownership concentration, and thus perhaps to efficiency gains,[13] the closed-end structure of the funds and the lack of prudential capital market regulation led to abuse and fraud. This proved sufficient to give the terms "privatization" and "fund" a bad name. Moreover, bank ownership of equity-holding investment funds was seen as a conflict of interest; it was thought that even indirect ownership of firms by banks would diminish their zeal for enforcing debt discipline, and thereby weaken the pressure on firms to restructure.

---

[11] The first MPP wave included 988 joint stock companies in the Czech Republic; the second, 861. They included some parts of several public utilities, iron and steel firms, metallurgy, chemicals, pulp and paper, consumer goods companies, and portions of the financial sector. The book value of shares offered was CZK200 and 155 billion in the first and second wave, respectively. The methods of privatization employed and the system of reporting adopted by the Czech authorities make it hard to state simply that X percentage of firms of the original state-owned enterprise stock has been divested. The measure of progress used by Czech authorities is the amount and percentage of assets privatized, using the initial book value of these assets as the baseline.

[12] A discussion of the legacy of the MPP in terms of its impact on corporate governance and on the structure and performance of the capital markets can be found in the recent report by the World Bank (1999), *Czech Republic Capital Market Review*. There is, as well, a large academic literature on this subject; for one recent example among many, see Michal Mejstrik, ed. (1997), *The Privatization Process in East-Central Europe: Evolutionary Process of Czech Privatization* (Boston: Kluwer Academic Publishers).

[13] This assertion is supported by two studies: Pohl *et al., op. cit.,* and R. Frydman *et al.* (1997), *Private Ownership and Corporate Performance: Some Lessons from Transition Economies* (World Bank: Policy Research Paper No. 1830) present evidence to show that privatized firms controlled by IPFs perform well and restructure. This conclusion is hotly contested. A. Weiss and G. Nikitin review financial performance in a set of Czech firms and find that while "ownership concentration in hands other than funds has a major (and positive) effect on performance" there is "no evidence of a positive effect of ownership shares by funds on the performance of operating companies." ("Performance of Czech Companies by Ownership Structure," unpublished draft, Boston University, 1997, p. 21.)

Since the MPP was completed in 1995, privatization of remaining enterprises has continued, but at a much slower pace, using non-voucher, traditional methods, including flotation of shares on the capital markets. Table 8.2, compiled mainly from information provided by the NPF and the Ministry of Industry and Trade provides details of the progress and results of privatization since it began, with a breakdown by method.

Table 8.2. Large Scale Privatization by Method

SHARES OF JOINT STOCK COMPANIES Nominal value *(CZK millions)*	1991-1997	1991-1997 As % of total
Sale (total)	85,322	16.43
of which		
Public offer	20,538	3.96
Direct sale to Czech citizens	26,860	5.17
Direct sale to foreigners	14,149	2.73
Employee shares	2,204	0.42
Public tenders	21,571	4.15
Free Transfer (total)	433,900	83.57
of which		
Vouchers	341,750	65.82
Restitution	1,760	0.34
Voluntary conveyance (to municipalities)	53,249	10.26
To Restitution Investment Fund (RIF)[1/]	19,739	3.80
Other	17,493	3.37
PRIVATIZED (total)	519,222	100.00
of which		
Privatization of RIF shares	7,540	1.45
PROPERTY OTHER THAN JOINT STOCK COMPANIES Book value *(CZK millions)*	1991-Jun/98	1991-Jun/98 As % of total
Public auctions	8,125	4.64
Public tenders	31,590	18.03
Direct sales	65,256	37.23
Free transfers	70,283	40.10
of which restitutions[2/]	4,455	2.54
PRIVATIZED (total)	175,253	100.00

1/ A fund established by the NPF for restitution purposes (indemnity in the form of RIF's shares for claimants whose Property cannot be returned).
2/ Including restitution combined with sale.
Source: National Property Fund.

By the end of 1997, approximately CZK700 billion of medium and large enterprise assets (at nominal value) had been privatized. Of this, about CZK350 billion, or half of medium and large enterprise assets, was privatized through voucher privatization; the other half was privatized by more conventional sales methods, or free transfers (to localities or former owners). Official figures to the end of 1996 show that privatization "projects" for 3,813 medium/large firms had been approved (of a total of 5,115 such projects submitted). There has been a marked slow-down of privatization after 1995.[14]

---

[14] Of the enterprise assets transferred to the NPF for privatization since 1990 by the NPF, around 44 percent have been in manufacturing, 18 percent in utilities, 10 percent in services and 10 percent in mining. Most of the remaining 18 percent were in agriculture, forestry and food processing, construction and housing.

NPF's total revenues from privatization by all methods up to the end of 1997 are estimated at around CZK176 billion at current prices or CZK246 billion in constant terms (this and all subsequent figures at constant 1997 prices). Revenues from small scale privatization accounted for approximately 23 percent of the total over the period, but small scale privatization was essentially completed in 1993. Around 81 percent of revenues were received from Czech nationals. Revenues from sales to foreigners fell from around 33-36 percent in 1992/3 to only 3-4 percent in 1996/7 -- in marked contrast to Hungary, which has generated substantial FDI through privatization, the bulk of it in 1995/96.

What's Left to Privatize?

A large amount of assets still remains in state hands: all of, or a majority stake in, the major utilities, a set of 40 firms and banks designated as "strategic," majority stakes in more than 30 non-strategic companies, and minority stakes in about 300 other such firms (see Table 8.3). As in other countries that used vouchers to spur a mass privatization effort, the Czechs have found it difficult to complete the sale of the residual holdings using cash or case-by-case methods -- though unlike other voucher-using countries, they did manage to stimulate secondary trading and ownership concentration. Nonetheless, the swift pace of initial divestiture slackened. Adding together the entities still fully owned by the state, and the shares held by the state in partially privatized firms, the state holds about a quarter of the shares of industrial firms, privatized, and privatizable. A revealing fact is that, as of the end of 1997, the Czech state still retained a substantial stake in nine of the country's ten largest firms.[15]

The Banks. The state retains substantial shares[16] in Ceska Sporitelna (45 percent), and Komercni Banka (49 percent), while the state's share in CSOB (65 percent) was privatized in July 1999.[17] The current government has indicated that it intends to complete bank privatization by the year 2000. This will mean that issues involving the Slovak Government ownership of shares in Komercni Banka, and managing the large portfolios of non-performing loans, will need finally to be resolved.

Strategic Enterprises. In some strategic enterprises, SPT Telecom and Unipetrol, for example, the state has initiated or concluded negotiations with joint venture partners for multi-billion CZK foreign investments. The NPF's 51 percent share (estimated value: CZK74 billion) in the telecommunications monopoly SPT Telecom is, by far, the state's largest single strategic holding.[18] Related to this is the state holding in Ceske Radiokomunikace (CZK9 billion). The Czechs have drafted a new telecommunications law that sets the legal and institutional regulatory framework to ensure competition, fair pricing and adequate service.[19] The need for a regulatory framework applies to other public utilities, such as the power generation monopoly CEZ (CZK33 billion) and to the regional power and gas distribution companies (CZK30 billion).

---

[15] As measured by sales. The state stake is either held directly through the NPF or indirectly through the Konsolidacni Banka.

[16] The Czech state's holdings are even more powerful than the numbers indicate: In Ceska Sporitelna, 14.75 percent of shares are held by Czech municipalities; they are neither traded nor voted. In Komercni Banka, 15 percent of shares are held by the Slovak State, and an additional 14 percent of share are in GDRS, and normally not voted.

[17] The Slovak government share of CSOB is expected to be privatized shortly to the same buyer.

[18] In 1995, 27 percent of SPT Telecom was sold to a Dutch-Swiss consortium, TelSource, for US$1.45 billion. TelSource received management control in return for investment and network expansion commitments, all of which have so far been more than met. SPT Telecom's monopoly officially ends in 2000, but already faces considerable competition from mobile phones and internet calls. In 1997, SPT Telecom reported a net profit of CZK6 billion.

[19] However, the new government is reconsidering portions of the framework, and may not submit the revised law to the legislature before the end of 1999.

Residual Holdings by the NPF in Non-Strategic Enterprises. The Czech state has already decided to divest itself of these holdings, particularly in the 236 enterprises where the NPF's share is less than five percent, expecting to obtain around CZK8 billion. These assets are a burden on the state which must maintain the structure within the NPF to manage or monitor them, while they are not a source of dividend revenue. Although the NPF has exercised its management role in minority holdings primarily in a passive way, it nonetheless still appoints members to the boards of some of these enterprises, thereby adversely affecting corporate governance.

Table 8.3. The Unfinished Privatization Agenda

STATE INSTITUTION	Book Value *CZK millions*	Market Value *CZK millions*	Number of Companies in Portfolio
NATIONAL PROPERTY FUND (as of June 30, 1998) Joint stock companies[1/]	170,748	207,853	369
of which			
Strategic companies	155,463	202,821	40
Non-strategic companies	15,285	5,032	329
Restitution Investment Fund (RIF) shares[2/]	1,243	1,161	1
Other property[3/]	3,941		569
CESKA FINANCNI (as of July 31, 1998) Assets obtained from technically nationalized banks by the CNB[4/]	13,942	4,000	Over 60
KONSOLIDACNI BANKA(as of June 30, 1998) Property participations taken over on the basis of government decisions[5/]	11,318	6,000	9

OTHER (Individual ministries, etc.)
Residual state-owned enterprises (as of December 20, 1997)[6/]
Property assigned for privatization, not yet transferred to the NPF
  Mainly:
  Part of the property Ceske Drahy (Ministry of Transport and Communications)[7/]
  Health care institutions (Ministry of Health Care)
			Number of firms
			1621

1/ Excluding companies in liquidation and bankruptcy proceedings (38 companies of book value CZK8.8 billions). Book value = nominal value of shares held by the NPF. Market value for traded securities is determined by their current price at the Prague Stock Exchange or RMS trading system; market value of non-traded companies is an estimate of NPF experts.

2/ Restitution Investment Fund was established by the NPF. Its shares serve as an indemnity for claimants whose property cannot be returned. The NPF still holds 13 percent of the RIF shares.

3/ Other property includes all businesses other than joint stock companies and individual assets to be privatized separately. The book value is taken from updated privatization projects.

4/ The book value is based on the price of securities when bought by Ceska Financni. Corresponding nominal value amounts to approximately CZK16 billions. Market value is a World Bank estimate based on available information.

5/ The book value is the nominal value of shares held by Konsolidacni Banka. Market value is a World Bank estimate based on information from the Ministry of Finance.

6/ The largest remaining state-owned enterprise is Ceske Drahy railroads company. In addition, there are over 160 state-owned enterprises in the sector of industry and construction.

7/ Part of the property of Ceske Drahy has been already assigned for privatization, but has not yet been transferred to the NPF.

Source: National Property Fund, Ceska Financni, Konsolidacni Banka, CSOB, Czech Statistical Office and Ministry of Finance.

Use of Privatization Revenues. Officially, the NPF is financially separate from the budget; in practice, however, the NPF has been obliged to finance government expenditures not related to its own privatization activities. This has included recapitalization of troubled banks, writing off bad debts of selected key enterprises, and providing loans and guarantees to what are termed the "transformation institutions" (see below). On several occasions, some of the NPF's resources have also been earmarked for the budget. From the perspective of promoting efficiency, some analysts would agree that the best use of privatization revenues is the retirement of state debt. Czech local consensus, however, is to use the revenues for improvement of infrastructure.

Portfolios of Ceska Financni (CF) and Konsolidacni Banka (KoB).[20] These two "transformation institutions" are mentioned here because, partly financed by the NPF, they have become holders of some CZK20 billion worth of enterprise shares,[21] some of them excellent candidates for privatization (Skoda Auto, the Czech airline (CSA), Zetor). Their purpose was to remove non-performing loans from supposedly viable banks, and to mount a vigorous collection effort on the non-performing credits. Later, they made new loans to enterprises in difficulty. By the end of 1997, KoB's assets amounted to CZK130 billion. As of the end of July, 1998, CF's loans and securities amounted to CZK32 billion.

The 1998 Ministry of Finance report on hidden debt concluded that the KoB is negatively affected by *ad hoc* decisions by the public authorities, the financial consequences of which are neither well analyzed nor reported. The report notes that KoB's losses and liabilities are financed largely by the NPF in a non-transparent manner. The loan portfolios taken over by CF are particularly risky: these institutions are encouraging fiscal instability, reducing the clarity of government financial policy and incurring high operational costs.[22] Through their non-transparent activities and their implicit promise of bail-outs, KoB and CF are also creating moral hazard and distortions within the incentive framework for the banking and enterprise sectors. At the same time, they have built a large amount of contingent liabilities that the State is likely to have to address.

By June of 1998, approximately three-quarters of the shares in the NPF's portfolio had been privatized. If privatization continues at the post-1995 speed, it will take six years or more to complete the process for the NPF's remaining portfolio -- and this does not take into account the substantial number of shares held by financial agencies other than the NPF.

Enterprise Restructuring and the Revitalization Agency

The Government has already made the first step in addressing the issue of enterprise restructuring, and accordingly approved in May 1999 a restructuring program with the creation of the Revitalization Agency (RA).[23] The Agency has been created as a joint-stock subsidiary company of KoB, with registered capital of CZK100 million provided by KoB. The key decision-making authority will be delegated to a renowned investment bank, chosen in an international tender to administrate the Agency's activity (KoB will prescribe the terms of the contract). The Administrator, assuming its duties by September 1999, will be required to contribute to the Agency's capital, and other banks in the Czech Republic that are creditors to selected enterprises will be encouraged to do likewise. It is expected that the state-owned stake in registered capital will gradually fall below 50 percent, so that KoB would retain no more than a blocking minority interest in RA (34 percent). The Administrator's share in revenues will be determined by its stake in the registered capital, and is regulated by a coefficient agreed on in advance.

---

[20] The workings and impact of CF and KoB are covered in more detail in the chapter on contingent liabilities of this report.

[21] KoB was created in 1991 to deal with the inherited stock problem of over-indebted firms; CF was created in 1996, to assist in dealing with a banking crisis, that is, to deal with the new flow. There is a third "transformation institution," Ceska Inkasni, subsidiary to the Ministry of Finance. Its activities are not discussed here since it does not own shares in enterprises.

[22] While the KoB is under responsibility of the government of the Czech Republic, CF was created by the Czech National Bank and is under its responsibility and jurisdiction.

[23] The program is a compromise between the programs proposed by the Vice-Premier and the Minster of Industry and Trade. The former promoted the industrial restructuring plan that would include the participation of involving creditors (from the private sector), while the latter called for a strong state role in the process.

Box 8.1. The Revitalization Agency: Its Structure and Selection Criteria

The Agency is governed by three fundamental bodies:
- *Board of Directors* (5 representatives of the Administrator, who has a majority, and major shareholders) presents proposals for asset realization methods to the Investment Committee;
- *Supervisory Committee* (representatives of government bodies, with the Minister of Industry and Trade as chairman) monitors the economic management and chooses the external auditor; and
- *Investment Committee* (9 members of the board, representatives of the participating banks, and a representative of EBRD or IFC) decides regarding the Board's proposals on methods of realizing assets, and on revitalizing programs.

Even though the role of state is minimized, compared to the initial proposal by Ministry of Industry and Trade; the State still maintains important functions, which include: (i) monitoring the Agency's activities through Supervisory Committee; (ii) creation of an adequate institutional environment (legislative and tax framework, stimulating demand, recapitalization and privatization decisions), and (iii) setting the date for the Agency's liquidation. The Government, in cooperation with the participating banks, assessed the enterprises that may be potential candidates for restructuring, based on the four criteria:

- Employ over 2,000 people; .
- Buy more than CZK1 billion (US$30 million) from the domestic suppliers in the past accounting period (multiplier effect);
- Have a positive operating profit before interest and tax; and
- Have debts in excess of CZK3 billion (US$90 million) with Komercni Banka, Ceska Sporitelna, and KoB.

For the information purposes, a non-binding indicative list of 59 companies has already been compiled, with the prime candidates consisting of the chemical conglomerate AliaChem, and engineering companies Skoda Pilsen, ZPS Zlin, CKD Praha, and Tatra Koprivnice.

The Administrator, however, is not limited to this list of the debtor companies in the selection of the portfolio of classified loans to be purchased from creditor banks, neither is the Administrator obliged to select any individual debtor company. The selection of the assets to be purchased by the RA is carried by the Administrator, and approved by the Board and Investment Committee, based on:

- Forward looking viability assessment of the debtor companies;
- Their willingness to cooperate with RA (including agreement of the existing shareholders with substantial wipe-out of their equity and debt for equity conversion);
- The agreement with other creditors on the restructuring plan.

The Administrator is allowed to choose any non-performing assets from KoB's portfolio, which might soon be enlarged by KoB's purchases of non-performing assets of some large Czech banks, and other creditors. The sale of banks' non-performing assets based on fair market value would in many cases result in looses as the commercial banks have not fully provisioned the individual credit exposures which would be transferred to the RA. In such a case, the Government would provide the necessary capital injection to the banks slated for privatization.

Given the nature of assets to be transferred, it is highly probable that RA will have to be actively involved in the restructuring of the industrial corporations. It is thus expected that the primary method of balance sheet restructuring of the debtor companies would be debt for equity swaps in order to obtain the control over debtor companies in RA' s portfolio, followed by restructuring. The main role of the program will be exercised by the Board and Investment Committee, which will determine the procedure to be used for resolving the debts owed by a particular debtor (capitalization/ asset management, or debt restructuring/loan management). The final solutions will range from revitalization of a debtor by a third party (chosen in a tender), sale of an enterprise or its debts to a strategic investor (public auction/ tender), or liquidation of an enterprise.

Source: Konsolidacni Banka.

The main objectives of the Agency are recapitalization and restructuring of selected enterprises, cleaning-up of loan portfolios of commercial banks and preparing them for privatization, and creation of an enabling environment for efficient enterprise performance in the Czech Republic (see Box 8.1). The Administrator will assist in finding a responsible strategic owner for restructured enterprises, including foreign investors. The troubled banks' bad assets will be partially carved out by the Agency, which will raise the interest of a strategic partner in the banks' privatizations, while also providing space for making new loans. The Agency will be financed by issue of shares, securitization of assets, subordinated debt, and other capital market instruments.[24]

While the government's effort is commendable, the program's benefits and weaknesses will derive from design specifications, some still to be determined. One of the key benefits include the provision of financial support to the largest state-owned banks, which will relieve them of burden, make them appealing for strategic partners and enable them to focus on the future rather than the past. Second, the restructuring decisions will be made by professionals in the private financial sector, instead of by government officials. Third, the limited time frame for the Agency's existence (until the Czech's entry into the EU) gives the process a clear sunset clause.[25] Fourth, the Agency will be used as a pilot for the future assets management and disposition by KoB itself. It will test and refine the valuation procedures, the incentive structure for the manager of the assets, the legal and political bottlenecks, as well as clarify public expectations about the process.

However, the weaknesses of the program need to be addressed as well. The lack of appropriate bankruptcy procedure legislation, and general legal environment that would provide security to international (and domestic) investors are the main obstacles to the success of the RA program. The need for speeding up the process of adoption of new legislation has already been emphasized by the authorities.

Another concern regarding the design of the program relates to the implicit limitations of the pool of available enterprises. Namely, even though the government-devised list of debtor enterprises is only an indicative one, it is very likely that the Administrator will focus on these largest debtors to KoB. As a result, the small and potentially viable enterprises might be left out of the restructuring efforts, since the personnel of the Administrator will not be able to cover the whole set of around 4,500 enterprises in KoB portfolio.

While the authorities focus on refining the program's parameters, they should not loose sight on setting the proper incentives and policies for effective corporate governance. The poor state of many large, domestically-owned industrial conglomerates has been a drag on the economy and banking sector. The overall objective of the revitalization program must be to advance the restructuring of the economy, not to protect insolvent enterprises from the harsh adjustments required by a market economy. Therefore, it should be carefully designed, targeted and implemented.

The re-privatization of revitalized firms needs to be targeted at strategic investors who can provide the required capital, management, and marketing expertise. The contract with the Administrator should be structured with the incentives for the Administrator to find the best strategic investor (in terms of management and not only in terms of sale price of the enterprise). The program must be strictly time-bound. Therefore, the enterprises taken over should be privatized in whole or in part within 1–2 years. Enterprises, or parts of these, for which no buyers can be found within that time frame, should be liquidated. It would be very dangerous for the state to face an outcome of the revitalization plan in which it is left as the owner of non-viable enterprises for any significant period of time.

The revitalization program will cover at most a small proportion of the industrial firms in serious financial difficulties. To deal with the remaining firms, as well as to ensure that privatized banks will operate in an appropriate business environment, it is critical to speed up corporate governance reforms,

---

[24] The funding will be based on a pass-through model, with junior subordinated debt (guaranteed by the Government or provided by KoB) serving as a second layer of risk capital in the event of future deterioration. KoB's management will work with the participating banks to secure their share in the provision of funds to the RA. It is expected that eventually the RA would be able to access the capital markets independently.

[25] The working assumption has been January 1, 2003.

particularly the preparation of an effective foreclosure and bankruptcy law. There is need for far-reaching reforms to the legal and institutional framework and for improving the enforcement of existing laws regulating economic activity.

To complement the revitalization program an accelerated divestment of non-financial strategic enterprises as well as the many stakes in smaller enterprises should be implemented. This would not only improve corporate governance and efficiency required to compete in the EU, but also send a strong signal of the commitment to the privatization process. There is no justification for the NPF to maintain the still large set of assets from privatized firms in its portfolio.

Statistical data shows that small and medium size enterprises (SMEs) are an important part of the Czech economy. Enterprises with less than 250 employees in industry, construction, trade and services employ 56.4 percent of employees of these sectors and generates 51.4 percent of value added.

SMEs development is strongly influenced by government financial support programs. The tools used by the Czech authorities to support SMEs include: guarantees on bank credits, guarantees on the development and risk for capital investors, contributions to interest payments, credits with subsidized -- lower than market -- interest rates, and state grants.

The volume of the financial resources from the state budget to SMEs support programs was doubled from CZK1.0 billion in 1998 to CZK1.9 billion in 1999. The programs' conditions approved by the government in 1999 and the increased volume of financial resources for their application will imply substantially more access to capital for SMEs.

In June 1999, the government approved a program called "Policy for the Promotion of the Small and Medium Size Enterprises from 1999 to 2002," which contains short-term and medium-term measures to assist SMEs, including the improvement of entrepreneurial environment. The attention in year 2000 will be given to advisory, information and education services, access to capital, support for innovation, simplification of legal instruments, reduction of the tax load, and to bringing down bureaucracy.

Recommendations

Accelerating and completing privatization is crucial for three major economic reasons. First, full privatization of the two large banks in which the state retains a substantial interest and equity holding is a critical pre-requisite for restoring domestic and foreign investor confidence, financial discipline, and transparency in relations between the state, the banks and the enterprise sector. Second, efficient, dynamic, privately owned, well-managed enterprises in telecommunication, energy, transportation, and heavy industry are necessary if the Czech Republic is to face competition within the open market of the EU. Third, privatized, dynamic large firms serve as the locomotive pulling small and medium suppliers into more efficient, higher quality production. A secondary financial objective is the generation of revenues from sales, estimated as of June 1998 at the market value of CZK230 billion (more than US$7 billion).[26]

The Government should focus on the following recommendations in order to improve enterprise performance:

---

[26] The current market value of these assets is likely to be lower as asset and share prices have felt throughout the region in part as a result of the Russian crisis.

- Complete privatization of most of its remaining assets in the enterprise sector to strategic investors. Any pre-privatization enterprise restructuring should only be passive in order to attract strategic investors, i.e., it should not include new capital investments; it should consist of unbundling conglomerates, creating an adequate social safety-net for affected workers, and possibly the restructuring of some enterprise debts.

- To ensure transparency and to correct past mistakes, the capital market and related policy reforms already embarked upon should be vigorously pursued and deepened. The government, however, should limit its role to establishing and enforcing fair and productive rules of the game, thus creating an enabling environment for sustainable development.

- New physical investments in those firms still in state hands should be avoided; these are best left to the new private owners, who will make decisions based on commercial judgments. Experience has shown that attempts to increase the selling prices of state enterprises by making pre-privatization investments are likely not to be recovered in the purchase price.

- The program under the auspices of the Revitalization Agency needs to be carefully tailored and executed with clear time-bounds and incentives that do not generate a negative environment for enterprises and banks.

Strategies and methodologies for privatizing state-owned assets will vary according to the type of asset. The sale of the state's interests in the two major banks to qualified strategic investors should be the first priority. Revenue generation should be very much a secondary consideration in these transactions, generally to be sacrificed to the promotion of long-term efficiency. The price obtained for the shares in these banks will reflect the quality of loan portfolios. For the remaining telecommunications stake and the public monopolies in energy and transport, work needs to begin immediately on structuring the markets to promote competitive forces, and on developing regulatory frameworks (for the remaining natural monopoly segments) that will encourage competition and ensure economic pricing and good service. Once these are in place, then privatization of these entities should go forward without delay. Privatization of the petrochemical, chemical, steel,[27] coal and other enterprises on the strategic list should be launched, and the assets divested by a combination of the methods that have been tried and tested in the Czech Republic. These include public offerings, tenders, direct sales and share sales on the capital markets.

The NPF should be instructed to divest its holdings in non-strategic enterprises as soon as possible by public offering to the highest bidders. In those cases where no bidders can be found, then proportional share giveaways by the NPF to existing shareholders, or cancellation of the NPF's shares (which amounts to the same thing) would be appropriate. Once the issue of the potential environmental liabilities taken

---

[27] It must be noted that in 1996 the government decided to privatize the State stakes in the steel industry -- Nová Hut 68.25 percent and Vítkovice 67.30 percent -- through its resolution No. 485 of September 18, 1996. In compliance with this resolution the NPF sold 1 percent of shares of those companies to their management and simultaneously signed with them contracts to sell them directly a larger percent before December 31, 2001. In those contracts, conditions were defined under which the management can obtain the shares. The programmed sale of 18.25 percent of Nová Hut shares and 17.30 percent of Vítkovice shares did not take place within the deadline fixed by the government's resolution, i.e. by June 30, 1997. New deadlines were fixed by a resolution, No. 608 of October 1, 1997. The new deadline was September 1, 1999 for Nová Hut and September 30, 2000 for Vítkovice. Moreover, in the context of the negotiations with IFC involvement in Nová Hut for the flat products plant, 18.25 percent of shares were transferred irrevocably to Credit Suisse First Boston which is to carry on the sale to a broad set of investors, thus reducing the stake of the State under 50 percent.

over by the NPF during the privatization process is resolved, a time horizon should be set for the closure of the NPF; its transformation into a state holding company should be avoided.

The roles of Ceska Financni and Konsolidacni Bank should be reviewed. Early corrective measures could include a full audit of the activities of the transformation institutions, followed by their consolidation into a single institution. It could include the clear separation of functions between their economic development role and the handling of non-performing loans, a clear financing policy for the consolidated institution, provision of incentives to deal with the non-performing loan portfolio, and implementation of clear financial reporting systems. Whatever decision is taken with respect to the future of these institutions, there is a strong case for selling to the highest bidders -- perhaps by the simple and transparent mechanism of an auction -- whatever marketable enterprise shares they possess, at the earliest opportunity.

Foreign Direct Investment

The investment climate in the Czech Republic, characterized by a well-educated labor force and an excellent location, is comparable to the other two or three most progressive nations of Central and Eastern Europe. The Czech Republic has managed to attract a significant amount of investment. Indeed, its average FDI/GDP ratio of 3.2 percent (for the period 1991 to 1997) is third in the region behind Hungary (5.5 percent) and Estonia (3.5 percent). Moreover, this Czech figure does not include divesting some of the "big ticket" FDI-generating items such as banks, airlines company and public utilities, the sales of which so heavily contributed to Hungary's leading position. In 1998, the Czech Republic was able to attract US$2.5 billion in FDI, the largest amount among the ten countries seeking EU accession. Nonetheless, there is a pervasive sentiment among both Czechs and investors alike that much more could, and should, be done to attract a larger amount of high quality FDI.

Present macroeconomic situation in the Czech Republic, with the prices on the stock exchange depressed, made some of the enterprises more attractive to the foreign investors. However, the deteriorating macroeconomic and financial conditions, and the lack of adequate legal environment are likely to detract some investors and impede larger FDI flows. The credit crunch in banks makes FDI generation even more important as a source of investment and restructuring capital, besides their general benefits of bringing new know-how, and other intangible attributes. Thus, the Czech Republic needs to improve the overall business and investment environment by two paths: completion of structural reforms, and FDI promotion.

Internal analysis and external observers alike have laid out the most important actions regarding incomplete status of reforms:

- Privatize banks, to assure availability of cheaper domestic credit.

- Strengthen corporate governance in order to facilitate negotiations between foreign investors and domestic management/ownership structures.

- Take steps to make managers responsible to owners.

- Protect minority investors.

- Fix bankruptcy laws and procedures.

- Strengthen capital markets regulation to decrease the risks of exit for foreign investors.

- Continue, and enforce, the recent legal, policy and institutional reforms aimed at improving capital market regulation and corporate governance procedures.

In addition to improving the business environment, the Czech Republic needs to be more effective in promoting FDI. To this end, three sets of actions are needed:

- Strengthen CzechInvest. It is one of the best investment promotion agencies in the region but has both insufficient budget and status.

- Further simplify and de-emphasize the incentive package announced in April 1998.

- Mount an all-out effort, from the highest echelons of government, to improve the country's image to investors.

Regarding the country's investment image, the objective is to construct a time-phased program that targets two or three problem areas identified by the investor community each year, with announced targets and evaluation of progress. This would be a practical way to make progress as well as a good marketing device. What is needed is some institutionalized system that sets standards and guidelines on business-friendly behavior, that rewards government officials who practice such behavior, and that sanctions and penalizes unnecessary and counter-productive interference or inaction with legitimate business investments and operations. This can be fairly easily designed; local knowledge on what needs to be done is abundant; the crucial first step is for the government to adopt such a system, let the public know it has been adopted, and then devote sufficient attention and resources seriously to implement it.

The incentive package to promote investment -- including FDI -- announced in the spring of 1998, had problems that the government has addressed in recent months. The problem of the minimum threshold, set initially at US$25 million has been resolved by reducing the minimum to US$10 million; the problem of the requirement that the investment be greenfield has also been removed (see Box 8.2.). The establishment of a minimum threshold and the restrictions to greenfield investments created bad feelings among smaller investors -- who are valuable to the Czech economy, particularly as suppliers to large investors. Moreover, large investors who make a series of investments, each of which is less than US$25 million, expected the same leveled playfield.

One way to convince potential investors that the Czech Republic really wants them and will assist them would be to strengthen CzechInvest. As opportunities to attract FDI to existing enterprises become fewer and fewer, and as other competing countries become stronger and more attractive, the Czech Republic needs a strong investment promotion agency, specifically:

- With a total budget of about US$2 million per year, CzechInvest is at the lower limit of resources for a promotion agency. Doubling the government contribution would be a good idea.

- To give CzechInvest more stature, more autonomy, but also as part of a move to make it speak for the entire Government, CzechInvest has already been served by a steering committee, with members coming from various relevant ministries and state agencies but also executives from private companies (financial, industrial, and legal).

- Such composition of the steering committee should enable the CzechInvest to ascertain if a particular investment meets stipulated criteria, and to certify those investments that do. The idea would be to eliminate the need for a draft proposal (see Box 8.2.) to go to one or more ministries or other agencies for separate reviews of their eligibility.

Box 8.2. Investment Incentives Program in the Czech Republic

The following incentives are offered to the manufacturing investors (selected services, such as telecommunications, might be eligible in the near future):
* Corporate tax relief for up to 10 years;
* Location in a customs-free zone;
* Duty-free imports of machinery and equipment;
* Job-creation grants (only in districts with high unemployment);
* Training grants (10-50 percent of training cost, depending on the unemployment rate of the particular district);
* Provision of low-cost building land and/or infrastructure.

In order to be eligible for any of the incentives, an investor has to meet all of the five criteria:
1. Investment of US$10 million into fixed assets;
2. The investment has to be made into a manufacturing sector, and at least 50 percent of the production line (in terms of cost) must consist of machinery listed under a Czech-government approved list of high-tech machinery;
3. Investment into machinery has to account for at least 40 percent of the total investment;
4. Investment must be made into the construction of a new production plant, or into the purchase or lease of existing production facilities to launch a new production activity. Acquisitions are not eligible;
5. The proposed production must meet all Czech environmental standards.

Each application for investment incentives has to be approved by the government. CzechInvest evaluates the investment projects and discusses them with the relevant ministries, prepares a draft proposal for the government resolution on granting the incentives, and passes the draft to all the ministries for the revision. After the draft proposal is reviewed, the revised proposal is sent for a final approval to the Government. If the incentives are granted, a Memorandum of Understanding is signed between the investor and representatives of the Government.

Investors who are not eligible for this national investment plan may apply for support directly to local authorities, which may offer job-creation grants, training and re-training grants, and provision of low-cost development land and /or infrastructure. All these incentives, however, are negotiated on a case-by-case basis, and the conditions may vary among the localities.

Source: CzechInvest.

Meeting EU Quality, Environmental, and Labor Safety Requirements

The Europe Agreement, signed by the Czech Republic and EU member states -- effective since February 1995 -- promotes the adoption of EU quality, technical, and environmental requirements, and seeks accession to EU standardizing bodies. It became clear, however, that many of the existing standards in Central and Eastern European countries would cause significant difficulties since several were idiosyncratic or were used to protect local producers. As a result of these problems, the European Commission started to negotiate Pan-European Conformity Assessment Agreements (PECAA). As a result, the Czech Republic will progressively adopt the complete EU standards regime -- the *acquis* in this area includes some 500 directives. The scope of these agreements will extend far beyond the Europe Agreements, which are much less specific on standards issues.

Technical and Quality Standards

In the Czech Republic, the system of obligatory technical regulations and the system of facultative technical standards were strictly separated by the legislation. An interim period during which a technical standard or its part can be obligatory will end on December 31, 1999. The Czech Republic committed itself to achieve full compatibility with EU normalization, technical regulations and procedures.

In the sphere of technical norms, the Czech Republic has made significant progress in the application of the procedures of the European normalization. By 1997 about 80 percent of the European norms have been introduced. Moreover, the Czech Normalization Institute became a fully-qualified member of the European normalization institutions.

Regarding the harmonization of technical regulations, significant progress has also been achieved, especially with respect to the transposition of the EU directives. In 1996 a program on technical harmonization was adopted to introduce a unified framework and enabling inter-departmental coordination by way of unified methodological instruments. The transposition of the *acquis* is progressing.

Results from surveys of manufacturing firms in the Czech Republic confirm these observations that significant harmonization has already occurred: 85 percent of those Czech firms sampled reported substantial harmonization efforts to adopt international standards.

In 1997 negotiations on the PECAA were opened. The aim is to support the process of transposition of EU directives and based on the achievement of an equivalent legislation, to eliminate technical barriers to trade. Until the Conformity Assessment Agreements between the EU and the Czech Republic are signed in the context of accession, products originating in the Czech Republic will be treated on an MFN basis.

With regards to the EU acceptance of national tests, Czech firms reported that, in the majority of cases, national (pre-shipment) test results were accepted. On the other hand, Czech firms reported that about 30 percent of imports were subject to testing or technical inspection by the Czech authorities. These findings suggest that the Czech Republic has proceeded relatively quickly in terms of harmonizing the standards regime with that of the EU. In March 1998, the EU Commission reported that the Czech Republic had achieved "approximation" in 9 out of 28 areas (as compared to 3 out of 28 for the next highest country, Hungary).

Environmental Requirements

Less progress, however, has been recorded in meeting EU environmental requirements. The European Commission estimates that the Czech Republic will need to devote a sizable amount of resources to bring its environmental standards up to EU, estimated at EUR5-7 billion without including industrial investment and EUR7-10 billion including industrial investment. About 30-35 percent will need to come from private sector: the rest will be incurred by public utilities and municipalities, most notably in dealing with water pollution and waste.[28] Czech companies, therefore will need to invest a very substantial EUR3 billion in environmental-friendly technology and clean-up efforts. Czech companies still produce considerable environmentally-hazardous waste though they also spend substantial amounts for dealing with environmental problems. On average, expenditures for environmental protection amounted to 2.5 percent of GDP between 1993 and 1997.[29]

---

[28] See environmental chapter in this report for a full analysis.

[29] This figure needs to be taken with caution. It is only an approximation since it is difficult to separate environmental investments from other type of investment. Generally, only the end-of-pipe investments are considered environmental, even though the process investments -- motivated by other considerations -- are usually the once with the most of the environmental impact. The most important EU legislation on industrial pollution stresses process improvement over end-of-pipe investments, which makes the compliance costs estimations extremely tricky. Even member countries have no estimates about how much it is costing them as they try to comply.

The 1996 Ministry of Environment survey of the 100 largest Czech enterprises found that these enterprises spent approximately US$300 million on environmental protection in 1996. The survey asked detailed questions about the costs of environmental clean up, including those of obtaining an EU Environmental Quality certificate. Approximately 27 percent of enterprises surveyed have either obtained, or are in the process of obtaining, an environmental quality certificate for their production process, usually the EU-specific Environmental Management Assessment Standard (EMAS) certificate. Finally, approximately 53 percent of the products of the surveyed Czech enterprises have obtained an environmental quality certificate, resulting from a national certification program called *Ecolabeling,* which officially states that the product meets certain environmental standards. In the 1994-97 period, approximately 230 products have been awarded the Czech ecolabel.

There has thus been some progress in addressing the environmental problems at the enterprise level. Nonetheless, several developments warrant consideration and attention:

- Expenditures on environmental protection at the enterprise level have gone towards "end of pipe" technologies rather than towards changes in the technological process *per se* -- only 30 percent of surveyed firms have invested in new technological processes.

- There is little scope for relocating existing facilities in cases when the enterprise was built inside the city limits. Relocation is nearly impossible because of the lack of infrastructure, transport, and the significant costs associated with building new facilities. Even large foreign investors concentrate on upgrading existing facilities rather than building new ones.

- Increased environmental pollution in the manufacturing sector is likely with the revived economic growth in Germany, where approximately 70 percent of all Czech exports are sold. Enterprise managers indicated that, unless they generate high export revenues (and in the process, all too often, increase pollution), they would be unable to invest in new technologies. On the other hand, if they manage to invest in the new process technology, they should be able to reduce their pollution intensity.

Factors contributing to these problems include the unavailability of bank credit and the excessive reliance on internal sources of finance for environmental upgrading projects in the manufacturing sector. Four of five enterprises in the sample reported substantial progress in the area of energy-saving technology, allowing them to relocate funds towards clean-up concerns. This indicates that the pursuit of enterprise restructuring measures can more generally result in improved environmental standards as internal resources are tapped for alternative uses.

The survey also indicated that the investment-promotion strategy of the Czech Environmental Office, while yielding positive results, could be further strengthened. Specifically, the Environmental Office grants enterprises grace periods for payment of environmental taxes if they are in the process of installing environmentally friendly technology. The extent of investment stimulated by this scheme is limited, as environmental taxes represent a small share of the overall corporate tax burden. This often results in smaller investments, particularly in "end of pipe" investment.

Another concern regarding the status of industrial environment is related to the clean up of the accumulated stock of industrial waste, particularly from processing and chemical industries. Although considerable effort has been put into dealing with this issue, both at the enterprise and government level, much remains to be done. While a concern for enterprises and the government, there is, however, no relevant EU environmental directive that deals with past liabilities explicitly. Studying the experience of EU member countries in this regard may provide innovative ideas and new solutions.

Labor Safety Standards

The EU accession agreement also requires compliance with Directive 89/391/EEC, which stipulates that employers are obliged to assess safety and health risks at work, and to provide employees with adequate training to maintain their safety. Legislation separate from the Labor Code should be drafted to include provisions regarding protective and preventive services, as well as health surveillance. A second stage in the accession process would involve compliance with 13 other EU Directives, which contain regulations on workplace equipment, safety signs, chemical exposure, etc.

Survey evidence in manufacturing enterprises collected by the World Bank suggests that enterprise managers are aware of the existing directives on labor safety standards in the Czech Republic. There is, however, little incentive for compliance, since such regulations are not strictly enforced at the moment. Particularly worrisome is the non-compliance with chemical exposure safety procedures: a large share of the equipment in chemical plants is still Soviet-made and does not contain instructions on safety at work. The new -- mostly German -- equipment has safety manuals but training is not common. The exceptions are enterprises with foreign participation -- enterprises which, in many cases, have reached the safety standards of their West European partners.

There has been, however, no attempt to quantify the likely costs of such compliance from the point of view of Czech firms. Such an exercise would provide a guideline for managers on how much they should expect to incur in safety expenditures over the next several years. Good comparators in this regard would be the three countries of the Southern EEC enlargement -- Greece, Portugal and Spain -- which also lacked proper safety regulations prior to accession, but took them on board during the first years of accession.

Chapter IX. Agriculture Sector in Transition

Agriculture in the Economy

Prior to the Second World War, the Czech Republic was one of the most industrialized countries in Central Europe. Agriculture played only a marginal role in the economy, largely because of the limited natural resources available for agricultural production. Based on family farming, Czech agriculture was solidly grounded in both private ownership and private enterprise. In the 1930's, Czech agriculture was well developed, with yields and livestock productivity comparable to those in Western European countries, though, on the whole, the country was a net importer of agricultural products. During the decades of socialism, Czech agriculture was both collectivized and managed under the principles of central planning. Although the yields and productivity in Czech agriculture continued to remain higher than the levels of other socialist countries, the country's agriculture fell behind the advances of Western countries.

The share of agriculture in the economy contracted without interruption during the transition. While agriculture represented about 6 percent of GDP and 10 percent of employment in 1990, by 1994 agriculture generated 4.7 percent of GDP and employed 6.9 percent of the civil labor force. This reflects two opposing trends, namely: a) a reduction in agricultural production; and b) after a sharp contraction in the first years of transition, recovery in the Gross Domestic Product (GDP) between 1994 and 1996. In 1998 the share of agriculture in GDP

Figure 9.1. Share of Agriculture in GDP and Employment

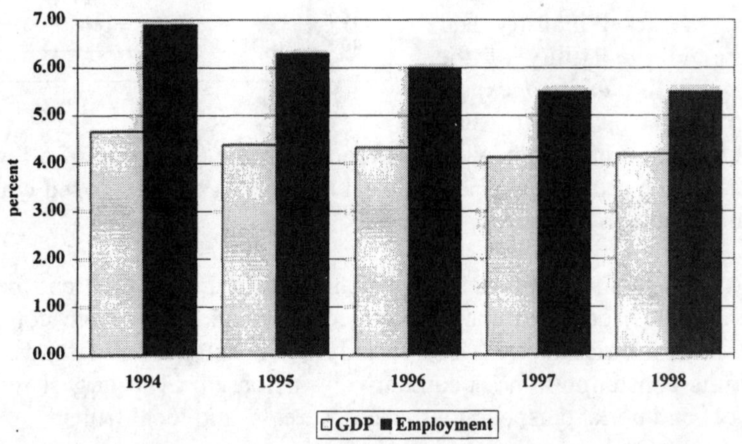

had dropped to 4.2 percent. With an active population of about 267,000 employed in agriculture, the share of employment in agriculture dropped to 5.5 percent in 1998 (see Figure 9.1). This reduction, facilitated by new opportunities for workers developed in non-agricultural activities, resulted in improved agricultural labor productivity. At world prices, productivity in the Czech Republic is more than two-thirds of the EU (15), nearly 60 percent higher than Austria but about 15 percent lower than in Germany (1996).

While the agricultural area has been relatively stable, agricultural production has experienced two parallel trends: a) a drastic reduction, year after year; and b) a slow switch from animal production to crop production. These changes reflect, in part, structural changes in the agricultural economy. However, their continuation also indicates that these changes have been slow, and as such primary agricultural production has not benefited from new and more efficient, market-oriented structures. The so-called "velvet revolution" in the political arena appears to have promoted a soft reform policy in agriculture -- a policy that one could qualify as the "velvet transition" of agriculture. But the downside of this policy is that the impact of the reforms, while milder on the agricultural sector, appears to have been stretched over a longer period. Under the current difficult international market conditions, this policy has not left breathing space in this continuous decline of Czech agriculture. With the exception of technical crops, which benefited from a specific policy in favor of the development of an industrial use of agricultural raw material, all crops and animal production fell drastically over the past eight years.

The Czech Republic is a net importer of agricultural and food products (see Figure 9.2). Its share of agriculture and food products in total exports has decreased by more than 50 percent, down to 5.4 percent in 1997, while the share in total imports decreased by about 25 percent down to 6.9 percent in 1997. The European Union (EU) is the main partner of the Czech Republic, with about 35 percent of the Czech agricultural and food exports and 50 percent of its imports. CEFTA countries constitute the second largest client for Czech exporters of agricultural and food products (about 33 percent of such exports). Prior to the 1998 crisis, countries from the former Soviet Union represented a growing clientele. Nonetheless, its land-locked position and the relatively poor product differentiation developed by the food industry had limited the ability of the Czech Republic to export to countries other than

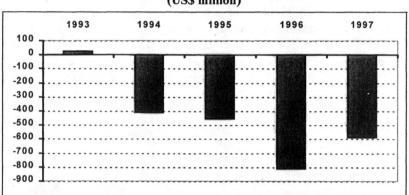

Figure 9.2. Balance of Agriculture and Food Trade, 1993-97 (US$ million)

those in its immediate neighborhood, with the exception of a few traditional Czech products (beer, ham, etc). The protection of agricultural markets in the developed countries represents a significant constraint to Czech agricultural exports.

The share of consumer expenditures going to food and beverages has decreased slightly over the past years, down to about 28 percent. Food prices have consistently increased less than the overall consumer price index (CPI). In only a few categories of foods, mainly poultry, vegetables and tropical fruits consumption has quantitatively increased. The largest reduction in per capita consumption is for beef and pork, eggs, potatoes, sugar, cereals, and local fruits.

Status of Sectoral Reforms

After the collapse of the socialist system at the end of 1989, a new government introduced a program of economic reform in 1991. This program included the transformation of agriculture based on the principles of ownership of land and other agricultural property. The aim was to create a market oriented and internationally competitive agricultural sector. During the first years of the transition, the agricultural policy of the Czech Republic focused on the implementation of an ambitious reform program to transform the food and agriculture sector. The most important measures generally fall into three categories:

- The creation of a macro-framework and an incentive system for producers, processors, and traders consistent with the requirements of a market-based food and agriculture system;

- The privatization of the major means of production, both in primary agricultural production and in agro-processing and input supply; and

- The changes in institutions and regulations to enhance the functioning markets.

Market Conforming Policy Framework with Increasing Intervention

The foundation of the current system of government intervention in agriculture was laid down in 1991-92. This framework was originally aimed at providing protection to farmers during the transition process as well as during the period of price liberalization. In recent years, different forms of market interventions were instituted, and the harmonization with the Common Agricultural Policy (CAP) has become an additional, but still not major, objective. The main instruments which have remained, more or less, unchanged since the early 1990s include:

- price support measures with "guaranteed" prices and export subsidies for the main commodities;

- financial support for the establishment of new private farms and for investments in the agro-food sector, in the form of direct subsidies, subsidized credits, and credit guarantees;

- direct payments or compensation to farmers in less favored areas, and areas with special features;

- support for socially and environmentally desirable farming practices, such as the transfer of arable land into meadows and pastures and other production extending practices; and

- support for more general agricultural services such as research, animal and crop breeding, information dissemination, training, and extension services.

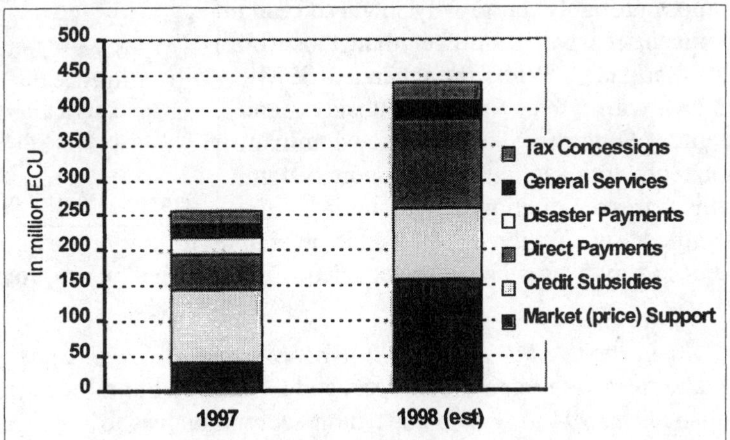

In the early years of the transition, the level of support, although having declined from the pre-reform period, nonetheless remained relatively high. By the mid-1990s, agricultural support and protection declined even further, although the objectives and basic instruments of the support system did not change. However, the Law on Agriculture, adopted in 1997, and other recent measures brought about an increase in the support and protection of agriculture. In 1998, the budgetary support to agriculture is expected to increase by 36 percent in nominal value. On the

Figure 9.3. Budget Expenditures in Agriculture, 1997-98

whole, however, the magnitude of budgetary expenditures related to agriculture, roughly equivalent to EUR437 million, cannot be considered excessive in comparison with most of the developed market economies (see Figure 9.3).

As was the case in many other countries in Central and Eastern Europe, agriculture in the Czech Republic experienced a cost/price squeeze because input prices increased more sharply than output prices early in the transition process. Input prices quickly rose to international levels -- more than doubling between 1990 and 1997. At the same time, prices paid to farmers remained relatively flat, increasing less than 50 percent over the same period. This sharply contrasts with the more than 2.5-fold increase in consumer prices during those years. Farmgate prices for practically all products are below those in the EU. Expressed in EUR, the domestic price rises have been, to some extent, mitigated by the depreciation of the Czech crown (CZK). The price gaps (at the farmgate level) with the EU have declined only modestly over time.

Direct Market Intervention: A Major Instrument of the Agricultural Policy. Direct market intervention is currently the major support instrument, which includes border measures as well as direct and indirect intervention in the market through the State Fund for Market Regulation (SFMR). In 1994-96, SFMR intervention was primarily limited to wheat and dairy products (see Box 9.1). In 1998, a broader system of intervention was introduced which covered wheat and pork. Interest rate subsidies were also introduced for the export of a broad range of agricultural commodities. As a result, the total magnitude of market intervention expenditures is expected to increase 2.3 times in 1998 when compared to 1997 levels. Although actual results for 1998 are not available, it is expected that effective government purchases will significantly increase relative to previous years. Expenditures of cereal market intervention will, most probably, be greatly increased, and domestic prices will be higher than those on world markets. With the change, SFMR together with the Credit Subsidy and Guarantee Schemes, became the dominant components of the agricultural support system. If this trend continues (assuming the

---

Box 9.1. State Fund for Market Regulation

The main objective of the State Fund for Market Regulation (SFMR) is to provide market stabilization by limiting excessive price movements and, as such, it tends to act as a safety net for agricultural producers by supporting guaranteed minimum prices for agricultural products within the budget allocation for a given year. More specifically, the SFMR can take the following steps to regulate markets:

- select a list of products to be regulated in any specific year;
- set a minimum price (guaranteed floor price) at which given quantities of the specific product are to be purchased by the government;
- stipulate the time period during which specific product markets are to be regulated;
- set the level of export subsidies for the regulated products; and
- influence the licensing of exports and imports of food and agricultural products through proposals in this respect, to the relevant state administrative bodies.

Source: Ministry of Agriculture.

---

constrained availability of all funds available to agriculture), these funds will channel significant resources away from other, more efficiency enhancing support programs.

An Elaborate but Financially Weak System of Credit Subsidies and Guarantees. Credit subsidies and guarantees -- through the Support and Guarantee Fund for Farmers and Forestry (SGFFF), which was established in 1994 to improve the farm sector's access to short- and longer-term credits -- represent the second largest component of support programs. The main function of SGFFF is to provide guarantees for loans (at commercial interest rates) already agreed upon between a food and agricultural entrepreneur and a commercial bank. The maximum level of guarantee ranges from 50 percent to 80 percent; in specific cases, it can be 100 percent. In addition, the SGFFF provides a subsidy to interest payments. In 1998, the interest payments were subsidized up to about 60 percent. Interest free loans are also provided to young farmers and for development in less favored regions. The 1998 agricultural budget envisages a decrease of almost 20 percent in credit-related support. The credit policy shifts away from providing interest-free loans to farmers towards loan guarantees, interest subsidies as well as increased support to larger-scale farming operations. The current situation of SGFFF is causing some concern for the mid- to longer-term budget outlook. Although the overall amount of outstanding credit guarantees does not seem excessively high (EUR524 million), the significantly increased amount of matured guaranteed loans in the last two years might undermine the financial sustainability of the whole program if this trend continues. At the same time, the value of the counterpart assets of the SGFFF has reportedly decreased to about one-sixth of its original, non-market based, value.

Direct Payments to Agriculture. In 1998, a generalized agricultural area payment was introduced, the level depending on the administrative land price. The payment was intended as a support to farming in general (maintenance of the landscape), and for organic farming and afforestation in particular, and, in less favored areas, livestock activities (beef, cattle, and sheep). The support for farms in less favored areas is conditional on an animal density between 0.1 and 1 livestock unit/ha (with pigs and poultry comprising not more than 50 percent of all livestock units).

A Relatively Liberal Trade Regime. The Czech Republic has a relatively liberal trading regime, governed by a number of multilateral and bilateral agreements. Border measures are, to a large extent, conditions imposed by the Czech Republic's WTO commitments. Most Czech tariffs are considerably lower than the EU *ad valorem* equivalents, with the exception of poultry, potatoes, and oilseeds, which enjoy higher protection, and also pork, which has a similar level of protection. On the export side, the Czech Republic is allowed to subsidize a limited range of products. The actual export subsidies in 1995-97 remained well below the value and quantity ceilings. The indirect export subsidies, introduced in 1997 through the SGFFF, might be breaching the Czech Republic's WTO commitments, in particular, for sugar. Automatic export and import licensing is applied mainly for registration purposes. Non-automatic export licensing is occasionally applied when world prices are significantly higher than domestic prices (e.g., cereals in 1995/96 when nearly no export licenses were issued).

The EU and CEFTA provide preferential markets for Czech agricultural products while, at the same time, the domestic Czech market must cope with increased competition from these countries. In general, Czech agriculture has benefited from these agreements, and the current liberal trading environment with these two groups of countries provides a good measure of how Czech agriculture might compete in an enlarged EU. Recently, the increased agricultural trade deficit and overproduction in some areas resulted in some trade policy measures, which do not fully conform with the existing EU and CEFTA trade agreements.

Incomplete Transition in the Farming Sector

The process of reform has been difficult and painful for many enterprises. In 1990, the country had no alternative other than to move to a market-based, privatized, agricultural sector if it wanted to compete in international markets. Due to the specific process used to privatize state assets, and due to the relative stability of the overall economy, the first years of transition in the Czech Republic brought relatively less disruption in the farming sector than that which occurred in many neighboring countries. These factors created a relatively favorable environment for reforms in the agricultural sector; at the same time, the pressure for radical transformation of inherited farming structures and other change was reduced. By the end of 1997, about 25 percent of agricultural land was in the hands of individual farmers; 35 percent was farmed by commercial companies, and 39 percent was still farmed by cooperatives. Czech farms differ, not only in terms of legal status from the traditional EU family-based structure, but in their larger size: about 90 percent of the farms cultivating more than 100 ha (about 40 percent in the EU). In addition, about 89 percent of the land they cultivate is not owned by the farm itself (versus 60 percent in the average EU country). This specific feature of the Czech farming sector has various implications in terms of land market and, financially, by the constraints it creates to mortgage lending. It appears that this farming structure is still not final, and requires further consolidation and restructuring.

The major features of the current farming structure include:

- *Dominance of Larger-Sized Farms.* The average size of farms, using about 75 percent of agricultural land, is around 1,000 ha. The average size of farms larger than three hectares, is over 100 ha;

- *Leasing of Land is a Major Form of Tenure.* Incorporated and collective farms use leased land almost exclusively. Larger individual farms also lease a significant amount of land. Most leases are only short to medium-term in length, inhibiting longer-term investment;

- *Low Profitability of Farming.* Most agricultural enterprises continue to show signs of continued low profitability. Economic results are rather unfavorable in the cooperative farming sector, which as a whole, operated with significant losses for the second consecutive year (1996-97). The economic results of agricultural companies also became negative in 1997. In contrast to larger farms, smaller individual farms significantly increased their profitability in recent years;

- *Significant Indebtedness.* The large-scale farming sector, especially the cooperative farms, carries a relatively large debt overhang, estimated at around CZK50 billion (nearly EUR1.7 billion). The bulk of the collective farm debt (approximately CZK12 billion) is due to the owners of the assets that were left with the cooperative farms by former cooperative members who left the farm (transformation shares). This debt, which is supposed to be settled in 1999, represents 20 percent of the value of the property of the farms concerned. The incorporated farms owe the government approximately CZK19 billion for non-land privatized property. Farms established in the framework of restitution still owe the government about CZK7 billion, which was provided in the early 1990s. The high indebtedness is a rather specific feature of farming in the Czech Republic, compared to many other Central European countries where pre-reform debts were settled during the transformation process and strictly enforced bankruptcy laws prevented the accumulation of new debt; and

- *Barely Restructured Collective Farms.* Most of the collective farms use about 38 percent of the agricultural land. Apart from the change in formal ownership relations (of land and assets) they still operate in the "old-fashioned" way -- with limited profitability and increasing financial difficulties. The majority of collective farms, in general, show a conservative and reluctant attitude to further restructuring. They are, to a large extent, still run as they were during the pre-transition period, with limited motivation on the part of the members.[1]

The Unfinished Agenda for Sectoral Reforms: Critical Issues for EU Accession

After a relatively successful launch of economic and sectoral reforms, some negative trends began to surface in 1995. Amid the worsening macro-economic framework, the importance of completing the remaining tasks of transition -- financial consolidation of the farms, privatization of remaining state-

---

[1] Farms, and in particular collective farms, benefited from various mechanisms of direct support and guarantees during the first years of the transition. Recently, there has been a trend to de-capitalize and dismember collective farms by members who take over the remaining good assets and leave the debts in the collective farms, creating in parallel another venture -- farm or other -- with the equipment and no debt.

owned land, improvement of competitiveness, and developing a market conforming institutional framework -- become more apparent. It is essential that the policy response to the demands of the agricultural sector for more support and attention to rural social problems, take an appropriate form. It is essential that such policy requirements not create new sources of inefficiencies and further gap with the requirements of EU accession. The current changes in international agricultural markets, the financial difficulties of completing the adjustment of the collective farming sector, as well as the increased social tensions in rural areas seem to lead to increased intervention and protection on the basis of the current set of instruments. This would be a misguided and artificial response to real problems; the intended financial protection would provide a misleading safeguard for an agricultural structure which still needs an overhaul, and improvement in competitiveness before EU accession takes place.

Refocusing the Policy Framework: Harmonization with the Common Agriculture Policy

Until recently, completing the transition to a market consistent agricultural policy environment, together with the provision of a certain safeguard of farming incomes, has been the focus of government attention. In recent years, different forms of market interventions were tried, and the harmonization with the CAP has become an additional, but still not major, objective. In general, agricultural policy framework and support systems need to focus on the following objectives:

- A more effective use of budgetary support to agriculture requires the revision of support programs to focus on efficiency enhancement rather than on price and export subsidies.

- The various instruments of government intervention in the sector, especially the various support programs, need to be integrated into a more consistent and predictable framework.

- Changes in the Czech agricultural policy framework need to take account of the evolving nature of the instruments and requirements of the CAP as a "moving target."

- The full adjustment of support to EU levels should be postponed until the time of actual accession.

- Measures to reduce social tensions and to provide social protection in rural areas need to be separated from the major instruments of agricultural policy aimed at improving efficiency and competitiveness.

The current agricultural support system definitely conforms with the principles of a market-based agriculture system. However, it does not fully correspond with the level of support and instruments of the CAP. Although there is pressure for immediate increases in support and protection on the farmer's side, and to converge at EU levels before accession, the level of support and border measures should remain at the current level in order to maintain pressure to complete reforms, and to remain within both budgetary constraints and WTO commitments. The level of support should, accordingly, be aligned only after the accession. At the same time, efforts should be concentrated on the adaptation of the same policy instruments as in the EU, but not yet necessarily applying them, or applying them at the same level. Agenda 2000 proposals for the reform of the EU's CAP should be used as a benchmark in this task. In particular, the following adjustment needs to be considered:

- The SFMR system needs to be adjusted into a transparent CAP-conforming framework incorporating the potential use of quotas in the case of some products, and changes the current intervention which is based on an *ex-ante* system (the intervention is based on short-term forecasts on production and consumption) to an *ex-post* CAP type intervention mechanism when market intervention decisions by private sector are based on the observed evolution of EU market prices. In addition, to be consistent with the principles of the CAP, price support would need to be transferred to the wholesale level instead of the farmgate for most products;

- The current credit guarantee scheme needs to be fully de-linked from government, and credit subsidies need to be discontinued in their present format. Credit subsidies might temporarily be replaced by investment grants for a transitory period to improve competitiveness, from national budgetary sources (or financed by the EU, if possible);

- Direct payments and other current structural support measures must be adapted to the EU format, while new ones, such as an agro-environmental program will have to be introduced. The generalized area payment scheme outside of the less-favored areas could be adapted and fitted into those national envelopes proposed for the dairy and beef sectors under the Agenda 2000;

- A more integrated regional and rural policy and related support programs have to be developed to utilize the EU's structural fund instruments; and

- The taxation system and the tax concessions provided need to be harmonized with EU practices and requirements.

Need for an Integrated Rural Development Approach

The balanced development of rural areas, as well as preparing for the full utilization of the emerging instruments of the evolving CAP, both require a complex and comprehensive approach which integrates agriculture into an overall rural development framework. Such an approach should include a set of specific measures to support:

- Emergence of competitive agriculture;

- Further development of the rural service sector and related industries to provide off-farm rural employment and additional demand for agricultural and other products;

- Improvement of rural infrastructure, including education and social services; and

- Development of an appropriate social policy to properly address specific social problems affecting rural populations;

Rural development, in particular in less-favored regions of the Czech Republic (mainly mountains) faces several challenges:

- *A Decentralized Approach.* In a country of relatively small dimensions and with a strong historical background in terms of central planning, the challenge here is to ascertain that the rural development program is conceived, developed, implemented and, in part, financed by local rural institutions -"the bottom-up approach." In other words, rural development needs to be driven by local demand as expressed by the ultimate stakeholders in rural development, the rural communities, and their inhabitants;

- *A Multi-Sectoral Approach.* The various and often complementary aspects of rural development imply the collaboration between various line Ministries (transport and infrastructure, health, education, environment, agriculture, etc.) to assess whether the decentralized programs would fit with the national policies and EU rules and regulations;

- *The Financial Engineering of Mostly Small to Medium-Size Projects.* The challenge here is to ensure the active participation of various financing institutions (Czech and foreign) to mobilize various sources of funds available to the country. These sources vary significantly depending on the type of project the local communities have prepared;

- *Fair Prioritization for Financing Based on Technical Criteria to Reduce the Risk of Preferential Treatment Given to Certain Communities Rather than Others on the Basis of Political Favoritism.* A strong technical analysis of priorities by local/regional policy-makers which would be screened by central government on the basis of simple technical criteria (e.g., un-employment, level of education in the region, private sector projects waiting for public infrastructure, etc.); and

- *Collaboration with Private Sector (Enterprises, NGOs, etc.).* This collaboration constitutes a challenge for public sector agencies like municipalities and villages although it also strengthens the sense of ownership in the region and facilitates implementation.

Another important objective of a program for rural development in the Czech Republic would be to support the government's efforts toward EU accession. By linking with the EU pre-accession (and accession) initiatives for rural development, environment, employment and agriculture, and rural development programs should also enable the government to use available resources (credits, grants, human capital) with maximum efficiency. In keeping with recent trends in EU member countries, such a program would need to assist the Czech Republic in making the fundamental shift from purely agricultural to mixed use of the countryside, reflecting new attitudes and needs of rural, urban and suburban communities. One of the important features to be incorporated in the program would be the special focus on less-favored regions.

Consolidation of the Farming Sector

While the initial issues of land privatization and restitution have been largely resolved, and while the new farming organizations are consistent with the principles of a market economy, the consolidation of ownership and the settlement of outstanding financial issues have yet to be achieved. These must be accomplished in order to create a viable farming structure under EU conditions. The critical areas for action are:

- *Further Transformation of Collective Farms.* There are many indications that cooperative farms, in their current state, would hardly be able to cope with the increased competitive pressure of the EU environment. Their methods of operation and management, and their handling of current resources, need to be further adjusted to the principles of market economy. A small number of cooperative farms have already entered the so-called "second transformation," which has often resulted in joint-stock companies or limited liability companies. This process involves the restructuring of ownership, management, and labor force; it often involves the splitting of activities and diversifying into downstream activities. Although the "second transformation" results in a more viable and profit motivated operations, it often leaves empty, skeleton cooperatives, which retain most of the debt; the transparency of such transformations is also often questionable. It is also important that the further transformation of collective farms takes place with adequate attention to the social consequences of the reduction in the labor force and streamlining of production;

- *Settlement of Farm Debts.* The huge debt overhang is a significant constraint on further consolidation of farming and would certainly be a handicap inside the EU. The so-called "transformation shares" represent a special case. It is obvious that the majority of collective farms are not able to settle this debt. Owners of these shares press for quick and full settlement, while the collective farms would prefer to have a settlement that involves long-term payment duration, based on special bonds issued by the cooperatives to the owners of the transformation shares. The speedy resolution of this issue remains critical to the further consolidation and restructuring of collective farms;

- *Sale of Remaining State-Owned Land.* The large amount of state-owned land awaiting privatization is an impediment to the emerging land market, as well as to the recapitalization of the sector. There is a draft law currently before parliament which would initiate the privatization of most of the state-owned land, providing preferences to current users. The individual farming sector, however, would prefer to restrict the right of purchase of state-owned land only to physical persons, in order to enhance the further development of the individual private farming sector. Since legally incorporated farms are genuinely privately-owned, it is hard to find another justification for preferences toward individual farmers other than to boost the development of individual private farms, which represent the most efficient part of the Czech agriculture sector; and

- *Access to Foreign Investors of Agricultural Land.* In principle, membership in the EU would require that agricultural land markets be opened to competitive forces from anywhere within the Union. Presently, foreign ownership of agricultural land is not allowed in the Czech Republic, and foreign agricultural land ownership is a rather sensitive issue, similar to other EU accession countries.

Strengthening of Factor Markets

Well functioning factor markets would constitute the basis for a good market-based structural adjustment of Czech agriculture. This would imply less distortive interventions from the state or from outdated laws. It would involve the development of modern instruments of exchange of land, labor, finance, and an element often forgotten in economies in transition: risk. At a time when Czech agriculture is faced with new challenges resulting from the accession to the EU, factor markets clearly constitute a significant constraint to be addressed by the Czech Republic to ensure reasonable chances to adjust to the new challenges with the proper instruments. It would be appropriate to:

- review the main legal reasons that prevent the land market, and mortgage lending based on agricultural land, from functioning;

- adjust and, if needed, create or improve those private and state institutions that can ensure a well functioning land market;

- review and adjust as needed the legal foundations of the warehouse receipts system, ensure that the private sector can operate properly under these laws, and assess the effectiveness of the performance guarantee given by the warehouses to deliver the product to their owner;

- reverse the recent tendency to promote credit guarantees and subsidies by SGFFF to cooperatives, a financially poor-performing category in the farming sector;

- nominate financial auditors (Czech and foreign) to review the evolution of the risks taken by the state through its activities in SGFFF, and assess whether and how this interest rate subsidy and guarantee by the state would be acceptable at the time of accession to the EU; and

- regarding labor transfers from agriculture, assess the social impact of the economic reforms in rural areas on poverty, migration to urban areas, and social services in less-favored rural regions and develop accordingly a program for facilitating the development of off-farm employment in rural regions. Such a program would need to be prepared in close coordination with foreign donors and, in particular, with the European Commission as part of its support programs to the Czech Republic.

Improvement of Wholesale Marketing Institutions

The review of the main agricultural services reflects an advanced system of private and state services. The network of private suppliers for mechanical equipment, fertilizers pesticides, as well as seeds is reportedly well-developed, its main constraints in terms of actual access to such inputs remains access to working capital, albeit in the form of various support schemes developed by SGFFF. In some sub-sectors, significant financing is provided by non-financial institutions, the warehouses and trading enterprises - in particular those of the former state monopoly. This pre-financing is quite an elaborate system in which the State Fund for Market Regulation (SFMR) plays a significant role. This partial pre-financing of the crop is provided at no financial cost to participating farmers unless these farmers fail to deliver at harvest the quantities contracted under the SFMR scheme. The SFMR operates through the local warehouses - mostly those from the previous state monopoly - and this creates an elaborate cross-support to participating intermediaries and farmers.

The network of wholesale agriculture marketing enterprises remains weak in several agricultural sub-sectors. This lack of competitive agricultural markets at the wholesale level significantly impedes the installation of CAP institutions in the Czech Republic.

With regard to agriculture services, the following actions are recommended:

- *A review of the legal framework of cooperatives* to assess the impediment it creates in the formation of marketing and processing cooperatives and in their effective management. In this regard, the analysis of cooperative laws should be performed from the view point of the agency theory;

- for fresh produce and livestock, *a network of private regional exchanges* with or without the support of local municipality, should be strengthened. Their role in terms of facilitating price information and developing competitive market intermediation should be developed. Such commodity exchanges could become elements of the information network that the CAP needs for products in the livestock, fruit and vegetable sub-sectors;

- a review of *the level of competition at the sub-sectoral level* and the implications of the market support policy on competition with the ultimate goal of alleviating this major constraint on future agricultural development is necessary;

- *the development of an analysis of price related risks taken by entrepreneurs in the agricultural and food marketing chain*, their costs, and the transfer to private sector from the SFMR of the management of such risks; and

- *the launching of training programs on agricultural marketing and price/risk management in agriculture.*

Accelerated Technical and Technological Development of Agroprocessing

The food industry is well diversified, with no single major sub-sector emerging as a leading outlet to agriculture. Considering the geo-climatic characteristics of the country, it would seem that the fruit and vegetables processing and dairy sub-sectors are less developed than one would expect. Moreover, small-scale food processing appears relatively under-developed in terms of both absolute numbers and contribution to the economy. Foreign direct investment (FDI) in food processing remains primarily limited to a few large enterprises. FDI is not playing a significant role in the transformation of the agri-food sector by bringing new technology, new know-how and substantial capital (including working capital) as part of the privatization process. The general problem that emerged in the Czech Republic in 1997 regarding the banking sector ownership (directly or via investment funds) of enterprises might also be observed in the food industry. The so-called "passive shareholder" syndrome, and the informal or formal coordination of enterprise strategies at the sub-sector level, could also affect the food industry. The restructuring of the industry in sub-sectors like dairy or meat processing has not, as a result, been accelerated. Most of the agro-processing in its current form, would likely have limited competitiveness under EU conditions. The accelerated development of this subsector is an essential precondition to coping with the challenge of EU accession.

Establishment of New Standards for Agricultural and Food Products

At each stage of the agricultural and food marketing chain, farmers and entrepreneurs have the important responsibility of ascertaining the quality of the products delivered to their clients, particularly in relation to potential health hazards, environmental impacts, and other services attached to the product. The Government of the Czech Republic is fully aware of the pending problems of harmonization with the EU system, of the legislation on these matters, and of its enforcement. Among the decisions that have not benefited from a similar level of attention, one could list the transfer to the private sector of a rather large number of tasks currently undertaken by numerous state agencies. One could also note a parallel reduction in the number, and a substantial reassignment, of the roles of implementing state agencies on standards, quality control, and health safety. This new approach would exercise a significant change in the incentives given to food processing enterprises while adjusting to this new set of responsibilities transferred to them. While the concerned departments of the Ministry of Agriculture have made great efforts in adjusting the whole set of legislation concerning food quality, standards, etc., it appears that the enterprises themselves have not benefited from the information, training and assistance to adjust to this new concept of quality management. The following program of actions is recommended:

- *A program of public information* -- awareness and data banks in real time open to scientists and lawyers, and in coordination with private trade association (see below). In addition, information for the rural population about the EU needs to be developed and/or strengthened;

- A *program of collaboration between the private sector and state agencies,* including the outsourcing of some of the activities of the public sector that could be easily undertaken either by the private sector or in collaboration with foreign state agencies;

- *The completion of the restructuring of state agencies* involved in consumer protection, animal and plant protection, agricultural research and extension, border control, farm registration, market information, market organization by sub-sector, and market intervention;

- *A review and adjustment of the salaries and benefits paid to civil servants in agriculture* so that they can remain competitive with private sector;

- *A detailed training program for existing staff in the various specialties concerned* and an exchange program of staff between Czech and EU institutions. This training program should not only be implemented for civil servants but should be designed, in collaboration with the concerned trade associations, to address the needs of the private sector in the various sub-sectors;

- A program of recruitment and adjustment of skills by the restructured state agencies (particularly in areas where the *acquis communautaire* imposes new types of activities on the country); and

- An investment program to strengthen technology related to quality control, and new food processing techniques incorporating technologies related to quality enhancement and environmental protection. The program could have two major components that would have to be consistent with each other: one for the financing of the private sector (e.g., five-year loans for priority actions for implementing the new legal framework); and one for the financing of the restructured state agencies (see above) in office technology, information networks, laboratory building and equipment, etc.

Strengthening Private Sector Representation in Agriculture and Food Economy Sub-sectors

Finally, the representation of private interests for each profession in the various agricultural and food subsectors constitutes an important missing element. This is a strikingly common feature in Central and Eastern European countries, with the exception of Hungary, where such representation is highly developed in a majority of agri-food sub-sectors. In the EU, such representation is a crucial element of the implementation of the CAP: it contributes to a better understanding of private interests by the European Commission and the governments in the EU, and of government policies by the concerned private sector. In addition, many decisions related to trade, research, and technology, market information, and training could proceed in common by operators belonging either to the same profession or to the same marketing chain (the so-called inter-professional associations, or, in Hungary, the "product councils"). The development of such organizations should be promoted and facilitated. Technical cooperation with similar foreign organizations could be explored to develop a sound understanding of the role of such organizations. When created, they should be sufficiently scrutinized in the light of competition laws to avoid possible sub-sectoral collusions. Among the services of general interest to be offered and performed along the various sub-sectoral marketing chains -- services at present primarily lacking in agriculture and agro-industries - one can list the following: (a) consultation with state agencies intervening in the sub-sector; (b) analysis and information on markets and regulations (domestic and foreign); (c) organization of technical and commercial training programs; (d) contracting for research on issues of common interest with domestic or foreign institutions; (e) organization of first instance arbitration of trade conflicts; and (f) development of facilitating procedures and instruments for the exchange of products.

Chapter X. Complying with the European Union Environmental Directives

Introduction

Joining the EU will require the Czech Republic to adopt and implement the whole body of EU legislation and standards -- the *Acquis Communautaire*. This chapter reviews the implications of complying with the environmental legislation of the Union. The chapter assesses the institutional changes, the cost of the required investment program, the scope for managing investments as efficiently as possible, and the impacts of these changes on households. The chapter starts with an overview, including a summary of the compliance costs. It then analyses the impact of compliance with the legislation on each of the environmental areas as well as the implications on utility tariffs; the chapter closes with recommendations for compliance strategies.[1]

Background

EU Environmental Legislation

The EU environmental directives touch all sectors of the economy. However, the EU does not assume that the Czech Republic or any of the other acceding countries will have implemented all of the environmental *acquis* before joining, but rather explicitly recognizes that extended transition periods will be necessary. Accordingly, the environmental *acquis* presents particular challenges for the Czech Republic for several reasons:

- *The Scale and Scope of EU Legislation Concerning Environment is Broad and Mandates Substantial Investment.* Even without the imperative of EU directives, the Czech Republic would choose to make the required or similar investments at some stage in the future. Accession, however, accelerates the investment program and reduces the scope for the Czech Republic to adopt different implementation policies.

- *The Benefits of the Necessary Investments will be Seen Only in the Long Term but the Costs will be Immediate.* The costs will affect each Czech household. Government at all levels will need to engage in systematic consultations with the public and will need to invest in awareness-raising campaigns. In the short term, environmental investment may have to be considered a price of joining the EU.

- *The Requirements of EU Directives do not Always Correspond with the Czech Republic's Immediate National Priorities.* The challenge is to identify actions that will have both domestic and transboundary benefits and, where this is not possible, to be clear about trade-offs.

- *The Investment Programs Required to Upgrade Infrastructure could Exacerbate Regional Disparities in Income and Employment.* Therefore, investment programs should be examined carefully for their local and regional impact, and appropriate transfer mechanisms implemented where necessary.

---

[1] A more detailed paper, outlying sources and assumptions on which this analysis is based, is available.

Environmental Protection in the Czech Republic

The Czech Republic's environmental legislation is based on the Environmental Protection Act of 1992 (No.17/1992, and the following acts on protection of specific parts of environment, such as nature and air) and the 1995 State Environmental Policy. In recent years, the country has made some progress in harmonizing its environmental laws and regulations with those of the EU; and is working hard to complete the process. The principal gaps relate to legislation on water, waste, integrated pollution prevention and control (IPPC), and genetically modified organisms (GMOs).

In terms of implementation, the country has made great progress since the early 1990s. The country has stopped the steady decline on environmental quality, and has even seen marked improvements in quality of air and surface water. It has invested heavily in achieving this. The level of environmental expenditures has stabilized at around 2.4 of GDP. This level exceeds that of most EU member states even at the height of their environmental investment programs. Environmental investment expenditure grew in real terms between 1990 and 1996, from EUR0.6 billion in 1990 to EUR1.2 billion (in 1996 prices). Overall, the share of central government expenditure has declined since 1992, while private sector investment increased due to the new environmental legislation. Environmental expenditures have focussed mainly on controlling and abating air and water pollution.

The Implications of the EU Approximation

Cost Estimates

Recent Government estimates have put the cost of fully implementing all EU environmental directives at approximately EUR 6.6-9.0 billion[2] (in 1998 prices). These estimates are highly optimistic, because they are silent about the cost of capital and high operating and maintenance expenditures in most sectors. The eight-year compliance period is also optimistic, as Section 5 will indicate. For the purpose of this study, we have assessed the overall cost for the Czech Republic of complying with EU environmental directives, including the operation and maintenance costs not covered elsewhere (see Table 10.1).

We estimate total investment costs, therefore, at between EUR5.0-6.8 billion. If the investments are annualized over their expected lifetime (20 years) using an interest rate of 12 percent and if O&M costs are included, the total annual costs are EUR1.2-1.7 billion or 2.5-3.7 percent of 1997 GDP. It is difficult to compare these figures with current environmental expenditures, but we estimate that this involves an increase of 120-150 percent over what the country would have spent without accession.

The timescale over which these investments are made is crucial. The current government policy appears to be to achieve full compliance by 2005. The present value of a stream of investments over seven years until 2005 is 30 percent higher than if the investments are spread until 2015. The present value of the benefits, however, is only 10 percent higher.[3]

---

[2] These estimates do not include costs related to cleaning up past pollution, estimated at about EUR2.2 billion.
[3] Note that this is not a full net present value calculation as we have used assumptions about the relative benefits, but have not estimated their value.

Table 10.1. Environmental Costs of EU Accession

	Investment Cost		Annual Capital Cost[1]		Annual O&M Cost		Total Annual Cost		Total per Capita		Total Annual Cost[2]	
	EUR Million		EUR Million		EUR Million		EUR Million		EUR		1997 GDP (%)	
	Low	High	Low	High	Low	High	Low	High	Low	High	Low	High
Air pollution[3]	1,074	1,628	114	218	164	274	308	492	30	48	0.7	1.1
Drinking water	811	1,668	109	223	81	148	190	371	18	36	0.4	0.8
Sewers	1,176	1,176	157	157	54	54	211	211	21	21	0.5	0.5
Wastewater treatment	878	1,075	118	144	62	100	180	244	17	24	0.4	0.5
Waste management	254	392	34	52	59	97	93	149	9	15	0.2	0.3
Others[4]	815	815	109	109	58	109	167	218	16	21	0.4	0.5
Total[5]	5,008	6,755	671	903	478	782	1,149	1,685	112	164	2.5	3.7
State Budget[6] percent	13	10	13	10	12	8	13	9				
Local Government[7]	61%	66%	61%	66%	57%	55%	59%	61%				

Note: Excluding nuclear safety, transport, industry and trade, and clean-up of past pollution, but including institutional costs.
1/ Investment costs are annualized over 20 years using an interest rate of 12 percent[4]. The cost recovery factor is estimated as follows: CRF=0.134= $r(1+r)^T/[(1+r)^T-1]$, where r=0.12 and T=20.
2/ Annual costs are represented as a ratio of 1997 GDP (EUR46 billion).
3/ Includes additional environmental investments by the main power company, CEZ, estimated at EUR182 million.
4/ Includes noise, environmental permitting (Integrated Pollution Prevention & Control (IPPC), EIA) and nature protection.
5/ We have rounded to the first decimal the totals of the last two columns.
6/ Mostly to cover administrative costs associated with noise control, environmental permitting, monitoring, etc.
7/ In some municipalities these costs will be covered by private investors or users.
Source: Assembled with information contained in recent studies supported by the Poland Hungary Assistance for Economic Reconstruction (PHARE) program, the 1997 CEZ Annual Report, the CarlBro study on accession in the water sector, and World Bank estimates for O&M costs.

Implications for the Public Sector

Compliance with the environmental *acquis* will affect the public sector through two channels: first, the costs of adjusting the institutional and regulatory framework; second, the investment requirements that must be made by the state and municipalities in different environmental areas.

The Czech Republic has made substantial progress in harmonizing its national legal acts. However, adapting its institutions poses an even greater challenge. The administration will have to change many of its public agencies that deal with environmental issues, including possibly creating some new bodies. Agencies will need to strengthen their administrative and technical capacities, and will have to possess staff with sufficient training and experience to enforce the new environmental legislation and standards, to implement effective policies, to monitor environmental quality accurately, and to report and disseminate information. A preliminary estimate indicates that the administration will need at least 820 new staff members. Moreover, enforcement will call for increased cooperation between the environmental ministry and the sectoral ministries, as well as a well-designed monitoring system. The Czech Republic has already established monitoring networks for air, water and waste, but it still requires additional investments for the construction of new stations and modern equipment to ensure effective enforcement of legislation.

In financial terms, incremental expenditures on salaries, office space, external expert services, and monitoring equipment have been tentatively estimated at EUR33 million, or 2-3 percent of total

---

[4] Real cost of capital in the Czech Republic has been estimated at 12 percent. This is based on the current experience of the water industry in the UK, where private investors are claiming between 6-9 percent as their cost of capital (OFWAT, 1998), and the fact that the water industry in the UK is perceived by investors as relatively low risk investment.

annualized costs associated with approximation. These estimates, however, underestimate the true institutional cost of approximation since they do not include expenditures associated with training of staff.

The public sector will play an important role in financing investments driven by the environmental *acquis*. The most important areas for public sector financing will be drinking water, sewerage, wastewater treatment, waste and improvement of ambient air quality. The responsibility for these areas lies mostly with *local governments or municipalities*. Although the 1993 Tax Law requires that seventy five percent of municipal budgets and investments must come from the municipalities' own resources, and the rest from the central government, in reality small municipalities rely mostly on the central government budget to finance their investments.[5] Many of the investments show substantial economies of scale, and require cooperation among municipalities. The fragmentation of large numbers of small municipalities hinders this cooperation. Thus, without central government support, small municipalities alone will not be able to develop projects or to finance the huge investment effort required in the near future.

The role of the central government will be different in the various environmental sectors:

- *Water Sector*. Municipalities are responsible for delivering service and for expansion, and can provide the services either through public or private companies. The central government should encourage the consolidation of smaller systems into larger units, in order to benefit from economies of scale, and they should ensure that issues such as drainage are given enough attention.

- *Waste Management*. Municipalities are responsible for household waste collection and, in most cases, disposal. At present, about 90 percent of investment expenditures have been financed from the municipalities' own resources.

- *Air Quality*. Central government support will probably be needed to deal with small pollution sources. Investments for conversion of local heating units from solid fuels to natural gas will most likely be subsidized by the state.

The European Union plans to make funds available to the accession countries to help finance the investments related to the environmental *acquis*. This represents a tremendous opportunity for the Czech Republic to meet their sectoral and environmental priorities and to relieve the burden of these investments on households, particularly on lower income groups. The country needs to plan carefully to make best use of these funds, as there is a significant danger that they may be used in an ad hoc manner, which would not allow them to realize these benefits.

Experience with similar funds in Spain, Portugal, Greece and Ireland (the "Cohesion Countries") provides some useful lessons for the Czech Republic in planning its investment priorities. Clearly, these resources enabled the poorer countries of the Union to meet both environmental requirements and their national environmental priorities earlier than would otherwise have been the case. Some problems encountered during implementation, however, highlight potential pitfalls[6]

- Some national submissions did not fit national priorities, as they were either based on short-term needs or were prepared in order to obtain the largest possible allocation of funds.

---

[5] See chapter on inter-government and local finance in this report.
[6] "Special Report No. 1/95 on the cohesion financial instrument together with the Commission's replies."

- Some submissions were groupings of apparently unrelated projects, which were difficult to implement in a coherent manner.

- High great levels appear to have hindered efforts to improve sector efficiency, particularly by improving levels of cost recovery in the water sector. This is, in part, because projected revenue streams from the project reduce the amount of grant that can be allocated.[7]

Main Environmental Areas

Internal Market

The 1995 EU White Paper on accession identifies the essential measures relevant to the internal market that the accession countries must adopt before they enter the EU. It covers legislation affecting the free movement of goods and services, which in the environment field covers only about 20 percent of the whole *acquis*. The major internal market related environmental areas are:

- Chemical substances: administrative procedures, risk assessments, classification, labeling, packaging, notification, transport, import and export;

- Waste management: waste oils, Polychlorinated Biphenyls (PCBs), Polychlorinated Terphenyls (PCTs), sewage sludge, batteries, packaging materials, incineration, landfills, recycling, and shipment;

- Air pollution: lead and benzene content of petrol and sulfur content of diesel fuel and gas oil, Volatile Organic Compounds (VOCs) and ozone depleting substances;

- Noise from vehicles and machinery; and

- Radioactive contamination of food stuffs and radiation protection.

The Czech Republic has already adopted significant elements of the White Paper relating to the internal market, whereas institutional capacity and enforcement require further development. Since all measures stated in the White Paper must be adopted by the time of accession, there are few strategic options. Formal adoption of White Paper measures relating to specific products will bring little financial cost to the public sector. Even though producers and users will bear most of the cost, they are likely to welcome the changes since the integration of EU standards into Czech standards relating to environment will ease their access to the EU internal market.

The new Chemical Substances and Preparations Act (157/98), compatible with EU regulations, has been in force since January 1999. It defines not only technical requirements on those chemical products that are put on the market, but also conditions for management of chemicals. The system is highly centralized, with responsibilities resting with government bodies rather than with producers. Average annual recurrent costs for the state administration have been estimated at about EUR3 million; annual costs for the private sector, in turn, have been estimated between EUR4-28 million. These overall expenditures represent 0.6-1.9 percent of overall annual compliance costs.

---

[7] "Special Report No. 3/98 concerning the implementation by the Commission of EU policy and action as regards water pollution accompanied by the replies of the Commission."

Compliance with EU legislation in other environmental areas, and its estimated investment costs, are addressed below in more detail.

Drinking Water

Directive 98/83/EEC on drinking water quality establishes strict standards for the quality of drinking water; it sets out a system of monitoring, sampling and testing of either tap water or bottled water. In the Czech Republic, drinking water quality is assessed under a draft Ministerial Decree, which is unlikely to be fully compatible with new EU standards and procedures. At present, drinking water quality is monitored in public piped water systems, which supply 40 percent of the population. Although no acute pollution problem has occurred, the Czech standards for some parameters, such as free chlorine, hardness, calcium, aluminum and iron, have been exceeded.

Raw water quality has been gradually deteriorating since the 1980s. In 1996, about 18 percent of surface water came from sources considered unsuitable for drinking purpose. Groundwater quality has also experienced a steady deterioration since the 1970s and 1980s, particularly in shallow aquifers. Some 86 percent of the total population is connected to the public water supply, and the rest of the population relies on water from individual shallow wells. Monitoring records of these systems indicate that 95-98 percent of all measures exceeds quality standards for drinking water. On the other hand, monitoring records of drinking piped water supplies that depend on groundwater indicate that less than 0.5 percent of the samples exceed quality standards.

Full compliance with the EU drinking water directive will require replacing the supply of water of those currently using shallow wells with an alternative supply that meets EU standards. This will require either building a new small water supply system or expanding existing systems. Per capita capital costs of alternative schemes have been reported in the range EUR470-2,800. The investment cost to comply with this directive is in the range of EUR0.8-1.7 billion. The first estimate assumes that piped water supply coverage will increase from 86 percent to 94 percent; the second estimate assumes 100 percent coverage. We estimate that annual operating and maintenance costs are EUR81-148 million. The institutional costs related to water protection have been estimated at EUR3.6 million per year.

Wastewater

By far the largest costs of implementing the environmental *acquis* are associated with the Urban Wastewater Treatment Directive (UWWT Directive). This specifies that all settlements with more than 2000 inhabitants have sewer systems and wastewater treatment plants. The level of treatment required depends on the characteristics of the receiving water. The directive gives a timetable for compliance depending on the size of settlements, but the Commission expects accession countries to negotiate their own timetables for compliance.

Since the beginning of the 1990s, the quality of surface water has improved. The country built 210 wastewater treatment plants between 1990 and 1996, and about 74 percent of the population are connected to the public sewerage system. On the other hand, about 10 percent of the wastewater discharged into the public system receives no treatment. The major challenges remaining are to ensure that all wastewater collected receives adequate treatment and to extend coverage and upgrade treatment for those 650 communities above 2000 inhabitants that lack facilities.[8] Very few entirely new systems are needed.

---

[8] Many of these communities lie inside the boundaries of larger municipalities.

As shown in Table 10.2, full compliance with the UWWT Directive will add an extra EUR1.6-1.8 billion to the capital investment program of the wastewater companies, and about EUR0.5 billion to industrial enterprises. In addition, the directive will add EUR88-109 million to the operating and maintenance costs of wastewater companies and EUR29-46 million to industrial enterprises.

Table 10.2. Investment and Operation and Maintenance (O&M) Requirements to Meet the Urban Wastewater Treatment Directive
(EUR million)

Component	Investment Costs	O&M Costs
Under All Country Non-Sensitive Scenario		
New sewerage system	1,176	54
Wastewater treatment plants (new and upgraded)[1]	383	34
Industrial wastewater treatment plants [1][2]	496	29
Total	2,054	117
Under All Country Sensitive Scenario		
New sewerage system	1,176	54
Wastewater treatment plants (new and upgraded) [1]	580	54
Industrial wastewater treatment plants [1][2]	496	46
Total	2,251	154

Notes: This assumes that all communities above 2,000 population equivalent must have collection and treatment systems. If the threshold is assumed at 10,000 p.e., then the investment costs will range between EUR1.1-1.2 billion and O&M costs between EUR62-94 million (see Table 10.3).

1/ Costs associated with sewage sludge disposal are included. Capital and operating costs are estimated at 20 percent of the total investment cost of wastewater treatment and 40 percent of the annual capital costs, respectively. Municipal sludge disposal investment costs range between EUR64-97 million, while operation and maintenance costs between EUR10-15 million per year.

2/ It includes future investment costs on securing treatment of industrial wastewater.

Source: Adapted from "Pre-Accession Planning to Meet the Requirements of EU Legislation in the Water Sector in the Czech Republic," Draft Final Report, March 1999.

Precise interpretation of the requirements is particularly important for the UWWT Directive, as different interpretations give varying costs. Article 3 of the directive gives dates by which member states must provide towns of more than 2,000 p.e. with sewer systems. It states, however, "where the establishment of a collecting system is not justified either because it would produce no environmental benefit or because it would involve excessive cost, individual systems or other appropriate systems which achieve the same level of environmental protection shall be used." It is unclear for how many Czech Republic towns between 2,000 and 10,000 p.e., the installation of sewers would either produce no environmental benefit or could involve excessive cost, but the proportions could be high. Septic tanks, for example, when properly maintained, can give satisfactory environmental results under many circumstances.

Table 10.3 compares the need for investment when different proportions of the towns between 2,000 and 10,000 p.e. are required to have sewer systems. It shows that more than EUR1 billion is at stake. It is, of course, highly unlikely that all towns can be considered exempt, because reducing their wastewater will bring positive environmental impacts, but nevertheless this issue does deserve attention as the Czech Republic plans its detailed compliance strategy.

Table 10.3. Impacts of Potential Exemptions from the Urban Wastewater Treatment Directive

Percent of towns 2,000 – 10,000 p.e. required to have sewer systems (percent)	Investment cost if all of territory is considered non-sensitive (EUR million)	Investment cost if whole territory is considered sensitive (EUR million)
0	619	726
60	912	1,056
100	1,558	1,775

Source: Adapted from "Pre-Accession Planning to Meet the Requirements of EU Legislation in the Water Sector in the Czech Republic", Draft Final Report, March 1999.

Waste Management

The overall EU structure for an effective waste management regime was set out in the 1975 Framework Directive on Waste, and the 1991 Hazardous Waste Directive. The key principles in the framework are prevention, polluter pays and the proximity principle, which states that waste should be disposed of as close as possible to its source. Specific directives define the requirements in more detail for products such as hazardous waste, waste oils, sewage sludge and packaging, and for particular activities such as movement of waste, incineration and disposal. In addition, two legislative initiatives will have important implications of the Czech Republic:

- The Packaging and Packaging Waste Directive (94/62/EC) aims to harmonize packaging waste management measures, and to avoid the erection of barriers to trade within the EU. It promotes recovery and collection from final users as well as reuse and recycling; it sets targets for 2001 (e.g., minimum recovery rate of 50 percent for all packaging and a minimum recycling and reuse rate of 15 percent for individual materials). Some EU member states have been granted a derogation from the packaging requirements on the grounds of the low level of packaging consumed, which would also appear to provide negotiating room for the Czech Republic.

- The Proposal on Landfill Directive (COM (97) 105) aims to reduce the adverse effects of landfills on the environment and to harmonize the technical standards for landfill. Prices for landfill disposal are expected to reflect the cost of current operations as well as site restoration.

The 1991 Law on Waste, and its regulations, governed the waste management sector in the Czech Republic until the New Act No. 125/1997 Coll., on Waste came into effect on January 1, 1998. This Act provides a more transparent legislation on waste management and is largely similar to that of the EU legislation. Implementation of the Act will cause an increased demand on the state administration at the district level to manage the upcoming transition period. The number of employees in the district offices will significantly increase between 1998 and 1999, from 273 employees to 410 employees.

Another requirement imposed by the EU legislation will be establishing a specialized advisory, public-relations, educational and coordination office, under the Ministry of Environment. This office will provide expert help to the district and municipal offices, and will unify the technical process in terms of equipment and methodology. This small unit would need about 100 employees.

Despite the positive trends in the waste management sector during recent years, there are some significant risks associated with the absence of a comprehensive strategy for waste management at the national, regional and local levels. This squanders resources. Hazardous waste infrastructure built by the private sector is having problems securing waste because of nearby landfill sites with much lower fees. At present, there is excesses capacity for landfills, and a deficit of recycling or related-activities producing energy from waste. The new approach towards packaging waste aims to encourage adoption of environmentally more friendly products and packaging; it passes responsibility of packaging reduction or reuse to the manufacture, importer or seller who introduces a product or package into the market. The new legislation, however, is not fully compatible with EU directives. Further amendments are expected in the year 2000.

Overall investment and annual recurrent costs associated with the transposition of the EU legislation into the Czech Republic have been estimated at EUR254-392 million and EUR59-97 million, respectively. As Table 10.4 shows, local governments will have responsibility for about 51 percent of the investment.

Table 10.4. Waste Management Investment and Recurrent Costs
(EUR million)

Element	Cost Type		Financed by[1]
	Investment[2]	Recurrent[3]	
General Directives			
- Reinforcement of State Administration		3.3	S
- Building	2.8		S
Waste Management Installations			
- Reconstruction of hazardous waste incinerators	15.2	1.5	P
- Process 50 percent of landfilled bio-degradable waste	84.6	11.7	M
Specific Types of Wastes (Inc. packing waste)			
- Elimination of oil waste – shutdown Ostrava Plant	8.3	1.7	P
- System for collection and landfilling of oil waste	13.8	1.2	P/M
- System for collection and landfilling of household waste	13.8	1.2	P/M
- Disposal of PCB waste	82.6	22.0	P
- Collection and recovery of packing waste	33.1	16.5	P/M
Total	**254.0**	**59.2**	
Municipal Budget (percent)	51	38	
Private Sector (percent)	48	56	

1/ It indicates source of financing, i.e., S means State Budget, P means Private, and M means Municipal or Local Government Budget.

2/ This represents a low estimate. A high estimate can bring the total investment cost to about EUR392 million, with the difference being borne by the private sector.

3/ This represents a low estimate. A high estimate can bring the total recurrent cost to about EUR97 million, with the difference being borne by the private sector.

Source: Assembled with information contained in the 1998 report prepared by the Environmental Management Office on "Economic Impacts of Implementing Legislation which Approximates European Union Environmental Legislation – Preparatory Study: Waste Management," and World Bank estimates for some recurrent costs.

Air Quality

The principal EU directives that aim to reduce air pollution are those dealing with stationary sources of emissions (energy and industry) and those that mandate levels of air quality in urban areas (which require reducing emissions from domestic heating, vehicles, industry and commerce). Apart from helping to control national air pollution problems, the EU directives address transboundary air pollution problems.

EU directives and technical standards inspired the 1991 Czech National Air Legislation. This legislation specifies pollution control and reduction via regulations and economic instruments, and defines emission limits on large combustion plants and waste incinerators. The Czech emission limits are in some cases more stringent than EU regulations, and according to the Czech authorities, about 98 percent of large sources and 90 percent of medium sources will fully comply with the regulations by the deadline. Controlling emissions from mobile sources will prove more difficult.

The Czech Republic has made an enormous effort to control pollution from stationary sources, and particularly from power plants. Overall emissions of SO_2, NO_x, and particulate matter have steadily declined since the early 1990s due to pollution control efforts, the overall decline of economic output and the reduced demand for energy. Current sulfur emissions on a per capita basis are still above the average of OECD countries, 68 kg./capita versus 39.5 kg./capita. Since large static sources are the major source of pollution, further efforts are needed to reduce the significant proportion of local brown coal with relatively high sulfur content. Current emissions of carbon dioxide on a per capita are slightly higher than the average for OECD countries, at 11.6 ton/capita versus 11.1 ton/capita.

These achievements are largely the result of passing and enforcing stringent air regulations. These have encouraged "end-of-pipe" investments and retrofitting of old production facilities.[9] The challenges ahead are to stabilize the current emission levels throughout the period of further economic growth and to address mobile source emissions, i.e., transport related pollution. The Czech Republic still needs to undertake preventive measures and introduce new and cleaner technological process.

As shown in Table 10.5, investment costs to the Czech Republic for complying with EU legislation in the area of air pollution have been estimated at between EUR1.0-1.6 billion. Less than 50 percent of the investment will be borne by local government. Overall annual expenditures for meeting EU requirements in the air sector, i.e., capital amortized over 20 years at 12 percent real interest rate, plus recurrent costs estimated at EUR308-492 million per year, would represent about 0.7-1.1 percent of 1997 GDP.

The above estimates include the costs to be incurred by the Czech Power Company (CEZ) -- the country's main power company and the provider of about 75-80 percent of electricity nationwide -- to fully meet its environmental targets set for the year 2000. The cost of the environmental component of the 1998-00-investment program of CEZ is CZK4.5 billion or about EUR182 million.

Despite considerable effort to meet targets for air pollution reduction, concentration of traditional pollutants tends to exceed standards in some urban areas. Using the Czech air quality classification system, about 23 percent of the population live in areas exposed to heavily polluted air. Adopted measures to prevent air pollution may be sufficient to reach values set down in standards for concentration of suspended particulate matter, SO_2, and even CO. Nonetheless, reaching valid standards for emission of nitrogen oxides will be difficult because of the expected increase in car traffic.

Control of transport-related pollutant emissions requires a large number of specific actions -- improving vehicle technical efficiency,[10] switching to fuel system with lower emissions, encouraging shifts toward modes with lower emissions, and managing transport demand. A national transport strategy for 2000 and beyond is under discussion, and will include broad objectives aiming to stabilize and reduce environmental burden.

[9] The 1996 survey of 100 industrial enterprises reveals that only 30 percent of the surveyed enterprises have invested in new technological processes. See the chapter on enterprise sector in this report.
[10] Such as gradual introduction of a new car fleet fitted with catalytic converters. The age of the car fleet is relatively high. In 1996, only about 18 percent of total vehicles equipped with catalytic converters.

Table 10.5. Cost Estimates for Improvements in Air Pollution Control
(In million EUR)

Item	Investment		Recurrent		Financed by[1]
	Low	High	Low	High	
Extension of the state administration	-	-	1	2	S
Monitoring improvement	-	-	6	6	S/M
Stationary pollution sources (adapting incinerators)[2]	28	28	6	6	P
Stationary pollution sources (new incinerators)[2]	275	413	55	83	P
Avoiding water pollution around incinerators	8	8	-	-	P
Improving oil production technology[3]	275	275	28	28	P
Elimination of asbestos	17	17	-	-	P
Elimination of ozone-damaging compounds	28	28	-	-	P
Finishing effective salvage network	14	28	-	-	P
Improving forest protection against air pollution	-	-	1	2	S
District heating[4]	220	623	44	125	P
Power sector[5]	182	182	27	27	P
Overall Cost	**1,074**	**1,628**	**164**	**274**	
of which financed by the local government (percent)	41	48			
of which financed by private sector (percent)	58	52			

1/ S means state budget, M means municipal or local government budget and P means private sector.
2/ Recurrent expenditures were estimated at 20 percent of capital costs.
3/ Recurrent expenditures were estimated at 10 percent of capital costs.
4/ These calculations are based on the need for 3,600 MW new generating capacity (380,000 households living in 60-square meter apartments consuming 0.16 KW per square meter). The high estimate assumes that all of this capacity will be coal-fired and the cost of fitting pollution control equipment is US$150 million /1,000 MW for SO_2 reduction and $20 million /1,000 MW for NO_x reduction. The low estimate assumes that half of the new generating capacity will be gas-fired, which requires no additional expenditure to comply with environmental standards, and that the cost of meeting both SO_2 and NO_x standards on the coal fired portion of the new plant will be $120 million/1,000 MW.
5/ It includes additional strictly environmental investments by the Czech Power Company, CEZ.
Source: Assembled with information from a recent study on "Economic Impacts of Implementing Legislation which Approximated European Union Environmental Legislation - Preparatory Study: Air," supported by the PHARE Program, the 1997 CEZ Annual Report, and World Bank estimates on district heating.

Industrial Pollution Control

The two principal directives that impact the industrial sector are:

- Directive 96/61/EC on Integrated Pollution Prevention and Control (IPPC), which encourages industries to prevent or minimize all emissions, rather than considering "end of pipe" solutions. It imposes permit obligations on manufacturing facilities. Emission limits on environmental permits are based on the application of Best Available Techniques (BAT). Member States are obliged to ensure that these requirement apply to new installations from October 1999, and to existing installation from October 2007.

- Regulation 1836/93/EEC on Environmental Management and Auditing Scheme (EMAS) encourages the voluntary participation of industrial plants in the development of both internal environmental management systems and audit programs as a means to improve their environmental performance.

Studies estimate that around 1,000 Czech industrial enterprises will have to obtain an integrated environmental permit under IPPC. There is wide variation among these enterprises in terms of their physical and technical lifetime, ranging from 6 to 25 years. Thus, the potential for gradual improvement of individual facilities varies substantially. Some companies may need to be allowed to operate the existing facilities at least until year 2010. Czech-enterprises are increasingly interested in EMAS, and applicable International Standard Office (ISO) Programs.

The public sector expenses related to the preparation, implementation and performance of the IPPC Directive are administrative and have been estimated at EUR3.3 million. This is an underestimate, as it does not include staff training, which will be necessary to develop necessary administrative and scientific knowledge.

While Czech companies still produce the most hazardous waste among the Central European countries, they also spend the most for dealing with environmental problems. A recent survey indicated that only around 14 percent of Czech companies expect to incur significant costs in complying with EU standards -- compared with 61 percent for Bulgarian, 40 percent for Polish, and 30 percent for Hungarian firms.[11] Nevertheless, the private expenses to be incurred have not been quantified and are expected to be large. Similar investment in Ireland, for example, was estimated at about ECU56 per capita (in 1990 prices). In implementing the directive, the authorities should encourage investments that reduce pollution before it is generated rather than treating pollution at the "end of the pipe". These "end-of-pipe" solutions tend to be more expensive than process changes, and thus have limited impact in enhancing the long-term sustainability of the production growth of Czech manufacturing.

Implications for Households

An investment program of the scale outlined above will necessarily involve an increase in the costs to consumers. Some utilities and municipalities may have access to EU grants and/or concessional finance, but many will have to borrow on commercial terms. Most of the investments have high operation and maintenance costs, which neither outside sources nor the central government will subsidize. Consequently, utilities and municipalities will have to pass a large part of the additional costs on to consumers.

We used the 1997 household budget survey to analyze the potential impact of these investments on households. The analysis assumes that all costs are passed onto the consumers, that demand for the services remains constant, and that household expenditure increases across all deciles by 3 percent. The impact of the timing of the compliance has been taken into account (year 2005 versus year 2015).

On average, the share of "environmental utilities"[12] in the household budget will rise. In the least costly scenario -- compliance by 2015 with the low cost, flexible interpretation of the requirements -- the share of utilities in the household budget rises from 10 percent to 12 percent. By contrast, the high cost, less flexible interpretation of the requirements increases the share of utilities in the household budget up to 13 percent. The major factor affecting household budgets is the timing for compliance. Under the low cost scenario, compliance by 2005 (as opposed to 2015) will take 16 percent of household expenditures (as opposed to 12 percent). Grant financing for capital, however, does not appear to make significant impact on the household budget, because operating costs are high.

The impact will be far larger on the rural populations than on urban areas. If compliance is phased in until 2015, utilities will actually take slightly less of the household budget for urban households but will take at least an additional five percent of rural household budgets. Compliance by 2005, however, has a major impact on both urban and rural consumers. It would mean that environmental utilities take 23

---

[11] See chapter on enterprise sector in this report.
[12] They include water and wastewater, electricity, gas, hot water, solid waste disposal, and heating.

percent of the expenditure of poor urban households and almost 30 percent of that of poor rural households. This option appears unlikely to be affordable.

This analysis points to three clear messages. First, increases in the prices of environmental utilities are inevitable even if significant concessional finance is available. Second, as the impacts on rural households will be greater than on urban groups, the government will need to establish transfer mechanisms to spread the burden between population groups. Third, early compliance will have a major impact on households, particularly low-income households. The government should consider phasing investments in slowly over a long transition period so that incomes can grow in line with price increases.

Recommendations for an Implementation Strategy

The backbone for any successful implementation strategy will be to strengthen institutional capacity in order to develop policies that bring the greatest environmental benefits for a given expenditure, and to develop policies that use public and external funds most wisely, both in terms of maximum environmental benefit and reducing distortions elsewhere in the economy. This will be particularly challenging because so many of the issues involved cut across sectoral areas of responsibility, as well as across different levels of government. Furthermore, building up capacity to enforce laws or set incentives for improving compliance will be essential in meeting many of the regulations that affect the private sector.

Clearly, all major sources of pollution will have to comply with relevant standards. There are, however, many areas of ambiguity in the EU legislation that allow for national circumstances. Many directives explicitly contain clauses that allow exemptions where environmental benefits are low or where costs are excessive, e.g., the UWWT Directive, which allows exemptions for certain small towns. It will be important to discuss either derogations where it is agreed that there is no environmental benefit, or very long transition periods for compliance with the most costly aspects of the directives for the smaller or less environmentally significant sources of pollution.

Furthermore, the analysis clearly shows the impact of different compliance timetables. The government will want to phase investments over a long period so as to let incomes rise sufficiently to be able to absorb the increased tariffs. Planning to comply with the UWWT Directive, the waste provisions and most of the air legislation by 2005 seems unrealistic as it could affect to a large degree the budget of a large proportion of households.

The government should use public and EU subsidies to direct investments towards strategic goals, during that long transition period. This is particularly important for wastewater collection and treatment, and for municipal solid waste. This prioritization has various aspects. First, large scope for improving efficiency in many utilities remains. Realizing this potential will reduce the upward pressure on tariffs; eligibility criteria for grants could be used to encourage utilities to improve their performance. In addition, limiting the proportion of grant funding, and thus requiring municipalities to contribute significantly from their own resources, will give an automatic incentive to municipalities to operate their utilities more efficiently. Technical assistance from the EU and other sources could also be used to help the less efficient utilities improve their performance.

Second, the costs of the investments themselves can be dramatically different, depending on some of the basic design parameters. For example, it will be important to ensure that wastewater treatment plants are large enough to take advantage of the substantial economies of scale, traded-off against the increased sewerage costs, even though multi-municipal co-operation may increase the institutional difficulties of the investments. Lastly, it will be important to remember that not all investments of the same size have the same environmental benefit. Benefits depend on the conditions in the receiving environment. Developing detailed plans so that authorities know which investments have the greatest environmental impact can be used as a further mechanism to direct investments strategically in the interim period towards full compliance.

Chapter XI. Public Administration

Introduction

An important aspect of the Czech Republic's candidacy for EU accession is bringing its public administration and governance capacities into line with EU member countries. This chapter examines the extent to which the Czech Republic is approaching EU standards and norms in these areas and suggests important steps the Government could take to move its public administration and governance capacities further along that path.

The Freedom House recently released rankings of Central and Eastern European countries and Newly Independent States (NIS) according to the governance and economic policies indices.[1] The Czech Republic has been placed among the better performers within this set of countries, both in terms of its governance institutions and its economic policies. Table 11.1 orders EU Accession candidate countries by their "Government and Public Administration" index values. The Czech Republic ranks among the top three EU accession candidates for both the "Governance" and "Economic Policies" indices, as well as the "Government and Public Administration" index, which is one component of the broader "Governance" index.

Table 11.1. Freedom House Governance Indices: EU Accession Countries, 1998

Country	Political Process	Civil Society	Independent Media	Rule of Law	Corruption	Government and Public Administration	Governance[1/]	Economic Policies[2/]
Poland	1.25	1.25	1.50	1.50	2.00	1.75	1.54	2.00
Hungary	1.25	1.25	1.50	1.75	2.00	1.75	1.58	1.63
Czech Republic	**1.25**	**1.50**	**1.25**	**1.50**	**3.00**	**2.00**	**1.75**	**1.88**
Estonia	1.75	2.25	1.75	2.25	3.00	2.25	2.21	2.13
Slovenia	2.00	2.00	1.75	1.50	2.00	2.50	1.96	2.38
Lithuania	1.75	2.00	1.50	2.00	3.00	2.50	2.13	2.50
Latvia	2.00	2.25	1.75	2.25	3.00	2.50	2.29	2.50
Slovakia	3.50	3.00	4.00	4.00	4.00	3.75	3.71	3.38
Bulgaria	2.75	3.75	3.50	3.75	4.00	4.00	3.63	5.38
Romania	3.25	3.75	4.00	4.25	4.00	4.00	3.88	4.63
Average	**2.08**	**2.30**	**2.25**	**2.48**	**3.00**	**2.70**	**2.47**	**2.84**
Median	**1.88**	**2.13**	**1.75**	**2.13**	**3.00**	**2.50**	**2.17**	**2.44**

1/ Simple average of the indices for political process, civil society, independent media, rule of law, corruption, and government and public administration.

2/ Simple average of indices (not reported here) for privatization, microeconomic policy and macroeconomic policy.

Source: Nations in Transit, Freedom House, 1999.

At the same time, the analysis in the rest of this chapter -- as well as in a separate study presently being undertaken by the World Bank of the public administration implications of EU accession --

---

[1] *Nations in Transit* (Freedom House: 1999). Index values range between 1 (best) and 7 (worst). The "Governance" index is the simple average of the first six indices (exclusive of the "Economic Policies" index). The corruption index values have been converted from alpha (A through D) to numeric (2 through 5), so as to permit their inclusion in the Governance index.

demonstrates that the Czech Republic still has a considerable way to go to meet governance, including public administration, standards of EU member countries and indeed to keep pace with some other acceding countries like Hungary and Estonia in specific -- and important -- sub-areas.[2] This is true both in terms of its human resource management capacities as well as its policy formulation and coordination capacities. The study evaluates key issues related to both of these areas; it assigns indicative numerical scores to facilitate assessment of each country's overall performance and highlights strengths and weaknesses in each area. As Figure 11.1 illustrates, the study findings show the Czech Republic lagging behind both Hungary and Estonia.

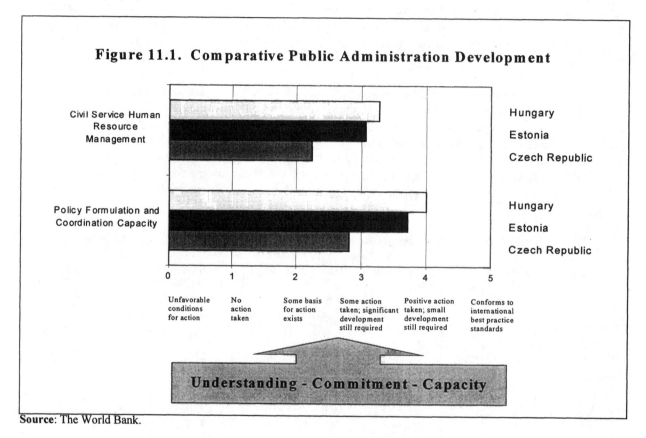

Figure 11.1. Comparative Public Administration Development

Source: The World Bank.

The rest of this chapter highlights the major considerations underlying these findings. After providing some background, the analysis examines each of the above three broad governance and public administration issues: civil service and human resource management, policy formulation and coordination and EU accession management. Two types of yardsticks are employed to assess each of those evaluative dimensions: comparisons with EU and OECD country norms, and consideration of the incentives likely to be created by the existing institutional arrangements. Considerations of incentive issues are woven throughout the analysis. Box 11.1 highlights some of the more significant findings regarding incentive effects identified in the chapter.

Finally, it should be noted that this chapter focuses on the central administrative machinery of government. Issues of public service delivery are not directly addressed or assessed. Insofar as this chapter touches on service delivery issues, it does so only by focusing on how well the central machinery of government helps to facilitate effective, responsive and efficient service delivery.

---

[2] See Nunberg et al. (1999), *Public Administration Development in the EU Accession Context*, mimeo, The World Bank.

Box 11.1. Summary of Incentive Effects according to the Area of Analysis

1) Civil service and human resource management

Legal and ethical framework: Absence of legal distinction between political appointments and civil servants creates strong incentives for narrowly focused, short-term political responsiveness, while making it difficult to create strong incentives for public servants to be responsive to cross-cutting and medium term policy objectives. In short, it undermines professionalism.

Institutional framework for human resource management: Absence of systematic mechanisms aimed at holding budget units and their employees accountable for effectively and efficiently achieving policy and program objectives makes it difficult to create strong incentives to meet performance targets.

Employment and pay policy and management: Ministry of Finance's practice of providing an overall wage budget envelope, while allowing substantial discretion to line ministries in its use (subject to various constraints imposed by existing regulations regarding remuneration) provides managerial discretion needed to effectively manage human resources while still maintaining effective aggregate fiscal discipline. Unfortunately, the absence of systematic mechanisms for holding budgetary units accountable for how effectively and efficiently they meet policy and program objectives undermines incentives to exercise that autonomy well.

Human resource management policies and practices: Absence of systematic mechanisms to ensure the existence of clear and widely shared organizational objectives and to focus organizational attention on meeting those objectives undermines incentives to effectively meet policy objectives. Second, an absence of systematic mechanisms to make a public sector career attractive undermines the public administration's capacity to attract, retain and develop needed human capital skills. Examples of systematic mechanisms that could be better designed to create stronger human capital accumulation incentives include: (i) career streams; (ii) pay policies; and (iii) performance-linked recognition and rewards. Finally, the absence of clear rules specifying the conditions under which competitive recruitment must be undertaken (discretion currently rests entirely with the budgetary unit) makes it difficult to build strong performance pressures among existing employees, since they have less cause to worry about meeting the competition in order to advance in their public sector career.

Training and career development: Again, the absence of systematic mechanisms for holding budgetary units accountable for, in this case, how effectively they deploy training resources makes it difficult to create strong incentives to use those resources well.

Service delivery and management culture: While the Administrative Code establishes basic standards for responding to citizen inquiries, systematic mechanisms have not been created to ensure the existence of standards governing service delivery and citizen responsiveness. For example, policies requiring that the public be involved in the development of service standards, as well as requiring publication of actual performance could help to create stronger incentives for budgetary units to improve their service delivery performance and become more responsive to the citizenry.

2) Policy formulation and coordination

Institutional arrangements: Existing Council of Ministers institutional arrangements, while aimed at facilitating policy formulation and coordination, appear to be creating a variety of counterproductive dynamics (i.e., problematic incentives). In particular, the existing arrangement that places four Deputy Prime Ministers (DPM) over collections of Ministers creates at least the following risks: (a) undermines the authority of line Ministers, since they are now subservient to not only the PM but also a DPM, (b) provides an organizational basis for stable coalitions of interests (each of the four groupings), which can be expected over time to make coordination across those four groupings more difficult, as it will become more difficult to build ad hoc coalitions that cut across DPM groupings, and (c) creates greater potential for challenges to the PM's authority by particularly effective DPMs, since the smaller number of DPMs, each possessing formal authority over roughly one-third of the Government's policy agenda, will be in a better position to demand cooperation from their groups of Ministers than would any individual Minister in the absence of such an arrangement.

Policy processes and procedures: Policy processes and procedures appear to be well designed and functioning smoothly.

Staffing arrangements: Despite the absence of an adequate legal framework to ensure the existence of a professional staff for handling these functions, the pivotal importance of this function appears to have ensured professionalism and stability in the staffing of the Department of Cabinet Agenda across changes in Governments. The same cannot, however, be said with respect to policy analysis staffing within the line ministries. These suffer from the same weaknesses noted above in the area of civil service and human resource management.

3) EU accession management

The chapter offers insights based largely on the experience of some recent EU accedes. Those lessons suggest, among other points, that creating a modern and professional civil service is not simply a requirement for EU accession. It is also a key means of ensuring that the Czech Republic will be able to mobilize a cadre of civil servants within its EU-dedicated institutions who will speak with a unified voice on policy matters affecting the Czech Republic's interests, and who will have the technical competence and EU-specific behavioral skills to effectively advance policy priorities. In short, the prospect of EU membership should provide a significant incentive for the Czech Republic to create a modern and professional civil service in order to ensure that the Czech Republic's policy agenda will be adequately represented within the EU. This task will require creating the sorts of incentive mechanisms noted above.

Source: The World Bank.

Administrative Transition since the Fall of Communism

As part of the now-dissolved Czechoslovak federal state, the Czech Republic made laudable progress after the *Velvet Revolution* of 1989 in changing the way government works. The communist party's supreme role in government and policy-making was quickly swept away. In 1990, the National Committee structure (the local arm of the central government) was abolished. At the same time, the Government reestablished local self-government and deconcentrated its own functions by creating district offices of the central state administration. The structure and functions of ministries and other central agencies were reoriented to better suit the emerging democratic system and free-market economy. Staff compromised by ties to the old regime left the administration, in part spurred by a lustration law that barred individuals who had collaborated with communist intelligence services from holding high level public posts.

In spite of these early steps, however, public administration reform in the Czech Republic remains in its early stages in several key areas. After years of heated debate an intermediate tier of government, comprised of 14 regions is to be established. While these regions are slated to come sometime in the future, many implementation issues (such as competencies and staffing) remain to be resolved. The exact date when the regions will be in operation has yet to be determined. Due to its prominence, the issue of regional reform has become almost synonymous with administrative reform, with the result that equally crucial components of reform -- including legislative and management frameworks for government staff -- have been relegated to the sidelines. Uncertainty regarding intergovernmental relations and the lack of specification of a vertical administrative structure has also resulted in central government bodies being free to establish what has become a complex web of deconcentrated offices (e.g., tax and employment offices, and a variety of inspectorates) at the subnational level. Despite often-stated intentions to create a uniform legal framework for government employees, human resource management remains the domain of individual ministries. Similarly, effective formulation and coordination of policy at the central level is complicated by the tendency of the line ministries to focus on narrow sectoral interests at the expense of broader cross-sectoral views.

While administrative reform is admittedly an arduous and long-term undertaking, several factors have intensified difficulties in the Czech case. In the aftermath of the fall of communism, the most pressing tasks were dismantling authoritarian state structures -- rather than building effective administrative machinery -- and replacing them with a new economic and political order. However, attention was quickly diverted toward fundamental issues of the survival of Czechoslovakia, as the future of the federal state became increasingly uncertain. Under these circumstances, it should come as no surprise that little political priority was given to administrative reform. After the dissolution of Czechoslovakia at the end of 1992, the newly-independent Czech Republic continued to focus heavily on macroeconomic reform and private sector development, almost to the exclusion of administrative reform. The privatization process -- particularly the high-profile "voucher privatization" program aimed at large state-owned enterprises -- captured government energy and public interest. In the general focus on dismantling or shrinking the role of government, elements of reform that would have necessitated strengthening administrative capabilities (for example, regulation of financial markets) tended to be left out of the spotlight.

The official programs of the two Governments formed after the general elections in 1992 and 1996 both cited some components of administrative reform as priority areas. Nonetheless, the primacy of economic matters and the prevailing mood of deep-rooted suspicion toward the bureaucracy de-emphasized, rather than promoted, the creation of an efficient administrative machinery. Rather than undertaking a comprehensive reform that would have treated administration as an integrated system, efforts tended to focus on discrete actions. This failure to adequately recognize early the role of a reliable administration as an important element of an enabling framework for economic and political/social development continues to resound in the complex problems now facing the Czech Republic.

Explicit responsibility for public administration issues has shifted among various organizations in recent years, and at one point was even left unassigned. In 1992, the Office of Legislation and Public Administration (OLPA) was created as a specialized unit reporting to a Deputy Prime Minister. Its public administration division served as an advisory body and a focal point for the development of reform proposals for human resources as well as all levels of government. The Government dissolved the OLPA in October 1996 with the stated expectation that, since administrative reform is a cross-sectoral issue, responsibility for its implementation should be decentralized to each individual agency rather than being concentrated within a single entity at the central level. This revealed either a low priority attached to administrative reform or a pervasive distrust of centralized bureaucracies or both. The inherent difficulty of such an approach was recognized five months later, when the Government assigned joint responsibility for drafting an administrative reform concept to the Ministries of Justice and Interior.

The caretaker government that was installed after the resignation of Prime Minister Vaclav Klaus at the end of 1997 again highlighted, in its official statements, the importance of administrative reform. In March 1998, a Cabinet decision was passed outlining necessary reform measures, including a target date of February 1999 for submission of a civil service act draft. These plans were, however, interrupted by the end of the government's mandate.

The new government that took office shortly after the general elections of June 1998 has taken steps to raise the profile of public administration reform. Both the policy paper presented to win a parliamentary vote of confidence and subsequent public pronouncements have stressed the importance of both reform in general as well as of the implementation of a legal framework for civil servants. The bulk of the responsibility for cross-sectoral public administration has been assigned to two newly-created entities: the Deputy Prime Minister (DPM) for legislation and the Ministry of Interior's public administration division. In addition, the deputy minister of Interior chairs a public administration reform committee composed of deputy ministers from line ministries, and, in the context of negotiations for accession to the EU, a special working group on public administration has been created. The DPM for legislation has a broad portfolio that includes the legal frameworks for the civil service (though actual drafting responsibility lies with the Ministry of Labor) as well as the creation of a regional tier of government, planned for the year 2000.

The Ministry of Interior was first assigned responsibility for public administration reform strategy in March 1997, as a means of filling the gap left by the dissolution of the Office of Legislation and Public Administration in late 1996.[3] In August 1998, a new division for Public Administration was created in the Ministry of Interior, with a deputy minister at its head. This division consists of departments for information technology in the public administration, human resources management and public administration reform, with the last being further divided into units for strategy, execution, and EU relations. At the time of writing, the division was in the process of achieving full staffing, and defining the scope of activities of each department.

Establishment and Wage Bill Control

The Czech Republic has been quite successful in maintaining control over both government employment and the aggregate wage bill.

---

[3] Responsibility for public administration reform was initially assigned jointly to the Ministries of Justice and Interior.

Establishment Control

Due to the absence of a Civil Service Act, data on government employment in the Czech Republic does not reflect the standard distinction between public servants and civil servants. Instead, employment is broadly divided between budgetary organizations (fully financed from the state budget) and those organizations that are to some extent self-financing but that also receive subsidies from the state budget. While no official definition of the civil service exists, unofficial estimates speak of between eighty and ninety thousand staff in core administrative positions who might form the basis of a future civil service. In 1998, total employment in both budgetary and subsidized organizations was 508,351. Of this number, 207,814 were employed by subsidized organizations, while 300,537 worked in budgetary organizations. Just over half of the budgetary organization staff worked for the state administration,[4] of whom 13,849 were employed directly in ministries and other central bodies.

Table 11.2. Employment in Budgetary and Subsidized Organizations, 1998

Type of Organization	Employees	Percent of Total
Subsidized organizations	207,814	40.9
Budgetary organizations of which:	300,537	59.1
State administration	154,073	30.3
In Central bodies	13,849	2.7
Total	508,351	100.0

Source: Ministry of Labor.

Relative to other EU accession candidates and to EU member countries, the Czech Republic's public employment levels are not excessively high. At 4.9 percent of population, public employment in the Czech Republic in 1997 placed it near the bottom of the range among its closest neighbors, and nearly at the bottom of the range of EU member countries (see Table 11.3).

Careful regulation of employment levels greatly diminishes the possibility of unrestrained employment increases while still allowing institutions some flexibility in managing the internal structure of employment. Currently, employment is regulated in three ways.[5] First, the cabinet sets binding employment limits based upon the recommendation of the Ministry of Finance (MoF). Second, the wage bill for each ministry or group of institutions is set by the MoF, with each ministry determining how this sum is distributed among subsidiary institutions. Finally, the volume of other personnel expenditures (for example for contract employees, elected or appointed officials) is also specified. However, unlike in the period from 1972 to 1986 when the existence of specific jobs in central bodies was pre-determined and could not be changed, organizations can decide the allocation of posts among units, and may choose to hire fewer staff than the maximum permitted. These arrangements appear to provide quite effective control over aggregate personnel expenditures and slots within each ministry or equivalent budgetary unit. They do not, however, provide an effective means for holding those agencies accountable for the effectiveness or efficiency with which they allocate their human resource budgets.

---

[4] The definition of state administration is complex and has undergone several changes, but generally includes ministries, selected other central bodies and their subsidiary organizations. It excludes the Supreme Audit Institution, the Radio and Television Broadcast Agency, parliamentary offices, the Grant Agency and the Academy of Science. For further information, see Volf et al. (1998), "Finance ve verejne sprave," in *Analyza verejne spravy Ceske republiky*, Odborne studie, National Training Foundation, July.

[5] This applies to budgetary organizations and those subsidized organizations for which the government subsidy is greater than the wage bill. When the subsidy is less than the wage bill, the organization is treated like a private organization.

Table 11.3. Government Employment in Selected Countries, 1997

	General Government[1]	
	Percent of Population	**Percent of Labor Force**
Czech Republic	**4.9**	**11.2**
Poland	4.9	9.3
Slovak Republic	8.6	19.4
Hungary	9.0	20.3
CEE sample Average	**6.9**	**15.1**
Greece	4.4	11.6
Germany	4.9	9.4
Portugal	5.7	11.1
Italy	6.0	14.6
United Kingdom	7.5	15.6
France	7.7	17.2
Belgium	8.1	19.5
Finland	13.0	25.5
Denmark	13.3	24.0
Sweden	18.1	34.7
EU Sample Average	**8.9**	**18.3**

1/ Includes general civilian government and armed forces.
Source: Ministries of Labor and Interior (Hungary); Ministry of Labor (Czech Republic);
"An International Survey of Government Employment and Wages," World Bank
1997.

Although the current government deliberated on reducing employment shortly after taking office, no formal downsizing plan has been undertaken. However, budgetary incentives for individual organizations to reduce staffing were recently increased, as explained below. There is reported to be some agreement within government that scope for employment reductions exists. The absence of mechanisms for holding budgetary units accountable for the effectiveness and efficiency with which they deploy their human resources, however, has made it difficult to generate and sustain the political will required to undertake such measures, whether government-wide or within organizations. While there are fears that cutting staff without rationalizing the employment structure will harm services, attempts in some ministries (for example, the Ministry of Foreign Affairs) to introduce targeted cuts in some departments have been successfully resisted in favor of across the board cuts. Resistance by those adversely affected by efforts to rationalize human resource usage is, of course, to be expected. It should come as no surprise, however, that the will and ingenuity required to overcome such resistance will be rare unless effective mechanisms exist for holding Ministries accountable for how well they manage their human resources.

Wage Bill Control

Spending on wages and salaries has been relatively stable over the past several years. The cost of wages and salaries in consolidated general government expenditure[6] constituted an estimated 9.1 percent of total expenditures in 1997. This appears somewhat low, though not excessively so, compared to the median of 11.2 percent for current EU member states, and 12.5 percent for a sample of eight EU applicant

---

[6] Consolidated central government in the Czech Republic includes the Cabinet office, parliament, ministries, president's office, supreme court, government agencies, local governments, extrabudgetary funds and health insurance organizations.

countries.[7] The preliminary figure for 1998 is even lower at 8.5 percent. Because of the great variability among countries in government functions and size, comparisons of this sort should be treated with caution. The comparison does demonstrate, however, that the Czech Republic is not facing an excessive wage bill burden.

As a percentage of total goods and service spending, the Czech Republic's wage bill is high relative to other EU accession candidates, but about average when compared to EC member countries (see Table 11.4). While this could indicate that the Czech Republic is approaching EU norms on the division of goods and services expenditures between labor and other inputs, it is not clear what sorts of conclusions one ought to draw from this.

Table 11.4. Wage Bill in Consolidated Central Government, 1993-98
(CZK billions)

Item	1993	1994	1995	1996	1997	1998[1/]
Total Revenue	446.7	504.3	578.4	634.4	662.1	706.0
Total Expenditure	420.1	495.0	573.6	638.7	682.0	733.5
Goods & Services	126.9	130.4	123.4	139.3	136.5	146.7
Wages & salaries	**37.1**	**48.6**	**50.3**	**57.4**	**62.3**	**62.6**
Other goods & services	89.8	81.8	73.1	81.9	74.2	84.0
GDP	1002.3	1182.7	1381.1	1572.3	1680.0	1820.7
Wage bill as:						
Percent total revenue	8.3	9.6	8.7	9.0	9.4	8.9
Percent total expenditure	8.8	9.8	8.8	9.0	9.1	8.5
Percent total goods and services	29.2	37.3	40.8	41.2	45.6	42.7
Percent GDP	3.7	4.1	3.6	3.7	3.7	3.4

1/ Preliminary.
Source: Ministry of Finance.

The Ministry of Finance controls the volume of the overall wage bill by setting the wage bill for individual chapters of the budget and by establishing the conditions under which savings from vacancies may be reallocated. As of 1997, organizations have been permitted to use all vacancy savings to "top-up" earnings of other employees through bonuses or other one-off allowances. Previously, only 3 percent of the organization's wage bill could be reassigned in this fashion, with excess savings being returned to the state budget. The impact of this measure thus far has been less than expected. This may partially reflect the novelty of this change. As noted previously, however, the absence of mechanisms that could create strong pressure on ministries or other budgetary units to effectively manage their human resources probably helps account for the modest use of this budgetary autonomy.

Human Resource Management

Civil Service Legislation

There is no Civil Service Act in place in the Czech Republic, and no official category of "civil servant". Like all other employed persons in the country, government workers are regulated by the Labor Code (Law 65/1965), and thus have a contractual relationship with the specific employing ministry rather than the state as a whole. While this lacuna is by no means solely responsible for the Czech Republic's lack of progress in establishing a modern and responsive public administration, it continues to pose a roadblock to Government efforts to meet EU accession norms in the area of public administration.

---

[7] Bulgaria, Czech Republic, Estonia, Hungary, Latvia, Lithuania, Poland and Romania.

Drafting of a civil service act has been underway since the break-up of the Czechoslovak State gave rise to the independent Czech Republic on January 1, 1993. While an inter-ministerial group has been established to review civil service act issues, principal drafting responsibility rests with a small team of staff in the Ministry of Labor, which has produced two draft documents. The most recent draft could have benefited from extensive and insightful comments by both foreign and Czech experts, including reviews by both SIGMA experts and the Ministry of Finance, in 1995. Opinions on the latest draft version vary within the Administration, with some individuals believing that the draft is ready for submission to the Government and with others pointing to serious shortcomings or omissions in substantive areas, as well as in the potential financial costs of proposed measures. Importantly, the extensive and valuable commentary provided by SIGMA and others back in 1995 has yet to be fully reflected in the draft version, despite the passage of approximately four years time. This impasse in both the preparation and enactment of a civil service law is worrying. It suggests that the various Governments over this four-year period have yet to be serious about civil service reform. They have not even managed to mount a technical team capable and willing to convert detailed and careful advice into a sensible draft law.

Recent political developments have seen several public pronouncements on the importance of a civil service act. At the very least, a significant number of government employees and senior politicians, as well as organizations like the National Training Fund[8] recognize that a civil service act is a necessary, though not sufficient, condition for meaningful reform. Both the National Program for EU integration and the current Government's position statement, issued in August 1998, assign top priority to passage of a civil service act, with implementation initially targeted for the year 2000[9] This schedule has subsequently been revised; as of mid-1999 there were plans to submit the draft law to Government by the end of the year, with implementation expected in 2002. However, the attention to this and related reform issues comes at a time of increased political uncertainty associated with the rule of a minority government. Producing and enacting a civil service act that fully resolves an array of highly complex issues (such as tenure, recruitment, promotion and appraisal systems, not to mention the ground rules for conversion of existing staff to "civil service" status) would appear to be a rather daunting challenge. This is particularly true given the sensitivities involved, the likely need for extensive reassessment of the current draft, and the complexity of reaching an agreement even under the best of political circumstances.

Nevertheless, the importance of creating a framework for the Civil Service is such that the Government of the Czech Republic would be well advised to devote significant resources and attention at the highest levels to the issue. This includes ensuring that appropriate expertise is allocated to produce a new draft law capable of successfully passing through rigorous internal review and parliamentary and cabinet processes. In addition to resolving some of the human resource management (HRM) complications addressed below, such an act should lay the groundwork for subsequent fine-tuning of issues related to the civil service in implementing regulations. Important examples of weaknesses that such an act should address include: inadequate protections against politicization of the civil service, insufficiently attractive conditions of employment, inadequate institutional arrangements to hold public servants accountable for their performance, and institutional arrangements that fail to create adequate pressures and mechanisms for holding agencies responsible for their performance.

---

[8] The National Training Fund, a foundation created under the auspices of the Ministry of Labor, is implementing several projects related to public administration reform.

[9] See "National Program for the Preparation of the Czech Republic for Membership in the European Union," as posted at http://www.czech.cz/english/national.htm and "Policy Statement of the Government of the Czech Republic," August 1998, posted at http://www.vlada.cz/vlada/dokumenty/prohlas.eng.htm. The previous "caretaker" government also cited civil service issues in its "Policy Statement" of January 1998, posted at http://www.vlada.cz/historie/vlada98/dokumenty/progrprohl.eng.htm.

Protections against politicization of the civil service are weaker in the Czech Republic than in most EU member countries. For instance, no Civil Service Law exists with provisions for a clear demarcation between political appointments and civil service appointments. Related to this, *institutional arrangements to foster a merit-based, professional civil service* are weaker than in EU member states. Again, there are presently no legal requirements for competitive recruitment, selection and promotion procedures.[10]

Employment Conditions

Conditions of employment appear to be less attractive relative to private sector options, as in EU member countries. Two major aspects of employment conditions deserve mention in this regard: the structure of remuneration and career options.

Structure of Remuneration. Two significant features of the structure of remuneration are worth particular attention: average levels relative to private sector comparators and how that relationship varies with the skill requirements of positions. Table 11.5 provides information that sheds light on both of these features. Two separate sources of data on private sector salaries are presented; they are compared with total remuneration likely to be put forward under the proposed 1999 public sector salary scale, so as to obtain as favorable a comparison for the public sector as possible.[11] The figures in the third column of that table reveals public salaries to fall between about 25 percent and 81 percent of their private sector comparators, and to decline in competitiveness as the human capital requirements of the position rise, at least within those positions below the levels normally staffed by political appointees. At the top of the human capital range encompassed by positions likely to be staffed by de facto "civil servants",[12] for instance, total monthly salaries hover around 25 percent to 32 percent of private sector equivalents for Director-level positions, but climb to the 58 percent to 81 percent range for lower skilled positions. These comparisons reveal a salary structure that becomes less competitive as skill level rises.

The Price Waterhouse Coopers data upon which these comparisons are based may, however, overstate the rapidity of the decline in public sector salaries relative to private sector comparators as skill requirements rise. This would be the case if the sample of firms covered by the Price Waterhouse-Coopers survey -- because it is skewed to more highly capitalized firms -- exhibits a steeper relationship between skill requirements and remuneration than is typical in the Czech private sector. Granting this qualification, it is still true that such a pattern is plausible among developing countries.[13] It is also corroborated by data revealing the compression ratio of highest to lowest salaries offered within the

---

[10] The Labor Code currently governing public employment relations provides some limited protections, but these are inadequate for a modern public administration, particularly since little exists in the way of institutional arrangements designed to ensure compliance with those protections.

[11] Public sector salaries have been estimated so as to incorporate the average level of salary supplements as a percentage of base salaries found in the Central Bodies of the State Administration (27.4 percent in 1998). They also reflect the 25 percent of highest base salary in grade available to the de facto civil service (see below).

[12] Article 73 of the Labor Code imposes extra responsibilities (including impartiality, confidentiality and avoiding conflict of interest) on certain categories of government employees. These individuals, who also receive a special wage supplement, are referred to in this text as "de facto" civil servants.

[13] See, for instance, Gary J. Reid and Graham Scott (1994), "Public Sector Human Resource Management: Experience in Latin America and the Caribbean and Strategies for Reform," Green Cover Report No. 12839, Public Sector Management Division, Technical Department, Latin America and the Caribbean Region (World Bank, Washington, DC: March 14), as well as Salvator Schiavo-Campo, Giulio de Tommaso and Amitabha Mukherjee (1996), "Civil Service and Economic Development: A Selective Synthesis of International Facts and Experience," background paper for the 1997 *World Development Report* (The World Bank: November 10).

public sector to be somewhere between 4.4 and 5.1.[14] This falls below most EU comparators, which tend to fall closer to the 6.0 to 10.0 range.[15] Such a pattern can be expected to undermine the public sector's capacity to recruit and retain qualified and motivated personnel in the ranks where quality and motivation matter most, namely, the professional and managerial ranks.

Table 11.5. Public/Private Monthly Salary Comparisons

Type of Private Sector Position	Private Sector Compensation (US$)	Public Sector Compensation (US$)	Public Compensation as percent of Private Sector	Type of Public Sector Position, Qualifications & Salary Point		
				Grade	Education Requirements	Min/Mid/Max of Salary Range
CEO	6,175	1,875	30.4	Minister		
Chief Financial Officer	3,803	1,406	37.0	First Deputy Minister		
Business Director	3,006	906	30.1	Director		
HR Director	2,816	784	27.9	12	5-yr. Univ. Degree	Max
Marketing Director	2,712	689	25.4	11	5-yr. Univ. Degree	Max
Info. Systems Director	1,897	603	31.8	10	5-yr. Univ. Degree	Max
Sales Representative	703	466	66.3	9	5-yr. Univ. Degree	Mid
Executive Secretary	729	421	57.7	8	3- or 5-yr. Univ. Degree	Mid
Accounting Assistant	470	380	81.0	7	Full High School	Mid

Source: Private sector data: Price Waterhouse/Coopers and KNO Worldwide Annual Worldwide salary survey, found in Hospodarske Noviny (Nov. 29, 1998) "Jak se v Cesku odmenuji lide".
Public sector data: Minister, First Deputy Minister and Director: estimates from Ministry of Finance. Others based on salary scale, adjusted to reflect 25 percent supplement for "civil servants" and average 27.3 percent additional pay from other salary supplements, bonuses, etc.

Regardless of the extent to which the competitiveness of public sector salaries declines as skill requirements rise, it is only half of the story on the structure of remuneration. The other half of the story is that average public sector salaries, while falling below private sector comparators, are probably still reasonably competitive. The Price Waterhouse/Coopers data, found in Table 11.5, almost surely overstate the relevant private sector comparators, since they tend to reflect the better capitalized firms in the Czech economy, such as international firms. The *Ekonom* magazine data, reported in Table 11.6, probably more accurately mirror the relevant domestic Czech labor market. Those data reveal that Ministers and First Deputy Ministers probably receive between about 25 percent and 30 percent less than plausible private sector counterparts.

---

[14] The 4.4 figure is based solely on the salary scale. The 5.1 figure compares the "Director" remuneration estimates found in Table 11.5 to the salary scale amount for the bottom of the lowest grade after adjustment for the 25 percent "civil service" supplement and average other supplements and bonuses of approximately 27.4 percent of base salary.
[15] Compression ratios from a number of EU countries include: France (5.7), Germany (7.5), Netherlands (8.2), U.K. (9.9).

Table 11.6. Chief Executive Officer Salaries Comparison

Type of Private Sector Position	Private Sector Compensation (US$)	Public Sector Compensation (US$)	Public Compensation as percent of Private Sector	Type of Public Sector Position, Qualifications & Salary Point		
				Grade	Education Requirements	Min/Mid/Max of Salary Range
500 + staff	2,656	1,875	70.6	Minister		
Smaller than 500 staff	1,875	1,406	75.0	First Deputy Minister		

Source: Private sector data: Ekonom magazine (No. 41, 1998), "Inventura penezenek", based on surveys by *Ekonom* magazine and Trexima (private co.) survey of 15,000 management staff.
Public sector data: Same as Table 11.5.

Career Prospects. Such a difference could leave the public sector reasonably competitive if other aspects of the employment relation were reasonably attractive. These somewhat lower salaries, however, are not counterbalanced by particularly attractive career prospects or tenure guarantees, which are found in many other countries, and could afford some non-pecuniary compensation in lieu of more competitive salaries. A compressed earnings structure provides little incentive to advancement, while introducing strong incentives to classify staff in higher grades in order to offer a more attractive salary. This is borne out both by anecdotal evidence as well as by the ratio of staff to managers, which averages 5.0 for central bodies, an unusually low level.[16] Such practices may provide a rational response by managers to a relatively uncompetitive salary scale. The absence of strong pressures on those managers to ensure that their units meet clear performance objectives, coupled with weak accountability for how well they manage their personnel, however, makes this a risky and less than transparent approach to managing pay and personnel.

Not surprisingly, somewhat lower earnings than those available in the domestic private sector, combined with uncertain career prospects, are reported to be responsible for an outflow of skilled staff from government, as well as for difficulty in attracting much-needed young professionals. This evidence is, however, anecdotal, as a lack of concrete information on staff turnover rates reveals a telling and ubiquitous lack of attention to human resource management throughout the Czech public sector. Anecdotal evidence also suggests that the new generation of career-oriented university graduates sees little appeal in government employment (with some notable exceptions such as the Ministry of Foreign Affairs) although recent rising unemployment is said to have spurred new interest. Overall turnover appears to be at a somewhat higher than optimal level. For example, MoF estimates its turnover to have been 11 percent in 1998, while turnover in some of the less favored ministries could easily exceed this level. Even the MoF's 11 percent turnover rate is somewhat higher than the range found in a number of EU countries -- from lows of around 2-3 percent in Canada to highs around 7-8 percent in France and the U.K. The deeper problem lies in the real possibility that disproportionate numbers of staff with valuable expertise are leaving government service for the private sector. This pattern may be exacerbated by informal norms that discourage firing of poor performers, and the absence of adequate mechanisms to foster effective human resource management, such as performance appraisal or attestation procedures and guidelines. Such informal norms and weak mechanisms for holding managers accountable for how well they manage their human resources may be perpetuating an entrenched culture of mediocrity.

Institutional Arrangements to Hold Public Servants Accountable for their Performance are Weak. Both the design and use of personnel performance evaluation processes are left to the discretion of each

---

[16] Analyza verejne spravy Ceske republiky, National Training Foundation, September 1998.

budgetary institution; in reality, few institutions have formal evaluation systems in place, and resistance to their implementation is high. Moreover, little appears to exist in the way of oversight of personnel performance evaluation practices. Recent efforts to lodge this responsibility within the Ministry of Interior appear unlikely to adequately address this need. Unless budgetary institutions given the authority and responsibility for personnel management and development are held accountable for how well they wield that authority, there is little reason to expect them to do a uniformly good job of meeting that responsibility.

Complementary to this, *institutional arrangements for holding agencies responsible for their performance* in implementing the policies and/or delivering the services entrusted to their care are also weak. Little in the way of systematic reporting on performance is required or enforced. Mechanisms do exist in some agencies and programs for setting basic performance standards (e.g., processing times for passports, drivers' licenses, etc.), but these could be strengthened. Again, in the absence of effective efforts to hold agencies accountable for meeting policy implementation and service provision objectives, it should come as no surprise if performance varies considerably across agencies and is not, on average, particularly impressive.

Policy Formulation and Coordination

Policy formulation and coordination capacities, while functional, are less than ideal. Czech officials familiar with their functioning appear to increasingly recognize those arrangements as needing reconsideration. The creation of four Deputy Prime Ministers (DPMs) without portfolio, but charged with coordinating policy formulation within each of their mutually exclusive collections of sectors, appears problematic. These arrangements pose risks of: (a) engendering irritation due to confusion about authority relations and hence a lack of cooperation among Ministers who have line authority but are nonetheless subject to the coordinating efforts of a given DPM; (b) increasing the difficulty of ensuring integrated and collaborative formulation of policies cutting across the lines established by the four mutually exclusive sets of sectors defined by the four DPM umbrellas; and (c) generating efforts by individual DPMs to build power bases sufficient to challenge the leadership of the Prime Minister. Efforts of some DPMs to expand the set of Ministers under their umbrellas suggest that some of these risks may already be recognized and/or materializing. In short, the current authority relations within the policy formulation and coordination apparatus appear unlikely to provide a stable and collaborative institutional basis for these processes. A unified and powerful Government leadership could possibly overcome these risks, at least for some finite period of time. It is unlikely, however, that the existing minority Government, buffeted by a divisive political environment, will be able to do so for very long.

Regarding the technical support needed for policy formulation and coordination, the structures, processes and capacities within the Czech Republic's Cabinet structure present a mixture of strengths and weaknesses. On the positive side, the Department of the Cabinet Agenda in the Prime Minister's Office appears to provide stable and capable support to the policy formulation process. Line Ministry staff report that the framework laid out in the Procedural Code and recently-revised Legislative Rules satisfactorily balances the need for review of policy proposals with that for timely processing. Furthermore, the process effectively resolves many, though not all, conflicts prior to Cabinet meetings, as it is intended to do. The Department of the Cabinet Agenda appears to be a well-managed unit held in high esteem by line ministry counterparts and plays an important role in the smooth functioning of this system.

At the same time, the absence of a professional cadre of policy analysts within the Cabinet itself with the capacity and mandate to provide technical assessments of the cross-cutting tradeoffs posed by policy and legislative proposals is an important weak link in the Cabinet's technical support structure.

While line Ministries appear to be able to provide technical assessments of such tradeoffs from the points of view of their own Ministries, it is important for the Cabinet to have an independent technical capacity to integrate (but not replicate) those various assessments. It is perhaps also worth noting that the creation of such a unit within the Prime Minister's Office could also form part of a medium-term strategy for creating a professional, merit-based civil service. The existence of such a unit could enhance the attractiveness of a civil service career by offering the possibility of landing a prestigious position within the Office of the Prime Minister as the potential apex of one's career as a civil servant.

Creation of this capacity within the Office of the Prime Minister should also help to obviate the perceived need to delegate to four DPMs the task of ensuring coordination of policy formulation within broad sets of sectors. Backed by solid and professional technical analysis, the Prime Minister should find the task of taking charge of the policy level deliberations himself/herself to be considerably more manageable. While it would still be useful and important to form committees and subcommittees of the Cabinet to deal with the policy substance of particular proposals before putting them before the full Cabinet, such a Committee structure need not pose the same major risks currently posed by the four-DPM arrangement. This would partly reflect the fact that the leadership and membership of such committees would: (a) be drawn from the Ministers with line responsibilities themselves; and (b) be interlocking (i.e., committee memberships would overlap, thereby creating a natural basis for informal communication across committees and hence across policy discussions). Such a structure would also have the additional integrating advantage of ensuring that all such committees would rely on a shared professional cadre to undertake the required technical analyses of the intersectoral tradeoffs posed by policy proposals under their consideration. Such a shared technical resource could be expected to provide the policy deliberation process with valuable inter-sectoral institutional memory.

Recommendations

Efforts to improve the Czech Republic's public administration since the "Velvet Revolution" do not appear to have been particularly serious. This is perhaps not too surprising, given that the Czech Republic's public administration functions relatively well when compared to some of its CEE neighbors (see Table 11.1 above). This "benign neglect" also appears to have reflected the higher priority given to private sector development than to public sector modernization. This prioritization was perhaps most stark under the Klaus Government. By now, however, undeniable progress in developing the domestic private sector is creating conditions that can be expected to be broadly supportive of public sector modernization. These would include such things as rising expectations on the part of the business community and the citizenry regarding the quality of public policy decision-making and its implementation. Examples of such rising expectations would include less ideological policy deliberations, greater transparency and predictability of the regulatory environment, reductions in the prevalence of corrupt practices, as well as improved quality, timeliness and client-friendliness of public services and their delivery. Modernization of the public administration could help to meet these rising expectations as well as reinforce gains made on the private sector development side of the equation.

The current Government has publicly stated, in its "Policy Statement" of August 1998, its intention to foster a more inclusive and less ideological policy-making process and to improve public administration. This is a welcome sign, but one which will need to be followed by concrete action. To meet these objectives, the Government will need to address the challenges of mounting a reform effort as well the challenges of adequately designing and implementing key elements of such an effort.

Mounting a Reform Effort

Mounting a public sector modernization effort is difficult, time-consuming and fraught with potential setbacks along the way.[17] An important element of a strategy for facing these challenges is reform leadership with adequate institutional authority, stature and stability, as well as organizational capacity and focus. The existing arrangements for leadership of the Government's public administration reform agenda do not appear adequate to meet these needs. Responsibilities for public administration reform have been divided between the Ministry of Interior and the Deputy Prime Minister (DPM) for Legislation. The Ministry of Interior is responsible for developing the concept of public administration reform and for its execution, as well as for drafting laws that fall under its competences and coordinating with other relevant ministries. Political-level leadership rests with the DPM for Legislation who is also chair of the legislative review council. The formal arrangements thus provide for the involvement of key actors, although two further points must be kept in mind. First, successful administrative reform requires integrated efforts in a number of areas, whereas there is a tendency in the Czech Republic as in other Central European countries to focus primarily on the legislative component. Second, it is important to ensure close coordination among all ministries, an activity that generally poses a challenge in the Czech administration. In this case, the coordinating role could be handled by the deputy minister-level committee for public administration reform that is chaired by the Deputy Minister of Interior. In the absence of a supra-ministerial leader for administrative issues, effective use of the committee would be an additional way to ensure that the Ministry of Interior's voice carries weight with other line ministries.

In addition to this division of responsibilities for mounting the Government's administrative reform agenda, the National Training Fund, an independent body funded largely by EU/PHARE grant money, appears to be providing much of the intellectual leadership for the various efforts at public administration reform within the Czech Republic. Finally, the Ministry of Finance unavoidably plays an important role in any public administration reform process, both because of its role in any decisions with budgetary implications as well as its role in holding budgetary institutions accountable for both financial and program or policy performance.

A somewhat more integrated leadership structure would probably be wise. One means of addressing this need would be to ensure that a public administration reform committee be established as an inter-ministerial commission headed by the Prime Minister and include organizational units representing all the disparate elements of the current reform leadership structure -- legislative, executive, intellectual, financial and programmatic. This would include the DPM for Legislation, the Department of Public Administration within the Ministry of Interior, the National Training Fund, as well as the Ministry of Finance. Such a body would need a technical unit to support its work, but the essential function of such a body would be to provide the authority, stature and stability, as well as the organizational capacity and focus required to mount a serious and prolonged public administration reform process.

Key Elements of the Reform Process

While an administrative reform process will need to address a wide variety of issues, the analysis presented in this chapter highlights a number of particularly important actions and issues that will need to be undertaken or addressed in the Czech Republic.

In the area of creating a firmer basis for civil service-human resources management, the following actions are particularly pressing:

---

[17] See Gary J. Reid, "Performance-Oriented Public Sector Modernization in Developing Countries: Meeting the Implementation Challenge," *Research in Public Administration*, edited by Jos. C.N. Raadschelders and James L. Perry (JAI Press, Inc.: Greenwich, Connecticut, forthcoming).

Draft and Enact a Civil Service Law. The existing draft Civil Service Law is quite problematic. Tellingly, virtually no progress has been made in revising it to address the serious problems identified in the incisive and detailed commentary provided by SIGMA in August of 1994. Given the lack of progress on improving that law over the last 4+ years, it would appear that the time is ripe for starting over with an entirely new team. While lawyers will certainly be required as members of such a team, that new team should be led by persons with substantive expertise in human resource management.

Prepare Subsidiary Civil Service Legislation. Once a Civil Service Law is in place, the balance of the legal framework for creating a professional, merit-based civil service will need to be established. This would include policies and guidelines aimed at ensuring, for instance, transparent and competitive recruitment, selection and promotion procedures; merit-oriented personnel performance appraisal policies and guidelines, mechanisms for administrative appeal of personnel actions, etc.

Revise Public Sector Remuneration Structure, Policies and Practices. The existing level and structure of remuneration in the public sector is not very competitive with the domestic private sector, especially within the more highly skilled ranks. In order to enhance the attractiveness of employment conditions within the public sector, the Government needs to prepare a fiscally sustainable strategy for making remuneration more competitive. That strategy should also address the need for enhancing the transparency of the processes and practices under which compensation decisions are made and their results monitored.

Strengthen Mechanisms for Holding Organizational Units Accountable for Policy and Program Implementation. Grants of autonomy (delegations of authority) are substantial but are perhaps provided under terms and practices that are a bit too laissez-faire to ensure that they will be used in ways that consistently and effectively meet policy objectives. While financial accountability appears to exist at an aggregate level for budgetary units (i.e., for broad budget category envelopes), little seems to exist in the way of mechanisms to ensure accountability for delivering results with those fiscal (as well as human) resources.

Strengthen the Administrative Units Responsible for Ensuring Good Civil Service/Human Resource Management. At the time of the writing, the Department of Public Administration within the Ministry of Interior was understaffed and under-resourced[18]. It had neither the capacity to provide helpful technical assistance on personnel management to budgetary institutions nor to ensure adequate oversight of personnel management policies. Moreover, analogous capacities in personnel departments of line ministries are apparently variable. In both cases, the efforts to strengthen these capacities should aim at building human resource management (HRM) units that are *facilitators* of good personnel management by line agencies and their managers, rather than HRM units that view their role as doing personnel management themselves.

Strengthen Mechanisms for Nurturing Public-Sector-Specific Human Capital by Fostering Career Development within the Public Sector. While general human capital skills can be directly recruited, given attractive conditions of employment within the public sector, important specific human capital skills and knowledge are unique to a given public sector and its public agencies. Examples include knowledge of specific policies, procedures and practices that are unique to, for instance, the Czech public sector and its public agencies. Institutional memory is a phrase that captures important aspects of such specific human capital. Because of this, it is important that human resource management policies and practices provide adequate mechanisms for building such human capital in-house. At least three broad types of such

---

[18] In mid-1999, the ministry reported having hired forty new staff, with plans to hire 20 more. Effective deployment of these staff will be key to developing the department's capabilities.

mechanisms are worth mentioning: (a) those that make a career in the public sector *attractive*; (b) those that *facilitate* career development; and (c) those that *protect* public employees from arbitrary impediments to their career growth. Examples of (a) include: career streams that permit professional growth, including increasing responsibility and authority; pay policies that permit progressively more attractive remuneration over the course of one's career; as well as management practices that provide public recognition and other rewards for work well done. Examples of (b) include: networks, both formal and informal, which facilitate labor mobility within the public sector; personnel performance evaluation policies and practices that encourage both fair evaluations and helpful feedback; as well as promotion policies and practices that incorporate transparency and competition devices so as to enhance the odds that promotion decisions will reflect career growth potential. Examples of (c) include: personnel performance evaluation policies that ensure both that personnel assessments are made frequently and by numerous evaluators (so as to reduce the likely impact of any inaccurate or unfair appraisal), and that evaluated employees are allowed to respond to evaluators' assessments; personnel information policies that ensure that each employee has ready access to all information in his/her permanent personnel file; as well as both administrative and judicial grievance procedures and mechanisms, which pose neither excessive transactions costs on the employee nor undue risk of retaliation by his/her superiors.

At least three actions are key to addressing the most pressing challenges to improving capacities for policy formulation and coordination at the center:

Revise the Current Cabinet Structure. The current DPM-based authority relations within the Cabinet appear unlikely to provide a stable and collaborative institutional basis for policy formulation and coordination. The Government should consider options for creating a Cabinet structure that would be more supportive of the Prime Minister taking charge of the policy level deliberations himself/herself. Such a structure would probably rely on a system of committees and subcommittees of the Cabinet, rather than DPMs, to deal with the policy substance of particular proposals before putting them before the full Cabinet. Those committees and subcommittees would be supported by a single, professional policy analysis unit within the Office of the Prime Minister (see next recommendation). Such a Committee structure could avoid the major risks currently posed by the four-DPM arrangement.

Create a Single, Professional Policy Analysis Unit within the Office of the Prime Minister. Such a unit would provide professional analyses of policy proposals, focusing particularly on inter-sectoral tradeoffs and coordination issues raised by them. The processes for staffing that unit should be integrated into an overall strategy for creating a professional, merit-based civil service, with these positions being part of the pinnacle of that civil service.

Strengthen Ministry-Level Policy Formulation Capacities. For Cabinet decision-making processes to function effectively, Ministry-level policy analysis capacities are essential. As such, one important priority of administrative reform will need to be the strengthening of capacities for sectoral policy analysis within line Ministries.

Chapter XII. Social Sector Development in the Transition

Introduction

The Czech Republic's social sectors have evolved during the transition. The changes have been promoted in order to meet two key objectives. First, the Czech authorities had to set an appropriate basis to support the transition to a market economy. An important part of this strategy was an extensive overhaul of the educational sector. The second objective -- closely related to the economic reforms in transition period -- has been establishing an adequate social safety net. Consequently, the Czech social security system has undergone fundamental restructuring during the 1990s with the objective of establishing a system that meets the needs of a market economy. The three main components of the social protection system consist of: (a) the pension scheme, (b) the unemployment compensation scheme, and (c) social assistance and support.

The Czech Government managed its pension system far more prudently than other transition economies. In particular, early retirement was not used as extensively as in other economies to provide an outlet for unemployment, which was relatively easy as the unemployment rate remained extremely low. Recently, a retirement age increase was enacted, but this long-run reduction in costs was offset by the re-adjustment of benefits, by provisions allowing for greater scope for early retirement, and by additional years of credited time for women providing for childcare. These changes are likely to increase costs of the pension system in the future.

Despite the initial adjustments of the unemployment compensation scheme at the beginning of the transition period, it is becoming clear that further improvements are necessary, particularly in order to meet the challenges of the growth in unemployment that is slowly becoming comparable to that found in other European countries. The challenge, however, increases with the effort to devise such a program that would minimize those work disincentives effects so frequently found in many countries.

Some of the key systemic improvements within the social protection net relate to the rationalization of social assistance through a system of income support that has reduced public expenditures and has targeted benefits towards the poorest members of the community. The targeting mechanism used is the minimum living standard (MLS) which is price-indexed and is adjusted periodically to ensure that it reflects the consumption baskets of lower income Czech families. This system is scheduled to be updated in the future to encourage work and to provide greater discretion on the part of social workers to deal with individual financial and personal circumstances.

As the Czech Republic prepares to enter the EU, it is incumbent that its social protection system and education sector are in line with other EU countries. Considerable effort has already been made in this direction. Nonetheless, it is equally important that the Czech Republic not be burdened by some of the problems inherent in the social protection systems of a number of EU countries, since these problems would be magnified in the Czech Republic, which lacks the income cushion to support overly expensive social entitlements.

This chapter analyses the social safety net in the Czech Republic. It focuses on the changes in the structure of benefits and eligibility of each component of the social protection system, the extent to which people rely on each part of the system, and the level of government expenditures. The implications of increasing unemployment on the social safety net will be assessed and recommendations proposed. A second part of this chapter looks at the status of Roma population, the principal ethnic minority in the

Czech Republic. Finally, the chapter addresses reforms in the education sector, looking at the gaps in the existing system and proposed policy recommendations to eliminate deficiencies.

Social Protection

The Pension System

Currently, the pension system provides three types of benefits: old-age pensions (for the retired), disability pensions (full and partial) and survivor pensions for widows, widowers and orphans. Old-age pensions have typically accounted for two-thirds of total expenditures, with a positive trend (64 percent in 1980 and 69 percent since 1990).[1] In January 1996, the new Pension Insurance Bill came into effect, which changed the retirement age, the conditions of early retirement and the calculation of pensions. Expenditures on pensions amounted to 9.0 and 9.1 percent of GDP in 1997 and 1998, respectively.

Retirement Age is Being Raised. Before 1996, men could retire with full pensions at the age of 60; for women the retirement age was between 53 and 57, depending on the number of children raised.[2] The 1996 pension bill raised the age of retirement incrementally, so that after Dec. 31, 2006, the retirement age will be 62 years for men and 57-61 years for women.

Incentives to Retire Later, While Early Retirement Discouraged. If a person wishes to continue working beyond the retirement age without collecting his/her pension, the pension rises by 4 percent for each year worked beyond the retirement age. The rather generous regulations concerning early retirement that were introduced in 1988 were tightened in 1993 and 1996. A person has to be registered as unemployed in the District Labor Office for at least 180 days before he/she can retire early. For those who retire less than two years before their legal retirement age, the pension benefit is lowered by 1 percent of the base for each 90 day period remaining between the age of retirement and the official retirement age. The pension benefit is then recalculated according to the general rules when the person reaches the official retirement age. For those who retire voluntarily one to two years prior to the official retirement age, the "regular" pension is lowered by 0.6 percent for each 90 days and its level is not changed once the retirement age is reached. No pensions are given to those who voluntarily retire more than three years prior to their retirement age.

Work Disincentives. Under the new comprehensive law, people who retire early cannot work and draw a pension simultaneously. During the first two years of retirement, a pension may be collected simultaneously with earnings from a secondary activity if the income earned in these activities does not exceed two times the MLS for a single person. The penalty is withdrawal of pension benefits. After the two years, there is no limit on the income earned simultaneously while collecting a pension.

Pension Benefit. Under this new system, the old-age pension consists of two parts which are both regularly indexed: a fixed lump sum to which every pensioner is eligible and a portion related to the pensioner's previous contributions. During the next ten years, the pension for a new retiree will be

---

[1] At the end of 1998, the old-age pensions amounted to CZK1,762 million, or around 69.9 percent of total pensions. The average monthly old-age pension for the same year was CZK5,717, and an average pension (including disability and other pensions) was CZK5,450.

[2] In accordance with other policies favoring maternity, the retirement age is lowered for women as a function of the number of children they have raised. Before 1995, a woman who did not have children could not retire until she was 57 (and in 2007, until she is 61) and a woman who raised five or more children could retire at 53 years of age in 1995 (57 years of age in 2007).

calculated according to both the new and the old rules; the retiree will receive whichever is higher. Pensions are not taxed.

As with the MLS, pensions (both parts) are regularly indexed whenever the consumer price index has risen by 5 percent since the last indexation. In practice, pension indexation exceeds consumer price inflation but is lower than the nominal wage growth. Between 1990 and 1998, pension levels were adjusted 14 times due to inflation. In 1998, the average old-age pension was equal to about 45.9 percent of the average gross wage, whereas in 1991 (the year of the highest inflation) the replacement ratio reached 57.4 percent -- comparable to ratios in the US, Canada and Great Britain but considerably lower than the ratios for the lower wage workers in West European economies. Nevertheless, the real value of the old age pension in 1998 was only 88.9 percent of what it was in 1989.

Since 1994, the Czech pension system has been based on two pillars: the original basic obligatory pension insurance ('pay-as-you-go') and the new supplementary state-contributory pension insurance which is voluntary and partially funded from individuals' savings. The supplementary pension insurance allows people to increase the pension level from the basic level and to retire earlier than they would with the basic system. In 1998, 30 private pension funds were registered, with a total of 1.7 million participants (35 percent of the economically active population). The contributors to the system systematically increase by age with the percentage of current contributors increasing slowly to a maximum of only 20 percent at around age 50 years. This pattern of contribution is to be expected in a voluntary system, as younger workers are less likely to think about retirement and their income and personal savings rates are likely to be lower. With a successful system of tax expenditures -- with contributions made by employers or employees in pre-tax crowns up to some reasonable limit -- the contribution rates among middle-aged workers could rise to between 50-70 percent of all employees.

The second peculiarity of the Czech voluntary pension system is the continuing contributions made by employees close to, or above, retirement age. This is a result of the very short time horizons required for the contributions of such employees to remain on deposit. These preferences should immediately be removed for the system to become a genuine pension system rather than simply a short-term savings plan supported by government revenues. Furthermore, the system should be reformed to become one in which contributions and earnings on pension accounts should not be taxed as current income.

Another constraint to the expansion of the voluntary pension system comes in the high replacement rate of the state pension system. Recent data indicate that while the gross replacement rate in 1998 was 45.9 percent of the average gross wage, the net replacement rate was 59.1 percent of the net wage -- and pensions are not taxable. An average 59.1 percent replacement rate is too high to encourage much voluntary pension saving, as it will take care of most consumption needs of workers in retirement. Pensioners will have lower consumption requirements than prime-age workers due to reductions in expenses derived from work, reductions in family expenses, and reductions in the need for individual savings. Other problems with the pension funds have been identified by the government.[3]

At the end of the day, the current pension system will need to be reformed, given the demographic structure of the country, otherwise the costs of the system will require a payroll tax that will not be supportable by the employed population. The government should be concerned about the demographic dynamics that are likely to destabilize the pension system soon after EU accession if appropriate measures are not taken. Now is the best time to initiate changes in the pension system to make it sustainable by scheduling further increases in the retirement age to take account of changes in life expectancy, improving the actuarial fairness of early retirement provisions, eliminating the accrual of benefits during periods when people are not in the labor force, and limiting the indexation mechanism only to inflation.

---

[3] See financial sector chapter in this report, and World Bank (1999), Czech Republic, Capital Market Review.

Further, the link between contributions and benefits should be strengthened, and consideration could be given to partially pre-funding the pension system to spread the burden of retirement financing more equally across generations and to enhance fiscal discipline.

Social Assistance and Social Support

A new and substantially revised social welfare system came into affect at the beginning of 1995, with some parts coming into effect in January 1996. One important thrust of these changes was that the number of means-tested benefits increased. In general terms, transfers today can be grouped as means- or income-tested *social assistance* and non-means tested *social support* to families with children, although some of the social support programs are also means-tested.

Social Assistance. In 1991, the right for everyone to have assistance essential for ensuring the basic living conditions was established. Minimum living standards (MLS) were set for different household types and served as a basis for providing means-testing. The MLS for each household was computed as a sum of two parts: the personal minimum, based on whether one is an adult or a child, and the household minimum, a function of the number of individuals considered to be living together as a household. Households can receive a cash benefit -- social assistance -- equal to the difference in their income and the MLS.

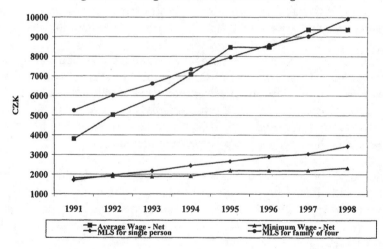

Figure 12.1. Wages and the Minimum Living Standard

The MLS levels are indexed on a regular basis. Until 1995, they were changed whenever inflation (measured by the CPI) had risen by more than 10 percent since the previous indexation. Since January 1995, the threshold of inflation was decreased to 5 percent. According to the law, the extent of indexation should "take into the account the extent of the cost-of-living increase," but no exact guidance is provided. The size of the increase is thus fully at the discretion of the government. Up to now, the rate of increase of the MLS has been equal to the changes in the CPI index.

Social Assistance and Support to Families with Children. Before 1996, all households with children (under the age of 20) were able to receive a package of family benefits irrespective of their level of income. Social support benefits were not taxable, but there was implicit taxation in that these benefits were included as part of total income of a household when applying for social assistance. Since 1996, most of these benefits (in terms of budget allocation) are means-tested. The most important elements of the family support benefits are described below, in descending order of importance:

- *Child Allowances* accounted for as much as 39 percent of the state social support budget in 1998. Currently, only those families whose income is less than three times the basic cost of living (or MLS) are eligible. The maximum and minimum benefits are 32 percent and 14 percent of the MLS for a child, and it is received by families whose income is less than 1.1 times or 1.8-3.0 times the MLS for that family. Benefits can be received for as long as the children are in school full time (including university studies).

- *Social Supplements* are additional benefits to help low-income families defray the costs associated with raising children. Hence, this benefit is only provided to families whose incomes are below 1.6 times the MLS for their household. The amount of the benefit varies by age of the child and the income of the family in the previous quarter. These supplements accounted for 21 percent of the budget for state social support in 1998.

- *Parental Contributions* are payments to a parent personally caring full-time for a child up to four years of age (or up to seven, if the child is handicapped or has a long-term illness). A parent receives 1.1 times the MLS of an adult. These benefits, which are not means tested, accounted for 26 percent of the budget for state social support in 1998.

- *Miscellaneous.* The remainder of the budget (approximately 14 percent in 1998) consists of housing and school transportation subsidies (which are means-tested) and benefits for foster care, funeral services, soldiers' families and maternity leave (for working women), which are not means-tested. Although not a large proportion of the budget for state social support, *maternity benefits* are of interest for their labor market incentive effects.[4] Working women can receive 28 weeks of maternity leave (37 weeks for single mothers) with a benefit equal to 69 percent of their gross daily wage for the full calendar month (30-31 days). In 1998, maternity grant for one child amounted to CZK6,240, which translated to 2.7 times the net minimum wage, or 67 percent of net average wage.

The data indicates that the relatively high level of income defining eligibility for the social support benefits results in a large number of benefit recipients: 3.37 million in May 1999. Given that this is one-third of the population, the original aim of targeting benefits primarily towards poorer families has thus been compromised. The most widely received benefit (over 1.9 million recipients) is child allowance. Approximately 74 percent of all the dependent children in the country received child allowances, of which 47 percent were eligible for the highest level of allowance, 41 percent were eligible for the middle level and 12 percent for the lowest one. Moreover, one-fifth of the families with children (about 561,000) qualified for the supplementary social allowance. The number of children eligible for this allowance clearly varies during the year whenever the MLS's are changed. According to the estimates of the Ministry of Labor and Social Affairs, the share of eligible children receiving these benefits should vary within 70-86 percent of all children.

Despite a stable downward trend in the number of newly born children since the start of the transition, the number of parents collecting a parental allowance rose as a result of the prolonged entitlement to this benefit when the cut-off age of the eligible child was raised from 3 to 4 years. While in January 1996 some 295,000 parents qualified for this benefit, the number rose to 309,000 by June 1996. This nearly 5 percent increase can be attributed solely to the prolonged entitlement. At the end of 1998, the average benefit (which is untaxed) represented 20 percent of the average gross monthly nominal wage.[5] The number of eligible parents, however, dropped to around 272,000 by May 1999. The data since the beginning of the transition suggest that women disproportionately fall into unemployment and tend to stay unemployed longer than men. The problem might be further exacerbated by the incentive for longer career breaks, which is likely to be used predominantly by lower-income, less-educated women.

The 1996 reform of the social support system was nevertheless a step in the right direction, as it attempted to target benefits towards the needy. In 1995, when the reform of the social support scheme

---

[4] Maternity benefits are considered as health care support.
[5] As of December 1998, the parental benefits were CZK2,343 a month. In cases when dependent child is more than 15 years old, the benefits amounted to CZK2,475 a month.

commenced, the non-tested benefits represented some 76 percent of the total spending on social support. By mid-1996, this share had fallen to 30 percent, and amounted to around 32 percent in 1998. The share of social transfers in the total household income changed over time, depending on the overall family income. While the share of social transfers to average income households with children fell during the last year by 1.4 percentage points to represent 9.6 percent in their total income, this share fell by 0.8 percentage points for the low-income households with children. For these low-income households, social incomes (defined to include social assistance, social support, pensions and sickness benefits) amounted to about 36.3 percent of their total income in 1998.

The structure of the social assistance and social support systems -- despite many recent changes -- exhibits many problematic signs in terms of the implied incentives for the recipients. The system has moved in the right direction by increasing the number of benefits that are means-tested, but the level at which the MLS is set is relatively high, especially for families with many children. The relatively high MLS means that: (a) targeting is not as narrow as might be desired; (b) social transfers represent a non-trivial part of the income for families with children; and (c) the scheme might have a serious work disincentive effect.

The Unemployment Compensation Scheme

A third important component of the social protection scheme in the Czech Republic is the unemployment compensation scheme. The characteristics of the scheme are described in more detail in the Chapter on Labor policy of this report. The unemployment benefits, however, are closely related to the social assistance and, in combination, both schemes can produce work disincetives.

First, the minimum living standards, as a measure of eligibilty for social assistance, sometimes allow the poor to rely on the social protection system, instead of securing a job. When the measure of minimum living standards (MLSs) is compared to the average economy-wide net wage and the net minimum wage, the analysis indicates that since 1992, the minimum wage has fallen below the MLS for a single-person household. Such a trend indicates that the level of the MLS may be set too high, for it enables a certain segment of the population to stay on welfare assistance rather than work. Also, the MLS for a family of four is nearly equal to the net average wage for the economy, or 6 percent higher at the end of 1998. The work disincentive effects are clear for low-skilled workers who are not likely to earn the average wage in the economy. Their choice is to have both parents work and perhaps make a little more than the MLS, or not work and live on the equivalent of one average net salary.

Second, a further analysis of comparing the unemployment benefits to social assistance programs, and their work disincentive reveal some interesting implications.[6] A simulation was constructed to examine the change in benefits as individuals move from unemployment benefits to social welfare assistance in 1996. In the single adult person family type, this transition to social assistance lowers the replacement rate only among those initially earning wages above the economy-wide average. Those who would earn 125 percent or less of MLS were receiving 80 percent or more of this income from the state, both during the time unemployment benefits are received, and when they are exhausted and only social assistance is received. Similarly, for the one-earner families with children, the replacement rate remains high at 75 percent.

In an analysis of exits from unemployment to a job using Labor Force Survey data, it is found that people in families with relatively more dependants, unemployed persons are less likely to leave unemployment for employment -- and more likely to remain unemployed. Moreover, people with these

---

[6] See Erbenova, Sorm and Terrell (1998).

characteristics are more likely to receive social assistance with higher replacement rates, indicating that the MLS is indeed having a work disincentive effect.

The problem of the poverty trap stemming from the means-tested social care cash benefits is well known. With a protected MLS income for a family of four, there will be little financial incentive for a parent to find a job[7] given the high implicit tax rate resulting from the post-employment reduction in the several layers of allowances. Moreover, there is little incentive for the working poor to look for better opportunities within the labor force, as any increase in pay would have a resulting reduction in benefits. The development of too flat an earnings structure will lead to the type of disincentives for advancement that were endemic in the pre-transition economies. The danger in ignoring the issue of work incentives is that, in an environment in which unemployment is likely to be maintained at higher European rates, a culture of poverty could be developed in which those at the lower end of the income spectrum have little incentive to escape.

Fiscal Consequences of Rising Unemployment on Social Protection System

The unemployment rate has been rising rapidly over the past several years, from an average rate of 3.0 percent in 1995, to 7.5 percent in 1998. As of January 1999, the unemployment rate increased to 8.1 percent, and is expected to reach over 10 percent by the end of 1999. The unemployment rate increase will have a direct influence on a social protection budget in a number of ways. Not only will unemployment compensation expenditures rise, but all other social programs will also be affected. Even marginal increases in each of the social protection program expenditures will be sufficient to add to an already sizable fiscal deficit. First, given the opportunity for early retirement, some individuals will select this option, thereby increasing expenditures on pensions from the already high 9.1 percent of GDP, and 30.4 percent of state expenditures (end-1998).[8] Second, given the fact that unemployment is more highly concentrated among women, the use of parental allowances may also increase. Already since 1991, the labor force participation rate of women under the age of 40 has substantially decreased, and parental allowances are equal to a large proportion of this numerical decrease.

Finally, between one-third and one-half of the newly unemployed could become long-term unemployed. This will directly lead to an increase in the number of individuals who will be qualified for the social protection program (either family benefits or unemployment benefits). While each of these programs represents expenditures of less than 2 percent of the state budget, any expansion in beneficiaries will still lead to marginal increases in program expenditures. These expenditures will increase regardless of the existence of another provider in the family, or regardless of wage growth in other areas of the economy. In addition, the MLS method of calculation of family allowance could increase social program expenditures by some CZK2 billion.

With the objective of achieving a balanced public budget, the possibilities of the social protection expenditure cuts need to be assessed. Social assistance and support expenditures form the smallest of the three programs, and cannot significantly affect public expenditures. However, within this budget, expenditures for persons with disabilities have been rising at a rapid rate, particularly in comparison with expenditures for the poor population. Accordingly, the government should reassess those programs which could better be provided as cash assistance in an equitable manner, reducing expenditures that are excessive and transferring some of the in-kind benefits to appropriate non-governmental organizations. Such rationalization would also free up the resources of the state administration to focus on poverty.

---

[7] See OECD (1998), Economic Survey: The Czech Republic.
[8] Share of pensions in consolidated general government expenditure amounted to 22.6 percent at the end of 1998.

Each of the social programs should be revisited in terms of the payroll tax rate used to finance the program. Currently, all social insurance programs -- pensions, employment programs, health insurance, and sickness and maternity benefits -- cost employers 35 percent of payroll, and employees 12.5 percent of payroll. In a situation of less than full employment, high payroll taxes will either discourage employment by increasing labor costs or will encourage informal market activity (non-taxpaying) in which employers can reduce their costs. Since payroll taxes are generally distortional, their use should be restricted as much as possible. In general, social security, health insurance, and unemployment insurance should be financed by earmarked taxes and run independently under a system that ensures fiscal controls -- that is, a system in which benefits are not subsidized by the state. Priority should be given to finding other taxes, such as the VAT, which can substitute for payroll tax revenues, possibly by some small rate adjustments in the future.

Coordination of Programs

With higher unemployment rates, the coordination of social programs becomes more important. The social allowance programs and the social care programs should be better coordinated. Even though both programs are income-tested and directed at families earning the lowest incomes, the families receiving social allowances are implicitly considered the 'worthy' poor, while those families receiving social assistance (excluding the aged and disabled) are implicitly considered the 'unworthy' poor. In fact, some proposals for program redesign would try to distinguish those who are willing to work from those who are not willing to work, which is increasingly a design criterion of welfare programs in Europe and the United States.

Nonetheless, there is likely to be a certain stigma throughout the population with regard to the receipt of social assistance cash transfers, particularly as it appears that the Romany population receive these benefits in a disproportionate number -- although they are a relatively small proportion of the population. Consequently, as the unemployment rate rises, the current program structure of the administrative separation of these benefits is likely to have one (or both) of two adverse consequences. First, many of the unemployed may decide not to apply for social assistance cash benefits because of the stigma involved. As such, they will fall below the MLS line to their detriment and that of their children. Second, those that do apply may lose their motivation to find work as they accept the stigma of failure (in conjunction with the normal poverty trap effects). Consequently, the combination and coordination of the administration of these programs into one structure would be advisable to ensure that work incentives are encouraged and services can be provided across the board to the newly unemployed.

The other area of program development should be between the social allowance and social assistance recipients and the employment offices. The challenge to the government is to improve the development of the active labor market programs (ALMP) and to increase their financing so that the newly unemployed and new entrants to the labor force can more easily find work. It would be preferable to cut certain traditional benefits -- such as maintenance allowance for families of soldiers, or the size of new benefits, such as the foster care grants -- than to let programs such as the ALMP program remain ineffective.

Ethnic Minorities and Social Exclusion

The principal ethnic minority in the Czech Republic is the Roma or Gypsies. Information on their number is imprecise, because many conceal their origin to minimize discrimination or social ostracism, and also because since 1989 it has been illegal to collect official data based on ethnic origin. Informed estimates from community leaders and social workers, however, suggest a Roma population in the order of 300,000, about 3 percent of the national population. They are particularly concentrated in the industrial and mining areas of northern Bohemia, where many of their ancestors migrated after World War II from the Slovak part of the former Czechoslovakia, attracted by plentiful opportunities of unskilled unemployment. With the break-up of Czechoslovakia, this history created a problem for many of the Roma settled in Bohemia, since many were initially denied Czech citizenship on the grounds of their Slovak origin. After some delay, this issue is now being addressed by the proper authorities.

Demographically, the Roma differ considerably from the majority Czech population in having a relatively high birthrate and a significantly lower life expectancy. The Roma are a "young" population, in contrast to the aging Czech population. Thus the two groups have very different dependency characteristics, elderly in the case of Czechs and juvenile in the case of Roma, implying different social policy needs.

Traditionally, the Roma were a community isolated from the majority. They had distinct economic roles before World War II, often linked to a nomadic lifestyle. In this situation, they were broadly tolerated because they seldom remained anywhere long enough to become the focus of majority hostility. During the Communist period many Roma were directed into unskilled jobs in state enterprises. At the end of this period the Roma were usually the first to be laid off when employment contracted. As a result, the Roma are now mostly in a very adverse situation. While unemployment among Czechs until recently remained below 5 percent, in Roma communities unemployment rates range from 70 percent to 90 percent, though there may be some informal or ephemeral economic activities to qualify this picture. There are some Roma entrepreneurs, especially in the construction sector, but employment there is mostly unskilled, seasonal, and foreign illegal workers are many times used, thus works do not necessarily employ Roma people.

Many of the Roma continue to live in isolated apartment blocks formerly associated with enterprises, but since they are mostly jobless, it is difficult for them to maintain the standard of their housing, and they survive on welfare payments. Since much of the welfare system is linked to family size, this pushes many Roma families into a "welfare trap" where their income from welfare is higher than they could earn from an unskilled job. Isolation also precludes easy access to health facilities, and this, together with an unhealthy lifestyle predisposes Roma to higher levels of illness. Communicable diseases could find fertile ground and lead to serious health problems due to the lack of public health intervention and unsanitary living conditions.

Many of the Roma coming from Slovakia had a version of the Romany language as their mother tongue, and have only limited knowledge of Czech. This impeded their children's access to the Czech education system, because they were mostly unable to perform well in the initial psychological assessment -- given in the Czech language -- required for all entrants to the system. The upshot is that most Roma children have been directed to special schools, intended for children with learning difficulties, which do not address their specific needs. Thus, educational progress has been poor, with many early drop-outs, and according to one estimate, only 2.5 percent of Roma children entering any form of secondary education.

The combination of limited education, high unemployment, unhealthy lifestyle, poor housing, and high birth and death rates has turned the Roma into a third-world enclave isolated and embedded as a series of small pockets of population among a first-world Czech nation. This unfavorable situation has been further reinforced by a growing prejudice and discrimination against Roma by the majority population. Roma are widely seen by non-Roma as feckless and prone to criminality. This discrimination has extended to frequent denial of access to employment, so that in practice Roma have had few legal opportunities for self-betterment, with the result that the popular prejudice against them has tended to become self-fulfilling, as they have lapsed into either apathy or petty criminality, for want of more productive options. Unemployment, lack of skills and opportunities, and discrimination have made Roma communities economically unviable.

Recently, following EU and other international concern, the national authorities have begun to address the situation of the Roma people, and a broad program of actions on many fronts has been drawn up, though initially with only limited resources allocated for its implementation. Moreover, at the local level where changes have to be implemented, there continue to be frequent manifestations of prejudice against Roma. Nevertheless, there have been promising initiatives to improve access to education for Roma children, and to eradicate prejudice among the police and judicial authorities. By 1998, about 41 elementary and special schools had established preparation classes for Roma children to ease their transition into primary education, and these have improved retention rates. A much greater effort is still needed to provide adult training to increase Roma access to employment and self-employment, and to facilitate increased use of medical and public health facilities by Roma, in order to improve their lifestyle and help them to become viable economic agents in a transition economy.

Education Sector Reform

Background

An important part of tackling the rising unemployment rate and promoting the human development of the Czech Republic, is the establishment and consolidation of a dynamic education system. Only education institutions adjusted to the aim of meeting the requirements of the market economy can assist the Czech Republic in successfully overcoming the transition period. From 1948 to 1989, the education system was subject to close ideological control, exercised through the Ministry of the Interior. After completing basic education, the majority of children were channeled into short-duration secondary vocational schools, where they took occupationally specific courses leading directly to jobs in production enterprises. Uniformity was stressed, not only in pupil performance, but also in the management and budgeting of education, and in teacher remuneration, which lead to the stagnation of the system.

A fundamental change occurred at the end of 1989 with the depoliticization and decentralization of education, the ending of the state monopoly, and the introduction of pupil and parental choice of study options. Other major changes included the introduction of normative financing, together with the diversification of sources of funding beyond the state budget, and the initiation of a significant degree of flexibility in curricula at the school level. The purpose of this section is to identify the changes, which have taken place since 1990, to analyze their implications, and to discuss the issues arising, particularly in the context of EU accession.

Educational Performance and Problems

In the context of the significant population decline, which is gradually reducing the size of entering school cohorts compared to the numbers of students graduating, the educational system faces an increasing need for rationalization and consolidation. However, the introduction of normative financing has complicated this process, since schools have an incentive to attract additional students in order to increase financial allocations. Similarly, the increasing under-employment of teachers in a contracting system exerts a downward pressure on wages, especially at the entry level, making it difficult to attract new young entrants, or to reward performance. Also, much of the personnel with long experience of the previous system have had difficulty in adjusting to the new conditions, largely due to inertia or lack of appropriate re-training. Reforms are needed in a number of directions if the education system is going to become a force for change in the process of the transition to a dynamic market economy.

Pre-School and Basic Education. By 1996, Czech pre-school enrollments compared favorably with most OECD countries, and were slightly above any other Central European country. There is universal enrollment for the nine-year period of compulsory education. Although the usual age for transition to upper secondary education is 15, there have been, since 1990, increasing opportunities for earlier transfer, at ages 11 or 13, into the gymnasium stream (academic secondary). However, this early loss of the more gifted pupils is beginning to adversely affect those remaining, especially in the city schools where the trend of early transfer is more common.

Upper Secondary Education. Besides general academic education (gymnasium), other upper secondary options at age 15 include technical, vocational, integrated and special secondary schools, and vocational training centers. At least 98 percent of pupils completing compulsory schooling continue their studies in some form of upper secondary education. The majority of upper secondary pupils is still found in the technical and vocational streams, though gymnasium enrollment has slowly increased from 10 percent to 20 percent of the total over the 1989-98 period. Technical school enrollments have increased from 30 percent to 45 percent of the total during the period, primarily accounted by the new private schools, while vocational enrollments have declined significantly, from 60 percent to 35 percent. In both technical and vocational schools, business and commercial studies are being favored at the expense of engineering-related fields. Some technical schools have moved to a broader curriculum closer to the general education stream. Another initiative has been the creation of vocational/technical integrated secondary schools which offer greater educational choice to students, and may lower costs as a single institution offers a greater diversity of programs. In addition, a few vocational training centers have been created, which offer retraining courses for job seekers.

While these initiatives are all potentially beneficial in various ways, they all supplement, rather than replace, existing types of institutions, thus tending to make a complex system even more so. According to the Ministry of Education, there are some 2000 different study options in technical and vocational education, many of them overlapping in content. Particularly for the less-demanded subjects, the provision of books and other materials thus becomes very expensive. Another problem relates to a decline in the average size of schools and classes due to the population decline and the growth of private institutions which tend to be significantly smaller than state schools. Also, the number of state technical schools, in part the result of conversions of former vocational schools, has increased. As a result, per student costs in technical education must have increased significantly, as the growth in both schools and teachers has outweighed the increase in pupil numbers, while teachers risk becoming under-utilized.

There is a serious and urgent need for a far-reaching rationalization of the technical and vocational secondary education structure, aiming to eliminate many of the outdated and narrowly-focussed courses which attract few enrollments, and broadening and re-orienting the curricula in remaining areas. These changes could both produce a more adaptable type of labor market entrant, and also significantly reduce the unit costs of delivery of an improved system.

At the completion of four-year upper secondary education, whether in the academic, technical, or vocational streams, all students take the *maturita* examination, for which the Ministry of Education lays down the general guidelines. However, schools individually determine the content of the examination for their students. As a result, employers do not have a common standard of achievement by which to evaluate school graduates entering the labor market, and universities impose an additional entrance examination in order to establish a standard of performance.

Post-Secondary and Higher Education. The most rapidly expanding sector of the Czech education system during the 1990s has been higher professional education. Introduced progressively from 1992 as a measure to supplement the limited number of university places, this is designed to offer three- or four-year courses leading to practical qualifications required for successful entry into middle- or even high-level positions in professional fields. Most of these courses have been located in technical secondary schools, which permits an effective use of otherwise redundant facilities. The demand for this type of education is reflected by the expansion of enrollments from 6,300 in 1995/6 to 23,500 in 1997/8, with applications still substantially exceeding the available places. Also, in 1996 the expenditure per pupil was less than half of that in higher education, and also slightly lower than in any form of upper secondary education. Conceivably, further expansion at this level could relieve future pressure to expand higher-cost university education.

New Higher Education Acts in 1990 and early 1998 changed the status of the higher education institutions. The 1990 Act restored academic freedom and institutional autonomy to universities, leading also to a renewal of international contacts. Teaching programs were revised, research reinvigorated, and new institutions created, leading to steady growth of student capacity. Between 1992 and 1997, undergraduate enrollments increased from 114,000 to 162,000, while figures of post-graduate students increased from 3,500 to 11,500. The 1998 Act allows the creation of private higher education institutions. However, higher education remained a state monopoly, and the state budget continued to be the main source of finance.

Each higher education institution is being provided with a Board of Trustees, with the members nominated by the Minister of Education after consultation with the university rector. Their role is to promote the public interest in the context of the management of higher education institutions, including the budget. The 1998 Act has also rationalized the internal management structure of higher education institutions by placing the component faculties under the central leadership of the rector, and by setting out the decision-making rights of the faculties within this structure.

The other main innovation of the 1998 Act is to clarify and strengthen the role of bachelor's degree courses as a shorter and complete form of higher education, aimed at direct preparation for a career, while not excluding the possibility of extending studies to prepare for a higher degree. Between 1992 and 1997, the number of students in bachelor programs increased from 12,500 to 39,000, i.e., from about 10 percent of undergraduates to about 25 percent. It has also become possible for non-university institutions to provide such courses, after going through an accreditation process. There are also active career centers within higher education institutions, further intended to ensure the relevance of educational services.

Although public higher education institutions continue to be substantially dependent on the state budget via provisions for normative financing, the 1998 Act increases their scope to generate funds from other activities, and also introduces the possibility of charging tuition fees. The fee income is intended to be used to provide a scholarship fund. Private higher education institutions determine their own fees, and may only receive any public subsidy if they operate on a non-profit basis.

Other types of higher education have been promoted at the beginning of a transition period. The range of adult education options has been diversified and now includes regular degree studies as well as requalification and special-interest studies. From 1990 to 1997, graduates doubled to 15,000. Distance education activities also grew during the period, with help from Phare, so that four well-equipped distance education centers have been established, and by 1997/98 24 programs in various specializations were offered. By contrast, part-time education appears not to be favored, though it is attractive to older students, and many fields of study are excluded from it.

Research. The Czechoslovak Academy of Sciences (1953-1992) had a broad responsibility for research, and post-graduate education, replacing the universities in this respect. The research structure was complemented by the research institutes belonging to various ministries and state enterprises (140 industrial research institutes in existence in 1989). In 1989, the Czech component of Czechoslovakia spent 2.2 percent of GDP on research and development (R&D), employing 140,000 people. However, much of this extensive institutional structure was unproductive in terms of research results, over-staffed and under-equipped.

Since 1989, this situation has been progressively changed, when 22 research institutes closed, with total staff declining by about 50 percent to 6,000, just over half of them researchers. The Academy of Sciences of the Czech Republic, created in 1992, continued to administer about 60 research institutes, while playing a more limited role in post-graduate education. Currently, universities are increasingly active in post-graduate education, with most of the instructional staff having both research and teaching roles. About 100 laboratories have so far been spun off from research institutes to universities, to make their research effort more effective. The industrial and agricultural research institutes attached to enterprises were privatized, with many subsequently closed.

By 1997/8, it was estimated that total employment in research had been stabilized at between 40,000 and 50,000, of whom some two-thirds were researchers. Total Research and Development (R&D) expenditure in 1998 was estimated to be about 1.1 percent of GDP, with the state budget for research representing 0.45 percent of GDP. An important initiative has been the creation, in 1992, of the Government's Research and Development Council, assigned to oversee all funding activities for R&D. Two types of support are provided: (a) targeted support for projects or programs; and (b) institutional funding of R&D institutions for both current and capital expenditures. While institutional funding grew steadily (in current terms) between 1993 and 1997, targeted support more than doubled and became the majority component by 1997 (56 percent). Thus, there is an increasing trend of focussing support on research projects, as distinct from research institutions.

In its policy-making role, the Council has developed successive Statements of Principles for R&D in the Czech Republic: (a) focussing on making the Czech system of R&D support compatible with EU practice, on reaching the target of 0.7 percent of GDP for state support to R&D; (b) developing the strategy of state support by strengthening industrial research, by linking defense research to NATO membership, and by expanding university research and international collaboration; (c) improving the remuneration of researchers and making it performance-related; and (d) initiating the fiscal steps needed to encourage private support of research, and the legal steps needed for EU compatibility.

This, in turn, led to the creation of the Grant Agency of the Czech Republic (GACR), which is the agency allocating research grants competitively across the R&D spectrum. In 1996, universities and the Academy each received just over 40 percent of GACR funds, with the balance shared between ministry laboratories and industry. By field of activity, technical and natural sciences each received some 30 percent of funds, and medicine, social sciences and agriculture 10-15 percent each. Many ministries act as channels of distribution for R&D funds awarded through the GACR.

Despite all of the ongoing efforts and initiatives, it is recognized that the present state of R&D in the Czech Republic still leaves room for improvement. In particular, the industrial sector so far shows little interest in using the results of research. A new program promotes partnerships between industry and the universities or the Academy, with 50 percent support from the Ministry of Industry, but this is languishing because industry is often unable to find its half of the funding.

At present, research tends to be over-concentrated on basic, as opposed to applied topics, while the popularity of social science studies is limiting the supply of students in technological fields who can become the next cohort of young researchers in these areas. Moreover, virtually no young people tend to become scientists due to the fact that the starting salary for a post-Ph.D. level researcher is below the average wage in the country. As a result, most researchers are older people -- trained under the umbrella of the old economic system. As yet, researchers derive little income from the intellectual property generated by their work, though a beginning has been made in this direction. The quality of university research also needs further strengthening, and to this end, an extensive evaluation process is being introduced in 1999 -- in the expectation that improved research will, in turn, lead to improved teaching.

Operational Aspects of Education - Management and Financing

Management of the Educational System

As a result of several Acts passed between 1990 and 1995, there is now (partly under the Ministry of Education) a very fragmented structure of management in the education system. There are also two distinct fields of state administration -- operational administration of schools, and pedagogical administration of the educational process. In addition, there is a hierarchy of organizations representing the "consumer" interest -- local communities, parents and students -- in the form of school councils, and the Education Committee of Parliament. Finally, the educational inspectorate, an independent budgetary unit reporting directly to the Ministry of Education, became an evaluator of educational results and the operating conditions in schools.

The Ministry of Education has a central role with respect to the pedagogical aspects of the educational process. In this domain, only the universities, by virtue of their academic autonomy, lie outside the competence of the Ministry. The operation of educational facilities -- payment of salaries and utilities, maintenance of facilities, provision of the inputs needed for education -- is a much more involved administrative process. The Ministry itself is concerned directly with these aspects only in the case of universities. For the gymnasia, secondary technical schools, and those vocational schools under its authority, the Ministry functions through the 86 local (district) education authorities. For kindergarten and basic schools, the situation is more complex still, because the Ministry operates through both the local education authorities and the municipalities.

In 1997/98, there were about 6,400 kindergartens and 5,000 basic schools, which implies that on average municipalities will each be responsible for one kindergarten and one basic school. In reality, there must be many municipalities with no educational facilities at all, and a minority in maintowns which operate much closer to the scale of a district education authority. Moreover, with the possibility for principals to assume managerial and administrative authority over their schools -- authority -- which covers economic and financial as well as personnel matters -- it is not clear what meaningful role is left to the municipalities. The possibility, since 1995, of establishing school councils representing the interests of parents, employees and the community, makes the role of municipalities appear even further attenuated.

Financing of the Educational System

The financing of education is formally decentralized, with the majority of funding coming from the national budget, and channeled through local education authorities. There has been some increase in parental contributions for special services such as extra-curricular activities, but education remains a publicly financed service, and even in the non-state sector, the institutions receive 60-90 percent of per student expenditures from the State. The allocation of funds to schools is done according to a system of per pupil norms, which vary by level and field of study. Higher education has, until now, remained an almost wholly state-funded activity, though the latest legislation opens the way to change in this respect.

As a share of GDP, public educational expenditure showed an increase from 4 percent to almost 6 percent between 1989 and 1994, but since then it has tended to decline. The distribution of expenditure within education has varied over the period, with the upper secondary level increasing from 16.6 percent to 25.9 percent, and tertiary education level falling from 16.6 percent to 13.5 percent. The proportion of total expenditure not specific to particular educational levels declined from 28.9 percent to 20.2 percent over the same period. The expansion of the share of upper secondary education in expenditures appears hard to justify, given that both enrollments and teachers at this level have shown slight overall declines, and that the growth of non-state education has been greatest at this level. By contrast, higher education enrollments have expanded about 50 percent during the period, with a declining share of the budget. This has been achieved by a more intensive use of personnel, leading to larger classes, and by limiting purchases of equipment. Given the pressure of demand for higher education, the scope for diversifying sources of financing, such as the sale of services, the hire of facilities, fees for tuition need to be urgently explored.

Although the education system serves a declining population -- so that there is no significant need for construction of new facilities -- capital expenditures for re-construction and major repairs are still required. In the 1998 education budget, capital expenditure accounts for some 5 percent of the total. Personnel expenses account for 55 percent of the budget, out of which approximately 3 percent goes to subsidies for staff costs in non-state schools. The remaining 40 percent is spent normatively (per pupil) for such items as textbooks and educational supplies, maintenance, utilities and heating, school meals and boarding. These figures are more a consequence of the low share of salaries, because of low remuneration levels of teachers, than an over-generous provision of services to schools. The low salary level, especially at the entry point, is a deterrent to the recruitment and retention of young teachers. The teaching force, which is about 75 percent female, is predominantly middle-aged, with a majority trained in the pre-1989 system.

Recommendations and EU Accession

The educational environment in the Czech Republic is dynamic in several respects: (i) overall enrollments are tending to decline as a function of the declining population; (ii) within this broad trend, university and other post-secondary enrollments have increased, along with technical secondary and to some extent gymnasia, whereas vocational secondary education has substantially decreased and kindergarten is slowly declining; (iii) private education has been introduced, especially at the technical secondary level; (iv) extensive decentralization took place, with district education authorities playing a key role, but even municipalities becoming involved in kindergarten and basic education; and (v) normative financing has become the dominant method of allocating educational expenditures.

In other respects, the system resists change: (i) the growth of private schools has not resulted in any significant decline of public schools; (ii) the number of teachers has declined slightly, but less than enrollments, so that teaching loads have declined further (the decline in teaching numbers is heavily concentrated among secondary vocational instructors and kindergarten teachers, while other categories have increased, sometimes substantially); (iii) there has been limited recruitment of young teachers with modern training, leaving the teaching force conservative and resistant to innovation; and (iv) the administrative fragmentation since 1989 makes it more difficult to introduce systemic improvements in education, e.g., standardized national examinations.

The level of education that appears the most problematic is *upper secondary*, especially the vocational stream. While this latter has been contracting in enrollment terms, not in the number of schools, it absorbs an increasing share of expenditures. Moreover, graduates of this stream have increasing difficulty in finding employment. There appear to be strong vested interests within the education system still wedded to the concept of training for specific vocational competencies, instead of making the switch to training for the occupational characteristic of a dynamic market economy. Since many of the programs in vocational education relate to industrial occupations no longer needed in an increasingly service-oriented economy, the inappropriateness of much current provision is thereby exacerbated. The expansion of non-state initiatives in this sector would offer scope to increase its relevance, except that this development has not been accompanied by any significant closure of the outdated facilities.

Two recommendations regarding the general and technical streams of upper secondary education relate to the need for greater economy in the use of resources, and the diversity of standards between the best schools and the rest. High overstaffing reflects the former norm of greater occupational specificity, so that every teacher tended to be subject-specific to a much greater degree than would be the case in a Western education system. Undoubtedly, there are several gymnasia and technical secondary schools in large cities, which dispense education of the best international standard, but elsewhere the quality of these institutions may not attain the same level. It is important that policy measures should give priority to improving the weaker performers, rather than further strengthening the best.

As noted earlier, *higher education* enrollments have expanded considerably since 1989, but expenditures have not increased commensurately. To some extent this can be justified, because this level was relatively favored financially under the previous system, and the expansion of enrollments has been strongest in faculties such as law and economics where equipment expenditures are lower. Nevertheless, in recent years the higher education system has not had the funds to update laboratory equipment and information technology to the extent needed. New legislation being introduced in 1999 gives the universities an independent public status, which will allow them more scope to generate their own income. But the slow transformation of industry may place limits on the effectiveness of this innovation, as it has on the development of research activities by the Research and Development Council.

The prospect of *EU accession* has significant implications for the Czech education system. EU membership will place the Czech Republic in a very competitive economic environment. This indicates the need to accentuate modernizing tendencies in the education system, in particular at the secondary and post-secondary levels, which will involve investments in staff retraining and equipment updating. Any further investment in the system presupposes savings in existing provisions in order to make room for new initiatives. There should be urgent attention to the closure of under-utilized and irrelevant facilities, especially in the vocational stream, with the concomitant staff reductions or redeployments. One possible channel of modernization will be the development of close institutional linkages with parallel schools or colleges in the present EU member states, with staff and student exchanges facilitating the adoption of innovations.

A more symmetrical *structure of educational administration* would enable the Ministry of Education to focus more attention on adaptation of the system to the pressures of the market-oriented EU environment. This will also require that the Ministry leads the effort to develop constructive partnerships at regional, district and school levels, in order that these levels become sources of initiative and innovation. Extensive retraining of administrators as well as principals and teachers will be necessary to achieve this new environment, and it will also require a continuing publicity effort directed to parents, students, and the local communities to engender their support for progress. There is likely to be an expanding component of non-state educational provision, which will also have to be brought into a changing environment as an active partner.

The likely constraints on future public resources for education will also place a premium on the expansion of *other sources of financing*, especially for post-secondary and higher education. With the initiation this year of opportunities to invest in non-state higher education, which will undoubtedly be fee-paying even if operated on a non-profit basis, the difficult issue of charging tuition fees for state higher education will come to the fore. The important point in any introduction of fees will be the simultaneous introduction of an equitable scheme of financial support to students from poorer backgrounds, who would otherwise be penalized by a tuition fee scheme.

Chapter XIII. The Challenges of Health Care Reform

Introduction

The health sector in Czech Republic has undergone a radical reform since 1990. Unlike the rest of the region, the Czech Republic initiated a sweeping reform that restructured, refinanced and reoriented its health system. Despite the gains associated with these changed, and in some cases because of them, fiscal pressures have persisted over this same period. Indeed, the challenges for the health system lie in establishing and ensuring clear and consistent policies in the health sector, coping with the existing debt overhang among providers, addressing the regulatory and enforcement weaknesses of the current system, and strengthening incentives for improved cost containment, including further downsizing. These elements will define the costs and effectiveness of the Czech Republic's health system.

The process of accession to the European Union (EU) is likely to impose sizable expenditure pressures on the Czech Republic. This will come precisely at the time that the country is facing the need to rationalize its expenditure policies, to consolidate the budget process and to impose real fiscal discipline on operations conducted outside the budget and by transformation institutions. While the transportation of the *Acquis Communautaire* will put little demand on the health sector, the EU has already expressed concern regarding the health financing system and its viability over the longer term. As the process of EU accession advances, an affordable and working health care system that does not compromise the government's expenditure envelope is necessary.

The current financing system is fragile. The percent of GDP devoted to health has remained relatively constant and current deficits have been manageable, although, underfinancing is emerging, particularly in the largest health insurance company. To complicate matters, highly indebted providers introduce instability into the sector. As the health system evolves, these issues will remain paramount and deserve to be carefully monitored along with the policy issues noted above.

Health Sector Reform

The Czech Republic's health reform totally revamped the Soviet-imposed system of public financing and provision that, as in the rest of the Soviet system, was based on input norms and resulted in an oversupply of physicians, hospital beds and other inputs. The system was characterized by low levels of efficiency and quality of service, and a lack of incentives to achieve either. Medical protocols and technology were decades-old, and management was largely an accounting practice.

The reform of the health care system touched every aspect of health care financing and delivery, and was driven by the same market principles that led reforms in other sectors after the *Velvet Revolution*. Financing arrangements were set out in the General Health Insurance Act (Act 550) of 1991, and shifted financing from the government budget to a payroll tax of 13.5 percent levied on employers and employees on a one-to-two ratio; that is a contribution of 4.5 percent of gross wages by employers and 9 percent by employees. The government contributes 13.5 percent of 80 percent of the minimum wage for those not working, the unemployed, the elderly and children under 18.[1] Government contributions are financed by the state budget.

---

[1] Originally, the government paid 65 percent of the minimum wage for those not covered by private health insurance, but this was raised in 1997 to 80 percent.

The concept behind the financing arrangement was to establish compulsory health insurance coverage, and to promote competition among non-profit health insurance funds. This arrangement was meant to discourage risk selection and to promote solidarity, in the anticipation that the government could eventually exit the system other than as regulator. The insurance companies were to provide not only a basic set of benefits (that was undefined) but were to compete in offering additional services; employers could also offer an enhanced set of health benefits for a higher premium. The government created a quasi-public General Health Insurance Fund (GHIF/VZP) under Act 551 to provide for those who could not purchase coverage from the private non-profit health insurers, but the government implicitly competes with any other insurance company.

Regulation (Act 280/1992) initially specified the rules of entry and exit into the insurance market, its organizational structure and how funds and information were to be established. The General Health Insurance Act (Act 550/1991) outlined health insurance entitlement, rights and obligations of premium payers and of the insured, health insurance contacts and methods of payment. Subsequent regulation (Act 48/1997) amended these, thereby reducing competition across the health insurance funds, among other groups. Although fundamental regulation of the non-profit insurance funds was virtually nonexistent, outside rights of the insured, government, particularly the Ministry of Health, nonetheless had a strong role in overseeing the GHIF and its practices.

Service providers -- hospitals, general practitioners, specialists and dentists -- have also gradually been privatized over the decade, starting with the newly created general practitioners and dentists, but increasingly affecting all providers to some degree. Indeed, hospitals in the Czech Republic are the most privatized in the region, although roughly 75 percent have remained public (national, county or municipal). A much higher percentage of beds are public. However, it is noteworthy that most public hospital physicians and staff are under contract to the hospital and are not civil servants, a major innovation and key to raising quality and controlling costs in the medium to long term. About 95 percent of pharmacies have been privatized.

The key to making a system with these characteristics work in the health sector is the payment mechanism and how resources flow from the payers insurance companies -- to the providers, in the interests of the patients. The key to controlling costs lies also in the payment system. Despite considerable advice to the contrary, the government initially established a fee-for-service arrangement that allowed providers to set prices and consumers to determine demand, with no disincentive to over-consume the free services, and with complete choice of what services to demand from any provider(s). The rapid growth in real per capita expenditures, from CZK7,112 per capita in 1993 to an estimated CZK12,744 in 1998 reflects the surge in both the volume of services and prices in the system, as well as the total absence of any brakes on the former.

By 1993, there were 27 non-profit insurance companies competing for patients in a population of roughly 10 million. The public providers, bloated under the previous regime, were simply absorbed into the private market. In health care, supply drives much of the demand for services as physicians act as "principle agents" for patients, determining what kind and how much care to provide. Where a third party, the insurance company, simply pays submitted billings, costs rise in any setting. In the context of the Czech Republic, this was exacerbated by too many physicians and beds, as compared to EU and OECD standards,[2] as well as by outdated medical protocols that required long lengths of hospital stays, roughly twice that of average OECD countries, and which constituted a major cost element of health care

---

[2] The number of beds per 1000 population in 1996 was 11.1, above the highest OECD country, Germany, with 9.7, and well above the 4.2-6.1 found in most of the OECD countries. The number of physicians was 3.5 per 1000 population, well above the OECD average of 2.7 per 1000.

systems. Moreover, the largest part of expenditures, those for hospitals, were run by physicians with no knowledge of management, and in any case facing no incentives to either control costs or ensure efficiency.

The structural transformation of the health care system was completed very quickly. A market driven system with virtually unlimited access to care appealed to the public, the professional providers and investors in health insurance funds. The major fallacy was the assumption that health care is a normal good and functions in a typical market. This is not the case, and the resulting cost spiral is consistent with similar results in other countries.

Recent Trends in Health Care Expenditures

Since 1993, overall expenditures on the health system have risen, particularly those of the health insurance funds that finance health care services and have absorbed an increasing proportion of all spending (see Table 13.1). Their share in total health expenditures has risen from 76 percent in 1993 to 81 percent in 1998. It is noteworthy that other sources of expenditure are modest by comparison, and constant over time; only "debt payments" have grown from zero in 1996 to less than 1 percent currently. Although these payments were meant to adjust for dislocations in the system, the amounts are miniscule relative to health insurance spending or their accumulated debts (see Figure 13.1).

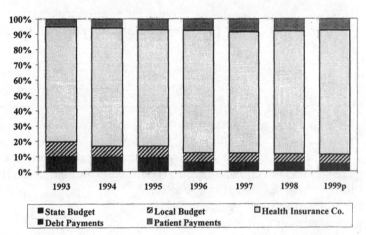

Figure 13.1. Health Expenditure Levels by Category, 1993-99

Table 13.1. Health Care Expenditures by Category, 1993-99
(CZK billion)

	1993	1994	1995	1996	1997	1998	1999[1]
Total Expenditure	73.5	89.6	102.4	112.4	122.8	131.1	141.8
State Budget	7.5	8.7	9.6	7.2	7.5	7.8	7.5
Local Budget	7	6.1	7.3	6.5	7.2	7.2	8.2
Health Insurance Co.	55.8	69.4	78.1	90.1	97.3	105.5	115.3
Debt Payments	..	..	..	0.3	0.9	0.4	0.3
Patient Payments	3.8	5.4	7.4	8.3	9.9	10.2	10.5

1/ Estimate.
Source: Ministry of Finance.

In contrast to absolute spending patterns, health has hovered around 7.5 percent of GDP between 1993 and 1998, and declined slightly as a proportion of national spending since 1995 (see Figure 13.2). Thus, as the country's economy bounded forward, health care spending was maintained constant levels. Indeed, if we compare rates of health care spending increases with that of consumer prices generally (see

Figure 13.2. Total Health Care Expenditures, 1993-98

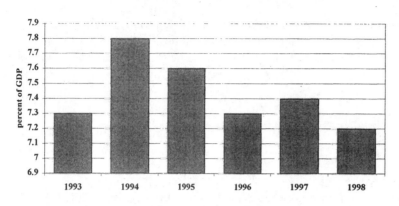

Table 13.2), health spending rose by over 16 percent in 1995, slowed in 1996 and declined further in 1997 to where increases were 2.2 percentage points below inflation.

The two largest components of the health sector budget are personnel and pharmaceuticals. Growth in health sector wages effectively mirrored wage growth in the economy at large, as indicated in Figure 13.3. Pharmaceuticals captured 23 percent of public expenditures in 1996, well above the OECD average of 11.8 percent.

Table 13.2. Growth Rates of Prices and Health Expenditures, 1995-98

	1995	1996	1997	1998[1]
Health Care Expenditures	16.5	9.9	6.3	6.7
Consumer Prices	9.1	8.8	8.5	10.7

1/ Preliminary.
Source: Ministry of Finance.

The public sector effectively dominates the health care market, as shown in Table 13.3; while public expenditures have risen, private expenditures have remained constant over the period 1995-98. Moreover, it is largely a central government-run arrangement. Co-payments are levied only for care not recommended or referred by a physician, and for upgraded hotel services (e.g., private rooms, and individual nursing care) in hospitals.

Health expenditure patterns are a product of the reforms, and of the (dis) incentives built into the evolving health care system. Future expenditure patterns hinge on the policies of the government toward the health sector, its management of resources, and the regulation of the major players.

Figure 13.3. Wage Growth in the Health Sector, 1993-97

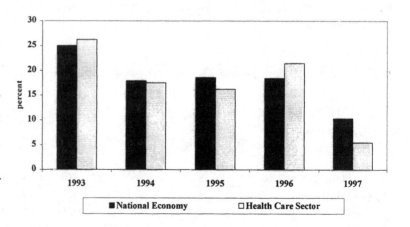

Table 13.3. Expenditures on Health Care, 1993-98
(in CZK billion)

		1993	1994	1995	1996	1997	1998[1]
1	Total Expenditure (4+5+6+7+8)	73.5	89.6	102.4	112.4	122.8	131.1
2	Total Public Expenditure	69.7	84.2	95.0	104.1	112.9	120.9
3	Expenditure from the state budget	29.4	28.9	30.0	31.5	35.2	39.5
	Ministry of Health	6.6	7.7	7.8	6.2	5.6	6.0
	• Ministry of Interior	0.9	1.0	1.4	0.9	0.8	1.5
	• General Treasury Administration	17.0	14.3	13.7	16.5	19.9	23.9
	• Payment of insurance of state insured citizens	16.0	14.3	13.3	16.4	18.3	23.5
	• Other appropriation + independent financial aid	1.0	0.0	0.0	0.0	0.5	0.1
	• Other direct & indirect expenditure in health care	0.0	0.0	0.4	0.1	1.1	0.3
	• Health insurance of state employees	3.7	4.7	5.6	6.4	6.7	6.7
	• Appropriation from state budget to local budgets	1.2	1.2	1.5	1.5	2.2	1.4
	Percent share in total health expenditure	40.0	32.3	29.3	28.0	28.7	30.1
4	Direct expenditure from the state budget (minus transfers)	7.5	8.7	9.6	7.2	7.5	7.8
	Percent share in total health expenditure	10.2	9.7	9.4	6.4	6.1	5.9
5	Expenditures from local budgets	6.4	6.1	7.3	6.5	7.2	7.2
	Percent share in total health expenditure	8.7	6.8	7.1	5.8	5.9	5.5
6	Expenditures in the system of health insurance companies	55.8	69.4	78.1	90.1	97.3	105.5
	• Health care costs	52.3	65.5	74.1	86.1	92.9	101.0
	• Operational/running/administration costs	2.8	3.9	3.9	3.8	4.2	4.3
	• Other costs in insurance companies	0.7	0.0	0.1	0.2	0.2	0.2
	Percent share in total health expenditures	75.9	77.5	76.3	80.2	79.2	80.5
7	Pay off debts to providers of bankrupt insurance companies				0.3	0.9	0.4
8	Private expenditures	3.8	5.4	7.4	8.3	9.9	10.2
	Percent share of private total health expenditures	5.2	6.0	7.2	7.4	8.1	7.8
9	Health care expenditure as percent of GDP	7.3	7.8	7.6	7.3	7.4	7.2
10	Expenditure in CZK per capita	7,112	8,671	9,922	10,903	11,923	12,744

1/ Preliminary.
Source: Ministry of Finance.

The rapidly rising costs discussed above were one of the most visible and predictable effects of the reform, but there were others, both positive and negative. First, the budgetary pressures became apparent early on, and efforts were explored to control them. Moreover, a series of amendments to the original legislation effectively undermined elements of the reform.

In 1995, the new insurance companies began to go bankrupt; by 1998, only 9 remained, down from the original 27, leaving behind CZK2 billion in unpaid debts to providers. The surge in utilization and costs associated with fee for service financing caught the newly-established insurance companies by surprise, and billings quickly outstripped their fixed revenues. Subsequent restrictions on the actions of insurance companies exacerbated the problem, thereby reducing their flexibility. In an effort to stave off bankruptcy, late payments of providers and other stalling mechanisms became common.

A major problem was the absence of appropriate insurance regulation. Without adequate regulation to establish or oversee financial standards, to advise insurance companies of impending problems and risks, or to intervene to restructure or oversee mergers among companies that are faltering, the government was impotent either staving off bankruptcy or in providing an orderly system for market exit. These functions are central to the government's ability to ensure continued health insurance coverage for the population and consumer confidence in the health insurance market. Moreover, there was no established method for dissolving bankrupt companies or for covering enrollees when their insurance company went out of business. As a result, consumers were left without coverage until they could reestablish themselves with a new company, and the debts of the bankrupt company were left unpaid, both to public and private providers. The debts were highest to hospitals, most of them public facilities.

Fiscal Problems under the Health Care Reform

Re-enrollment of consumers from bankrupt companies was heavily biased to the GHIF, where the central role of government was seen as a protection against future bankruptcy. In 1994, GHIF enrolled 6.5 million people; by 1997, they had 7.8 million enrollees. The Ministries of Interior and Defense established their own health insurance companies in 1992 to serve their employees: these were outgrowths of the parallel health care systems from the pre-1990 era. The Ministry of Health instituted restrictions on the health insurance industry, mostly having to do with equalizing benefits and expenditures, but in the process it undermined efforts by those companies to discourage overuse of services and to introduce other cost control measures. The expanded benefits and supplementary premiums anticipated under the reforms never materialized and were discouraged by the subsequent amendments to the Act. In the end, competition was not permitted on benefits or price, and the disintegration of the competitive insurance market effectively undermined the concept of a market-driven reform.

There were other shifts as well. The payment system for providers was modified, and by 1998, four different payment arrangements were in place. Dentists were effectively privatized and only serious, medically indicated dental care was subsidized. General practitioners were paid on a "capitated basis", whereby individuals select their primary care physician who coordinates care and arranges access to specialists and inpatient care. The single fee covers all basic outpatient services, and establishes an incentive to provide only basic care without unnecessary additional services. The U.K. and U.S. health maintenance organizations employ these arrangements and they are associated with effective, but considerably lower cost care. Specialists are paid on a "point system" where the elements of treatment are paid by an allocation of "points" with a predetermined price for each point, allowing payment to reflect the severity and scope of services provided. Germany and other OECD countries rely heavily on this type of payment, but it entails onerous, individual pricing for hundreds of outpatient services.

Figure 13.4. Claims and Obligations of Hospitals

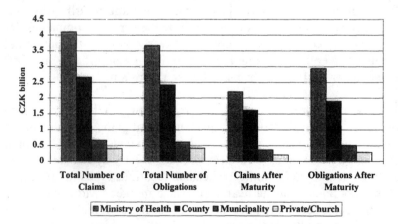

Hospital payment is evolving, and represents the single biggest source of overspending and debt. Initially, hospitals were financed by a patient-based fee-for-service system. Budgetary financing based on historical allocations was introduced in 1997. There is, of course, a mixed arrangement in some pilot hospitals where the facility receives a budget, but it is adjusted by a prospective reimbursement arrangement that accounts for the mix of patients and the severity of their condition -- know as Diagnostic Related Groups (DRGs).

Rising hospital costs and accumulating debt have been the major sources of budget overruns. Hospital debts stem from unpaid billings due to insurance company bankruptcy, slow contraction of infrastructure (both hospitals and beds), lack of accountability for cost overruns, and impediments to efficiency improvements. The relative importance of these factors is tied, to some extent, to hospital ownership, but debt overhang from the bankruptcies earlier in the decade are particularly important. Figure 13.4 shows the status of accumulated financial claims (mostly unpaid billings) and obligations of hospitals by type of ownership and type of claim. The Ministry of Health hospitals have the largest value of outstanding debt at over CZK400 million. Municipal and private facilities have much lower debt, partly because they are often smaller, but also because there is greater accountability and less access to discretionary, supplementary funds from the Ministry of Health. Reliance on such "just in time" allocations certainly undermines financial discipline. Cost overruns are unviable for private facilities, and counties have lower revenues and more limited ability to finance gaps.

Figure 13.5 shows the revenue and cost comparisons for different hospital ownership categories. For 1997, financial management appears much improved from that of previous years: if debts are taken out of the equation, at least in 1997, both public and private hospitals balanced their books. But it is important to keep the debt problems in mind. Hospitals do not have adequate revenues to pay off debt, and any additional debt jeopardizes their ability to purchase inputs from suppliers. Insurance companies can remain solvent by transferring their costs to providers who are effectively price takers. Hence, hospitals may be at greater risk of insolvency than those insurance companies that have survived the shake out of the mid-1990s.

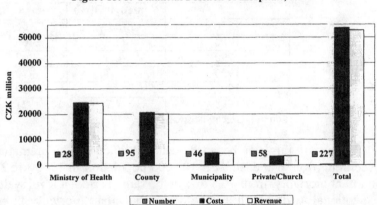

Figure 13. 5. Financial Position of Hospitals, 1997

Public hospitals are political, as well as the medical, concerns of government. These hospitals represent the bulk of inpatient beds and are saddled with hundreds of beds (many of which are unnecessary). They guarantee access for emergency care, which private facilities typically do not offer, and provide tertiary care services, often in sprawling campuses that are difficult to control given the prominence and the political importance of the researchers, physicians and directors who run these institutions. Cost overruns lead to neither reprimand nor dismissal, thereby leading to a disregard for financial rules: these factors also contribute to high expenditures. One overriding problem facing hospitals is the lack of adequate managers and management training. Typically, physicians operate the hospitals with input from administrative staff, and this further complicates solving efficiency and management problems.

The early bankruptcies of the health insurance funds have tapered off, but the debt overhang of providers remains as its legacy. Resolving the structural and financial problems entails debt restructuring to give providers a clean slate; it entails a strengthened regulation of payers and providers, improved oversight of providers, particularly in the public sector, and clearer policies and priorities in the sector.

Achievements of the Reform

The health reform agenda and subsequent actions, as well as the systematic search for answers to medical, managerial and financial problems, all reflect the Czech health community's growing awareness of international experience. The Czech experience is not unique, and there is rich experience elsewhere, despite the fact that there is no clear guide to the preferred answer. Each of the OECD countries treats its health care system differently, so there is much to consider but nothing that defines the answer. Such search has led to some highly positive outcomes which balance to some extent, the financial difficulties that continue to plague the health sector.

Improvements in health status indicators have been impressive. Table 13.4 summarizes the shifts in life expectancy for women and men at birth during 1970-98, and for men at age 40 until 1996. Between 1970 and 1980, improvements were negligible, and except for women remained stagnant for the following decade. The sharp increases between 1990 and 1996 were 1.2, 3.0 and 2 years, respectively for women, men, and men at age 40. Such dramatic increases are rare, and certainly did not occur in other OECD countries over the same time period.

Table 13.4. Life Expectancy, 1990-96

	Women at Birth	Men at Birth	Men at Age 40
1970	73.0	66.1	30.2
1980	73.9	66.8	30.2
1990	76.0	67.5	30.3
1996	77.3	70.4	32.3
1997	77.5	70.6	..
1998	77.7	71.0	..

Source: Czech Statistical Office.

Part of this can be attributed to reductions in premature deaths from cardiovascular disease (declining from 645 deaths per 100,000 population in 1990 to 529.7 in 1996), and partly to a sharp drop in infant mortality, from 10.8 to 6 in the same period, a level well below rates in most of the OECD. It is exceptional to find such a large decline in infant mortality in such a short period of time. Moreover, reductions at this range for infant mortality are linked entirely to improved medical care for mothers and infants, and entail both better technology, and improved monitoring and accountability for medical quality. Better cardiovascular care is likely related to more modern (and expensive) interventions, the only possibility since preventive efforts would not have had time to affect mortality of adult men.

While no systematic study has pinpointed the reasons for the impressive improvements, more resources, improved technology, rapid embracing of new medical protocols and techniques, and better quality of care all play a role. In effect, additional expenditures allowed for the upgrading of equipment, the purchasing of expensive new technologies and generally the raising of the level of medical care closer to OECD standards. When comparing expenditures and outcomes in Czech Republic, the overspending had a positive health impact.

Despite the persistent oversupply of health inputs, there has been some contraction in the overall number of beds, and a reduction in average lengths of hospital stays, two important indicators of efficiency. The number of beds have been reduced by over 13,500, declining almost 20 percent from 13.5 to 11.2 beds per 1,000 population; however, this remains well above OECD levels. The average length of stay has dropped from 12 to 9.1 days, at the high end of OECD countries. Thus, progress in reducing excessive inputs has modestly improved, but persistently high numbers of beds and long lengths of stay drive up costs. It also suggests that there has been inadequate improvement in outpatient treatments that increasingly offer a lower cost and higher quality alternative treatment for many illnesses.

Finally, the pattern of extensive informal and illegal payments to providers, apparent in most of the other countries of Eastern Europe, has largely disappeared in the Czech Republic. Informal payments effectively promote corruption and are difficult to dislodge once in place. Moreover, it remunerates physicians and other medical personnel, but fixed costs of administration and maintenance, and capital costs of infrastructure and technology are neglected. The level of investment and the expanded choice of services, both outpatient and inpatient, are the reasons put forward for this phenomena.

Conclusion and Recommendations

The Czech Republic's health reform had important effects on both health care and its financing. It was highly successful in dismantling the previous system of delivery and finance, and increasing spending to improve medical care. However, there remains a serious debt overhang, as well as the lack of incentives in the system to continue the needed improvements to raise both efficiency and effectiveness of health care, both of which will be required to satisfy the professionals in the system and the financial imperatives of the Ministry of Finance.

Because of the nature of the health care market, controlling public expenditures entails clear policies, regulations that define and enforce the rules of the game, appropriate incentives in the system to foster desirable behavior, and strategies to keep the volume and cost of services in check.

First, a major problem is the highly fragmented nature of health policy in the Czech Republic. Policy shifts and implementation have been led by multiple actors often not working in concert, including the Ministry of Health, the GHIF and Parliament, among others. There is no clear leadership in the sector, and the myriad of amendments to the original Act is testament to the lack of a clear vision. This lack of vision affects both the nature of the system and its costs. Without more concerted leadership, progress will be difficult if the past is any guide. Legislation and regulations proliferate to address narrow issues without regard for the broader concerns of the system or its finances. Roles of accountability, however, are ambiguous.

Second, the policy toward the health insurance companies and their regulation needs greater consistency. As of 1998, wage increases of 7 percent were instituted by Parliament for all government workers, thereby raising health care costs without commensurate increases in premiums, or controls on costs and volume of health care under health insurance. Although technically this did not affect all health workers, it raised wages in public facilities, and implicitly forced private hospitals to follow suit to retain staff. Given the already strapped finances of the health insurance companies, this move undermined the financial order achieved in 1997. If this is not monitored, insurance companies will revert to past practices of under and late payments to providers, thereby risking renewed hospital debt accumulation. Strengthening regulation of insurance companies, as discussed above, is essential. Nonetheless, allowing some product competition and differentiation of benefits and policies across insurance companies, while maintaining financial stringency, can yield benefits and at the same time contain costs.

An important means of fostering clearer policies and greater internal consistency is through policy analysis to advise policymakers and guide policymaking. Tracking costs, assessing the effectiveness of incentives, evaluating regulatory measures or determining how to foster both quality and cost containment are examples of the kinds of issues that policy analysis can inform. Many of the issues raised below could be addressed, monitored and evaluated through such efforts. Some countries use grants to solicit such analysis from universities or private research groups, and this could be applied in the Czech Republic. Such analysis allows adjustment to the health system and its financing through a more transparent and consistent assessment, and could lead to more coherency in health policy.

Third, some of the incentives under the current system effectively control costs -- alternative payment system for physicians (e.g., capitated primary health care), adoption of new medical protocols, reimbursement only for basic services or technologies, commission to control acquisition of medical technology -- should be maintained.

There is, however, a need to improve cost containment efforts where they are inadequate. Areas of particularly high priority would be: (i) further reduce beds and hospitals, and continuing to shift services to outpatient settings where quality and efficiency are enhanced; (ii) tracking the number of physicians being trained to control oversupply, which raises overall costs; (iii) increasing the role of the general physician versus access to ambulance specialists; (iv) improving the drug pricing and reimbursement regulations to encourage cost consciousness, enhancing information systems of drug use and pricing to inform policymakers as well as providers, payers and consumers, and reducing the public subsidy from 80 percent of costs to proportions closer to other OECD countries; (v) allow some product competition and differentiation by insurance companies while maintaining financial requirements; (vi) permitting greater cost sharing by consumers for items where there is a likely ability to pay, such as pharmaceuticals, or upgraded quality (e.g., more expensive diagnostic or treatment technologies or high quality medical materials), as is done for hospital hotel services now. This maintains a basic level of subsidized care, and retains patients who contribute to the health insurance funds, but are willing to pay a premium for small increments in quality; and, (vii) dealing with the debt overhang of hospitals. Commensurate with paying off debts, financial stringency in the health care system, which should be required to avoid the problems of the past and to signal the seriousness of the issue for the sector.

Finally, longer term projects that deserve attention in the short run are information and quality: a high quality, interactive management information system to assist the government, insurers and managers track the volume and costs of care is needed. Some elements of MIS already exist, but systematizing and broadening it would lead to improved overall management. Upgraded MIS would allow monitoring of hospital management performance, and would enhance the role of hospital managers. Quality assurance, clearly something that has been given attention in some areas, deserves higher priority, because such practices not only raise quality, but they can often reduce costs.

The Czech Republic's health care system is still evolving, and its financial circumstances are key to continued progress in quality and coverage. These recommendations are meant to provide a menu of possible areas for intervention to strengthen the observed weaknesses in the health financing system. However, as is evident from the recommendations, financing and medical practice issues cannot be addressed separately: the challenge is how to merge the two and ensure a consistent Czech government policy.

Chapter XIV. Reform in the Infrastructure Sectors

Introduction

In the last few years, the Czech Republic has implemented far-reaching structural reform and privatization programs in key sectors of its economy. While the experience varies across industries, by-and-large these reform programs have brought about the expected social benefits of market liberalization and private enterprise: enhanced productivity and cost-effectiveness, improved output quality, greater responsiveness to consumer and business needs, and increased investment driven by market incentives rather than bureaucratic preference. These improvements in performance, however, will be limited and are unlikely to be sustainable in the long run, unless the movement towards reform is accompanied by appropriate policies to promote competition and to regulate monopoly. Therefore, the next phase is crucially important to ensure that the benefits of privatization and competition are maintained.

The policy outcomes from several countries reveal quite clearly that the organization and architecture of the post-privatization market and governance structures are critical to the ongoing success of the privatization process and the overall reform program. Indeed, both economic analysis and policy experience show that any program for restructuring the relationship between government and industry, and developing effective regulatory policy, should be explicitly based on the underlying economic characteristics of the industry and the technological conditions of its production, the country's institutional endowment, structural legacy, character of special-interest coalitions, and so on. Thus, the reform process must include an appropriate mechanism of post-privatization governance, as well as guideposts for the substantive content of that governance.

The objectives of this chapter are to: (i) provide a diagnostic assessment of recent and ongoing structural and regulatory reforms in the infrastructure sectors -- telecommunications, electricity, gas, and transportation -- of the Czech Republic; (ii) identify priorities for additional competitive restructuring and regulatory decontrol measures, their expected impact, as well as policies designed to minimize the transition costs of deregulation and market liberalization; (iii) assess the progress made towards compliance with the EU accession requirements and identify areas that might benefit from special attention to accelerate the transition to a liberalized regime; and (iv) identify the major regulatory issues that need to be addressed in the medium term by the Czech regulatory agencies and suggest a strategy for addressing these issues

The chapter's focus on the structural and regulatory issues of the infrastructure sectors is motivated by two factors. First, it is widely recognized that the efficient functioning of these sectors is vital to both sustained economic growth and international competitiveness. The infrastructure sectors provide services that are critical inputs in manufacturing, transportation and commerce. They also provide services that are essential to boosting economic activity and to increasing competition through the expansion of product lines and geographic spheres of distribution. Second, during the last decade, there has been a major reassessment of public policy towards the infrastructure sectors and of the proper role of the state in the provision of these services. Governments throughout the world have been actively pursuing institutional, regulatory, and structural reforms aimed at improving operating efficiency and service quality. Countries that have implemented such reforms have realized substantial economic benefits.

Several policy measures, which will be identified, if properly adapted, would accelerate the restructuring process in the Czech infrastructure sectors. Moreover, would minimize the costs of accession to the EU as well as the transition to a fully liberalized regime. One of the fundamental tenets of the chapter is that for privatization to unleash the forces of private enterprise, regulation cannot be simply another form of state control. Therefore, it underscores the importance of limiting the discretionary exercise of regulatory power and of establishing mechanisms that can contain and deter arbitrary and discriminatory interventions by the government. It places particular emphasis on the rational determination of prices of end-user services; it underscores the critical importance of rebalancing the traditional rate structures in the infrastructure sectors from the standpoint of economic efficiency. Finally, the chapter also emphasizes the critical need for developing an effective interconnection policy that ensures nondiscriminatory access to essential infrastructure facilities by prospective entrants. This is particularly important in view of the vertical unbundling and market liberalization policies that are being promoted by the EU in the network utilities of its member states.

Status of Key Infrastructure Sectors

There is no doubt that sustained economic growth and prosperity require basic infrastructure sectors that are responsive to consumer and business needs and demands, as well as to marketplace opportunities for innovation. It is also clear today that network utilities, organized and controlled according to the monolithic monopoly model, must be restructured in order to effectively contribute to the economy and to avoid being a significant impediment to growth and prosperity. Set forth below is an overview of the key structural developments in the telecommunications, electricity, gas, and transportation sectors of the Czech Republic.

Telecommunications

According to experts, by the late 1980s, the Central and Eastern European countries (CEECs) were roughly twenty years behind the countries of Western Europe in the provision of basic and advanced (data transmission and value-added) telecommunications services. This technological backwardness was due to the fact that the existing telephone networks of these countries, like those of the former Soviet Union, were designed primarily to meet the needs of government, the military, and state security structures rather than the needs of ordinary customers and businesses. The absence of customer orientation also reflected political leaders' fears of the subversive potential of unregulated communications. Moreover, because of technology export controls imposed by the United States and its allies, the former Comecon countries were often unable to purchase advanced telecommunications equipment. As a result, not only did the CEECs' telephone industries suffer from a longstanding government policy of underinvestment, but the telecommunications networks in these countries were substandard and poorly maintained.

The situation in the Czech Republic was no better than in Poland or Hungary. In 1991, more than half of all switching facilities were over 30 years old, and much of the remainder were technologically outdated. Less than 5 percent of the access lines were digital, which vastly impaired provision of advanced data services. Penetration rates were also significantly below western standards.[1] Long hook-up waiting lists added to the dissatisfaction with telecommunications services. On the eve of privatization, 600,000 people were on the waiting list for service. Those lucky enough to obtain service paid low rates by international standards, but like in most countries, the rates were highly unbalanced: while local calling and monthly charges were low, long distance and international rates were high.

---

[1] For example, in 1989, penetration (measured by the ratio of main access lines divided by the total population) was only 15 percent, and by 1995 (the year SPT Telecom was privatized) grew to only 24 percent. By comparison, in the early 1990's, penetration in advanced western countries averaged about 40 percent.

Policy Initiatives for Industry Structure and Network Development. In 1991, the government launched a network development program, known as the First Telecommunications Project. This development plan sought to expand the capital stock of SPT Telecom in order to implement a comprehensive investment program. It also sought to reform and modernize the company's management structure and practices under continued public ownership. The ultimate goal of the program was to expand and modernize the country's outdated telecommunications network and to improve the quality of service.

During the first phase of the project (1992-94), a national digital overlay network was successfully completed. However, the project achieved only modest success in terms of its remaining objectives. Network expansion remained sluggish until 1995. This lack of success perhaps confirms the general difficulty of truly reforming public sector enterprises that are protected by exclusivity. It also highlighted the formidable advantages to a major rebalancing of the private-public sectors' roles in the telecommunications industry. Indeed, it was the privatization of SPT Telecom and the introduction of local service competition in select regions that provided strong incentives and a secure basis for a rapid expansion of the Czech telecommunications system.

Privatization of SPT Telecom. In January 1993, Sprava Post a Telekomunikaci Praha was restructured. Postal and telecommunications services were separated, and Czech Posts and SPT Telecom were created. A number of non-core commercial, construction and assembly, and production activities were also spun off and privatized. This restructuring represented the Czech government's first serious attempt to modernize its outdated telecommunications network and to make the industry more responsive to the demands of a growing entrepreneurial economy for better and more varied information services. Subsequently, and in preparation for privatization, SPT Telecom was transformed into a joint stock company on January 1, 1994.

The centerpiece of the Czech government's liberalization program has been the privatization of SPT Telecom. Without successful privatization of the incumbent monopoly telecommunications carrier, it is unlikely that the Czech Republic would have been able to modernize its telecommunications networks, increase penetration, and improve the quality of services, while substantially reducing the waiting lists for the installation of service. The cash infusion from the privatization allowed SPT Telecom to substantially increase annual main line installation. In addition to financing, the strategic partners also brought substantial operational expertise, modern management skills, and an emphasis on customer service. These were factors that the previous monolithic state-owned entity generally lacked despite the efforts under the First Telecommunications Project.

The government timed the privatization of SPT Telecom to coincide with the second wave of voucher privatization. In early 1995, vouchers previously distributed to citizens were permitted to be exchanged for SPT Telecom common shares representing 26 percent of the company's outstanding stock. The remaining 74 percent was held by the Czech National Property Fund (70 percent) and the specialized restitution and endowment funds (4 percent). Widespread ownership, providing the company with a broad shareholder base was a central goal of the voucher plan in general, and of the SPT Telecom privatization in particular. In addition, the government believed that the liquidity provided by the shareholdings was critical to the overall privatization plan. Accordingly, SPT Telecom's shares were listed on the Prague exchange, and trading began in June 1995. SPT Telecom shares are the largest issue on the exchange.

Concurrently with the voucher component of the SPT Telecom privatization plan, the government organized the sale of a further stake in the company to a strategic investor-cum-operator. The main qualities that the government was looking for in a strategic operator were the ability and commitment to undertake investments in upgrading the network, the ability to meet the penetration goals, and the transfer of technology and managerial skills. Five qualified consortia competed for the transaction. In July 1995, the tender for a strategic joint venture partner with a 27 percent stake in SPT Telecom was completed. The winning consortium was TeleSource -- representing KPN, the Dutch operator, Swiss Telecom, and AT&T as a non-equity partner.[2]

Although the minimum bid was US$1 billion for the 27 percent stake, the final price was US$1.45 billion. Proceeds from the sale of the newly-issued stock were paid to the company, not to the government, as was the case in Hungary or certain other Czech privatizations. The result was a better capitalized company. Of the total bid price, $131 million was to be paid in kind through management services, software and other investments. Telesource's winning bid was not the highest: as in Hungary, STET's was the highest. Ultimately, officials making the final decision were also interested in non-monetary factors, and the fact the TeleSource consortium consisted of smaller, but nonetheless reputable operators, may have tipped the scale in its favor.

The divestiture of SPT Telecom differed significantly from other Czech privatizations, which were characterized by low participation of strategic investors. Indeed, the strategic entry of TeleSource into SPT Telecom is widely considered to be one of the few successful major investment deals in the Czech Republic since the collapse of communism. The state earned a substantial amount of revenue from the sale and significantly increased the value of its remaining stake in the company. In addition, the privatized entity made a substantial leap in terms of network development. Between 1995 and 1998, the number of fixed telephone lines in the Czech Republic increased by more than 1.7 million to over 3.8 million. By the end of 1999, it is expected that the country will have over 4 million telephone lines, covering 74 percent of households.

Electricity

At the time of the Velvet Revolution in 1989, the Electricity Supply Industry (ESI) was organised as a single, vertically integrated utility -- the Czech Power Works -- generating about 90 percent of total electricity, the balance being generated by auto power producers (APPs), which consumed 90 percent of their own output. The Czech Power Works also owned the transmission and all distribution grids and was the exclusive supplier to final consumers. The Czech Power Works was unbundled in 1990, six months after the Velvet Revolution (and just before the first elections), when the 8 Regional Electricity Companies (RECs) were established as independent state enterprises. During 1991 and 1992, the combined heat and power units (CHP) were separated and established as independent heat and power producers. The most attractive of these, Opatovice Energy Company (Elektrarny Opatovice, EOP), was created as a company in 1992, the same year that the remaining power stations and the high voltage grid were placed in the single company, CEZ (Ceske Energeticke zavody, a.s.).

Ownership Structure. CEZ was created in May 1992; 27 percent of the shares were sold to the public in the first wave of large-scale privatisation in May 1993, with further sales in 1995 thereby bringing the share up to 32 percent.[3]

Opatovice Energy Company (Elektrarny Opatovice, EOP) produced 1.4 TWh and 5,500 TJ of heat in 1993 (2.3 percent of total generation and about the same percentage of total heat). It was described as one of

[2] The current ownership structure of SPT Telecom is as follows: National Property Fund (NPF) has 51percent; Telsource has 27 percent; individual shareholders and investment funds have 19 percent; foundation and restitution funds have 0.27 percent. SPT Telecom's holdings include a mobile joint venture, EuroTel, in which SPT Telecom holds 51 percent, and a consortium of Bell Atlantic and US West, 49 percent.
[3] As of June 2, 1998, NPF held 67.6 percent of CEZ, individuals held 3 percent, other legal persons held 28.5 percent and the Restitution Investment Fund held just under 1 percent. 24 percent of the shares were held by foreign investors.

the most technically and economically viable companies in the Czech Republic because it relies mainly on (cheap) coal as fuel, it produces thermal energy in an energy-efficient cogeneration configuration, and it benefits from having a major share of its thermal energy output required as base-load energy for industrial purposes. It was established as a joint-stock company in May 1992 and was subsequently privatised.[4] The 8 regional electricity companies (Prague; Middle-Bohemian; South-Bohemian; West-Bohemian; North-Bohemian; East-Bohemian; South-Moravian; North-Moravian) were established as joint-stock companies on January 1, 1994. The Bohemian companies form a doughnut around Prague, with Middle-Bohemian (STE, or Stredoceská energetická, a.s.) surrounding the capital. The Moravian companies lie to the east and abut Slovakia.[5]

Organization of ESI. This piecemeal restructuring left some ambiguity about where the obligation to supply lies, though CEZ appears to assume that it has the final obligation to ensure adequate supplies of electricity and that the RECs have the obligation to meet demands in their regions, though they can call on CEZ to meet their demand. Short-term dispatch is handled by the transmission grid dispatch, which was part of CEZ until July 31, 1999. From August 1, 1999 it is a part of Czech Transmission Systems (CEPS, a.s.), joint-stock company, which is 100 percent owned by CEZ. Under the 1994 Energy Act, the Central Electric Dispatching Organisation (CED) was founded in April 1997 as an association of legal bodies (as CEZ, IPPs plus APPs, RECs and the Ministry of Industry and Trade (MIT)). The Act states that "suppliers and licence holders operating generating equipment above 50MW are obliged to set up central dispatching facilities on the basis of contracts of association." This association of power producers and distributors deals with long-term balance and proposes rules for the electricity market. The CED appears to play a largely advisory role, and has nothing to do with the daily dispatch of generating plant.[6]

The RECs own the 110kV system, and are free to buy direct from IPPs and APPs over this system, apparently without regard to the merit order. They can also import (but only via the 110kV lines they own). They buy the balance from CEZ at regulated prices, and sell at regulated prices to different consumer classes in their regional franchise.[7] In June 1998, the National Property Fund as majority shareholder of CEZ required the Directors of CEZ to place the high tension grid into a separate legal body able to discharge its responsibilities from January 1, 1999, with a challenging timetable to meet in preparing the Grid Code and other operational rules.

---

[4] About 76 percent of the shares were sold in the voucher privatization, 15 percent were allocated to municipalities, 3 percent went to the State Restitution fund and 6 percent remained in the NPF. National Power bought 48 percent of the shares in early 1998, and subsequently increased its stake to 51 percent and thereafter to 90 percent by October 1998.

[5] Taking STE as an example, the company dates its current name back to 1941, though the Prague company was spun off in 1982 and became an independent state enterprise in 1990. Its ownership structure in 1997 was NPF 59.11 percent, municipalities 26.33 percent, employees 0.78 percent, voucher coupon holders 1.51 percent, and other investors (mainly RWE but including mutual funds) 12.27 percent. STE has a long term agreement with RWE signed in 1992, and RWE bought shares in the company in 1997. RWE also has shares in the Prague gas company but not in any other RECs, as the 1994 Energy Act forbids one owner of two RECs or one owner of the same regional REC and LDC. STE's area excludes Prague and hence meets this condition. By August 1998, RWE had increased its shareholding from 10.33 percent to 11.61 percent and the NPF had reduced its holding to 58.34 percent but most other shareholdings remained unchanged. The state, therefore, continues to have a majority ownership, even discounting the municipal shares (where the voting rights are at risk of being transferred to private owners) and has yet to decide whether to proceed with the previous Government's plans for eventual privatization.

[6] CEZ has 20 percent of the voting shares in the CED, as do the 18 IPPs and APPs together, and MIT, while the 8 RECs have the remaining 40 percent. A super majority of 80 percent of the votes is required for a change.

[7] CEZ has three power purchase agreements with IPPs (one of which is EOP), who are scheduled for dispatch ahead of time, but do not take part in short-run system balancing. IPPs are free to enter the industry and contract either directly with the RECs or with CEZ.

Natural Gas

Gas is of growing importance as a fuel in the Czech Republic. Its share in primary energy more than doubled from 8 percent to 18 percent over the past decade and is growing while the consumption of most other fuels is rapidly falling. Since this trend is likely to continue, and since almost all gas is imported from Russia, the Czech Republic is naturally concerned about its energy dependence and energy security. Accession to the EU and access to a liberalized western European gas market would go some way to alleviating these concerns.

The Czech Gas Works Group (CPP Group) was established as a state-owned enterprise on January 1, 1989. In 1990, the company was internally restructured into nine subsidiaries (six gas distribution subsidiaries, the transmission company which later became Transgas, and two others). In 1993, South Bohemian Gas Works split away from West Bohemian Gas Works, and Prague Gas Works split away from Central Bohemian Gas Works to form the 8 regional gas distribution companies (GDCs). As part of the subsequent privatisation process, all the subsidiaries' assets were transferred from CPP into separate companies. In 1994, the eight GDCs were partially privatised, primarily to foreign investors such as Ruhrgas and RWE, but with 34 percent of the shares distributed free of charge to the municipalities with restrictions on resale, and 47 percent retained in the National Property Fund.[8]

By the end of 1997, CPP retained only the assets of Transgas; in December 1997, Transgas was created as a unified state-owned company, Transgas, s.p. Transgas is involved in gas purchase, storage, sale, transit of Russian gas through the country to the west, and transmission to the GDCs. In 1997, 8.4-8.6 bcm of gas was purchased under an existing three-year contract with Gazexport (Russia) and Wintershall (Germany). Wintershall is part owned by Gazprom, the Russian gas monopoly producer and exporter of gas, so that effectively all this gas came from the monopoly Russian supplier. In April 1997, a long term contract was signed with Norway for a total of 53 bcm under a twenty year agreement with volumes increasing up to 3 bcm after 2002. Delivery started in 1997 and accounted for 7.5 percent of total gas imports. 1998 saw the end of the three-year contract with Russia and a new 15-year contract was signed with Gazexport on October 15, 1998 for 9 bcm under a take-or-pay contract linked to the price of HFO and LFO.

The maximum monthly demand in 1997 was just below 1500 million cm/month in January, and the minimum monthly demand came in July and August at about 300 mcm/month. The swing was, therefore, 5 to 1, requiring considerable flexibility to vary supplies and draw from storage. Transgas owns 5 underground storage facilities in the Czech Republic and is developing an additional peak shaving site. Total storage in the Czech republic in 1997 was 1.74 bcm, with a maximum delivery rate of 20.7 million cm/day.[9]

---

[8] The ownership stakes by the municipalities reflect the investments that they made in the past in creating the local distribution system. Some of these municipalities were persuaded to sell their voting rights to existing private shareholders, raising the threat that the GDCs would become majority private controlled companies, with the state holding only a minority share of 47 percent through the NPF, without the state enjoying the control premium from selling majority stakes initially.

[9] In addition, Transgas leases capacity in the Slovak Republic and Germany amounting to 0.99 bcm with a delivery capacity of 10.1 mcm/day, accounting for slightly more than one-third of the total storage of 2.73 bcm. Transgas also has short-term flexible gas purchase agreements with German companies (Wintershall, Rurhgas, BEB and VNG) to manage the swing. Storage thus amounts to 107 days average consumption, somewhat above the IEA/EU target level of 90 days. This ought to be adequate given the large share of industry (42 percent in 1993) and the relatively smaller share of household demand (22 percent).

Transportation

Economic decisions in the Czech Republic's transportation system are made by private companies for some modes and by the state for others. Thus, a fundamental question that needs to be addressed is whether changes in decision making authority and service provision could lead to efficiency improvements in their transportation system. Economic decisions about transportation infrastructure, roads and airports, are made by the state. The central issue that needs to be addressed is whether changes in the state's policy could improve allocation of limited infrastructure resources.

Air Transportation. Domestic flights in the Czech Republic are provided by a private carrier, Czech Airlines (CSA). In contrast to some other European carriers, CSA does not receive any direct subsidies from the state. Only a fraction (less than 1 percent) of domestic travel in the Czech Republic is made by air. Domestic fares and service are regulated by the Ministry of Transport. Most of CSA's operations are international. Fares, entry, and exit in these markets are determined by IATA accords. Since 1996, CSA has had a partnership agreement with Continental Airlines, enabling it to serve 24 U.S. cities through Newark airport.

Rail Transportation. Freight and passenger railways are owned and operated by the state in the form of Czech Railways. Future plans call for Czech Railways to become a joint stock company consistent with EU guidelines. Freight rates are not regulated *per se* but are determined through negotiations with shippers. Intermodal competition from trucking provides some competitive discipline on these rates. Entry and exit of freight markets is determined by the state. Entry by private companies (e.g., coal companies) that wish to provide their own rail service by leasing track is allowed in some instances. Lease prices for the track are determined by the Ministry of Finance based on cost information provided by the Czech Railways. Passenger fares are regulated by the state and explicitly subsidized in accordance with social obligations to provide mobility for the public. Finally, although the state owns the rail infrastructure, the state typically solicit bids from 10-12 private companies for large maintenance and construction projects.

During 1993-97, the railway cut back its physical capital (track, tractive stock, and passenger and freight cars) as well as its labor force. But passenger and freight traffic have also declined during this period. Thus, Czech Railways' total losses have grown, although freight operations have been profitable during the past few years. Of course, the profitability of freight operations depends on the volume and type of commodities that the railways transport. Its principal traffic consists of coal, lignite, and iron. Sharp declines in the transport of these commodities could have a significant effect on the profitability of rail freight operations.

Truck Transportation. Truck transportation is provided by private unregulated carriers. Less than 1 percent of truck transportation is state owned. Shippers can use for-hire carriers who provide their own trucking service ("private" trucking). Private trucks can operate in a for-hire capacity, and some for-hire companies also provide bus transport as noted below. Most for-hire trucking companies consist of a few employees and vehicles. Although the failure rate in for-hire trucking is high, entry appears to be easy.

Bus Transportation. Bus transportation is provided by private companies, but this service is explicitly subsidized in accordance with social obligations to provide mobility for the public. International and long distance trips are not subsidized. District/regional transport departments administer the subsidies.

Bus service is provided by bus companies and by companies that also provide truck service. Although there are thousands of these companies, they can only enter routes if they are given approval by the district/regional transport departments.

Highway and Airport Infrastructure. The Czech Republic has an extensive system of highways, major roads, and local thoroughfares that is used by millions of cars, buses, and trucks. Revenues for highway maintenance and construction are generated from fuel taxes on cars, trucks, and buses. In addition, trucks pay a fixed fee based on gross vehicle weight and a user charge based on categories of gross vehicle weight. It is claimed that diesel fuel taxes paid by railroads are partly diverted to highway projects. Some 20-30 companies bid for large road construction projects.

The state owns and operates most of the airports including the major airport in Prague. Airlines pay user fees based on aircraft weight.

Public Policy Issues in the Czech Infrastructure Sectors

During the past decade, Czech policy makers have been confronted with the dilemma of weighing the short-term political costs of implementing appropriate sectoral policies (especially in the areas of pricing, investment, and structure of ownership) against the long-term economic benefits likely to result from an aggressive program of market liberalization, deregulation, and privatization. (For a description of the worldwide trend towards competitive restructuring, regulatory decontrol, and privatization in the infrastructure sectors, see the Annex.) In the Czech Republic, as in many other transition economies, these choices became especially agonizing in view of the country's difficult transformation from centralized direction to a market-driven economy and in view of its delicate macroeconomic condition. Furthermore, the standard internal inefficiency problems that normally plague public enterprises became acute in the infrastructure sectors due to the rapidly changing market conditions and the growing importance of these sectors in the context of a global, information-based economy.

This section focuses on the current and forthcoming regulatory policies and determinations in the Czech network utilities. The challenge facing Czech policy makers centers around their ability to: (i) establish a framework that promotes undistorted and effective competition; (ii) create mechanisms that enforce substantive and procedural restraints on arbitrary administrative intervention and regulatory discretion; (iii) put in place pricing structures that provide signals and incentives for efficient actions by consumers, suppliers of complementary and substitute services, suppliers of inputs, and investors; (iv) remove the regulatory impediments to revenue adequacy; (v) establish rules that ensure open, non-discriminatory access to bottleneck infrastructural facilities; and (vi) design competitively neutral mechanisms to foster desirable social goals and positive economic externalities.

Telecommunications

Despite significant progress, the Czech republic still faces significant policy challenges in the telecommunications sector during the process of accession to the EU. It is not enough to establish a liberalization timetable. Beyond this narrow focus, the Czech Republic must: (i) further re-balance its traditional rate structure to prepare for full competition; (ii) establish an effective interconnect policy; and (iii) adopt measures that harmonize competition with regulation and create a level playing field.

Tariff Re-balancing and Competitive Pricing Flexibility. The telecommunications tariffs in the Czech Republic did not change from 1979 to 1993. Therefore, during that period, they were basically unrelated to the underlying costs of providing service. This pricing policy effectively decapitalized the system. It was consistent, however, with the government's policy of benign neglect towards the country's telecommunications system. As was noted above, the promotion and facilitation of efficient information exchange was clearly not an integral part of the communist regime's program. In 1994, the government introduced a general tariff framework for regulated services. Until the year 2000, regulated telecommunications tariffs will be adjusted according to a price cap formula.

The primary purpose of price caps was to provide incentives to SPT Telecom and the other regulated entities to minimize costs and to adopt efficient technological improvements. The price cap mechanism also has the advantage of being clear and predictable. However, there have been some practical problems with its implementation. SPT Telecom has complained that the price cap formula, as applied by the regulator, does not accurately reflect inflation.

The structure of telecommunications tariffs is unbalanced. For historic and other reasons, rates for local calling and access are low relative to underlying long-term costs. In contrast, rates for domestic long-distance and international calls are high relative to underlying long-term costs. The monthly access (rental) fee is CZK135 for both residential and business customers. SPT Telecom claims that a fee of CZK400 would be needed to cover costs. The Ministry of Finance, on the other hand, estimates the compensatory access fee to be approximately CZK250. The price for local calls is CZK2.6 per pulse (each pulse corresponds to 3 minutes of calling during peak hours and to 6 minutes of calling during off-peak hours). Installation charges, by contrast, are relatively high (CZK3,500 for both residential and business customers). International PSTN tariffs are also high.

In February 1998, the TeleSource consortium announced that the maximum tariff increases that were authorized by the government for 1998 were not sufficiently high to justify TeleSource's investments in SPT Telecom and were in violation of the joint venture agreement. While the SPT Telecom-TeleSource contract called for an annual tariff increase of up to 4 percent, the maximum increase that was approved by the Ministry of Finance was only 1.9 percent. The TeleSource consortium threatened to reduce its planned US$1 billion investment in SPT Telecom for the year 1998 unless the government revised its tariff schedule for the following year. One of the main areas of contention was the monthly residential access fee which was raised from CZK90 (US$2.60) to CZK100 (US$2.90). By contrast, the monthly access fee charged by MATAV, the Hungarian national operator, was US$6. SPT Telecom proposed: a 30 percent increase in the monthly rental fee -- although TeleSource claimed that proper level was CZK350 (US$10); a 26 percent increase in local rates; a 13 percent reduction in domestic long distance rates; and a 20 percent reduction in the international rates. In October 1998, the Ministry of Finance approved a 25 percent increase in local rates, an increase in public payphone call costs, and moderate reductions in domestic long-distance calls. Rates were also increased in January 1999.

Distorted telephone rates impose significant costs on the Czech economy by providing the wrong economic signals to the users of the telephone network. Low rates for local calling over-stimulate local usage while long-distance calling is inefficiently repressed because of excessive rates. In addition, unbalanced rates create incentives for uneconomic bypass. Unbalanced tariff structures are not sustainable in a competitive environment: entrants will divert the overpriced business, but will not relieve the incumbent operators from the financial burden of serving unprofitable customers.

The introduction of the price cap mechanism was coupled with a program of tariff rebalancing. The aim of the Czech government has been to achieve a rebalanced tariff structure that will promote greater efficiency within SPT Telecom and reduce the cross-subsidy from domestic and international long distance to local service. However, rebalancing has proven to be a politically sensitive issue. The adjustment of the monthly rental and local rates is problematic since it is a very visible process and it is perceived as being unfair to the poor. Moreover, SPT Telecom is considered to be a very profitable company that does not need any additional revenue from increased local rates.

Although SPT Telecom negotiates new tariffs each November, the company has been hampered in its ability to increase the monthly line rentals and local rates primarily by the reluctance of the Ministry of Finance to permit large increases. SPT Telecom's annual report for 1997 states that, while the company welcomes the possibility of a fully liberalized environment in 2001, it needs to re-balance domestic tariffs quickly because post-liberalization, competing operators who are targeting the international market will depress margins and will undermine SPT Telecom's total margins.

With rate re-balancing, the incumbent operator will lose its ability to cross-subsidize the underpriced local services, including network access, with revenues from over-priced services (such as international calling). Different subsidy sources must be found, or the rates below incremental costs must be raised to compensatory levels.

SPT Telecom further claims that the existing rate structure will not allow it to compete fairly with its wireless rivals. Its problems will be aggravated after the introduction of full wire-line competition. As the Czech Republic moves towards a fully liberalized telecommunications market in accordance to the harmonization requirements of accession to the EU, this rate structure must be further rationalized. Re-balancing will be necessary -- in the interests of SPT Telecom, other operators, and the public interest -- as full competition draws near, as international call-back and other arbitrage mechanisms spread, and as value-added services become closer substitutes for basic services.

Because the local licensees must compete with subsidized SPT Telecom rates until tariff re-balancing is complete in the year 2000, they remain small and uncompetitive. For the same reason, they are unable to obtain financing. The failure to deal with the issue of rate re-balancing has, therefore, had an adverse impact on the development of local competition in the Czech Republic.

Czech policy makers should continue the transition to a competitive telecommunications pricing structure. The primary issues that need to be addressed should include the standard for further rebalancing (e.g., revenue neutrality, adjusted revenue neutrality, or profit neutrality), how fast to proceed, and how to continue the promotion of universal service in a competitive environment.

For the Czech economy to receive the benefits of market liberalization, SPT Telecom and the other operators must be permitted to compete with flexibility on prices and terms. In order to cover their fixed costs, sunk cost, costs of various obligations, as well as the revenue requirements of privatization agreements, the operators' prices will best serve the public interest if regulators permit prices to vary among users and classes of users in accordance with value of service (or elasticity of demand), as well as in response to marginal costs of service. Within the boundaries determined by the avoidance of cross-subsidization, the need to set some prices aggressively low in order to retain the business means that other prices should be permitted to take up the slack to secure adequate returns.

Without appropriate pricing flexibility, the incumbent operator will find it difficult to raise the capital needed, not only to meet demand for traditional telephone services, but to provide an array of new services. The Czech Republic must adopt policies relating to future price regulation that will enable SPT Telecom to function and to raise capital in the newly competitive environment in which new entrants will include some of the world's largest and best capitalized telecom operators.

SPT Telecom would favor an acceleration of competition if it were released from some build-out obligations and if it were afforded more pricing flexibility. It is now confronting significant pressure to accelerate the timetable for liberalization. The GSM cellular operator, Radiomobil, in which Deutsche Telekom is an investor, has begun to provide international services over the internet in connection with its GSM service. Thus, it is challenging SPT Telecom's exclusive right to provide international voice telephone service, which represents the very core of SPT Telecom's exclusive rights under its concession.

Regulated telecommunications prices should be permitted to vary in response to forward looking marginal and incremental costs, as well to the relative values of service, subject to the stipulation that they yield sufficient revenues to cover total costs.

As in many countries, price setting policy in the Czech Republic is a political process because of the traditional role of the Ministry of Finance as a price control agency; it will not be easy to increase tariffs for local services. Although there is political pressure from all quarters of the market, including the incumbent operator, to accelerate the timetable for liberalization, it is not clear that the Czech government has accepted the importance of accelerated pricing solutions to enable the market to become truly competitive.

Thus, the real challenge facing the Czech Republic is not merely its ability to adopt a liberalization timetable and to establish independent regulatory institutions. The real challenge, rather, centers on its ability to put in place effective price re-balancing and price regulation for the future. The fastest and most effective way of doing so will be to introduce not only timetables and regulatory institutions, but also effective consultative processes involving regulatory officials and industry participants that will facilitate re-balancing and future price regulation.

Interconnection Policy. No transparent regulation of access and interconnection currently exists. A clear set of principles governing the terms on which operators may connect to each other's networks is critical to the successful transition to competition after SPT Telecom's statutory monopoly expires by 2001. The absence of clear interconnection rules may stymie the development of local competition and competition in the provision of long-distance and international services. Indeed, experience from several countries indicates that the removal of legal barriers to competitive entry is not sufficient in itself to create effective competition in the telecommunications sector. Competitors must have access to essential network facilities on non-discriminatory terms if they are to compete.

Regulatory intervention may be necessary to assure access, particularly when incumbent operators control essential facilities, and have little incentive to give rivals access on fair terms. Several internet service providers have already filed several complaints relating to SPT Telecom's actions. Licensed local operators like Kabel Plus and Ram Global Networks have repeatedly attempted to negotiate their terms of interconnection with SPT Telecom. They have met with little success, resulting in high fees or no agreement at all. If interconnection rates for fixed network competitors are not reduced, competition may be impeded. SPT Telecom has resisted the idea of interconnection based on long run incremental cost principles on the ground that its cost structure reflects its license requirement to build out the Czech telecom infrastructure on an accelerated time schedule.

One of the primary challenges facing the Czech regulators is to establish a transparent and effective interconnection policy. This involves setting a level and structure of access prices which promote dynamic efficiency through efficient entry and investment decisions, while enabling network owners to obtain a fair return on their invested capital. Access regulation should, therefore, provide adequate pressure on the infrastructure owner to operate in an efficient manner, so that no unnecessary duplication of network construction takes place.

The implementation of an access regime is an on-going process in which difficult issues of interpretation must be resolved.

The Czech regulatory authorities must articulate a set of fundamental principles governing regulation of access and interconnection, must establish clear guidelines by which the behavior of bottleneck monopolists and their rivals can be judged, and must develop a set of standards and procedures to apply if private negotiations fail.

In today's fast changing technological and marketing environment, it is difficult to predict which network elements are essential to the efficient provision of particular services. Opportunities for effective competition that bring innovative offerings to consumers would be enhanced by the availability on an unbundled and non-discriminatory basis of any basic network element, or any collection of functions.

Competitively Neutral Mechanisms for Funding Universal Service. In the Czech Republic, as in most countries around the world, traditional telecommunications policy has led to prices reflecting cross-subsidization. Both economic theory and regulatory experience suggest that, with open entry and no remedial policy, maintaining cross-subsidies in price structure is impossible. Thus, with market liberalization, either new sources of subsidy must be found, or rates below incremental costs must be raised to compensatory levels.

Deregulation of key sectors of the U.S. economy was based on the promulgation of competitively neutral mechanisms to foster desirable social goals and positive economic externalities. The need to adopt support explicit mechanisms sufficient to advance certain publicly articulated universal service principles, and to assist consumers who would otherwise be disadvantaged, is more pronounced in the Czech Republic (relative to the United States) in view of the socioeconomic characteristics of its telephone users.

While the U.S. and E.U. experiences are instructive, policies for pursuing universal service goals must be sensitive to an individual country's political and institutional endowment, fiscal condition, consumer incomes and preferences, as well as the industry's economic characteristics. Policy makers in the Czech Republic must understand how these factors affect the optimal design of support mechanisms: whether support for universal service should be funded out of general tax revenues, or perhaps out of a broadly-based tax on revenues derived from the industry's products and services; the extent and scope of subsidies; and methods for delivering the subsidy without distorting competition. So far, it is unclear how the new Telecommunications Act will deal with the question of universal service funding.

The Czech regulatory authorities should articulate principles that pay efficient and neutral attention to the sector's social goals. If revenues are to be collected to support social goals, the surcharges or taxes should leave the relationship between the competitors' prices undistorted. If subsidies are to be conferred on particular services earmarked for particular consumers, then the subsidy payments should be offered to any supplier who is able to commit to performing the requisite services.

The Need to Minimize Regulatory Intervention. Technology is very rapidly eliminating natural monopoly in the telecommunications sector. The inter-exchange markets are already structurally competitive. The natural monopoly characteristics of local service are also being continuously modified by technological change. The only areas which will ultimately require continued regulatory oversight are: access and interconnection to essential network facilities; dispute resolution; and spectrum allocation. During the transition to a fully competitive system, the pricing of local exchange services will also require regulatory oversight.

Experience in other countries has shown that the effectiveness of regulation is enhanced by the implementation of processes to arbitrate and resolve commercial controversies arising in the marketplace. Such processes will become increasingly essential as a means for dealing with industry developments that are truly cross-border in scope and beyond the effective influence of national regulators. Therefore, the emphasis should be less on statist or institutional regulatory mechanisms than on developing effective consultative mechanisms involving market participants as well as regulators. Competitive entry is ultimately the most effective regulatory tool. Ideally, the market, and not the regulator, is the impetus for change.

Regulatory intervention in the telecommunications sector should ultimately be limited to enforcing an efficient access pricing and interconnection policy, to resolving disputes, and to allocating the spectrum. The pricing of local exchange services will require regulatory oversight only during the transition to a fully liberalized market.

Electricity and Gas

The most important accession requirement in the electricity sector is compliance with Directive 96/92/EC concerning rules of the internal market in electricity, adopted on December 19, 1996, and effective from February 19, 1997. Most member states have two years to bring this into effect. The Directive establishes common rules for generation, transmission and distribution of electricity, and offers a variety of alternative ways of meeting the criteria. It aims to achieve a competitive market in electricity. The Directive lays down that procedures should be objective, transparent and non-discriminatory -- a phrase that recurs so often it is useful to refer to it as OTND.

Pricing Policy. Czech gas and electricity prices are highly unbalanced, with industrial and commercial customers cross-subsidizing domestic consumers for both electricity and gas. Thus, the ratio of the household to industry price for electricity was 0.56 in 1996 and 0.64 in 1997, compared to 1.1 in Hungary, 1.6 in Poland, and 2.1 in the EU. Heat was subsidized until June 1998, and coal price regulation was removed some time ago. The Ministry of Finance view appears to be that energy prices are not subsidized because the electricity and gas companies are cash positive. Perhaps surprisingly, given the evident reluctance to raise domestic electricity and gas prices, the previous Government raised VAT on energy (gas, electricity and district heat) from 5 to 22 percent on January 1, 1998; on July 1, it raised pre-tax electricity prices to domestic customers by 24 percent compared to its previous level.

Since 1991, real domestic prices have remained moderately constant before tax until 1997, when real prices rose by 24 percent, and the after-tax price returned to 97 percent of its 1989 level. The new Government took office in August 1998 and immediately decided to hold 1998 prices constant through 1999. The original target announced in 1992 was that energy prices would be brought up to a reasonable level by 1998, but this target has now slipped to 2000 or later. Pre-tax electricity prices are now 60 percent of commercial prices, and if they were to be brought up to the current real commercial level with annual price increases from January 2000 to January 2002, prices would have to increase 28 percent p.a. faster than the CPI.

The government should plan for a smooth transition to competitive market pricing in the electricity and gas sectors by adopting a timetable for rebalancing the existing rate structures.

Supply Competition. The Directive allows eligible customers to choose their supplier, where an eligible customer is defined by consumption on one site. Eligibility is rather indirectly defined in terms of the share of the market that must be open to competition at each benchmark date after the Directive comes into force. In the first step starting from February 1999 "the share of the national market shall be calculated on the basis of the Community share of electricity consumed by final consumers consuming more than 40 GWh per year (on a consumption site basis and including autoproduction." (Article 19 (1)). The estimate is that this will open up 23 percent of total consumption to competition, and it is this share that applies in each market, regardless of the level of demand. The later thresholds are that, one year later, customers with 20 GWh (a market share of 28 percent) and, three years later in 2003, any one taking 9 GWh becomes eligible. These are minimum requirements, and each country can move faster.[10]

---

[10] Each country can decide whether RECs count as eligible customers (though the Commission has stated clearly that it would prefer this to be the case), and whether e.g., municipalities can aggregate domestic customers in the town and buy on their behalf. Any country that chooses to make RECs eligible should ensure that the benefits are passed on to their

Access to Transmission. The Directive offers two main methods of organizing access to transmission - the Single Buyer Model (SBM), and third party access (TPA). "The first paragraph of Article 3 stipulates that the two approaches to system access (SBM and TPA) must lead to equivalent economic results and hence to a directly comparable level of opening-up of markets and to a directly comparable degree of access to electricity markets." In both forms, the country must designate a Transmission Operator (TO) to ensure the provision of adequate and well maintained transmission, and a Transmission System Operator (TSO) responsible for dispatch within the area controlled and interconnection with other systems. Both forms require that transmission is functionally unbundled from generation and distribution, with separate accounts and "Chinese walls" to prevent the flow of information from generation and distribution to the TSO. The Directive does not require vertically integrated utilities to legally separate transmission, though clearly it reduces the need for intrusive regulatory oversight. CEZ has started the process of functionally unbundling transmission by placing the transmission assets into a separate wholly owned subsidiary company, but there are no plans at present to divest this company.

The criteria for dispatch must be OTND and published, so that the TSO is not allowed to favor dispatch from its own generation. While the TSO is required to dispatch in merit order taking account of transmission constraints, it may also take account of environmental objectives even if plant with these characteristics (e.g., equipped with Flue Gas Desulphurisation, generating from renewables, or having lower green house gas emissions as with nuclear power) cost more than generation which does not possess these environmental advantages. In addition, preference can be given to electricity produced from indigenous fuels -- up to 15 percent of the total. There are a variety of ways in which these obligations can be imposed on customers, even in a liberalized market. These environmental and strategic objectives could be pursued without disrupting the liberalization of the electricity market.

Third Party Access and the Single Buyer Model. Third Party Access is set out in Article 17 and may take two forms: negotiated TPA (nTPA) or regulated TPA (rTPA). Regulated TPA requires that tariffs for use of the transmission system be published and that eligible customers have right of access. Negotiated TPA requires the parties to negotiate transport charges, and for the TSO to publish indicative prices, which will normally be based on the average price agreed in the previous 12 months. The Single Buyer Model is set out in Article 18, and requires the designation of a single buyer within the territory of the TSO. The SB can either buy on behalf of customers or allow them to negotiate directly, in which case electricity is effectively traded under either rTPA or nTPA. If the SB buys on behalf of customers, then the TO must publish non-discriminatory tariffs for the use of the transmission and distribution system. The SB is required to pay the producer a price equal to the price paid by the customer less the published transmission and distribution tariff. Clearly, the effect is exactly the same as rTPA (as it is intended to be).

Whatever access method is chosen, the TSO or the SB (in the SBM) can refuse access if there is inadequate transmission capacity, although it is required to give reasons. CEZ would clearly like the Government to adopt the SBM, but whatever the choice, there are good arguments for choosing to publish transmission and distribution tariffs and hence rejecting nTPA. Published tariffs are required for both the SBM and rTPA. The transmission and distribution systems will both clearly require regulatory oversight as natural monopolies, and their owners will need to demonstrate that their tariffs are cost-justified and non-discriminatory. Publication makes the process obviously OTND, and forces the owners to propose and defend tariffs to the satisfaction of the regulator. Negotiation would be far harder to monitor for discrimination, and would make foreign investors doubtful about their terms of access to transmission, and hence reluctant to invest in generation.

---

customers. The main regulatory concern here is that RECs may buy from IPPs in which they have an ownership stake at above market prices. Regulators will have to be vigilant in protecting the REC's franchise customers from such exploitation.

Pricing Wholesale Electricity. Liberalizing some fraction of the market has dramatic consequences for the way in which electricity and various ancillary services are priced. If customers contract directly with producers for raw electricity (MWh), they will also need to pay the TSO, not just for transmission facilities, but also for the services required to maintain voltage and frequency stability and system security, which are supplied to the system as a whole. The customer and producer will also need to be metered and their half-hourly production and consumption levels measured.[11]

The spirit of the Directive is that markets should be competitive: this means confining regulation to the natural monopoly transmission and distribution business, while allowing competition in generation and supply (contracting, metering and billing), and possibly also in the provision of ancillary services. This is best achieved by rTPA, legally unbundling transmission from generation, and ensuring adequate competition between generators. At present, CEZ has a completely dominant position in generation, though it would face competition from imports provided the Slovak Republic and Poland were given TPA rights (or suppliers like Czechpol were allowed to buy from these countries and obtain access to the transmission system). Without modeling the import transmission capacity and the way in which CEZ's bidding strategies may create possible transmission constraints, it is hard to say how effective that competition might be, but there must be a serious worry that CEZ would still retain excessive market power.

In order to promote competition in generation, the government should require CEZ to divest a reasonable fraction of mid-merit generation -- either sold, or leased on long leases to independent companies.[12]

If an adequately competitive structure for the generating industry is created, then the logical way to encourage competition is by creating a wholesale market or electricity pool. This could provide for dispatch, pricing and hence payment for generation. As a result, it would automatically have a mechanism for pricing imbalances. This route is open to the Czech Government as it still retains a majority ownership stake in CEZ, and can therefore decide to restructure the company as part of its preparations for meeting the Electricity Directive. As the grid is an important part of the asset value of CEZ, and as transmission charges must be set anyway, it is desirable to consider the entire restructuring plan for CEZ at the same time.

The alternative route in which CEZ retains its dominant position is less satisfactory. It is far more demanding from a regulatory point of view, as wholesale electricity prices would require regulation, or at least price capping. It would be difficult to make CEZ the SB, as this is a role better suited to the TSO. The Hungarian approach has been to create a strong grid company (MVM) owning the single nuclear power station, and buying from the power companies (of which six once belonged to the predecessor of MVM, and three are IPPs) under long-term power purchase agreements. If CEZ were to follow this route, then it would divest at least the fossil generating plant; this would leave transmission as the core of the new company (much like Transgas). It might also keep pumped storage and nuclear power within the company (but in a generating subsidiary), if the former were felt important for system balancing and the latter were unlikely to

---

[11] In the event that contracted supply and demand are not exactly equal in each half-hour, the TSO will need to secure other supplies or reduce the amount generated by other producers, and these imbalances will have to be settled at a suitable price. Some mechanism for determining this half-hourly price for settling imbalances will therefore be needed, and the choice will depend on the philosophy behind the organization of generation.

[12] CEZ has five coal-fired stations of 800 MW or above that are, or will be, brought up to environmental standards (940 MW at Melnik, 800 MW at Detmarovice, 800 MW at Tusimice, 1490 MW at Prunerov and 1000 MW at Pocerady), each of which would be of adequate size to form a viable generating company, judging from the experience of OEP. There are three pump storage stations totaling 1,145 MW, various smaller stations that might be combined with the larger stations, and, of course, the nuclear stations of Dukovany and the as-yet unfinished Temelin. Simulations studies suggest that five roughly equal size (and cost) companies create a very competitive market (provided they do not collude).

be properly valued by the market. It could also be state owned, on the model of Transgas, if that were thought a suitable and possibly transitional stage to a final equilibrium.

This model has the obvious attraction: it allows the previous system of regulating the wholesale price to be preserved and, with it, some (more limited) cross-subsidy to domestic consumers, though eligible customers would leave if the wholesale price were too high. It also allows a system of tendering for new generation, and provides the greatest continuity from the former system of a centrally planned ESI. As such, it suffers from the tensions and inefficiencies that liberalization was designed to address. Its defenders might argue that it would preserve some of the benefits of coordination that motivated vertical integration in the past, while introducing competition in generation (and eligible supply).

Requirements of the EU Gas Directive. The 1998 European Gas Directive was the outcome of nine years of painful negotiations between countries, some of which were highly protective of their present arrangements. They have succeeded in inserting various exemptions for public-service obligations, consumer and environmental protection, and for stranded investments and contracts, none of which are clearly defined and which, therefore, give the countries opposed to change the power to delay reform. Indeed, the Directive states that these rules are no more than general principles providing a framework, the detailed implementation of which should be left to Member States. Nevertheless, the Directive clearly signals the intention of creating competitive markets. It therefore encourages the emerging pressures for competition created by surplus pipeline capacity, falling gas prices, and the demand of independent power producers for access to cheap gas. An optimistic view is that countries will increasingly recognise that their competitive position will be improved by liberalising the gas market.

Third Party Access (TPA) is defined by the European Commission as "a regime providing for an obligation, to the extent that there is capacity available, on companies operating transmission and distribution networks for gas to offer terms for the use of their grid, in particular to individual consumers or to distribution companies." (EC, 1992). TPA thus imposes no obligations on the pipeline owner to provide access if the capacity has been already allocated. Under Article 17 of the 1998 Gas Directive, pipeline owners may also refuse access where this would prevent them from carrying out public-service obligations; they may also refuse on the basis of serious economic and financial difficulties with take-or-pay contracts -- though in both cases, "duly substantiated reasons shall be given for such a refusal."

Eligible customers will be free to contract directly for gas supplies with producers in any of the EU countries, and that effectively means directly for import. Gazprom has supply companies registered in most EU countries and will surely be happy to contract directly with eligible customers, as no doubt will other producers and traders. The definition of eligible customers includes all gas-fired power stations, and CHP plants above a threshold level (determined for electricity security reasons, but at least as low as for other eligible customers). Customers taking more than 25 mcm/yr will automatically be eligible; the threshold level must be set low enough to ensure that at least 20 percent of the market is opened initially and 28 percent after 5 years, rising to 33 percent after 10 years. Elsewhere in the EU, the rate of market opening appears to be faster than that required by the Directive. Britain, for example, had liberalised the entire market down to domestic households by mid-1998.

The most important step to liberalise gas markets is the functional unbundling of transmission from supply or marketing, yet this is not required by the Gas Directive. As there are no Europe-wide regulatory agencies or any agreements on the methodology for determining access prices, it will be difficult for competitors to demonstrate the abuse of incumbent market power. Gas companies are, however, required to unbundle the functions and management of transmission and marketing. An aggressive pro-competitive regulator can use this to encourage legal unbundling, as happened in the case of British Gas.

The Directive offers two alternative forms of TPA: negotiated and regulated TPA. Negotiated TPA under Article 15 requires countries to allow eligible customers and other gas undertakings inside and outside the country to negotiate voluntary commercial agreements "in good faith;" and under published commercial conditions. Regulated TPA (Article 16) requires gas undertakings to publish "tariffs and/or other terms and obligations of use," though as mentioned above, Article 17 allows access to be denied in specified cases (public-service obligations, stranded assets, etc). The trend within the EU appears to be away from negotiated TPA to regulated TPA.

To meet these requirements, Transgas and the GDCs will have to publish (or prepare to defend) tariffs for using the transmission system and storage facilities. Transgas would need to functionally unbundle the transmission system (perhaps including storage, but preferably with storage in a separate subsidiary) from the trading activity of buying and selling gas. The GDCs would similarly have to create subsidiaries for operating the local distribution systems, and supplying customers (billing, meter reading etc). The supply business would then have to compete with the trading arm of Transgas and other gas suppliers once eligible customers were free to choose their supplier.

Transportation

The Czech Republic has made remarkable strides since 1989 to develop a market oriented economy. This progress is reflected in several aspects of its transportation system including the development of a competitive unregulated trucking industry, the growth of a profitable unsubsidized airline, and the maintenance of an extensive network of highways and rail lines. The main concern with the Czech Republic transport system is that its current pricing policies and subsidies discourage efficiency in certain services.

Rail Service. Czech Railways provides freight and passenger service. Freight transportation appears to be profitable, but passenger transportation loses money and is subsidized. The loss from passenger transportation in 1997 amounted to CZK6 billion, inclusive of grants and roughly CZK11.5 billion if these grants are not included.

Subsidies are a sign of social economic inefficiency if they are less than the social benefits of the service. Even if the subsidies are socially justified, they could suggest that railway service is generally not as efficient as it could be. To stress this point, we first note that the cost of rail freight transportation is 5.5 cents per ton-mile (freight rates per ton-mile are slightly lower, but Czech Railways derives freight income from other sources). By contrast, the cost of rail freight transport in the U.S. is roughly 2 cents per ton-mile. Part of this difference can be explained by U.S. railroads' greater trip distances and freight car utilization, but much of this difference is likely to be explained by Czech Railways' cost inefficiencies.

First, the Czech rail network appears to be over built. The network consists of 10,200 miles of track to carry roughly 13,402 (million) ton-miles of freight or roughly 1.3 million ton-miles per mile of track. By contrast, the U.S. rail network consists of 180,000 miles of track to carry 1,305,688 (million) ton miles of freight or roughly 7.25 million ton-miles per mile of track. Thus, the U.S. rail network's traffic density is 6 times greater than Czech Railway's traffic density. Recently, the Czech rail system has been rationalizing its operations, which will improve traffic density. In addition, policy makers in the Czech Republic have recognized that their rail system is in need of considerable pruning as demonstrated by attempts of the previous government to cut some 30 percent of rail lines by selling or abandoning them. Unfortunately, community and trade union resistance halted the abandonment process.

Low density lines constitute a serious impediment to the attainment of static and dynamic efficiency in the Czech rail system.

Czech Railways should be accorded considerable structural flexibility and be permitted to eliminate unproductive and redundant track and other facilities.

Second, Czech Railways' costs appear to be inflated because it has low labor productivity. The U.S. rail freight system produces nearly 5 million ton-miles per employee. Although it is difficult to unambiguously distinguish freight employees from passenger employees in the Czech system, it appears that Czech Railways' labor productivity is no more than 0.5 million ton-miles per employee, which is roughly 10 times lower than U.S. rail labor productivity. Czech Railways is reducing its labor force in this sector, but this has not significantly increased labor productivity because the amount of freight shipped by rail has also fallen.

The government should carefully articulate the inevitability of staff reductions in the railroad sector and formulate a program of labor adjustment which is based on the cooperation of organized labor. It might be socially desirable for the methods of adjustment to focus on voluntary separation based on incentive schemes, and redeployment combined with retraining.

Third, the U.S. railway system has made substantial investments in computerized operations. For example, Norfolk Southern railway once tracked its cars and locomotives by posting a video camera at the entrance to each rail yard; now, an electronic scanner automatically tracks each car's arrival. Czech Railways is increasingly using computers as modern systems replace older ones, but much more progress needs to be made.

Finally, the Czech freight system is characterized by very little intermodal (truck/rail) operations. Under this form of transportation, a shipper's freight is picked up by a truck and put in a container, which is then placed on a rail car for the linehaul part of the journey and delivered by truck to its final destination. The lack of specialized infrastructure and technical equipment in the Czech Republic has been identified as the reason why these operations are not in greater use. Nonetheless, intermodal operations are essential for an efficient freight transport system -- indeed, intermodal traffic in the U.S. has grown from roughly 3 million trailers and containers at the time of deregulation in 1980 to nearly 9 million trailers and containers today.

The freight segment of Czech railways has been able to make money by charging rates that cover its inflated costs. But as noted, rail output has been declining in the past decade. In addition, it is anticipated that coal production will slow down, which will have serious implications for rail revenues because coal accounts for nearly 15 percent of the tonnage that rail transports. Thus, Czech railways will have to find ways to improve the efficiency of its freight operations to maintain profitability.

Although it is acknowledged that rail passenger transportation is subsidized, the extent of rail passenger inefficiencies may not be entirely clear. The cost of rail transport per passenger mile is 12.2 cents. As in the case of freight transport, these costs are undoubtedly inflated by operating inefficiencies. Moreover, current fares of 2.6 cents per passenger mile only cover a fraction of the costs. As noted, the annual loss from passenger transportation that must be covered by the public amounts to CZK11.5 billion or more than US$400 million. This required subsidy approaches the subsidy that is given to Amtrak, the U.S. intercity passenger railroad, to cover losses from its entire operations. Given that the Czech Republic spends nearly as much as the United States to subsidize travel on railroads, a relatively high cost mode, it is reasonable to suggest that the Czech Republic may be over-subsidizing rail passenger transportation.

As noted, passenger service receives some CZK11.5 billion in annual subsidies and has high costs per passenger mile. Freight service does not receive explicit subsidies but it also has high costs. If the costs of rail operations were reduced by a plausible amount and if subsidies were eliminated, then the Czech Republic would save considerably more than CZK20 billion annually. These objectives could be accomplished if steps are taken to privatize rail operations.

To be sure, rail privatization has been explored before and has been rejected on political grounds. But this policy should be reconsidered for a number of reasons. First, the share of freight transported by rail has declined over time, and continual declines could threaten rail freight profitability and force freight service to receive subsidies or to exploit monopoly power in the shipment of some commodities. Second, rail passenger subsidies are hardly justified given the existence of a viable lower cost mode, bus. It would be more efficient to divert some of rail's subsidies to bus, if the Czech Republic is committed to subsidizing passenger service. Rail passenger service could be provided by private rail carriers in markets that have sufficient passenger density to support such service. Finally, and most important, the Czech Republic's entry into the EU offers an opportunity to encourage competition with rail carriers from EU countries. It has been argued that the capital requirements would prevent anyone from the Czech Republic from purchasing a rail carrier (i.e., Czech Railways). But it is conceivable that a Czech concern could combine with an EU transportation firm and own a private rail carrier that would compete with other EU rail carriers within the Czech Republic. The effects of this intensified rail competition would be to lower rail costs and rates and improve service.

The complexity of the proposed policy should not be underestimated. But if the U.S. experience with railroad deregulation is any guide -- and it appears to be for other countries -- then privatization is a promising way for the Czech Republic to develop a much more efficient rail system that would regain traffic from truck and provide a high quality service for those passengers who are willing to pay for it.

In order to induce cost-effectiveness, responsive output quality, and creative productivity in the operations of the railroad industry, the government should consider the option of privatization.

Efficient Pricing of and Investment in Highway Infrastructure. Policy makers in the Czech Republic are concerned about the growing level of highway congestion and damage to their roads. Annual highway expenditures are roughly CZK10 billion. Some may believe that the problems of congestion and damage can be solved by increasing highway expenditures. But it is becoming clear in many industrialized countries that additional expenditures will only postpone these problems. The efficient solution is to charge motorists and truckers for their use of scarce peak-period highway capacity and limited road durability. These charges could substantially improve travel times and reduce maintenance costs, as well as generate revenues that will be needed to improve thoroughfares at border crossings. Although precise estimates are difficult to make, based on estimates for the U.S., annual benefits from efficient pricing and investment could easily amount to 30 percent of current highway expenditures, or CZK3 billion.

In order to deal with the growing problem of highway congestion, the government should introduce a pricing scheme that charges motorists and truckers for their use of scarce peak-period highway capacity.

Eliminating Subsidies and Promoting Competition in Bus Transport. Bus transport receives roughly CZK2 billion in annual subsidies. But the administration of these subsidies is contentious. Subsidies from the state have declined so local governments are increasingly forced to contribute more funds. This has provoked arguments between local governments, which want a high level of service, and bus companies, which claim that more money is needed to provide the desired service. For example, the Minister of Transport states that common carrier obligations call for 6 daily bus trips on each line. But the current subsidy does not cover this level of service.

It can be plausibly argued that it would be more efficient to use some of rail's subsidies to support bus service, but it would be even more efficient to phase out subsidies and encourage the development of a fully competitive unregulated bus service. Currently, there are market entry restrictions on bus service. These restrictions should be eliminated, and any carrier wishing to provide service should be allowed to do so. This would accomplish two objectives. First, the enhanced competition would lead to greater efficiency, which would reduce costs and the need for subsidies. Second, services would be tailored to travelers' preferences.

There would be a mixture of bus sizes and services with prices that reflect the costs of providing particular services.

If Czech policy makers believe that low-income and elderly travelers need a safety net, then it would be more efficient for the state to give these travelers transportation vouchers instead of subsidizing bus companies. These travelers could use public funds to obtain the transportation service that best suits them if these funds are directly given to carriers they will delay efforts to minimize costs.

All statutory restrictions on entry into bus transport should be eliminated, regulatory intervention should be limited to enforcing safety standards.

Truck Transportation. Truck transportation in the Czech Republic is very competitive. Some might say it is too competitive because there are a large number of bankruptcies in this industry. Nonetheless, shippers have the choice of providing their own truck service (private trucking) or hiring commercial carriers. It appears, however, that private carriers' relatively large share of freight may be partly a result of inflated costs and restrictions on for-hire operations in international markets.

Data from a large for-hire trucking company, Cetrans, indicates that its average rates and costs are roughly 14 cents per ton-mile. This is consistent with average rates of 14.2 cents per ton mile for all for-hire companies reported in the Tranis 1994-1995 report. This figure can be decomposed into average truck rates for international shipments of 9 cents per ton-mile, and average rates for domestic (Czech Republic) shipments of 18 cents per ton mile. Presumably, average rates are lower for international shipments than domestic shipments because they have lower costs from economies of distance and traffic density. The costs of the for-hire trucking industry can, therefore, be reduced if it serves international and domestic markets. Nonetheless, for-hire trucking companies need permits to operate in international markets, and it has been claimed that an insufficient number of permits are available. Private trucks do not need permits to operate in international markets, thus they have an unfair competitive advantage over for-hire trucks because they can realize the cost savings from freely operating in these markets.

The Czech Republic's entry into the EU should ease entry restrictions on its for-hire carriers into EU markets and should facilitate entry of foreign carriers into the Czech Republic. For-hire truck competition for international shipments should thus become much more intensive and possibly enable shippers to place less reliance on private trucking. All regulatory impediments to entry by for-hire carriers into international markets should be eliminated.

Air Transportation. In contrast to some other European carriers, CSA does not receive state subsidies. Thus, it is somewhat encouraging that although the carrier lost money in the early 1990s, it is now starting to earn a profit. In addition, CSA continues to improve its service and has good safety practices as indicated by a recent audit by the U.S. Federal Aviation Administration.

On the other hand, it is important to recognize that CSA primarily operates in international markets that are characterized by high regulated fares and entry restrictions. CSA's average fare in 1997 was 20 cents per passenger mile, which is considerably above U.S. carriers' 1997 average fare of 13 cents per passenger mile. This difference can be partly explained by U.S. carriers' lower costs from greater average trip distances (surprisingly, U.S. carriers and CSA have similar average load factors). In all likelihood, however, regulation is largely responsible for raising CSA's costs and its fares. First, CSA's average labor productivity of roughly 44,000 ton-miles per employee is 3 times lower than U.S. carriers' average labor productivity of roughly 130,000 ton-miles per employee. CSA's lower labor productivity undoubtedly derives from operating in an environment that does not provide sufficient competitive discipline to optimize the use of labor. Second, CSA is not free to optimize its network because it is constrained from operating at capacity controlled airports in Europe such as London's Heathrow airport. Until CSA has the ability and competitive incentive to minimize its costs and until it is subject to unregulated price competition, citizens of the Czech Republic will continue to pay excessive airline fares.

Prices in the domestic Czech airline industry should be fully deregulated. Air transport will become more competitive as travelers within the EU are able to choose among carriers from member countries. But slot restrictions at major airports in Europe can prevent some carriers, such as CSA, from optimally developing their networks. Prague airport does not have slot restrictions or much congestion, but the growth of air traffic within the EU will put pressure on Prague airport's capacity. If congestion develops, slot controls should be resisted in favor of efficient take-off and landing tolls.

Table 1.1. Total and Active Population, 1990-97

	1990	1993	1994	1995	1996	1997[1]
			(In persons, end of year)			
Population, total	10 304 607[3]	10,334,013	10,333,161	10,321,344	10,309,137	10,299,125
I. Economically active, total	5,435,695	5,194,010	5,137,138	5,176,453	5,210,789	5,245,410
a) Workers (manual and non-manual)[2]	5,106,223	4,783,310	4,766,051	4,830,694	4,846,898	4,806,018
b) Women on						
- maternity leave	70,273	47,573	41,848	40,245	37,766	38,371
- child-care leave	219,820	177,911	162,759	152,473	139,786	132,119
c) Job applicants registered by Labor Offices	39,379	185,216	166,480	153,041	186,339	268,902
II. Not economically active	4,868,912	5,140,003	5,196,023	5,144,891	5,098,348	5,053,715
a) Under 15	2,175,638	2,009,752	1,948,024	1,893,259	1,842,679	1,795,032
b) Pupils and students 15 plus (incl. secondary vocational schools	573,122	628,821	653,174	675,078	660,869	658,431
c) Others	2,120,152	2,501,430	2,594,825	2,576,554	2,594,800	2,600,252

1/ Preliminary data.

2/ With the only or main job, excluding foreign nationals (including Slovaks).

3/ On 1 January 1991 (adjusted according to the 1991 Population and Housing Census).

Source: Czech Statistical Office.

Table 1.2. Population by Gender and Age Group, 1995-97

Age	31 December 1995			31 December 1996			31 December 1997		
	Men	Women	Total	Men	Women	Total	Men	Women	Total
Total	5,013,413	5,312,284	10,325,697	5,012,085	5,297,052	10,309,137	5,008,730	5,290,395	10,299,125
0	62,141	58,622	120,763	46,217	43,797	90,014	46,347	43,918	90,265
1 - 4	261,777	249,490	511,267	226,809	215,043	441,852	210,988	200,257	411,245
5 - 9	338,465	321,957	660,422	327,739	312,107	639,846	324,204	308,569	632,773
10 - 14	395,348	376,745	772,093	343,334	327,633	670,967	338,522	322,227	660,749
15 - 19	465,372	445,288	910,660	414,974	395,884	810,858	395,296	377,201	772,497
20 - 24	371,927	355,233	727,160	456,377	437,912	894,289	465,084	446,673	911,757
25 - 29	358,226	343,120	701,346	359,334	343,826	703,160	373,698	357,710	731,408
30 - 34	324,429	313,881	638,310	356,067	342,119	698,186	359,521	344,706	704,227
35 - 39	390,786	384,112	774,898	333,010	323,700	656,710	324,580	314,643	639,223
40 - 44	414,120	412,116	826,236	396,290	393,009	789,299	387,627	383,474	771,101
45 - 49	382,069	388,240	770,309	412,009	415,327	827,336	406,441	409,892	816,333
50 - 54	278,264	291,684	569,948	346,173	360,953	707,126	368,811	383,674	752,485
55 - 59	231,260	256,246	487,506	249,674	272,713	522,387	262,214	285,367	547,581
60 - 64	239,451	287,070	526,521	215,150	253,709	468,859	209,475	246,144	455,619
65 - 69	205,932	284,782	490,714	204,924	269,976	474,900	205,145	267,495	472,640
70 - 74	137,653	214,001	351,654	163,150	255,873	419,023	161,864	251,290	413,154
75 - 79	75,894	137,691	213,585	83,112	148,046	231,158	95,824	172,412	268,236
80 - 84	57,653	124,070	181,723	48,853	104,813	153,666	42,393	91,037	133,430
85+	22,646	67,936	90,582	28,889	80,612	109,501	30,696	83,706	114,402
0 - 14	1,057,731	1,006,814	2,064,545	944,099	898,580	1,842,679	920,061	874,971	1,795,032
15 - 59	3,216,453	3,189,920	6,406,373	3,323,908	3,285,443	6,609,351	3,343,272	3,303,340	6,646,612
60+	739,229	1,115,550	1,854,779	744,078	1,113,029	1,857,107	745,397	1,112,084	1,857,481

Source: Czech Statistical Office.

Table 1.3. Unemployment Rates by Region, 1994-98

	1994				1995				1996			
	QI	QII	QIII	QIV	QI	QII	QIII	QIV	QI	QII	QIII	QIV
Total	1.00	1.00	1.00	1.00	1.00	1.00	1.00	1.00	1.00	1.00	1.00	1.00
Prague	0.74	0.63	0.60	0.66	0.60	0.61	0.67	0.63	0.48	0.47	0.54	0.53
Center Bohemia	1.02	0.87	0.83	0.85	0.93	0.96	1.00	0.94	0.86	0.81	0.78	0.78
South Bohemia	0.81	0.78	0.74	0.71	0.65	0.62	0.61	0.62	0.71	0.74	0.74	0.70
West Bohemia	0.99	1.04	0.99	0.98	0.96	0.89	0.83	0.83	0.77	0.78	0.78	0.72
North Bohemia	1.20	1.37	1.41	1.37	1.39	1.51	1.53	1.75	1.99	2.03	1.84	1.80
East Bohemia	0.80	0.76	0.77	0.73	0.76	0.84	0.89	0.81	0.77	0.85	0.91	0.86
South Moravia	0.94	0.95	0.91	0.86	0.91	0.89	0.86	0.85	0.89	0.87	0.89	0.84
North Moravia	1.31	1.36	1.45	1.53	1.47	1.38	1.33	1.31	1.28	1.26	1.28	1.44
Memo:												
Total Unemployment Rate (percent)	4.2	4.2	4.5	4.3	4.3	4.0	4.0	3.7	3.7	3.8	4.0	4.1

	1997				1998			
	QI	QII	QIII	QIV	QI	QII	QIII	QIV
Total	1.00	1.00	1.00	1.00	1.00	1.00	1.00	1.00
Prague	0.46	0.50	0.52	0.50	0.48	0.52	0.52	0.49
Center Bohemia	0.81	0.86	0.77	0.72	0.76	0.83	0.87	0.86
South Bohemia	0.73	0.71	0.69	0.76	0.80	0.69	0.80	0.69
West Bohemia	0.78	0.92	0.97	0.96	0.94	0.87	0.97	0.90
North Bohemia	1.71	1.73	1.74	1.68	1.60	1.62	1.49	1.65
East Bohemia	0.86	0.75	0.77	0.77	0.84	0.79	0.85	0.90
South Moravia	0.80	0.79	0.82	0.82	0.83	0.90	0.87	0.88
North Moravia	1.52	1.47	1.46	1.52	1.48	1.44	1.41	1.37
Memo:								
Total Unemployment Rate (percent)	4.3	4.5	5.0	5.4	5.9	5.9	6.8	7.3

Source: Czech Statistical Office, Labor Force Survey Data.

Table 1.4. Civil Employment by Sector, 1993-98

	1993	1994	1995	1996	1997[1]	1998[1]
	(In thousands, annual average)					
Agriculture	333	340	314	303	278	267
Industry	1,710	1,620	1,628	1,614	1,598	1,596
Construction	453	444	450	452	433	398
Trade and catering	720	839	891	931	958	903
Transportation and communication	385	353	355	363	345	337
Financial services	65	76	85	89	93	87
Real estate	303	341	389	382	388	394
Public administration	133	146	162	168	175	175
Education	324	321	322	322	309	305
Health service	263	258	262	268	267	263
Other services	159	147	154	152	149	146
Total employment	4,848	4,885	5,012	5,044	4,993	4,871
	(Share in total employment, in percent)					
Agriculture	6.9	6.9	6.3	6.0	5.5	5.5
Industry	35.3	33.1	32.5	32.0	32	32.8
Construction	9.3	9.1	9.0	9.0	8.7	8.2
Trade and catering	14.9	17.2	17.7	18.4	19.1	18.5
Transportation and communication	7.9	7.2	7.1	7.2	6.9	6.9
Financial services	1.3	1.6	1.7	1.8	1.9	1.8
Real estate	6.3	7.0	7.8	7.6	7.8	8.1
Public administration	2.7	3.0	3.2	3.3	3.5	3.6
Education	6.7	6.6	6.4	6.4	6.2	6.2
Health service	5.4	5.3	5.2	5.3	5.4	5.4
Other services	3.3	3.0	3.1	3.0	3.0	3.0
Total employment	100	100	100	100	100	100

Note: Includes private entrepreneurs and workers in enterprises of all size groups.

1/ Preliminary data.

Source: Czech Statistical Office.

Table 1.5. Civil Employment in Large Enterprises by Sector, 1993-98

	1993	1994	1995	1996	1997[1]	1998[2]
			(In thousands, annual average)			
Agriculture	300	262	210	183	215	197
Industry	1,416	1,351	1,206	1,147	1,321	1,296
Construction	226	236	236	227	263	234
Trade and catering	212	241	162	159	322	305
Transportation and communication	302	292	288	288	292	281
Financial services	63	73	80	84	82	79
Real estate	133	138	144	143	181	181
Public administration	131	146	161	167	172	174
Education	314	312	309	308	298	293
Health service	238	220	220	218	215	211
Other services	99	98	107	106	104	104
Total employment	3,434	3,369	3,123	3,030	3,465	3,355
Memorandum items:						
State sector	n.a.	n.a.	1,131	926	870	817
Cooperatives	n.a.	n.a.	186	161	165	144
Private sector[2]	n.a.	n.a.	831	765	1,349	1,297

Note: Until 1996, all firms with 25 employees or more (in 1995-96, firms in industry, trade, and catering only with 100 employees or more). In 1997, firms in the entrepreneurial sphere with 20 employees or more (all firms of financial intermediation and all budgetary and subsidized sphere organizations.
1/ Excluding foreign-owned enterprises.
2/ Preliminary.

Source: Czech Statistical Office.

Table 1.6. Structure of Employment by Public-Private Ownership, 1989-97

	1989	1993	1994	1995	1996	1997
			(In percent of total)			
Private	1.3	47.1	53.0	57.2	58.9	61.6
Private/State Mixed	..	6.4	5.9	13.4	14.3	13.0
Collective (coops)	12.9	5.7	4.8	4.2	3.7	3.3
Civic Organization	1.5	0.6	0.5	0.7	0.6	0.7
State & Local	84.3	40.1	35.8	24.5	22.4	21.4
Total percent	100.0	100.0	100.0	100.0	100.0	100.0

Source: Czech Statistical Office, data from Establishment Survey.

Table 2.1. Gross Domestic Product, 1992-98

	1992	1993	1994	1995	1996	1997	1998
	\multicolumn{7}{c}{(In billions of CZK, at current prices)}						
Total consumption	605.9	717.9	861.6	976.8	1123.2	1222.8	1301.6
Government consumption	166.7	227.4	255.5	275.1	312.5	331.3	351.8
Private consumption	439.2	490.5	606.1	701.7	810.7	891.5	949.8
(as a share in GDP)	51.9	48.9	51.2	50.8	51.6	53.1	52.2
Gross capital formation	226.3	269.1	352.8	470.0	549.5	557.1	544.7
Gross fixed investment	241.3	280.8	339.8	442.4	500.6	506.9	501.4
Change in stocks	-15.0	-11.7	13.0	27.6	48.9	50.2	43.3
(as a share in GDP)	26.7	26.8	29.8	34.0	34.9	33.2	29.9
Net export of goods and nonfactor services	14.6	15.3	-31.7	-65.7	-100.4	-99.9	-25.6
Gross domestic product	846.8	1002.3	1182.7	1381.1	1572.3	1680.0	1820.7
	\multicolumn{7}{c}{(In billions of CZK, at constant 1995 prices)}						
Total consumption	..	..	947.5	976.8	1021.8	1047.0	1027.0
Government consumption			286.2	275.1	271.8	281.5	283.3
Private consumption	..	..	661.3	701.7	750.0	765.5	743.7
Gross capital formation	..	..	382.4	470.0	524.9	504.6	475.6
Gross fixed investment	..	..	369.0	442.4	478.5	457.9	440.7
Change in stocks	..	..	13.4	27.6	46.4	46.7	34.9
Net export of goods and nonfactor services	..	..	-32.2	-65.7	-112.8	-113.1	-97.6
Gross domestic product	1106.6	1118.4	1297.7	1381.1	1433.9	1438.5	1405.0

Note: Data for 1990-1993 is in the process of revision, which will be completed by the third quarter of 1999. Data for 1997-1998 come from quarterly estimate.

Source: Czech Statistical Office.

Table 2.2. Composition of Gross Domestic Product, 1992-98

	1992	1993	1994	1995	1996	1997	1998
	(Share in GDP at current prices, in percent)						
Total consumption	71.6	71.6	72.9	70.7	71.4	72.8	71.5
Government consumption	19.7	22.7	21.6	19.9	19.9	19.7	19.3
Private consumption	51.9	48.9	51.3	50.8	51.6	53.1	52.2
Gross capital formation	26.7	26.8	29.8	34.0	35.0	33.2	29.9
Gross fixed investment	28.5	28.0	28.7	32.0	31.9	30.2	27.5
Change in stocks	-1.8	-1.2	1.1	2.0	3.1	3.0	2.4
Net export of goods and nonfactor services	1.7	1.5	-2.7	4.7	-6.4	6.0	-1.4
Gross domestic product	100.0	100.0	100.0	109.5	100.1	111.9	100.0
	(Share in GDP at constant 1995 prices, in percent)						
Total consumption	..	..	73.0	70.7	71.3	72.8	73.1
Government consumption	..	..	22.0	19.9	19.0	19.6	20.2
Private consumption	..	..	51.0	50.8	52.3	53.2	52.9
Gross capital formation	..	..	29.5	34.0	36.6	35.1	33.9
Gross fixed investment	..	..	28.5	32.0	33.4	31.8	31.4
Change in stocks	..	..	1.0	2.0	3.2	3.3	2.5
Net export of goods and nonfactor services	..	..	-2.5	-4.7	-7.9	-7.9	-7.0
Gross domestic product	..	..	100.0	100.1	100.0	100.0	99.9
	(Percentage change, at constant 1995 prices)						
Total consumption	..	..	..	3.1	4.6	2.5	-1.9
Government consumption	..	..	..	-3.9	-1.2	3.6	0.6
Private consumption	..	..	..	6.1	6.9	2.1	-2.8
Gross capital formation	..	..	..	22.9	11.7	-3.9	-5.7
Gross fixed investment	..	..	..	19.9	8.2	-4.3	-3.8
Change in stocks	..	..	..	106.0	68.1	0.6	-25.3
Net export of goods and nonfactor services	..	..	..	104.0	71.7	0.3	-13.7
Gross domestic product	-3.3	1.1	2.7	6.4	3.8	0.3	-2.3

Note: Data for 1990-1993 is in the process of revision, which will be completed by the third quarter of 1999.
Data for 1997-1998 come from quarterly estimate.

Source: Czech Statistical Office.

Table 2.3. Gross Domestic Product by Origin, 1994-98

	1994	1995	1996	1997	1998
	(In billions of CZK, at current prices)				
Agriculture, hunting, forestry, and fishing	55.2	60.6	68.1	69.2	76.4
Industry[1]	378.8	429.6	470.1	526.7	586.0
Construction	82.7	111.6	121.4	129.7	127.7
Wholesale and retail trade, restaurants and hotels	150.4	193.7	236.7	231.7	223.3
Transport, storage and communication	94.1	104.8	116.5	120.1	160.0
Financial services	64.8	60.9	59.1	74.7	84.7
Business services	137.9	149.8	168.6	198.4	220.4
Public administration, education and health	154.3	179.6	210.5	213.9	228.5
Taxes minus subsidies	133.2	157.3	181.7	182.7	187.3
FISIM	68.7	66.8	60.4	67.1	73.6
Total GDP (at market prices)	1,182.7	1,381.1	1,572.3	1,680.0	1,820.7
	(In billions of CZK, at 1995 prices)				
Agriculture, hunting, forestry and fishing	63.5	60.6	60.6	62.1	67.1
Industry[1]	406.0	429.6	473.0	510.9	502.6
Construction	94.1	111.6	86.3	84.7	65.3
Wholesale and retail trade, restaurants and hotels	163.2	193.7	223.1	212.6	193.9
Transport, storage and communication	106.2	104.8	103.4	103.5	117.8
Financial services	55.8	60.9	80.3	89.4	92.7
Business services	152.9	149.8	159.3	147.1	146.3
Public administration, education and health	179.7	179.6	157.7	144.1	134.0
Taxes minus subsidies	136.4	157.3	168.2	167.1	169.4
FISIM	60.1	66.8	78.0	83.0	84.1
Total GDP (at market prices)	1,297.7	1,381.1	1,433.9	1,438.5	1,405.0

1 / Includes mining, manufacturing industry, electricity, gas and water.

Source: Czech Statistical Office.

Table 2.4. Industrial Production, 1992-98

	1992	1993	1994	1995	1996	1997	1998
	(Annual percent change, at constant prices)						
Mining and quarrying	-12.8	-7.1	0.6	-1.4	1.4	-2.9	-5.7
Manufacturing	-14.6	-7.7	0.1	8.2	1.7	6.4	2.6
Food products and beverages	-7.0	-4.4	-2.2	4.0	4.1	4.3	-0.3
Textiles and textile products	-13.7	-14.2	-1.7	0.5	-7.2	-2.0	-1.5
Leather and leather products	-14.0	-2.0	-1.2	-10.2	-4.8	-24.8	-29.5
Wood and wood products	-21.4	-14.0	3.0	2.4	-0.9	4.9	-2.3
Pulp, paper, publishing, and printing	-3.2	-7.1	18.2	1.4	2.8	12.2	9.0
Coke, refined petroleum products, and nuclear fuel	0.9	-8.1	8.0	7.2	3.2	-0.1	-16.1
Chemicals and chemical products	-9.3	-6.2	3.8	-1.2	3.5	0.9	2.8
Rubber and plastic products	-4.9	-2.0	1.7	14.5	10.9	16.2	11.2
Nonmetallic mineral products	-6.0	-11.4	5.6	6.6	3.6	8.2	1.2
Basic metal and metal products	-18.6	-6.5	2.8	12.3	-7.2	4.1	-4.3
Machinery and equipment, n.e.c.	-24.9	-16.6	-4.7	9.4	6.8	15.1	3.6
Electrical and optical equipment	-29.0	-8.1	12.3	21.8	12.5	24.6	41.5
Transport equipment	-26.7	-3.4	-14.1	24.3	18.0	16.3	6.6
Other manufacturing, n.e.c.	-13.6	-10.4	-5.8	9.8	8.3	4.6	10.7
Electricity, gas, and water supply	-3.0	-4.8	-2.8	3.4	3.7	-2.7	-1.5
Industry (large enterprises)[1]	-13.7	-7.4	-0.1	7.1	..	..	..
Industry, total	-7.9	-5.3	2.1	8.7	2.0	4.5	1.6

Note: For 1992-95, changes in industrial sales. From 1996, changes in index of physical production (IPP).
1/ In 1992-94, enterprises with 25 employees or more. In 1995 enterprises with 100 employees or more. In 1996-98, enterprises with 20 employees or more.

Source: Czech Statistical Office.

Table 2.5. Gross Fixed Capital Investment in Tangible Goods, 1993-98

	1993	1994	1995	1996	1997[1]	1998[2]
	(In millions of CZK, current prices)					
Total	**256,107**	**332,629**	**461,343**	**585,240**	**557,815**	**547,230**
Sector:						
Non-financial corporations	160,026	207,972	280,798	359,180	386,082	365,909
Financial corporations	26,730	34,353	52,232	57,894	16,816	13,437
General government and non-profit institutions	49,855	66,712	97,173	131,116	100,983	111,806
Households	19,496	23,592	31,140	37,050	53,934	56,078
Type of management:						
Private	61,671	93,026	120,266	169,260	199,821	195,347
Cooperative	8,643	9,545	11,958	13,438	10,461	7,597
State	110,760	113,526	97,523	105,091	100,047	91,875
Municipal	15,112	25,974	41,311	67,310	47,807	50,831
Other	59,921	90,558	190,285	230,141	199,679	201,580
	(In millions of CZK, constant 1994 prices)					
Total	**283,889**	**330,208**	**430,180**	**508,245**	**454,999**	**429,233**
Sector:						
Non-financial corporations	176,148	206,286	262,997	315,018	320,277	294,334
Financial corporations	29,639	34,195	49,534	52,741	13,691	10,626
General government and non-profit institutions	56,034	66,227	88,862	109,028	77,945	81,676
Households	22,068	23,500	28,787	31,458	43,086	42,597
Type of management:						
Private	68,369	92,347	112,081	146,727	163,763	155,215
Cooperative	9,569	9,476	11,155	11,630	8,558	5,980
State	122,872	112,702	89,978	89,740	79,374	69,038
Municipal	17,070	25,795	37,457	55,818	36,234	35,962
Other	66,009	89,888	179,509	204,330	167,070	163,038

1/ Preliminary data.
2/ Converted into constant prices by quarter through quarterly price indices.

Source: Czech Statistical Office.

Table 2.6. Household Current Incomes and Expenditures, 1996-98

	1996	1997	1998
	(Index against the same period of previous year)		
Current incomes	115.2	108.8	105.7
of which:			
- employee remuneration	117.8	106.9	106.3
- mixed income	105.6	100.8	105.4
- property income	109.1	121.0	107.4
- social benefits	117.0	113.5	109.9
- other current transfers	124.0	128.2	87.9
Current expenditures	116.7	108.0	106.3
of which:			
- property income	100.2	100.5	95.9
- current taxes on income and wealth	118.1	109.8	107.6
- social contributions	115.5	107.1	105.8
- other current transfers	132.4	113.6	111.2
Disposable income	114.5	109.2	105.5
Changes in net share of households in pension fund reserves	160.6	95.8	82.4
Expenditures on individual consumption	115.6	110.0	106.5
Savings	109.7	102.2	95.5
Household savings ratio (savings/disposable income - ratio in percent)	95.8	93.5	90.6

Source: Czech Statistical Office.

Table 2.7. Structure of the Money Income of Households
by Social Group, 1998

	Households		Self--employed	Farmers	Pensioners
	Employees	including: Families with children			
	(per household member)				
Money income, total (CZK)	**100,544**	**85,791**	**87,077**	**80,363**	**70,152**
Structure (percent):					
Income					
from employment	85.4	85.0	87.8	83.9	3.2
including:					
From main					
employment					
Head of household	55.1	54.8	53.6	52.0	0.0
Wife	24.7	25.4	28.8	26.4	0.0
Other members	2.8	2.0	3.3	2.6	0.0
Social income	8.2	7.9	6.6	11.2	93.4
including:					
Pensions	3.3	1.4	2.3	3.2	93.0
Sickness benefits	1.3	1.1	0.7	2.0	0.0
Children's allowance	1.4	2.2	1.3	2.4	0.0
Other income	6.5	7.1	5.6	4.9	3.4
Deposits withdrawn (CZK)	30,022	26,361	21,782	16,460	10,864

Source: Czech Statistical Office (Family Budget Statistics).

Table 2.8. Structure of the Money Expenditure of Households by Social Group, 1998

	Households				
	Employees	including: Families with children	Self--employed	Farmers	Pensioners
	(per household member)				
Money expenditure, total (CZK)	**96,067**	**82,282**	**88,807**	**78,879**	**71,076**
Structure (percent):					
Food	20.4	21.2	22.0	21.2	31.7
including:					
Meat and meat products	4.4	4.3	4.7	4.0	8.5
Fats and oils	0.8	0.8	0.8	1.0	1.8
Eggs, milk, cheese	3.2	3.5	3.4	3.3	5.0
Bread, pastries, cereal products, rice	2.5	2.7	2.5	3.3	4.2
Potatoes, vegetables and products therefrom	1.2	1.2	1.3	0.9	2.1
Fruits and fruit products	1.1	1.1	1.2	1.0	1.9
Sugar and confectionery	1.1	1.1	1.2	1.4	1.9
Non-alcoholic beverages	1.2	1.3	1.4	1.2	1.3
Public catering	3.3	3.5	3.6	3.2	1.7
Alcoholic beverages, tobacco	2.7	2.5	3.1	3.1	3.1
Clothing and footwear	6.1	6.6	7.6	6.3	4.5
Housing	14.7	14.4	18.5	12.6	26.0
including:					
Rent and municipal services	3.9	3.8	4.2	1.7	7.3
Central heating, hot water	2.8	2.6	2.6	0.5	5.4
Electricity and gas	3.5	3.5	4.4	5.1	6.9
Household equipment and operation	7.0	6.6	7.9	9.2	8.3
Personal and medical care	4.3	4.5	4.8	3.9	4.8
including:					
Personal care products	3.1	3.2	3.4	2.6	2.9
Transport and communications	9.6	9.6	9.6	10.8	6.2
including:					
Purchase and operation of personal transport equipment	6.6	6.5	6.5	8.0	3.1
Culture, education, sports, recreation	8.5	9.3	11.1	7.1	6.4
including:					
Pastime related equipment	2.8	3.2	3.3	2.6	1.3
Leisure services	1.4	1.5	1.6	1.2	1.8
Recreation in CR and abroad	2.6	2.7	4.1	1.7	1.4
Taxes, insurance, payments	26.7	25.4	15.4	25.8	9.0
including:					
Income tax	8.7	8.2	3.1	7.0	0.4
Health and social insurance	10.7	10.6	3.9	10.1	0.0
Deposits (CZK)	34,007	29,492	19,847	17,471	9,406

Source: Czech Statistical Office (Family Budget Statistics).

Table 2.9. Gross Agricultural Output, 1990-98

	1990	1993	1994	1995	1996	1997	1998
				(at constant 1989 prices)			
Gross agricultural output, total (CZK thousand)	106,142,680	83,058,765	78,090,204	82,030,749	80,916,103	76,802,916	77,350,760
Crop production	44,416,849	37,387,204	34,679,038	35,693,854	36,438,241	35,137,980	34,534,747
including:							
Cereals	19,563,447	14,673,539	14,929,573	14,446,535	14,508,426	15,178,163	14,568,975
Industrial crops	4,431,530	4,302,075	4,503,012	5,916,627	5,359,640	5,025,557	5,946,712
Fodder and feed root crops	9,155,939	7,216,856	6,520,574	6,704,598	6,640,065	6,380,907	5,576,531
Potatoes	3,159,522	4,312,458	2,215,865	2,394,214	3,240,490	2,522,993	2,735,582
Vegetables	2,007,414	1,891,765	1,733,134	1,808,684	2,023,672	1,786,778	1,824,422
Fruit and grapes	2,415,028	2,307,160	2,132,992	1,856,284	2,180,052	2,013,580	2,094,620
Hops	912,300	945,300	949,000	988,900	1,012,500	741,500	489,600
Livestock production	61,725,831	45,671,561	43,411,166	46,336,895	44,477,862	41,664,936	42,816,013
including:							
Livestock for slaughter	29,498,634	25,745,612	22,750,897	23,637,483	23,297,898	21,849,757	20,323,049
including:							
Cattle	14,283,780	11,118,716	8,905,148	8,942,640	8,604,428	7,955,416	6,617,660
Pigs	14,807,100	14,390,340	13,639,260	14,515,720	14,539,900	13,597,560	13,398,100
Milk	21,611,351	15,076,112	14,107,838	13,639,910	13,676,805	12,165,719	12,223,427
Eggs	3,703,977	3,043,183	2,950,828	2,894,715	2,800,682	3,156,191	3,434,213
Gross agricultural output per 1 person engaged in agriculture (CZK)	191,039	291,303	270,587	316,786	325,172	333,930	348,983
Crop production	79,943	131,124	120,165	137,842	146,432	152,776	155,810
Livestock production	111,096	160,179	150,422	178,944	178,740	181,154	193,173
Gross agricultural output per 1 hectare of agricultural land (CZK)	25,040	19,395	18,239	19,164	18,907	17,946	18,064
Crop production	10,478	8,730	8,100	8,339	8,514	8,210	8,065
Livestock production	14,562	10,665	10,139	10,825	10,393	9,736	9,999

Source: Czech Statistical Office.

Table 2.10. Agricultural Production, 1993-98

	1993	1994	1995	1996	1997	1998
	(Annual percentage change; at constant prices)					
Total gross agricultural production	-2.3	-6.0	5.0	-1.4	-5.1	0.7
Crop production	4.6	-7.2	2.9	2.1	-3.6	-1.7
Of which:						
Grains	-0.1	1.7	-3.2	0.4	4.6	-4.0
Fodder and root crops	5.7	-9.6	2.8	-1.0	-3.9	-12.6
Potatoes	21.7	-48.6	8.0	35.3	-22.1	8.4
Vegetables	18.6	-8.4	4.4	11.9	-11.7	2.1
Animal production	-7.3	-4.9	6.7	-4.0	-6.3	2.8
Of which:						
Livestock for slaughter	-2.0	-11.6	3.9	-1.4	-6.2	-7.0
Of which:						
Cattle	-5.7	-19.9	0.4	-3.8	-7.5	-16.8
Pigs	1.2	-5.2	6.4	0.2	-6.5	-1.5
Milk	-9.5	-6.4	-3.3	0.3	-11.0	0.5
Eggs	-10.7	-3.0	-1.9	-3.2	12.7	8.8

Source: Czech Statistical Office.

Table 3.1. Balance of Payments, 1993-98

	1993	1994	1995	1996	1997	1998[1]
	(In millions of US Dollars)					
A. Current Account	**455.8**	**-786.8**	**-1,369.1**	**-4,292.2**	**-3,211.0**	**-1,046.1**
Trade balance[2]	-525.3	-1,381.2	-3,677.9	-5,877.3	-4,540.4	-2,580.7
Exports	14,229.0	15,929.0	21,462.5	21,690.6	22,776.7	26,358.3
Imports	14,754.3	17,310.2	25,140.4	27,567.9	27,317.1	28,939.0
Balance of services	1,010.8	488.3	1,842.0	1,923.0	1,763.3	1,882.3
Credit	4,722.9	5,156.5	6,717.8	8,179.4	7,162.2	7,406.1
Transportation	1,241.2	1,242.5	1,460.5	1,333.9	1,313.4	1,345.9
Travel	1,558.5	2,229.7	2,875.2	4,075.2	3,647.4	3,718.9
Other services	1,923.2	1,684.3	2,382.1	2,770.3	2,201.4	2,341.3
Debit	3,712.1	4,668.2	4,875.8	6,256.4	5,398.9	5,523.8
Transportation	734.1	852.8	799.3	699.3	629.7	608.8
Travel	527.1	1,584.6	1,632.8	2,953.4	2,380.1	1,868.7
Other services	2,450.9	2,230.8	2,443.7	2,603.7	2,389.1	3,046.3
Income balance	-117.5	-20.2	-105.6	-722.5	-791.3	-750.4
Credit	547.2	789.1	1,194.5	1,170.2	1,409.1	1,484.7
Debit	664.7	809.3	1,300.1	1,892.7	2,200.4	2,235.1
Current transfers	87.8	126.3	572.4	384.6	357.4	402.7
Credit	241.0	296.1	664.4	617.2	863.9	773.3
Debit	153.2	169.8	92.0	232.6	506.5	370.6
B. Capital Account	**-554.8**	**..**	**6.8**	**0.6**	**9.9**	**2.1**
Credit	205.0	..	11.6	1.0	15.5	14.1
Debit	759.8	..	4.8	0.4	5.6	12.0
C. Financial Account	**3,024.8**	**3,371.1**	**8,225.9**	**4,184.3**	**1,081.9**	**2,630.7**
Direct investment	563.3	748.9	2,525.6	1,275.5	1,275.2	2,484.6
Abroad[3]	-90.2	-119.6	-36.6	-152.9	-25.2	-55.0
In the Czech Republic	653.5	868.5	2,562.2	1,428.4	1,300.4	2,539.6
Portfolio investment	1,600.5	854.6	1,362.0	725.5	1,085.7	1,012.8
Assets	-229.3	-46.1	-322.8	-47.5	-189.4	-80.0
Equity securities	-229.3	-46.1	-322.8	-47.5	0.6	74.5
Debt securities					-190.0	-154.5
Liabilities	1,829.8	900.7	1,684.8	773.0	1,275.1	1,092.8
Equity securities	1,117.2	499.3	1,234.6	602.0	434.5	1,079.9
Debt securities	712.6	401.4	450.2	171.0	840.6	12.9
Other investment	861.0	1,767.6	4,338.3	2,183.3	-1,279.0	-866.7
Assets	-2,878.2	-2,417.7	-2,489.0	-2,381.5	-4,499.4	-1,573.9
Long-term	457.6	418.6	52.2	-396.7	-350.5	-770.6
Short-term	-3,335.8	-2,836.3	-2,541.2	-1,984.8	-4,148.9	-803.3
Liabilities	3,739.2	4,185.3	6,827.3	4,564.8	3,220.4	707.2
Long-term	347.5	690.2	3,314.9	3,506.8	758.1	-135.9
Short-term	3,391.7	3,495.1	3,512.4	1,058.0	2,462.3	843.1
D. Net errors and omissions, valuation changes	**103.5**	**-212.7**	**594.5**	**-720.7**	**352.5**	**353.8**
E. Change in reserves (-increase)	**-3,029.3**	**-2,371.6**	**-7,458.1**	**828.0**	**1,766.7**	**-1,949.5**
Memo:						
	(percent of GDP)					
Current Account Balance	1.3	-1.9	-2.6	-7.4	-6.1	-1.9
Trade Balance	-1.5	-3.4	-7.1	-10.1	-8.6	-4.9
Direct Foreign Investment	1.6	1.8	4.9	2.2	2.4	4.7

1/ Preliminary data.

2/ Based on data published by the Czech Statistical Office - according to methodology for customs statistics in effect from 1.1.1996.

3/ Adjusted outflow of direct investment capital (based on the results of a survey of the corporate sector).

Source: Czech National Bank. Based on the 5th edition of the Balance of Payments Manual (IMF 1993).

Table 3.2. Geographical Composition of Exports and Imports, 1994-98

	1994	1995	1996[1]	1997[2]	1998[3]	1994	1995	1996	1997	1998
	(In millions of U.S. dollars)					(In percent of total)				
Imports, f.o.b.	16,206	21,657	21,906	22,777	26,351	100.0	100.0	100.0	100.0	100.0
Former planned economies	4,677	6,185	6,728	6,802	7,007	28.9	28.6	30.7	29.9	26.6
Of which:										
China	90	95	71	48	45	0.6	0.4	0.3	0.2	0.2
Former CMEA										
Bulgaria	58	76	67	61	97	0.4	0.3	0.3	0.3	0.4
Hungary	371	378	391	428	501	2.3	1.7	1.8	1.9	1.9
Poland	557	966	1,205	1,307	1,490	3.4	4.5	5.5	5.7	5.7
Slovak Republic	2,366	3,005	3,120	2,941	2,806	14.6	13.9	14.2	12.9	10.6
Former Soviet Union	866	1,090	1,203	1,321	1,254	5.3	5.0	5.5	5.8	4.8
Industrial countries	10,454	14,295	13,939	14,856	18,320	64.5	66.0	63.6	65.2	69.5
Of which:										
EU	9,584	13,198	12,755	13,650	16,914	59.1	60.9	58.2	59.9	64.2
Austria	1,158	1,425	1,411	1,463	1,658	7.1	6.6	6.4	6.4	6.3
France	395	569	626	724	890	2.4	2.6	2.9	3.2	3.4
Italy	675	806	720	834	991	4.2	3.7	3.3	3.7	3.8
Germany	5,616	8,134	7,890	8,141	10,153	34.7	37.6	36.0	35.7	38.5
United Kingdom	540	687	552	690	895	3.3	3.2	2.5	3.0	3.4
Netherlands	392	517	454	551	596	2.4	2.4	2.1	2.4	2.3
Switzerland	222	286	260	276	329	1.4	1.3	1.2	1.2	1.2
United States	333	415	465	586	589	2.1	1.9	2.1	2.6	2.2
Other, Developing Countries	1,065	1,161	1,218	1,106	1,011	6.6	5.4	5.6	4.9	3.8
Of which:										
India	58	81	84	65	48	0.4	0.4	0.4	0.3	0.2
Hong Kong, China	118	71	104	66	69	0.7	0.3	0.5	0.3	0.3
Egypt	125	81	93	90	95	0.8	0.4	0.4	0.4	0.4
Singapore	72	122	70	73	78	0.4	0.6	0.3	0.3	0.3
Exports f.o.b.	17,427	25,265	27,716	27,167	28,788	100.0	100.0	100.0	99.9	99.9
Former planned economies	4,779	6,668	6,811	6,744	6,579	27.4	26.4	24.6	24.8	22.9
Of which:										
China	106	209	298	377	499	0.6	0.8	1.1	1.4	1.7
Former CMEA										
Bulgaria	15	18	23	22	22	0.1	0.1	0.1	0.1	0.1
Hungary	179	218	276	355	396	1.0	0.9	1.0	1.3	1.4
Poland	449	682	807	870	969	2.6	2.7	2.9	3.2	3.4
Slovak Republic	2,317	2,984	2,650	2,272	2,072	13.3	11.8	9.6	8.4	7.2
Former Soviet Union	1,494	2,226	2,361	2,187	1,931	8.6	8.8	8.5	8.0	6.7
Industrial countries	11,819	17,476	19,497	19,058	20,842	67.8	69.2	70.3	70.2	72.4
Of which:										
EU	10,381	15,431	17,297	16,701	18,281	59.6	61.1	62.4	61.5	63.5
Austria	1,403	1,746	1,594	1,647	1,687	8.0	6.9	5.8	6.1	5.9
France	626	1,016	1,161	1,119	1,289	3.6	4.0	4.2	4.1	4.5
Italy	839	928	1,633	1,494	1,507	4.8	3.7	5.9	5.5	5.2
Germany	5,250	8,003	8,261	8,666	9,941	30.1	31.7	29.8	31.9	34.5
United Kingdom	619	952	1,042	1,054	1,096	3.6	3.8	3.8	3.9	3.8
Netherlands	470	664	630	655	689	2.7	2.6	2.3	2.4	2.4
Switzerland	362	485	488	449	513	2.1	1.9	1.8	1.7	1.8
United States	549	852	939	1,029	1,077	3.2	3.4	3.4	3.8	3.7
Other, Developing countries	823	1,112	1,390	1,335	1,328	4.7	4.4	5.0	4.9	4.6
Of which:										
India	50	61	83	64	74	0.3	0.2	0.3	0.2	0.3
Hong Kong, China	74	104	109	84	89	0.4	0.4	0.4	0.3	0.3
Egypt	7	9	16	8	11	0.0	0.0	0.1	0.0	0.0
Singapore	40	70	54	54	59	0.2	0.3	0.2	0.2	0.2

1/ Final figures referring to the revision of July 15, 1997.
2/ Preliminary figures referring to the revision of January 15, 1998.
3/ Final figures referring to the revision of July 20, 1999.

Source: Czech Statistical Office.

Table 3.3. External Trade by Destination, 1993-98 (Continued)

	1993	1994	1995	1996[1]	1997[2]	1998[3]
			(In millions of CZK, FOB)			
Imports, total	426,084	501,549	670,445	752,344	861,770	928,939
Imports excl. Slovakia	358,338	434,851	591,268	630,398	789,689	862,073
OECD	273,547	341,552	490,378	542,473	655,518	732,519
Developed market economies	273,392	340,145	463,751	529,252	604,540	672,540
EU	239,297	298,758	409,484	469,514	529,765	589,880
Germany	124,102	151,108	212,379	224,244	274,908	320,782
Austria	32,756	40,367	46,327	43,273	52,238	54,438
EFTA	10,583	12,108	15,070	15,215	18,695	21,198
Other market economies	23,512	29,279	39,197	44,523	56,080	61,462
Developing economies	19,177	23,681	29,504	37,720	42,339	42,843
European transition and CIS economies	130,614	134,245	170,937	176,253	200,894	194,891
CEFTA	85,844	89,174	109,534	109,567	128,648	130,372
Slovakia	67,746	66,692	79,177	71,946	72,081	66,866
Others transition economies and economies with a state trade system	2,522	3,291	6,017	8,642	13,040	17,390
China	2,308	3,053	5,552	8,096	11,971	16,087
Unspecified	379	187	236	477	958	1,275
Exports, total	421,601	466,403	574,722	594,629	722,501	850,308
Exports excl. Slovakia	338,401	398,322	494,966	509,935	629,197	759,761
OECD	244,816	300,400	415,772	421,292	530,593	655,195
Developed market economies	242,352	300,865	379,334	378,363	471,232	591,164
EU	222,260	275,834	350,231	346,239	432,978	545,767
Germany	127,406	161,632	215,860	214,163	258,251	327,610
Austria	25,427	33,320	37,810	38,312	46,420	53,504
EFTA	4,107	7,827	9,651	9,635	12,141	14,905
Other market economies	13,985	17,204	19,452	22,489	26,113	30,492
Developing economies	33,023	30,642	30,818	33,053	35,086	32,617
European transition and CIS economies	137,519	131,454	160,712	179,937	213,414	223,467
CEFTA	107,296	99,529	122,713	135,678	159,424	172,282
Slovakia	83,200	68,081	79,756	84,694	93,304	90,547
Others transition economies and economies with a state trade system	8,448	3,147	3,410	2,706	2,365	2,620
China	7,373	2,587	2,509	1,938	1,537	1,457
Unspecified	259	295	448	570	404	439
Balance, total	-4,483	-35,146	-95,723	-157,715	-139,269	-78,631
Balance excl. Slovakia	-19,937	-36,529	-96,302	-120,463	-160,492	-102,312
OECD	-28,731	-41,152	-74,606	-121,181	-124,925	-77,324
Developed market economies	-31,040	-39,280	-84,417	-150,889	-133,308	-81,376
EU	-17,037	-22,924	-59,253	-123,275	-96,787	-44,113
Germany	3,304	10,524	3,481	-10,081	-16,657	6,828
Austria	-7,329	-7,047	-8,517	-4,961	-5,818	-934
EFTA	-6,476	-4,281	-5,419	-5,580	-6,554	-6,293
Other market economies	-9,527	-12,075	-19,745	-22,034	-29,967	-30,970
Developing economies	13,846	6,961	1,314	-4,667	-7,253	-10,226
European transition and CIS economies	6,905	-2,791	-10,225	3,684	12,520	28,576
CEFTA	21,452	10,355	13,179	26,111	30,776	41,910
Slovakia	15,454	1,389	579	12,748	21,223	23,681
Others transition economies and economies with a state trade system	5,926	-144	-2,607	-5,936	-10,675	-14,770
China	5,065	-466	-3,043	-6,158	-10,434	-14,630
Unspecified	-120	108	212	93	-554	-836

Note: In the whole series, the economic groupings include countries belonging there now. The German Democratic Republic and West Berlin are included in Germany.
The statistics are based on customs declarations.
1/ Final figures referring to the revision of July 15, 1997.
2/ Preliminary figures referring to the revision of January 15, 1998.
3/ Final figures referring to the revision of July 20, 1999.

Source: Czech Statistical Office.

Table 3.3. External Trade by Destination, 1993-98

	1993	1994	1995	1996[1]	1997[2]	1998[3]
	(as percent of GDP, FOB)					
Imports, total	42.5	42.4	48.5	47.8	51.3	51.0
Imports excl. Slovakia	35.8	36.8	42.8	40.1	47.0	47.3
OECD	27.3	28.9	35.5	34.5	39.4	40.2
Developed market econ	27.3	28.8	33.6	33.7	36.0	36.9
EU	23.9	25.3	29.6	29.9	31.5	32.4
Germany	12.4	12.8	15.4	14.3	16.4	17.6
Austria	3.3	3.4	3.4	2.8	3.1	3.0
EFTA	1.1	1.0	1.1	1.0	1.1	1.2
Other market economie	2.3	2.5	2.8	2.8	3.3	3.4
Developing economies	1.9	2.0	2.1	2.4	2.5	2.4
European transition						
and CIS economies	13.0	11.4	12.4	11.2	12.0	10.7
CEFTA	8.6	7.5	7.9	7.0	7.7	7.2
Slovakia	6.8	5.6	5.7	4.6	4.3	3.7
Others transition economies and						
economies with a state	0.3	0.3	0.4	0.5	0.8	1.0
China	0.2	0.3	0.4	0.5	0.7	0.9
Unspecified	0.0	0.0	0.0	0.0	0.1	0.1
Exports, total	42.1	39.4	41.6	37.8	43.0	46.7
Exports excl. Slovakia	33.8	33.7	35.8	32.4	37.5	41.7
OECD	24.4	25.4	30.1	26.8	31.6	36.0
Developed market econ	24.2	25.4	27.5	24.1	28.0	32.5
EU	22.2	23.3	25.4	22.0	25.8	30.0
Germany	12.7	13.7	15.6	13.6	15.4	18.0
Austria	2.5	2.8	2.7	2.4	2.8	2.9
EFTA	0.4	0.7	0.7	0.6	0.7	0.8
Other market economie	1.4	1.5	1.4	1.4	1.6	1.7
Developing economies	3.3	2.6	2.2	2.1	2.1	1.8
European transition						
and CIS economies	13.7	11.1	11.6	11.4	12.7	12.3
CEFTA	10.7	8.4	8.9	8.6	9.5	9.5
Slovakia	8.3	5.8	5.8	5.4	5.6	5.0
Others transition economies and						
economies with a state	0.8	0.3	0.2	0.2	0.1	0.1
China	0.7	0.2	0.2	0.1	0.1	0.1
Unspecified	0.0	0.0	0.0	0.0	0.0	0.0
Balance, total	-0.4	-3.0	-6.9	-10.0	-8.3	-4.3
Balance excl. Slovakia	-2.0	-3.1	-7.0	-7.7	-9.6	-5.6
OECD	-2.9	-3.5	-5.4	-7.7	-7.8	-4.2
Developed market econ	-3.1	-3.3	-6.1	-9.6	-7.9	-4.5
EU	-1.7	-1.9	-4.3	-7.8	-5.8	-2.4
Germany	0.3	0.9	0.3	-0.6	-1.0	0.4
Austria	-0.7	-0.6	-0.6	-0.3	-0.3	-0.1
EFTA	-0.6	-0.4	-0.4	-0.4	-0.4	-0.3
Other market economie	-1.0	-1.0	-1.4	-1.4	-1.8	-1.7
Developing economies	1.4	0.6	0.1	-0.3	-0.4	-0.6
European transition						
and CIS economies	0.7	-0.2	-0.7	0.2	0.7	1.6
CEFTA	2.1	0.9	1.0	1.7	1.8	2.3
Slovakia	1.5	0.1	0.0	0.8	1.3	1.3
Others transition economies and						
economies with a state	0.6	0.0	-0.2	-0.4	-0.6	-0.8
China	0.5	0.0	-0.2	-0.4	-0.6	-0.8
Unspecified	0.0	0.0	0.0	0.0	0.0	0.0

Note: In the whole series, the economic groupings include countries belonging there now. The German Democratic Republic and West Berlin are included in Germany.
The statistics are based on customs declarations.
1/ Final figures referring to the revision of July 15, 1997.
2/ Preliminary figures referring to the revision of January 15, 1998.
3/ Final figures referring to the revision of July 20, 1999.

Source: Czech Statistical Office.

Table 3.4. Commodity Composition of Exports, 1994-98

(In millions of US Dollars)

SITC[4]	Description	Former Planned Countries					Advanced Market Countries					Total				
		1994	1995	1996[1]	1997[2]	1998[3]	1994	1995	1996[1]	1997[2]	1998[3]	1994	1995	1996[1]	1997[2]	1998[3]
0	Food and live animals	304	486	462	485	530	445	556	419	347	348	749	1,043	883	833	880
1	Beverages and tobacco	104	109	134	168	174	54	65	89	122	115	158	174	223	290	289
2	Crude materials inedible, except fuels	165	216	174	157	145	813	899	887	759	766	978	1,118	1,063	919	912
3	Minerals, fuels, lubricants, and related materials	386	404	409	349	347	410	510	574	502	486	800	924	992	855	839
4	Animal and vegetable oils, and fats	26	19	27	25	31	21	15	11	11	11	47	34	38	36	42
5	Chemicals	633	825	946	944	958	854	1,188	1,031	1,060	1,072	1,487	2,013	1,977	2,005	2,030
6	Manufactured goods, classified chiefly by material	1,165	1,726	1,906	1,816	1,999	3,753	5,253	4,397	4,278	4,973	4,923	6,979	6,310	6,096	6,974
7	Machinery and transport equipment	1,379	1,734	1,890	2,175	2,137	3,267	4,849	5,278	6,415	8,735	4,646	6,584	7,168	8,591	10,873
8	Miscellaneous manufactured articles	513	665	774	680	683	1,886	2,101	2,447	2,446	2,798	2,399	2,766	3,222	3,127	3,481
9	Miscellaneous transactions and commodities not classified	2	2	6	5	4	16	19	23	22	27	18	21	29	26	31
Total	SITC 0-9	4,677	6,185	6,728	6,802	7,007	11,519	15,456	15,156	15,962	19,331	16,206	21,657	21,906	22,777	26,351

1/ Final figures referring to the revision of July 15, 1997.
2/ Preliminary figures referring to the revision of January 15, 1998.
3/ Final figures referring to the revision of July 20, 1999.
4/ Standard International Trade Classification.

Source: Czech Statistical Office.

Table 3.5. Commodity Composition of Imports, 1993-98

(In millions of US Dollars)

SITC[4]	Description	Former Planned Countries						Advanced Market Countries						Total					
		1993	1994	1995	1996[1]	1997[2]	1998[3]	1993	1994	1995	1996[1]	1997[2]	1998[3]	1993	1994	1995	1996[1]	1997[2]	1998[3]
0	Food and live animals	188	227	283	306	328	369	639	832	1,117	1,279	1,077	1,052	828	1,060	1,400	1,586	1,406	1,422
1	Beverages and tobacco	49	62	50	44	51	53	87	130	149	198	236	195	136	192	198	242	287	248
2	Crude materials inedible, except fuels	435	461	587	509	498	557	289	352	537	507	512	563	726	814	1,128	1,020	1,012	1,122
3	Minerals, fuels, lubricants, and related	1,276	1,263	1,776	2,061	1,912	1,440	112	227	202	355	437	427	1,387	1,490	1,978	2,416	2,348	1,867
4	Animal and vegetable oils, and fats	6	8	12	12	11	14	42	49	65	69	55	74	48	57	78	81	66	88
5	Chemicals	472	541	746	717	702	656	1,158	1,532	2,239	2,553	2,618	2,835	1,631	2,073	2,986	3,270	3,321	3,491
6	Manufactured goods, classified chiefly by material	993	1,127	1,679	1,540	1,480	1,667	1,422	2,084	3,444	3,802	3,766	4,331	2,420	3,212	5,123	5,345	5,250	6,006
7	Machinery and transport equipment	806	723	1,004	1,079	1,097	1,188	4,756	5,585	8,357	9,488	9,218	10,150	5,565	6,309	9,363	10,572	10,324	11,351
8	Miscellaneous manufactured articles	340	366	529	543	664	634	1,471	1,831	2,458	2,627	2,465	2,530	1,813	2,200	2,989	3,175	3,143	3,179
9	Miscellaneous transactions and commodities not classified	2	2	2	1	1	2	60	18	20	8	8	13	62	20	22	9	9	15
Total	SITC 0-9	4,567	4,779	6,668	6,811	6,744	6,579	10,037	12,642	18,587	20,887	20,393	22,170	14,617	17,427	25,265	27,716	27,167	28,788

1/ Final figures referring to the revision of July 15, 1997.
2/ Preliminary figures referring to the revision of January 15, 1998.
3/ Final figures referring to the revision of July 20, 1999.
4/ Standard International Trade Classification.

Source: Czech Statistical Office.

Table 3.6. Foreign Direct Investment by Industry and Country, 1993-98

	1993	1994	1995	1996	1997	1998
	(In millions of US Dollars)					
Nonmanufacturing						
Agriculture, hunting, and forestry	2	1	8	0	7	4
Mining and quarrying	14	21	23	7	0	0
Electricity, gas, and water supply	24	87	40	160	375	197
Construction	65	108	68	121	38	48
Trade, hotels and restaurants	40	35	147	283	124	562
Transport, storage and communications	3	10	1,350	184	1	295
Financial intermediation	55	132	65	33	298	472
Real estate and business activities	..	..	0	0	42	142
Education	..	..	0	0	0	0
Health and social work	..	..	0	0	7	19
Other social and personal services	..	..	0	0	0	0
Total	**203**	**394**	**1,701**	**788**	**892**	**1,739**
Manufacturing						
Food and tobacco	229	71	122	73	94	129
Textiles, wearing apparel, and leather	1	1	2	23	15	89
Wood, paper and publishing	0	0	0	81	102	90
Refined petroleum and chemicals	19	44	90	334	51	61
Nonmetallic products	49	60	177	61	17	34
Basic metals and metal products	0	0	0	0	79	267
Machinery and equipment	67	292	466	68	16	48
Recycling and other manufacturing	..	..	..	..	34	83
Total	**365**	**468**	**857**	**640**	**408**	**801**
Country						
Western Europe						
Belgium	32	33	25	57	56	45
Denmark	2	5	12	11	3	3
France	34	77	168	20	102	97
Germany	82	418	567	249	391	538
United Kingdom	0	38	53	84	196	337
Italy	12	12	736	90	-36	27
Netherlands	30	6	1	259	134	608
Austria	55	80	87	208	95	245
Sweden	12	19	22	56	89	3
Switzerland	14	39	679	55	47	83
Canada	20	0	0	0	0	3
United States	255	39	101	253	99	258
Japan	0	5	0	39	11	25
Other	20	91	107	47	113	268
Total	**568**	**862**	**2,558**	**1,428**	**1,300**	**2,540**

Source: Czech National Bank.

Table 3.7. International Investment Position, 1993-98

	1993	1994	1995	1996	1997	1998[1]
	(In millions of US Dollars)					
ASSETS	18,023.8	20,300.3	29,283.3	30,577.5	29,662.9	36,035.0
Direct investment abroad	182.6	298.6	344.7	497.8	546.8	656.6
Equity capital[2]	182.6	298.6	344.7	497.8	529.4	636.5
Other capital[3]	..	..	..	..	17.4	20.1
Portfolio investment	277.5	430.1	753.1	1,372.0	1,029.0	1,247.7
Equity securities	265.8	332.1	691.0	748.0	415.8	500.6
Debt securities	11.7	98.1	62.1	624.0	613.2	747.1
Other investment	13,666.6	13,366.0	14,193.1	16,276.0	18,339.7	21,599.6
Long-term	8,373.6	8,115.7	8,043.1	8,590.0	8,437.6	9,416.3
CNB	825.7	870.8	981.7	955.5	752.2	869.0
Commercial banks[4]	62.2	62.5	191.9	921.0	1,067.9	2,130.5
Government[5/6]	6,282.5	6,193.6	5,924.6	5,887.0	5,871.7	5,815.9
Other sectors	1,203.2	988.9	944.9	826.5	745.8	601.0
Short-term	5,293.0	5,250.2	6,150.0	7,686.0	9,902.1	12,183.3
CNB	0.2	0.2	0.2	0.2	0.0	0.0
Commercial banks[4]	2,793.5	2,863.9	3,269.9	4,699.4	7,217.7	9,055.9
gold and foreign exchange[7/8]	2,376.6	2,524.2	2,855.5	3,490.6	4,961.2	5,846.7
Government	184.9	..	..	..	..	..
Other sectors	2,314.5	2,386.1	2,879.9	2,986.5	2,684.4	3,127.4
Reserves	3,897.2	6,205.6	13,992.4	12,431.7	9,747.3	12,531.0
Gold[7]	82.9	81.8	83.8	83.8	43.8	12.3
SDR	8.3	..	0.2	..	..	..
Foreign exchange	3,806.0	6,123.8	13,908.4	12,348.0	9,703.5	12,518.8
LIABILITIES	14,221.7	17,978.0	27,123.1	33,140.9	32,774.2	40,145.3
Direct investment in the Czech Rep.	3,445.5	4,519.3	7,334.1	8,569.9	9,208.8	13,365.5
Equity capital[2]	3,445.5	4,519.3	7,334.1	8,569.9	8,196.8	12,196.3
Other capital[3]	..	..	..	..	1,012.0	1,169.2
Portfolio investment	1,968.5	2,892.2	4,686.2	5,296.5	4,867.1	5,526.6
Equity securities	1,108.4	1,323.0	2,636.2	3,396.8	3,019.4	3,767.4
Debt securities	860.2	1,569.2	2,050.0	1,899.8	1,847.7	1,759.2
Other investment	8,807.6	10,566.5	15,102.9	19,274.5	18,698.4	21,253.3
Long-term	6,465.9	7,345.5	10,479.7	13,709.4	12,273.8	13,044.3
CNB	1,132.3	60.1	93.5	83.1	63.0	62.7
Commercial banks[4]	543.5	922.8	3,387.1	5,247.0	4,120.9	4,134.6
Government[5]	2,765.3	2,712.0	1,995.5	1,609.5	1,094.2	798.2
Other sectors	2,024.8	3,650.6	5,003.7	6,769.7	6,995.7	8,048.8
Short-term	2,341.7	3,221.0	4,623.1	5,565.1	6,424.6	8,209.0
CNB	153.9	1.3	4.3	2.0	1.3	1.3
Commercial banks[4]	747.6	1,464.9	2,607.0	3,714.1	4,864.0	6,432.9
Government[5]	0.0	177.7	41.4	11.5	8.3	3.4
Other sectors	1,440.1	1,577.1	1,970.4	1,837.5	1,551.0	1,771.4
NET INVESTMENT POSITION	3,802.1	2,322.3	2,160.2	-2,563.4	-3,111.3	-4,110.3

1/ Preliminary data.

2/ Data on initial capital updated to include holdings in associated companies; since end 1997, initial capital has included reinvested profits.

3/ Starting with the position at end 1997, part of the credits stemming from credit relations between direct investors and companies have been transferred from other investment (other sectors) to direct investment (other capital).

4/ In connection with the introduction of CZK convertibility (1 October 1995), CZK assets and liabilities towards non-residents are included in the bank position. Non-resident CZK deposits are included in commercial bank short-term liabilities as of December 1994.

5/ During January 1993, part of the receivables and payables in convertible and non-convertible currencies were transferred from the CSOB position to the Ministry of Finance.

6/ Including foreign exchange shares in international non-monetary organizations (The World Bank, EBRD, IBEC, IIB).

7/ Gold worth USD42.22 per ounce.

8/ Foreign exchange - convertible currencies.

Source: Czech National Bank

Table 3.8. Official External Reserves and Other Foreign Assets, 1980-98

	1980	1985	1990	1991	1992	1993	1994	1995	1996	1997	1998
	(In millions of US Dollars, end of period)										
Gross external reserves	1,739	745	1,056	2,611	3,587	6,244	8,892	16,981	16,097	15,002	18,903
Gold	86	107	72	87	96	83	83	85	85	44	12
Foreign exchange	1,653	638	984	2,431	3,462	6,153	8,809	16,896	16,012	14,958	18,890
Held by central bank	368	433	236	730	727	3,781	6,161	13,939	12,352	9,730	12,605
Held by other banks	1,285	205	748	1,701	2,735	2,372	2,649	2,957	3,660	5,228	6,286
Holding of SDRs	..	..	..	93	28	8	0	0	0	0	0
Other foreign assets in convertible currencies	1,549	2,582	3,835	4,250	4,877	4,777	4,743	5,895	10,444	10,698	13,410
Held by enterprises	1,104	1,598	2,089	2,422	2,884	2,652	2,589	3,054	3,683	3,313	3,658
Held by government institutions	433	923	1,687	1,758	1,742	1,931	1,935	2,057	1,974	1,970	1,983
Long-term assets of other banks [1]	11	61	59	70	91	62	63	597	3,585	4,362	6,598
Direct investment abroad	..	..	..	..	160	132	156	186	1,203	1,053	1,171
Foreign assets in nonconvertible currencies [2]	1,638	1,545	2,187	6,146	5,242	4,596	4,538	4,044	4,047	4,044	3,969
Held by central bank	45	82	15	1	0	0	0	0	0	0	0
Held by other banks	343	310	1,060	3,888	3,161	2	1	10	0	0	0
Held by enterprises	517	681	474	528	307	277	240	154	132	127	96
Held by government institutions	732	472	639	1,728	1,770	4,310[3]	4,297	3,880	3,915	3,918	3,873
Direct investment abroad	..	..	..	..	4	7	0	0	0	0	0
Claims on the Slovak Republic in nonconvertible currencies [4]	..	..	..	..	..	2,289	2,252	2,427	0	0	0
Total	4,925	4,872	7,078	13,006	13,706	17,906	20,425	29,346	30,588	29,743	36,282

1/ Assets in CZK included from 1995.
2/ Excluding the Slovak Republic.
3/ Reflects assumption by the government of assets in nonconvertible currencies previously held by the Ceskoslovenska Obchodni Banka (CSOB).
4/ Effective 1996, these are treated as foreign assets in convertible currencies.

Source: Czech National Bank.

Table 4.1. External Indebtedness, 1993-98

	1993 beginning	1993	1994	1995	1996	1997	1998[1]
	(In millions of US Dollars, end of period unless otherwise specified)						
Debt in convertible currencies	**7,082.4**	**8,495.7**	**10,694.2**	**16,548.8**	**20,844.6**	**21,352.4**	**24,046.4**
of which:							
Long-term	**5,283.7**	**6,493.9**	**7,805.8**	**11,504.2**	**14,823.1**	**14,293.2**	**15,464.7**
by debtor:							
CNB	1,224.9	1,964.1	814.5	837.1	409.0	333.4	366.9
Commercial banks	501.4	540.0	984.7	3,587.5	5,516.6	4,576.2	4,467.5
Government	2,115.9	1,985.6	2,202.0	1,958.5	1,710.1	1,237.9	1,109.8
Other sectors	1,441.5	2,004.2	3,804.6	5,121.1	7,187.4	8,145.7	9,520.5
by creditor:							
Foreign banks	2,149.6	2,765.8	4,428.9	8,206.6	11,009.5	10,414.7	10,853.7
Governments	231.4	245.3	266.7	264.6	242.6	209.9	147.7
Multilateral institutions	1,734.5	1,765.7	709.1	713.8	645.6	401.1	241.9
Suppliers and direct investors	1,004.3	862.5	1,162.3	923.5	992.1	1,341.6	1,819.7
Other investors	163.9	854.6	1,238.8	1,395.7	1,933.3	1,925.9	2,401.7
Short-term	**1,798.7**	**2,001.8**	**2,888.4**	**5,044.6**	**6,021.5**	**7,059.2**	**8,581.7**
by debtor:							
CNB	0.3	152.9	1.4	4.3	2.0	1.3	1.3
Commercial banks	616.6	705.0	1,162.6	2,703.3	3,909.5	4,912.4	6,477.1
Government			339.9	568.2	101.9	235.7	0.7
Other sectors	1,181.8	1,143.9	1,384.5	1,768.8	2,008.1	1,909.8	2,102.6
by creditor:							
Foreign banks	394.6	743.0	1,014.9	2,213.2	3,125.4	4,113.1	5,744.6
Multilateral institutions							
Suppliers and direct investors	1,144.3	990.3	1,216.9	1,578.3	1,679.9	1,669.7	1,886.2
Other investors	259.8	268.5	656.6	1,253.1	1,216.2	1,276.4	950.9
Debt in non-convertible currencies	**679.9**	**1,109.2**	**1,515.5**	**641.5**	**335.9**	**264.1**	**301.3**
of which:							
Long-term	362.4	784.5	823.3	394.1	324.4	255.8	297.9
Short-term	317.5	324.7	692.2	247.4	11.5	8.3	3.4
TOTAL EXTERNAL DEBT	**7,762.3**	**9,604.9**	**12,209.7**	**17,190.3**	**21,180.5**	**21,616.5**	**24,347.7**
of which:							
Long-term	5,646.1	7,278.4	8,629.1	11,898.3	15,147.5	14,549.0	15,762.6
Short-term	2,116.2	2,326.5	3,580.6	5,292.0	6,033.0	7,067.5	8,585.1

1/ Preliminary data.

Source: Czech National Bank.

Table 4.2. External Debt in Convertible and Nonconvertible Currencies, 1980-98

	1980	1985	1990	1992	1993	1994	1995	1996	1997	1998
					(In millions of US Dollars, end of period)					
Debt in convertible currencies										
Medium- and long-term	1,936	1,835	3,557	5,284	6,494	7,806	11,504	14,823	14,293	15,464
By maturity										
1-5 years	473	854	1,321	2,094	2,530	4,170	7,155	..	..	..
Over 5 years	1,463	981	2,236	3,190	3,964	3,636	4,349	..	..	..
By creditor										
Banks	1,373	1,273	2,193	2,298	2,766	4,429	8,207	11,009	10,414	10,854
Governments	5	0	0	231	245	267	265	243	210	148
Multilateral institutions	0	0	0	1,594	1,766	709	714	646	401	242
Suppliers' credits	322	488	1,192	1,020	863	1,162	923	992	1,342	1,819
Other investors	236	74	172	141	855	1,239	1,396	1,933	1,926	2,402
By debtor										
Banks	n.a.	n.a.	n.a.	n.a.	2,504	1,799	4,425	5,926	4,910	4,834
Of which: commercial banks	n.a.	n.a.	n.a.	n.a.	540	985	3,588	5,517	4,576	4,468
Government	n.a.	n.a.	n.a.	n.a.	1,986	2,202	1,959	1,710	1,238	1,110
Corporations and other	n.a.	n.a.	n.a.	n.a.	2,004	3,805	5,121	7,187	8,146	9,520
Short-term	3,790	1,539	2,400	1,798	2,002	2,888	5,045	6,022	7,059	8,582
Of which: liabilities in CZK	n.a.	n.a.	n.a.	n.a.	n.a.	n.a.	757	1,783	..	..
Total	5,726	3,374	5,957	7,082	8,496	10,694	16,549	20,845	21,352	24,046
Debt in nonconvertible currencies[1]										
Medium- and long-term	125	54	39	344	770	812	357	324	256	298
Short-term	659	750	1,032	27	7	245	0	0	0	0
Total	784	804	1,071	371	776	1,057	357	324	256	298
Total debt[2]	6,510	4,178	7,028	7,453	9,605	12,210	17,190	21,181	21,608	24,344
Medium- and long-term	2,061	1,889	3,596	5,627	7,278	8,629	11,898	15,148	14,549	15,762
Short-term	4,449	2,289	3,432	1,826	2,327	3,580	5,292	6,033	7,059	8,582

1/ Excluding the Slovak Republic. Total debt to the Slovak Republic at the end of 1995 was US$285 million, of which US$247 million was short-term, and the remainder medium- and long-term. At end-September 1997, this figure had fallen to US$8.4 million, all of which was short-term.
2/ Includes debt vis-a-vis the Slovak Republic from 1993.

Source: Czech National Bank.

Table 4.3. External Debt Service Obligations in Convertible Currencies, 1992-2003

	1992	1993	1994	1995	1996	1997	1998	1999	2000	2001	2002	2003
					(In millions of US Dollars)							
Principal	1,130	841	2,072	2,014	2,221	3,826	4,085	4,258	3,082	2,334	1,506	1,066
By creditor												
Foreign banks	n.a.	n.a.	n.a.	n.a.	n.a.	n.a.	n.a.	2,839	2,182	1,594	861	703
Official	n.a.	n.a.	n.a.	n.a.	n.a.	n.a.	n.a.	43	15	15	15	15
Multilateral institutions	n.a.	n.a.	n.a.	n.a.	n.a.	n.a.	n.a.	30	31	30	30	30
Suppliers	n.a.	n.a.	n.a.	n.a.	n.a.	n.a.	n.a.	780	450	293	278	19
Other	n.a.	n.a.	n.a.	n.a.	n.a.	n.a.	n.a.	566	404	402	322	299
By debtor												
Banks	n.a.	n.a.	n.a.	n.a.	n.a.	n.a.	n.a.	1,384	1,039	866	635	338
CNB	n.a.	n.a.	n.a.	n.a.	n.a.	n.a.	n.a.	8	312	8	8	8
Commercial banks	n.a.	n.a.	n.a.	n.a.	n.a.	n.a.	n.a.	1,376	727	858	627	330
Official	n.a.	n.a.	n.a.	n.a.	n.a.	n.a.	n.a.	491	102	144	103	136
Corporations and other	n.a.	n.a.	n.a.	n.a.	n.a.	n.a.	n.a.	2,383	1,941	1,324	769	592
By instrument												
Financial credit	216	172	1,315	359	658	791	1,066	984	617	592	253	312
Commercial banks	216	50	15	85	397	385	747	846	562	537	200	259
CNB	..	..	1,110	..	..	12	7	8	8	8	8	8
Government	..	122	190	274	261	394	312	130	47	47	45	45
Bonds	73	116	126	212	375	727	147	430	393	145	323	93
Commercial banks	34	..	..	..	..	229	..	20	17	1	265	..
CNB	39	..	126	..	375	24	..	..	304			
Government	..	114	..	194	..	128	147	361	55	97	58	91
Corporations and other	..	2	..	18	..	346	..	49	17	47	..	2
Export credit	123	133	115	445	236	137	134	62	53	72	48	33
Commercial banks	119	133	115	445	236	137	134	62	53	72	48	33
CNB	4	..	..	..	..	..	..	..	..	..	..	
Deposits	..	17	..	..	..	556	892	448	95	248	114	38
Commercial banks	..	17	..	..	..	556	892	448	95	248	114	38
Trade credit	718	403	516	998	952	1,615	1,846	2,334	1,924	1,277	768	590
Corporations	718	403	516	998	952	1,615	1,846	2,334	1,924	1,277	768	590
Interest	308	316	397	611	1,021	881	1,039	741	554	405	331	232
By creditor												
Foreign banks	n.a.	n.a.	n.a.	n.a.	n.a.	330	n.a.	522	384	286	213	179
Official	n.a.	n.a.	n.a.	n.a.	n.a.	6	n.a.	7	5	5	4	3
Multilateral institutions	n.a.	n.a.	n.a.	n.a.	n.a.	19	n.a.	20	18	14	13	9
Suppliers	n.a.	n.a.	n.a.	n.a.	n.a.	12	n.a.	47	33	20	13	
Other	n.a.	n.a.	n.a.	n.a.	n.a.	120	n.a.	145	114	80	68	41
By debtor												
Banks	n.a.	n.a.	n.a.	n.a.	n.a.	163	n.a.	204	158	102	79	39
CNB	n.a.	n.a.	n.a.	n.a.	n.a.	12	n.a.	23	22	2	2	1
Commercial banks	n.a.	n.a.	n.a.	n.a.	n.a.	151	n.a.	181	136	100	77	38
Official	n.a.	n.a.	n.a.	n.a.	n.a.	42	n.a.	60	32	27	19	16
Corporations and other	n.a.	n.a.	n.a.	n.a.	n.a.	282	n.a.	453	316	228	165	126
By instrument												
Financial credit	195	191	164	109	158	146	129	118	83	57	39	29
Commercial banks	80	3	3	11	78	82	92	86	58	36	21	15
CNB	70	69	37	4	4	3	3	3	2	2	2	1
Government	45	119	124	93	76	61	34	29	23	19	16	13
Bonds	56	44	94	148	390	352	364	123	91	67	55	34
Commercial banks	39	..	1	30	149	145	172	26	24	22	21	..
CNB	17	13	62	53	50	11	17	20	20			
Government	..	31	26	45	115	70	67	31	9	8	3	3
Corporations and other	..	..	5	20	76	126	108	46	38	37	31	31
Export credit	23	30	32	49	38	28	28	36	33	29	25	23
Commercial banks	23	30	32	49	38	28	28	36	33	29	25	23
Deposits	..	1	3	76	87	123	59	33	21	13	10	3
Commercial banks	..	1	3	76	87	123	59	33	21	13	10	3
Trade credit	34	50	104	229	348	232	459	431	326	239	182	143
Corporations	34	50	104	229	348	232	459	431	326	239	182	143
Total debt service	1,438	1,157	2,469	2,625	3,244	4,707	5,124	4,999	3,636	2,739	1,817	1,298

Source: Czech National Bank.

Table 5.1. Operations of the General Government, 1995-99

	1995 Actual	1996 Actual	1997 Actual	1998 Actual	1999 Budget	1995 Actual	1996 Actual	1997 Actual	1998 Actual	1999 Budget
	(In billions of CZK)					(In percent of GDP)				
Total revenue	**622.5**	**679.4**	**701.8**	**756.1**	**796.0**	**45.1**	**43.2**	**41.8**	**41.5**	**40.7**
Tax revenue	536.1	594.6	626.2	670.1	721.1	38.8	37.8	37.3	36.8	36.9
Direct taxes	135.9	143.5	142.6	162.2	170.6	9.8	9.1	8.5	8.9	8.7
Corporate profits tax	67.3	63.0	54.9	67.3	64.0	4.9	4.0	3.3	3.7	3.3
Personal income tax	68.6	80.5	87.7	94.9	106.6	5.0	5.1	5.2	5.2	5.5
Indirect taxes	168.9	190.2	196.7	200.8	214.5	12.2	12.1	11.7	11.0	11.0
VAT	94.8	109.3	117.6	119.4	131.7	6.9	7.0	7.0	6.6	6.7
Excise	56.7	61.2	64.2	67.8	70.2	4.1	3.9	3.8	3.7	3.6
Customs duties	17.4	19.7	14.9	13.6	12.6	1.3	1.3	0.9	0.7	0.6
Social insurance contributions	213.3	242.3	266.2	284.6	312.1	15.4	15.4	15.8	15.6	16.0
Social security	154.3	174.3	191.0	203.9	226.9	11.2	11.1	11.4	11.2	11.6
Health funds	59.0	68.0	75.2	80.7	85.2	4.3	4.3	4.5	4.4	4.4
Other budgetary tax revenue[1]	18.0	18.6	20.7	22.5	23.9	1.3	1.2	1.2	1.2	1.2
Non-tax revenue	86.4	84.8	75.6	86.0	74.9	6.3	5.4	4.5	4.7	3.8
Total expenditure	**620.1**	**685.3**	**724.8**	**782.0**	**843.9**	**44.9**	**43.6**	**43.1**	**43.0**	**43.2**
Current expenditure	518.4	580.8	632.4	672.2	738.4	37.5	36.9	37.6	36.9	37.8
On goods and services[2]	294.2	330.9	337.0	360.2	390.5	21.3	21.0	20.1	19.8	20.0
Interest Payments	16.2	16.2	20.6	22.1	27.2	1.2	1.0	1.2	1.2	1.4
Transfers	208.0	233.7	274.8	289.9	320.7	15.1	14.9	16.4	15.9	16.4
Enterprises and banks	42.4	46.8	54.7	50.2	58.1	3.1	3.0	3.3	2.8	3.0
Households[3]	163.3	185.4	216.3	235.9	254.1	11.8	11.8	12.9	13.0	13.0
Others[4]	2.3	1.5	3.8	3.8	8.5	0.2	0.1	0.2	0.2	0.4
Capital expenditure[5]	96.2	102.5	92.1	93.5	97.2	7.0	6.5	5.5	5.1	5.0
Net lending	5.5	2.0	-0.7	1.8	-1.7	0.4	0.1	0.0	0.1	-0.1
Bank restructuring costs[6]	0.0	0.0	1.0	14.5	10.0	0.0	0.0	0.1	0.8	0.5
Balance including privatization revenues	2.4	-5.9	-23.0	-25.9	-47.9	0.2	-0.4	-1.4	-1.4	-2.5
Balance excluding privatization revenues and bank restructuring costs	**-35.1**	**-35.8**	**-39.0**	**-29.4**	**-55.0**	**-2.5**	**-2.3**	**-2.3**	**-1.6**	**-2.8**
Memo item:										
Nominal GDP	1,381.1	1,572.3	1,680.0	1,820.7	1,954.0					

Note: Comprises Central Government, Local Authorities, Extra-budgetary Funds (excluding Fund for Market Regulation; including Czech Land Fund), State Financial Assets, the National Property Fund, and Health Funds.

1/ Includes property, gift and inheritance taxes, motor vehicle tax, and other tax revenues.

2/ Includes government consumption, current spending by extra-budgetary funds, transfers to subsidized organizations, and health fund expenditures.

3/ Includes social security, unemployment, and general income support benefits.

4/ Includes transfers abroad and other transfers.

5/ Includes capital transfers to enterprises and subsidized organizations as well as other transfers from local governments.

6/ Financed by the Central Government and the NPF.

Sources: Ministry of Finance and IMF staff estimates.

Table 5.2. Operations of the Central State Budget, 1995-99

	1995 Actual	1996 Actual	1997 Actual	1998 Actual	1999 Budget	1995 Actual	1996 Actual	1997 Actual	1998 Actual	1999 Budget
	(In billions of CZK)					(In percent of GDP)				
Total revenue	**444.4**	**476.3**	**499.5**	**530.1**	**565.9**	**32.2**	**30.3**	**29.7**	**29.1**	**29.0**
Tax revenue	409.7	457.4	478.5	509.7	549.9	29.7	29.1	28.5	28.0	28.1
Direct taxes	72.7	78.3	74.8	87.4	89.3	5.3	5.0	4.5	4.8	4.6
Corporate income	64.2	48.6	41.6	51.1	48.4	4.6	3.1	2.5	2.8	2.5
Personal income	8.5	29.7	33.2	36.3	40.9	0.6	1.9	2.0	2.0	2.1
Indirect taxes	168.9	190.2	196.7	200.8	214.5	12.2	12.1	11.7	11.0	11.0
VAT	94.8	109.3	117.6	119.4	131.7	6.9	7.0	7.0	6.6	6.7
Excise	56.7	61.2	64.2	67.8	70.2	4.1	3.9	3.8	3.7	3.6
Customs duties	17.4	19.7	14.9	13.6	12.6	1.3	1.3	0.9	0.7	0.6
Social security contributions	154.3	174.3	191.0	203.9	226.9	11.2	11.1	11.4	11.2	11.6
Other taxes[1]	13.8	14.6	16.0	17.6	19.2	1.0	0.9	1.0	1.0	1.0
Nontax revenue[2]	34.7	18.9	21.0	20.4	16.0	2.5	1.2	1.3	1.1	0.8
Total expenditure	**437.2**	**477.8**	**515.2**	**559.3**	**606.9**	**31.7**	**30.4**	**30.7**	**30.7**	**31.1**
Current expenditure	369.6	423.2	466.2	492.9	539.5	26.8	26.9	27.8	27.1	27.6
On goods and services	95.7	103.6	96.2	101.4	110.1	6.9	6.6	5.7	5.6	5.6
Wages and Salaries	40.4	45.5	47.8	47.4	53.0	2.9	2.9	2.8	2.6	2.7
Other[3]	55.3	58.1	48.4	54.0	57.1	4.0	3.7	2.9	3.0	2.9
Interest payments	13.3	14.0	17.9	19.8	25.1	1.0	0.9	1.1	1.1	1.3
Transfers	271.3	305.6	352.1	371.7	404.3	19.6	19.4	21.0	20.4	20.7
To enterprises	27.8	26.2	37.8	30.4	33.2	2.0	1.7	2.3	1.7	1.7
To households	155.6	180.7	211.0	228.7	247.0	11.3	11.5	12.6	12.6	12.6
Social security benefits[4]	153.2	178.0	207.6	224.5	241.0	11.1	11.3	12.4	12.3	12.3
Unemployment benefits	2.4	2.7	3.4	4.2	6.0	0.2	0.2	0.2	0.2	0.3
Other[5]	87.9	98.7	103.3	112.6	124.1	6.4	6.3	6.1	6.2	6.4
Capital expenditure	55.6	57.0	49.7	64.6	67.8	4.0	3.6	3.0	3.5	3.5
By budgetary organizations	21.4	25.8	16.3	16.5	20.2	1.5	1.6	1.0	0.9	1.0
Transfers	34.2	31.2	33.4	48.1	45.1	2.5	2.0	2.0	2.6	2.3
Net lending[6]	1.3	-2.4	-0.7	1.8	-0.4	0.1	-0.2	0.0	0.1	0.0
Balance	**7.2**	**-1.5**	**-15.7**	**-29.2**	**-41.0**	**0.5**	**-0.1**	**-0.9**	**-1.6**	**-2.1**
Memorandum item:										
Defense spending[7]	24.6	26.9	28.3	33.4	..	1.8	1.7	1.7	1.8	..
Nominal GDP	1381.1	1572.3	1680.0	1820.7	1954.0	100.0	100.0	100.0	100.0	100.0

1/ Includes property, gift and inheritance tax, and motor vehicle tax.
2/ Includes transfers from the State Financial Assets and Liabilities account with the central bank and from the National Property Fund.
3/ Includes transfers to the health fund on behalf of nonproductive individuals.
4/ Includes general income support.
5/ Includes transfers to local authorities, subsidized organizations, and extrabudgetary funds.
6/ Includes bank related costs of CZK14.5 billion in 1998 and CZK10 billion in the budget for 1999 (officially assumed under SFA).
7/ Includes expenditure on the armed forces (excluding nonmilitary expenditures) and civil defense.

Sources: Ministry and Finance and IMF staff estimates.

Table 5.3. Functional Classification of Subsidies from the State Budget, 1995-99

	1995 Actual	1996 Actual	1997 Actual	1998 Actual	1999 Budget
	(In billions of CZK)				
Total subsidies[1]	28.6	27.3	34.3	49.1	34.9
Producer	28.6	27.3	34.3	43.9	30.6
Agriculture and foodstuffs	6.2	6.9	7.2	10.3	11.9
Prices and other fees	..	..	..	..	..
Fund for Market Regulation[2]	0.9	1.1	1.0	1.1	1.6
Other	4.9	5.3	5.9	8.5	9.7
Forestry and water	0.4	0.5	0.3	0.7	0.6
Mining	4.8	5.1	4.3	4.4	4.0
Uranium	1.3	1.4	1.2	1.3	1.2
Ore	0.2	0.2	0.1	0.2	0.2
Coal	3.3	3.5	3.0	2.9	2.6
Residential heating	7.3	7.0	5.2	0.1	0.0
Transportation	6.7	5.4	5.5	5.9	5.8
Railways	5.2	5.2	5.3	5.8	5.7
Bus, urban transport, and airlines	1.5	0.2	0.2	0.1	0.1
Housing	..	..	..	..	..
Energy savings	0.2	0.2	0.2	0.1	0.2
Export promotion	0.9	0.9	0.9	1.3	1.5
Called loan guarantees	0.8	0.1	1.6	6.7	1.5
Employment of handicapped	0.3	0.3	0.3	0.3	0.3
Small business development	1.5	1.2	0.9	0.8	1.3
Other non-investment	..	0.2	13.1	20.2	8.4
Private education	0.0	0.0	0.0	1.5	1.4
Subsidies the embargo	0.0	0.0	0.1	0.1	0.3
Property detriment	0.0	0.0	4.8	3.6	2.6
Other	0.0	0.2	8.2	15.0	4.1
Memorandum items:					
Nominal GDP	1,381.1	1,572.3	1,680.0	1,820.7	1,954.0
Total subsidies (percent of GDP)	2.1	1.7	2.0	2.7	1.8

1/ Differences from the totals are due to classification.
2/ Includes transfers to and deficit of Fund for Market Regulation in agriculture.

Source: Ministry of Finance and IMF staff estimates.

Table 5.4. Operations of the Local Authorities, 1995-99

	1995	1996	1997	1998	1999	1995	1996	1997	1998	1999
	Actual	Actual	Actual	Actual	Budget	Actual	Actual	Actual	Actual	Budget
	(In billions of CZK)					(In percent of GDP)				
Total revenue	130.7	135.0	147.4	162.4	163.3	9.5	8.6	8.8	8.9	8.4
Tax revenue	67.4	69.2	72.5	79.7	86.0	4.9	4.4	4.3	4.4	4.4
Direct taxes	63.2	65.2	67.8	74.8	81.3	4.6	4.1	4.0	4.1	4.2
Corporate income	3.1	14.4	13.3	16.2	15.6	0.2	0.9	0.8	0.9	0.8
Personal income	60.1	50.8	54.5	58.6	65.7	4.4	3.2	3.2	3.2	3.4
Property taxes	3.8	4.0	3.9	4.1	4.0	0.3	0.3	0.2	0.2	0.2
Other taxes	0.4	0.0	0.8	0.8	0.7	0.0	0.0	0.0	0.0	0.0
Non-tax revenue	22.3	25.0	27.1	28.3	29.8	1.6	1.6	1.6	1.6	1.5
Entrepreneurial and property income	13.8	15.9	10.3	12.3	11.5	1.0	1.0	0.6	0.7	0.6
From budgetary and subsidized organizations	12.8	14.6	8.4	9.9	9.6	0.9	0.9	0.5	0.5	0.5
Interest	1.0	1.3	1.9	2.4	1.9	0.1	0.1	0.1	0.1	0.1
Fees and Fines	3.3	3.5	3.6	3.6	4.2	0.2	0.2	0.2	0.2	0.2
Other	5.2	5.6	13.2	12.4	14.1	0.4	0.4	0.8	0.7	0.7
Transfers[1]	36.5	33.6	37.9	41.0	38.0	2.6	2.1	2.3	2.3	1.9
Capital revenue	4.5	7.2	9.9	13.4	9.5	0.3	0.5	0.6	0.7	0.5
Total expenditure	132.3	144.4	151.8	160.3	164.9	9.6	9.2	9.0	8.8	8.4
Current expenditure	81.4	91.0	100.2	106.9	115.9	5.9	5.8	6.0	5.9	5.9
On goods and services	53.1	60.3	66.0	70.9	79.3	3.8	3.8	3.9	3.9	4.1
Wages and salaries	9.7	12.2	13.0	13.8	14.4	0.7	0.8	0.8	0.8	0.7
Other	43.4	48.1	53.0	57.1	64.9	3.1	3.1	3.2	3.1	3.3
Interest payments	1.3	1.7	2.4	2.3	2.1	0.1	0.1	0.1	0.1	0.1
Transfers	27.0	29.0	31.8	33.7	34.5	2.0	1.8	1.9	1.9	1.8
To enterprises	6.0	7.2	8.9	9.0	9.2	0.4	0.5	0.5	0.5	0.5
To subsidized organizations	15.1	17.2	17.7	17.5	18.3	1.1	1.1	1.1	1.0	0.9
To extrabudgetary funds	0.0	0.0	0.0	0.0	0.0	0.0	0.0	0.0	0.0	0.0
To households	5.9	4.6	5.2	7.2	7.0	0.4	0.3	0.3	0.4	0.4
Capital expenditure	50.9	53.4	51.6	53.4	49.0	3.7	3.4	3.1	2.9	2.5
By budgetary organizations	41.7	45.0	43.5	42.7	40.5	3.0	2.9	2.6	2.3	2.1
Transfers	9.2	8.4	8.1	10.7	8.5	0.7	0.5	0.5	0.6	0.4
To enterprises	3.3	3.6	3.3	4.6	3.8	0.2	0.2	0.2	0.3	0.2
To subsidized organizations	5.9	4.8	3.9	4.2	3.8	0.4	0.3	0.2	0.2	0.2
Other	0.0	0.0	0.9	1.9	0.9	0.0	0.0	0.1	0.1	0.0
Balance of local budgets	-1.7	-9.4	-4.4	2.1	-1.6	-0.1	-0.6	-0.3	0.1	-0.1

1/ Includes transfers from the central government, extrabudgetary funds, and the National Property Fund.

Sources: Ministry of Finance and IMF staff estimates.

Table 5.5. Operations of the Extrabudgetary Funds, 1995-99

	1995 Actual	1996 Actual	1997 Actual	1998 Actual	1999 Budget	1995 Actual	1996 Actual	1997 Actual	1998 Actual	1999 Budget
	(In billions of CZK)					(In percent of GDP)				
Revenue	5.1	5.3	5.5	4.1	2.8	0.4	0.3	0.3	0.2	0.1
Own revenue	3.5	3.3	3.9	3.9	2.8	0.3	0.2	0.2	0.2	0.1
Transfers	1.6	2.0	1.6	0.2	0.0	0.1	0.1	0.1	0.0	0.0
Expenditure	5.0	4.7	3.4	3.0	2.7	0.4	0.3	0.2	0.2	0.1
Current	1.2	0.7	0.2	0.6	1.3	0.1	0.0	0.0	0.0	0.1
Capital	1.2	1.9	1.4	1.5	1.4	0.1	0.1	0.1	0.1	0.1
Transfers to local authorities	2.6	2.1	1.8	0.9	1.3	0.2	0.1	0.1	0.0	0.1
Net lending	..	..	..	..	-1.3	0.0	0.0	0.0	0.0	-0.1
Balance (excluding Czech Land Fund)	0.1	0.6	2.1	1.1	0.1	0.0	0.0	0.1	0.1	0.0
Czech Land Fund	1.1	0.6	-1.6	0.1	-0.6	0.1	0.0	-0.1	0.0	0.0
Balance (including Czech Land Fund)	1.2	1.2	0.5	1.2	-0.5	0.1	0.1	0.0	0.1	0.0

Note: Excluding Fund for Market Regulation.

Sources: Ministry of Finance and IMF Staff estimates.

Table 5.6. Extrabudgetary Expenditures of the Central Government, 1995-99

	1995 Actual	1996 Actual	1997 Actual	1998 Actual	1999 Budget	1995 Actual	1996 Actual	1997 Actual	1998 Actual	1999 Budget
	(In billions of CZK)					(In percent of GDP)				
State Financial Assets										
Revenue	0.9	1.0	5.6	11.8	1.2	0.1	0.1	0.3	0.6	0.1
Total spending	13.4	4.8	8.1	8.8	1.2	1.0	0.3	0.5	0.5	0.1
Consumption	0.6	0.0	0.1	0.0	0.0	0.0	0.0	0.0	0.0	0.0
Transfers	10.6	4.8	7.3	8.0	1.2	0.8	0.3	0.4	0.4	0.1
To enterprises	2.4	0.9	0.0	0.0	0.0	0.2	0.1	0.0	0.0	0.0
To central government	6.4	3.8	7.2	8.0	1.1	0.5	0.2	0.4	0.4	0.1
To households	1.8	0.1	0.1	0.0	0.1	0.1	0.0	0.0	0.0	0.0
Capital expenditure	0.0	0.0	0.0	0.0	0.0	0.0	0.0	0.0	0.0	0.0
Net lending	2.0	0.0	0.0	0.0	0.0	0.1	0.0	0.0	0.0	0.0
Other	0.2	0.0	0.7	0.7	0.0	0.0	0.0	0.0	0.0	0.0
Balance	**-12.5**	**-3.8**	**-3.5**	**3.0**	**0.0**	**-0.9**	**-0.2**	**-0.2**	**0.2**	**0.0**
National Property Fund										
Total revenues	37.5	29.9	17.0	18.0	17.1	2.7	1.9	1.0	1.0	0.9
o/w proceeds from large privatizations	33.5	25.7	12.5	14.1	16.5	2.4	1.6	0.7	0.8	0.8
Total spending	25.7	20.3	16.5	21.1	22.9	1.9	1.3	1.0	1.2	1.2
Consumption	0.0	0.0	0.0	0.0	0.0	0.0	0.0	0.0	0.0	0.0
Interest	1.6	0.5	0.3	0.0	0.0	0.1	0.0	0.0	0.0	0.0
Transfers	21.2	15.5	14.5	20.3	21.5	1.5	1.0	0.9	1.1	1.1
To enterprises	6.2	12.6	1.5	2.7	6.2	0.4	0.8	0.1	0.1	0.3
To financial institutions	0.0	-0.1	6.5	8.1	9.5	0.0	0.0	0.4	0.4	0.5
To central government	12.2	0.0	0.0	0.0	5.8	0.9	0.0	0.0	0.0	0.3
To local governments	1.2	0.0	0.0	0.0	0.0	0.1	0.0	0.0	0.0	0.0
To extrabudgetary funds	1.6	2.0	1.5	0.0	0.0	0.1	0.1	0.1	0.0	0.0
To State Financial Assets	0.0	0.0	5.0	9.5	0.0	0.0	0.0	0.3	0.5	0.0
To Health Fund	0.0	1.0	0.0	0.0	0.0	0.0	0.1	0.0	0.0	0.0
Other	0.7	-0.1	0.7	0.8	1.4	0.1	0.0	0.0	0.0	0.1
Net lending	2.2	4.4	0.0	0.0	0.0	0.2	0.3	0.0	0.0	0.0
Capital injections	0.0	0.0	1.0	0.0	0.0	0.0	0.0	0.1	0.0	0.0
Balance	**11.8**	**9.6**	**0.5**	**-3.1**	**-5.8**	**0.9**	**0.6**	**0.0**	**-0.2**	**-0.3**

Sources: Ministry of Finance and IMF staff estimates.

Table 5.7. State Subsidies to Local Budgets, 1998-99

	1998 Actual			1999 Budget			Index 1999		
	Total	District	Municipal	Total	District	Municipal	Total	District	Municipal
	(In millions of CZK)						(1998=100)		
Subsidies to District Offices and Municipalities	17,912.4	8,517.4	9,395.0	20,977.0	9,546.3	11,430.7	117.1	112.1	121.7
Social benefits	4,940.0	949.9	3,990.1	6,920.0	1,303.5	5,616.5	140.1	137.2	140.8
Social welfare institutions	1,027.0	807.7	219.6	1,047.5	821.0	226.5	102.0	101.6	103.1
Home for the elderly	1,716.6	1,041.1	675.5	1,719.3	1,026.6	692.7	100.2	98.6	102.5
Education	1,558.2	..	1,558.2	1,696.6	..	1,696.6	108.9	..	108.9
Transport service	1,012.8	1,012.8	..	1,114.1	1,100.9	13.2	110.0	108.7	..
Selected medical facilities	132.1	97.4	34.7	128.9	96.4	32.5	97.6	99.0	93.7
State administration functions	2,255.5	..	2,255.5	1,962.4	..	1,962.4	87.0	..	87.0
Spatial planning	..	..	0.0	514.9	..	514.9	..	..	..
Spatial planning	2,818.0	2,201.6	616.4	3,121.0	2,445.7	675.3	110.8	111.1	109.6
Equalization subsides	2,406.9	2,406.9	..	2,750.2	2,750.2	..	114.3	114.3	..
Funds for increase in social benefits	2,387.0	977.1	1,409.9	120.0	120.0	..	..	..	..
Contribution to district offices towards state administration functions	..	..	..	..	..	..	..	..	..
Land adjustments	850.4	824.2	26.2	847.0	820.8	26.2	99.6	99.6	100.0
Administration expenses in connection wit benefit distribution	189.7	168.7	21.0	240.0	219.0	21.0	126.5	129.8	100.0
Comprehensive co-operation program of crime and drug prevention at local level	110.0	..	110.0	110.0	..	110.0	100.0	..	100.0
Museum of T. G. Masaryk in Lany	3.0	..	3.0	..	..	..	..	..	..
Fire safety severance and salary compensation	3.9	3.9	..	50.0	50.0	..	1,282.1	1,282.1	..
Non-capital subsidies from the general budget	20,854.0	9,933.9	10,920.1	22,344.0	10,756.1	11,587.9	107.1	108.3	106.1
o/w excl. benefits	13,527.0	8,006.9	5,520.1	15,424.0	9,452.6	5,971.4	114.0	118.1	108.2
Capital subsidies from the general budget	2,417.0	1,210.5	1,206.5	2,743.5	1,524.9	1,218.6	113.5	126.0	101.0
Subsides from the general budget total	23,271.0	11,144.4	12,126.6	25,087.5	12,281.0	12,806.5	107.8	110.2	105.6
o/w Non-capital	1,421.3	748.8	672.5	695.3	421.6	273.7	48.9	56.3	40.7
Capital	6,437.7	1,555.0	4,882.7	7,602.7	1,521.9	6,080.8	118.1	97.9	124.5
Other subsides accepted from Ministries	7,859.0	2,303.8	5,555.2	8,298.0	1,943.5	6,354.5	105.6	84.4	114.4
Subsidies from the state budget, total	31,130.0	13,448.2	17,681.8	33,385.5	14,224.5	19,161.0	107.2	105.8	108.4
Subsidies from State Environmental Fund	1,100.0	..	1,100.0	1,300.0	..	1,300.0	118.2	..	118.2
Total subsidies	32,230.0	13,448.2	18,781.8	34,685.5	14,224.5	20,461.0	107.6	105.8	108.9

Source: Ministry of Finance.

Table 5.8. Transfers to Households, 1993-99

(In billions of CZK)

	1993 Actual	1994 Actual	1995 Actual	1996 Actual	1997 Actual	1998 Actual	1999 Budgeted	1999 Expected
Pensions	76.6	88.2	109.8	127.6	150.2	166.1	176.0	172.9
Old age	53.1	62.2	77.3	89.8	106.1	118.4	...	...
Disability	14.0	15.7	20.4	24.1	28.2	31.0	...	...
Widow	8.6	9.4	10.4	12.2	13.9	14.6	...	...
Other[1]	0.9	0.9	1.7	1.5	2.0	2.1	...	...
Sickness and maternity	12.0	16.6	18.4	20.4	19.8	18.6	20.7	20.7
Traditional state allowances	14.5	18.3	17.6	1.1	0.0	0.0	0.0	0.0
Per child allowances	9.6	12.5	12.5	1.1	...	...	...	...
Parental allowances	4.4	5.2	4.8	...	...	...	...	...
Other	0.5	0.6	0.3	...	...	...	...	...
Compensatory income support	13.1	10.6	6.0	0.5	...	...	...	...
Other state benefits[2]	0.8	0.7	1.4	1.6	2.8	3.4	4.2	4.2
Social state support	0.0	0.0	1.2	26.7	29.2	29.6	32.0	31.6
Per child allowances	...	...	...	11.1	12.5	11.5	13.5	13.5
Parental allowances	...	...	1.0	7.3	7.6	7.8	8.0	8.0
Other (including housing)	...	...	0.2	8.3	9.0	9.9	10.1	9.8
Flat benefits	...	...	...	...	0.1	0.4	0.4	0.3
Benefits provided by								
Local authorities	3.0	3.6	4.1	4.2	5.2	6.6	6.9	7.4
State policy of employment	2.2	2.6	2.4	2.7	4.0	5.1	7.5	7.5
Of which:								
Unemployment benefits	1.4	1.8	1.8	2.1	3.4	4.2	6.0	6.0
Total	122.2	140.6	160.9	184.8	211.2	229.4	247.3	244.3

(In percent of GDP)

	1993 Actual	1994 Actual	1995 Actual	1996 Actual	1997 Actual	1998 Actual	1999 Budgeted	1999 Expected
Pensions	7.6	7.5	8.0	8.1	8.9	9.1	9.4	9.3
Old age	5.3	5.3	5.6	5.7	6.3	6.5	...	...
Disability	1.4	1.3	1.5	1.5	1.7	1.7	...	...
Widow	0.9	0.8	0.8	0.8	0.8	0.8	...	...
Other[1]	0.1	0.1	0.1	0.1	0.1	0.1	...	...
Sickness and maternity	1.2	1.4	1.3	1.3	1.2	1.0	1.1	1.1
Traditional state allowances	1.4	1.5	1.3	0.1	0.0	0.0	0.0	0.0
Per child allowances	1.0	1.1	0.9	0.1	...	...	...	...
Parental allowances	0.4	0.4	0.3	...	...	...	...	...
Other	0.0	0.1	0.0	...	...	...	...	...
Compensatory income support	1.3	0.9	0.4	0.0	...	...	...	...
Other state benefits[2]	0.1	0.1	0.1	0.1	0.2	0.2	0.2	0.2
Social state support	0.0	0.0	0.1	1.7	1.7	1.6	1.7	1.7
Per child allowances	...	...	...	0.7	0.7	0.6	0.7	0.7
Parental allowances	...	...	0.1	0.5	0.5	0.4	0.4	0.4
Other (including housing)	...	...	0.0	0.5	0.5	0.5	0.5	0.5
Flat benefits	...	...	...	...	0.0	0.0	0.0	0.0
Benefits provided by								
Local authorities	0.3	0.3	0.3	0.3	0.3	0.4	0.4	0.4
State policy of employment	0.2	0.2	0.2	0.2	0.2	0.3	0.4	0.4
Of which:								
Unemployment benefits	0.1	0.2	0.1	0.1	0.2	0.2	0.3	0.3
Total	12.2	11.9	11.7	11.8	12.6	12.6	13.2	13.1

Notes: Totals differ slightly from consolidated budget because of classification, especially restitutions in 1994.
1/ Includes pensions of police and military.
2/ Includes special allowances for soldiers, policemen, etc.

Sources: Ministry of Finance, Ministry of Labor and Social Affairs and staff estimates.

Table 5.9. Financial Balance of the Public Health Insurance System, 1996-98

(In millions of CZK)

	1996			1997			1998		
	Total	General Health Ins. Co. [1]	Other Health Ins. Co. [2]	Total	General Health Ins. Co. [1]	Other Health Ins. Co. [2]	Total	General Health Ins. Co. [1]	Other Health Ins. Co. [2]
Health Insurance System Revenues									
1. Collection of Premiums after redistribution	84,413	62,382	22,031	93,425	71,562	21,863	102,934	78,683	24,251
2. Payments from State budget for premiums paid by state	16,059	19,448	-3,389	18,475	21,298	-2,823	22,886	24,749	-1,863
3. Economic active payer and self-employer	68,354	42,934	25,420	74,950	50,264	24,686	80,048	53,934	26,114
4. Fine, penalty, and damages	1,474	1,338	136	1,095	994	101	880	600	280
5. Other yields linked to public health insurance	937	169	768	972	222	750	1,732	87	1,645
6. Subsides from public budgets (not included in row 2)	0	0	0	0	0	0	0	0	0
A1. Health Insurance System Revenues total (2 to 6)	86,824	63,889	22,935	95,492	72,778	22,714	105,546	79,370	26,176
7. Commercial activities (Taxed, not by means of deduction)	80	15	65	50	22	28	431	155	276
8. Commercial insurance and supplementary insurance	225	225	0	285	285	0	445	445	0
Total health system revenue (1 to 8)	87,129	64,129	23,000	95,827	73,085	22,742	106,422	79,970	26,452
Health insurance system expenditures									
9. Health care costs	86,088	65,336	20,752	92,893	72,765	20,128	101,450	79,612	21,838
10. Public health insurance operations costs	3,244	1,816	1,428	3,456	1,959	1,497	4,817	2,063	2,754
B1. Total insurance expenditure	89,332	67,152	22,180	96,349	74,724	21,625	106,267	81,675	24,592
11. Operations overheads (operation costs-written off & capital expenditure)	3,844	2,139	1,705	4,266	2,485	1,781	5,355	2,412	2,843
B2. Modified public health insurance costs (9+11)	89,932	67,475	22,457	97,159	75,250	21,909	106,805	82,124	24,681
12. Taxable activities costs	50	11	39	49	16	33	362	301	61
13. Contractual and supplementary insurance compensation costs	38	38	0	75	75	0	93	93	0
14. Contractual & supplementary insurance operation costs	116	116	0	108	108	0	238	238	0
B. Total insurance costs (B1 +12 to 14)	89,536	67,317	22,219	96,581	74,923	21,658	106,960	82,307	24,653
C. Modified total insurance costs (B2+12+13+14)	90,136	67,640	22,496	97,391	75,449	21,942	107,498	82,756	24,742
Total balance (A-B)	-2,407	-3,188	781	-754	-1,838	1,084	-538	-2,337	1,799
Balance of insurance operations	-2,508	-3,263	755	-857	-1,946	1,089	-721	-2,305	1584
Balance adjusted by business operational cost (A-C)	-3,007	-3,511	504	-1,564	-2,364	800	-1,076	-2,786	1,710
Balance adjusted by operational overhead cost (A1-B2)	-3,108	-3,586	478	-1,667	-2,472	805	-1,259	-2,754	1,495

1/ G.H.I.C. - General Health Insurance Company
2/ Others - other insurance companies including merged and liquidated health insurance companies.

Source: Ministry of Finance.

Table 5.10. Operations of the Health Funds, 1995-99

	1995	1996	1997	1998	1999	1995	1996	1997	1998	1999
	Actual	Actual	Actual	Actual	Budget	Actual	Actual	Actual	Actual	Budget
	(In billions of CZK)					(In percent of GDP)				
Revenue	73.7	88.1	96.2	108.0	116.3	5.3	5.6	5.7	5.9	6.0
Health contributions	59.0	68.0	75.2	80.7	85.2	4.3	4.3	4.5	4.4	4.4
Transfers from government	13.5	16.4	18.7	23.4	27.6	1.0	1.0	1.1	1.3	1.4
Other	1.2	3.7	2.3	3.9	3.5	0.1	0.2	0.1	0.2	0.2
Expenditure	77.3	90.1	97.6	107.9	115.3	5.6	5.7	5.8	5.9	5.9
Payment of claims	72.2	86.1	93.0	102.0	110.5	5.2	5.5	5.5	5.6	5.7
Operating expenditures	4.2	3.8	4.5	4.0	4.5	0.3	0.2	0.3	0.2	0.2
Other	0.9	0.2	0.1	1.9	0.3	0.1	0.0	0.0	0.1	0.0
Balance	-3.6	-2.0	-1.4	0.1	1.0	-0.3	-0.1	-0.1	0.0	0.1

Sources: Ministry of Finance and IMF staff estimates.

Table 5.11. Central Government Debt Outstanding, 1993-98

End of period	Total Debt	Securities Total	of which			Direct Credits
			T-Bills	T-Bonds	Other	
			(In billions of CZK)			
1993 December	**158.9**	37.2	17.0	19.5	0.7	121.6
1994 March	**159.4**	42.3	22.0	19.6	0.7	117.1
June	**159.1**	43.6	24.0	18.9	0.7	115.4
September	**159.4**	49.6	25.0	23.9	0.7	109.7
December	**157.3**	52.8	23.8	28.3	0.7	104.5
1995 March	**157.6**	64.0	30.0	33.3	0.7	93.6
June	**157.2**	70.8	31.8	38.3	0.7	86.4
September	**159.1**	82.7	41.8	40.2	0.7	76.3
December	**154.4**	84.4	42.0	41.7	0.7	70.0
1996 March	**154.5**	98.8	51.4	46.7	0.7	55.7
June	**165.1**	111.8	64.3	46.8	0.7	53.3
September	**158.6**	107.5	62.9	43.9	0.7	51.1
December	**155.2**	107.3	62.6	43.9	0.7	47.9
1997 March	**165.9**	123.7	72.9	50.0	0.7	42.3
June	**178.7**	133.7	82.9	50.0	0.8	45.0
September	**172.1**	129.3	70.8	57.7	0.8	42.8
December	**173.1**	135.6	76.9	57.9	0.8	37.5
1998 January	**164.6**	127.0	68.3	57.9	0.8	37.5
February	**173.3**	136.7	74.0	62.0	0.8	36.6
March	**168.0**	137.3	72.9	63.6	0.8	30.8
April	**168.0**	137.6	73.1	63.6	0.9	30.5
May	**173.5**	143.1	78.7	63.6	0.9	30.4
June	**170.8**	143.2	78.6	63.6	1.0	27.6
July	**165.3**	139.5	74.9	63.6	1.0	25.8
August	**166.6**	139.7	70.1	68.6	1.0	26.8
September	**164.6**	139.8	70.1	68.6	1.0	24.8
October	**164.3**	139.8	70.2	68.6	1.0	24.5
November	**170.1**	145.9	74.9	70.0	1.0	24.2
December	**194.7**	170.8	99.8	70.0	1.0	23.9

Source: Ministry of Finance.

Table 6.1. Monetary Survey, 1993-98

	1993	1994	1995	1996	1997	1998
	(In billions of CZK, end of period)					
TOTAL ASSETS	**720.4**	**870.4**	**1,039.6**	**1,120.5**	**1,217.6**	**1,280.8**
A. NET FOREIGN ASSETS	115.7	194.4	311.4	281.9	338.5	410.0
- assets	213.6	275.8	493.2	538.0	670.7	746.1
- liabilities	97.9	81.4	181.8	256.1	332.2	336.1
B. NET DOMESTIC ASSETS	604.7	676.0	728.2	838.6	879.1	870.8
1. Domestic credits	713.9	817.5	929.5	1,029.7	1,137.7	1,121.8
a) Net credit to the government sector	18.4	5.1	10.1	12.6	24.8	38.6
- net credit to government	35.1	23.1	25.4	28.5	37.9	47.9
- net credit to NPF	-16.7	-18.0	-15.3	-15.9	-13.1	-9.3
b) Credits of commercial banks and CNB	695.5	812.4	919.4	1,017.1	1,112.9	1,083.2
ba) CZK credits	669.6	768.9	822.3	888.6	912.6	869.6
- businesses	576.8	661.1	720.5	785.1	808.2	765.6
- households	92.8	107.8	101.8	103.5	104.4	104.0
bb) foreign currency credits	25.9	43.5	97.1	128.5	200.3	213.6
2. Other net items	-109.2	-141.5	-201.3	-191.1	-258.6	-251.0
MONEY SUPPLY	**720.4**	**870.4**	**1,039.6**	**1,120.5**	**1,217.6**	**1,280.8**
A. MONEY	359.9	421.8	453.3	475.3	445.1	433.4
1. Currency in circulation	59.8	84.0	104.3	118.9	119.3	127.2
2. Demand deposits	300.1	337.8	349.0	356.4	325.8	306.2
- households	109.3	131.5	148.8	155.7	153.2	144.0
- businesses	185.1	201.1	195.6	195.6	168.2	158.9
- insurance companies	5.7	5.2	4.6	5.1	4.4	3.3
B. QUASI MONEY	360.5	448.6	586.3	645.2	772.5	847.4
1. Time deposits	303.1	387.8	498.8	559.5	634.0	674.7
- households	206.8	244.7	306.5	366.0	474.4	550.8
- businesses	60.0	102.9	150.2	172.7	133.9	91.8
- insurance companies	36.3	40.2	42.1	20.8	25.7	32.1
2. Certificates of deposit, deposit bills of exchange and other bonds [1/]	..	..	..	..	..	30.2
3. Foreign currency deposits	57.4	60.8	87.5	85.7	138.5	142.5
- households	45.7	42.2	35.8	40.1	68.8	73.6
- businesses	11.7	18.6	51.7	45.6	69.7	68.9
Adjusted M2 [2/]	704.6	845.1	1,012.3	1,105.8	1,217.6	1,280.9
Monetary aggregate L [5/]	704.6	845.5	1,019.0	1,138.9	1,241.8	1,329.9
For information:						
Increase against the same month of the previous year						
1. M1 [3/]						
- in CZK billion	53.6	61.9	31.5	22.0	-30.2	-11.7
- percent	17.5	17.2	7.5	4.9	-6.4	-2.6
2. M2 [4/]						
- in CZK billion	116.5	140.5	167.2	93.5	111.8	63.3
- percent	19.8	19.9	19.8	9.2	10.1	5.2
3. L						
- in CZK billion	116.5	140.9	173.5	119.9	102.9	88.1
- percent	19.8	20.0	20.5	11.8	9.0	7.1

1/ Because of changes in statistical reporting, deposit bills of exchange, certificates of deposit and other bonds are excluded from CZK deposits.

2/ Adjusted for float in 1993 and 1994, short-term operations of some banks in 1994 and for SPT Telecom deposit with CNB in 1995 and 1996.

3/ Currency in circulation, demand deposits.

4/ Currency in circulation, demand deposits, time deposits, residents' foreign currency deposits.

5/ Adjusted M2 plus T-bills, CNB bills and NPF bills in the portfolios of domestic non-bank institutions.

For credits and deposits individuals were replaced by the household sector (according to SNA - individuals + traders).

Source: Czech National Bank.

Table 6.2. Minimum Reserve Requirements, 1990-99

Category of Deposits	Date of Change											
	1990 Jan.[1]	1991 May	1992 Feb.	1992 Nov.	1993 Feb.[2]	1993 July	1994 Aug.	1995 July	1996 Aug.[3]	1997 May[3]	1998 July[3]	1999 Jan.[3]
	(In percent of eligible deposits, beginning of period)											
Demand deposit	5	8	8	9	9,12	9	12	8.5	11.5	9.5	7.5	5
Savings and time deposits	5	8	2	3	3,4	3	3	8.5	11.5	9.5	7.5	5
Remuneration (per annum)[4]	4	4	4	..	..	..	..	..	..	..	..	..
Maintenance period[5]	month	month	month	month	month	fortnight	fortnight	fortnight	fortnight	fortnight	fortnight	fortnight

1/ Required reserves were first introduced in 1990. Prior to February 1992, foreign exchange deposits were not subject to reserve requirements.

2/ The lower rates apply to banks with primary liabilities of less than CZK25 billion.

3/ A lower rate of 4 percent applies to deposit of nonbanks with building societies and the Czech and Moravian Guarantee Bank.

4/ A penalty of three times the discount rate is applied on shortfalls in required reserve obligations.

5/ Required reserves are calculated on deposits in the three-week period ending three weeks before the maintenance period: for banks whose required reserves are less than CZK1 billion, a daily balance of up to CZK100 million in excess of the minimum required reserve may be averaged out. For other banks, daily balances of up to 10 percent in excess of the minimum required reserves may be used for averaging purposes. On shortfalls, a penalty rate of 3 times the discount rate is applied.

Source: Czech National Bank.

Table 6.3. Balance Sheet of the Czech National Bank, 1995-98

	1995	1996	1997 Mar.	Jun.	Sep.	Dec.	1998 Mar.	June	Sep.	Dec.
			\multicolumn{10}{c}{(In billions of CZK, end of period)}
Net foreign assets	311	300	298	244	282	249	279	287	300	300
Foreign assets[1][2]	359	342	356	335	342	311	320	337	337	337
Foreign liabilities (-)	-49	-42	-58	-91	-60	-62	-41	-50	-38	-37
Net domestic credit	-133	-82	-79	-93	-85	-67	-101	-110	-166	-157
Net claims on government	-31	-43	-40	-44	-39	-32	-31	-32	-26	-36
Credits	442	484	106	237	367	509	121	254	395	535
Liabilities	-473	-527	-146	-281	-405	-541	-151	-286	-421	-571
Net claims on the economy	-41	-48	-43	-42	-22	-17	-34	-15	-5	14
Credits	1	4	4	8	22	19	19	30	33	33
Nongovernment securities	1	2	4	4	4	6	4	4	4	17
CNB's bills with non-banks	0	-13	-17	-13	-12	-2	-21	-13	-13	-5
Other government deposits[1]	-44	-40	-35	-41	-37	-41	-35	-36	-29	-30
Net claims on banks	-61	9	4	-7	-24	-18	-37	-63	-136	-136
Refinancing credit	6	15	16	25	24	29	22	13	3	0
Other claims on banks	2	8	6	8	13	17	15	34	15	19
Redistribution credits	62	56	56	56	55	53	44	43	43	32
Inseparable reserves	-2	-3	-3	-4	-2	-5	-4	-4	-2	-3
Other deposits of banks	-8	-5	-3	-10	-3	-8	-4	-24	-21	-20
CNB bills with banks	-121	-62	-68	-53	-109	-103	-111	-126	-173	-164
Other liabilities to banks[3]	0	-2	-1	-29	-1	-2	0	0	0	0
Other net assets	16	32	33	68	39	45	54	57	93	89
Other unclassified domestic assets	25	47	45	93	99	125	67	77	104	85
Reserve money	194	249	252	220	236	227	231	234	226	232
Currency, incl. Vault cash	119	136	134	131	134	138	131	138	136	145
Reserve deposits	75	113	118	88	102	90	99	96	89	87
Required reserves	76	116	116	97	101	101	101	102	85	84
Excess reserves	-1	-3	2	-9	2	-11	-2	-6	5	2

1/ Excluding the foreign exchange deposit of SPT with the Czech National Bank.
2/ Excluding pre-1993 claims on Slovakia amounting to CZK26 billion at end-1997 which are classified under other assets.
3/ Since June 1998, includes a deposit by GE in connection with the sale of Agrobanka.

Source: Czech National Bank and staff calculations.

Table 6.4. Structure of Domestic Currency Deposits, 1992-98

	1992	1993	1994	1995	1996	1997	March	June	Sept.	Dec.
									1998	
					(In billions of CZK, end of period)					
Total	518.8	648.4	771.3	899.8	960.7	1006.2	969.9	992.8	1009.9	1022.6
By maturity[1]										
Short-term	373.1	467.4	555.6	648.5	727.9	784.8	756.3	789.4	807.1	817.2
Medium-term	106.2	136.1	174.0	201.0	173.6	140.0	129.3	111.6	107.9	107.6
Long-term	39.5	44.9	41.7	50.3	59.2	81.4	84.3	91.8	94.9	97.8
					(In percent)					
By maturity (share of total deposits)										
Short-term	71.9	72.1	72.0	72.1	75.8	78.0	78.0	79.5	79.9	79.9
Medium-term	20.5	21.0	22.6	22.3	18.1	13.9	13.3	11.2	10.7	10.5
Long-term	7.6	6.9	5.4	5.6	6.2	8.1	8.7	9.2	9.4	9.6
					(In billions of CZK, end of period)					
By type of holder										
Non-financial organizations	138.9	158.3	207.5	231.4	282.5	219.3	187.0	186.5	200.1	188.1
Finance	0.9	8.8	10.4	19.4	23.4	26.9	14.1	15.3	12.4	16.0
Insurance	40.3	42.0	45.5	46.7	25.8	30.1	31.9	30.5	31.8	35.4
Public organizations	50.2	76.5	77.8	81.4	78.7	71.7	67.7	69.3	60.3	61.7
Non-profit organizations	5.7	6.7	7.9	10.1	11.2	12.4	13.3	13.3	14.3	13.0
Small enterprises	20.9	25.1	33.4	34.5	37.4	40.2	34.4	40.2	41.4	34.7
Households	239.3	291.0	342.8	420.9	484.4	587.4	605.0	622.2	636.2	660.2
Non-residents	0.8	1.7	2.7	7.7	8.6	12.1	11.5	11.2	10.5	11.0
Others	21.9	38.3	43.3	47.7	8.7	6.1	5.0	4.2	2.9	2.5

1/ Short-term: up to and including one year; medium term: more than one and up to and including four years; long-term: over four years.

Source: Czech National Bank.

Table 6.5. Interest Rates on Interbank Deposits, 1993-98

| | 1993 | 1994 | 1995 | 1996 | 1997 | 1998 | | | | | |
	12	12	12	12	12	3	6	9	10	11	12
						(in percent)					
1. AVERAGE PRIBOR RATE [1]											
- 1 day	5.47	10.75	10.83	12.44	12.55	13.91	13.63	14.05	13.18	12.00	10.84
- 7 day	5.90	12.28	11.17	12.61	16.64	14.95	15.26	13.99	13.43	11.97	10.56
- 14 day	6.14	12.38	11.20	12.61	16.77	15.01	15.34	13.99	13.42	11.95	10.54
- 1 month	6.68	12.55	11.01	12.63	17.49	15.18	15.63	13.90	13.35	11.70	10.46
- 2 month	7.34	12.61	10.97	12.62	17.54	15.36	15.77	13.86	13.26	11.46	10.27
- 3 month	8.00	12.65	10.93	12.67	17.50	15.52	15.81	13.82	13.20	11.31	10.08
- 6 month	9.21	12.65	10.89	12.55	17.41	15.85	15.83	13.59	12.94	10.82	9.56
- 9 month	10.69	12.65	10.89	12.25	17.39	15.98	15.84	13.44	12.69	10.59	9.38
- 12 month	11.90	12.66	10.90	12.23	17.36	16.08	15.84	13.39	12.60	10.51	9.31
2. AVERAGE PRIBID RATE [1]											
- 1 day	4.51	10.01	10.52	12.19	10.75	13.19	12.60	13.63	12.66	11.68	10.48
- 7 day	4.92	11.48	10.82	12.35	15.37	14.56	14.87	13.73	13.17	11.72	10.30
- 14 day	5.16	11.55	10.84	12.36	15.45	14.62	14.94	13.72	13.16	11.70	10.27
- 1 month	5.68	11.72	10.63	12.35	16.26	14.80	15.22	13.60	13.07	11.43	10.18
- 2 month	6.34	11.76	10.59	12.34	16.33	14.95	15.34	13.56	12.98	11.18	9.99
- 3 month	7.00	11.80	10.53	12.39	16.35	15.14	15.39	13.52	12.92	11.04	9.79
- 6 month	8.21	11.81	10.48	12.26	16.31	15.45	15.40	13.29	12.65	10.53	9.26
- 9 month	9.56	11.82	10.47	11.96	16.27	15.59	15.40	13.13	12.39	10.30	9.08
- 12 month	10.89	11.83	10.48	11.94	16.23	15.69	15.41	13.09	12.31	10.22	9.02

1/ Commercial banks quoting their rates daily on the interbank deposit market.

Source: Czech National Bank.

Table 6.6. Czech National Bank Monetary Policy Instruments, 1995-99

	Repo rate (percent)		Discount rate (percent)	Lombard rate (percent)	Minimum reserve requirement for primary deposits (percent)	
	1 week	2 week			banks	building societies and ČMZRB
1995						
26 June			9.5	12.5		
3 August						4.0
8 December	11.25	11.30				
1996						
29 March	11.50	11.50				
29 April	11.60	11.60				
9 May	11.80	11.80				
21 June	12.40	12.40	10.5	14.0		
1 August					11.5	
1997						
8 May					9.5	
16 May	12.90			50.0		
19 May	45.00					
23 May	75.00					
27 May			13.0			
2 June	45.00					
4 June		39.00				
6 June	39.00					
11 June	31.00	29.00				
13 June	29.00					
18 June	25.00	25.00				
20 June	22.00	22.00				
23 June	20.00	20.00				
24 June	18.50	18.50				
27 June				23.0		
30 June	18.20	18.20				
1 July	17.90	17.90				
7 July	17.00	17.00				
8 July	16.50	16.50				
9 July	16.20	16.20				
15 July	16.00					
16 July		16.00				
22 July	15.70	15.70				
23 July	15.20	15.40				
24 July		15.20				
28 July	14.90	14.90				
1 August		14.70				
4 August	14.50	14.50				
31 October		14.80				
1 December	19.00	18.50				
2 December	18.50	18.00				
3 December	17.75	17.50				
4 December	17.00	16.75				
9 December	15.50	15.50				
10 December		15.00				
11 December	15.00					
17 December		14.75				
1998						
23 January				19.0		
20 March		15.00				
17 July		14.50				
30 July					7.50	
14 August		14.00	11.50	16.00		
25 September		13.50				
27 October		12.50	10.0	15.0		
13 November		11.50				
4 December		10.50				
23 December		9.50	7.5	12.5		
1999						
18-Jan		8.75			5.0	
28-Jan						
29-Jan		8.00				
12-Mar		7.50	6.0	10.0		

Source: Czech National Bank.

Table 6.7. PRIBOR Interest Rates, 1993-98

	Nominal rates				Real rates based on CPI				Real rates based on PPI		
	PRIBOR		short-term		PRIBOR		short-term		PRIBOR		short-term
	1W	1Y	new credits	time deposits	1W	1Y	new credits	time deposits	1W	1Y	new credits
					(In percent)						
1/93	9.0	14.8	14 5	9 2	-12 2	-6.4	-6.7	-12.0	-3.2	2.6	2 3
2/93	11.3	15.5	14.5	9 4	-10.6	-6.4	-7.4	-12.5	-2 8	1 4	0 4
3/93	13.1	16.0	15 2	9 7	-8 8	-5.9	-6.7	-12.2	-1.4	1.5	0 7
4/93	17.9	18.5	15.6	10.1	-3.9	-3.3	-6.2	-11 7	3.7	4 3	1 4
5/93	14.6	17.2	15.2	10 4	-7.2	-4.6	-6.6	-11.4	1 5	4 1	2.1
6/93	13.3	15 7	15.1	9.4	-8.5	-6.1	-6.7	-12.4	0.5	2 9	2 3
7/93	9.7	14.4	14.2	9 4	-11.6	-6.9	-7.1	-11.9	-3 2	1.5	1.3
8/93	10.5	14.2	14.5	9.6	-10.9	-7.2	-6.9	-11.8	-2.5	1.2	1.5
9/93	9.2	13.8	15.1	9.6	-11.7	-7.1	-5.8	-11.3	-3.8	0.8	2.1
10/93	7.7	13.5	14.8	9.7	-12.2	-6.4	-5.1	-10.2	-5.3	0.5	1.8
11/93	6.0	12.8	13.1	9 6	-11.9	-5.1	-4.8	-8.3	-5.9	0.9	1 2
12/93	5.9	11.9	14.0	9.6	-12.3	-6.3	-4.2	-8.6	-5.5	0.5	2.6
1/94	7.8	10.9	11.9	9.7	-3.1	0.0	1.0	-1.2	-0.4	2.7	3.7
2/94	7.7	10.5	12.2	9 6	-2.0	0.8	2.5	-0.1	2 4	5.2	6.9
3/94	8.4	10.4	12.2	9.7	-1.0	1.0	2.8	0.3	3.4	5.4	7.2
4/94	7.2	9.9	12.9	9.5	-2.0	0.7	3.7	0.3	2.3	5.0	8.0
5/94	6.7	9.1	12.3	9.3	-2.6	-0.2	3.0	0.0	1.7	4.1	7.3
6/94	6.1	8.3	12.1	9.7	-3 7	-1 4	2.4	0.0	0.8	3.0	6.8
7/94	7.5	8.4	12.3	9.2	-2.2	-1.3	2.6	-0.5	2.6	3.5	7.4
8/94	8.1	8.5	11.9	9.3	-2.1	-1.7	1.7	-0.9	3.3	3.7	7.1
9/94	8.7	9.0	13.1	9.1	-1.8	-1.5	2.6	-1.4	3.8	4.1	8.2
10/94	10.0	10.4	12.2	9.2	-0.7	-0.3	1.5	-1.5	5.3	5.7	7.5
11/94	11.1	11.3	13.0	9.2	0.4	0.6	2.3	-1.5	6.0	6.2	7.9
12/94	12.3	12.7	13.3	9.6	2.1	2.5	3.1	-0.6	6.7	7.1	7.7
1/95	11.2	11.5	13.5	9.6	2.3	2.6	4.6	0.7	4.2	4.5	6.5
2/95	10.7	10.8	13.2	9.5	1.2	1.3	3.7	0.0	3.3	3.4	5.8
3/95	10.3	10.4	13.3	9.5	0.7	0.8	3.7	-0.1	2.6	2.7	5.6
4/95	10.3	10.4	12.7	9.5	0.1	0.2	2.5	-0.7	2.6	2.7	5.0
5/95	10.3	10.4	12.4	9.6	0.1	0.2	2.2	-0.6	2.7	2.8	4.8
6/95	10.7	10.8	12.9	9.6	0.7	0.8	2.9	-0.4	3.3	3.4	5.5
7/95	11.6	11.7	12.8	9.7	1.9	2.0	3.1	0.0	4.0	4.1	5.2
8/95	11.0	11.4	13.3	9.8	2.0	2.4	4.3	0.8	3.2	3.6	5.5
9/95	10.9	11.1	13.1	9.8	2.3	2.5	4.5	1.2	3.1	3.3	5.3
10/95	11.1	11.2	12.9	9 8	3.0	3.1	4.8	1.7	3.3	3.4	5.1
11/95	11.3	11.2	13.1	9.7	3.3	3.2	5.1	1.7	3.6	3.5	5.4
12/95	11.2	10.9	12.9	9.7	3.3	3.0	5.0	1.8	4.0	3.7	5.7
1/96	11.1	10.5	12.7	9.6	2.1	1.5	3.7	0.6	4.8	4.2	6.4
2/96	11.1	10 7	12 7	9.6	2.5	2.1	4.1	1.0	5.4	5.0	7.0
3/96	11.3	11.0	12.7	9.6	2.4	2.1	3.8	0.7	6.1	5.8	7 5
4/96	11.6	11.3	12.7	9.4	3.1	2.8	4.2	0.9	6.4	6.1	7.5
5/96	11.8	11.8	13.0	9.3	3.1	3.1	4.3	0.6	6.7	6.7	7.9
6/96	12.1	12.2	13.1	9.2	3.7	3.8	4.7	0.8	7.3	7.4	8.3
7/96	12.6	12.9	13.7	9.4	3.2	3.5	4.3	0.0	8.2	8.5	9.3
8/96	12.6	12.8	13.8	9.3	3.0	3.2	4.2	-0.3	8.4	8.6	9.6
9/96	12.6	12.4	13.8	9.4	3.7	3.5	4.9	0.5	8.7	8.5	9.9
10/96	12.6	12.3	13.7	9.5	3.9	3.6	5.0	0.8	8.5	8.2	9.6
11/96	12.6	12.3	13.8	9.4	4.0	3.7	5.2	0.8	8.4	8.1	9.6
12/96	12.6	12.2	13.6	9.3	4.0	3.6	5.0	0.7	8.2	7.8	9.2
1/97	12.5	11.8	13.5	9.1	5.1	4.4	6.1	1.7	8.0	7.3	9.0
2/97	12.5	11.4	13.4	9.4	5.2	4.1	6.1	2.1	8.3	7.2	9.2
3/97	12.5	11.8	13.4	9.3	5.7	5.0	6.6	2.5	8.2	7.5	9.1
4/97	12.5	11.8	13.4	9.3	5.8	5.1	6.7	2.6	8.2	7.5	9.1
5/97	42.3	15.8	23.8	15.5	36.0	9.5	17.5	9.2	38.2	11.7	19.7
6/97	33.8	19.0	21.1	13.0	27.0	12.2	14.3	6.2	29.3	14.5	16.6
7/97	17.3	15.9	17.0	11.7	7.9	6.5	7.6	2.3	12.2	10.8	11.9
8/97	14.7	14.4	15.8	11.1	4.8	4.5	5.9	1.2	9.0	8.7	10.1
9/97	14.6	14.8	15.7	11.0	4.3	4.5	5.4	0.7	8.8	9.0	9.9
10/97	14.9	15.0	15.5	10.8	4.7	4.8	5.3	0.6	9.3	9.4	9.9
11/97	15.4	16.6	15.6	11.2	5.3	6.5	5.5	1.1	9.9	11.1	10.!
12/97	16.6	17.4	16.5	11.6	6.6	7.4	6.5	1.6	10.9	11.7	10.8
1/98	15.3	16.7	15.8	11.9	2.2	3.6	2.7	-1.2	9.2	10.6	9.7
2/98	14.9	16.4	15.8	11.9	1.5	3.0	2.4	-1.5	8.3	9.8	9.2
3/98	15.0	16.1	16.2	11.9	1.6	2.7	2.8	-1.5	8.5	9.6	9.7
4/98	15.1	15.9	16.3	11.9	2.0	2.8	3.2	-1.2	8.9	9.7	10.1
5/98	15.2	15.6	15.8	11.6	2.2	2.6	2.8	-1.4	9.0	9.4	9.6
6/98	15.3	15.8	16.0	12.0	3.3	3.8	4.0	0.0	9.7	10.2	10.4
7/98	14.8	14.0	15.3	11.8	4.4	3.6	4.9	1.4	9.6	8.8	10.1
8/98	14.4	13.5	15.1	11.6	5.0	4.1	5.7	2.2	10.2	9.3	10.9
9/98	14.0	13.4	14.5	11.4	5.2	4.6	5.7	2.6	10.3	9.7	10 9
10/98	13.4	12.6	14.3	11.1	5.2	4.4	6.1	2.9	10.1	9.3	11.0
11/98	12.0	10.5	12.9	10.1	4.5	3.0	5.4	2.6	9.2	7.7	10.1
12/98	10.6	9.3	11.7	9.2	3.8	2.5	4.9	2.4	8.4	7.1	9.5

Note: Real Rates = nominal rates - actual index (CPI and PPI) in given month.

Source: Czech National Bank.

Table 6.8. Forward Rate Agreement, 1997-98

(monthly averages in percent)

	1997				1998											
	3	6	9	12	1	2	3	4	5	6	7	8	9	10	11	12
3 * 6	11.82	14.60	14.53	16.70	16.28	16.00	15.62	15.46	15.21	15.38	13.78	13.39	13.16	12.36	10.27	9.02
3 * 9	11.52	14.22	14.53	16.70	16.29	16.10	15.80	15.56	15.22	15.39	13.67	13.20	13.02	12.21	10.15	8.99
6 * 9	11.00	13.33	14.02	16.03	15.63	15.63	15.43	15.07	14.66	14.81	13.08	12.60	12.46	11.68	9.82	8.79
6 * 12	10.97	13.13	13.97	16.01	15.63	15.72	15.52	15.14	14.67	14.82	13.06	12.51	12.37	11.57	9.75	8.79
9 * 12	10.57	12.63	13.52	15.47	15.08	15.17	15.09	14.67	14.18	14.34	12.62	12.07	11.94	11.17	9.47	8.62
12 * 24	10.44	12.16	13.00	15.28	14.74	15.04	14.95	14.56	13.75	13.78	12.13	11.70	11.45	10.85	9.71	9.03
9*12 - 3*6 spread	-1.25	-1.97	-1.01	-1.23	-1.19	-0.83	-0.53	-0.79	-1.03	-1.04	-1.16	-1.31	-1.23	-1.19	-0.81	-0.40
6*12 - 3*9 spread	-0.55	-1.09	-0.55	-0.69	-0.67	-0.38	-0.28	-0.42	-0.55	-0.57	-0.61	-0.69	-0.65	-0.64	-0.40	0.20
offer - bid spread (3*6)	0.10	0.21	0.21	0.21	0.20	0.18	0.16	0.14	0.11	0.12	0.11	0.15	0.16	0.15	0.16	0.19
offer - bid spread (12*24)	0.17	0.36	0.35	0.30	0.28	0.20	0.19	0.15	0.15	0.12	0.18	0.19	0.18	0.30	0.66	0.58

Source: Czech National Bank.

Table 6.9. Interest Rate Swaps, 1997-98

(monthly averages in percent)

	1997				1998											
	3	6	9	12	1	2	3	4	5	6	7	8	9	10	11	12
1Y	11.89	18.07	14.92	17.54	16.91	16.67	16.32	16.06	15.71	15.97	14.16	13.65	13.44	12.68	10.68	9.52
2Y	11.17	15.34	13.94	16.58	15.92	15.93	15.69	15.39	14.83	15.00	13.24	12.77	12.53	11.77	10.02	9.13
3Y	11.05	14.34	13.26	15.93	15.37	15.40	15.20	14.83	14.01	14.17	12.58	12.24	12.07	11.32	9.80	9.06
4Y	11.01	13.79	12.84	15.54	15.01	15.06	14.78	14.33	13.27	13.49	12.11	11.85	11.76	11.05	9.69	8.99
5Y	10.98	13.28	12.50	15.25	14.67	14.81	14.49	13.88	12.75	12.98	11.67	11.55	11.51	10.85	9.63	8.93
6Y	10.97	12.81	12.28	15.19	14.81	14.64	14.28	13.55	12.25	12.43	11.32	11.28	11.26	10.64	9.38	8.73
7Y	10.91	12.64	12.09	14.88	14.34	14.42	14.11	13.33	11.88	12.08	11.03	11.06	11.09	10.51	9.29	8.71
8Y	10.94	12.47	12.03	14.90	14.24	14.27	14.01	13.18	11.69	11.85	10.83	10.85	10.90	10.36	9.23	8.67
9Y	10.90	12.31	11.92	14.29	14.14	14.14	13.93	13.05	11.55	11.65	10.68	10.73	10.72	10.24	9.17	8.63
10Y	10.88	12.20	11.81	14.24	13.86	14.02	13.83	13.01	11.45	11.60	10.51	10.60	10.61	10.15	9.06	8.61
2Y - 1Y spread	-0.72	-2.73	-0.98	-0.97	-0.99	-0.75	-0.64	-0.67	-0.88	-0.97	-0.92	-0.87	-0.91	-0.90	-0.66	-0.39
5Y - 1Y spread	-0.91	-4.78	-2.42	-2.30	-2.24	-1.86	-1.83	-2.18	-2.96	-2.99	-2.49	-2.09	-1.94	-1.82	-1.05	-0.60
10Y - 1Y spread	-1.01	-5.87	-3.11	-3.30	-3.05	-2.65	-2.50	-3.04	-4.27	-4.37	-3.64	-3.04	-2.84	-2.53	-1.62	-0.92
offer - bid spread (1Y)	0.12	0.38	0.13	0.23	0.21	0.14	0.13	0.13	0.12	0.11	0.12	0.14	0.13	0.12	0.18	0.25
offer - bid spread (2Y)	0.12	0.54	0.19	0.30	0.22	0.20	0.18	0.17	0.12	0.16	0.16	0.20	0.19	0.18	0.21	0.28
offer - bid spread (5Y)	0.17	0.60	0.24	0.37	0.30	0.23	0.17	0.18	0.20	0.19	0.19	0.21	0.20	0.21	0.34	0.31
offer - bid spread (10Y)	0.35	0.76	0.29	0.46	0.48	0.37	0.35	0.32	0.26	0.29	0.22	0.28	0.28	0.28	0.21	0.20

Source: Czech National Bank.

Table 6.10. Lending and Deposit Rates of Commercial Banks, 1993-98

		All Loans				New Loans				Deposits					
		Total	Short-term	edium-term	Long-term	Total	Short-term	Medium-term	Long-term	Total	Demand	Total	Term Deposits		
													Short-term	Medium-term	Long-term
								(In percent per annum)							
1993	March	14.00	15.70	16.17	10.35	14.55	14.76	16.02	9.40	6.95	2.09	11.22	9.45	12.22	14.05
	June	14.40	16.27	16.03	10.55	15.49	15.31	16.99	11.71	7.25	2.27	11.27	9.97	11.99	13.66
	September	14.10	15.43	15.91	10.36	15.29	14.64	17.35	16.47	6.99	2.35	10.85	9.51	11.54	13.64
	December	13.90	15.10	15.57	10.44	14.42	13.97	16.36	13.31	6.93	2.44	10.87	9.61	11.51	13.62
1994	March	13.24	13.87	15.08	10.55	12.80	12.10	15.17	13.24	7.26	2.58	10.93	9.68	11.84	12.83
	June	13.25	13.52	15.24	11.02	12.86	12.37	14.28	14.69	7.14	2.51	10.80	9.47	11.78	13.14
	September	13.12	13.25	14.99	11.10	13.02	12.51	14.21	14.10	7.02	2.64	10.49	9.19	11.37	12.62
	December	12.86	12.86	14.57	11.13	13.30	12.89	14.71	14.00	6.87	2.53	10.34	9.35	11.17	11.75
1995	March	12.76	12.71	14.37	11.16	13.47	13.33	14.26	13.36	6.94	2.55	10.29	9.55	11.04	11.16
	June	12.77	12.71	14.28	11.31	12.94	12.67	14.31	12.99	6.99	2.49	10.27	9.57	11.12	10.52
	September	12.88	12.81	14.41	11.43	13.30	13.08	14.43	13.82	6.97	2.48	10.25	9.74	10.98	10.07
	December	12.79	12.68	14.26	11.49	13.21	12.98	14.33	13.60	6.94	2.62	10.10	9.73	10.79	9.36
1996	January	12.57	12.49	14.14	11.40	12.86	12.67	14.17	13.18	6.90	2.54	9.93	9.64	10.66	8.65
	June	12.38	12.31	13.59	11.37	13.36	13.13	14.38	13.78	6.70	2.55	9.25	9.24	10.01	6.71
	September	12.67	12.43	13.95	11.96	13.96	13.83	14.52	14.30	6.72	2.51	9.30	9.40	9.94	6.35
	December	12.48	12.40	13.50	11.76	13.61	13.65	14.34	12.48	6.68	2.52	9.32	9.33	9.85	6.24
1997	January	12.07	12.02	12.67	11.64	13.59	13.53	14.29	13.59	6.62	2.44	8.98	9.10	9.82	5.70
	February	11.93	11.95	12.46	11.47	13.54	13.43	14.01	14.03	6.66	2.33	9.11	9.38	9.79	5.70
	March	11.93	11.78	12.67	11.51	13.53	13.41	14.51	13.57	6.68	2.38	9.10	9.26	9.84	5.73
	April	11.92	11.81	12.59	11.51	13.43	13.37	13.58	13.93	6.63	2.33	9.01	9.29	9.83	5.26
	May	15.75	17.08	16.27	13.39	21.56	23.83	16.59	13.73	9.89	2.28	13.53	15.55	11.14	5.48
	June	14.56	14.37	15.27	14.24	20.35	21.09	17.40	16.91	8.87	2.25	11.83	12.98	11.32	5.26
	July	13.84	13.62	14.37	13.70	17.02	17.04	16.51	17.39	8.21	2.29	10.88	11.68	10.82	5.55
	August	13.19	12.91	13.90	13.01	15.81	15.83	15.49	15.91	7.78	2.10	10.42	11.06	10.97	5.19
	September	12.93	12.60	13.63	12.81	15.98	15.72	15.98	16.22	7.74	2.08	10.35	10.98	10.99	5.36
	October	13.17	13.03	14.02	12.66	15.51	15.51	15.38	15.67	7.58	2.13	10.18	10.79	10.91	5.36
	November	13.30	13.21	14.08	12.80	15.78	15.59	16.45	16.77	7.84	2.06	10.51	11.22	11.12	5.36
	December	13.87	14.13	14.61	12.98	16.54	16.53	16.99	16.03	8.05	2.15	10.90	11.58	12.15	5.24
1998	January	13.68	13.76	14.47	12.97	15.68	15.84	16.50	13.93	8.47	2.10	11.09	11.88	12.20	5.09
	February	13.57	13.58	14.41	12.90	15.73	15.83	15.45	14.94	8.47	2.13	11.08	11.91	12.15	5.04
	March	13.45	13.47	14.31	12.75	16.13	16.23	17.11	14.12	8.47	2.06	11.06	11.87	12.22	4.93
	April	13.46	13.77	14.12	12.58	16.16	16.28	15.08	15.91	8.46	2.08	10.99	11.89	12.14	4.72
	May	13.48	13.80	14.23	12.51	15.76	15.75	15.61	16.08	8.20	2.04	10.73	11.60	11.86	4.73
	June	13.46	14.08	13.91	12.37	15.95	16.02	15.17	16.22	8.40	2.04	10.98	11.97	11.88	4.69
	July	13.03	13.55	13.54	12.05	15.27	15.33	14.76	15.12	8.39	2.02	10.87	11.83	11.84	4.64
	August	12.93	13.51	13.41	11.87	14.81	15.13	14.39	12.48	8.18	2.04	10.67	11.60	11.71	4.56
	September	12.72	13.37	13.24	11.58	14.57	14.55	14.48	15.02	8.18	1.91	10.55	11.42	11.69	4.57
	October	12.24	12.76	12.86	11.17	14.25	14.29	14.02	14.31	7.97	1.89	10.28	11.10	11.59	4.42
	November	11.62	11.99	12.31	10.70	12.85	12.88	12.78	12.65	7.33	1.97	9.46	10.12	11.11	4.19
	December	10.51	10.61	10.66	10.29	11.87	11.65	13.35	11.74	6.66	1.88	8.73	9.15	10.94	4.20

Note: For 1993-96, figures are quarterly averages. Short-term: up to and including one year; medium term: more than one and up to and including four years; long-term: over four years.

Source: Czech National Bank.

Table 6.11. Selected Interest Rates, 1994-98

		Discount Rate[1]	Lombard Rate[1]	2-week Repo Rate	T-bills[2] bills (Average)	Interbank[3]				Credits[4]				Deposits[4]	
						Overnight	7-day	30-day	3-month	Total Enterprizes	State Enterprizes	Private[5]	Households	Total	useholds
						(In percent per annum)									
1994	March	8.0	11.5	..	..	7.37	7.93	8.42	8.93	13.24	13.04	14.35	7.08	7.26	7.75
	June	8.0	10.5	..	..	5.88	6.64	7.23	7.77	13.25	13.50	13.87	7.78	7.14	7.89
	Sept.	8.0	10.5	..	..	7.86	8.14	8.27	8.36	13.12	12.85	13.88	7.59	7.02	7.68
	Dec.	8.5	11.5	..	..	10.41	11.11	11.28	11.36	12.86	12.32	13.62	7.84	6.87	7.83
1995	March	8.5	11.5	..	8.01	10.21	10.74	10.84	10.86	12.76	12.26	13.42	8.12	6.94	7.94
	June	9.5	12.5	..	8.20	10.27	10.40	10.46	10.50	12.77	12.35	13.40	7.50	6.99	7.98
	Sept.	9.5	12.5	..	8.71	10.96	11.17	11.27	11.31	12.88	12.29	13.56	6.20	6.97	7.93
	Dec.	9.5	12.5	11.3	8.96	11.01	11.19	11.15	11.11	12.79	12.19	13.41	6.39	6.94	7.92
1996	March	9.5	12.5	11.5	9.03	11.27	11.26	11.23	10.86	12.47	11.74	13.11	6.63	6.92	7.82
	June	9.5	14.0	12.4	9.70	11.10	12.07	12.10	11.82	12.38	11.46	12.87	6.94	6.70	7.24
	Sept.	10.5	14.0	12.4	12.11	11.79	12.59	12.58	12.69	12.67	11.82	13.17	7.26	6.71	7.38
	Dec.	10.5	14.0	12.4	11.92	12.46	12.61	12.63	12.68	12.48	11.72	13.02	7.67	6.68	7.33
1997	March	10.5	14.0	12.4	9.00	12.46	12.48	12.46	12.38	11.93	10.79	12.47	7.89	6.68	7.30
	June	13.0	23.0	27.6	11.85	31.52	33.84	31.54	19.67	14.56	13.36	15.09	9.13	8.87	8.93
	Sept.	13.0	23.0	14.5	11.15	13.49	14.59	14.71	15.42	12.93	12.31	13.30	9.04	7.74	8.21
	Dec.	13.0	23.0	15.5	11.40	12.55	16.64	17.49	16.46	13.87	12.80	14.47	9.30	8.05	9.00
1998	Jan.	13.0	19.0	14.8	16.22	13.48	15.31	16.22	16.59	12.11	12.89	14.18	9.26	8.47	9.06
	Feb.	13.0	19.0	14.8	15.50	13.95	14.88	15.44	15.92	12.05	12.77	14.08	9.29	8.47	9.07
	March	13.0	19.0	14.8	15.48	13.91	14.95	15.18	15.52	11.97	12.64	13.93	9.35	8.47	9.05
	April	13.0	19.0	15.0	15.25	14.76	15.07	15.19	15.47	11.97	12.62	13.93	9.36	8.46	9.01
	May	13.0	19.0	15.0	15.07	14.44	15.23	15.38	15.55	11.95	12.48	13.97	9.39	8.20	8.84
	June	13.0	19.0	15.0	15.49	13.63	15.26	15.63	15.81	11.91	12.28	13.95	9.49	8.40	8.88
	July	13.0	19.0	14.8	14.33	14.99	14.83	14.72	14.50	11.65	12.01	13.46	9.49	8.39	8.83
	Aug.	11.5	16.0	14.2	13.75	13.70	14.37	14.36	14.23	11.61	11.97	13.40	9.47	8.18	8.69
	Sept.	11.5	16.0	13.9	13.48	14.05	13.99	13.90	13.82	11.48	11.85	13.10	9.50	8.18	8.61
	Oct.	10.0	15.0	13.4	12.00	13.18	13.43	13.35	13.20	11.13	11.29	12.59	9.52	7.97	8.47
	Nov.	10.0	15.0	11.9	10.53	12.00	11.97	11.70	11.31	10.76	11.04	11.86	9.40	7.33	7.88
	Dec.	7.5	12.5	10.4	9.83	10.84	10.56	10.46	10.08	10.34	10.61	10.85	9.56	6.66	7.48

Notes: For 1993-97, figures are quarterly averages.
1/ End of period.
2/ Average rate on 91-day bills.
3/ Offer rates.
4/ Weighted average on total outstanding stocks.
5/ Includes private corporations and cooperatives.

Source: Czech National Bank.

Table 6.12. Distribution of Bank Credits to the Nongovernment Sector, 1992-98

(In billions of CZK, end of period)

	1992	1993	1994	1995	1996	1997	1998 March	June	Sept.	Dec.
Total credits[1]	567.8	672.9	776.5	826.0	895.6	914.6	915.2	912.6	916.5	869.2
By maturity[2]										
Short-term	217.2	277.0	315.9	346.0	387.9	384.1	378.0	390.6	370.3	357.2
Medium-term	155.0	194.1	233.6	240.3	232.0	223.2	221.5	209.0	226.4	195.6
Long-term	195.6	201.8	227.0	239.7	275.7	307.3	315.7	313.0	319.9	316.4
By sector										
State sector[3]	276.4	223.8	212.3	167.9	151.8	143.4	142.5	120.1	117.4	117.4
Private sector[4]	212.4	353.1	450.4	551.1	637.1	649.9	648.4	653.5	663.6	591.0
Enterprises under foreign control	15.0	20.1	42.1	47.3	55.7	59.5	60.8	70.3	62.6	60.7
Households	46.5	46.5	46.4	35.5	38.0	48.5	50.1	53.7	57.1	62.3
Non-residents	0.2	3.2	2.7	2.9	5.8	9.0	9.8	12.0	14.0	36.2
Others	17.2	26.2	22.6	21.3	7.2	4.3	3.6	3.0	1.8	1.6
By branch of industry										
Agriculture, hunting and fishing	27.3	26.4	25.7	30.9	32.5	30.0	32.6	30.9	28.4	25.7
Forestry and logging	2.6	0.9	1.4	1.3	2.5	1.8	1.9	1.6	1.5	1.3
Mining and quarrying	11.1	11.8	10.9	10.6	10.2	13.3	10.1	10.9	10.6	11.6
Manufacturing	186.5	198.1	238.6	253.5	282.7	254.2	252.3	256.9	231.6	223.3
Production and distribution of electricity	17.2	18.9	15.9	19.5	29.3	34.1	32.6	30.8	32.2	30.4
Construction	16.6	22.9	26.9	29.3	30.5	31.3	32.7	33.1	31.4	29.8
Trade, sales, catering, and accommodation	125.5	153.8	198.3	213.7	216.5	209.6	213.8	201.0	196.6	185.9
Transport, storage, tourism, and communications	12.6	14.8	22.5	21.0	22.1	27.5	26.5	28.4	29.3	28.7
Others	168.3	225.3	236.3	246.2	269.3	312.8	312.7	319.0	354.9	332.5

1/ Excludes foreign currency denominated credits.
2/ Short-term: up to and including one year; medium-term: more than one and up to and including four years; long-term: over four years.
3/ Including CNB credits to the National Property Fund.
4/ Including cooperatives.

Source: Czech National Bank.

Table 6.13. Distribution of Classified Loans by Maturity, 1994-98

	1994				1995				1996			
	March	June	Sep.	Dec.	March	June	Sep.	Dec.	March	June	Sep.	Dec.
	(In billions of CZK, end of period)											
Total	156.6	176.6	264.0	293.1	298.5	316.0	321.6	318.0	332.8	338.6	337.7	348.9
Short-term	80.9	78.9	133.9	125.2	125.5	125.5	133.5	137.4	135.1	138.3	137.5	136.1
Medium-term	29.6	41.5	73.0	98.7	103.9	110.7	107.2	106.1	108.6	110.9	108.0	111.5
Long-term	46.1	56.2	57.1	69.2	69.1	79.8	80.9	74.5	89.1	89.4	92.2	101.3
	(In percent of total credits)											
Total	21.8	23.5	34.1	36.0	36.2	37.0	36.3	34.5	35.2	34.8	34.0	34.4
Short-term	11.3	10.5	17.3	15.4	15.2	14.7	15.1	14.9	14.3	14.2	13.8	13.4
Medium-term	4.1	5.5	9.4	12.1	12.6	13.0	12.1	11.5	11.5	11.4	10.9	11.0
Long-term	6.4	7.5	7.4	8.5	8.4	9.3	9.1	8.1	9.4	9.2	9.3	10.0

	1997				1998			
	March	June	Sep.	Dec.	March	June	Sep.	Dec.
	(In billions of CZK, end of period)							
Total	352.9	364.8	364.4	373.8	380.9	388.5	403.7	382.4
Short-term	139.0	139.7	133.4	136.3	135.6	141.7	130.2	127.5
Medium-term	105.8	115.2	114.9	119.2	120.3	115.5	127.0	107.9
Long-term	108.1	109.9	116.1	118.4	125.0	131.3	146.5	146.9
	(In percent of total credits)							
Total	34.0	33.5	33.5	32.8	33.3	33.1	34.2	33.0
Short-term	13.4	12.8	12.2	11.9	11.8	12.1	11.0	11.0
Medium-term	10.2	10.6	10.6	10.4	10.5	9.8	10.8	9.3
Long-term	10.4	10.1	10.7	10.4	10.9	11.2	12.4	12.7

Note: Short-term: up to and including one year; medium term: more than one and up to and including four years; long-term: over four years. Konsolidacni Banka is included.

Source: Czech National Bank.

Table 6.14. Distribution of Classified Loans by Type, 1994-98

	1994				1995				1996				1997				1998			
	March	June	Sept.	Dec.	March	June	Sept.	Dec.	March	June	Sept.	Dec.	March	June	Sept.	Dec.	March	June	Sept.	Dec.
(In billions of CZK, end of period)																				
Total	156.6	176.7	264.1	293.1	298.6	316.0	321.6	318.0	332.8	338.6	338.7	348.9	352.9	364.8	364.4	373.8	380.9	388.5	403.7	382.4
Watch	17.0	18.5	56.2	54.8	53.4	53.1	50.1	48.4	50.9	53.7	49.4	52.6	56.9	56.5	61.0	68.9	61.5	71.9	65.2	59.0
Sub-standard	40.1	43.8	41.5	42.7	39.0	39.5	39.8	35.6	35.6	35.3	35.4	29.6	35.5	32.8	30.8	30.3	36.7	36.8	40.1	49.5
Doubtful	48.3	46.8	51.6	56.3	51.6	48.3	41.9	36.7	37.2	30.6	32.2	39.0	42.2	37.4	36.4	38.3	34.8	32.9	49.1	43.0
Loss	51.2	67.6	114.8	139.3	154.6	175.1	189.8	197.3	209.2	219.0	221.6	227.6	218.2	238.1	236.1	236.3	247.9	246.9	249.3	230.8
(In percent of total classified loans)																				
Total	100.0	100.0	100.0	100.0	100.0	100.0	100.0	100.0	100.0	100.0	100.0	100.0	100.0	100.0	100.0	100.0	100.0	100.0	100.0	100.0
Watch	10.9	10.5	21.3	18.7	17.9	16.8	15.6	15.2	15.3	15.9	14.6	15.1	16.1	15.5	16.8	18.4	16.1	18.5	16.2	15.4
Sub-standard	25.6	24.8	15.7	14.6	13.1	12.5	12.4	11.2	10.7	10.4	10.5	8.5	10.1	9.0	8.5	8.1	9.6	9.5	9.9	13.0
Doubtful	30.9	26.5	19.5	19.2	17.3	15.3	13.0	11.5	11.2	9.0	9.5	11.2	12.0	10.3	10.0	10.2	9.1	8.5	12.2	11.2
Loss	32.7	38.2	43.5	47.5	51.8	55.4	59.0	62.1	62.9	64.7	65.4	65.2	61.8	65.3	64.8	63.2	65.1	63.6	61.7	60.4
(In percent of total loans)																				
Total	21.8	23.6	34.2	36.0	36.1	37.0	36.3	34.6	35.2	34.7	34.1	34.3	34.0	33.5	30.9	32.8	33.3	33.1	34.2	33.0
Watch	2.4	2.5	7.3	6.7	6.5	6.2	5.7	5.3	5.4	5.5	5.0	5.2	5.5	5.2	5.2	6.0	5.4	6.1	5.5	5.1
Sub-standard	5.6	5.9	5.4	5.3	4.7	4.6	4.5	3.9	3.8	3.6	3.6	2.9	3.4	3.0	2.6	2.7	3.2	3.1	3.4	4.3
Doubtful	6.7	6.2	6.7	6.9	6.2	5.7	4.7	4.0	3.9	3.1	3.2	3.8	4.1	3.4	3.1	3.4	3.0	2.8	4.2	3.7
Loss	7.1	9.0	14.8	17.1	18.7	20.5	21.4	21.5	22.1	22.5	22.3	22.4	21.0	21.9	20.0	20.7	21.6	21.1	21.2	19.9

Note: Konsolidacni Banka is included.

Source: Czech National Bank.

Table 6.15. Capital Markets Indices and Trade Volumes, 1997-98

A. SHARE MARKET INDICES

	1997				1998					
	3	6	9	12	3	6	9	10	11	12
	(last day of the month in points)									
PX-50	558	489	536	495	505	467	360	388	390	394
PX-GLOB	670	592	652	599	615	568	460	474	476	478
PK-30	748	649	740	664	698	656	521	549	554	564

B. BOND MARKET

	1997				1998					
	3	6	9	12	3	6	9	10	11	12
	(monthly averages in percent)									
YIELDS OF TAXED GOVERNMENT BONDS										
Maturity in years										
1Y	..	..	..	..	..	14.51	12.81	12.10	10.11	8.88
2Y	..	14.35	13.65	16.23	14.95	14.39	12.55	11.82	9.96	8.77
3Y	..	13.84	13.30	15.67	14.64	13.58	11.98	11.35	9.67	8.57
4Y	..	14.72	12.94	15.10	14.38	13.13	11.59	11.01	9.48	8.52
5Y	..	12.97	12.63	14.85	14.41	13.03	11.51	10.90	9.49	8.64
6Y	..	12.88	12.39	14.84	14.43	..	..	..	..	..
YIELDS OF CORPORATE BONDS										
Maturity in years										
1Y	11.57	16.38	15.14	17.93	16.29	..	..	..	..	..
2Y	11.34	15.23	14.19	16.57	15.63	14.57	12.92	12.46	11.50	..
3Y	11.05	14.10	13.50	15.70	15.41	14.21	12.86	12.70	11.75	..
4Y	11.08	13.71	13.37	15.20	15.21	13.82	12.48	12.31	11.47	..
5Y	11.14	13.45	12.97	15.07	14.87	13.33	11.86	11.54	10.93	..
6Y	11.12	13.30	12.71	15.06	14.55	12.95	11.86	11.65	11.14	..
7Y	11.35	13.42	12.72	14.92	14.86	12.86	12.23	12.05	11.44	..
8Y	11.13	13.11	12.83	14.69	14.68	12.62	12.15	11.99	11.37	..
9Y	11.07	12.94	12.64	14.42	14.35	12.37	12.08	11.94	11.31	..
10Y	11.07	12.77	13.03	14.98	15.02	12.31	..	..	..	..
11Y	11.03	12.53	..	..	..	..	..	..	..	..

C. TRADE VOLUMES

	1997				1998					
	3	6	9	12	3	6	9	10	11	12
	(In millions of CZK)									
PSE										
Total trade volume	51,225	73,413	48,545	63,249	52,525	88,271	87,771	96,643	93,902	92,553
of which:										
a) automated system	2,358	1,125	1,589	1,368	1,718	6,210	11,892	9,886	8,347	6,772
b) outright and block trades	48,867	72,288	46,956	61,881	50,807	82,061	75,879	86,757	85,555	85,781
RM-SYSTEM										
Total trade and transfer volume	10,517	5,239	13,662	36,870	17,562	22,163	11,271	17,075	20,244	20,837
of which:										
a) running auction	692	392	742	547	1,036	643	552	467	505	491
b) outright and block trades	9,814	4,841	12,915	36,290	16,520	21,425	10,715	16,603	19,737	20,334
c) transfers with declared price	10	6	4	33	6	95	4	5	2	12
SC										
Total volume of charged transfers	100,019	125,576	93,634	150,980	138,738	153,081	159,095	142,123	151,337	141,892

Source: Czech National Bank.

Table 7.1. Inflation Development, 1995-99

year-on-year change in %

1995

	1	2	3	4	5	6	7	8	9	10	11	12
Consumer prices	8 9	9.5	9.6	10 2	10.2	10.0	9 7	9 0	8 6	8 1	8 0	7 9
Regulated prices[1]	5 0	4.8	4.9	6.7	6 7	7.2	9.4	9 4	9.7	10.0	10.1	10.2
(contribution to CPI inflation)[1]	1.17	1.13	1.15	1.56	1 57	1.69	2.19	2.19	2 25	2 28	2 30	2 29
Influence of indirect tax growth on unregulated prices (contribution to CPI inflation)	0.00	0.00	0.00	0.00	0.00	0.00	0.00	0 00	0.00	0.00	0 00	0 00
Net inflation	10.2	10 9	10.9	11.2	11.3	10 8	9.8	8 8	8.2	7.5	7 3	7.3
(contribution to CPI inflation)[1]	7.86	8 38	8.41	8.59	8.68	8.33	7 54	6.80	6.32	5.86	5 72	5 65
of which: food[1]	13.7	14.7	14.7	14.4	14 1	12.6	10.0	7.8	6 8	5 9	5.5	5 4
(contribution to CPI inflation)[1]	4.38	4.71	4.69	4.63	4.53	4 08	3 22	2 55	2.23	1 95	1.82	1 80
adjusted inflation[1]	7 8	8.3	8.3	8.9	9.3	9.6	9.7	9.6	9.3	8.9	8.9	8.7
(contribution to CPI inflation)[1]	3.48	3.67	3.71	3.96	4.15	4 26	4.31	4.26	4.09	3.91	3 90	3 85
Inflation rate[2]	9.9	9.8	9.8	9.9	10.0	10.0	10.0	9.9	9.8	9.6	9.3	9.1

1996

	1	2	3	4	5	6	7	8	9	10	11	12
Consumer prices	9.0	8.6	8.9	8.5	8.7	8.4	9.4	9.6	8.9	8 7	8.6	8.6
Regulated prices[1]	12.6	12.5	12.5	11.3	11.4	9.9	11.8	14.1	13.0	13.0	13.6	13.8
(contribution to CPI inflation)[1]	2.85	2.82	2.81	2.57	2.59	2.27	2.74	3.28	3.05	3.02	3.16	3.17
Influence of indirect tax growth on unregulated prices (contribution to CPI inflation)	0.34	0.34	0.34	0.34	0.34	0.34	0.34	0.34	0.34	0.34	0.34	0.34
Net inflation	7.4	7.0	7.4	7.3	7.4	7.4	8.2	7.8	7.1	7.0	6.6	6.6
(contribution to CPI inflation)[1]	5.73	5.40	5.72	5.61	5.74	5.75	6.29	5.96	5.47	5.37	5.09	5.09
of which: food[1]	6.6	5.9	7.0	7.5	8.1	8.4	9.9	9.1	7.9	8.0	7.4	7.4
(contribution to CPI inflation)[1]	2.20	2.00	2.34	2.50	2.71	2.79	3.21	2.93	2.56	2.60	2.41	2.41
adjusted inflation[1]	8.0	7.7	7.7	7.1	6.9	6.7	6.9	6.8	6.6	6.3	6.0	6.1
(contribution to CPI inflation)[1]	3.53	3.40	3.38	3.10	3.03	2.96	3.07	3.03	2.91	2.78	2.68	2.68
Inflation rate[2]	9.1	9.1	9.0	8.9	8.7	8.6	8.6	8.6	8.7	8.7	8.8	8.8

1997

	1	2	3	4	5	6	7	8	9	10	11	12
Consumer prices	7.4	7.3	6.8	6.7	6.3	6.8	9.4	9.9	10.3	10.2	10.1	10.0
Regulated prices[1]	12.6	12.7	12.6	13.0	13.3	13.3	25.6	22.7	23.2	23.0	22.6	22.7
(contribution to CPI inflation)[1]	2.49	2.49	2.47	2.55	2.59	2.58	5.15	4.68	4.78	4.72	4.63	4 62
Influence of indirect tax growth on unregulated prices (contribution to CPI inflation)	0.00	0.00	0.00	0.00	0.00	0.00	0.00	0.00	0.00	0.00	0.00	0.00
Net inflation	6.1	5.9	5.3	5.2	4.6	5.2	5.3	6.6	6.9	6.9	6.9	6.8
(contribution to CPI inflation)[1]	4.93	4.76	4.29	4.18	3.72	4.17	4.20	5.25	5.51	5.50	5.48	5.42
of which: food[1]	6.0	5.5	4.2	3.6	2.6	3.4	3.5	5.6	6.1	5.8	5.8	5.6
(contribution to CPI inflation)[1]	1.98	1.79	1.39	1.20	0.86	1.14	1.13	1.80	1.97	1.87	1.88	1.82
adjusted inflation[1]	6.2	6.3	6.1	6.3	6 1	6.4	6.5	7.3	7.5	7.7	7.6	7.6
(contribution to CPI inflation)[1]	2.96	2.97	2.90	2.98	2.87	3.03	3.07	3.44	3.54	3.63	3 60	3.60
Inflation rate[2]	8.7	8.6	8.4	8.2	8.0	7.9	7.9	7.9	8.1	8.2	8.3	8.5

1998

	1	2	3	4	5	6	7	8	9	10	11	12
Consumer prices	13.1	13.4	13.4	13.1	13.0	12.0	10.4	9.4	8.8	8.2	7.5	6.8
Regulated prices[1]	30.7	30.8	30.8	30.1	29.8	29.7	21.1	20.9	20.4	20.6	20.5	20.4
(contribution to CPI inflation)[1]	6 36	6.38	6.38	6.26	6.20	6.11	5.00	4.91	4.79	4.81	4.78	4.73
Influence of indirect tax growth on unregulated prices (contribution to CPI inflation)	0.73	0.73	0.73	0.73	0.73	0.73	0.73	0.73	0.73	0.73	0.73	0.73
Net inflation	7.5	7.9	7.9	7.6	7.6	6.5	6.1	4.9	4.3	3.4	2.6	1.7
(contribution to CPI inflation)[1]	6.00	6.31	6.32	6.08	6.07	5 19	4.66	3.73	3.31	2.64	1.96	1.32
of which: food[1]	5.0	6.8	7.2	7.2	7.5	5.8	5.4	3.8	3.1	1.9	0.4	-1.2
(contribution to CPI inflation)[1]	1.97	2.22	2.40	2.44	2.88	1.96	1.75	1.21	1.00	0.60	0.14	-0.38
adjusted inflation[1]	8.5	8.6	8.4	7.9	7.7	6.9	6.6	5.6	5.1	4.5	4.0	3.7
(contribution to CPI inflation)[1]	4.03	4.09	3.92	3.64	3.19	3.22	2.91	2.53	2.30	2.04	1.82	1.70
Inflation rate[2]	8.9	9.5	10.0	10.5	11.1	11.5	11.6	11.5	11.4	11.2	11.0	10.7

1999

	1	2	3	4	5	6	7	8	9	10	11	12
Consumer prices	3.5	2.8	2.5	2.5	2.4	2.2	1.1					
Regulated prices[1]	12.1	11.9	11.7									
(contribution to CPI inflation)[1]	2.97	2.90	2.87									
Influence of indirect tax growth on unregulated prices (contribution to CPI inflation)	0.00	0.00	0.00									
Net inflation	0.7	-0.1	-0.4	-0.3	-0.5	-0.6	-0.5					
(contribution to CPI inflation)[1]	0.54	-0.06	-0.33									
of which: food[1]	-2.0	-3.1	-4.0									
(contribution to CPI inflation)[1]	-0.61	-0.98	-1.25									
adjusted inflation[1]	2.6	2.1	2.1									
(contribution to CPI inflation)[1]	1.15	0.91	0.92									
Inflation rate[2]	9.8	8.9	8.0	7.1	6.3	5.5	4.7					

1/ CNB Calculation.
2/ Moving average of CPI for last 12 months against previous 12 months.

Source: Czech Statistical Office.

Table 7.2. Net Inflation, 1995-99

(change in percent)

1995

	1	2	3	4	5	6	7	8	9	10	11	12
a) From previous month	1.2	1.0	0.3	0.7	0.5	0.8	-0.6	-0.1	0.9	0.7	0.8	0.7
b) From same period of previous year	10.2	10.9	10.9	11.2	11.3	10.8	9.8	8.8	8.2	7.5	7.3	7.3
c) From December of previous year	1.2	2.3	2.6	3.3	3.8	4.7	4.0	4.0	4.9	5.7	6.6	7.3

1996

	1	2	3	4	5	6	7	8	9	10	11	12
a) From previous month	1.4	0.6	0.7	0.6	0.6	0.8	0.1	-0.4	0.3	0.6	0.5	0.7
b) From same period of previous year	7.4	7.0	7.4	7.3	7.4	7.4	8.2	7.8	7.1	7.0	6.6	6.6
c) From December of previous year	1.4	2.0	2.7	3.3	4.0	4.8	4.9	4.5	4.8	5.4	5.9	6.6

1997

	1	2	3	4	5	6	7	8	9	10	11	12
a) From previous month	0.8	0.3	0.1	0.5	0.1	1.4	0.2	0.8	0.6	0.6	0.5	0.6
b) From same period of previous year	6.1	5.9	5.3	5.2	4.6	5.2	5.3	6.6	6.9	6.9	6.9	6.8
c) From December of previous year	0.8	1.2	1.3	1.8	1.9	3.3	3.5	4.4	5.1	5.7	6.2	6.8

1998

	1	2	3	4	5	6	7	8	9	10	11	12
a) From previous month	1.5	0.7	0.1	0.2	0.1	0.4	-0.2	-0.3	0.1	-0.3	-0.3	-0.3
b) From same period of previous year	7.5	7.9	7.9	7.6	7.6	6.5	6.1	4.9	4.3	3.4	2.6	1.7
c) From December of previous year	1.5	2.2	2.3	2.5	2.6	3.0	2.8	2.5	2.6	2.4	2.0	1.7

1999

	1	2	3	4	5	6	7	8	9	10	11	12
a) From previous month	0.5	-0.1	-0.2	0.4	-0.1	0.2	0.0					
b) From same period of previous year	0.7	-0.1	-0.4	-0.3	-0.5	-0.6	-0.5					
c) From December of previous year	0.5	0.4	0.2	0.5	0.4	0.6	0.6					

Source: Czech Statistical Office.

Table 7.3. Consumer Price Index, 1994-98

Period	Aggregate consumer price index numbers	including:									
		Food, beverages, tobacco	Clothing, footwear	Housing water, electricity, gas	Furnishings, household, equipment and mainten. of house	Health	Transport	Leisure	Education	Hotels, cafes and restaurants	Miscellanous goods and services
					(1994 average = 100)						
1994	100.0	100.0	100 0	100.0	100 0	100 0	100.0	100.0	100.0	100.0	100.0
1995	109.1	110.3	110.3	110.1	105 5	102 9	106.2	108.8	118.7	112.0	108.1
1996	118.8	119.4	121.7	123.5	110.1	106.1	114 3	116.1	163.9	118.5	117 2
1997	128.8	125.2	132.4	146 6	116 0	111.5	124.8	124.0	180.3	126.3	127.3
1998	142.6	132.0	140.6	190 9	123.0	116.3	134.3	132.4	208.7	137.6	136.7
1994 - 1st quarter	97.3	95.9	96.8	97.9	98 6	99.3	98.4	98.4	93.3	96.4	98.7
2nd quarter	98.5	97.6	98 9	99.2	99.3	99.7	99.4	99.0	94.3	97.5	99 4
1st half	97.9	96.7	97.9	98.6	99.0	99.5	98.9	98.7	93.9	97.0	99.1
3rd quarter	100.7	100.8	100.5	101.1	100.3	100.3	100 6	101.2	99.6	100.4	100.4
1st-3rd quarters	98.9	98.1	98.8	99.4	99.4	99.8	99.4	99.5	95.8	98.1	99 5
4th quarter	103.6	105.8	103.6	101.8	101.6	100 8	101.6	101.6	112.8	105.9	101.3
1995 - 1st quarter	106.3	109.6	106.1	105.2	103 4	100.9	103.2	104.5	114.6	109.4	102.4
2nd quarter	108.5	110.9	109.1	106.8	105.1	101.9	106.2	108.0	116.4	111.5	108 4
1st half	107.4	110.3	107.6	106.0	104.2	101.4	104.7	106.3	115.5	110.5	105.4
3rd quarter	109.8	109.0	110.9	113.3	105.9	103.8	107.2	111.2	119.3	113.2	109.9
1st-3rd quarters	108.3	109.8	108.7	108.4	104.7	102.2	105.5	107.9	116.8	111.4	106.9
4th quarter	111.9	111.8	114.9	115.0	107.4	105.1	108.3	111.5	124.4	114.1	111.6
1996 - 1st quarter	115.7	117.2	117.4	117.1	108.7	105.5	111.8	114.0	159.4	116.1	113.4
2nd quarter	117.8	120.4	120.5	117.7	109.9	105.7	113.6	115.1	161.3	117.4	117.4
1st half	116.8	118.8	119.0	117.4	109.3	105.6	112.7	114.5	160.4	116.7	115.4
3rd quarter	120.0	119.3	122.8	128.4	110.6	106.1	115.1	118.2	164.1	119.2	118.3
1st-3rd quarters	117.8	119.0	120.3	121 1	109.7	105.8	113.5	115.8	161.6	117.5	116.4
4th quarter	121.5	120.8	126.1	130.5	111.4	107.2	116.7	116.9	170.7	121.4	119.6
1997 - 1st quarter	124.0	123.3	127.9	132.8	112.7	108.0	121.9	118.8	176.0	122.8	121.6
2nd quarter	125.5	124.3	131.1	133.6	114.6	110.9	122.8	120.3	176.9	124.4	127.1
1st half	124.8	123.8	129.5	133.2	113.7	109.5	122.4	119.5	176.4	123.6	124.4
3rd quarter	131.9	125.4	133.1	159.4	117.1	113.2	126.5	128.7	180.5	127.7	129.1
1st-3rd quarters	127.1	124.3	130.7	142 0	114.8	110.7	123.7	122.6	177.8	125.0	125.9
4th quarter	133.8	127.8	137.4	160.4	119.5	114.0	128.2	128.2	187.9	130.2	131.5
1998 - 1st quarter	140.5	132.7	138.5	180.2	121.6	115.5	135.8	130.9	203.1	135.2	133.4
2nd quarter	141.5	134.0	140.4	181.2	122.9	116.1	133.9	131.2	206.3	137.4	136.9
1st half	141.0	133.4	139.5	180.7	122.3	115.8	134.9	131.0	204.7	136.3	135.2
3rd quarter	144.4	131.8	141.0	200.5	123.7	116.8	134.1	134.7	209.7	138.6	137.9
1st-3rd quarters	142.1	132.8	140.0	187.3	122.7	116.1	134.6	132.3	206.4	137.1	136.1
4th quarter	143.8	129.4	142.5	201.7	123.7	117.0	133.3	132.7	215.8	139.1	138.6

Source: Czech Statistical Office.

Table 7.4. Developments in Wholesale and Consumer Prices, 1995-98

	Weights[1]	1995	1996	1997	1998	1997				1998			
						Q1	Q2	Q3	Q4	Q1	Q2	Q3	Q4
						(average 1994 = 100)							
Wholesale prices (Industry)		107.6	112.7	118.2	124.0	116.2	117.2	119.2	120.4	123.6	124.1	124.3	123.8
Consumer Prices	100.0	109.1	118.8	128.8	142.6	124.0	125.6	131.9	133.8	140.5	141.5	144.4	143.8
		9.1	8.9	8.4	10.7								
Foodstuffs[2]	29.4	111.8	120.5	126.1	133.0	124.2	125.0	126.2	129.0	134.1	135.3	132.6	130.2
Other goods	50.4	107.6	116.0	125.8	140.3	120.9	122.4	128.9	130.8	138.1	138.6	141.9	142.4
Of which:													
Beverages and tobacco	8.6	106.3	115.6	122.9	133.8	120.3	121.8	124.3	125.0	131.5	133.6	135.0	135.2
Fuel and electricity	6.3	112.6	124.1	148.0	203.9	132.5	132.3	163.0	164.2	195.1	194.7	212.1	213.7
Services, excluding rent	14.6	109.7	123.0	137.3	153.1	130.8	134.3	141.5	142.4	149.4	151.5	156.1	155.3
Rent	5.6	107.5	122.7	146.6	182.2	131.5	132.9	160.6	161.5	169.5	171.5	193.5	194.4
Net inflation	n.a.	109.5	117.5	124.4	131.4	121.5	123	125.4	127.7	131.9	131.7	130.9	128.6

Note: Period average.

1/ 1993 constant weights.

2/ Including restaurant meals, but excluding beverages and tobacco.

Source: Czech Statistical Office.

Table 7.5. Exchange Rates, 1990-99

	U.S. Dollar		Deutsche Mark		Currency Basket[1]		Nominal Effective Exchange Rate	Real Effective Exchange Rate	
	End of period	Average	End of period	Average	End of period	Average		ULC Based[2]	CPI Based[3]
	(CZK per unit of foreign currency)						(Jan.-Sep. 1990 = 100)		
1990	24.19	17.95	16.23	11.08	n.a.	n.a.	91.67	91.93	93.45
1991	28.55	29.49	18.78	17.77	n.a.	n.a.	55.50	72.90	85.80
1992	28.59	28.18	17.76	18.06	n.a.	n.a.	55.50	85.60	91.10
1993	29.95	29.15	17.35	17.63	0.995	0.996	57.85	99.40	110.33
1994	28.05	28.79	18.11	17.74	0.999	0.995	57.75	108.36	117.88
1995	26.60	26.54	18.56	18.52	0.998	0.996	57.22	112.86	124.62
1996	27.34	27.15	17.63	18.05	0.973	0.986	57.77	119.48	134.35
1997[4]	34.73	31.71	19.52	18.28	1.133	1.050	55.63	119.17	137.76
1998	30.00	32.26	18.00	18.33	1.019	1.059	55.29	129.25	149.46
1997[4] Q1	29.20	28.28	17.22	17.09	0.981	0.965	59.90	131.93	142.87
Q2	32.38	31.11	18.75	18.16	1.076	1.039	56.04	118.59	135.97
Q3	33.59	33.82	18.79	18.72	1.092	1.092	53.73	114.34	136.17
Q4	34.73	33.63	19.52	19.14	1.133	1.105	52.85	111.80	136.05
1998 July	30.81	31.85	17.29	17.72	1.004	1.032	56.97	129.67	155.11
August	32.68	32.23	18.46	18.04	1.069	1.048	56.42	135.37	154.14
September	30.29	30.62	18.08	17.98	1.026	1.026	56.44	134.73	154.15
October	28.87	29.17	17.46	17.80	0.986	1.002	57.22	139.86	156.10
November	30.75	29.85	18.02	17.76	1.029	1.009	57.52	135.85	156.84
December	30.17	30.00	18.01	18.00	1.022	1.019	56.25	135.81	153.64
1999 January	32.01	30.69	18.67	18.24	1.068	1.036	56.48	148.50	154.88
February	34.40	33.80	19.40	19.35	1.124	1.115	51.20	131.28	141.40
March	35.80	34.91	19.63	19.43	1.150	1.131	..	..	..
April	35.51	35.44	19.26	19.40	1.133	1.137	..	..	..
May	35.91	35.44	19.21	19.27	1.136	1.132	..	..	..

1/ The currency basket represented fixed amounts of U.S. dollars and Deutsche marks, with a weight of 65 percent for the Deutsche mark and 35 percent for the U.S. dollar. Increase denotes a nominal depreciation.

2/ Unit labor cost deflator. Increase denotes appreciation.

3/ Consumer price deflator. Increase denotes appreciation.

4/ Effective May 27, 1997 the peg of the CZK to the basket was abolished.

Sources: International Financial Statistics, and IMF staff calculations.

Table 7.6. Average Monthly Earnings, 1993-98

	1993	1994	1995	1996	1997	1998
	(In CZK)					
Agriculture	5,107	5,874	6,878	7,808	8,519	9,240
Industry	5,893	6,888	8,148	9,587	10,733	11,853
Construction	6,529	7,622	8,837	10,166	11,225	12,065
Trade and Catering	5,154	6,274	7,226	8,497	10,164	11,449
Transport and Communication	5,672	6,807	8,241	9,853	11,320	12,628
Financial Services	10,336	12,081	14,017	16,407	18,658	21,168
Real Estate	6,032	7,404	8,896	10,494	11,734	13,070
Public Administration	6,914	8,321	9,608	11,460	11,788	12,062
Education	5,249	6,325	7,426	8,994	9,422	9,852
Health Service	5,525	6,475	7,529	9,068	9,626	9,945
Other Services	5,023	5,806	6,720	8,097	9,266	9,997
All Sectors	5,817	6,894	8,172	9,676	10,696	11,688
Memorandum Items:						
State Sector	5,873	6,920	8,040	9,710	10,539	11,168
Cooperatives	4,771	5,484	6,382	7,293	8,039	8,664
Private Sector[1]	5,901	6,795	7,994	9,243	10,123	10,995

Notes: Until 1996, all firms with 25 employees or more (in 1995-96, firms in industry, trade and catering only with 100 employees or more). In 1997, firms in the entrepreneurial sphere with 20 employees or more (all firms of financial intermediation and all budgetary and subsidized sphere organizations).
1/ Excluding foreign-owned enterprises.

Source: Czech Statistical Office.

Table 7.7. Index of Average Monthly Gross Salaries by Economic Sector
A Comparison to Agricultural Sector, 1993-98

	1993	1994	1995	1996	1997	1998
			(In percent)			
Agriculture, Hunting and Forestry	100.0	100.0	100.0	100.0	100.0	100.0
Industry	115.4	117.3	118.5	122.8	126.0	128.3
Construction	127.8	129.8	128.5	130.2	131.8	130.6
Trade and Catering	100.9	106.8	105.1	108.8	119.3	123.9
Transport and Communication	111.1	115.9	119.8	126.2	132.9	136.7
Financial Services	202.4	205.7	203.8	210.1	219.0	229.1
Real Estate	118.1	126.0	129.3	134.4	137.7	141.5
Public Administration	135.4	141.7	139.7	146.8	138.4	130.5
Education	102.8	107.7	108.0	115.2	110.6	106.6
Health Service	108.2	110.2	109.5	116.1	113.0	107.6
Other Services	98.4	98.8	97.7	103.7	108.8	108.2
All Sectors	113.9	117.4	118.8	123.9	125.6	126.5
Memo:			(In nominal CZK)			
Agriculture, Hunting and Forestry	5,107	5,874	6,878	7,808	8,519	9,240

Source: Czech Statistical Office.

Table 7.8. Quarterly Average Monthly Earnings, 1994-98

(In CZK)

	1994				1995				1996				1997				1998			
	Mar.	Jun.	Sep.	Dec.	Mar.	Jun.	Sep.	Dec.	Mar.	Jun.	Sep.	Dec.	Mar.	Jun.	Sep.	Dec.	Mar.	Jun.	Sep.	Dec.
Agriculture	5,056	5,589	6,131	6,746	5,895	6,617	7,147	7,859	6,734	7,523	8,078	8,898	7,501	8,342	8,844	9,439	8,134	9,050	9,635	10,158
Industry	6,090	6,819	6,854	7,834	7,235	8,233	8,007	9,142	8,556	9,660	9,409	10,757	9,590	10,808	10,540	12,043	10,806	11,993	11,674	12,997
Construction	6,611	7,448	7,794	8,667	7,803	8,662	9,013	9,841	8,795	9,926	10,457	11,464	9,791	11,095	11,481	12,553	10,868	12,048	12,365	13,180
Trade and catering	5,411	6,094	6,358	7,040	6,266	7,114	7,246	8,227	7,471	8,410	8,411	9,794	9,038	10,003	10,167	11,495	10,500	11,234	11,304	12,680
Transport and communication	5,855	6,661	6,772	7,884	7,035	8,156	8,202	9,552	8,775	10,023	9,666	10,942	10,062	11,508	11,165	12,575	11,260	12,553	12,530	14,262
Financial services	9,150	13,432	10,758	14,753	11,076	15,037	12,938	16,906	13,828	17,023	15,412	19,327	15,920	19,654	17,328	21,790	18,750	22,610	19,739	23,696
Real estate	6,345	6,987	7,263	8,779	7,727	8,635	8,699	10,628	9,001	10,447	10,233	12,355	10,379	11,666	11,550	13,389	11,233	12,775	12,757	14,973
Public administration	7,183	7,836	8,666	9,529	8,233	9,571	9,111	11,445	9,013	12,480	10,355	13,833	9,960	13,672	11,200	12,290	10,465	12,625	11,294	13,796
Education	5,509	6,172	6,221	7,390	5,986	7,262	7,077	9,227	7,093	9,903	8,341	10,600	7,786	10,799	9,115	9,990	8,209	10,103	9,404	11,759
Health services	5,873	6,428	6,542	7,066	6,566	7,601	7,321	8,718	7,400	9,867	8,455	10,571	8,522	10,934	9,278	9,781	8,791	10,357	9,570	11,102
Other services	5,186	5,562	5,694	6,591	5,950	6,677	6,604	7,899	7,076	8,344	7,580	9,455	8,285	9,758	8,905	10,116	8,905	10,101	9,622	11,247
All sectors	6,001	6,773	6,889	7,899	7,072	8,157	8,037	9,435	8,335	9,909	9,402	11,082	9,410	11,030	10,525	11,855	10,438	11,797	11,482	13,041
Memorandum items:																				
State sector	6,028	6,840	6,921	8,066	7,033	8,047	7,896	9,627	8,075	10,337	9,186	11,271	9,116	11,597	10,231	11,228	9,737	11,416	10,809	12,756
Cooperatives	4,706	5,225	5,742	6,253	5,518	6,166	6,699	7,199	6,305	7,042	7,603	8,312	7,055	7,872	8,360	8,923	7,632	8,502	9,093	9,413
Private sector 1/	5,958	6,640	6,808	7,654	7,108	7,887	8,039	8,964	8,159	9,120	9,285	10,424	9,016	10,023	10,155	11,338	10,022	10,921	11,037	12,051

Notes: Until 1996, all firms with 25 employees or more (in 1995-96, firms in industry, trade, and catering only with 100 employees or more). From 1997, firms in the entrepreneurial sphere with 20 employees or more (all financial intermediaries and all budgetary and subsidized sphere organizations). Excluding armed forces.
1/ Excluding foreign-owned enterprises.

Source: Czech Statistical Office.

Table 7.9. Average Monthly Gross Salaries of Employees by Region, 1990-1997

	1990	1992	1993	1994	1995	1996	1997
			(In CZK per Month)				
Total	3286	4644	5817	6894	8172	9676	10696
Prague	3474	5322	7145	8731	10520	12541	14073
Center Bohemia	3259	4395	5743	6778	8042	9495	10522
South Bohemia	3225	4410	5519	6484	7635	9052	9991
West Bohemia	3228	4371	5655	6687	7957	9407	10225
North Bohemia	3261	4682	5874	6860	7987	9401	10276
East Bohemia	3124	4262	5343	6288	7376	8709	9663
South Moravia	3216	4284	5443	6436	7613	9025	9930
North Moravia	3391	4709	5856	6763	8034	9479	10372
			(As Percent of Average Salary in East Bohemia)				
Total	105.19	108.96	108.87	109.64	110.79	111.10	110.69
Prague	111.20	124.87	133.73	138.85	142.62	144.00	145.64
Center Bohemia	104.32	103.12	107.49	107.79	109.03	109.03	108.89
South Bohemia	103.23	103.47	103.29	103.12	103.51	103.94	103.39
West Bohemia	103.33	102.56	105.84	106.35	107.88	108.01	105.82
North Bohemia	104.39	109.85	109.94	109.10	108.28	107.95	106.34
East Bohemia	100.00	100.00	100.00	100.00	100.00	100.00	100.00
South Moravia	102.94	100.52	101.87	102.35	103.21	103.63	102.76
North Moravia	108.55	110.49	109.60	107.55	108.92	108.84	107.34

Source: Czech Statistical Office.

Table 7.10. Subsistence Level Rates

In Force Since

(In CZK per month)

	29-Oct-91	1-Mar-93	1-Feb-94	1-Jan-95	1-Jan-96	1-Oct-96	1-Jul-97	1-Apr-98
For Personal needs of								
Child < 6 years	900	1,020	1,120	1,230	1,320	1,410	1,480	1,560
Child 6-10 years	1,000	1,130	1,240	1,360	1,460	1,560	1,640	1,730
Child 10-15 years	1,200	1,360	1,500	1,620	1,730	1,850	1,940	2,050
Child 15-26 years	1,300	1,470	1,620	1,780	1,900	2,030	2,130	2,250
Other persons>26 years	1,200	1,360	1,500	1,680	1,800	1,920	2,020	2,130
For Collective needs of household of:								
Individual	500	600	660	760	860	970	1,020	1,300
2 persons	650	780	860	1,000	1,130	1,270	1,330	1,700
3-4 persons	800	960	1,060	1,240	1,400	1,570	1,650	2,110
>4 persons	950	1,140	1,260	1,400	1,580	1,770	1,860	2,370

Source: Law of the Czech Republic.

Table 8.1. Overall Energy Balance Sheet, 1990-97

Indicator	1990	1994	1995	1996	1997
	(In Petajoule)				
Domestic natural resources	**1,730.5**	**1,379.6**	**1,409.5**	**1,403.0**	**1,346.4**
Solid fuel	1,571.7	1,218.1	1,253.6	1,241.0	1,189.2
Liquid fuel	2.1	5.4	6.1	6.4	6.7
Gaseous fuel	8.4	8.0	8.3	7.6	7.1
Primary heat and electricity	148.4	148.1	141.5	148.0	143.4
Imports	**592.1**	**674.7**	**726.1**	**802.9**	**770.7**
Solid fuel	45.3	45.2	63.3	80.8	62.4
Liquid fuel	317.1	365.3	350.7	369.4	360.8
Gaseous fuel	209.8	244.7	270.0	320.5	323.1
Exports	**158.9**	**373.8**	**397.3**	**388.9**	**376.1**
Solid fuel	105.1	306.8	341.0	313.2	292.4
Liquid fuel	21.8	45.8	33.6	42.1	45.0
Gaseous fuel	24.1	0.1	0.0	1.9	1.9
Drawing on inventories (+), supplies to inventories (-) and other resources	67.0	3.4	10.8	6.4	-2.1
CR-SR balance	-154.6	..	..	..	..
Gross consumption of primary energy resources	**2,076.1**	**1,683.9**	**1,749.7**	**1,823.4**	**1,746.9**
Solid fuel	1,348.2	984.4	1,005.8	1,015.8	978.7
Liquid fuel	355.5	312.3	321.6	341.5	305.3
Gaseous fuel	226.4	240.7	279.3	318.1	323.8
Primary heat and electricity	146.0	146.5	143.0	148.0	139.1
Total losses	**688.5**	**597.4**	**594.5**	**602.4**	**587.0**
Mining and preparation of fuel	16.7	20.6	22.1	19.8	15.6
Fuel upgrading	86.5	81.4	68.4	55.8	54.5
Heat generation	106.6	66.0	78.8	57.4	46.1
Power generation	443.6	393.4	388.2	430.0	431.7
Distribution	35.1	36.0	37.0	39.4	39.1
Balance differences	24.4	7.3	2.3	-3.8	2.2
Final consumption, total	**1,303.2**	**1,038.2**	**1,091.3**	**1,151.5**	**1,098.1**
Non-energy materials	59.9	55.6	66.5	65.7	64.0

Source: Czech Statistical Office.

Table 8.2. Electricity Production and Consumption, 1992-98

	1992	1993	1994	1995	1996	1997	1998
	(In millions of kilowatt hours)						
Production (gross)	59,131	58,882	58,705	60,847	64,257	64,598	65,112
Of which:							
Thermal	45,243	44,659	43,952	46,343	49,004	50,024	50063
Hydro	1,638	1,596	1,776	2,274	2,403	2,080	1871
Nuclear	12,250	12,627	12,977	12,230	12,850	12,494	13,178
Imports	6,156	5,952	5,415	6,722	8,811	9,013	8,383
Exports (including to Slovak Republic)	9,192	8,056	5,860	6,304	8,814	10,201	10,844
Losses	3,860	4,793	4,660	4,768	5,154	5,088	4,953
Domestic consumption	52,235	51,985	53,600	56,497	59,100	58,322	57,698
Of which:							
Industry	29,029	28,054	27,933	28,502	29,009	29,000	..
Agriculture	2,054	1,793	1,595	1,575	1,598	1,258	..
Households	10,343	11,399	13,184	14,847	16,011	15,503	14506
Other	10,809	10,739	10,888	11,573	12,482	12,561	..

Source: Czech Statistical Office.

Table 8.3. Environment -- Specific Emissions of Main Pollutants, 1990-97

Area, region	Year	Solids	Sulphur dioxide	Nitrogen oxides	Carbon monoxide	Hydrocarbons
			(Tonnes/Km2)			
Czech Republic	1990	8.0	23.8	6.7	8.6	1.9
	1993	5.6	18.0	4.6	9.6	1.7
	1994	4.4	16.1	3.0	9.4	1.6
	1995	2.5	13.7	2.8	7.7	1.2
	1996	2.1	11.9	2.6	7.5	1.2
	1997	1.5	8.8	2.4	6.7	1.1
Capital Prague	1990	42.1	84.8	23.8	89.6	20.5
	1993	26.8	66.5	19.3	53.6	13.1
	1994	22.8	61.1	15.7	54.8	13.4
	1995	14.7	49.8	15.2	49.4	12.1
	1996	12.6	31.3	10.6	33.5	8.6
	1997	7.4	21.3	9.6	23.7	6.5
Central Bohemia	1990	9.1	17.8	4.8	8.5	1.8
	1993	5.2	14.5	3.5	5.7	1.3
	1994	4.0	13.2	2.5	5.5	1.4
	1995	2.7	12.2	2.6	4.5	1.2
	1996	2.5	12.7	2.4	5.2	1.3
	1997	1.6	14.2	2.3	4.6	1.2
South Bohemia	1990	2.3	5.5	1.4	3.6	0.8
	1993	1.9	4.4	1.0	3.5	0.8
	1994	1.8	3.8	0.9	3.4	0.9
	1995	0.9	2.4	0.7	2.6	0.6
	1996	0.8	2.4	0.7	3.1	0.8
	1997	0.6	2.0	0.6	2.6	0.6
West Bohemia	1990	5.8	16.7	4.3	6.7	1.5
	1993	4.2	10.0	3.9	5.5	1.3
	1994	3.6	8.7	1.9	6.1	1.3
	1995	1.7	6.2	1.5	4.1	0.9
	1996	1.7	6.7	1.9	4.5	1.1
	1997	1.3	5.0	1.7	3.5	0.9
North Bohemia	1990	18.7	109.8	27.5	12.8	3.1
	1993	12.8	82.1	16.8	9.2	2.6
	1994	9.2	79.1	10.2	9.0	2.5
	1995	5.8	71.5	9.5	7.0	2.1
	1996	5.6	56.1	9.0	7.5	1.9
	1997	3.2	29.3	8.7	6.1	1.9
East Bohemia	1990	6.1	19.9	5.1	7.8	1.7
	1993	4.3	15.2	3.0	6.5	1.5
	1994	3.7	12.4	1.9	6.4	1.5
	1995	2.0	10.8	1.9	5.0	1.1
	1996	1.5	9.3	1.5	4.8	1.1
	1997	1.1	9.4	1.6	4.1	1.1
South Moravia	1990	5.1	8.3	2.3	7.5	1.6
	1993	3.4	6.7	1.6	6.1	1.4
	1994	2.8	5.0	1.1	5.7	1.4
	1995	1.2	3.2	1.0	3.8	0.9
	1996	0.9	3.1	1.0	3.5	0.8
	1997	0.8	2.3	0.9	3.2	0.8
North Moravia	1990	11.7	16.9	8.7	11.6	2.7
	1993	9.3	13.9	6.6	29.9	2.7
	1994	6.9	11.4	4.8	28.9	2.3
	1995	3.9	9.2	4.1	26.5	1.2
	1996	3.0	8.6	3.9	24.6	1.4
	1997	2.4	7.1	3.0	23.4	1.2

Source: Czech Statistical Office.

Table 9.1. Real GDP Growth in Europe and Central Asia, 1990-98

	1990	1991	1992	1993	1994	1995	1996	1997	1998
	(In percent change)								
ECA Region[1][2]	**-2.3**	**-6.3**	**-9.5**	**-5.2**	**-8.9**	**-1.3**	**-0.1**	**2.0**	**-0.3**
Central Europe and Baltic States[1][2]	**-7.4**	**-10.8**	**-4.5**	**0.4**	**3.6**	**5.5**	**3.6**	**1.9**	**1.6**
Albania	-10.0	-27.7	-7.2	9.6	9.4	8.9	8.2	-7.0	8.0
Bosnia						33.0	69.1	29.5	17.7
Bulgaria	-9.1	-11.7	-7.3	-1.5	1.8	2.1	-10.9	-6.9	3.5
Croatia			-2.1	-2.5	6.0	2.6	4.3	6.5	2.9
Czech Republic[3]	-1.2	-14.2	-3.3	1.1	2.7	6.4	3.8	0.3	-2.3
Estonia	-8.1	-11.0	-25.8	-8.5	-2.7	4.3	4.0	11.4	4.3
Hungary	-3.5	-11.9	-3.1	-0.6	2.9	1.5	1.3	4.6	5.1
Latvia	-3.5	-8.0	-35.0	-16.0	0.6	-0.8	3.3	8.6	3.6
Lithuania	-6.9	-5.7	-21.3	-16.2	-9.8	3.3	4.7	6.1	4.4
FYR Macedonia				-9.4	-1.7	-1.2	0.8	1.5	2.9
Poland	-11.6	-7.0	2.6	3.8	5.2	7.0	6.1	6.9	4.8
Romania	-5.6	-12.9	-8.8	1.5	3.9	6.9	4.1	-6.6	-7.3
Slovak Republic	-2.5	-14.6	-6.5	-3.7	4.9	6.8	6.9	6.5	4.4
Slovenia	-4.7	-8.1	-5.4	2.8	5.3	4.1	3.1	3.8	3.9
Community of Independent States[1]	**-2.9**	**-6.2**	**-15.0**	**-10.5**	**-14.8**	**-6.0**	**-3.3**	**0.7**	**-1.7**
Armenia	-8.5	-8.8	-52.3	-15.0	5.4	6.9	5.8	3.1	6.9
Azerbaijan	-11.7	-0.7	-35.2	-23.1	-19.7	-13.3	1.2	5.8	10.0
Belarus	-1.9	-1.2	-9.6	-7.6	-12.6	-10.4	2.8	11.4	8.3
Georgia	-11.1	-28.1	-43.4	-39.4	-11.4	2.4	10.5	10.7	2.9
Kazakhstan	-1.1	-11.8	-13.0	-12.9	-18.0	-8.2	0.5	1.7	-2.5
Kyrgyz Republic	3.2	-5.0	-19.0	-16.0	-20.0	-5.4	5.6	9.9	1.8
Moldova	-1.5	-18.7	-29.1	-1.2	-31.2	-2.9	-8.0	1.3	-8.6
Russia	-3.6	-5.0	-14.5	-8.7	-12.6	-4.1	-3.5	0.8	-4.6
Tajikistan	-0.6	-8.7	-28.9	-11.1	-21.4	-12.5	-4.4	1.7	5.3
Turkmenistan	1.5	-5.0	-5.0	-10.0	-19.0	-8.2	-8.0	-26.0	5.0
Ukraine	-3.8	-8.4	-9.7	-14.2	-23.5	-12.2	-10.0	-3.2	-1.7
Uzbekistan	4.3	-0.9	-9.5	-2.3	-4.2	-0.9	1.6	2.4	3.4
Turkey	9.3	0.9	6.0	8.0	-5.5	7.2	7.0	7.5	2.8

1/ Population-weighted averages.

2/ Averages exclude Bosnia, Croatia and Macedonia.

3/ Data for 1990-93 is in the process of revision, which will be completed by the third quarter of 1999.

Sources: National Authorities, World Bank Staff Estimates and Czech Statistical Office.

Table 9.2. Real GDP Index in Europe and Central Asia, 1990-98

	1990	1991	1992	1993	1994	1995	1996	1997	1998
					(Index 1990 = 100)				
ECA Region[1/][2/]	**100**	**93.7**	**84.8**	**80.4**	**73.3**	**72.3**	**72.2**	**73.6**	**73.4**
Central Europe and Baltic States[1/][2/]	**100**	**89.2**	**85.2**	**85.5**	**88.6**	**93.4**	**96.8**	**98.7**	**100.3**
Albania	100	72.3	67.1	73.5	80.4	87.6	94.8	88.2	95.2
Bosnia					100.0	133.0	225.0	291.4	343.1
Bulgaria[3/]	100	88.3	81.9	80.7	82.1	83.8	74.7	69.5	71.9
Croatia[4/]		100.0	97.9	95.5	101.2	103.9	108.3	115.4	118.7
Czech Republic[5/]	100	85.8	83.0	83.9	86.1	91.7	95.1	95.4	93.2
Estonia	100	89.0	66.0	60.4	58.8	61.3	63.8	71.0	74.1
Hungary	100	88.1	85.4	84.9	87.4	88.7	89.8	94.0	98.8
Latvia	100	92.0	59.8	50.2	50.5	50.1	51.8	56.2	58.3
Lithuania	100	94.3	74.2	62.2	56.1	57.9	60.7	64.4	67.2
FYR Macedonia[6/]			100.0	90.6	89.1	88.0	88.7	90.0	92.6
Poland	100	93.0	95.5	99.1	104.3	111.6	118.4	126.6	132.7
Romania	100	87.1	79.4	80.6	83.8	89.6	93.2	87.1	80.7
Slovak Republic	100	85.4	79.9	76.9	80.7	86.2	92.1	98.1	102.4
Slovenia	100	91.9	86.9	89.4	94.1	98.0	101.0	104.8	108.9
Community of Independent States[1/]	**100**	**93.8**	**79.7**	**71.4**	**60.8**	**57.2**	**55.3**	**55.8**	**54.8**
Armenia	100	91.2	43.5	37.0	39.0	41.7	44.1	45.4	48.6
Azerbaijan	100	99.3	64.3	49.5	39.7	34.4	34.9	36.9	40.6
Belarus	100	98.8	89.3	82.5	72.1	64.6	66.4	74.0	80.2
Georgia	100	71.9	40.7	24.7	21.9	22.4	24.7	27.4	28.2
Kazakhstan	100	88.2	76.7	66.8	54.8	50.3	50.6	51.4	50.1
Kyrgyz Republic	100	95.0	77.0	64.6	51.7	48.9	51.7	56.8	57.8
Moldova	100	81.3	57.6	56.9	39.2	38.0	35.0	35.5	32.4
Russia	100	95.0	81.2	74.2	64.8	62.2	60.0	60.5	57.7
Tajikistan	100	91.3	64.9	57.7	45.4	39.7	37.9	38.6	40.6
Turkmenistan	100	95.0	90.3	81.2	65.8	60.4	55.6	41.1	43.2
Ukraine	100	91.6	82.7	71.0	54.3	47.7	42.9	41.5	40.8
Uzbekistan	100	99.1	89.7	87.6	83.9	83.2	84.5	86.5	89.5
Turkey	100.0	100.9	107.0	115.6	109.3	117.1	125.3	134.8	138.5

1/ Population-weighted averages.

2/ Averages exclude Bosnia, Croatia and Macedonia.

3/ Index in Bosnia is based on 1994=100.

4/ Index in Croatia is based on 1991=100.

3/ Data for 1990-93 is in the process of revision, which will be completed by the third quarter of 1999.

6/ Index in FYR Macedonia is based on 1992=100.

Source: National Authorities, World Bank Staff Estimates and Czech Statistical Office.

Table 9.3. Annual Inflation in Europe and Central Asia, 1990-98

	1990	1991	1992	1993	1994	1995	1996	1997	1998
	(Change in period-average Consumer Price Index, percent)								
ECA Region[1]	**10.1**	**91.9**	**677.9**	**355.0**	**136.8**	**33.5**	**24.1**	**14.4**	**10.7**
Central Europe and Baltic States[1]	**16.1**	**120.2**	**211.2**	**85.0**	**35.9**	**19.3**	**15.2**	**10.0**	**9.3**
Albania	0.0	35.5	226.0	85.0	22.5	7.8	12.7	33.2	21.9
Bosnia	..	..	..	..	..	7.2	-7.7	11.2	3.1
Bulgaria	64.0	238.9	82.6	72.8	96.0	62.6	123.0	1,082.3	22.3
Croatia	..	122.6	663.6	1,517.1	97.5	2.0	3.6	3.7	5.8
Czech Republic	9.6	57.0	11.0	21.0	10.0	9.1	8.9	8.4	10.7
Estonia	23.1	210.6	1,069.0	89.0	47.7	28.8	23.1	11.2	10.6
Hungary	28.9	35.0	23.0	22.5	18.8	28.2	23.6	18.3	14.3
Latvia	10.5	172.2	958.7	109.2	35.9	25.0	17.6	8.4	4.7
Lithuania	16.1	224.0	1,162.7	291.4	72.2	39.6	24.6	8.9	5.1
FYR Macedonia	..	..	1,975.0	355.0	55.0	8.6	-0.7	2.7	1.5
Poland	585.8	70.3	43.0	35.3	32.2	27.8	19.9	14.8	11.7
Romania	4.7	161.1	211.2	255.2	136.8	32.3	38.8	154.8	40.6
Slovak Republic	10.4	61.2	10.0	23.2	13.4	9.9	6.9	6.0	6.7
Slovenia	549.7	117.7	201.3	32.3	21.1	13.5	9.9	8.4	8.0
Community of Independent States[1]	**5.2**	**89.3**	**1,108.5**	**1,221.8**	**1,497.9**	**246.8**	**43.4**	**16.6**	**17.6**
Armenia	10.1	80.1	677.9	3,731.9	5,273.4	176.7	18.6	14.0	9.4
Azerbaijan	7.5	82.8	1,350.9	980.9	1,427.7	411.7	24.6	4.0	-0.8
Belarus	4.5	94.1	970.0	1,188.0	2,221.0	709.3	52.7	63.9	73.0
Georgia	3.3	78.7	637.3	3,125.0	15,606.5	162.7	39.4	7.1	3.6
Kazakhstan	18.9	87.4	1,622.6	1,255.5	1,158.3	34.7	39.3	17.4	7.0
Kyrgyz Republic	4.8	113.7	1,007.0	782.1	228.0	52.4	31.4	25.4	9.5
Moldova	14.8	136.1	1,780.4	2,707.2	2,404.6	23.8	15.1	11.2	18.3
Russia	5.6	92.6	1,354.0	895.3	305.2	188.5	47.5	14.8	27.7
Tajikistan	..	..	..	..	350.4	635.0	443.0	88.0	64.0
Turkmenistan	..	..	..	..	1,748.0	1,005.0	992.0	84.0	17.0
Ukraine	4.2	91.2	1,210.0	4,735.0	891.1	376.8	80.2	15.9	20.0
Uzbekistan	3.1	82.2	645.0	534.0	1,568.0	305.0	53.7	71.0	29.0
Turkey	60.3	65.9	70.1	66.1	106.3	93.6	78.8	85.6	83.7

1/ Median of countries included.

Source: National Authorities and World Bank Staff's Estimates.

Table 9.4. Current Account Balances in Europe and Central Asia, 1990-98

	1990	1991	1992	1993	1994	1995	1996	1997	1998
					(As a share of GDP, percent)				
ECA Region[1]	0.4	-2.5	-1.0	-3.3	-2.2	-4.4	-7.1	-6.1	-7.8
Central Europe and Baltic States[1]	-1.9	-4.5	0.0	-1.6	-1.9	-5.0	-7.5	-6.8	-7.8
Albania	-5.8	-25.7	-62.3	-29.7	-14.3	-7.5	-9.2	-12.1	-6.1
Bosnia	..	..	..	..	..	-10.3	-27.3	-32.3	-24.4
Bulgaria	-5.9	-7.2	-9.3	-12.8	-2.1	-1.0	-0.8	4.1	-2.2
Croatia	..	-10.1	5.3	0.9	0.7	-9.5	-7.6	-12.5	-7.6
Czech Republic	..	..	-1.7	1.3	-1.9	-2.6	-7.4	-6.1	-1.9
Estonia	..	..	-1.0	1.3	-7.1	-4.4	-9.1	-12.0	-8.7
Hungary	1.0	0.8	0.9	-9.0	-9.5	-5.6	-3.7	-2.1	-4.8
Latvia	..	..	15.2	19.7	5.5	-0.4	-5.5	-6.1	-11.0
Lithuania	..	..	5.4	-3.1	-2.1	-10.2	-9.2	-10.2	-12.1
FYR Macedonia	..	..	..	..	-9.4	-5.7	-6.5	-7.4	-8.4
Poland	1.1	-1.0	-0.3	-0.1	2.3	3.3	-1.0	-3.1	-4.5
Romania	-4.7	-4.5	-7.5	-4.7	-1.7	-5.6	-7.8	-6.7	-7.9
Slovak Republic	..	..	0.4	-5.0	4.8	2.3	-11.1	-6.9	-9.7
Slovenia	3.0	1.5	7.4	1.5	3.8	-0.1	0.2	0.2	0.0
Community of Independent States[1]	0.4	2.8	-4.6	-4.9	-5.1	-4.0	-6.5	-5.5	-7.8
Armenia (excluding grants)	..	..	-84.1	-54.6	-35.5	-16.9	-15.0	-15.8	-17.3
Azerbaijan	..	9.8	..	-2.8	-15.8	-10.1	-18.2	-23.7	-33.1
Belarus	..	..	..	-11.9	-9.1	-4.3	-3.7	-5.9	-7.1
Georgia (excluding grants)	..	..	-21.0	-11.0	-22.3	-7.5	-6.0	-7.6	-8.4
Kazakhstan	..	..	-0.4	-1.8	-6.0	-2.7	-3.6	-4.1	-5.6
Kyrgyz Republic	..	..	-4.6	-3.4	-3.3	-7.0	-15.5	-6.2	-15.1
Moldova	..	..	-1.4	-6.3	-4.2	-3.7	-9.1	-14.9	-20.1
Russia	0.4	2.8	0.1	0.7	2.7	1.9	2.1	0.6	0.3
Tajikistan	..	..	-18.0	-31.0	-21.0	-15.0	-7.0	-5.0	-10.2
Turkmenistan	..	..	..	18.5	8.0	1.3	0.5	-4.7	-6.8
Ukraine	..	-3.9	-0.7	-1.2	-2.2	-2.3	-2.7	-2.2	-3.1
Uzbekistan [2]	..	..	-11.8	-8.4	0.5	-0.2	-7.2	-4.0	-1.4
Turkey	..	0.2	-0.6	-3.5	2.0	-1.4	-2.6	-2.5	0.0

1/ Median of countries included.

2/ Figures for 1995-96 includes estimate of non-registered trade surplus.

Source: National Authorities and World Bank Staff Estimates.

Table 9.5. Fiscal Balances in Europe and Central Asia, 1990-98

	1990	1991	1992	1993	1994	1995	1996	1997	1998
	(As a share of GDP, percent)								
ECA Region[1/]	**0.8**	**-4.6**	**-7.2**	**-7.0**	**-6.1**	**-3.7**	**-4.2**	**-2.8**	**-3.2**
Central Europe and Baltic States[1/]	**0.5**	**-4.6**	**-4.9**	**-3.4**	**-2.9**	**-2.8**	**-1.7**	**-1.5**	**-2.4**
Albania	-3.7	-43.7	-20.3	-14.5	-12.9	-10.4	-12.1	-12.6	-10.4
Bosnia	..	..	..	..	..	-7.0	-27.0	-25.0	-20.0
Bulgaria	-9.1	-8.2	-7.2	-10.9	-6.4	-5.2	-15.4	2.1	2.5
Croatia	..	-4.6	-3.4	-1.5	1.7	-0.7	-0.4	-1.1	0.9
Czech Republic	..	..	-1.0	2.7	0.8	0.3	-0.4	-1.2	-1.5
Estonia	..	..	..	-0.7	1.3	0.4	-1.9	2.0	-0.2
Hungary	0.5	-2.1	-5.4	-6.6	-7.5	-3.1	0.8	-1.8	-4.0
Latvia	..	..	..	0.6	-4.0	-2.9	-1.2	1.7	0.0
Lithuania	..	..	..	-5.5	-5.0	-4.7	-4.5	-1.8	-5.9
FYR Macedonia	..	..	..	-13.8	-2.9	-1.2	-0.4	-0.4	-1.7
Poland	3.7	-6.7	-4.9	-3.4	-3.2	-3.3	-3.6	-3.3	-3.0
Romania	1.2	3.2	-4.6	-0.4	-1.9	-2.7	-4.1	-3.9	-3.3
Slovak Republic	..	..	-11.9	-7.0	-1.3	0.2	-1.4	-4.5	-5.5
Slovenia	..	2.6	0.2	0.3	-0.2	0.0	0.3	-1.1	-1.2
Community of Independent States[1/]	**1.8**	**-3.4**	**-15.8**	**-11.1**	**-8.9**	**-5.5**	**-5.2**	**-4.1**	**-3.8**
Armenia	..	-1.8	-8.1	-56.1	-16.4	-9.0	-8.6	-5.5	-5.5
Azerbaijan	-5.5	-5.0	-4.1	-14.0	-16.4	-4.1	-4.3	-1.7	-4.5
Belarus	..	..	-2.0	-5.6	-3.6	-2.8	-2.0	-2.3	-1.1
Georgia	..	..	..	-26.2	-16.5	-5.2	-4.5	-4.6	-4.5
Kazakhstan	..	-9.0	-6.9	-0.7	-6.5	-3.2	-3.2	-3.7	-3.7
Kyrgyz Republic	..	4.0	-17.4	-13.5	-7.7	-17.3	-9.5	-9.0	-8.1
Moldova	2.8	0.0	-27.3	-8.4	-9.7	-5.7	-6.3	-6.2	-2.9
Russia	..	..	-21.8	-8.7	-11.3	-5.8	-8.7	-7.6	-7.9
Tajikistan	..	..	-30.3	-24.8	-10.2	-11.2	-5.8	-3.3	-3.8
Turkmenistan	1.8	2.5	..	-0.4	-2.0	-3.0	-1.0	0.0	-3.0
Ukraine	..	-13.8	-14.3	-11.8	-8.2	-7.0	-4.4	-6.7	-2.7
Uzbekistan	..	-4.9	-18.5	-10.4	-6.1	-4.1	-7.3	-2.1	-3.0
Turkey	-7.5	-9.6	-10.7	-12.4	-7.7	-4.8	-9.0	-8.7	-10.2

1/ Median of countries included.

Source: National Authorities and World Bank Staff Estimates.

Table 9.6. Foreign Direct Investment in Europe and Central Asia, 1991-98

	1991	1992	1993	1994	1995	1996	1997	1998
				(As a share of GDP, percent)				
ECA Region [1]	**0.5**	**0.5**	**0.9**	**0.7**	**1.1**	**1.6**	**2.6**	**3.2**
Central Europe and Baltic States [1]	**0.3**	**0.7**	**1.0**	**1.2**	**1.2**	**2.0**	**2.5**	**3.4**
Albania	..	3.1	3.7	3.3	3.6	3.5	1.8	1.4
Bosnia	..	..	..	..	0.0	0.0	0.0	2.4
Bulgaria	0.5	0.4	0.5	1.1	0.8	1.4	4.9	2.9
Croatia		0.1	0.7	0.7	0.5	2.6	1.2	3.8
Czech Republic	2.5	3.9	2.1	1.9	5.0	2.5	2.5	4.5
Estonia	0.0	1.3	3.9	5.3	4.2	2.5	2.7	2.4
Hungary	4.4	4.0	6.1	2.8	10.0	4.4	3.6	3.0
Latvia	..	0.0	1.0	5.1	5.0	7.4	9.0	3.4
Lithuania	..	0.5	1.1	0.7	1.2	1.9	3.7	8.7
FYR Macedonia	..	..	..	0.7	0.2	0.3	0.4	3.6
Poland	0.2	0.3	0.7	0.6	1.0	2.0	2.3	3.4
Romania	0.1	0.3	0.3	1.2	1.3	0.8	3.8	5.4
Slovak Republic	..	0.9	1.1	1.2	0.8	0.7	0.4	1.8
Slovenia	0.3	0.9	0.9	0.9	0.9	0.9	1.6	0.8
Community of Independent States [1]	**0.6**	**0.3**	**0.4**	**0.3**	**1.1**	**1.2**	**3.3**	**3.7**
Armenia	..	..	..	0.2	1.5	1.1	2.9	7.0
Azerbaijan	..	..	1.3	0.5	7.3	16.7	27.2	28.0
Belarus	..	..	0.1	0.1	0.1	0.4	1.0	0.6
Georgia	..	..	..	0.2	0.2	1.2	4.6	4.4
Kazakhstan	..	0.4	1.9	4.2	4.9	5.5	5.9	5.1
Kyrgyz Republic	..	..	0.4	1.5	2.9	1.7	3.7	3.1
Moldova	0.6	0.6	0.3	0.7	2.4	3.3	4.4	5.4
Russia	..	0.2	0.3	0.2	0.6	0.6	1.4	0.8
Tajikistan	..	..	..	0.0	0.6	1.0	1.8	..
Turkmenistan	..	0.2	1.4	2.3	5.3	6.3	4.5	..
Ukraine	..	0.2	0.3	0.3	0.5	1.2	1.0	1.7
Uzbekistan	..	0.5	0.9	0.3	-0.2	0.7	1.2	1.6
Turkey	0.5	0.5	0.3	0.4	0.4	0.3	0.3	0.3

1/ Median of countries included.

Source: National Authorities and World Bank Staff's Estimates.

Table 9.7. Tax Rates in Selected Countries

	PIT	CIT	VAT	Total pension to to total labor cost[1]	Total payroll tax for SS to total labor cost[1]
Czech Republic	40.0	35.0	22.0	20.1	35.9
Hungary	48.0	20.5	25.0	20.5	40.6
Poland	45.0	40.0	22.0	30.4	32.4
Slovakia	42.0	40.0	23.0	19.6	34.1
Slovenia	50.0	25.0	N/A.	25.2	37.2
OECD average	43.9	40.6	8.2	12.9	24.9
EU 15 average	43.9	39.5	18.1	15.3	32.5

1/ OECD and EU averages do not include Denmark.

Sources: Individual taxes-A Worldwide Summary. Price Waterhouse, 1996;
Corporate Taxes-A Worldwide Summary. Price Waterhouse, 1996; IMF.

Distributors of World Bank Group Publications

Prices and credit terms vary from country to country. Consult your local distributor before placing an order.

ARGENTINA
World Publications SA
Av. Cordoba 1877
1120 Ciudad de Buenos Aires
Tel: (54 11) 4815-8156
Fax: (54 11) 4815-8156
E-mail: wpbooks@infovia.com.ar

AUSTRALIA, FIJI, PAPUA NEW GUINEA, SOLOMON ISLANDS, VANUATU, AND SAMOA
D.A. Information Services
648 Whitehorse Road
Mitcham 3132, Victoria
Tel: (61) 3 9210 7777
Fax: (61) 3 9210 7788
E-mail: service@dadirect.com.au
URL: http://www.dadirect.com.au

AUSTRIA
Gerold and Co.
Weihburggasse 26
A-1011 Wien
Tel: (43 1) 512-47-31-0
Fax: (43 1) 512-47-31-29
URL: http://www.gerold.co/at.online

BANGLADESH
Micro Industries Development Assistance Society (MIDAS)
House 5, Road 16
Dhanmondi R/Area
Dhaka 1209
Tel: (880 2) 326427
Fax: (880 2) 811188

BELGIUM
Jean De Lannoy
Av. du Roi 202
1060 Brussels
Tel: (32 2) 538-5169
Fax: (32 2) 538-0841

BRAZIL
Publicacões Tecnicas Internacionais Ltda.
Rua Peixoto Gomide, 209
01409 Sao Paulo, SP.
Tel: (55 11) 259-6644
Fax: (55 11) 258-6990
E-mail: postmaster@pti.uol.br
URL: http://www.uol.br

CANADA
Renouf Publishing Co. Ltd.
5369 Canotek Road
Ottawa, Ontario K1J 9J3
Tel: (613) 745-2665
Fax: (613) 745-7660
E-mail: order.dept@renoufbooks.com
URL: http://www.renoufbooks.com

CHINA
China Financial & Economic Publishing House
8, Da Fo Si Dong Jie
Beijing
Tel: (86 10) 6401-7365
Fax: (86 10) 6401-7365

China Book Import Centre
P.O. Box 2825
Beijing

Chinese Corporation for Promotion of Humanities
52, You Fang Hu Tong,
Xuan Nei Da Jie
Beijing
Tel: (86 10) 660 72 494
Fax: (86 10) 660 72 494

COLOMBIA
Infoenlace Ltda.
Carrera 6 No. 51-21
Apartado Aereo 34270
Santafé de Bogotá, D.C.
Tel: (57 1) 285-2798
Fax: (57 1) 285-2798

COTE D'IVOIRE
Center d'Edition et de Diffusion Africaines (CEDA)
04 B.P. 541
Abidjan 04
Tel: (225) 24 6510; 24 6511
Fax: (225) 25 0567

CYPRUS
Center for Applied Research
Cyprus College
6, Diogenes Street, Engomi
P.O. Box 2006
Nicosia
Tel: (357 2) 59-0730
Fax: (357 2) 66-2051

CZECH REPUBLIC
USIS, NIS Prodejna
Havelkova 22
130 00 Prague 3
Tel: (420 2) 2423 1486
Fax: (420 2) 2423 1114
URL: http://www.nis.cz/

DENMARK
SamfundsLitteratur
Rosenoerns Allé 11
DK-1970 Frederiksberg C
Tel: (45 35) 351942
Fax: (45 35) 357822
URL: http://www.sl.cbs.dk

ECUADOR
Libri Mundi
Libreria Internacional
P.O. Box 17-01-3029
Juan Leon Mera 851
Quito
Tel: (593 2) 521-606; (593 2) 544-185
Fax: (593 2) 504-209
E-mail: librimu1@librimundi.com.ec
E-mail: librimu2@librimundi.com.ec

CODEU
Ruiz de Castilla 763, Edif. Expocolor
Primer piso, Of. #2
Quito
Tel/Fax: (593 2) 507-383; 253-091
E-mail: codeu@impsat.net.ec

EGYPT, ARAB REPUBLIC OF
Al Ahram Distribution Agency
Al Galaa Street
Cairo
Tel: (20 2) 578-6083
Fax: (20 2) 578-6833

The Middle East Observer
41, Sherif Street
Cairo
Tel: (20 2) 393-9732
Fax: (20 2) 393-9732

FINLAND
Akateeminen Kirjakauppa
P.O. Box 128
FIN-00101 Helsinki
Tel: (358 0) 121 4418
Fax: (358 0) 121-4435
E-mail: akatilaus@stockmann.fi
URL: http://www.akateeminen.com

FRANCE
Editions Eska; DBJ
48, rue Gay Lussac
75005 Paris
Tel: (33-1) 55-42-73-08
Fax: (33-1) 43-29-91-67

GERMANY
UNO-Verlag
Poppelsdorfer Allee 55
53115 Bonn
Tel: (49 228) 949020
Fax: (49 228) 217492
URL: http://www.uno-verlag.de
E-mail: unoverlag@aol.com

GHANA
Epp Books Services
P.O. Box 44
TUC
Accra
Tel: 223 21 778843
Fax: 223 21 779099

GREECE
Papasotiriou S.A.
35, Stournara Str.
106 82 Athens
Tel: (30 1) 364-1826
Fax: (30 1) 364-8254

HAITI
Culture Diffusion
5, Rue Capois
C.P. 257
Port-au-Prince
Tel: (509) 23 9260
Fax: (509) 23 4858

HONG KONG, CHINA; MACAO
Asia 2000 Ltd.
Sales & Circulation Department
302 Seabird House
22-28 Wyndham Street, Central
Hong Kong, China
Tel: (852) 2530-1409
Fax: (852) 2526-1107
E-mail: sales@asia2000.com.hk
URL: http://www.asia2000.com.hk

HUNGARY
Euro Info Service
Margitszgeti Europa Haz
H-1138 Budapest
Tel: (36 1) 350 80 24, 350 80 25
Fax: (36 1) 350 90 32
E-mail: euroinfo@mail.matav.hu

INDIA
Allied Publishers Ltd.
751 Mount Road
Madras - 600 002
Tel: (91 44) 852-3938
Fax: (91 44) 852-0649

INDONESIA
Pt. Indira Limited
Jalan Borobudur 20
P.O. Box 181
Jakarta 10320
Tel: (62 21) 390-4290
Fax: (62 21) 390-4289

IRAN
Ketab Sara Co. Publishers
Khaled Eslamboli Ave., 6th Street
Delafrooz Alley No. 8
P.O. Box 15745-733
Tehran 15117
Tel: (98 21) 8717819; 8716104
Fax: (98 21) 8712479
E-mail: ketab-sara@neda.net.ir

Kowkab Publishers
P.O. Box 19575-511
Tehran
Tel: (98 21) 258-3723
Fax: (98 21) 258-3723

IRELAND
Government Supplies Agency
Oifig an tSoláthair
4-5 Harcourt Road
Dublin 2
Tel: (353 1) 661-3111
Fax: (353 1) 475-2670

ISRAEL
Yozmot Literature Ltd.
P.O. Box 56055
3 Yohanan Hasandlar Street
Tel Aviv 61560
Tel: (972 3) 5285-397
Fax: (972 3) 5285-397

R.O.Y. International
PO Box 13056
Tel Aviv 61130
Tel: (972 3) 649 9469
Fax: (972 3) 648 6039
E-mail: royil@netvision.net.il
URL: http://www.royint.co.il

Palestinian Authority/Middle East
Index Information Services
P.O.B. 19502 Jerusalem
Tel: (972 2) 6271219
Fax: (972 2) 6271634

ITALY, LIBERIA
Licosa Commissionaria Sansoni SPA
Via Duca Di Calabria, 1/1
Casella Postale 552
50125 Firenze
Tel: (39 55) 645-415
Fax: (39 55) 641-257
E-mail: licosa@ftbcc.it
URL: http://www.ftbcc.it/licosa

JAMAICA
Ian Randle Publishers Ltd.
206 Old Hope Road, Kingston 6
Tel: 876-927-2085
Fax: 876-977-0243
E-mail: irpl@colis.com

JAPAN
Eastern Book Service
3-13 Hongo 3-chome, Bunkyo-ku
Tokyo 113
Tel: (81 3) 3818-0861
Fax: (81 3) 3818-0864
E-mail: orders@svt-ebs.co.jp
URL:
http://www.bekkoame.or.jp/~svt-ebs

KENYA
Africa Book Service (E.A.) Ltd.
Quaran House, Mfangano Street
P.O. Box 45245
Nairobi
Tel: (254 2) 223 641
Fax: (254 2) 330 272

Legacy Books
Loita House
Mezzanine 1
P.O. Box 68077
Nairobi
Tel: (254) 2-330853, 221426
Fax: (254) 2-330854, 561654
E-mail: Legacy@form-net.com

KOREA, REPUBLIC OF
Dayang Books Trading Co.
International Division
783-20, Pangba Bon-Dong,
Socho-ku
Seoul
Tel: (82 2) 536-9555
Fax: (82 2) 536-0025
E-mail: seamap@chollian.net

Eulyoo Publishing Co., Ltd.
46-1, Susong-Dong
Jongro-Gu
Seoul
Tel: (82 2) 734-3515
Fax: (82 2) 732-9154

LEBANON
Librairie du Liban
P.O. Box 11-9232
Beirut
Tel: (961 9) 217 944
Fax: (961 9) 217 434
E-mail: hsayegh@librairie-du-liban.com.lb
URL: http://www.librairie-du-liban.com.lb

MALAYSIA
University of Malaya Cooperative Bookshop, Limited
P.O. Box 1127
Jalan Pantai Baru
59700 Kuala Lumpur
Tel: (60 3) 756-5000
Fax: (60 3) 755-4424
E-mail: umkoop@tm.net.my

MEXICO
INFOTEC
Av. San Fernando No. 37
Col. Toriello Guerra
14050 Mexico, D.F.
Tel: (52 5) 624-2800
Fax: (52 5) 624-2822
E-mail: infotec@rtn.net.mx
URL: http://rtn.net.mx

Mundi-Prensa Mexico S.A. de C.V.
c/Rio Panuco, 141-Colonia Cuauhtemoc
06500 Mexico, D.F.
Tel: (52 5) 533-5658
Fax: (52 5) 514-6799

NEPAL
Everest Media International Services (P.) Ltd.
GPO Box 5443
Kathmandu
Tel: (977 1) 416 026
Fax: (977 1) 224 431

NETHERLANDS
De Lindeboom/Internationale Publicaties b.v.-
P.O. Box 202, 7480 AE Haaksbergen
Tel: (31 53) 574-0004
Fax: (31 53) 572-9296
E-mail: lindeboo@worldonline.nl
URL: http://www.worldonline.nl/~lindeboo

NEW ZEALAND
EBSCO NZ Ltd.
Private Mail Bag 99914
New Market
Auckland
Tel: (64 9) 524-8119
Fax: (64 9) 524-8067

NIGERIA
University Press Limited
Three Crowns Building Jericho
Private Mail Bag 5095
Ibadan
Tel: (234 22) 41-1356
Fax: (234 22) 41-2056

PAKISTAN
Mirza Book Agency
65, Shahrah-e-Quaid-e-Azam
Lahore 54000
Tel: (92 42) 735 3601
Fax: (92 42) 576 3714

Oxford University Press
5 Bangalore Town
Sharae Faisal
PO Box 13033
Karachi-75350
Tel: (92 21) 446307
Fax: (92 21) 4547640
E-mail: ouppak@TheOffice.net

Pak Book Corporation
Aziz Chambers 21, Queen's Road
Lahore
Tel: (92 42) 636 3222; 636 0885
Fax: (92 42) 636 2328
E-mail: pbc@brain.net.pk

PERU
Editorial Desarrollo SA
Apartado 3824, Ica 242 OF. 106
Lima 1
Tel: (51 14) 285380
Fax: (51 14) 286628

PHILIPPINES
International Booksource Center Inc.
1127-A Antipolo St, Barangay, Venezuela
Makati City
Tel: (63 2) 896 6501; 6505; 6507
Fax: (63 2) 896 1741

POLAND
International Publishing Service
Ul. Piekna 31/37
00-677 Warzawa
Tel: (48 2) 628-6089
Fax: (48 2) 621-7255
E-mail: books%ips@ikp.atm.com.pl
URL: http://www.ipscg.waw.pl/ips/export

PORTUGAL
Livraria Portugal
Apartado 2681, Rua Do Carm o 70-74
1200 Lisbon
Tel: (1) 347-4982
Fax: (1) 347-0264

ROMANIA
Compani De Librarii Bucuresti S.A.
Str. Lipscani no. 26, sector 3
Bucharest
Tel: (40 1) 313 9645
Fax: (40 1) 312 4000

RUSSIAN FEDERATION
Isdatelstvo <Ves Mir>
9a, Kolpachniy Pereulok
Moscow 101831
Tel: (7 095) 917 87 49
Fax: (7 095) 917 92 59
ozimarin@glasnet.ru

SINGAPORE; TAIWAN, CHINA MYANMAR; BRUNEI
Hemisphere Publication Services
41 Kallang Pudding Road #04-03
Golden Wheel Building
Singapore 349316
Tel: (65) 741-5166
Fax: (65) 742-9356
E-mail: ashgate@asianconnect.com

SLOVENIA
Gospodarski vestnik Publishing Group
Dunajska cesta 5
1000 Ljubljana
Tel: (386 61) 133 83 47; 132 12 30
Fax: (386 61) 133 80 30
E-mail: repansekj@gvestnik.si

SOUTH AFRICA, BOTSWANA
For single titles:
Oxford University Press Southern Africa
Vasco Boulevard, Goodwood
P.O. Box 12119, N1 City 7463
Cape Town
Tel: (27 21) 595 4400
Fax: (27 21) 595 4430
E-mail: oxford@oup.co.za

For subscription orders:
International Subscription Service
P.O. Box 41095
Craighall
Johannesburg 2024
Tel: (27 11) 880-1448
Fax: (27 11) 880-6248
E-mail: iss@is.co.za

SPAIN
Mundi-Prensa Libros, S.A.
Castello 37
28001 Madrid
Tel: (34 91) 4 363700
Fax: (34 91) 5 753998
E-mail: libreria@mundiprensa.es
URL: http://www.mundiprensa.com/

Mundi-Prensa Barcelona
Conseil de Cent, 391
08009 Barcelona
Tel: (34 3) 488-3492
Fax: (34 3) 487-7659
E-mail: barcelona@mundiprensa.es

SRI LANKA, THE MALDIVES
Lake House Bookshop
100, Sir Chittampalam Gardiner Mawatha
Colombo 2
Tel: (94 1) 32105
Fax: (94 1) 432104
E-mail: LHL@sri.lanka.net

SWEDEN
Wennergren-Williams AB
P.O. Box 1305
S-171 25 Solna
Tel: (46 8) 705-97-50
Fax: (46 8) 27-00-71
E-mail: mail@wwi.se

SWITZERLAND
Librairie Payot Service Institutionnel
C(tm)tes-de-Montbenon 30
1002 Lausanne
Tel: (41 21) 341-3229
Fax: (41 21) 341-3235

ADECO Van Diermen EditionsTechniques
Ch. de Lacuez 41
CH1807 Blonay
Tel: (41 21) 943 2673
Fax: (41 21) 943 3605

THAILAND
Central Books Distribution
306 Silom Road
Bangkok 10500
Tel: (66 2) 2336930-9
Fax: (66 2) 237-8321

TRINIDAD & TOBAGO AND THE CARRIBBEAN
Systematics Studies Ltd.
St. Augustine Shopping Center
Eastern Main Road, St. Augustine
Trinidad & Tobago, West Indies
Tel: (868) 645-8466
Fax: (868) 645-8467
E-mail: tobe@trinidad.net

UGANDA
Gustro Ltd.
PO Box 9997, Madhvani Building
Plot 16/4 Jinja Rd.
Kampala
Tel: (256 41) 251 467
Fax: (256 41) 251 468
E-mail: gus@swiftuganda.com

UNITED KINGDOM
Microinfo Ltd.
P.O. Box 3, Omega Park, Alton,
Hampshire GU34 2PG
England
Tel: (44 1420) 86848
Fax: (44 1420) 89889
E-mail: wbank@microinfo.co.uk
URL: http://www.microinfo.co.uk

The Stationery Office
51 Nine Elms Lane
London SW8 5DR
Tel: (44 171) 873-8400
Fax: (44 171) 873-8242
URL: http://www.the-stationery-office.co.uk/

VENEZUELA
Tecni-Ciencia Libros, S.A.
Centro Cuidad Comercial Tamanco
Nivel C2, Caracas
Tel: (58 2) 959 5547; 5035; 0016
Fax: (58 2) 959 5636

ZAMBIA
University Bookshop, University of Zambia
Great East Road Campus
P.O. Box 32379
Lusaka
Tel: (260 1) 252 576
Fax: (260 1) 253 952

ZIMBABWE
Academic and Baobab Books (Pvt.) Ltd.
4 Conald Road, Graniteside
P.O. Box 567
Harare
Tel: 263 4 755035
Fax: 263 4 781913

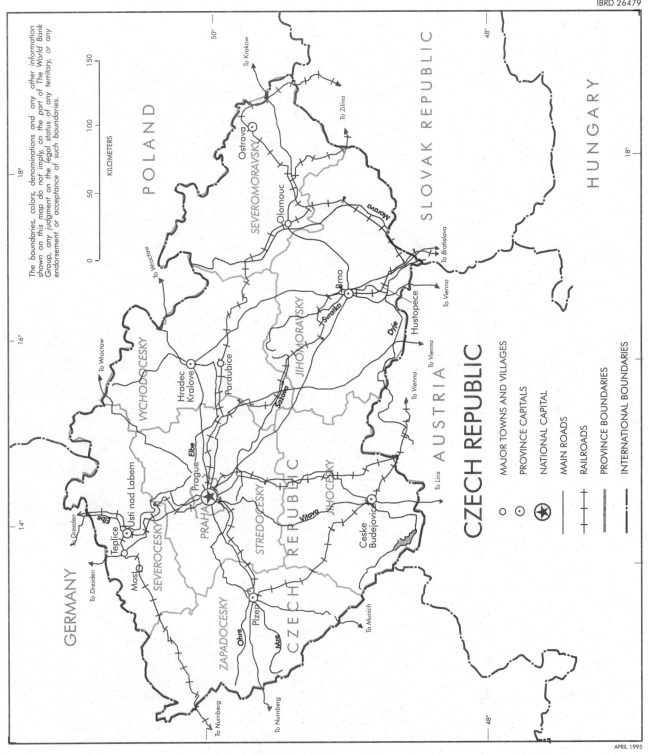

IBRD 26479

The boundaries, colors, denominations and any other information shown on this map do not imply, on the part of The World Bank Group, any judgment on the legal status of any territory, or any endorsement or acceptance of such boundaries.

KILOMETERS

0   50   100   150

POLAND

GERMANY

SLOVAK REPUBLIC

HUNGARY

AUSTRIA

CZECH REPUBLIC

CZECH REPUBLIC

○   MAJOR TOWNS AND VILLAGES
⊙   PROVINCE CAPITALS
✪   NATIONAL CAPITAL
      MAIN ROADS
╫╫╫   RAILROADS
      PROVINCE BOUNDARIES
      INTERNATIONAL BOUNDARIES

SEVEROMORAVSKY
Ostrava
Olomouc
Morava
JIHOMORAVSKY
Brno
Svratka
Dyje
Hustopece
VYCHODOCESKY
Hradec Kralove
Pardubice
Sazava
STREDOCESKY
PRAHA
Prague
Elbe
Usti nad Labem
Teplice
Most
SEVEROCESKY
Ohre
ZAPADOCESKY
Plzen
Mze
Vltava
JIHOCESKY
Ceske Budejovice

To Krakow
To Zilina
To Bratislava
To Vienna
To Vienna
To Vienna
To Vienna
To Linz
To Munich
To Nurnberg
To Nurnberg
To Dresden
To Dresden
To Wroclaw
To Wroclaw

14°   16°   18°

48°

50°

48°

18°

APRIL 1995